NAPOLEON BONAPARTE

NAPOLEON BONAPARTE

J. M. THOMPSON

Honorary Fellow of St. Mary Magdalen College

BARNES
&NOBLE
BOOKS
NEW YORK

1996 Barnes & Noble Books

ISBN 0-76070-094-X

Printed and bound in the United States of America

M 9 8 7 6 5 4 3 2 1

FG

PREFACE

ANY HISTORIAN may well hesitate to attempt a Life of Napoleon. The mass of material is so immense, the field of inquiry so vast, the verdicts of previous biographers so various. Kircheisen spent ten years compiling a list of some 100,000 works dealing with Napoleon and his times. His biography ran to nine volumes: his bibliography has never been published in full. A *catalogue spécial à Napoléon et à son temps* recently issued by a Paris bookseller contained 1765 items. The *Revue des études napoléoniennes*, founded in 1912, has published hundreds of articles and documents: a *Societé des études napoléoniennes* and (within the last two years) an *Académie Napoléon* devote themselves entirely to the study of Napoleon's career.

A distinguished Dutch historian who spent his time of internment during the second World War reading lives of Napoleon was impressed less by their agreement as to the facts of his career than by their disagreement as to its interpretation. It needs no philosophy of history to tell us that every historian has a point of view, partly due to his mental make-up and experience, and partly to the country, the society, and the age to which he belongs. He is not to apologize for it. It is his business as a historian to understand an alien age, and to enter into characters and ideas which are not his own; but he cannot do this if he ceases to be himself. He can make the dead bones live only if he has a life of his own to breathe into them. There never was and there never can be such a person as everybody's Napoleon. 'No human intelligence [says Professor Geyl] could hope to bring together the overwhelming multiplicity of data and factors, of forces and movements, and from them establish the true, one might almost say the divine balance. That is literally a superhuman task.'

The biographer of Napoleon, then, need not have read the 100,000 books in Kircheisen's catalogue: such labour might only earn him the rebuke of Festus: *multae te litterae ad insaniam convertunt.* Let him concentrate on the best evidence—above all on Napoleon's correspondence; let him use what he knows of the background and setting of the story, and rely on his own skill and judgment to construct a life-like portrait. There cannot be too many likenesses of a great man in the picture-gallery of history. It is in any event difficult for one who has studied the French Revolution up to 1794 not to wonder what happened afterwards; and well-nigh impossible

to resist the temptation to match his wits against so magnificent a subject
—a subject which will always be alive:

> Death makes no conquest of this conqueror,
> For now he lives in fame.

It will be noticed that, in order to simplify a field that covers all Europe
and the Near East, this book, at the cost of occasional overlapping, treats
separately each country with which Napoleon had to do. If some topics
receive more and others less attention than is customary, it is due to the
wish to concentrate on the things which matter most for the understanding
of Napoleon himself. It is for a similar reason that the turning-point between his 'rise' and his 'fall' has been placed in 1802, the year of the Peace
of Amiens, the Concordat, and the Life Consulate, rather than in 1804, the
year of Empire, or 1807, the year of Tilsit.

There is no bibliography: an excellent one can be found in Villat's *La
Révolution et l'Empire,* Tom. II (1936). The Notes give references to
Napoleon's Correspondence, and to secondary sources that have been found
specially useful. It is hoped that the Appendix will lead to more study of
the Correspondence. 'Bonaparte's own letters (wrote Mrs. Arbuthnot, and
her opinion was probably that of her friend Wellington) are most interesting, and have every mark of being the production of a most superior mind.
They are concise and *dictatorial* to the greatest degree; the political arrangements discussed in them are all of the most daring kind, and they
prove also that he paid as much attention to the most trivial details of the
army and the accommodation of the soldiers as to the more important
arrangements for the general success of their arms. It is sad that a mind
thus highly gifted should invariably have bent all its energies to the destruction of the human race.'

But this last sentiment, natural enough in 1820, has been given too much
popularity by historians and artists who prefer to picture Napoleon on the
battle-field. It is not likely to be the final opinion of those who read his
correspondence or who consider his government of France and the French
Empire. His greatest conquest was not Europe, but the French Revolution.
His most lasting monument is not the Arc de Triomphe or the flags at the
Invalides, but the laws and institutions in which he adapted the ideas of
1789 to the traditions of the monarchy, and enabled France to survive three
invasions and a century and a half of political unrest.

CONTENTS

NAPOLEON BONAPARTE

I

CORSICA

(1769-1793)

I

NAPOLEONE BUONAPARTE was born at Ajaccio in Corsica on August 15th, 1769.

The biographer who wishes to know the scene and society on which he opened his eyes is fortunate in possessing a contemporary account of Corsica and the Corsicans by an intelligent and observant young Scot. In October 1765 James Boswell crossed in a Tuscan vessel from Leghorn to Centuri. Since he had parted from his venerable friend Samuel Johnson on the quay at Harwich two years before, he had surveyed the Universities of the Netherlands, the courts of Germany, and the picture galleries of Italy. He believed that, in order 'to escape from the gloom of dark speculation,' it was necessary to make some 'excursions into the field of amusement and perhaps of folly': but his romantic eye was almost as quick to recognize wisdom in a man as beauty in a woman; and he was anxious to admire heroism wherever he could do so with public credit.

There were three great Europeans in 1764 whom no adept of the Grand Tour could afford to omit from his memoirs. Frederick the Great was only seen by Boswell, as anyone might see him, on the parade-ground at Potsdam; but he forced his company on Voltaire, and spent a night at Ferney arguing about religion; and he had five interviews with Rousseau, introducing himself as an ancient Scots gentleman of a kindred melancholy, at his retreat near Neuchâtel. One of the subjects they discussed was Corsica, whose liberty-loving people had at last succeeded in freeing themselves from the control of the Genoese, and whose heroic leader Paoli had invited Jean-Jacques to visit what he had described in his *Contrat Social* as the only country in Europe capable of setting up a free constitution. The Liberator had, indeed, invited the *homme sage* not to legislate for the island (he was confident he could do that himself) but to publicize it; and Rousseau had declined the invitation. Boswell fancied

3

himself for the part. A chance meeting in Italy with another champion of liberty, John Wilkes, may have fixed his resolve to visit the island. Rousseau provided an introduction to Paoli, and this letter was in Boswell's pocket when he stepped ashore at Centuri.

The Corsican peasants, he found, went armed; the roads were bad, and there were hardly any inns; but the traveller was hospitably entertained in religious or private houses with excellent fare, home grown, and the country women carried his luggage on their heads. Tourists were almost unknown, and Boswell was taken for some kind of British emissary. At Solacaro he presented Rousseau's letter to Paoli, 'a tall strong well-made man, of a fair complexion, a sensible, free, and open countenance, and a manly and noble carriage.' Paoli soon became friendly with an ingenuous young man who flattered his love of liberty, and capped his quotations from Vergil. He let him ride on his own horse, 'with rich furniture of crimson and velvet, with broad gold lace,' and confided to him his personal and political ambitions.

Corsica, he said, would revive like the Shunammite's daughter, when the new Elisha stretched himself upon her dead body. The Corsicans, if lawless and cruel, were as famed for patriotism as for personal courage. If they fought, they would fight like the Romans of old, despising the impedimenta of a modern army. Boswell, who had begun by flattering, ended by admiring: where shall I find (he reflected) a man greater than Paoli? As for his followers: 'the peasants and soldiers were all frank, open, lively, and bold, with a certain roughness of manner' which reminded him of his own Highlanders. He complimented them by dressing as a native, and playing them Scots airs on the flute: he even sang to them 'Hearts of oak are our ships.' [1]

Corsica and its affairs were not unknown in England before the time of Boswell's visit. No reader of the *Gentleman's Magazine* during the previous thirty years need have been unaware of the ups and downs of the islanders' struggle against Genoa. The frequent appeals of the Corsicans for foreign help; their overthrow by the king of Spain (1734); the intervention of Baron von Neuhof, *alias* King Theodore, in 1737; their temporary repression by French troops under Maillebois (1739); and the confusing Franco-Genoese disputes and inter-Corsican feuds of the next fifteen years; till at last Paoli came forward (1756), and by the victory of Pedicoste six years later established the right of his countrymen to independence—all this was known at least in outline to educated Englishmen. Moreover, since the loss of Port Mahon in 1756, there was the realization of the naval value of Corsica. The failure of Admiral Osborne's fleet to help the rebels at San Pellegrino in 1757 had been bitterly commented upon; and that same year the *Magazine* had published for the benefit of its readers a description and map of the island, 'as some late

Measures have given Reason to imagine that by assisting the Corsicans against the Tyranny of the Genoese we intended to obtain the Advantage of using Corsica as a Mediterranean Port instead of Minorca.'

Nevertheless Paoli had good reason to be grateful for the impulse which took Boswell to Corsica. Two years after the traveller's return to England the publication of *An Account of Corsica* did more than any other single work to put the island on the map of Europe. It was prefaced by a letter from Lord Lyttelton, comparing Paoli to the Greek liberators Timoleon and Epaminondas. Its Introduction opened with a laudation of Liberty, coupled with the name of Corsica: 'There a brave and resolute nation has now for upwards of six and thirty years maintained a constant struggle against the oppression of the republick of Genoa'; and the Corsicans are now 'on the eve of emancipating themselves for ever from a foreign yoke.'

From this preface Boswell passes into a geographical, economical and historical account of the home of freedom. Corsica, he says, is 150 miles long by 40 or 50 wide. It is a 'most agreeable island . . . charmingly situated in the Mediterranean from whence continual breezes fan and cool it in summer, and the surrounding body of water keeps it warm in winter, so that it is one of the most temperate countries in that quarter of Europe.' The Greeks rightly called it Calliste ('the fairest of the fair'), and Callimachus puts it second only to Delos, the sacred gem of the Aegean. It has, besides, plenty of good harbours, a number of 'poor fishing villages,' and 'hamlets prettily situated,' generally on hill-tops, amongst the lakes, rivers, mountains and mineral springs of the interior. The landscape culminated in Gradaccio or Monte Rotondo, a peak of 'amazing height,' commanding a view of France and Italy, but seldom ascended, 'for the upper part of the montain is almost a perpendicular rock, so that a man must climb two miles with the help of his hands and knees.'

Boswell ends with an account of 'the present state of Corsica.' Paoli's government, 'even as it is now,' he looks upon as 'the best model that hath ever existed in the democratical form.' The five Catholic bishops are suffragans of Pisa. There are sixty-five convents of friars, dependent on the charity of the faithful, but no nunneries. The country priests are pious and militant. The people, whose number he puts at 220,000, are illiterate, but have a talent for music and poetry. They speak Italian with some Genoese corruptions and a coarse accent. They resemble Tacitus's famous account of the ancient Germans, except that they are not addicted to drink. The men are good fighters, but poor workers. They love, like the American Indians, to lie round a fire and talk, whilst their work is done by hired labourers from Lucca or Sardinia. 'They are no doubt (he concludes) a people of strong passions, as well as of lively and vigorous minds . . . These islanders have abilities for anything; but their fortune

has been such, that they have been conspicuous only for the hard and resolute qualities.'

By an ironical stroke of history, carried out in the very year (1768) in
which Boswell publicized Paoli's hopes for the permanent freedom of
Corsica, the islanders once more lost their independence: this time to
France, this time finally. A force of 4000 men landed at Ajaccio; the island was put under an *Intendant*; and the hostility of the natives was diverted from the old Genoese to the new French oppressor. But guerrilla
warfare which had defied the ill-disciplined levies of Genoa found itself
powerless against the professional army of the French king and the skill
of French engineers, who carried a military road from Ajaccio to Bastia
over obstacles as high as Snowdon. Under the dilatory Chauvelin, indeed,
and his transient successor Marbeuf (August 1768-March 1769), little
progress was made in the reduction of the rebels; but de Vaux's arrival
in April with young Mirabeau, and (if we are to believe his *Memoirs*)
the courage and initiative of Dumouriez, made it effective, and Paoli was
driven from the island, protesting that no claim to its possession was valid
without the free consent of its people.[2]

If this claim had been upheld, Napoleone Buonaparte, who was just a
fortnight old at the time, would not have been born a French citizen.

2

'Buona-Parte' (as he is called in General Dugommier's letter of 10 Frim.,
An. II, which first got his name into the *Moniteur*), 'Buonaparte' (as it is
on his marriage register), or 'Bonaparte' (as he began to sign himself
soon after his appointment to the Italian command in 1796): what does
it signify? Napoleon himself proudly claimed that the house of Bonaparte dated from the 18th Brumaire—the day when he rebuilt it upon the
foundation of his own career. Nevertheless the family history was not
without bearing on the career, and retains some interest for a biographer.

That the Buonapartes were of noble origin, and could claim two hundred years' residence as Corsican nobility, was formally established by the
Conseil Supérieur of the island in 1771. But on what kind of genealogy
did this claim rest? Was the family of Italian or of Greek origin? Was it
merely aristocratic, or was it perhaps royal? When Bonaparte came to
Treviso in October 1797, the magistrates of the town sought to commend
it to his favour by telling him that members of the Buonaparte family
had played an important part in local history. When he passed through
San Miniato at the end of June 1796, he stayed (as his father had done
thirty years before) with a surviving member of the Tuscan branch of the
family, an ecclesiatic, named Philip Buonaparte. The roll of Doctors of
the University of Pisa contains the names of fifteen Buonapartes between

1633 and 1754. There are other indications of the Italian origin and connections of the family, pointing to Florence and Venice; so that one biographer does not hesitate to print a complete genealogy through seventeen generations of Italian nobles, beginning with a certain Conrad son of Tedice in the early tenth century.

But there were times (as for instance during his Adriatic campaign of 1797) when it might be advantageous for Bonaparte to exploit a Greek ancestry; and other biographers have traced his descent either from Manuel II, the Palaeologue Emperor of Byzantium, and the Macedonian Princess whom he took to wife at the end of the fourteenth century, or from David Comnenus, the last Emperor of Trebizond, deposed by the Turks in 1471.

Napoleon was the child of a love-match. The father was only 18 at the time of his marriage in March 1764, the mother only 14. Charles (Carlo-Maria) Buonaparte was a handsome, attractive and gifted young man, an eloquent speaker, with a knowledge of French unusual among Corsicans: he could write Voltairian verses in Italian, and turn a pretty sonnet for a courtship or a wedding. But he was flighty, extravagant and easy-going, except only where the claims of his family were concerned, or the creed of his political party. He had been destined by his cautious great-uncle, Lucien Buonaparte, Archdeacon of Ajaccio, for a rich marriage, which would re-establish the family fortunes. For the Buonapartes passed for a family of some importance in a society of half-Italian *cittadini* and *condottieri*, in which villages played the part of towns, and local feuds assumed the proportions of civil war (Bocognano and Bastelica were to Ajaccio what Lucca or Pistoia were to Florence), and in which the possession of a few acres of land, a flock of sheep, a mulberry-plot and a town house denoted gentility.

It was therefore something of a disappointment when Charles fell in love with Maria-Letizia Ramolino, the pretty daughter of an Inspector of roads and bridges, and the niece of a canon of the cathedral of Ajaccio. Her dowry of £300 was not large. But the girl's mother came of a family, the Pietra-Santas, as 'noble' as the Buonapartes; and Letizia herself, with every domestic virtue, had enough character to keep her volatile husband in order. Though she never outgrew her Corsican origin, and spoke French (as Bonaparte himself did) with *ou* for *eu* or *u*, Letizia's signature, with its ornamental initial and final flourish, is that of a woman of some education.

Though her father had, twenty years before, held a military command at Genoa, Letizia easily accepted her husband's party, which by tradition and choice was that of Paoli, and accompanied him in the field, in the fashion of 'Resistance' warfare, during the campaigns of 1768 and 1769 against the French. That of 1768 ended in the victory of Borgo, that of 1769 in the final defeat of Ponte Nuovo: after this Paoli fled to the continent with a part of his followers. The remainder, after painful wanderings in the mountains, were allowed by their enemies to return home. Letizia, carrying Joseph in her arms, reached Ajaccio in time to give birth to Napoleon there, three months after the battle.

Napoleon was the fourth child of the marriage. The first two children had died in infancy. The third, born on January 8th, 1768, was named Joseph (Giuseppe) according to family custom: the next inherited the name Napoleone, or took it from the obscure saint on whose day he was born. But whereas Joseph, born before the annexation of 1768, was a Corsican, Napoleon, born after it, was a French citizen; and, like St. Paul, he was always proud to say, 'I was born free.' Other children came later: Maria-Anna in 1771 (she died in 1776), Lucien in 1775, Maria-Anna, called Elisa, in 1777, Louis in 1778, Pauline in 1780, Maria-Nunciata, called Caroline, in 1782, and Jérôme in 1783. Letizia was by then 33: she lived to be 87, and to survive all but five of her large family: *Une maîtresse mère*, her son rightly called her.

It is easy, looking at Gérard's portrait of Letizia Buonaparte, to see where Napoleon got his fine eyes and his pouting upper lip. It might not be difficult, if there were a family portrait gallery, to trace his features back into earlier generations of Buonapartes and Ramolinos. With the mental and moral make-up of the child this is not possible, and perhaps not worth attempting. It is more profitable to consider the general character of the family and society from which Bonaparte sprang, and in which he was brought up.

Its geographical isolation and its long history of wars and feuds had deprived Corsica, as it had deprived Scotland or Wales, of opportunities of culture and education, but had not robbed the Corsicans of their natural taste and intelligence. Put aside the specious propaganda, 'I am a Frenchman,' and reckon the 'nobility' of Napoleon's family for what it was really worth: pride in an old name, and in the story of ancestors who held high positions in more civilized societies; a scrap of property; some influence with the government; and a disposition to stand aside from the vulgar concerns of the *bourgeoisie*. Imagine what it meant for a society of proud clansmen and poor peasants to be the prey of successive conquerors, and how many talents for the amenities and arts of peace were diverted, not for six years, but for five times six, to the degrading practices of war.

Boswell was right when he said 'These islanders have ability for anything.' Rousseau was right when he saw in them the raw material of a democratic state. If they had to fight, they would know how to die; but they also knew how to live; they had ability for administration and the arts; they wished to be educated; they could behave and converse in the society of gentlemen. The French *Ministre de la Marine* who addressed the Mayor and citizens of Ajaccio at the unveiling of a statue of Napoleon at his birthplace in 1938 might be excused for some exaggeration: but there was truth in his claim that 'In Napoleon there can be retraced the character of a people whose rare qualities have been proved by their history. His ambition, his clannishness, his impetuous will, his sudden acts of violence—why! gentlemen, are they not at the root of our Corsican temperament? Will, courage, sense of authority, taste for action—those are pure Corsican. Add genius, and you have Napoleon!'

Boswell, full of memories of his childhood at Auchinleck, and conscious of his attempts to turn himself into an Englishman, can hardly have missed the likeness between the society of Corsica and that of the Highlands. Five years after writing his book he embarked with Dr. Johnson on another tour which produced two masterpieces—*Journals* worth reading side by side with *An Account of Corsica*. The same contrast of squalor and plenty, the same mixture of feudal traditions and democratic ideas, the same juxtaposition of ignorance and enlightenment, the same taste for music, dancing and poetry, the same coarseness of manners and aspirations towards gentility that Boswell found in Corsica he rediscovered in the Hebrides.[3]

3

Bonaparte's earliest education was that of the home and the street. The home was ruled by women; and his first and longest loyalties were for his wet-nurse, Camilla Carbone, his 'nanny' Caterina, and a maid-servant named Saveria, who remained with Letizia all her life, helped to bring up her children, and died in her service in 1825. Legend was soon busy inventing stories of the boy's infant precocity, and of his predilection for games of war. All that seems certain is that he was a masterful, troublesome child, inclined to dominate his brothers and sisters. One story will suffice. When quite young, Napoleon and Joseph were sent to a boys' school kept by the abbé Rocco, a *professeur* at the *collège d'Ajaccio*. Joseph's *Memoirs* record that the pupils sat on opposite sides of a room, on one wall of which hung a Roman flag, and on the other a Carthaginian. Joseph, as the elder brother, was put under the Roman flag, but nothing would content Napoleon until he too was allowed to sit on the victorious side. He left the abbé £1000 in his will; 'he was the first man,' he said, 'who taught me to read.'

One result of the French annexation of Corsica was that Corsican nobles qualified for French nobility, and that their children became eligible for educational endowments at certain French schools. An *Ordonnance* of 1770, of which Charles Buonaparte, along with several of his friends, hastened to take advantage, directed that claims to nobility were to be verified by the *Conseil Supérieur* of the island. This certificate Charles obtained the following year.

As part of the military reforms initiated by Saint-Germain, when Minister of War for Louis XVI, twelve schools had been set apart for the education of 600 sons of poor nobles at the royal expense. Each school was to admit 50 or 60 of these scholars (*boursiers*) between the ages of eight and nine—the scholarships were worth the standard pay of a *vicaire* (curate), £35 a year—along with an equal number of boarders (*pensionnaires*) paid for by their parents. The candidates had to prove their noble birth, their poverty, and their ability to read and write. In return they were kept for six years, and taught history, geography, languages, mathematics, drawing, fencing and dancing.

As soon as he heard of these scholarships, Charles Buonaparte set about securing one of them for his second son. Not his first; for he had decided that Joseph would never make a soldier, and had better be put into the Church. His friend Marbeuf, the *Intendant* of Corsica, undertook to pay for Joseph's education, and recommended that both boys should be sent to learn French—it was almost a foreign language to them—at the Oratorian *collège d'Autun*, where his relative the bishop could keep an eye on them. No time was wasted. The grant of Napoleon's scholarship was dated December 31st, 1778. He began his schooling at Autun on January 1st, 1779—nearly twelve years after a boy with whom he would have much to do in the future, Lazare Carnot.

He was at this school three months, and only two pieces of evidence have survived as to his time there. His name appears in the school accounts as M. Neapoleonne de Bonnaparte'; his schoolmaster, writing to a clerical friend forty years afterwards, said that the boy soon 'learnt enough French to speak it fluently, and even to write short essays and translations.'

Meanwhile Charles had registered his Corsican certificate of nobility in Paris, and had succeeded in getting his second son's scholarship transferred from the comparatively obscure school at Autun to the more central and fashionable establishment at Brienne; and there he took Napoleon in May 1779, leaving Joseph to continue his education alone at Autun.

Bonaparte was at Brienne from May 1779 till October 1784, and these five and a half years fixed his character and career. He was at an impressionable age. He was completely cut off from the outside world, whether French or Corsican. He had to hold his own, as the half-foreign champion of an obscure island and of an unknown 'Liberator,' in a school full of French royalists. He went through the experience of his first Communion. He discovered that he had brains, and became ambitious to do well. In a word, it was at Brienne that young Bonaparte 'found himself,' and set the course from which he never afterwards diverged.

Too much has been made of his home-sickness, and of the 'ragging' he had to put up with on account of his Corsican accent and opinions. Too little has been allowed for the steady pressure of a school system unrelieved by holidays, and undisturbed by parental visits: Bonaparte only saw his mother (in 1782) and his father (in 1784) once in more than five years. Legend has invented or embroidered incidents as irrelevant and unreal as those in any of our school romances. What is certain is that Bonaparte recognized all his life a debt of gratitude to Brienne as a turning-point in his development, pensioning or promoting his teachers, visiting the *curé* who gave him his first Communion, and even finding employment at Malmaison for the school porter.

But Brienne did not turn him into a *dévot*; rather, as the engineering College of Mezières turned Carnot—a not unlikely result of a mathematical and scientific training—into an agnostic.

Here is the passing-out certificate given to Bonaparte by the visiting Inspector of Military Schools. 'M. de Buonaparte (Napoléon),' wrote Keralio, 'born Aug. 15, 1769; height 4 feet 10 inches; has reached the fourth class. Constitution and health, excellent; character, obedient, amenable, honest, grateful; conduct, perfectly regular; he has throughout distinguished himself by his steady work at mathematics. He knows his history and geography pretty well. Fencing and dancing (*exercises d'agrément*) very poor. He will make an excellent sailor, and is fit for admission to the school at Paris.'

It is not certain how Bonaparte's career, which at the end of his time at Brienne seemed to be directed towards the navy, was diverted into the army. One letter from his father suggests that there was some fear of the mathematical teaching from which he had benefited so much being no longer available. Another says that the cause was Keralio's replacement by an *Inspecteur* less keen on the navy; together with his mother's understandable objection to his going to sea. In any case mathematics was as essential for the artillery or the engineers as for the navy; and both these services—the most efficient in the army—offered great opportunities to young men who were prepared to work, and to win advancement by merit. So at any rate it was decided; and in October 1784 the boy received a nomination to a place in the *École militaire* of Paris, signed by Louis XVI and countersigned by de Ségur, as Minister of War.

Napoleon revisited Brienne in 1805 and in 1814. In 1805 it was the scene of peaceful and complimentary celebrations, and he bought the Château de Pont, not far away, as a country residence for his mother. In 1814 it was a battlefield on which the Emperor experienced his first defeat on French soil, and owed his life to the presence of mind of the faithful Gourgaud. The place is now Brienne-Napoléon, and is embellished with a statue of its most famous cadet, meditating, with a book in his left hand, and his right already thrust into his half-open waistcoat. So history is improved by legend.[4]

4

On receipt of his summons to Paris Bonaparte set out along with four other boys in charge of one of the teachers, and arrived at the Military School (*École militaire*) on October 19th, 1784.

The French Sandhurst had been founded by the Maréchal de Belleisle and Paris Duverney in 1751, and re-established in 1777 as a school for the *Corps des Cadets Gentilshommes*. The beautiful building lies at the south-east end of the Champ de Mars, side by side with the Invalides. Gabriel's finest design, and the happy juxtaposition of school and hospital, the beginning and end of a military career, recall the Queen's House and Naval Hospital at Greenwich, the masterpiece of Inigo Jones.

The school had been intended to attract the sons of the poorer nobility to the service of Louis XV. As at Brienne, royal scholars (*élèves*) and boarders (*pensionnaires*) lived together under the same regime. All were to be trained as good royalists, fine gentlemen and efficient officers. The establishment was on a royal scale. The Governors were distinguished men, headed by the Minister of War himself. The staff included some of the ablest teachers of the day: and to the teachers were added doctors, nurses, cooks, grooms and a hairdresser. There was a chapel, a library, a riding school reputed to be the best in Europe, and wide grounds for drilling and recreation. Every boy had a room to himself, two uniforms a year (in blue and red, with white facings and silver and gold braid), and three changes of linen a week. The food and service were in a style familiar enough, perhaps, to the *pensionnaires*, who came from rich homes, but strange and almost shocking to a Corsican fresh from the Spartan existence of Brienne. 'We were fed and served magnificently,' said Bonaparte; 'we were treated in every respect like officers accustomed to do themselves well, in a style much better than most of our families were accustomed to, or than most of us were likely to enjoy in future life.'

The principal subjects taught to all the cadets were mathematics, history, geography, French and German grammar, fortification, drawing, fencing and dancing. English was taken by boys going into the navy, writing classes were prescribed for such as needed them, and lectures on ethics and law for those who might serve as officers in foreign courts. Riding, shooting and drill-book instruction were taken 'out of school.' Religion, as might be expected in a Bourbon foundation, was the background of everything. There were three chapel services a day, beginning with mass at six in the morning; catechism on Sundays, confession on Saturdays, and Communion six times a year.

Bonaparte, having learnt to work at Brienne, made good use of his single year at Paris. His history master prophesied that 'with luck he would go far.' His French master, Domairon, was never able to eradicate his Corsican accent, or the Italianisms of his 'volcanic' style; but the boy acquired a taste for the classical poetry of Racine and Corneille which he never outgrew; and recommended his teacher's *Principes généraux* all his life. Bonaparte did not take Latin and escaped English, which he tried to learn for the first time, too late, and with very little success, on the voyage to St. Helena. None of his schoolmasters taught him to write legibly.

The royalist and aristocratic tone of the *École militaire* is shown by the fact that most of Bonaparte's two hundred contemporaries there deserted their country during the Revolution. Bonaparte was still marked out, as he had been at Brienne, by his Corsican origin and opinions. They were a school joke; and there survives a crudely drawn caricature of him by one of his friends, in cadet's uniform, setting out for the defence of Paoli: but it was no longer safe to laugh openly at his oddities.

It is difficult to be sure how far contemporary changes of manners and ideas found their way into the classrooms and playgrounds of Autun, Brienne, or Paris. What did young Bonaparte ever hear of James Cook's first voyage round the world, begun in the year of his birth; of the great scientific discoveries of the age—the spinning-mill (1769), nitrogen (1772), oxygen (1774); of the first iron bridge (1773), the first efficient steam-engine (1775), or the first air balloon (1782)? Did his teachers ever tell him about the *Sorrows of Werther* (1774), the *Wealth of Nations* (1776), the *Decline and Fall* (1776), *Evelina* (1778), Rousseau's *Confessions* (1781), or Kant's *Critique* (1781)? Did he ever hear Gluck's *Iphigeneia* (1779), or Mozart's *Il Seraglio* (1782)? Did he suck revolution from the flowers of Beaumarchais's *Mariage de Figaro* (1784)? A modern biographer would know all about such contacts with the outside world, and weigh their influence upon his young hero. With Bonaparte one can only reconstruct the beginning from the end; can only notice, looking through his library, which books have been most thumbed, and infer that they are old favourites; can only (and that precariously) guess from the fixed rounds of manhood what may have been the unplanned excursions of youth.[5]

5

Bonaparte took the passing-out examination from the *École militaire* with seven other boys in September 1785, and was placed 42nd out of a total of 58 candidates. This was no discredit, seeing that he had only one year for a course to which most of his rivals had given two or three. He was gazetted to a second lieutenancy in the *Régiment de la Fère du corps royal d'artillerie*, stationed at that time at Valence. He was the first Corsican boy to have passed through the Military School; and only one other during this period held a commission in the artillery.

At Valence he took military lodgings with a Mlle Bou, whom he remembered and rewarded on his return from Egypt thirteen years later. He found himself posted to the 1st Company of the 5th Brigade of the regiment, that of the *bombardiers*. The station was exceptionally well found, and the regiment reputed one of the smartest in the army. The officers were a hardworking and well-disciplined lot, taking their profession seriously, and making themselves popular with the townspeople. Their training had hitherto been theoretical: now they had to learn the practical side of soldiering. For three months they were on probation, and did sentry-go and other duties of a common soldier. Thereafter the routine of classes and lectures left a certain amount of time which the young officer might spend as he chose.

Bonaparte's pay, £55 a year, did not leave much margin, after board and lodging, for private expenses. A shy and still half-foreign boy of sixteen, he might not easily find friends. But one family at least befriended him, and with Caroline Colombier, a girl of something like his own age, he seems to have carried on a mild flirtation. He would not lose his head over Caroline as his friend Des Mazis did over his Adelaide; but he kept up his friendship with her in after life when she became Mme Bressieux.

Any time that could be spared, and any money that could be saved, was devoted to books. Rousseau's *Confessions*, the most exciting work of the eighteenth century, had been published five years before; it was still half-heartedly forbidden to young people, whole-heartedly admired by them. With Rousseau Bonaparte would associate, as Boswell did, Corsica and national liberty. He is found writing to a bookseller at Geneva, asking for the *Memoirs* of Mme de Warens to read as a sequel to the *Confessions*; for Germanes's *Histoire des révolutions de Corse*; and for any other books on Corsican history that may be available. Three years later he would be sending to the philosopher-historian Raynal his own first draft of a book on his native island. Indeed there exist some manuscript notes on the subject, dated April 26th, 1786, in which he vindicates the right of the Corsicans under Paoli to revolt against their Genoese and French oppressors; and a *Lament of a young patriot absent from his country*, written a year earlier (May 3rd, 1785), in which the young romantic professes to envy the natural life of the mountaineer who spends his days in *affaires publiques*, and his nights *dans les tendres bras d'une épouse chérie*.

More significant of the way his mind was forming at this time is a *Defence of Rousseau*, dated (with characteristic meticulousness) May 9th, 4 p.m. (1786). The argument goes throughout upon the Catholic assumption that the Roman Church *is* Christianity in being. Only when he is in-veighing against the wealth and warlikeness of the church does Napoleon catch a glimpse of the Sermon on the Mount; and lets it go again. To him Christianity is an international society working against the national inter-ests of the state; diverting the citizen from his duty in this world to his preparation for a world to come; corrupting his loyalty to the nation in the name of fidelity to the faith; putting the directions of the priest above the commands of the magistrate; in short, undermining the whole authority of government. 'The Church's empire is not of this world: the churchman is never a citizen.' 'Wherever the priesthood is an international body it is the master of the government. Its decisions override those of all other embodi-ments of the state. By its rule over the conscience it makes the law. Its every act is that of a tyrant.'

The way out of this *impasse* by the subordination of the church to the state was not yet apparent to the young controversialist: it had to be learnt from experience of Jacobinism in Paris, of Mohammedanism at Cairo and of Papalism in Italy. Yet the hot contentions of the boy of sixteen forecast the cool convictions of the man of thirty-three; and one can already see in this manuscript the rough draft of a Concordat.

Before his year at Valence was up, on September 1st, 1786, Bonaparte was due for leave. On August 7th there broke out at Lyon one of the periodical *émeutes* for which it was notorious—a strike for better wages amongst the silk-workers, complicated by complaints of the inn-keepers about a tax on wine. Bonaparte's battalion was dispatched to restore order: three work-men were hanged, and the rest sent back to their duties. This early ex-perience of mob-violence and its suppression he never forgot. The affair only took a week; but as the whole regiment was due to change its quarters to Douai next month, the battalion stayed on at Lyon to be joined there by the rest. So Bonaparte returned alone to Valence, left there again on Sep-tember 1st, and was at Ajaccio by the 15th.[6]

<h2 style="text-align:center">6</h2>

He was now seventeen, and it was nearly eight years since he had been at home. Then he had been a child; now he was a man. 'His return home,' wrote Joseph afterwards, 'was a great pleasure to my mother and me . . . His habits were those of a serious and studious young man.' Of the two pieces of luggage he brought with him, the smaller sufficed for his clothes and toilet, the larger was crammed with French translations of the classics—Plutarch, Plato, Cicero, Cornelius Nepos, Livy and Tacitus; with Montaigne, Montesquieu, Raynal and Ossian. Officially, he should have been recruiting likely Corsican youths for the French army, and went so far as to draw up a form of enlistment: actually his hope was to write a history of the Corsican revolutions; and for this he must re-learn Italian, the nursery language which both he and his brother had half forgotten.

But, as always happened when he was at home, Bonaparte found himself shouldering the affairs of a big and penurious family. Lucien, the arch-deacon, the trustee of the Buonaparte estate, was now, at the age of sixty-eight, bedridden. The local doctors could do nothing for him. Bonaparte wrote a long letter, flavoured with discreet flattery and a quotation from Fontenelle, to the famous Dr. Tissot, F.R.S., of Lausanne, an admirer of Paoli, and author of a *Traité de la santé des gens de lettres*, asking for a better opinion.

Then there was the complicated and tiresome affair of the *pépinière de muriers* to deal with. Three years before his death Charles Buonaparte had accepted a contract from the government for the management of a mulberry plantation, expecting that at the end of five years the sale of the fully grown trees would leave him a good profit. But the government had just cancelled the contract, leaving the family heavily in debt, and with claims which it might take years to recover from a dilatory *Contrôle général*. Bonaparte went into the matter with characteristic thoroughness; wrote a *Mémoire sur la culture du murier*; and, on the ground that he was suffering from an at-tack of malaria, applied for and obtained six months' extension of his leave (from May 16th to November 1st) in order that he might travel to Paris, and press the family claims in person on the government.

He stayed in Paris at the modest Hotel de Cherbourg, rue Four Saint-Honoré. He was alone in the city for the first time. He wrote letters to the *Contrôle* explaining the matter of the *pépinière*; he went out to Versailles to interview the *Contrôleur*; but he was left with most of his time upon his hands. One cold night he went to the Italian opera. When he came out he strolled into the Palais-Royal, the meeting-place of every idler and scamp in the capital. His head was full of echoes of the opera; but when he turned under the colonnade, where the prostitutes picked up their customers, he was struck by the figure and face of a girl. She seemed pale and shy like himself. He talked with her, made her tell him her story, and took her back to the hotel. His own account of the incident, though intended to suggest that he was merely studying human nature, leaves little doubt that it ended in the way of nature. It was, he would persuade us, his first experience of *le sexe*.

There is perhaps an echo of this adventure in an *Essay on Love* written about this time for 'Mademoiselle.' But it is to be remarked that *mademoiselle* is interchanged with *messieurs*, and that the real subject of the discourse is not *l'amour des femmes* but *l'amour de la patrie*—patriotism, and its distinction from *l'amour de la gloire*, ambition. 'I have hardly reached the age of the dawn of passion': such are his first words; and the rest is a catalogue of heroic names and heroic acts which shows clearly enough where his real affections are engaged.[7]

Bonaparte returned home again on New Year's Day, 1788. His mother was now alone, with four young children on her hands (Louis 10, Pauline 8, Caroline 6, Jérôme 4), and with no servants to help her. Joseph was away at Pisa, studying for his doctorate in law. Once more he took up the question of the *pépinière* with the *Intendant*, and visited him at Bastia. Here there was a garrison of artillery, whose mess he frequented. One of the officers, his senior by two years' service, remembered it in later days, and said in his *Souvenirs* that they had found him dull and opinionated (*sec et sententieux*), too fond of airing his views in a donnish way (*ton doctrinal*) on political questions, and criticizing the French government.

The fresh extension of leave which Bonaparte had obtained ran to September 1st: he could not decently ask for more. But it seems that he left Ajaccio on June 1st. Where did he spend the interval? A possible answer is given in Metternich's *Memoirs*. He records that he and his younger brother were at Strasbourg University in the summer of 1788, just when Bonaparte had left there, after attending an artillery school with the local garrison. Metternich admits that he did not discover this until he revisited the place eighteen years later, when he found Napoleon's old fencing-master talking about his now famous pupil. But there would be nothing improbable in Bonaparte's going there, supposing he could afford it, to attend the lectures of Lombard, the artillery expert, and perhaps to receive private instruction (for his public lectures were in Latin) from J. M. Lorenz, another teacher in the same circle.[8]

7

Bonaparte now remained at Auxonne for just a year (September 1788-September 1789). 'I have nothing to do here (he writes) except work. I only get into uniform once a week. I sleep very little since my illness. You would hardly believe it; but I go to bed at ten and get up at four. I only have one meal a day, and it suits my health very well.' He was living in barracks now, not in lodgings. He had to catch up the year's instruction he had missed in Paris. Under its commandant, Maréchal Du Teil, the school at Auxonne was reputed the most efficient and hard-working in the service. There were frequent field practices in the country round. But this left plenty of time for the reading of manuals and monographs bearing on the principles and technicalities of gunnery, and for the general reading in which Bonaparte was by now so absorbed.

That he did not lead a solitary or obscure life is shown by his being chosen by his brother officers to draft a constitution and rules for the *Calotte*, or Junior Officers' Club, in which they maintained their *esprit de corps* and their rights against officers of the rank of Captain upwards (Carnot belonged to a similar institution at Mezières). The *Projet de constitution de la Calotte du régiment de la Fère* is a solemn and long-winded affair, in which it is easy to see a by-product of its author's constitutional studies. It takes for granted the soldier's duty of blind obedience to orders; it lays it down that the Equality of all members of the *Calotte* is an irrefragable law deriving directly from the nature of the Original Contract (*pacte primitif*); and it places the control of the *Calotte* in the hands of a senior Lieutenant and two comrades, rather as the government of France ten years later was entrusted to a First Consul and two associates.

Of the group of writings dealing with artillery subjects belonging to this period the most important is a *Mémoire sur la manière de disposer les canons pour le jet des bombes*: not for technical reasons, but because Buona-Parte (he signed the report 'B.P.') had been picked out by Du Teil to pre-pare and report on these experiments, although he was the youngest and most junior in rank of a commission of seven. He was making his mark.

The manuscript notes on Bonaparte's general reading which have sur-vived need not be detailed here: but they show that he studied Plato's *Republic*, probably in Grou's French translation (1762), and analysed the discussion between Socrates, Cephalos, Polemarchos and Thrasymachus on the subject of Justice; that he was interested in the government, religion and antiquities of Egypt, as described in Rollin's *Histoire ancienne*, and in the constitutional development of the Greek city-states; that he read part of Raynal's *Histoire des deux Indes*; that he studied a Life of Frederick the Great; that the *Mémoires* of the abbé Terray provided him with in-formation on industry and finance, particularly in connection with the Compagnie des Indes; and that he returned to Egypt and Syria in the *Mémoires* of the Baron de Tott.

There are notes on Mirabeau's *Lettres de cachet*, on Boulainvilliers and Blackstone; and those on the sensational *L'espion anglais* (1784) show an interest in all kinds of matters dealing with the *ancien régime*, the provin-cial *états*, the *parlements*, the clergy, the *tiers état*, Louis XVI and his minis-ters, the American colonies, and the theatrical world of Paris. He seems also to have read parts of Mably's *Histoire de France*, Marigny's *Histoire des arabes*, and Amelot de la Houssaie's *Gouvernement de Venise*.

His gleanings from Barrow's *History of England* were extensive and peculiar. He draws up an elaborate table of the kings of Wessex, Essex and the rest from the fifth to the eighth century; the provisions of Magna Carta, the origins of Parliament, the battles of the Civil War all have their place: his patience does not give out till he reaches the revolution of 1688.

There exists, besides these notes, a six-page manuscript entitled the *Comte d'Essex*: it is a melodramatic account of the mysterious death of Essex after the Rye House plot against the life of Charles II, and of his wife's prophetic dream. In somewhat the same vein is *Le Masque prophète*, an episode perhaps from Marigny's Arab history, in which Napoleon drama-tizes himself as the prophet Hakem.

History, then, both for its administrative and financial side, and for its romantic possibilities, was Bonaparte's favourite reading: but there are also notes on geography, meteorology, and marriage customs, mostly taken from Buffon, and ending with an interesting computation of the expectation of life in the eighteenth century; and on Lacroix's *Géographie*, the standard work of the time. What chiefly interested him here seems to have been the British possessions in various parts of the world: he makes notes on our colonial defences, and on the revenues of Bengal. The principal manuscript breaks off, prophetically enough, with the words *Sainte-Hélène, petite île.* . . .

8

Born in 1769, Bonaparte belonged to the generation which inherited the French Revolution, not to that which made it. Three out of every four deputies of the Third Estate in the National Assembly of 1789 were born at least twenty years before him: if he had sat in the Convention of 1792, he would have been two years junior to the youngest member, Saint-Just. But it is not irrelevant to inquire what impression may have been made upon his mind by the events which were passing in France during the twenty years preceding the outbreak of the Revolution: provided always that it is remembered that he was a foreigner, and a schoolboy, in a position (perhaps) analogous to that of an Irish boy put to school in England during the time of the American rebellion, the Wilkes controversy, and the Gordon riots.

His first six years of life coincided with the last six decadent years of the reign of Louis XV. By the time he went to school at Autun, Louis XVI had initiated reforms which he had not the will to carry out, and engaged his country in a war as disastrous in final results as it was superficially successful: Adam Smith and Tom Paine had pointed the economic and political morals of the American rebellion; Voltaire and Rousseau, the prophets of Reason and Instinct, had died in giving birth to the Revolution. Did the future Emperor hear talk of these things?

During his five and a half years at Brienne Bonaparte was effectively cut off from the outside world; yet it cannot be supposed that the masters at a military school left him in complete ignorance of the Siege of Gibraltar (June 1779), the League of Armed Neutrality (March 1780), the Anglo-Dutch war (November 1780), the capitulation of Cornwallis at Yorktown (October 1781), the battle of Les Saintes (April 1782), or the Treaty of Versailles (September 1783). It was a time of national self-congratulation already tinged with doubts and omens of disaster: the capital which the young cadet saw for a few days in 1785 and a few weeks in 1787, and the country which he talked about in the Officers' Mess at Valence, or Bastia, or Auxonne, was already moving towards revolution.

Three of the Auxonne manuscripts show in what direction Bonaparte's mind was pointing. On October 23rd, 1788, he sketched the outline of a *Dissertation sur l'autorité royale*, in which he intended to discuss 'some of the general ideas on the origin and growth of the name of King in men's minds'; the military government with which monarchy is most closely associated; and the 'usurpation of authority enjoyed by the actual sovereigns in the twelve kingdoms of Europe'; for 'there are few monarchs,' he holds, 'who do not deserve to lose the thrones they occupy.' When Necker's *Rapport* of May 5th, 1789 (his speech at the opening of the States-General), is published Bonaparte analyses it, and copies down all the main figures of the minister's financial statement. He studies, too, such foreign news as is contained in publications taken in by the regimental library; and his *Notes diverses tirées des gazettes ou autres papiers publics* (dated June 1789) include a summary of Wilberforce's report and proposals on the Slave Trade.

This interest in the political situation might have been purely academic, had it not been that Bonaparte became involved in two practical instances of the revolutionary spirit which was spreading over the face of French society. In April 1789, at Seurre, a small town on the Saône down-stream from Auxonne, two corn-dealers were lynched on a charge of hoarding—a not uncommon occurrence in the spring following the bad harvest and hard winter of 1788; and Bonaparte was second in command of a detachment of soldiers sent to suppress the riot. Three months later, five days after the Fall of the Bastille (July 19th-20th), the common people of Auxonne itself, backed by 'brigands' (as it became the fashion to call them), from the country round, rose against the town officials, especially the collectors of rates and taxes, of *octroi* and *gabelle*, broke up their offices, and held to ransom some of the well-to-do citizens.

The garrison at first looked the other way, but were at last ordered to load their muskets, drive out the 'brigands,' and close the gates of the town. They showed little zeal for the task, and a month later themselves mutinied against their officers, demanding a share-out of the regimental funds (*trésor*). This was just such an incident as led, a year later, to the more serious Nancy mutiny, and the ferocious punishment of the Châteauvieux regiment. At Auxonne the officers gave way; the money was squandered in drink; and one Second Lieutenant at least drew ominous conclusions as to the incompatibility of mob-rule with army discipline.

Yet this was no ordinary mutiny, but rather a forcible Declaration of the Rights of the common soldier. Democracy was now the only wear. Within a few days (August 23rd) the whole regiment, officers and men alike, took an oath of allegiance to the New Order. The Revolution was an accepted fact. Louis was 'the King of the French.' France was a nation.[9]

9

As a soldier Bonaparte disapproved of the riot and mutiny at Auxonne: as a Corsican he realized the possibility of organizing something of the same kind at Bastia or Ajaccio. Already at Paris in 1788 his mind had been full of the grievances of his countrymen under the French rule. Already he was planning a series of *Letters on Corsica* which should rouse public concern. Now, in the summer of 1789, the outbreak of revolution in Paris and the provinces brought all his hopes to a head. It is impossible, he thinks, for the new France, the country of Liberty and Equality, any longer to reject the just demands of the Corsican patriots. They must be pressed with a fresh urgency: they may even be supported if need be, by an appeal to force. 'Remember,' he wrote to Pozzo di Borgo about this time, 'that fine saying of Montesquieu that Mirabeau contests in vain: The law is like those statues of the gods that are occasionally veiled.' But first Paoli had to be consulted. Bonaparte's letter, dated Auxonne, June 12th, 1789, is a highly rhetorical composition. 'I was born,' he begins, 'when my country was dying. Thirty thousand Frenchmen disgorged upon our shores, drowning the throne of liberty in a sea of blood—such was the hateful spectacle that offended my infant eyes.' During Paoli's exile his government (the government that Boswell admired) has been traduced, and the country cruelly oppressed. Unable to visit Paris, and sceptical of private appeals, he has decided to write a book, and to publish the misfortunes of his country. 'I am still young, and may be rash to undertake this: but I am upheld by my love of truth, of my country, and of my compatriots, and by the enthusiasm I never cease to derive from the prospect of an improvement in our state . . . Whether my book is successful or not, I am aware that it will raise up against me a whole battalion of French officials who govern our island, and whom I am attacking. But what matter, if it is in my country's cause? I shall hear the thunder of ill-will; and if the bolt falls, I shall take refuge in my conscience, recall the rightness of my motives, and be encouraged to face the storm.'

It was in this heroic mood that Bonaparte landed at Ajaccio at the end of September 1789. He must have felt as though he had stepped back into the reign of Louis XV. Corsica had hardly so much as heard that there was a revolution. The French *Intendant* had suppressed the decrees of the National Assembly. His troops still sported the white cockade. There was no National Guard; no Abolition of Feudalism; no Declaration of the Rights of Man.

The arrival of a Corsican officer in a smart French regiment who had first-hand knowledge of the situation, and could expound the foundation-deeds of the revolution, soon resulted in the wearing of the tricolor, the opening of a patriotic club, and the formation of a National Guard. An attempt by the *Intendant* to suppress the movement with the help of Swiss mercenaries was defeated. Bonaparte drew up an eloquent Address to the National Assembly, which he signed, together with his family and friends, and dispatched to Paris. 'For twenty years,' he declared, 'we have lived without hope, weighed down by the yoke of an arbitrary government. Now the happy revolution which has restored to mankind its rights and to France its Fatherland has revived our courage, and hope is born again in our oppressed hearts.' The Corsicans have heard that their claim to liberty has hitherto been rejected. They dispute the grounds of this judgment, and appeal for its reconsideration. 'Do you, the champions of liberty, deign for a moment to turn your gaze on us who have been for so long its most zealous defenders.'

This address was dated October 31st. Its dispatch was followed immediately by action. Within a few days Bonaparte appeared at Bastia, the capital of the island. He distributed a cargo of tricolor cockades which he had ordered from Leghorn, and headed a deputation to the *Intendant*, asking him to authorize the wearing of the revolutionary colours. This was at first refused; but an attempt to prevent it led to trouble; and when the troops fired on the armed citizens who formed the nucleus of a National Guard, public indignation was so great that the *Intendant* was forced to give way, and to admit the people to a share in the control of the town.

When a letter from the *commune* of Bastia reporting these events to their deputies was read in the National Assembly at Paris on November 30th, a decree was passed on the motion of Mirabeau declaring that Corsica was henceforth part of the French Empire, that its inhabitants should enjoy the same constitutional rights as other Frenchmen, and that all future legislation should apply to the island. It was a complete if temporary triumph for the Bonapartists.

It was a happy time for Bonaparte. He took his place in the ranks of the National Guard. He worked at his *Corsican Letters*, which might now be less propagandist, and more historical: not the sad lament of a land of oppression, but the proud epic of a land of freedom. He went for long walks about the island with Joseph and Lucien. He was even able to turn to good account a bout of fever which resulted from one of these excursions; for he extracted another four months' leave on medical grounds from a complacent Colonel; leave which he overstayed by many extra weeks, so that he did not finally rejoin his regiment at Auxonne until February 1791.

The return of the exiled patriot-dictator Paoli within less than a month of the rising at Ajaccio brought temporary peace into the troubled scene of Corsican politics. But would it last? Fêted in Paris, presented to the King, harangued at the Jacobin Club and the Town Hall, Paoli was welcomed at Ajaccio (whose deputation had included Joseph, and whose address had been drawn up by Napoleon) as an almost mythical liberator. He was now a man of sixty-five; he had not seen the island for more than twenty years; he had imbibed during his exile in England the opinions of a country at war with republicanism, and of a society which even the enthusiasm of 'Corsican' Boswell could hardly save from conservatism. He might well prove to belong to a world of lost causes and out-moded ideas. It was inevitable that Bonaparte's *Letters*, once more revised at a time of doubt and suspicion, should be propagandist and partisan.

10

Bonaparte left Corsica at the end of January 1791 to return to his regiment at Auxonne, taking with him his twelve-year-old brother Louis, and armed with certificates of patriotic zeal from his friends at Ajaccio which he rightly calculated would serve as well as a doctor's letter to justify his overdraft of leave, and to claim his arrears of pay. It pleased him, in his present mood, to travel Rousseau-like from Valence (February 8th), through the hill country of Drôme on foot, and to pen a letter to Fesch from a peasant's cottage at the little village of Serve, describing the spirit of the countryside: the people resolute, the soldiers patriots (but their officers aristocrats), most of the clergy assenting to the Civil Oath, and defying their bishops, a local club of 200 members, including women, but 'society' mostly partisans of an English constitution.

At the next stopping-place, Saint-Vallier, he is in another mood, and outlines *Reflexions on Love* which seem to derive from some *amour de voyage*: for this is a love which is not satisfied by friendship, and clings, like the ivy, to the first human being it encounters. But it leaves him still a young cynic. At thirteen, he thinks, the boy has his friend; at twenty-three the youth loves his mistress; at forty the man loves his fortune; and at sixty nothing but himself.

It may well have been more for the sake of his brother's education than his own comfort that he protested (in a letter to Le Sancquer, of the War Ministry), against his transfer to Valence which was gazetted on June 1st; for this coincided with his promotion to a First Lieutenancy in the Grenoble regiment, and involved his return to a station which he knew well, and where he had many friends.

Arrived at Valence, Bonaparte hired two small and barely furnished rooms from his old landlady Mlle Bou, for himself and his brother, whose education he was taking in hand, and about whom he wrote to Joseph (Easter Day, 1791) reporting good progress, and his popularity in local society. He soon became an enthusiastic member of the local Jacobin Club, and a regular reader at M. Aurel's *cabinet de lecture*; and though his old friend the abbé Saint Ruf was dead, and the Colombier family had moved away, he had many friends amongst the younger officers of the La Fère regiment, who shared his revolutionary views, and appreciated his readings from the Paris papers. Within two months of his arrival came the news of the King's Flight to Varennes—the event which more than any other divided republicans from monarchists, and decided the course of the Revolution. It decided Bonaparte's course, too. Hitherto divided between monarchy and republic, he can now doubt no more: he becomes a confirmed Republican.

A letter to M. Naudin at the same period (July 27th), adds a personal postscript: 'The southern blood in my veins runs as swiftly as the Rhone. So forgive me, if you find my scrawling hand difficult to read.' (It was the reason he always gave for his illegibility, that his thoughts moved too fast for his pen.) It must have been with no formal acquiescence that Bonaparte took the new oath of allegiance to the National Assembly replacing that taken in the name of 'Nation, King, and Law' two years before.

But however stirring the times, nothing will drag Bonaparte for long from his books; and the notes that remain of his reading at Valence are still the best indication of the way in which his mind was developing.

From Eustache de Noble's classical exposition of the Gallican answer to Bellarmine's Ultramontanism (*Esprit de Gerson*, 1691) he tabulates the arguments of either side, and shows that his sympathy is with Gallicanism. Some propositions from Rousseau's *Discours sur l'origine de l'inégalité* are punctuated with the refrain 'I don't believe a word of it' (*Je ne crois rien de cela*), and followed by his own *Réflexions sur l'état de Nature*, in which he denies that there was ever a time in the history of man when the faculty of feeling and reasoning did not involve some beginning of family life, society and morality—and therefore of inequality. He also takes up again the argument about Love which had been in his mind for months past, and composes an imaginary dialogue with Des Mazis, in which he contrasts his friend's devotion to his Adelaide with his own devotion to Corsica, and maintains that love of woman is incompatible with one's life-work and duty to society. Des Mazis replies, like any young lover, that Adelaide at any rate is not the sort of girl to interfere with her man's career; and that it is only too evident Bonaparte has never been in love. That was true enough. Bonaparte might love Corsica, but only as one can love an island. He had yet to meet Joséphine.

One product of Bonaparte's pen remains, and it is the most significant: that so-called *Discours de Lyon*. This was an Essay written to compete for a prize offered by Raynal through the Academy of Lyon. The subject set was: How can men be educated for happiness? (*Quelles vérités et quels sentiments il importe le plus d'inculquer aux hommes pour leur bonheur*). The essay is a sentimental, rhetorical, romantic effusion, but shows a genuine enthusiasm for 'the good, the beautiful, and the true' still unspoilt by personal ambition and worldly careerism. Morals and politics, Bonaparte asserts at the outset (with an eye on his judges), languished under kings, but have made a fresh start in an age of freedom. Man was born for happiness, and happiness consists in the satisfaction of his natural needs—physical and spiritual. He may be prevented from attaining it by lack of property and means: hence the value of the Spartan legislation of Lycurgus, or the Corsican regime of Paoli, which secured for everyone an opportunity for self-realization.

As for sentiment, there are moments in life—on a sea beach at sunset, under the stars at midnight, in the taper-lit gloom of St. Peter's, or as a castaway on the romantic isle of Monte Cristo—when one is overwhelmed with the beauty and the sadness of life, *l'électricité de la nature*; feelings only less powerful than those of home, of family, of young love, of laughter and of tears . . . No man can be truly happy unless he feels deeply. Yet sentiment must be ruled and ordered by reason, as it is (Bonaparte illustrates his point) in the great dramatists; and the reign of reason implies freedom to hold and express one's opinions. Here the essay loses sight of its argument awhile, and embarks on a fresh treatment of the theme of the dialogue on Love, to end with a death-bed discourse of an old man who has achieved happiness.

There is nothing original in all this, hardly a turn of thought or choice of words that would tempt the examiner for a College scholarship, to wonder whether there might not be a scrap of genius in the boy, and to put *alpha query* in the margin. But it shows an inquisitive and acquisitive mind; ideas (too many of them, perhaps) jostling for priority; an uncertain balance of sentiment and reason. One might fairly conclude that if some creative purpose were to come into this second-hand world it might strike order out of chaos, and produce greatness.

II

Bonaparte returned to Ajaccio for the fourth time early in October 1791, just before the election of deputies to the French Legislative Assembly—the body which took the place of the Constituent Assembly under the Constitution of 1791. His presence in the island had so often meant trouble that Paoli, at least, may well have regarded it with apprehension. 'The Corsicans as a whole,' he reported to Delessart, the Minister of the Interior, 'in spite of the insinuations and intrigues of a few malcontents [amongst whom no doubt he included the Bonapartes], are in favour of the laws involving the liberty of the monarchy [i.e. the Constitution of 1791], and are loyal to the sacred person of the King.' The news of the Flight to Varennes encouraged the rebels; but they were soon depressed by the report of the King's recapture; and when Paoli marched on Bastia with the National Guard the ringleaders fled by sea, and the rest submitted to disarmament and the garrisoning of the capital. When the elections came on three months later, Paoli was strong enough to secure the appointment of his own nominees,

Peraldi (commandant of the National Guard) and Pozzo di Borgo, and to exclude the Bonapartist candidates; but he had the tact to console Joseph, the least hostile of them, with a place on the Departmental Directory. The stage might now seem to be cleared for the second act of the benevolent dictatorship of which the first had been played twenty years ago.

But once more Paoli's plans were upset by the irreconcilable feuds of his Corsican subjects. The *émeute* of April 8th-12th, 1792, seems to have begun as an unpolitical quarrel amongst some of the waterside citizens (*quelques mariniers*) of Ajaccio; but when a detachment of a battalion of the National Guard, recently moved into the town under the command of Quenza and Bonaparte, tried to restore order, one of their officers was killed; and on the following days the affair developed into street-fighting between *mariniers* and *volontaires*, in which houses were set on fire, and civilians killed.

A number of reports of the affair reached the capital. That drawn up by Bonaparte in the name of his brother officers exonerates himself and his men, and places the blame on certain *malintentionnés* who incited the citizens against them, on the inactivity of the municipal officials, and on the refusal of Maillard, the commandant of the garrison in the citadel, to help the beleaguered National Guardsmen. But the almost unanimous agreement of other reports that the chief provocation came from the National Guard puts Bonaparte's version of the affair in a different light. If it is true that he and his superior Quenza barricaded themselves in the Seminary, carried off cattle and grain belonging to the citizens, shot down civilians in the streets, and refused to negotiate with a municipal deputation under a white flag, their action was deservedly repudiated by the military governor, and condemned by the *commissaire* of the Department, who ordered the 'compromised battalion' to leave Ajaccio, and to await further orders at Corte.

As soon as these hostile reports on the affair became public, Bonaparte saw that he was seriously compromised. Joseph wrote to him on May 14th saying that he had made his peace with Paoli, but that the general would not employ Lucien, or have anything more to do with the Buonaparte family (*il ne veut pas s'amalguer avec nous*); and he advised Napoleon to remove himself to France as soon as possible. He had in fact already started. Only in Paris could he hope to meet the charges that were being brought against him, to regularize his double employment as a Lieutenant of Artillery and an Adjutant-Colonel of the National Guard, and to be excused for once more outstaying his leave.

He could now better afford the journey. On October 15th, 1791, old Lucien Buonaparte had at last died, with the family round him, and the family gold under his bed, ready for distribution. He may not have said to

Bonaparte (as Joseph asserts) *Tu poi sarai un omone*—'you will be a great man'—but he left him enough cash to invest something in local *biens nationaux*, and to eke out his officer's pay.

12

Bonaparte arrived in Paris on May 28th. It was an interesting and exciting moment. The declaration of war against the Emperor on April 20th had united the people of France, but it had exasperated the quarrels of the politicians. The King's immediate supporters were either defeatists like Lamarck, who hoped for a successful foreign intervention, or careerists like Dumouriez, who planned to erect a military dictatorship on the ruins of the throne. The followers of Brissot were working for the fall of the King and a monopoly of power for their party. The Robespierrists prophesied defeat, and were equally afraid of a royalist, a military, or a *Brissotin* dictatorship. The initial defeats on the Belgian frontier (April 28th) turned public anger, exploited by the Robespierrists, against the *Brissotin* ministers, and they passed it on to the King. Two days after Bonaparte's arrival in Paris the Assembly decreed the disbanding of the Household troops which were the King's only protection against popular violence; and it was certain that some demonstration against the Tuileries would soon follow.

'Paris,' writes Bonaparte on May 29th, 'is in a state of great commotion. It is crowded with foreigners, and there is a great deal of discontent . . . The news from the frontiers is the same as before [*he means, it is news of defeat*]. We shall probably retire, and make it a defensive campaign. There is an enormous amount of desertion amongst the officers. The position is critical in every respect.' He is going to attend a session of the Legislative Assembly; 'it doesn't enjoy the same reputation (he notes) as the Constituent'; and it is clear that he already inclines towards the Robespierrist party, which had originated in opposition to Brissot's war policy during the winter of 1791-92, and consolidated itself during the disasters of the spring of 1792.

A fortnight later (June 14th) he writes again. He reports the fall of Brissot's ministry (June 13th), and its replacement by royalist nonentities; but notes that the new Minister of Foreign Affairs is De Naillac, a Valence acquaintance, who may be able to help him on. 'The country (so he sums up the situation) is being sniped at (*tiraillé*) by intense party spirit. It is difficult to follow the thread of so many policies. I don't know how it will all end, but I expect in something pretty revolutionary.' This impression is repeated with more detail on June 18th. The ministerial crisis mentioned on the 14th still continues. Dumouriez, *l'intrigant*, the King's accomplice in the dismissal of the *Brissotins*, has now shared their fall. The Assembly, alarmed at the weakness of the Executive, has appointed a Committee of Twelve 'to save the Republic.' An attempt on the part of the working-class *faubourgs* to force the King to accept decrees establishing a *fédéré* camp near Paris, and penalizing the refractory priests, and to restore the *Brissotin* ministers, has been stopped by the National Guard.

Two days later this attempt was renewed, with the connivance of the Mayor of Paris and the National Guard. Bonaparte was there, and described the scene in a letter to Joseph on the 22nd. 'The day before yesterday (he writes) seven or eight thousand men armed with pikes, hatchets, swords, muskets, spits and pointed stakes, marched to the Assembly to present a petition. From there they went on to the royal palace. The Tuileries garden was closed, and protected by 15,000 National Guards. The mob battered down the doors, forced an entrance into the palace, turned their guns on the royal apartments, razed four gates to the ground, and presented the King with two cockades—one white, and the other red, white and blue. They gave him the choice: "Make up your mind," they said, "whether you will reign here or at Coblentz." The king showed up well. He put on the *bonnet rouge*: so did the Queen and the Dauphin. They gave the king a drink. They stayed in the palace four hours. This event (he concludes) has provided plenty of material for aristocratic harangues at the Feuillants' Club. None the less, it is unconstitutional, and sets a very dangerous precedent.' Like many others of his age and temper he believed in the patriotic sincerity of the people but shrank from its excesses in action. He did not, he could not believe in the King; but he resented any attack upon the crown. He was accustomed to military discipline, and all his soldier's training revolted against the spectacle of a mob in arms.

The scene inside the palace, just described, he had at second hand; he had been sufficiently shocked by what he saw himself of the attack outside preceding the entry of the crowd. 'This June 20th' wrote the lawyer Lavaux, many years afterwards, 'I was walking aimlessly in the Tuileries gardens amidst the din of the armed mob invading the Tuileries, when I was accosted by M. Perronet, the engineer of roads and bridges. We were both deploring such an outrage to the royal dignity, when we were interrupted by a young man, whom I should have distrusted, but for M. Perronet's reception of him. He looked like a soldier: his eyes were piercing, his complexion pale; he had an uneducated accent, and a foreign name. He spoke his mind freely about the disorderly scene before us, and said that if he were king such things would not be tolerated. I paid little attention to this remark at the time: but later events recalled it to my mind; for the speaker was Bonaparte.'

If he were King. Was Bonaparte already looking so far ahead? His letter at least shows that he was a Government man and a careerist. He could not afford to make enemies. 'As things are,' he says, 'I see only one thing clear; I must keep on the right side of (*ménager*) those who have been and can be my friends.' He is, in this careful calculating mood, worried about his brother Lucien, who at the irresponsible age of seventeen is compromising the family by his indiscreet republicanism. He has written (Bonaparte hears from Louis) a *lettre sanguinaire* attacking one of the Corsican deputies, and wants to send a copy to Paoli. He pens a proclamation, to which his elder brother's answer is anything but sympathetic. 'It has too many words in it,' he says, 'and too few ideas . . . This is not the way to address the people.'

On July 3rd follows a letter (probably to his brother Joseph), containing Bonaparte's second thoughts about the Revolution. 'You know the history of Ajaccio,' he goes on: 'that of Paris is exactly the same, though perhaps people here are pettier, viler, more abusive, and more censorious. You have to look closely before you realize that enthusiasm is still enthusiasm, and that the French are still an ancient and independent people . . . Every individual is out for his own interests, and will forward them if he can, by insult and outrage; intrigue is as underhand as ever. All this (he confesses) discourages ambition . . . A quiet life, spent in the enjoyment of one's own tastes and of the affection of one's family—that, my dear friend, is the happiest choice, especially (he is cautious enough to add) if one has an income of £200 to £250 a year, and is between the ages of twenty-five and forty, when imagination torments one no longer, but is at rest.'

But this was only a passing mood of disillusionment. Bonaparte's family knew him too well to be taken in by it. Almost on the same day Joseph received a letter from Lucien (dated Ucciani, June 24th), in which this precocious youth spoke quite candidly of his elder brother. 'I can tell you in complete confidence,' he wrote, 'that I have always discerned in Napoléon a purely personal ambition (*une ambition tout à fait égoiste*), which overrules his patriotism (*son amour pour le bien public*). I am convinced that he is a dangerous man in a free state . . . He seems to me to have a strong leaning towards tyranny: I think that if he were a king he would certainly be a tyrant, and that by posterity and by every good patriot his name would be held in detestation.' Prophetic discernment!

A week after his letter of July 3rd Bonaparte's mood changed again. He heard from Lajard, the Minister of War (July 10th) that the *Comité d'artillerie* had reported in favour of his rehabilitation, and that he had better report for service, with a step up in rank, as Captain. It now mattered little that Lajard had also written (July 8th) to Maillard, the commandant of the regular troops at Ajaccio, agreeing that Quenza and Bonaparte were seriously to blame, and saying that he had put the case into the hands of the Minister of Justice. Justice moved so slowly that Bonaparte had little to fear from Dejoly, and nothing from Danton, who succeeded him after the fall of the throne. A letter to Joseph on August 7th shows that he is pleased with the outcome of the affair, and that life is once more interesting, even exciting. He is taking up astronomy, 'a splendid distraction, and a noble science,' easily mastered by a mathematician. He has finished his 'work'—he means the *Letters on Corsica*—corrected it, and made a fair copy: but it is not the time to print; and anyhow (he says) 'I have given up the petty ambition of authorship': in fact, he is off to his regiment, and active service.

Three days after this letter (1792) the event which he already foresaw took place. On the morning of August 10th—so Las Cases makes him tell the story—the tocsin rang and news came of the assault on the Tuileries. He hurried from his lodgings in the rue du Mail (it was not far, past the Palais-Royal and across the rue Saint-Honoré) to the Carrousel, the open space to the east of the royal palace. On his way, in the rue des Petits-Champs, he met a group of men carrying a head on a pike, who made him cry *Vive la nation!* ('and I made no bones about it, you can be sure'). Facing onto the Carrousel was a furniture shop kept by one Fauvelet, an old school-fellow of Brienne; and from this house he watched the whole attack on the Tuileries.

The defenders, he judged, had more force on their side, and the attackers less, than in the affair of Vendémiaire, in which he took part three years later; and if Louis XVI had only appeared on horseback, and appealed to the people (so Joseph reports him as saying), he would have won the day. After the palace was evacuated, and the King had taken refuge in the Assembly, Bonaparte ventured at some risk (*je me hasardai*) into the Tuileries gardens. It was cumbered more thickly than any battlefield with the dead bodies of the Swiss Guard, which were being outraged by decently dressed women. In the neighbouring *cafés*, crowded with citizens of better class, he found anger on every face and in every heart.

Las Cases is rightly suspect for his fashion of working up casual or scattered remarks of his hero into connected literary narratives: but there are details here—the correct names of the streets Napoleon would pass through, his unheroic behaviour, the scenes in the garden, or in the *cafés*—which bear the stamp of truth; and it can hardly be doubted that the experiences of the day (along with those of June 20th) had much to do with his lifelong distrust—yes, and fear—of civilian crowds, and anything resembling mob-rule.

One result of the revolution of August 10th was that the royal school of St. Cyr closed down on the 16th, and Bonaparte had to take his sister Elisa, whom his father had placed there, back to Corsica. If they started (as he told Joseph) on September 9th, he was in Paris at the time of the Prison massacres of September 2nd, which Las Cases makes him describe—though not as an eye-witness; and the date of his arrival at Ajaccio (probably October 15th) allows for considerable delay both at Paris and at Marseille, where he had to wait for a passage, and perhaps also for the draft of £260 which he received on account of pay due for the past year's service.[10]

13

As soon as he landed in Corsica, Bonaparte wrote to Lieutenant Costa (October 18th) about taking up his commission again in the National Guard. Though proud of the French victories reported from the Ardennes, Nice and Savoy ('the soldiers of liberty are triumphing everywhere over the mercenary slaves of tyrants'), he has for the moment given up his own military ambitions in the country of his adoption, and will strike one more blow for the country of his birth. This means attacking Paoli, who is now virtual dictator of Corsica, with control both of the regular troops and of the National Guard, and whose policy is as consistent with an English as with a French allegiance. He soon hears from his friend Saliceti in Paris (January 9th, 1793) that the *Conseil Exécutif* (the Provisional Ministry set up after August 10th), has considerable grounds of complaint against Paoli's regime, but that it is hoped that Corsica will share in the 'consolidation of liberty' to which he looks forward.

This rather mysterious phrase is explained by what follows. France has already been at war for nine months with the Emperor and his Prussian ally. It will soon be at war with England, perhaps the whole of Europe. The nation 'is fixed in a noble enthusiasm to win freedom at all costs'; but the politicians are engaged in deadly personal quarrels. The war is very expensive, but the country can carry on for another year. What Saliceti looks forward to is a popular rising, under Jacobin guidance, against the majority in the Convention, which will bring new life into the national effort: just such a rising as took place four months later, and swept the Brissotin party out of power. If Paoli is counting on the fall of the French Republic, then he will be completely deceived. On the contrary, once France is at war with England, Corsica will assume fresh importance as a possible naval base and source of supplies for the blockade of Toulon, and the republican government will have to make sure of their hold on it.

Bonaparte's first impulse, on receipt of this letter, was to go to Paris, and to join in the political campaign against Paoli; but he was diverted from this to a naval and military expedition against Sardinia which was being planned by the French Republic. Its objects are nowhere better expressed than in his own *Mémoire sur la nécessité de se rendre maître des îles de la Magdelaine*. The small islands called Maddalena and Caprera lie off the north-eastern point of Sardinia, and command the Strait of Bonifacio that separates it from the southern point of Corsica. This strait is on the short route from Marseille to Naples, and the long route from the Gulf of Lyon to the eastern Mediterranean: it was a key-point of naval strategy. The power which held the islands could protect South Corsican coasting vessels, secure the provisioning of Corsica from Sardinia, and prey on British shipping passing to and from the Levant. In order to secure this position Admiral Truguet was to bring a fleet from Toulon, and Paoli was to contribute troops of the line and National Guards from Corsica.

The affair was however mismanaged throughout, and ended in complete failure. The arrival of Truguet's fleet of Ajaccio led to quarrels and bloodshed between his marines and Paoli's National Guards. The Corsican detachment was withdrawn in the moment of success, in spite of the protests of Bonaparte and other officers. Twice in ten days (February 18th-27th) the expedition sailed, and twice it returned, leaving nothing but ill blood and a bundle of protests behind it.

The Maddalena fiasco furnished the Republican government with a fresh charge against Paoli. Already on February 1st Saliceti and two other commissioners had been empowered to investigate his conduct. When he pleaded ill-health as a reason for not leaving the island, the Commissioners sailed for Corsica (April 5th), the day after Lucien Buonaparte had induced the *société populaire* of Toulon to address to the Convention an attack on Paoli's regime. Unluckily for the Corsican this was the very moment of Dumouriez's treachery, and he easily fell under the same suspicion of intended dictatorship. The commissioners, to Lucien's pride (it was a triumph for a boy of eighteen), were instructed to arrest Paoli, and to bring him to Paris.

Napoleon, not as yet knowing his brother's part in the affair, and fearing (whether for Corsica or for his career) a premature break between Paoli and the Republic, had penned a rhetorical appeal from the Ajaccio club to the Convention defending Paoli against the charge of wishing to hand over the island to the British. But this did not prevent him from engaging in an attempt to recapture the citadel of Ajaccio from the Paolists. The adventure failed. He had to go into hiding at Ajaccio, whilst his mother and her children took refuge at their country estate of Milelli, leaving their town house to be sacked by the partisans of Paoli and Peraldi. The failure of a final attempt to recapture Ajaccio made it inevitable that the Buonapartes should fly again to Calvi, and thence make sail for Toulon. They landed there on June 13th, 1793. So, at the age of twenty-four, Napoleon ended his apprenticeship as a Corsican, and began his professional career as a Frenchman.

II

TOULON AND NICE

(1793-1795)

I

BONAPARTE had done with Corsica; but as the island of his birth faded from sight his active mind was still busy with the problems it presented. Not content with a series of Plans for a new attack on Maddalena, for the defence of the Gulf of Ajaccio or of St. Florent, he spent some hours, either his last on the island or his first on the mainland, composing a report on the *Position politique et militaire du département de Corse.*

But even professional soldiers cannot escape the ties of family and property; and the position of a party of Corsican refugees in a foreign land during a time of civil war and food shortage—though they had a small relief allowance from the French government—was almost desperate. Bonaparte's first care was to settle his mother and her children, first at La Valette, a small village east of Toulon, and then, when Toulon became dangerous, at Bausset, Mionnac and finally Marseille. His second anxiety was to obtain promotion and better pay for himself in the army, so as to be in a position to support his family and forward their interests. Fortunately he was able to get in touch with Du Teil, a brother of his old artillery instructor, who commissioned him to provide forges (*fours à réverbère*) for heating cannonballs to fire from the coastal batteries at passing British ships.[1]

Within a month occurred an even better opportunity for advancement. On July 11th Couthon reported to the National Deputies at Paris that a departmental congress held at Lyon had chosen to repudiate the authority of the Convention, and had passed a sentence of outlawry on the *Montagne*, the Jacobin party that controlled the government. Almost at the same time it was heard that Marseille was also in arms against the Paris government, and was sending troops to the help of Lyon. A force was at once mobilized near Lyon to deal with this threat, and was placed under the orders of Jean-François Carteaux, once a soldier, but of recent years a painter of military pictures and portraits, and now adjutant-general in the republican army. Bonaparte was ordered to report for service with this force.

He arrived at Carteaux's headquarters near Avignon on July 15th, and found himself in command of the artillery attached to the expedition. Within ten days (July 26th) Carteaux had driven the Marseillais out of Avignon—a success said to have been due to Bonaparte's guns posted at a point on the west bank of the Rhone from which they silenced the rebel artillery in the town. During the next three days Bonaparte, rejoining the force on the east bank, took part in the operations which drove the enemy across the Durance, and occupied Tarascon and Beaucaire. On August 20th he was probably present at the decisive victory of Salon, from which Carteaux pressed on to occupy the rebel headquarters at Aix, and, only five days later, to enter Marseille.

From Aix Bonaparte seems to have returned to Beaucaire, Arles and Avignon, and to have stayed at this last place for several weeks, before going north again to add his guns to the artillery bombarding Lyon. It was while at Avignon (August 25th) that he wrote to the Jacobin Minister of War, Bouchotte, asking for a lieutenant-colonelship in the army of the Rhine. He did not get it: but Bouchotte brought his name to the notice of the *Commissaires* of the army of the Midi.

It was at this moment, too, that he published the most considerable of his political pamphlets, *Le Souper de Beaucaire*. Its sub-title sufficiently explains its form: *Dialogue entre un Militaire de l'armée de Carteaux* (that is, Bonaparte himself), *un Marseillais, un Nîmois et un Fabricant de Montpellier, sur les évènements qui sont arrivés dans le çi-devant Comtat à l'arrivée des Marseillais.*

The scene of the dialogue is Beaucaire, and the date July 29th, 1793, the last day of the annual fair for which that small town on the Rhone, half way between Arles and Avignon, was famous. It was intended to record the exploits of Carteaux's army at Avignon, and to warn the Marseillais that they had better surrender, not fight it out. Bonaparte already saw that the best political argument was a victory in the field.

In the first pages of the pamphlet the *militaire* tells the man of Nîmes what really happened at Avignon: how the rebel levies from Marseille, marching to the help of Lyon, were forced to retreat by Carteaux's smaller and weaker force of republican troops. He goes on to warn Marseille that its boasts will come to nothing: it had better think again, remembering the superiority of Carteaux's artillery(here the writer speaks as an expert), the inferiority of defence to offence (a favourite maxim of Bonaparte's), and the recent subjugation of the Corsicans (a piece of personal experience). Marseille does not stand alone; but there is no more prospect of success for a league of the whole Midi: it would be beaten in the field, and riddled by factions at home. Finally, backed by the men of Nîmes and Montpellier, the *militaire* turns on the people of Marseille, sweeps aside their fear of the Jacobin regime, exposes their royalism and treachery (with a telling comparison to Paoli), and forces their representative, willy-nilly, to admit the desperate condition of his town, whose only hope lies in the mercy of the republican army. *Vous voilà enfin raisonnable*, remarks the *militaire*; and the dialogue ends happily with the prophesy that a repentant and republican Marseille *sera toujours le centre de gravité de la liberté*; whilst the man of Marseille, as the losing side, pays for the considerable number of bottles of champagne consumed during the evening.[2]

2

The French Portsmouth (as Marseille was Southampton), the headquarters of the Mediterranean fleet, and the home of a large population of dock-yard workers, Toulon had been sharply divided, since the early days of the revolution, between the aristocratic and popular points of view, the monarchical and the republican interests. In March 1789, a dockers' revolt, aided by volunteers from Marseille, had been put down by the *bourgeois* National Guard, and the town had seemingly acquiesced in the constitu-tional government of the National Assemblies of 1789 and 1791. On July 28th, 1792, when the *fédérés* from the Midi, singing the *Marseillaise*, were within sight of Paris, a working-class revolt under the *société populaire* of Toulon murdered the departmental *directeurs*, and set up a *clubiste* regime at once republican and proletarian. This only lasted a year. In July 1793 a coalition between the royalists and the *bourgeoisie*, controlling the National Guard, organized permanent meetings of the eight *sections* of the town, with a central executive *comité général*, supplanting the *société populaire*, and purging the municipal and departmental bodies. The new regime was nominally republican; but its sympathy with Marseille, and its half Girondin, half royalist leanings, soon threw it onto the side of the *fédéraliste* revolt against the Jacobin government at Paris. Six weeks after the expul-sion of the Girondin deputies from the Convention (June 2nd) the Toulon Committee joined with the similarly constituted *comité général* of Marseille in declaring against the Jacobins, and listening to overtures from the na-tional enemy, the English.

The ruling fact in the economic life of both ports at this time was the British blockade. A fleet under Lord Hood, based on Gibraltar, 700 miles to the south-west, but with a safe anchorage in the roads of Hyères, only fifteen miles east of Toulon, and drawing supplies from Genoa, Leghorn and Naples, could prevent any ship going in or out of their harbours. This was damaging enough, even when the townspeople could rely upon getting the necessities of life from the neighbouring coast-lands. But when republican troops, under orders from Paris, advanced upon them from east and west, consuming or stopping their supplies, there was no help for it: they must either make terms with the blockading fleet, or starve. Thus from the middle of July both towns were in communication with the enemy. When the *comité général* of Toulon first considered Lord Hood's terms it did not think the position so critical as to justify their acceptance. But within a week the arrival of *commissaires* from Marseille with authority to treat with the British forced the issue. On the night of August 23rd Hood's terms were accepted, and the surrender carried out, in spite of the opposition of the republican Saint-Julien, the *de facto* commander of the French fleet in the harbour (its nominal commander, the royalist Trogoff, remained on shore).

In view of the sequel it is not unimportant to note the terms of this surrender. 'If a candid and explicit declaration in favour of the monarchy,' Hood had said, 'is made at Toulon and Marseille, and the standard of Royalty hoisted, the ships in the harbour dismantled, and the ports and forts provisionally put at my disposition . . . the people of Provence shall have all the assistance and support His Britannic Majesty's fleet under my command can give . . . And whenever peace takes place . . . the port, with all the ships in the harbour, and forts of Toulon, shall be restored to France, with the stores of every kind.' The reply of the Toulon committee was that it was the unanimous wish of the inhabitants to adopt the monarchy set up by the Constituent Assembly of 1789 (that is, the monarchical Constitution of 1791 abolished by the revolution of 1792), and that they had therefore proclaimed the Dauphin king as 'Louis XVII.' They would fly the white flag of the Bourbons. They would hand over the citadel and forts to the British, whom they trusted to provide for the victualling of the town, and for its defence against the republican armies. The ships and forts were to be restored at the re-establishment of peace.

The few realists within Toulon who suspected British designs on their port and fleet had good reason for distrusting this agreement. Burke wrote to Sir Gilbert Elliot that it was 'worth twenty victories.' 'What an event this has been for Lord Hood' wrote Nelson to his wife from Naples: 'such a one as History cannot produce its equal; that the strongest place in Europe, and twenty-two Sail of the Line, etc. should be given up without firing a shot. It is not to be credited.' The best part of the enemy fleet was now *hors de combat* for the remainder of the war. In the event of peace being signed, its return to a Bourbon king, set on his throne by allied arms, would be no great danger. In the more likely contingency of the recapture of Toulon by the republicans, the promise to restore the ships would not hold.

The town and port of Toulon stood at the north-east corner of a bay, the small roadstead (*petite rade*), three miles long from east to west, and one mile wide from north to south; the southern exit, three-quarters of a mile wide, led into the big roadstead (*grande rade*), a bay of the same shape and size as the *petite rade*, but open to the sea south-eastwards. The town and port of Toulon were overlooked by the great ridge of Mt. Faron (1800 feet high) to the north-east. On the east shore fortifications had been provided against attack from the Italian side. The more open west side had not been so protected; and Carteaux's troops, advancing from Marseille, would find it easy to occupy the hills of Ollioules, four miles to the north-west, and to advance up to the western shore of the *petite rade*. This inner harbour, the only safe anchorage for the allied fleets, was reasonably secure so long as its enclosing arms were held by the batteries of Fort la Malgue on the east (described by Bonaparte as 'one of the most carefully constructed forts' in France) and Balaguier and l'Éguillette on the west. The town itself could be held, so long as the forts on Mt. Faron and to the immediate east (St. Catherine) and west (Malbosquet—a weak but well sited defence) could beat off attacks, and so long as the fleet, its only source of supply, could remain at anchor in the roads, and keep up communications with the garrison.

It was from the first the opinion of the navy that this could be done, and of the army that it could not. Hood was an optimist. But of the generals—Mulgrave, O'Hara, Dundas—each seemed more pessimistic than his predecessor. How indeed could so extended a position be held by so few men, and most of them untrustworthy? The only troops fit to fight beside the 2000 British, they believed, were 1500 (ultimately 2200) Sardinians. The 4000 (ultimately 7000) Neapolitans were well equipped and well intentioned, but had never been under fire before and 'did not like danger.' Austrian troops to the number of 6000 had been promised, and might have turned the scale; but they never arrived. The 6000 Spaniards were a poor substitute for them. They refused, up to the time of O'Hara's appointment, to take orders from the British commander, considering that their numbers entitled their commander, Gravina, to be generalissimo; and they 'always ran away, officers and men together.' If only two battalions of British troops could have been sent from Gibraltar, the situation might have been saved. But they, too, never arrived. It was in fact impossible, with 12,000 or 15,000 mixed troops, and a fleet under fire from the shore, to hold a scattered line of forts on a fifteen mile front, against a force always equal in numbers, and in the end far superior, fighting with the enthusiasm of one nation and one cause.[3]

3

On August 29th, only four days after the capture of Marseille, Carteaux arrived at Ollioules, five miles west of Toulon, and Lapoype at La Valette, half that distance east of it, in order to isolate the town from its sources of supply in the surrounding country. Soon the town, though open to the slopes of Mt. Faron on the north, was closely invested to the east and west, whilst the Anglo-Spanish fleet, uncomfortably crowded within the *petite rade*, came under long-range fire from French guns at the west end of the bay.

What happened next is best told in the words of the chief republican representative. 'The plan that we have adopted,' writes Saliceti on September 26th, 'is to burn or drive away the enemy fleet from the roads, and, so far as Toulon itself is concerned, to cut all communications inwards or outwards. This was the only practicable plan, in view of the small numbers of men we have.' As for the fleet, that was a job for the artillery, and the artillery alone. 'We had some heavy artillery at Marseille; but it was in a bad state, there are few means of transport in this district, and repairs and transport together have caused us a week's delay. Dommartin's injury (*he was wounded in the first day's fighting at Ollioules*) left us without anyone to command the artillery. Then we had a wonderful stroke of luck: we stopped citizen Buonaparte, an expert captain of artillery (*capitaine instruit*) on his way to the army of Italy, and ordered him to take Dommartin's place.'[4]

Meanwhile the seriousness of the threat to the fleet, if the French established guns commanding the inner harbour, was appreciated by the British, who on the night of the 25th occupied the high ground on the western point of the *rade*, established there Fort Mulgrave (which the French called *Petit Gibraltar*), and brought up floating batteries to support the position. There would still have been time for the French to throw this defence back, if strong enough forces had been employed; but the few men sent forward were repulsed; and next day it was too late. Thus, when Saliceti wrote on the 26th, he could only report that his plan had miscarried, and that the siege must now become a matter of time and numbers.

But within three days of his arrival Bonaparte established a battery half a mile west of Fort Malbosquet, and drove away some British gunboats that had approached the shore. Two days later he advanced his guns to the shore, and drew a heavy counter fire from the fleet. His intention was to provide artillery cover for a fresh attack on the western promontory, the occupation of which would force the British fleet to retire.

But this plan required an able and enterprising general. Carteaux, who was neither, and who had made matters worse by quarrelling with Lapoype, was superseded, first by Doppet, the captor of Lyon (an ex-doctor and journalist in place of an ex-artist), and a few days later, when Doppet admitted that the affair was beyond his powers, by Dugommier, who had returned to France from distinguished service in the West Indies, and was described by Napoleon as 'a real soldier, covered with scars, and as dauntless as the weapon he carried.' The Committee also considered it advisable to give Saliceti the help of a civilian with some military experience, and sent Barras from Lyon (October 29th). He did not arrive at Toulon until the end of November, when the plans for the final assault were far advanced, and took no large part in it: but this did not prevent his claiming the credit.

With Dugommier in command, and reinforcements arriving, the plan for the final assault was energetically pushed on. At 5 a.m. on the dark and wet morning of December 17th, after forty-eight hours' bombardment by Bonaparte's heavy guns, an infantry attack was launched, and within two hours the critical positions of Fort Mulgrave, l'Éguillette, and Balaguier were captured, with 500 prisoners. The rest of the garrison were either killed or forced to re-embark. Bonaparte himself took part in the assault, and was wounded in the thigh by a British bayonet: he showed the scar and told the story of it at St. Helena.

Simultaneously Lapoype's troops scaled the heights of Mt. Faron to the north of the town, and captured its forts; but the attack on Fort la Malgue, on the east side of the harbour, which would have completed the success of the plan, seems to have been abandoned. The allies were therefore able to use the eastern beaches to take off the remains of their land forces. For, at a council of war held early on the 18th, it was decided that the positions lost on land could not be recovered, and that, since their loss, the fleet could not longer remain safely in the roads. It was necessary to acknowledge defeat, and to evacuate the town.

What, in any case, was Toulon worth to the British cause, deprived of the help of Lyon and Marseille, and cut off from all the surrounding districts? It was still worth the one thing for which, in professional eyes, it had always stood: its fleet. The admirals, Hood and Langara alike, were realists. They must withdraw their troops before they were driven into the sea. They might rescue as many of the royalists as possible from republican vengeance. They would at any rate carry away or destroy whatever they could of the French ships and naval stores. Land power would once more be defeated by sea power.

The decision was quickly taken, and promptly acted upon, not so much because the situation had grown suddenly desperate, as because it had been so long foreseen. But for the same reason some blame attaches to the disorders which attended its execution. The retreat became almost a flight. 'There has seldom been crammed more misery and more horror in a short space than we have witnessed these last four days,' wrote Elliot on December 20th; nor is it difficult to see that he holds his own friends partly responsible. If the troops had been more slowly withdrawn—in particular, if the Neapolitans had remained on shore till the evening of the 19th, as ordered— more of the civil population might have been saved, and more of the French ships destroyed.[5]

4

Such was the stage—a small one but set with all the characteristic features of revolutionary warfare—on which Bonaparte played his first big part. What exactly did it amount to?

Several fortunate accidents determined the conditions of his service at Toulon. He was given temporary command of the artillery, always an independent arm in a French army, owing to the fact that Dommartin was wounded—one of only three casualties—in the first action of the siege. He was given it by Saliceti, who was his friend, and a fellow-Corsican, and who by good chance had been attached to the army before Toulon whilst waiting for the reinforcements he was to take to Corsica. Never more than a *chef de battalion* (October 18th) he might at any moment be superseded by a senior artillery officer. General La Salette of the army of the Eastern Pyrenees had been ordered to take over the command; but owing to the miscarriage of a letter he did not arrive at Toulon until it was all over.

By another stroke of good fortune, the representative who shared with Saliceti the burden of the siege was Gasparin, a fellow-Corsican; and it can easily be read between the lines of the official reports that the three men were good friends and good comrades, sharing the same ideas as to the conduct of the operations. Generals and representatives might come and go: Carteaux, Doppet, Dugommier, Ricord, Robespierre, Barras, Fréron: but these three, until Gasparin's illness and death in November, bore most of the responsibility; though, being Corsicans, and men of second rank in the republican hierarchy, they got least of the credit.

Bonaparte's correspondence, which is always more trustworthy than the *Memoirs* Napoleon dictated thirty years later, gives ample evidence of the energy with which he organized the artillery during the two months of waiting between the failure of September 15th and the success of December 17th. A series of letters shows him impressing upon the Committee of Public Safety (October 25th) the necessity of a proper siege train; asking Sucy, the war commissioner at Valence, for horses, oxen and drivers for his guns (November 3rd); and again, next day, for spare parts, etc.; explaining to the Minister of War (November 14th) his plan for the reduction of the town, and reporting the consequential decisions arrived at; even giving Dupin, an official at the War Office, an account of the action of November 30th, and (December 24th) of the retreat of the British fleet, four hours before his guns were in position to open fire on it.

It has been seen that the *coup de main* which so nearly succeeded on September 15th-19th followed immediately on Bonaparte's arrival at Toulon, and may be fairly attributed in part to his insight and energy. How much was due to him of the plan which finally brought about the fall of the town? Except for some despairing talk, after the failure of the *coup de main*, of undertaking formal siege operations, it seems to have been agreed from the first both by the men on the spot and by the directing mind at Paris, which the correspondence shows to have been Carnot's, that the only way to capture Toulon was by establishing batteries on the high ground on the western arm of the bay, and so driving away the enemy fleet. This was the plan mentioned by Saliceti's letters of September 10th and 26th. This was the idea behind the attack of September 15th. It is reasonable to suspect that, after its failure, Bonaparte was behind Saliceti's and Gasparin's efforts to have Carteaux superseded, and their reiterated demands (backed on October 23rd by a memorandum from Bonaparte himself) for men, guns and ammunition.

The crucial decrees of the Committee of Public Safety dated October 28th and November 4th resurrect the original plan of September 10th, with additions made possible by the greater resources now available, and Barras is sent with fresh authority to see that it is carried out. But it is clear from Saliceti's letter of November 9th that the plan has been anticipated, and that the preparations for carrying it out are well advanced, before his arrival at the end of the month. Dugommier accepts the situation as he finds it, approves of the dispositions made by Bonaparte, and carries through a Council of War on November 25th the plan which Saliceti had forecast in his letters ever since the affair of September 15th.

This was in fact the plan which Bonaparte, as anxious as any other young republican officer to keep his name before the authorities in Paris, had sent to the Minister of War on November 14th, the plan which Saliceti had adopted, on his advice, for the capture of the town by what was essentially an artillery operation. There is no reason to deny him the credit for this, nor for the consequential orders passed at the council of war on the 25th, and forwarded by him as its secretary the same day; nor for the energetic and skilful disposition of the artillery which made success possible. But the plan was not new, nor was it his own: it had been drawn up originally by the generals and representatives before Bonaparte arrived at Toulon. Nor was it different from the plan favoured at Paris. The plan of September 26th (says Saliceti in his account of that operation) 'was exactly the same as the one you had sent us from Paris'; and it was a revised form of this plan that Carnot drafted on November 4th, ten days before Bonaparte sent 'his' plan to the Minister of War.

In view of these facts it is not difficult to account for the failure of the real captors of Toulon to get the credit for what they had done. True, General Dugommier's dispatch on the action of November 30th, read in the Convention on December 6th, said that 'Amongst those who most distinguished themselves, and helped me most to rally our men and lead them on, were citizens Buona-Parte, commandant of artillery, and Arena and Cervoni, adjutants-general.' (They too were Corsicans.) But in his dispatch of December 19th reporting the capture of L'Éguillette, whilst saying that 'the representatives of the people, Robespierre, Saliceti, Ricord, Fréron, were with us; they set our brethren an example of the most devoted heroism,' he made no mention of Bonaparte.

As for the representatives themselves, each was so anxious to figure well before the Convention that he would hardly allow any merit to another—still less to any of the soldiers. Augustin Robespierre's letter to his brother Maximilien is mainly concerned with his own bravery. Fréron's report to the Committee made out that he had played as large a part in the affair as Robespierre or Saliceti. The hero of Barras's report to the Convention (October 15th, 1795) was, as one would expect, Barras himself; as he was again of Merlin's official report the following day. Four days later Berruyer was mentioned, and further names refused: though later in the same sitting Barras signalized Bonaparte's services, probably to justify his appointment as second in command of the army of the Interior. This may seem an ungracious treatment of one who had played so big a part, and so recently, in the reduction of the rebel seaport. But it must be remembered that it was a moment when everyone who was not a proved patriot was a possible traitor; and that the first question asked before a military appointment was made would be, not, Is he a good soldier? but, Is he a good Jacobin?

The politicians might be suspicious, jealous and self-important. The Representatives who had experience of Bonaparte's work saw to it that he was promoted to the rank of general (December 22nd, confirmed by the *Conseil Exécutif* six weeks later), as a recognition of 'the zeal and intelligence of which he had given proof in his part in the surrender of the rebel town.' But the most convincing testimony is that of Bonaparte's brother officers, who knew a good soldier when they saw one. Doppet, a straightforward and modest man, spent a week with the Toulon army in the middle of November. 'I had brought with me,' he writes in his *Memoirs*, 'from the army of the Alps a senior general of artillery, and an excellent man, named Du Teil. He visited with me the batteries established before my arrival, and I noticed with as much satisfaction as surprise that this old artilleryman praised all the dispositions made by young Bonaparte, then no more than a lieutenant-colonel of artillery. It gives me pleasure to say that this young officer combined with plenty of talent an unusual degree of courage, and quite tireless activity. Whenever I visited the positions held by the army I always found him at his post. If he needed a moment's rest, he took it on the ground, wrapped in his cloak. He never left the batteries.' The Chevalier Du Teil himself, the brother of Bonaparte's old instructor, who might have taken over the command, professed himself unequal to the task. In any case there was no need for him to do so. 'Words fail me,' he wrote to the Minister of War, Bouchotte, 'to describe Bonaparte's merits. He has plenty of knowledge, and as much intelligence and courage; and that is no more than a first sketch of the virtues of a most uncommon officer (*ce rare officier*).'

Nor would Bonaparte himself hesitate to exploit his success, if he could. 'Even if his country were to be ungrateful to him (wrote Dugommier), this officer would see to his own promotion.' He knew, as he said in after life, that Toulon was the beginning of his military reputation. But hero-worship has done no service to history by exaggerating his exploits or antedating his greatness.[6]

5

It was by now becoming more evident every day that all operations on the southern front of the Republic, naval as well as military, depended on the question of supply. Marseille and Toulon had been reduced by the threat of starvation; whilst the forces which reduced them were themselves half starved. The armies of the Pyrenees to the west and the armies of Italy and the Alps to the east were alike perilously short both of food and of munitions. The political and economic discontents of the Midi were both a cause and a result of lack of food: farmers would not grow or sell for the doubtful gains of a depreciated paper currency; munitions could not be produced by undernourished workers. The Jacobin government was blamed for the inevitable results of economic causes. Both in order to suppress disorder and to supply the armies it was essential that food should be imported by sea—from Genoa, from Leghorn, from Tunis, from Malta. The minutes of the Committee of Public Safety and the correspondence of the *commissaires* are full of these preoccupations.

In view of the danger of the direct route from Tunis, Malta, or Naples through the straits of Bonifacio, supply ships bound for Nice, Toulon, or Marseille hugged the west coast of Italy: from Leghorn and Genoa onwards they might hope for some protection from the French navy and shore batteries. This was where Bonaparte's services would be useful. His skill in positioning batteries, and his expert knowledge of the 'new weapon,' cannon-balls heated in *fours à réverbère*, qualified him for the inspection and improvement of the coastal defences. With his headquarters first (January-February 1794) at Marseille and Toulon, and then (March) at Toulon and Nice, he travelled up and down the coast, trying to make the route from Nice to Marseille safe for food-ships.

His letters show how busy he is. On January 4th he writes to the Minister of War on the need of bringing the defences of Marseille up to date: they were laid out, he says, in complete ignorance of the principles of fortification. He is installing *fours à réverbère*, and manning the guns with National Guardsmen rather than sailors, who had better be at sea. On February 12th he sends a similar report on the coastal defences generally; and on the 28th writes again insisting on the need of fortifications to protect the convoys. When the Committee of Public Safety leaves his letters unanswered he writes to Mazurier, *adjoint au Ministère de la Guerre*, or to Maignet, *représentant du peuple*, pressing his demands.

Of the activities behind this correspondence let one instance suffice, which has been recorded in some detail. A month after the evacuation of

Toulon part of the British fleet was still using the anchorage within the islands of Hyères as a base from which to impede French access to the port. This was to be the scene of an attempt to repeat the tactics which had driven the fleet out of the Toulon roads. 'In agreement with General Mouret,' wrote Saliceti to the Committee of Public Safety on January 28th, 'and with Buonaparte, Commandant of the artillery, we considered that the only thing to do was to attempt a night landing on the islands, taking mortars with us, in order to bombard the fleet and force it to quit the anchorage. With this intention we had moved some troops towards Hyères, and made every preparation which could contribute to the success of our design, which, however difficult to carry out, was nevertheless possible, and involved gains of the highest value. Whilst I was busy ordering all these dispositions I was informed that the fleet was showing signs of leaving the roadstead. I went at once to Hyères with generals Mouret and Buonaparte. We found that the fleet, consisting of fifty-six vessels, sixteen of them warships and the rest transports, were under sail, and heading for Italy. We embarked for the islands, with a battalion, which we left there to prevent any further landings by the enemy. The English, on their departure, had set fire to the small forts, and broken up the fourteen or fifteen guns contained in them. This small mishap was remedied by the guns which I at once had landed on the islands, and by the batteries in whose construction we are at present occupied.'

The day following this dispatch (January 29th) Bonaparte himself wrote to Dupin at Toulon, saying 'I am back from the islands of Hyères, where I am constructing a number of batteries to put these islands in a state of defence, and to enable them to furnish a safe base for our ships against a superior fleet.' A month later (February 28th) he sent details of the work. In this action Saliceti and Bonaparte anticipated the orders of the Committee of Public Safety (January 29th) to the Minister of Marine, to send officers to Toulon, and to take steps to drive the British ships away from Hyères: another instance of Corsican initiative and enterprise.[7]

6

With Marseille re-fortified, Toulon freed from the enemy, Hyères secure against attack, and the coastal batteries ready for action, it was possible to make plans for a forward move on the Italian front, where two armies, those of Italy and of the Alps, had been stationary ever since the autumn of 1792. There were good reasons for their failure to advance. In the spring of 1793 the government's attention had been concentrated on the Belgian front. The dismissal of Girondin officers, as a result of the political revolution of the summer, and the difficulty of replacing them; the constant changes in the higher command—the Army of the Alps had seen five Commanders-in-chief come and go in three months; the diver-

sion of troops and reinforcements to Lyon and Toulon; the needs of
coastal defence; and with it all the hold-up of supplies, had disorganized
and discouraged operations. Only the unreadiness of the Austrians, and
the approach of winter, rendering the Alpine roads impassable, enabled
the Republicans to hold the line they had won. Obviously things could
not remain so, when the snows melted, and the enemy began to move
along the coast, and towards the crest of the Alps.

During the winter Nice became the headquarters for a reorganization
of the armies on the *amalgame* principle (stiffening the recruits of 1793
with a proportion of seasoned veterans), and for setting up a proper system of commissariat. The Jacobin government, inspired by Carnot, was
determined to end the stalemate on this front, and to carry out an offensive campaign, as soon as the season allowed. The discipline of the army
would be improved if it had something to do: the problem of commissariat would be solved (paradoxical as the notion might seem) if the army
lengthened its backward communications, and reached forward to the in-
exhaustible supplies awaiting it in the rich lands of northern Italy. Every
step eastwards along the coast shortened the supply route from Genoa.
Every inch gained beyond the crest of the Alps brought the snow-bound
and starving troops of the Little St. Bernard and Mt. Cenis nearer the
smiling plains of Lombardy, upon which so many generations of travellers before them had gazed with delighted anticipation.

Operations were to begin earlier than anyone, especially the Austrians,
had expected. On January 25th the Committee of Public Safety dispatched
orders to General Dumas, who had only just taken over the command
of the army of the Alps, to capture the enemy forts on the Little St.
Bernard and the Great and Little Mt. Cenis. This was no light matter.
There were some 47,000 raw and half-armed troops on this front: the line
of demarcation between the armies of the Alps and Italy had not been
fixed: the reorganization (*embrigadement*) ordered by the Committee
had not yet been completed (February 25th). It was not until March 26th
that Dumas was able to report that he was ready to move. In the middle
of April the Mt. Cenis was attacked, but without success. But on the
24th Gaston, his *commissaire*, wrote again, reporting, in the flamboyant
terms usual on such occasions, the capture of the Little St. Bernard; and
that of the Mt. Cenis followed on May 12th.

These successes were in great part due to the co-operation of the army
of Italy, whose advance on the right drew off Austrian troops that might
have defended the passes on the left. On this southern front the key point
was the little port of Oneglia, situated in a Piedmontese *enclave* within
Genoese territory between Nice (forty miles west) and Genoa (sixty miles
east). As early as January 23rd Saliceti, Moltedo and Ricord, writing from
Toulon to the Committee of Public Safety, had enclosed a letter from

Tilly, the French Resident at Genoa, recommending an attack on Oneglia, whose seizure would be easy, and would be welcomed by the Genoese anti-Austrian party. Carnot (January 30th) approved. On March 9th the Committee, seeing the present impossibility of succouring Corsica, authorized the diversion of troops intended for this purpose to the army of Italy, and gave orders for an expedition to attack Oneglia by sea, so as to avoid the violation of Genoese territory. Saliceti, who was at this moment submitting plans for an Italian campaign, was transferred to the army of Italy to supervise these operations. With his usual energy and independence he soon decided that it would take too long to organize an attack by sea, and that it was necessary to risk the difficult land march, and the violation of Genoese neutrality, in order to anticipate a possible counter-move on the part of the Austrians.

Once more Bonaparte was summoned to carry out the details of a plan which he may very well have recommended. 'I have ordered *général d'artillerie* Buonaparte,' writes Saliceti, 'to go to Nice, so that when I arrive there I may find all the necessary dispositions made to ensure the triumph of the Republican arms in the expedition with which we have been entrusted.' His confidence in the young artilleryman was completely justified. On April 6th the *commissaires* at Nice reported to Paris that the attack had begun. Two days later they wrote from Oneglia itself announcing the capture of the town—a success so rapidly won that 'the republican gunners had no time to open fire on the brigands of Oneglia; but they performed prodigies of courage and skill in dragging their guns over inaccessible mountain country.' This was, in fact, the first time that a French army was accompanied by a properly organized mountain artillery.

It was at this moment, and doubtless in view of this exploit (April 4th), that Augustin Robespierre, who had shared with Ricord and Saliceti the supervision of the campaign, wrote to his brother Maximilien in Paris, at the end of a long letter about the political temper of the army and of the country: 'I add to the names of patriots whom I have mentioned to you citizen Buonaparte, an exceedingly meritorious general in command of the artillery (*général chef de l'artillerie d'un mérite transcendant*). This last is a Corsican. My only ground for trusting him (*Il ne m'offre que la garantie*) is that he is a Corsican who has resisted Paoli's flattery, and whose property has been devastated by that traitor.' Such a testimonial from the brother of the most powerful man in France was a reward that many of Bonaparte's fellow-officers would have envied; but it was to prove dangerous a few months later, when anyone known to be in favour with the Robespierres was in danger of proscription.[8]

7

The seizure of Oneglia and of the crest of the Alps was only a preliminary move; but it was part of a preconceived plan the further steps of which were now to be put into operation. To invade Austria by way of Lombardy was a classical manœuvre, as old as Catinat, Vendôme and Maillebois. The best method of attack had been worked out by Bourcet, the teacher of Guibert and Du Teil, before the Revolution, and had been embodied in the scheme drawn up by Carnot in January 1794. The St. Bernard and Mt. Cenis passes were the gates to the valleys converging on Turin. Oneglia was not merely a nest of pirates, but the first step on the road to Saorgio, which guarded the Col di Tenda on the right flank of the valleys by which the advance from the passes towards Coni and Turin would have to be made.

No time was lost in pressing on, after the easy capture of Oneglia (defended by no more than 500 men), towards the more difficult objective of Saorgio, whose garrison of 8000, now warned about the French advance, might be expected to put up a strong resistance against the army of 'heroes, republicans and philosophers'; but the place was taken, at the cost of considerable losses, on the 28th, within less than three weeks of the fall of Oneglia.

After this exploit there was a fortnight's pause. On May 13th Dumerbion wrote to the Committee that he was ready to advance again, but that he needed another 20,000 men, and 6000 horses. On May 15th Robespierre and Ricord called a conference at Colmars, at which the commanders of both armies were present, to discuss plans for their combined operations, as enjoined upon them by a letter from the Committee dated May 8th, and probably just received. The basis of their discussion was a scheme drawn up by Bonaparte, of which the main feature was a drive by the army of Italy into the valley of the Stura, where alone (he held) it would be possible to join forces with the army of the Alps. This *Plan pour la seconde opération préparatoire à l'ouverture de la campagne de Piémont* was forwarded to Paris by Ricord and Laporte on May 21st. It was followed on June 20th by a revised Plan providing for an advance of the army of Italy down the Stura valley (the head of which was now cleared by the capture of the Col d'Argentière) to its junction with the Tanaro, whilst the army of the Alps was to follow its advance via Château-Dauphin from the north-west, to prevent any outflanking moves by the enemy.

Bonaparte's revised plan was never carried out. Although Carnot had sanctioned the preparatory moves for an invasion of Italy, there is reason to think that he was not happy about the undertaking. As a soldier he disliked the risk involved in denuding the Midi of troops to strengthen

an army fighting beyond the French frontier. As a statesman he shrank
from the policy of conquest, and feared the political consequences of an
invasion of foreign soil. His attitude towards territorial gains on the lower
Rhine had shown itself in the remark that 'aggrandizement of that kind
would only weaken France, and land her in interminable warfare.' He
would feel even more strongly about the invasion of territory 400 miles
from Paris, and on the wrong side of the Alps. At any rate he persuaded
the Committee to write to the *commissaires* of the two armies on July 3rd,
countermanding Bonaparte's plan, and prescribing a 'limited offensive.'
The army of Italy was to make a demonstration against Coni with all its
available forces, 'in order to terrify the enemy, and bring about an insurrection which may lead to our possession of the place; and if these tactics
are successful at Coni they are to be repeated at Demonte and Ceva.
Nothing more was to be attempted until the communications of the
armies were sufficiently secured by strong garrisons at Nice, Oneglia and
Toulon.'

It has been suggested that Carnot's rather sudden distaste for the Italian
offensive was due to political differences with Maximilien Robespierre,
whose brother Augustin was its most prominent exponent; and that the
change of policy at the front was the first shot in the duel between the
Robespierrists and the anti-Robespierrists in the Jacobin government
which ended in the proscription of Maximilien, along with his brother,
three weeks later. But this theory seems to read too much back into
events which carry their own explanation. The reasons given by Carnot
for stopping the Italian offensive are adequate, and need carry no political
implications. There is no sign in the many dispatches that passed between
the Committee and the armies of two policies, or two allegiances. There
are none of the jealousies and quarrels that impeded the operations at
Toulon. Augustin Robespierre might write to his brother about the
Hébertist and Dantonist factions; but the generals seem to have been
singularly uninterested in the politics of Paris; and the news of Thermidor
came to them with a shock of surprise.[9]

8

Since his letter of April 4th, Augustin Robespierre had worked with
Bonaparte at every turn of the campaign: Tilly, the French resident at
Genoa, regarded the general as the intimate adviser (*favori et conseiller
intime*) of the *commissaire*. His brother Joseph had taken advantage of
the credit he enjoyed with the government to obtain an appointment in
Corsica. There is no hint in the correspondence of the Committee of any
charge against either Robespierre or Bonaparte until after Thermidor.
Then, of course, suspicion attached to all Robespierrists, and treachery lay
concealed beneath their most innocent acts.

The evidence for what follows is taken from the correspondence of Bonaparte's fellow-countryman and fellow-worker, Saliceti. The most trusted of the representatives (or *commissaires*) in the Midi, he had been summoned from Toulon, where he was supervising the preparations for the Corsican expedition, to take part in the Oneglia-Saorgio operation. Before this was finished, at the moment of the capture of Ormea (April 18th) news came from Toulon that Admiral Martin had three times disobeyed orders to put to sea, from fear of superior British forces. Saliceti was ordered to return, and investigate. On his arrival (April 30th) he found that the orders to sail had been countermanded. With his usual independence of mind and liking for active operations, he wrote to the Committee of Public Safety criticizing this decision. Now if ever, he maintained, was the moment to make a naval demonstration. *Il faut de l'audace* (though Danton, who coined the phrase, had just been guillotined); and they could trust him not to take unnecessary risks, even in succouring his own countrymen of Corsica. On May 29th the fleet left harbour, and Saliceti with it; and again on June 5th. On the 9th he reports, from on board the *Sans-Culotte*, an action off St. Tropez. On July 8th he is back at Toulon, and under orders to rejoin the army of Italy. He fears it is too late to expect further successes in the Piedmont campaign, and says that his health has been so ruined by the hard work of the last ten months that he would like to be recalled. It is clear that he is discouraged as well as exhausted; and he may be feeling (though there is no direct evidence of this) a change of tone in the letters from Paris, as opposition grows within the government to the Robespierrist party which has hitherto supported him.

It is against this background that Saliceti's two letters of August 6th have to be read. They were written from Barcelonette (a small town in the Basses-Alpes department, about half way between Nice and Grenoble) which he had reached after a difficult and dangerous journey from Nice, and where he had found Albitte and Laporte. In his first (covering) letter he begins by congratulating the surviving members of the Committee of Public Safety on the fall of Robespierre. He then explains his part in the business of one Haller, a banker whom he had orders to arrest at Nice, but who (he found) had left for Genoa, with a passport granted by Ricord. Haller was suspected of embezzlement of national funds, and Ricord was a friend and colleague of Augustin Robespierre; both, then, might be involved in a 'Robespierrist intrigue.'

Saliceti's second (official) letter, written on the same day, in collaboration with Albitte and Laporte, elaborates the suspicions that were now spreading from Paris to the army. Augustin Robespierre and Ricord, it is alleged, had persisted in ignoring the advice of the other representatives. The 'secret' plan of campaign (that is, Bonaparte's plan of June 20th) was known not only to everyone in the army of Italy, but also to the enemy: how else is one to account for the counter-attack which held up the advance over the passes, or for the three months' delay of the army of the Alps? Then comes the passage which concerns Bonaparte. 'Lastly,' write the representatives, 'you should be informed that Buonaparte and Ricord himself admitted to Saliceti that the siege of Coni was only a feint (*qu'on ne ferait que semblant d'assiéger Coni*), but that nothing was to be said about this to the representatives with the army of the Alps. So we conclude (the letter goes on) that we were deceived by intriguers and hypocrites.' There has been a defeatist plot amongst the commanders on this front, inspired by Ricord and Robespierre; and their tool had been Bonaparte: *Buonaparte était leur homme, leur faiseur de plans, auxquels il nous fallait obéir.*

Further evidence for this plot was not lacking. An anonymous letter from Genoa had warned the representatives that a sum of a million *livres* (£250,000) was being conveyed there 'to bribe a general.' Saliceti had already reported the suspect Haller's hurried departure from Nice to Genoa with a passport from Ricord; now he remembered that Bonaparte too had gone there with a similar passport on July 11th, and had remained there till the 21st. This was enough to shift attention to the Corsican. 'All our suspicions were concentrated on him . . . The first step to be taken (they end) is to get rid of (*écarter*) Ricord and Buonaparte: we shall take the responsibility of arresting them, seizing their papers, and sending them to you at Paris.'

More 'evidence' was quickly forthcoming. Lyon was said to be a Robespierrist centre. Augustin Robespierre had his creatures everywhere in the army of Italy, and had plotted to raise the whole Midi against the Convention. From Nice on August 11th Albitte encloses 'a letter about Ricord and Bonaparte,' and joins Saliceti in advising that, in view of the Robespierrist plot, the lateness of the season, and the Anglo-Spanish threat to the Midi, the army should remain on the defensive. Subsequent letters (August 19th, 1793) reported further details of the Haller affair: but nothing emerged to implicate Bonaparte, except the coincidence of their presence at Genoa. What the Committee at Paris made of these revelations is not recorded; but they gave Carnot a good occasion to reassert his dislike of the Italian adventure, and to reiterate his orders for a 'limited offensive' (August 13th).

Bonaparte had returned from Genoa to Nice on July 23rd, in order to be present at the marriage of his brother Joseph to Mlle Clary (August 1st). Arrested on August 9th, he was imprisoned in Fort Carré near Antibes. Two letters have survived written during his fortnight's incarceration. The first was addressed to his friend Junot, who had apparently offered to help him to escape from prison: 'Mankind may be unjust to me (he wrote), but it is enough that I am innocent. My conscience is the court before which my conduct is to be tried. My conscience is calm, when I question it. Take no action, therefore: you would only compromise me.'

The other letter is addressed to the representatives Albitte, Saliceti and Laporte. Sending them, as requested, what information he can as to the coastal defences and the artillery, his two special charges, he adds: 'I had begun a written account of the coastal defences, but I do not feel able to finish it. Now that I have apparently lost the respect of free men (*âmes libres*) my soul is kept calm by the feeling of my conscience; but the feelings of my heart are overwhelmed; and I feel that with a cool head and a hot heart one cannot reconcile oneself to living on long under suspicion.'

This letter was written on August 14th. Ten days later Bonaparte was again a free man. In their report to the Committee explaining his release Albitte and Saliceti mentioned the 'serious suspicions we had as regards Ricord and Buonaparte,' and continued: 'We told you that both men would be sent (to Paris): Ricord you recalled; Buonaparte, as we have already informed you, we placed under arrest. As a result of examining his papers, and of all the evidence that we have collected, we have come to the conclusion that there is no positive ground to justify his further detention; especially now that we have found the *arrêt* issued by Ricord, in virtue of which this representative sent General Buonaparte to Genoa; and we are convinced how useful this soldier's talents can be—talents which, we cannot deny, are becoming very necessary in an army which nobody else knows so well, and in which men of his type are extremely difficult to find. We have accordingly set him at liberty, but without restoring him to his post, in order to get from him all the information we need, and to ensure that by his devotion to the state, and the use made of his knowledge, he may regain credit and be given a fresh post which he is fully capable, after a time, of filling successfully, and in which the circumstances and critical position of the army of Italy might oblige us to reinstate him provisionally, whilst waiting for any instructions you may give us with respect to him.'

There can be little doubt that the cautious and involved terms of this letter were meant to guard the representatives against the possible displeasure of the Committee. If Bonaparte's colleagues had really believed him guilty, they would have sent him under arrest to Paris: the reason for his journey to Genoa (the only ground of suspicion against him) was found upon inquiry to be perfectly innocent: his services were indispensable to the army: the best thing to do was to keep him in prison long enough to satisfy the alarmists, and then to restore him to the responsibilities (though without the rank or pay) that were his before.

In fact within six days of his release Bonaparte is found sending Berlier a budget of complaints, and demanding an answer. 'It is not for those who are not at the controls (*au centre*),' he goes on, 'to criticize the work-ing of the marchine.' On August 1st he writes with equal assurance of his position to Deschamps, the *commissaire*, 'They made a great mystery out of my journey to Genoa: it even gave me a few moments of boredom [*he means, ten days in prison*]; but that's all over now.' As for the Com-mittee, it seems to have accepted the action of the representatives without question. The 'Robespierrist plot' was good for political propaganda: it could not be allowed to compromise the military situation.

Such were the circumstances which, if Nice had been nearer Paris, or the representatives less sensible men, might have cost Bonaparte his career, if not his life.[10]

9

Saliceti was the more anxious to release Bonaparte from prison, and to restore him to the army, because, with his usual enterprise, he intended to use what remained of campaigning weather in 1794 to improve the positions of the army of Italy, with a view to next year's invasion of Italy. The 'defensive' strategy that he and Albitte had recommended to the Committee on August 11th included the capture of Demonte, perhaps Coni, and certainly Ceva; and for this purpose they asked for reinforce-ments, and for a new general to take the place of Dumerbion. To explain their plans they enclosed a map showing all the positions held by the army of Italy. This letter crossed one written by Carnot on August 14th, enjoin-ing a complete cessation of active operations on the Italian front, and ordering the army to settle down in winter quarters; another letter a week later arranged for the garrisoning of the coastal towns, evidently at the expense of the army of Italy.

To these orders the representatives apparently turned deaf ears. In their second letter from Nice on August 24th, by which time they would have received Carnot's orders of the 14th, they announce the opening of an offensive by the army of the Alps against Demonte and Coni which will enable the army of Italy to take Borgo and Ceva, and threaten Savona; for they have just heard that 4000 Piedmontese troops are on their way to seize Savona, and it is essential to anticipate them. 'We shall do our duty zealously (*chaudement*),' they add, 'up to the very moment of our re-call'; words which seem to show that they know they are acting against orders. They ask for sanction, indeed, but do not intend to wait for it. On September 23rd Saliceti and Albitte were able to write triumphantly that, after releasing 6000 men for the garrison of Toulon, they led 10,000 against the enemy, drove them out of Cairo onto the heights of Dego, defeated them there, and camped on the battlefield. The enemy have re-treated towards Alexandria, and cannot now occupy Savona. The repre-sentatives are satisfied with what they have done, and are coming home. In a letter written from Nice a few days later Saliceti takes credit for an offensive which has saved a dangerous situation, assured Genoese neutrality, and put the army in a favourable situation for next year's campaign.

What was Bonaparte's share in this brilliant little campaign? His first plan, accepted by the representatives at the conference at Colmars, and sent to the Committee on May 21st, had been made unnecessary by the capture of the Col d'Argentière on June 8th. His second plan, dated 'Nice, June 20th,' had been countermanded by the Committee on July 3rd, and indefinitely postponed by the fall of the Robespierrist faction. Augustin Robespierre, who had gone to Paris at the end of June, took with him not only this plan, but also an explanatory 'Note on the political and military position of our armies of Piedmont and of Spain,' in which Bonaparte insisted on the need of giving priority to the Piedmont campaign: that was to be the underlying principle of the next three years' operations. He does not propose a winter campaign; but he is dissatisfied with the front at present held by the armies, and ends by saying that 'if they can secure winter quarters on enemy territory, and force the Emperor to make a diversion in strength, the campaign will have achieved its object, and paved the way' for the final defeat of the Austrians.

Bonaparte's mission to Genoa, which brought him under suspicion of Robespierrism, was no doubt connected with this forward move of the army of Italy. His release from prison was due to the need of a plan for the limited offensive which Saliceti substituted for the unlimited defensive ordered by Carnot, in view of the Austrian threat to Savona; and it was this plan, based upon Maillebois's campaign of 1745, which led to the victory of Dego on September 21st. 'It is to the ability of the general of artillery,' wrote Dumerbion to the Committee of Public Safety, reporting the action, that I owe the clever combinations which have secured our success.'

10

All the operations of 1794 on the southern front had been based upon the triangle formed by Toulon, Corsica and Nice. At each point an enemy force had to be encountered: at Toulon, the disaffection of the Midi, at Nice the hostility of Piedmont and Austria, in Corsica the Paolists and the British fleet. The British occupation of rebel Toulon had forced the republican government to concentrate its first measures upon that point. The necessity of provisioning the army of Italy, and securing its position on the Alpine frontier, had directed most of their efforts, during the summer and autumn, upon Nice and its supply lines.

But the *raison d'être* of Toulon was Corsica, and the command of the western Mediterranean, without which any advance eastwards from Nice was dangerous, if not impracticable. It was therefore always part of the French plan to equip and safeguard Toulon as a naval base, to construct and man a fleet, to relieve the French garrison in Corsica, to secure the coastal supply line, and to drive the British out of the western Mediterranean. In Bonaparte's letter of September 23rd, 1794, to Moltedo reporting the success of the Dego campaign he ends by saying that it has opened the way for an expedition against Corsica, which will be nothing more than a walk-over (*une promenade militaire*), and will drive the British from their last foothold in the Mediterranean.

Orders written by Carnot directed that an expedition for the conquest of Corsica was to be undertaken *dans le plus court délai*; and that 12,000 men were to be drafted for this purpose from the army of Italy. Sailing with a northwest wind from Toulon, the expedition would land at S. Fiorenzo or Ajaccio. It was to avoid unnecessary action until the arrival of the ships from Brest, which were due to sail soon; when they had joined company, it should seek battle, and destroy the British fleet in the Mediterranean.

The weakness of this scheme was that it put the cart before the horse. Whatever the strength of the French ships (and Nelson, writing from Leghorn on October 31st, admitted that 'although many of them are old, yet they have fitted them well enough for an Action, if it should be necessary'), it would be impossible to land troops on the island without first defeating the British fleet. It was at any rate just such an adventure as required the trusted energy of Saliceti; and it is no surprise to find him at once (November 9th) charged, under the *commissaire* at Toulon, Jeanbon St. André, to accompany the expedition, and to use his local knowledge in the occupation of Corsica.

This was the more important, as Saint-André was dissatisfied with the strength of the forces available (November 12th), especially in view of the reported return of the British fleet (fourteen or fifteen ships of the line) to S. Fiorenzo (December 3rd). Whilst Saliceti writes optimistically (December 24th) that the British, even if superior in numbers, will not risk an action so far from their bases, Saint-André with equal pessimism (December 29th) refuses to send the fleet out so long as the enemy keep up the blockade of Toulon. 'He disapproves of the expedition,' wrote Saliceti on January 5th; 'he complains openly that the Committee has not adopted his plan; and assuredly that is not the way to encourage the crews.'

It is at this point that Bonaparte once more comes to the front. Writing from Nice on December 5th he instructs Monceaux at Toulon as to the arrival there of both field and mountain artillery, the first by land, the second by sea, obviously intended for the Corsican expedition: and by January 12th he is informing Deschamps, a *commissaire des guerres* who has asked for employment *à l'expédition maritime*, that his application comes too late. Evidently he is once more at Saliceti's side, all the more indispensable because he too is a Corsican.

But the clash between Saliceti and Saint-André was so serious that the Committee had to make up its mind between them. Ritter urged that Saint-André, *le moderne Neptune*, a man whose head had been turned by too much power, should be recalled (January 6th); but he was too influential to be sacrificed; and the opportunity was taken of the technical ending of Saliceti's mission (January 29th) to summon this *cher collègue* politely to Paris, and to send Le Tourneur to report on the situation. Le Tourneur reported (February 18th) in favour of Saliceti, and advised the adoption of his plan for a naval offensive; with the sensible proviso that the fleet should not be encumbered by a convoy, but should aim simply at seeking out and destroying the British ships, either by action at sea, or, if they took refuge at S. Fiorenzo or Leghorn, by artillery bombardment from the shore, as at Toulon.

This was Bonaparte's speciality. Accordingly he sailed with his fellow-officers Junot and Marmont on his first naval expedition, and took part in the only naval action of his career. Le Tourneur took the fleet to sea under Admiral Saint-Martin, after many delays (the Sirocco was not after all under the control of the Committee) on March 5th. After one success, the capture of H.M.S. *Berwick*, seventy-four guns (March 8th), he was brought to action off Genoa, and after a three days' running fight had to take refuge again in the Golfe Juan, after losing his biggest ship, the famous *Ça Ira*, and the *Censeur*; whilst *Victoire* and *Timoléon* were too badly damaged to fight again (March 15th). Though this defeat might pass for a victory, and be *considéré comme très glorieux pour la marine française*, it ended a chapter of Mediterranean history, and left British predominance unimpaired. By an ironical stroke the Brest squadron of six ships of the line, three frigates and one corvette, whose help might have turned the scales in the French favour, arrived at Toulon (though in a battered condition) on April 2nd, only a week after Le Tourneur's ships had limped back to port.[11]

On April 30th, 1795, Bonaparte wrote to J-J-B. Gassendi, an ex-aristocrat artillery officer, regretting that he had not been able to get him the promotion he had hoped; but he was moving (*je passe*) to Paris, and there he would try to secure him the management either of the Arsenal at Toulon, or of the munitions factory at Valence. There may have been some boastfulness in this; but it seems hardly consistent with the idea that Bonaparte's summons to Paris was a mark of disapproval or a threat of degradation. He may have been suspected, as a report about this time by General Schérer alleged, of 'too much ambition and intriguing habits for advancement.' But he knew that he had friends in high position in Paris, and possessed professional talents that were not too common in the republican armies. He was confident that he would make good. After staying with Marmont's family at Châtillon-sur-Seine, he reached the capital, in the company of his brother Louis and his friends Marmont and Junot, at the end of May.

II

Paris in May 1795 was at the height of the Thermidorian Reaction. During the six months since the closing of the Jacobin Club (November 12th, 1794) a series of measures had marked the return of the moderate republicans to power. A committee had been appointed to draw up a constitution; the seventy-three Girondin 'protesters' and the survivors of their twenty-two prescribed leaders had been restored to the Convention; Carrier, the terrorist of Nantes, had been guillotined; the *maximum* (price-control) had been abolished; and the anti-Girondin fête of May 31st had been struck off the calendar. A month ago Barère and other Jacobin leaders had been deported as a result of the rising of the 12th Germinal. Two days before Bonaparte left Marseille for Paris (April 6th) Fouquier-Tinville, the Jacobin Public Prosecutor, had been condemned and executed. Less than a week before his arrival at the capital the rising of the 1st Prairial (May 20th), had been decisively defeated by the Convention and the army, and the spectacular suicide of seven of the last Jacobin leaders showed how complete was the overthrow of a party which did not reappear in the streets of the capital for more than thirty years.

Bonaparte's letters to his brother Joseph describe the state of Paris at this time. The first, dated May 28th, speaks of the terribly high prices which were one of the underlying causes of political discontent; 'it will soon be impossible to live: people are awaiting the harvest with impatience.' Six weeks later (July 12th) he writes again, describing the hectic life of fashion which sparkled against the drab background of poverty and discontent: 'here in Paris, luxury, enjoyment, and the arts are resuming their sway in surprising fashion. Yesterday *Phèdre* was put on at the Opera—a benefit performance for a retired actress. Though the seats cost three times as much as usual, the house was crowded out as early as two o'clock. Smart carriages and fashionably dressed people are once more in the streets; they have the air of waking up after a long dream, and forgetting that they ever ceased to display themselves. The book shops are open again. There is a succession of lectures on history, chemistry, botany, astronomy and so forth. The place is crammed with everything that can distract, and make life agreeable. No one is given time to think. Anyhow, who could be a pessimist in this mental workshop, this whirlwind of activity? Women are everywhere—applauding the plays, reading in the book shops, walking in the Park. The lovely creatures even penetrate to the professor's study. Paris is the only place in the world where they deserve to steer the ship of state: the men are mad about them, think of nothing else, only live by them and for them. Give a woman six months in Paris, and she knows where her empire is, and what is her due.'

It is not difficult to read between the lines of this letter Bonaparte's pre-occupation with two interests of which his life had been starved during the years of campaigning in the south—books and women. It is hardly too fanciful (provided fancy be not taken for fact) to imagine him turning over books at the second-hand counter, attending scientific lectures, and penetrating into some professor's study: everywhere with an eye for the inaccessible beauties who shared his tastes. Sometimes he is so bored with his idle life that he would as lief be quit of it. 'Life,' he writes to Joseph on June 24th, 'is an unsubstantial dream that soon fades away': or, on August 12th, 'I hardly care what happens to me. I watch life almost indifferently . . . Since a chance meeting with death may end it all at any minute, it is stupid to worry about anything. Everything disposes me to face my destiny without flinching. At this rate, my friend, I shall end by not stepping out of the way of a passing carriage.' But a few days later a stroke of good fortune ended this state of indifference and fatalism.

On June 22nd Napoleon had told his brother that he was appointed a Brigadier-General in the army of the West, but not in the artillery. 'I am ill,' he added, 'and must take two or three months' leave. When I am fit again, I shall see what is to be done.' The illness (it can hardly be doubted) was a convenient excuse for refusing an unwelcome command, which would keep him away from the capital—the centre of political influence and the market for military talent. He was still in Paris at the end of July, when he told Joseph that he was interesting himself in his brother's possible appointment as *chargé d'affaires* for the Republic in Italy. A few days later he wrote again, reporting the victory over the royalists at Quiberon; and again sending Joseph a passport, and a letter from the Foreign Office to the French minister at Genoa, asking his assistance in his brother's affairs.

He is still in Paris in mid-August, when quite suddenly his luck changes. On the 17th he is once more explaining (to Sucy, the *commissaire ordonnateur*) why he has not taken up his command in the army of the West: 'I am refusing the job: plenty of soldiers will make better brigadiers than myself, but very few can command artillery more successfully. I am keeping in the background, confident that those who can appreciate my services will be aware how unjustly they are being rewarded.' Three days later his calculations had their reward. On August 20th he tells Joseph that he has just been 'attached to the *bureau topographique* of the *Comité de Salut Public*, to direct the movements of the armies, in place of Carnot. The appointment is a great compliment (*très flatteur pour moi*).'

At once his world is changed. Joseph has only to ask for the Turkish Consulate, and a ship will be ready to sail from Genoa to Constantinople. He is thinking already of buying a country estate. Soon (August 25th) he is *accablé d'affaires* all the afternoon, attends a meeting of the Committee at five, and another at eleven which may go on till three in the morning. It is the young artilleryman who sends the veteran victor of Valmy plans for his new campaign (August 23rd), and writes out, for Doulcet's signature, his Instructions from the Committee. What more could ambition desire?

Nevertheless he did not give up the attractive idea of foreign service—it might be in Russia, or in British India (both ideas had previously attracted him), or of becoming military attaché to the Porte: and it is worth pausing a moment to consider what estimate Bonaparte made of himself at the moment of his unexpected success, and what was thought of him by his colleagues.

There remains amongst his papers a *Note du général Buonaparte*, drawn up on August 30th, applying for the Turkish appointment. 'General Buonaparte (it runs) who has acquired a certain reputation during his command of the artillery of armies in different circumstances, and particularly at the siege of Toulon, offers to go with a government mission to Turkey. He will take with him six or seven officers, each an expert in some special branch of the art of war. If, in this new career, he can render the Turkish armies more formidable, and the fortresses of the Turkish empire impregnable, he will consider that he has rendered a signal service to his country, and, when he returns, to have merited her gratitude.'

Bonaparte was not content to put his own case: he asked the most influential of his friends to support it. In the margin of his confident proposal Doulcet de Pontécoulant, a new member of the Committee of Public Safety, has written: 'Brigadier-General Buonaparte served with distinction in the army of the Alps, in which he commanded the artillery. Seconded for duties with the Committee of Public Safety, he has worked zealously and accurately in the part of the war section entrusted with plans of campaign and the supervision of land operations; and I have pleasure in stating that I am indebted to his advice for the greater part of the useful measures that I have proposed to the Committee with regard to the army of Italy and the Alps. I recommend him to my colleagues as a citizen who can be profitably employed in the service of the Republic, either in the artillery, or in any other branch of the army, or even in the department of Foreign Affairs.'

Debry, another prominent Thermidorian, adds a further note: 'I agree with the views of my colleague Doulcet about Brigadier-General Buonaparte, whom I have seen and interviewed. I think that for the reasons which have determined both his opinion and mine the Committee of Public Safety should hesitate to banish (*éloigner*) from the Republic, particularly at this moment, so distinguished an officer. My opinion is that the Committee should recompense him for his services in the first instance by promoting him in the artillery; but without prejudice to a subsequent consideration of his proposal, if he persists in it.'

As a result of these recommendations, Bonaparte's appointment to the army of the West was cancelled (September 15th), and he remained in the *bureau topographique*. 'The Committee has decided,' he wrote to Joseph on September 5th, 'that it is impossible for me to leave France whilst the war continues. I am going to be reinstated in the artillery, and I shall probably stay where I am at the Committee.' Again, next day, 'Whatever happens, I have nothing to fear. All the important people, of whatever party or opinion, are friendly to me. Mariette would do anything for me—you know what he thinks of me. I am on intimate terms with Doulcet. If my hopes are matched by the good luck (*ce bonheur*) which never deserts my undertakings, I shall be able to make you happy, and give you all you desire. Tomorrow (he adds) I shall have three horses; then I shall be able to go about a bit in my private carriage, and get through all the business I have in hand. Bear my interests in mind, for I am set on having a house of my own.' And only two days later his mood of elation breaks out again; 'I see nothing ahead of me but occasions of pleasure. Even were it otherwise, it would still be right to live in the present: a brave man recks nothing of the future.'

Seeing life so rosily, and able for the first time to indulge himself in an establishment, and perhaps a wife, it was not likely that Bonaparte would long regret the loss of a more adventurous commission. Soon he would be involved in a fresh political crisis, giving a new turn to his career. Three years later the expedition to Egypt fulfilled more than he had ever dreamed of an independent command in the Levant.

12

A more important motive than his distaste for service with the infantry was at this time keeping Bonaparte in Paris. He was shrewd enough, and sufficiently in touch with public opinion, to know that a political crisis was at hand which might put new men into power, and would certainly bring opportunities for advancement of which full advantage could only be taken by those who were on the spot.

The National Convention was at its last gasp. The Commission nominated on April 18th to draw up a new Constitution had reported on June 23rd. After two months' debate the Constitution of the Year III was voted on August 22nd. It only remained for the Convention to be dissolved, and for the new Assemblies—the *Anciens* and the *Cinq-Cents*—to take its place. That the Assembly which had 'saved the country' should disappear before the war ended was a rash expedient justified only by the long-standing demand for a constitution, and by the recurrent hope that with a change of government would come an improvement in the two great afflictions of the day: inflation and food-shortage.

The men of 1789 had never forgotten the quixotic and disastrous measure which in 1791 excluded the deputies of the Constituent Assembly from membership of the Legislative Assembly: but whilst as statesmen they wished to avoid a repetition of this mistake, as politicians they sought for a means of retaining their power and their pay. It was accordingly proposed, as a corollary of the new constitution, that the Lower House of the new Legislative, the Five Hundred, which was to be renewed as to one-third of its members every year, should be composed in the first instance, as to one-third, of new members, and as to two-thirds, of ex-members of the outgoing Convention. The 'Decree of the Two-thirds' which embodied this proposal was published on August 22nd; and in case the electors failed to respond, and returned less than the two-thirds required, a further decree arranged for its co-option by those who were so elected.

The *assemblées primaires* (parliamentary constituencies) all over the country were now asked to vote for or against the acceptance of the Constitution; it was left uncertain whether their votes would also cover the two-thirds decree. After a troublesome month of dissension and disorder it was announced on the first day of the new year (September 21st, 1795) that the constitution had been accepted by 914,000 votes to 41,000, and the two-thirds decree by 167,000 votes to 95,000. (The 'final' figures a few days later made it 1,000,000 against 50,000 and 205,000 against 108,000.)

If the high proportion of abstentions showed that many people were indifferent to all constitutional change, there had been plenty of evidence throughout the country of a royalist desire for a Restoration, of a religious campaign for the re-establishment of the Catholic Church and of Jacobin resentment against the attempt of the Thermidorians to remain in power. In Paris eighteen Sections demanded a recount: crowds gathered in the streets; shots were fired; and the Convention prepared to deal with one more insurrection. After four days of indecision Barras was entrusted with the defence of the Convention: under him were Bonaparte (not officially, but effectively, second in command) and four other generals. The Louvre and Tuileries were strengthened with artillery; but orders had been given not to fire first. It was not till the evening of October 5th (13th Vendémiaire) that, after beating off several attacks, Barras took the offensive.

One of the last posts held by the insurgents was the church of Saint-Roch in the Rue Saint-Honoré; but Carlyle's famous 'whiff of grape-shot' by which Bonaparte dislodged them is described by the latest historian of the day as a legend. Thibaudeau's account is that the attackers, confident of success, made the mistake of advancing in columns down the open

streets, but had none of the *élan* of their predecessors of 1792, and took to
their heels when fired upon. None the less it was a miraculous deliverance. Bonaparte's own account of the affair to his brother Joseph (dated 2
a.m. on October 6th) runs as Caesar might have written it. 'At last,' he
says, 'it is all over. My first thought is to give you news of myself. The
Royalists, organized in Sections, were becoming more aggressive every
day. The Convention gave orders that the Lepelletier Section should be
disarmed. The troops sent to do this were repulsed. Menou, it was said,
was a traitor. He was at once dismissed. The Convention appointed Barras to command the armed forces of the Government: the Committees
chose me as second in command. We disposed our troops. The enemy attacked us at the Tuileries. We killed a large number of them. They
killed thirty of our men, and wounded sixty. We have disarmed the Sections, and all is quiet. As usual, I haven't had a scratch.' [12]

13

There was a last and a non-political motive which determined Bonaparte
not to persist in his application for foreign service. He was seriously thinking of getting married. Soon after the Toulon episode, when both business and family affection frequently took him to Marseille, he had
formed an attachment to the younger of two daughters of a rich silk
merchant, Desirée Clary: in August 1794 his brother Joseph had married
the elder daughter, Julie. The affection seems to have been mainly on the
girl's side; and her father is said to have thought that one Corsican
in the family was enough. But when Bonaparte became fixed in Paris,
and had a comfortable income, he thought again of the girl at Marseille.
'If I remain here,' he wrote to Joseph on September 5th, 'it is not impossible that a craze for marriage may seize me. Send me a line about this.
Perhaps it would be well if you spoke to Desirée's brother on the subject
(not her father?). Let me hear the result: that is all that matters.'

But whatever the reply may have been, and although this courtship
may have inspired the romance *Clisson et Eugénie* which was found in
manuscript among his papers at St. Helena, he was soon thinking of another bride—and with the calculating caution of a shy man who has to
make his way in society turned his thoughts towards his old friend Mme
Permon, recently widowed and now living in Paris with two children,
one of whom afterwards became the Duchesse d'Abrantès, and recorded
the affair in her *Memoirs* with an abundance of picturesque detail which
it would be unsafe to treat as historical. When she refused his offer, he
transferred it, again unsuccessfully, to a Mme de la Boucharderie.

Bonaparte's fourth attempt at matrimony satisfied both prudence and
passion. On March 11th, 1798, Letourneur, who was then President of the
Executive Directory, received this letter.

I have already authorized citizen Barras to inform the Executive
Directory of my marriage with *citoyenne* Tascher Beauharnais. The
confidence which the Directory has placed in me at every turn makes
it my duty to keep it informed of all my actions. This is a fresh tie
between myself and my country: it is an additional pledge of my
fixed resolve to entrust all my fortunes to (*de ne trouver de salut que
dans*) the Republic.

BUONAPARTE

Général en chef of the Army of the Interior.

Such is the only reference to Bonaparte's marriage in the Official Correspondence. From letters excluded by the editors, and from the researches
of historians, the main outlines of the affair can be filled in, without com-
plicating it with the more or less untrustworthy embellishments of the
memoir-writers.

In 1779, the same year that the ten-year-old Bonaparte went to school
at Autun, a girl of sixteen landed in France from Martinique to marry a
boy of nineteen whom she had not seen since he was five and she was
two. He was Alexandre de Beauharnais, son of a rich Orléans landowner
who had seen service as a marine at Martinique: she was Marie-Joséphine-
Rose, daughter of Joseph Gaspard Tascher de la Pagerie, a member of an
old but impoverished Martinique family. Two children were born of her
marriage to Beauharnais: Eugène (1781) and Hortense (1783).
Beauharnais had not wanted to marry; he looked down on the colonial
manners of his bride, and soon tired of her charms: and within a few
years they were legally separated. Joséphine returned for two years to
Martinique and did not come back to Paris till the second year of the
Revolution, in October 1790.

Meanwhile her husband had been elected for the *noblesse* of Blois to
the National Assembly, and had made some mark as a Liberal aristocrat.
Eight months after her return, at the time of the King's flight to
Varennes, he was President of the Assembly. When its session ended, he
served as Colonel with the army of the North under Custine, and commanded the camp at Soissons. In 1793 he resigned his appointment as
général-en-chef of the army of the Rhine, and retired to his country estate. Unfortunately his connection with Custine, together with his aristocratic birth, made him suspect in that year of suspicions, 1794: he was
arrested, condemned, and executed only four days before Robespierre,
whose death might have saved his life. The Revolution brought Alexandre
and Joséphine together again. When he was arrested she did all she could
to get him released, and was rewarded by being thrown into the same
prison: the illness into which the shock of his death threw her saved her
own life: she could not be brought to trial before Thermidor, and was
released soon afterwards.

Joséphine, now a widow of thirty-one, found herself alone in Paris with no relations, living beyond her means (for her husband's estate was forfeit), and with two children in her care. Ill-educated and unbusinesslike, but graceful, charming and generous, it was not to be wondered at that she made full use of acquaintances whom the latest turn of the revolutionary wheel had placed in power: Barras (who perhaps had her for mistress), Tallien and his lovely but scandalous wife; and now Bonaparte. Bonaparte was making money, and thinking of settling down. A professional soldier, whose life had been spent in barracks or in the field, he had yet to learn the ways of polite society. A shy man, who knew little of women, he had already shown a partiality for the protective colouring of widowhood. His inexperience was flattered and his sensuality indulged by the complacent art of a still seductive beauty. At one stroke he could secure a mistress and a partner; indulge a passion and forward a career.

There is no need to disbelieve Bonaparte's own account of his first acquaintance with Joséphine; for though the story is contradicted in the memoirs of Barras and Ouvrard, it is corroborated by those of Eugène and Hortense. Three days after the 13th Vendémiaire Bonaparte left the lodgings in the rue Vivienne which he had shared with his aide-de-camp Junot for an official residence in the hôtel de la Colonnade. The next day an *arrêté* was issued ordering the disarmament of the Sections Lepelletier and Théâtre français; everyone living in those quarters had to surrender within three hours any arms they possessed. Joséphine was at that time living at No. 62, rue de la Chaussée d'Antin, with her daughter Hortense and Eugène, a boy of fourteen. She sent Eugène to Bonaparte's headquarters with his father's sword, asking that they might be allowed to keep it, as a memento of a republican general: Bonaparte, moved by the boy's manner, agreed. Next day (October 10th) Joséphine called to thank him. He was attracted by her, and called back (October 15th). A fortnight later we find her writing to him. 'You no longer come to see a friend who is fond of you (*une amie qui vous aime*): you have abandoned her completely; and you are much to blame, for she is very fond of you (*tendrement attachée*). Come to *déjeuner* with me tomorrow. I want to see you and to talk to you about your concerns. *Bonsoir*, my friend, *je vous embrasse*. Veuve Beauharnais.' He replied, and went. The friendship prospered; and before the end of the year ended in the way it would.

'I awake all filled with you,' writes Bonaparte on the morning of December 29th, 1795. 'Your image, and the intoxicating pleasures of last night, allow my senses no rest. Sweet and matchless Joséphine, how strangely you work upon my heart! Are you angry with me? Are you unhappy? Are you upset? . . . My soul is broken with grief, and my love for you forbids repose. But how can I rest any more, when I yield to the feeling that masters my inmost self, when I quaff from your lips and from your heart a scorching flame? Yes! One night has taught me how far your portrait falls short of yourself! You start at midday: in three hours I shall see you again. Till then, a thousand kisses, *mio dolce amor*: but give me none back, for they set my blood on fire.'

This was not how Barras would write. Joséphine was not too old to be stirred by genuine passion. Yet it is not so easy to account for her willingness to marry a gauche little Corsican six years younger than herself, who was still on the fringe of the government circle, and had barely begun to make money and a career. At the moment he had a future; but an unsuccessful campaign, or another turn of the political wheel, might reverse all his fortunes, and hers too. Perhaps she was touched by his boyish infatuation, and determination to marry her; perhaps she was too indolent to refuse; certainly (though there is some evidence that he thought he was marrying money), she was too poor to throw away what might be her only chance of a permanent settlement. So a night's generosity became the sacrifice of a life-time, and the apartment in the rue d'Antin an antechamber to the Tuileries.

On March 9th, 1796, they were married, at the Registry Office of the Section; and Barras was one of the witnesses. Joséphine took four years off her age, giving her birthday as June 23rd, 1767 instead of 1763; and Bonaparte, by adopting his brother Joseph's birthday, February 5th, 1768, added eighteen months to his. He settled upon her, in case of his death, £900 a year, which he had yet to make, and paid £320 on account (it was all he had) for a house in the rue Chantereine, in which they now lived.

Their marriage was a modest affair, and must have caused some amusement to their friends. But it was probably the most sensible thing either of them ever did. Bonaparte represented to Joséphine just what she lacked: not merely money, but energy, enthusiasm, businesslike ways, an active interest in life. She gave him at first passion, afterwards affection, with all the social virtues of which she was mistress: charm, tact, generosity, goodness of heart. Wholly feminine, at once primitive and polished, uneducated, amoral, she was the perfect foil to his hard efficient masculinity. They might often be at cross purposes: but they could always be honest and natural with one another.

Married life in the rue Chantereine only lasted two days. On March 11th Bonaparte left Paris for Nice. He had been given the command of the army of Italy, and nothing could keep him back from the campaign for which his whole military life had been a preparation. But at every stage of the journey—from Nice on March 31st, from Port-Maurice on April 3rd, from Albenga on April 5th, he sent back love-letters whose language is as romantic as their passion is real. 'My only consolation,' he says, 'is in writing to you: the thought of you is the lode-star of my moral ideas: you are the confidante of all my troubles.' [13]

III

ITALY

(1796-1797)

I

AN INVASION of Italy was the traditional outcome of every forward move in France's classical anti-Austrian policy. Every traveller knew how tempting were the valley-approaches from the Durance and the Isère to the crest of the western Alps. Every schoolboy had been told how Hannibal and his elephants crossed the St. Bernard. Every historian was familiar with the French invasions of Italy in 1494, 1515, 1733 and 1745. Pezay and Bourcet were text-books at every military academy. Every archaeologist and man of taste knew the wealth of printing and sculpture, the gold and the jewels that made Italy the museum of Europe. Every householder realized that whilst the necessities of life were provided by the fields and coasts of France, the luxuries came from across the Alps, by the Savoy passes or by the sea-route from Naples and Genoa to Nice and Marseille. For this was the final consideration which the soldiers always had in mind: north Italy not only provided a 'low road' to Vienna which could be used at the same time as the 'high road' of the Danube valley; but it had accommodation for three lines of traffic—across the Alpine passes, along the Riviera coast-road, and by sea.

The fall of Robespierre in July 1794 had begun a period of inactivity on the Italian front which lasted until the autumn of 1795. All that summer, operations were held up on the Italian front by the stringency of the British blockade. In spite of the exceptional efficiency of Joseph Bonaparte, whom Chiappe, the representative with the army of Italy, described (May 12th) as a first-class *commissaire des guerres*, yet the need of cash, the prevalence of desertion, political troubles at Toulon, discouraging rumours of peace, lack of transport, failure of reinforcements, depredations by 'brigands' behind the lines, lack of food and forage, and constant changes in the command, so disheartened the troops that the *commissaires* were in despair. 'We can put it in two words (write Peyre and Maisse on July 26th); the army of Italy is in a totally different position from that of other

65

armies. It is fighting in country which provides a soldier with nothing he wants. He holds a position on a mountain-top. Nothing is to be found there. Behind him is a country that provides the bare subsistence of its own inhabitants. Before him is a country whose citizens make profits out of our difficulties, and will not give us a thing except for cash. Great as our needs are, they are no greater than the difficulty of supplying them.' To make matters worse (they add a month later), 'brigands' behind the lines, not Piedmontese, but Frenchmen, attack convoys, murder volunteers and *gendarmes*, and attack the army in the back.[1]

In the summer of 1795 an Austrian offensive had forced the French, in a month's fighting, to yield some important miles of coastline, and had given the British fleet the use of the valuable port of Vado. Bonaparte, now at the *bureau topographique*, was quick to realize from his knowledge of the ground how serious this retreat was, and drew up a *Note sur l'armée d'Italie* urging and outlining a forward move on Vado and Savona, as a necessary preliminary of the Italian campaign which so many considerations made advisable. If the army of Italy, he said, remained inactive during February as it had done during January, the Italian campaign would be as good as lost. Once across the crest of the Alps the army need not fear a winter campaign, but welcome it as an opportunity to win great success on this front. The first objective should be the Piedmontese camp before Ceva; this must be seized before the Austrians at Acqui can send help to the garrison. Then Ceva itself must be besieged; siege guns (twenty-four to thirty will suffice) can go by sea to Vado, where there is plenty of transport. Ceva taken, the army will concentrate, invest Coni, and march on Turin. The King of Sardinia will sue for peace; if his terms are too stiff, we must burn Turin, citadel and all. Turin in our hands, Alexandria and Tortona are useless to the enemy, and nothing can stop our advance on Milan. 'We shall find carts, clothing and food for the brave army as soon as it occupies the plains of Piedmont and the Milanais.' 'Summarily,' he concludes, 'since war in Italy depends entirely on the weather, each month demands a different plan of campaign. The government must have complete confidence in its general, and must leave him wide discretion (*une grande latitude*), prescribing nothing but the aim he is to fulfil. It takes a month to get an answer to a dispatch from Savona to Paris, and everything may change in the interval.'

This ambitious and prophetic memorandum had its hoped-for effect: when Schérer read it he said the plan was impracticable, and resigned. Before the end of February Bonaparte knew that the appointment was his: it was gazetted on March 2nd. A week later he was married; within ten days he left Paris; before the month was out he had reached his headquarters (Nice, March 26th), held his first review (March 31st), and changed his signature (the first instance in the official correspondence is on the 24th) from Corsican *Buonaparte* to French *Bonaparte*. He was soon busily employed with the real and immediate worries of a commander-in-chief; writing for money to the municipal authorities of Marseille; to Chauvet, head of the commissariat at Genoa, about contracts for the supply of fresh meat, fodder, grain and baggage animals ('Come to Nice as quickly as you can: I want you'), or to Sucy, also of the Genoese supply-base, ending *Adieu mon cher ordonnateur. Activité et courage!*; or to Faypoult, the French political representative at Genoa, urging the necessity of avoiding any clash with the local authorities whilst their supplies are so essential, but breathing threats against any infringement of their friendly neutrality.

The solitary fame of Napoleon's later career has obscured the fact that up to the time (at least) of his capture of Milan he owed most of his successes to the opportunities and help given him by a civilian and a fellow-countryman whom history has condemned to comparative obscurity. Antoine-Christophe Saliceti was, like Bonaparte himself, a Corsican of the Bastia district: he too boasted aristocratic Italian blood, and had, like Charles Buonaparte, taken a law degree at Pisa. But whilst Bonaparte had been training for the army he had represented Corsica in the States General of 1789; and three years later he sat on the Left of the Convention —the only Corsican to be marked out as a regicide and a terrorist. Having thus proved that he could be trusted, he was able to associate his friend Bonaparte with his missions to Corsica, Marseille, Toulon, and the army of Italy. It was he who secured the publication of the *Souper de Beaucaire*, he who gave Bonaparte command of the artillery at Toulon, and he who prepared the way for his victories in Italy. Described by the Duchesse d'Abrantès, whose mother, Mme Permon, knew both Corsicans intimately, as a tall thin man, with a long, pock-marked yellow face, Saliceti was full of ideas, initiative and ambition; and he never allowed himself to be overshadowed by the fellow-countryman whom he had imprisoned and released from prison, with whom he had shared the suspicion of the Thermidorians, and the success of Vendémiaire, and whose partner he had now become in the Italian adventure.

Yet Saliceti was never more than *Laertes* to *Hamlet*; and it would be impossible to omit here the portrait of Bonaparte as seen by his new command. 'When he arrived in Italy (writes Chaptal) none of the generals knew him; and Masséna has told me that the first time they went to see him they formed a pretty poor opinion of him. His few inches and weak physique were not impressive. They imagined, from the way he carried about his wife's portrait and showed it to everyone, and still more from his extreme youth, that he owed his appointment to yet another bit of intrigue. But in a minute or two (added Masséna) he put on his general's hat, and seemed two feet taller. He asked us where our divisions were stationed, how they were equipped, what was the spirit and fighting value of each corps; he gave us our marching orders, and announced that tomorrow he would inspect the whole army, and the day after tomorrow it would march and deliver battle against the enemy. He spoke with such dignity, preciseness and competence that his generals retired with the conviction that at last they had a real leader.'[2]

2

The enthusiasm of military historians for the strategical and tactical triumphs of the Italian campaign has a little obscured the importance of Bonaparte's other activities. No general is unaware that most battles are won off the battlefield. No reader of Napoleon's correspondence (the one indispensable authority) can fail to see that he was an indefatigable organizer, or miss the rhythm of the campaign, in which each sharp and momentary stroke of battle is preceded by a period of preparation and followed by an interval of recuperation. Victories were won, not by heroic contests against odds, but by carefully planned moves and quick marches which ensured that, when the fight came, the French troops engaged outnumbered their opponents. In a pitched battle between the whole available forces on both sides, such as the enemy, with his old-fashioned ideas, expected and desired, Bonaparte might well have been defeated. In the successive actions of small detachments which history has linked into the battles of Montenotte, Millesimo, Dego and Mondovi, he was invariably victorious.

This is vividly reflected in the correspondence. From March 26th, when he arrives at Nice, till the end of the month Bonaparte's letters are nearly all concerned with reinforcements and commissariat; indeed, these subjects are never wholly out of his mind. On the 31st come the first orders for troop movements, which are issued with increasing fullness of detail (such in particular is the group written to Masséna, Laharpe and Serrurier on April 11th) up to the eve of the battle of Montenotte (April 12th). From the 12th to the 21st, when this group of engagements ended in the battle of Mondovi, 54 out of 60 letters are addressed to his generals in the field: on the 14th there are 17 in one day, 3 of them written after 10 p.m.; on the 20th there are 9, of which 3 are headed '1 a.m.' As soon as he has won a military success, he must turn his attention again to the prevention of private looting, the organization of the public looting called requisitioning, and the administration of towns and districts occupied during the advance. The troops must be thanked as well as fed, and reports must be sent home to the Directory on the state of the army and the progress of the campaign.

The famous proclamation of March 27th, so often quoted, was invented at St. Helena; but the generals were led to feel that they had their commander's confidence, and the troops were told what they were fighting for. 'The government,' Bonaparte wrote to Chauvet on March 27th, 'expects great things of this army: we must achieve them, and save the country from its present crisis.' After his first general review of the 29th he issued an *Ordre du jour* in which he said that 'he was satisfied with the bearing of the troops, their feeling of devotion to the Republic, and their strong will to victory. He had found throughout their ranks soldiers accustomed to conquer and to endure, soldiers devoted both to liberty and to discipline, the mainspring of an army. They would find in him (he went on) a brother in arms, strong in the trust of the government, proud of the esteem of patriots, and determined to win for the army of Italy the destiny that it deserved. On the morning of Montenotte he wrote to Masséna 'Everything tells us that today and tomorrow will leave their marks on history'; and on the second day of the action, to Dommartin, 'Today will be as glorious for the arms of the Republic as yesterday.' The *Ordre du jour* announcing the victory of Mondovi on the 22nd is accompanied by another *Ordre* congratulating the troops on their 'courage and success,' but at the same time condemning the horrible looting (*pillage affreux*) by which some of them have dishonoured their victory: for Bonaparte had no illusions as to the indiscipline which made the liberators of Italy only less unpopular than the Austrians they displaced, and which could be used by the civil *commissaires*, by his enemies at home, or by any discontented subordinate, to set the government against him, and to ruin his career.

'You can have no idea [he wrote to the Directors on April 24th] of the military and administrative condition of the army. When I got here it was under the influence of disaffected agitators, without bread, without discipline and without order. I made some examples, I took every step I could to reorganize the commissariat; and victory did the rest. All the same, our lack of wagons, the badness of our horses, and the greed of the contractors keep us in a state of absolute penury. I can't tell you the life I lead: I come in tired out, and then have to be up all night hard at work, or hurrying here, there, and everywhere to restore order. When the men have no bread they indulge in outrages which make one blush for human nature . . . But I will either restore discipline or give up my command over these brigands.'[3]

Specially interesting and important, in view of these difficulties, are Bonaparte's letters to the government in Paris. There are seven official dispatches to the Directory during the period March 26th to April 22nd, and two of them are accompanied by private letters to individual Directors or Ministers; for there were things then, as there are now, which a general in command cannot put into an open dispatch.

The first dispatch is from Nice on March 28th; it is concerned chiefly

with questions of pay and commissariat, but contains a generous apprecia-
tion of the *franchise et honnêteté* of General Schérer, from whom Bonaparte has just taken over the command. With it goes a private letter to
Carnot, the Director who can best understand the military situation, and
to whom he can speak most freely. 'I have been very well received,' he
writes, 'by the army, and I cannot but feel a lively gratitude for the confidence it shows in me.' A week later (April 6th) he sends another dispatch from Albenga, reporting the first enemy reactions to the advance
on Genoa, and estimating the Piedmontese forces at 40,000 and the Austrians at 37,000, as against the French 45,000. Actually by April 9th Bonaparte had 57,000 men under his command; the Piedmontese had 25,000
men in the field out of a paper strength of 70,000, and the Austrians
28,000: Bonaparte was already adopting the useful device of misrepresent-
ing the relative strength of the forces engaged on each side. But there is
no pretence in his concern for the army's lack of equipment. Though the
commissariat is better than it was, 'the army is in an alarming state of
destitution (*un dénûment à faire peur*). I have still great obstacles to
surmount; but they can be surmounted. Bad conditions here have naturally led to indiscipline, and without discipline victory is impossible.'

On April 14th Bonaparte sent his first report of successful hostilities—
the victory of Montenotte: the opening of a series of small engagements
in which he skilfully threw back an Austrian advance from the north on
Savona and Genoa, and drove a wedge between the Austrian and
Sardinian armies. 'The Italian campaign has begun (he wrote). The generals, officers, and soldiers, on this memorable day, all upheld the honour
of the French name.' Next day another dispatch tells of the victory of
Millesimo; and another next day adds further details. With it goes a letter
for Carnot's eyes alone: 'I cannot pretend that I get the support I should
either from the Engineers or the Artillery: in spite of the orders you gave
about it, I have not got with me a single one of the officers I asked for.'
In particular, he has no one who knows how to attack or defend a fortified position. The fault lies with the Ministry of War. 'The engineer
and artillery services are ruined by backstairs intrigue, and military considerations are sacrificed to the interests of individuals. The Minister's
subordinates sprinkle holy water, and the country is the sufferer.' Perhaps
Bonaparte fears that this letter may be suppressed before it reaches Carnot:
anyhow he sends another the same day reiterating the demand for field
artillery and engineers, particularly urgent at a moment when the army
is debouching from the mountain country into the plain of Lombardy.

On April 22nd another dispatch reports the capture of Ceva, the battle
of Mondovi, and the occupation of that town. It includes praise for all
ranks of the army, especially of Berthier, 'Chief of the General Staff,

whose talents are as great as his activity, patriotism and courage.' The capture of Cherasco three days later determined and gave a name to the armistice by which the King of Sardinia admitted the final defeat of his armies in the field.[4]

3

The negotiations for the armistice raised questions of a new kind between Bonaparte and the Directory. Already on the 22nd Colli, the Sardinian commander, had reported that his army could only be saved by an armistice, and a council was held at which he was authorized to approach Bonaparte with this object, whilst envoys were sent to Genoa to treat with Faypoult, the French diplomatic representative there, for terms of peace with the Directory. Bonaparte's answer to Colli (April 23rd) was that the Directory had reserved to itself the right to treat for peace, and that the Sardinian negotiators must either travel to Paris, or wait at Genoa for the arrival of a French plenipotentiary. Meanwhile no armistice would be granted, unless the Sardinians handed over two out of the three fortresses of Coni, Tortona and Alexandria. It was in order to turn the screw on these hard terms that Bonaparte ordered the further hostilities which led to the capture of Cherasco on the 25th.

Meanwhile (on the 24th) he had sent off his brother Joseph to Paris with an account of the military situation, and of the proposed armistice terms; and with him went Junot carrying a trophy of twenty-one captured flags. These were not only a proof of victory, but also a pledge of political loyalty: 'The army of Italy,' wrote its commander, 'whilst presenting you with these flags as a proof of its courage, charges me to assure you of its devotion to the constitution and to the magistrates whose strong arm suppresses the different factions that would still tear in pieces the bosom of the fatherland.' Was this a reference to the troubles which were to lead, a fortnight later (May 10th) to the arrest of Babeuf? The language used is at any rate significant as one of the first political manifestos of a republican general and army in the field. Bonaparte's increasing self-confidence is further illustrated by the accompanying letter, this time addressed not to Carnot (whom he knew to be prejudiced against the use of light artillery), but to the Minister of War, complaining of the failure to supply him with field guns, officers and engineers. If he had had field artillery, he says, Stengel (his best cavalry leader) would not have been killed at Mondovi, and the attack would not have been held up by the superiority of the enemy's cavalry.

He is by now looking further, indeed far ahead. 'If we can get peace or an armistice on the terms I have demanded,' he declares (April 26th), 'I shall pass into the Tyrol, join hands with the army of the Rhine, and carry the war into Bavaria.' Again, on the 28th: 'if you don't come to terms with the King of Sardinia, I shall keep the places (the fortresses mentioned in the armistice terms), and march upon Turin . . . Meanwhile, I am marching tomorrow, I force him to cross the Po, I cross it immediately after, I occupy the whole of Lombardy, and before a month is out I hope to be in the mountains of the Tyrol, to make contact with the army of the Rhine, and to join arms with it in carrying the war into Bavaria. This is a plan worthy of you, and of the army, and of the destiny of France. If you keep your confidence in me,' he ends, 'and approve of these proposals, I am certain of success: Italy is yours.'

It may be noted that there was nothing to prevent Bonaparte resuming his advance against the Austrians without waiting for the conclusion of terms with Sardinia—he knew that it might be fatal to remain inactive, and to give the enemy an opportunity for recovery, during the fortnight that would elapse before a decision could be got from Paris; on the other hand the suggestion of an advance into the Tyrol resuscitated an idea which had been in Bonaparte's mind for six months past, but which he had refrained from mentioning in his notes of December 11th and January 19th, and which had been deliberately ignored in the Instructions he had received from the Directory.

The facts were these. During the autumn of 1795, before the Directory came into power (November 3rd), a group of young officers in the *bureau topographique*, of whom Bonaparte was one, had drawn up two unsigned memoranda outlining plans for the Italian campaign. In these documents it was urged that a successful campaign in Lombardy, and the capture of Mantua, should be followed by an advance into the Trentino, a junction with the army of the Rhine, and a concerted invasion of Austria. In due course both memoranda came up for consideration by the Directors: they consulted Saliceti; and on March 2nd they formulated the *Instruction pour le général en chef de l'armée d'Italie* which was handed to Bonaparte on the 6th. The French (said the document) have two enemies in Italy—Piedmont and Austria. Piedmont has the larger fighting force; but Austria is the more dangerous, because it is more hostile, has better resources, is friendly with England ('our natural enemy'), and controls the policy of the court of Turin. It is only necessary, therefore, to defeat the Austrian army, and to offer compensation, such as Milan, for Piedmont to collapse: whereas a direct attack on that country, and the destruction of its forts (even if we had the artillery to do it) would antagonize Piedmont without damaging Austria. The Directors therefore favour, first, a sufficient offensive against Piedmont to induce it to make terms with France, and, secondly, a main and persistent campaign against Austria.

The detailed execution of this attack is left to the general in command; but its main lines are laid down clearly enough. 'Every consideration bids us use all the means in our power to force the enemy back across the Po, and to aim our principle blows in the direction of Milan.' But this 'essential operation' cannot be undertaken until Ceva is captured, and the Piedmontese driven back upon Turin. Once this is done, the army will strike in two directions—its left (the main attack) across the Po towards Milan: the right (a subordinate attack) towards Tortona and Genoa: the first aiming at the destruction of the Austrians, and the second at coercing the Genoese government to supply more money and food for the expedition.

Three remarks may be made about these Instructions. First, they are based upon an assumption which was common property of all students of previous campaigns in the western Alps, and had been prominent in the memoranda of the *bureau topographique*, namely, that Ceva was the clue to the conquest of Lombardy. Secondly, they show that it was generally anticipated that Piedmont would come to terms without a military defeat. True, the court was more in sympathy with the Austrian Empire than with the French Republic; but not the ministers, not the merchants, not the people; and in fact when Turin surrendered it was not due to the non-existent siege artillery of Bonaparte, nor even to the partial defeat of Colli's troops, but to 'defeatist' influences within the city. Thirdly, the Instructions are silent as to anything that may follow the advance on Milan; and this silence could not be taken as approving (though it need not be taken as disapproving) of the junction with the army of the Rhine, and a combined campaign in the Tyrol, suggested in the Bonapartist memorandum already mentioned.

Bonaparte's return to this idea in his dispatches of the 26th and 28th was, then, a deliberate challenge to the Instructions under which he was acting; and a challenge which he would not have made unless he had felt that his success in the field enabled him to put a wide interpretation on the discretionary powers he had claimed in his Note of January 19th. He must have reckoned that Carnot, and the older heads on the Directory, would think him presumptuous: but he had enough self-conceit to believe that he would soon make himself so necessary to the government that they would give him a free hand. The main interest in the story of the next few months lies in the working out of this situation—a development far more important, in the long run, than the course of the campaign.[5]

4

Bonaparte's anxiety to stand well with the Directory explains two features of his correspondence during these early months of the campaign: his zeal to suppress looting and other misconduct in the army, and his care to make the campaign self-supporting, and to send home as much cash and other valuables as possible.

In his *Ordre* of April 22nd condemning looting he had called for a report on the conduct both of officers and of civil *commissaires*. Divisional generals were empowered to arrest and send to the rear any officers authorizing pillage, and to shoot out of hand any officer or man caught in the act. Two days later, finding mere threats insufficient, Bonaparte published his intention to substitute official for unofficial looting by levying contributions on occupied territory equal to half the pay of his troops, and by taking over stolen horses for the use of the army. In his dispatch of the 26th he informed the Directors that he had the problem well in hand (*Tout va bien*). 'There is less looting than there was. The first thirst of a famishing army is being assuaged. There are excuses for the guilty men; they have arrived in the Promised Land for which they sighed for three years on the summit of the Alps, and they want to enjoy it.' A few have been shot, more put to hard labour behind the lines. Soon (May 9th) he is able to report that 'we are all getting fat: the men eat none but the best bread (*pain de Gonesse*), plenty of good fresh meat, excellent wine, and so forth. Discipline is improving every day, though we still have to shoot a good many men, for there are some intractable characters incapable of self-restraint.' So this problem gradually solved itself.

The Directors, though they had not said so in their Instructions, were frankly concerned to make as much money out of the campaign as possible. As early as April 12th they had written to Bonaparte suggesting that he should raid the treasury of Nôtre Dame de Loretto, which was valued at ten million sterling. This place, fifteen miles south of Ancona, was, they admitted, forty-five leagues within Papal territory, and it would involve a difficult march of some 250 miles across the Apennines: but it was worth risking the lives of not more than 10,000 men. Later, when Ancona was in his hands, Bonaparte took the hint.

In the early days of the campaign his army was so short of supplies, and the necessity of stopping private looting so urgent, that everything that he could lay hands on, whether by capture from the defeated enemy, or by requisitioning from friendly towns liberated during the advance, was used to supply his needs. The municipality of Mondovi (April 21st) was required to provide 8000 rations of fresh meat, 4000 bottles of wine immediately, another 8000 rations of bread and meat, and another 4000 bottles of wine the following day. The municipality of Frabosa (April 26th) was asked to prove its attachment to the French Republic by feeding the French troops, and handing over Piedmontese arms. The municipality of Acqui (May 1st) has not only to hand over all clothes and boots left behind by the retreating Austrians, but also the inhabitants' own boots—which will be paid for; if they are not offered for sale they will be confiscated.

Individuals, too, are plundered. General Pelletier (May 4th) is given instructions to levy £12,500 from the *seigneurs* of the Imperial fiefs, besides cattle and mules; and £2500 from the *seigneur* of Arquata: 'if he fails to pay up you are to pull down his house and destroy his property; for he is a mad oligarch, an enemy of France and the army.' It is not long before such plunder is being set aside for transport to Paris. As soon as Bonaparte is able to settle down amidst the art treasures of Piacenza (May 9th) he thinks of his greedy masters at home: 'I will send you as soon as possible Correggio's finest pictures, including a St. Jerome which is said to be his *chef d'œuvre*'; and he suggests that art experts should be sent out to pick over the galleries. Official looting thus became an organized part of the campaign, and forged a link of gold between the general and the government which was not easily broken.

5

Whilst the Directors were considering their reply to Bonaparte's proposals of March 28th, he was doing his best to make any reply out of date. Between the end of April and the end of May he traversed the whole length of the plain of Lombardy from Acqui to Verona, occupied Milan, and drove back the Austrian army into Mantua and behind the Adige. It is enough to follow his journey on the map. On April 30th he was at Acqui, on May 2nd at Bosco, on the 3rd at Tortona, directing the crossing of the Po at Piacenza, which he reached on the 7th; on the 10th he crossed the Adda at Lodi; on the 15th he was at Milan, and summoned the Governor of the castle to surrender; on the 26th at Pavia, on the 27th at Brescia, on the 30th at Borghetto on the Mincio, almost within sight of Mantua; on June 3rd he reached Verona, some 150 miles in a straight line from his starting-point. It was a campaign of a speed almost unknown before the days of motor transport.

The fighting, it is true, had not been severe; for Bonaparte's advance on the south bank of the Po had outflanked in turn every position that Beaulieu might have defended against an advance on the north bank. It was all the more tempting to exaggerate the rear action at the bridge of Lodi into a major battle, and to advertise the bravery of the young commander and his troops. But it must be allowed that the 'legend of Lodi' which (in a contemporary print published by Faipoult at Genoa) showed Bonaparte himself seizing a standard and leading the troops across the bullet-swept bridge—a legend which he was not unwilling to confirm in later days—did not originate in the dispatches announcing the victory. In the *Ordre du jour* of May 10th Bonaparte spoke only of the courage of the rank and file. In his dispatch to the Directors the next day, though giving a highly coloured picture of the action, he named Berthier, Masséna, Cervoni, and three others as the officers who rallied the column that stormed the bridge. Saliceti's dispatch confirms his general's, and adds that Bonaparte was under fire whilst placing the guns at the bridge, but did not lead the troops across it.

When Bonaparte sent his next formal report to the Directors, it was dated from Peschiera, June 1st. After describing the operations since Lodi, he was able to say, without much exaggeration, 'Thus the Austrians have been utterly expelled from Italy. Our advance posts are on the mountains of Germany'; and he added a picturesque account of the spirit of the army which has also become part of the 'legend': 'They gamble with death with a smile on their lips . . . Their courage is only equalled by the cheerfulness with which they face forced marches of the hardest kind. Sometimes they sing of Love and sometimes of their Fatherland. Do you suppose that when they arrive in camp all they can do is to sleep? Not a bit of it. Every one has adventures to tell, or plans for tomorrow's operations; and often enough their views are very sound.' There was a *chasseur*, for instance, whom Bonaparte snubbed for offering advice; but afterwards he told him that he had carried out just what the man suggested. Miot de Melito, who met him at Brescia on June 5th, described in his *Mémoires* his surprise at Bonaparte's appearance. He was 'below common height and very thin. His hair, powdered and cut square below his ears, fell on his shoulders. He was dressed in a tight tunic buttoned to the top, with narrow gold facings; and he had a tricolor feather in his hat. My first impression was that he was anything but good-looking; but his strong features, keen questioning look and quick decisive gestures revealed a flame-like spirit (*âme ardente*); his broad and reflective forehead were those of a deep thinker.'

A controversial incident during this advance was Bonaparte's violation of the neutral territory of Parma-Piacenza. His dispatch of May 19th to the Directors described how, after making a feint to cross the Po at Valenza, he marched rapidly along its south bank to Piacenza, and crossed there. Bets had been offered, he said, that they would not cross the river under two months; but if the Austrians were so simple as to suppose he would respect the neutrality of a defenceless state, 'French republicans are not such fools as Francis I.' A crossing was forced in face of negligible opposition; the Duke of Parma agreed to an armistice, and a selection of his finest works of art started on their long journey to Paris. Thus Austrians and Italians alike learnt the realities of the new warfare.

6

Any anxiety which Bonaparte may have felt about the Sardinian armistice was set at rest by a letter (May 7th) which he received on entering Milan approving of the terms he had proposed on April 23rd, provided they had the approval of Saliceti; 'for (and a snub could not have been more politely expressed) urgent transactions of this kind, about

which the Director cannot be consulted, fall specifically within the sphere
of the government *commissaires* attached to the armies. The French generals are indeed the only representatives whom the enemy generals will
recognize; but it is proper that they should not have power to conclude
any transaction or negotiation in circumstances such as those above-
mentioned without previous orders from the Directory, or conditions
transmitted to them by the government *commissaires*.'

The same letter went on to deal with future plans for the campaign
in a manner which showed that the Directors were far from accepting
dictation from their victorious general. The proposed advance into the
Tyrol, they said, 'presents serious obstacles and difficulties that might be
called insuperable,' in view of the small size of Bonaparte's army, the
length of its communications, and the necessity of finishing the campaign
this year. 'The Italian powers summon you to your right,' especially to
deal with Corsica, and with the British forces in the Mediterranean.
Bonaparte must therefore first occupy Milan, then drive the Austrians
back into the Tyrol; when that is done he is to lead the major part of his
forces upon Genoa, Leghorn, Rome and Naples, whilst the rest, with the
help of the Sardinians and Kellermann's troops, all under Kellermann's
command, exploit the situation in the Milanais: perhaps later on they
might invade the Tyrol.

The rest of the letter is taken up with instructions as to Bonaparte's
policy towards the city-states: Genoa is to be gently treated until the time
comes for demanding compensation for the loss of the *Modeste* (a French
ship captured and burnt by the British under the guns of the Genoese
forts); Lucca to be told we have no hostile intentions against her; Parma
to pay for her neutrality in requisitions; Milan to be mulcted of contributions in cash at once, 'during the first fears inspired by the approach of
our arms'; and Venice to be treated as a neutral, but not as a friend—'she
has done nothing to merit our regard.' Naples must give up her fleet, and
close her port against enemy or neutral shipping; and, if Rome makes
overtures to us, our first demand must be that the Pope shall order prayers
for the success of the French arms. With this bit of republican humour
the Directors pass (in a second letter of the same date) to instructions
as to the plundering of Italian galleries to 'repair the ravages of Vandal-
ism' in the museums of Paris.

The insistence on the southward turn of Bonaparte's invasion which is
the burden of this letter is stiffly maintained in the correspondence of the
Directors with their victorious general during the next three months. It
is not until August 12th that the reader at last finds a letter authorizing
the march on Innsbruck. What was Bonaparte's reaction to this persistent
rejection of his pet plan? His immediate reply to the letter of May 7th,
in the form of two letters to the Directors and a third to Carnot, all dated

May 14th, is of crucial importance in this respect. The first (in order of printing in the official correspondence) reports the fall of Cremona, asserts that 'the whole of Lombardy now belongs to the Republic,' and raises once more the idea of combined operations with the army of the Rhine, i.e. in the Tyrol. This letter may perhaps have been dispatched before he received that of the Directors quoted above.

The second letter, after saying that Beaulieu has taken refuge in Mantua, where his troops will die of malaria, deals vigorously with the two main topics of the Directors' letter, but without protesting against the rejection of the Tyrol plan. 'I think it very bad policy,' he says, 'to divide the army of Italy in two: it is equally contrary to the interests of the Republic to appoint two separate generals in command.' As for the southern advance, Bonaparte made light of it (*très peu de chose*), and thought it should be subordinated to the Austrian campaign. 'For that,' he went on, 'it is necessary not only that the general should exercise undivided command, but also that there should be no interference with his movements or operations. I have conducted this campaign without consulting anyone. I should have done no good if I had had to square my views with someone else's. If I have won successes over forces very much superior to my own, and in spite of complete lack of resources, it is because, confident that you trusted me, my troops have moved as rapidly as my thoughts. If you trammel me in all sorts of ways, if I have to refer every step to the government *commissaires*, and if they have the right to alter my dispositions and to send me troops or take them away from me at will, then you need not expect anything more of me. If you weaken your strength by dividing your forces, or if you break, so far as Italy is concerned, the unity of direction (*l'unité de la pensée militaire*), then I tell you, with regret, that you have thrown away a golden opportunity of imposing your will on Italy . . . Everyone has his own way of fighting. General Kellermann has more experience than I have, and will do the work better: but if we both act together we shall make a thorough mess of it. I cannot give the country the service it sorely needs unless you have entire and absolute confidence in me. I am aware that it needs much courage to write you this letter: it would be so easy to accuse me of ambition and pride!'

With this dispatch went a covering letter to Carnot, asking him for friendship's sake to make what seems to him the best use of it, and to support Bonaparte's contentions. 'Kellermann,' he says again, 'would command the army as well as myself; for no one could be more convinced than I am that our victories are due to the courage and dash (*audace*) of the army: but I think that to give Kellermann and myself joint command in Italy would mean ruining everything. I can't agree to serve with a man who believes himself the best general in Europe; and in any case I am sure one bad general is better than two good ones. War, like government, *est une affaire de tact.*'

The appeal to Carnot was well calculated, and carried the day. When the Directors wrote again on May 18th, Bonaparte's letter had not yet reached them (the courier must have been delayed, taking more than nine days instead of the usual seven); and their congratulations on the victory of Lodi are followed by a repetition of the instructions of May 7th, both as to the appointment of Kellermann and as to the invasion of central Italy; though they take pains to soften the blow by emphasising the importance of the southern command: the attack on Leghorn 'will make London shake in its shoes, and strike a mortal blow against the English'; and the advance on Rome 'will shake the throne of the so-called head of the universal church.' But the next letter, dated May 21st, and evidently in reply to Bonaparte's protest of the 9th, says that the division of the command may wait until the final defeat of Beaulieu, and that meanwhile Kellermann will stay at Chambéry, and do no more than occupy the places handed over by Sardinia under the peace treaty.

Bonaparte had, therefore, at this turning-point in his relations with the Directory, won his point against the division of command, and lost his point for the Tyrol campaign. It has been argued that, of the two adventures before them, the Directory chose the more dangerous. 'The Po Valley is a mouse-trap,' and an invading army finds itself encircled there both by nature and man—by the Alps, the Apennines, and the sea; Piedmont behind, Venice ahead, and Austria on the left flank: and if Bonaparte turns south, he becomes involved in the quarrels of the small states, the hostility of the Papacy, and the threat of a Neapolitan army nearly twice the size of his own. Bonaparte must have been aware of all this. He had read the campaigns of Charles VIII and Louis XII. He knew that he was running a great risk. Why did he not protest?

The answer lies partly in his love of adventure, and in the self-confidence of a military gambler who is enjoying a run of luck. But there was a more important consideration which the argument has overlooked. The communications of the French army in north Italy were threatened every day by the British occupation of the western Italian ports, and of bases in Corsica from which they could raid every convoy sailing through the Gulf of Lyons. Bonaparte was as well aware of this as Carnot: it had been one of his most harassing pre-occupations ever since the campaign began. Genoa, Leghorn and Naples were as important to him as Turin, Milan and Mantua. There were further attractions about the southern expedition. Genoa was already under the French heel; the occupation of the southern ports would make its resistance even more difficult. Leghorn would supply a stepping-stone to Corsica. The Pope was in no position to resist a military invasion. The Neapolitan army was far away. There would be plenty of time to do.what was necessary in central Italy, and to turn north again, before the slow-moving Austrians could reinforce Beaulieu sufficiently to threaten the French position in the Po valley, whose circuit of mountains was less a danger than a defence. Finally there was the question—always vital to the Directors, and therefore to any general who would retain their confidence—the question of loot. What were the small towns of Lombardy, for all their St. Jeromes and Loretto Madonnas, to the great art treasures of Florence and Rome? Such were doubtless the reasons which decided Bonaparte to barter his Tyrol scheme for the undivided command of the army in Italy.[6]

7

The difficulties of the southern campaign had not been under-rated. Within less than a month it was all over. Bonaparte's speed matched the expressed impatience of the Directory (June 15th, 30th). From Brescia, on June 5th, he settled the terms of an armistice with Naples. Leaving Milan again about the 11th, he was at Pavia on the 12th, Tortona on the 13th, Modena on the 19th, and Bologna on the 20th. Within three days he had concluded an armistice with the Papacy, in five he was across the Apennines at Pistoia, in seven at Leghorn, and in nine at Florence. On July 1st he turned back to Bologna, and found time to revisit Verona before arriving at Milan on the 13th. The threat of arms had been enough. Half the Italian peninsula was now under tribute to the French Republic.

There was one disappointment. Pope Pius VI, negotiating through Azara, the Spanish ambassador, had consented to the cession of Ancona, Bologna, and Ferrara, and had handed over cash and valuables worth a million and a quarter sterling; but he had avoided the pressing demand of the Directory that he should discipline the 'refractory' clergy: Bonaparte's hurry or over-confidence had missed the chief benefit expected of his victory—the benefit which he himself exacted from Pius VI's successor by a greater victory a few years later. He was, in fact, more concerned with the military situation than with the political possibilities of the settlement. He was primarily concerned to make such terms as would enable him to write off southern Italy, and advance eastwards from Lombardy without fear of attack on his right flank. It was of little concern to him whether or not the diplomatists would be able to secure terms of peace comparable to those of the armistice; and in fact it turned out to be impossible.

The Directors had begun the Italian adventure without any clear Italian policy; but the unexpected sweep of Bonaparte's victories forced them to consider the future of the country as a whole. Towards the end of July 1796, Delacroix submitted a memorandum headed *Projets d'ar-*

rangements en Italie, in which he argued against the setting up of republican governments either in the Milanese or in the Papal states, let alone for the whole of Italy, on the ground that this would involve France in a difficult and dangerous Protectorate; instead he outlined a scheme for the re-partition of the Italian states under a federal government in which France should be represented. The decisions of the Directory based on Delacroix's memorandum were, as he admitted in a marginal note, 'completely changed by the course of events'; but they played some part in the negotiations carried on in Italy, Germany and Spain during the succeeding six months—negotiations which obtained nothing from the Pope, and next to nothing from the King of Naples. Austria could not be brought to negotiate so long as Mantua was untaken and Wurmser in the field. England was as determined as ever to go on fighting. Only the treaty with Spain offered openings which might lead to a settlement. Bonaparte's instinct was right. Italy was a diversion. The direct road to peace led through Vienna.

Bonaparte's preoccupations during the campaigns of 1796 were more those of a statesman than of a general. Milan, the Paris of this new France, and a possible source of insurrection, had to be kept quiet and submissive by a blend of indulgence and threats: Lombardy had to be pacified and governed; Genoa coerced; Verona and Venice bullied into neutrality. A letter of June 21st explained to the Directors the main lines of this policy. 'Italy,' wrote Bonaparte, 'is now all in French hands: but with such a small army we must be ready for anything; hold the Austrian armies, besiege the fortresses, protect our communications, impose our will on Genoa, Venice, Tuscany, Rome, Naples. We must be strong everywhere. There must, therefore, be a single policy in military, diplomatic, and financial matters. In one place we have to burn and shoot to intimidate people and make a striking example, in another things happen which we must pretend not to see and be careful not to mention, because the time is not ripe. For the moment, here in Italy, diplomacy is a business for soldiers (*toute militaire*).'

The Directors could hardly deny this; but Saliceti was instructed (May 31st) to insist on his right as *commissaire* to sign all documents dealing with armistices or requisitioning; Bonaparte was reminded that he ought to have consulted Saliceti before concluding his negotiations with Naples (June 15th); letters full of detailed advice and instructions followed him wherever he went; and there were complaints that he had been irregular in the dispatches which the Directors expected to receive from him every ten days (July 25th). There was no disposition on the part of the government to abdicate its authority, nor any sign that Bonaparte thought himself strong enough to defy it.

If a civil *commissaire* tried to overstep his functions, Bonaparte would be the first to remind him of their common duty to the government. Saliceti knew his general. Garrau, who was sent out to assist him, was soon put in his place. 'We are all what we are,' Bonaparte wrote to him (July 20th), 'in virtue of the law. Anyone who tries to give orders and to usurp functions beyond his legal powers is no republican. When you were a Representative of the people, there were no limits to your powers; it was everyone's duty to obey you. Now you are a government commissioner, holding a very important position; but your duties are regulated by definite instructions, and you must keep to them.'

8

But much more was at stake than the relations between the general and his *commissaires*. It was because he suspected that they represented a different policy from his own for the settlement of Italy that Bonaparte grudged them their diplomatic independence. When he first entered Lombardy he had accepted Delacroix's ban on republicanising north Italy: but ever since his entry into Milan he had come round to the opposite view.

What Milan thought today Lombardy would think tomorrow. It was essential that the French policy should be defined there, and the character of the French occupation illustrated, for all to see. 'Milan,' wrote Bonaparte on May 17th, 'is strongly inclined for liberty: it has a club 800 strong, all lawyers and merchants. We are going to let the traditional forms of government carry on: we shall only change the personnel, who are unworthy of our trust'; then (after speaking of the contributions to be exacted from the place), 'it is from Milan that journals and writings of all kinds spread throughout Italy, which is in a state of panic.' The question is, shall Milan be republicanized, and if so to what degree?

Bonaparte already had instructions on this point. 'The Milanese,' the Directors had written on July 11th, 'are to be encouraged to regard the capture of their citadel, so long held by the Austrian garrison, as the fall of another Bastille, a symbol of the destruction of feudalism.' But there must be a limit to this policy. When Bonaparte asked for further instructions on October 1st, the reply (October 11th) was that there could be no harm in allowing the Milanese to agitate for liberty and republicanism, so long as it made the position of the French army of occupation safer: but they must not be indulged so far as to make that of the Austrians less so, in the event of their resuming possession of western Lombardy; for the Directors do not want to commit themselves to a republican settlement of the Milanese, which might make it more difficult to restore it to Austria at the peace in exchange for the Rhine frontier.

This applied not only to Milan, but also to Bologna, Ferrara, Modena, and any other Italian states under French control. 'Our wish is that you should allow them real independence until the political horizon clears up, and enables us to make a definite settlement for Italy as part of a general peace.' Again on October 18th: 'You will take care that France is not committed to any guarantee, so that she can reserve for herself the widest possible liberty to make peace with the Emperor if things turn out badly.' And again, ten days later, 'It would be unwise to kindle too strong a revolutionary fire in Italy: it might become fatal to the peoples whom we want to encourage to achieve their own freedom.' If the war had gone according to plan (the Directors continue), it would have been possible to give Italy complete freedom: but now that part of our gains (north of the Alps) has been lost, and the country is tired of war, we must think seriously of peace, and of the possible future of the Italians under the restoration of Austrian rule.

But this policy considered only the diplomatic consequences of the oc-cupation of north Italy, without reference to the position of the occupying army. For six months the impact of the French arms was such as to stun and silence the internal feuds of the country. It was not until Bonaparte had returned from his dash to the south, and was being held up by the resistance of Mantua and the hostility of Venice from pursuing his ad-vance eastwards, that the governments of the states which he had hitherto retained in power found themselves unable to keep order between the reactionaries and the republicans; or that Bonaparte himself fully realized the difficult position of his small army, if it had at once to defeat the Aus-trians and to defend the impotent and unpopular rulers of the liberated states of Italy. It was the development of this danger, towards the end of September, which induced Bonaparte, whilst sending home (October 2nd) urgent demands for reinforcements, to direct the thoughts of the Italians towards republicanism and nationalism, as the best means of diverting their attention from the weakness of the French army to the crimes of their own governments, and of encouraging them to set up popular re-gimes more capable of keeping order and supplying the French troops with the necessities of war.

Thus he writes to the Senate of Bologna on September 26th: 'Woe to those who attract the indignation of the French army! Woe to Ravenna, Faenza and Rimini, if they are ever so misled as to forget the respect they owe to the victorious army, and to the friends of popular liberty! . . . The time has come for Italy to take an honourable place amongst the Powers. Lombardy, Bologna, Modena, Reggio, Ferrara, perhaps the Romagna too, if she shows herself worthy, will one day astonish Europe, and will recapitulate the finest hours of Italian history. To Arms! The free part of Italy is rich and populous. Put fear into the enemies of your rights and of your freedom. I shall not forget you. The republicans will point you the way to victory. You will learn with them to beat down the tyrants.'

Such language, Bonaparte might well feel, required some explanation to the Directory. He wrote to them on October 17th: 'Bologna, Modena, Reggio and Ferrara have met in congress, each sending about 100 deputies to Modena. They are animated by the liveliest enthusiasm and the purest patriotism. Already they envisage a revival of ancient Italy. Their imagination has caught fire, their patriotism is stirred, and citizens of every class are standing together. I shall not be surprised if this district and Lombardy rouse a real and important movement throughout Italy. Revolution (he goes on) bears a different character here from that it bore amongst us, principally because it has not the same obstacles to surmount, and because these people can profit by our experience. We can at any rate be confident that we have nothing to fear in this district from fanaticism, and that if Rome thinks it well to declare a war of religion she will have no success in the conquered territories.'

'There are at the moment in Lombardy,' he explains to the Directors on December 28th, 'three parties: (1) that which allows itself to be led by the French, (2) that which would like liberty, and even shows its desire for it with a certain amount of impatience, and (3) that which is friendly to the Austrians and hostile to the French. The first I support and encourage, the second I restrain, the third I suppress.'

It is not necessary to find in Bonaparte's declarations a deliberate traversing of the Directorial policy; it is rather that he is trying to interpret his instructions as liberally as he dares in view of a military situation not fully understood in Paris; indulging the republican movement in the Italian states without recognizing republican governments; giving it a twist towards a nationalism strong enough to be a threat to Rome and Naples without becoming a danger to the invader; and arming the liberated states to keep order and organize supplies on the lines of communication of his army. He is not in a position to dictate a policy to his masters at home; but he is hopeful that they will come to acquiesce in a modification of it dictated by circumstances beyond their control.

9

So much for Lombardy and central Italy. Bonaparte's real anxiety all the time was the gathering of fresh Austrian armies on his left front, and the hostility of Venice, which lay between him and any advance east of Verona. It had been part of his Instructions on May 7th to treat Venice as a neutral, but not as a friend. He had been informed by the Directors on June 2nd that the Venetians were helping the Austrian army with supplies, and he had been authorized to seize any such convoys. On the 11th he was instructed, in view of their complaints of French action at Brescia, to put the screw on the Venetians, but not to declare open war. 'In the present delicate situation your moves must do nothing to hasten a rupture.'

Bonaparte's message of May 29th to the Venetian Republic shows how he applied this policy. 'The French army,' he wrote, 'in its pursuit of the Austrians, is advancing into territory of the Venetian Republic; but it will not forget that the two republics are united by a long-standing friendship. Religion, government, customs, and property will be respected. The General in command relies upon the officers, magistrates, and priests of the Venetian Republic to make his sentiments known to the people, so that confidence may cement the friendship which has so long united the two nations.' A few days later (June 4th) Lallement was instructed to read the Venetian 'Sages' a lecture on their action in allowing the Austrians to hold Peschiera; at the same time he was told that Bonaparte could not afford to quarrel with a republic whose alliance was so useful to him.

But Bonaparte's dispatch of June 7th suggests another and more dishonest policy. 'If it is your intention to extract 5 or 6 millions from Venice,' he writes, 'I have provided just the rupture you need for the purpose; you could demand an indemnity for the battle I had to fight in order to take Borghetto. If your intentions go beyond this, I think we ought to keep this opportunity for dissension alive.' Meanwhile Lambert is instructed (June 10th) to exact the maximum of supplies from Venice, not paying for anything, but giving I.O.U.s.

This technique of extortion was more than approved by the Directory, who wrote again on June 15th, and told Bonaparte that he should now demand an advance of 12 million *livres tournois* on the security of a Dutch loan to France. His reply (July 12th) was to suggest that the Directors should 'pick a small quarrel with the Venetian minister in Paris, so as to facilitate the demand.' He described how he was squeezing supplies out of the unwilling Venetians, but said that he must defer the demand for the two millions until the fall of Mantua enabled him to risk a definite break with Venice. When the Directors (August 12th) showed a little impatience on this score, he wrote at greater length (August 26th): 'I have begun to open negotiations with the Venetians, by demanding food for the army. The very moment I have cleared the Tyrol, negotiations in conformity with your instructions will be started. But at the moment they would be no use. These fellows have a strong fleet, and they are safe from any coercion in their capital. It might be very difficult to force them to sequestrate English and Imperial property.' Again, on October 2nd, he remarks that Venice hates us more than any other city in Italy, and is arming for defence; but that nothing can be done till the fall of Mantua.

Such indeed, had by now become the refrain of all Bonaparte's dispatches. Never was there a clearer case in military history of a campaign, and all that depended on it, being held up by the failure to capture a solitary fortress. Ever since its investment at the beginning of July the Directors had insisted (July 17th) that its capture must precede both the defeat of Wurmser and the advance on Venice. An unsuccessful sortie by the garrison, which was decimated by sickness (so Bonaparte reported to the Directors on July 22nd) encouraged them to hope that this would soon come about. But it did not; and they accepted philosophically the general's decision, reported by Saliceti on August 2nd, to raise the siege for the moment, in order to deal with fresh Austrian attacks from the north. Mantua, which was an embarrassment to the French, was also a snare for the Austrians: if Bonaparte's army was too weak to contain it, Wurmser's was not strong enough to relieve it.

The victory of Castiglione (August 5th) freed Bonaparte's hands again. The victory of Arcola (November 16th)—the climax of a fortnight's campaign against Wurmser's second attempt to raise the siege—made the ultimate fall of Mantua a foregone conclusion: this at last, after four months' anxious expectation, the Directors were able to assume in their letter to Bonaparte of December 1st. No wonder that Paris began to count on the long-expected news, and that the Rouen potters designed bowls representing the commander of the garrison handing over the key of the town to the victor of Arcola, inscribed in imperfect French *Prises et capitulation du fort de Mentout per les Francois*, 1786. In fact it was not until February 1797 that the place finally fell, as a result of the further victory of Rivoli (January 15th-16th): and by that time new plans were already well advanced.

The Austrians, aided by the failure of the French armies north of the Alps to contain their reinforcements, had shown unexpected powers of recovery. As long ago as May 31st, Bonaparte might remember, he had said in an *ordre du jour* 'The Austrians have been completely driven out of Italy'; and on June 21st he had told the Directory 'All Italy is French.' Two months later, after the set-back which involved the retreat from Mantua, and which Bonaparte himself described as a defeat (*nous avons essayés des revers*, August 2nd), he was able to boast again (August 8th) 'The Austrian army . . . has disappeared like a dream,' and was planning an advance to Trieste which would open the road to Vienna (August 14th, September 6th). But still Austrian reinforcements flowed over the Brenner, outnumbering his depleted troops, and it might take another three months to reduce Mantua (October 1st). On the eve of Arcola (November 13th) he admits 'We may be on the point of losing Italy,' and uses terms almost of despair. When the battle is won, he praises his generals, but does not boast that he has destroyed the enemy. A month later (December 27th) he is wondering whether the Emperor may not be preparing a fresh attack for the New Year.

He was; and it was not till the middle of March (17th), after the battle of Rivoli, that he could write confidently to the Directory: 'The last campaign has destroyed the Emperor's resources . . . he has no more troops in the interior of his states.' This hydra-headed regrowth of the Imperial armies, rather than any predilection for a further advance eastwards, or even dislike of the government's central Italian designs, was the chief cause of Bonaparte's unwillingness to commit himself to any prolonged campaign on the far side of the Apennines.

10

But when the spring came, and Mantua was at last in his hands, it must have been a sad disappointment to Bonaparte to find himself diverted for a second time from Vienna to Rome, from the pursuit of the Emperor to the punishment of the Pope.

Four months ago (October 15th, 18th) the Directors had suggested that, if he thought it a good moment ('and we think that you will apply to this question the capacity for a bird's eye view [*coup d'œil*] for which you are well known') he might now deal with Rome; and they had given him full powers to make a fresh armistice with the Pope, or even to conclude the treaty of peace which had been hanging fire all the summer. If the Pope refuses to sign, he may take military measures, and march on Rome.

Negotiations with the Papacy had already begun, before Bonaparte received this letter. On October 21st he had made a final appeal to Cardinal Mattei to prevent war. 'Go to Rome, see the Holy Father, enlighten him as to his real interests; rescue him from the intrigues of those who desire the ruin of himself and of the court of Rome.' Three days later, perhaps on the receipt of the Directors' letter of the 15th, he had instructed Cacault, the French ambassador to the Holy See, to take advantage of the favourable position of French affairs in Naples, Genoa, Sardinia and the Mediterranean to press on the negotiations. But Bonaparte is only waiting for a suitable moment to 'make a dash for Rome, and avenge the national honour by seizing Ancona; so Cacault must play for time, and keep the ball in the air (*se jeter réciproquement la balle*), so as to outwit that old fox' (the Pope). On the 28th Cacault is further authorized to assure the Pope 'that I have always been opposed to the treaty hitherto proposed to him, and particularly to the style of the negotiations, and that it is as a result of my special and repeated representations that the Directory has authorized me to open fresh negotiations. My ambition is to be called the saviour, not the destroyer of the Holy See.'

Hitherto nothing had come of this nicely blended policy of flattery and force. But on January 22nd, 1797, within ten days of the victory of Rivoli, Cardinal Mattei received just such a letter as had reached him on October 21st, 1796, preparing him for a French occupation of Rome; and Cacault had his instructions the same day. This time it was serious. On February 1st Bonaparte was at Bologna, and issued a characteristic proclamation: The French army is entering Papal territory: it will be faithful to the principles it professes: it will protect religion and the people. But (1) any village that sounds the tocsin on the approach of the French will be burnt down, and its municipal officers shot; (2) any commune on whose territory a Frenchman's life is attacked will be subjected to martial law, hostages taken, and fines levied; and (3) if priests 'conduct themselves according to Gospel principles' they will be well treated and reinstated, but if not they will be treated with more severity than ordinary civilians. Another proclamation the same day accused the Pope of violating the armistice.

Then the advance began. On February 2nd Bonaparte was at Sant' Antonio; on the 3rd at Faenza and Forli; on the 4th at Rimini, and demanding that the Republic of San Marino should surrender its bishop, who had taken refuge there; on the 7th at Pesaro; on the 9th at Sinigaglia; and on the 10th he reports from Ancona the capture of that port, together with £350,000 worth of treasure from Loretto, and the friendly welcome given to the French troops by people tired of Papal misrule. At Naples on February 7th the news of his advance prevented the annual liquefaction of the blood of St. Januarius: but the omen was in vain. On the 14th, about the time he received secret instructions from the Directory (February 3rd) for the opening of the campaign, it was practically over, and he was writing from Macerata about the terms that he proposed to dictate to the Pope.

The treaty of Tolentino, which Bonaparte dispatched home on the 19th, did not accord with his instructions, and he was at pains to excuse his deviations from them. 'The Roman religion,' the Directors had written, 'will always be an irreconcilable enemy of the Republic,' and, to defeat it, propaganda must be backed by force. Bonaparte must, therefore, do all he can to destroy the Papal government; if possible, by setting up a French government which by its good rule will make the regime of the Papacy doubly unpopular.

This Bonaparte had neither the will nor the resources to undertake: he had no wish to tie up a large part of his army policing the Papal states. He therefore contented himself with forcing the Pope to surrender his claims to Avignon and the Legations, to pay a huge indemnity, and to close his ports to all hostile navies. It was better (he explained to the Directors) to have three Papal states in the hand than all in the bush; as it was better to have 30 millions in cash than to occupy a city which would not yield 5 millions. Besides, the king of Naples might intervene, and make the position at Rome untenable. It was, once again, a choice between diplomatic and military interests, and military interests won the day. Next day Bonaparte was back at Ancona, and reached Bologna on the 24th. The second march on Rome had lasted no longer than the first: just three weeks.

II

At last Bonaparte was free to begin his advance north-eastwards from the Lombardy plain towards Villach, Bruck and Vienna. He was not likely to underrate the difficulties of this new adventure. His troops had already covered some 500 *kilomètres*, 'as the crow flies,' from the Italian frontier to the head of the Adriatic: they had as far again to go, before they could hope to see the Danube. Though the army had been reinforced by two divisions from the Rhine front, two had to be detached into the Tyrol to guard the left flank of the advance. It was by no means certain that they could do so, in difficult country, and against the threat of a fresh Austrian advance over the Brenner Pass. Besides, if the march on Vienna were delayed, or, if it did not force the Emperor to make terms quickly, fresh dangers might be expected to arise from the direction of Venice, Milan, or Genoa.

On the other hand, it was the best and last opportunity likely to offer itself, and the risk was not greater than the prize. England, the chief ally of Austria, had evacuated the Mediterranean, and now grudged subsidies which seemed to yield no return. The new Tsar (Paul had succeeded Catherine on November 16th, 1796) was unfriendly to the Allies. The Archduke Charles, the most popular and competent general that Austria could put in the field, had visited the Italian front, and reported against further resistance. At court only Thugut still stood out for a fight to the finish. Patriotism might still be roused by the singing of Haydn's *Gott erhalte Franz der Kaiser* (1797), which became a national anthem, or by the resistance of guerrilla forces in the Tyrol: but it was not anticipated that serious opposition would be offered to Bonaparte's advance, or that peace negotiations could be long delayed.

This advance was as rapid as the world had now come to expect. It was heralded by a proclamation 'to the soldiers of the army of Italy' issued from Bassano on March 10th. By the 14th the French troops were across the Piave, and Bonaparte slept at Sacile on the Livenza. His generals were ordered to receive no Austrian *parlementaires*. Two days later he was beyond the Tagliamento, and on March 20th reported to the Directory that he had crossed the Isonzo: he sent Kellermann home next day (was he glad to be rid of a rival?) with twenty-four flags captured during the advance. Now he was in German-speaking territory, and could publish from Gorizia the promises and warnings that accompanied every French army in a foreign land: nor was it insignificant that he chose this moment for inscribing on the flags of the Fifty-seventh *La terrible 57e demi-brigade que rien n'arrête*. Nevertheless he was not entirely easy. On the 22nd he wrote home, 'All the Emperor's forces are on the move, and steps are being taken in every state of the House of Austria to oppose us.' In a week he hopes to be at Klagenfurt, within fourteen stages of Vienna. But unless Moreau moves up quickly from the Rhine, and anticipates any Austrian flank attack from Innsbruck, it will be impossible to maintain his advance.

Bonaparte reached Klagenfurt, as he had said he would, on March 30th. The next day he wrote to the Archduke Charles suggesting that he should ask for terms; meanwhile pushing on to Leoben (April 7th), and even posting an advance guard on the Semmering Pass, almost within sight of Vienna. This was the end of the war party in the capital. The same day Austrian envoys arrived in the French camp; and after a week's talk, preliminary terms of peace were signed at Leoben on April 18th. The campaign had lasted just five weeks.

12

Nevertheless six months were to elapse before the final terms of peace were signed on October 17th. Why was there this interval? What issues were at stake? Summarily speaking, the delay was due to differences of opinion not only between Paris and Vienna, but also between Paris and Milan.

In Paris the position of the government, between April 18th and October 17th, 1797, underwent a profound change. The trial of Babeuf coincided with the beginning of the elections for the renewal of one-third of the national representatives. In the reaction from *Babouvisme* the Royalists gained a majority, and, the day after Babeuf's execution, secured a place on the Directory for their nominee, Barthélemy. Their general, Pichegru, President of the Council of the Five Hundred, was found to be intriguing with the royalist Clichy Club for a Bourbon restoration. The evidence for this came from Italy. The Comte de Provence, having been refused permission by the British government to go to Toulon as Regent in 1793, retired from Turin to Verona, where he joined in every plot against the Directory. Since the death of the Dauphin in the Temple he had assumed the title of 'Louis XVIII,' but was passing incognito as the 'Comte de Lille.' One of Bonaparte's first acts in Italy (April 13th, 1796) had been to demand his expulsion by the government of Venice: he then thrust his embarrassing company on Condé and the royalist army in the Rhineland. But his agents were still in Italy a year later, and in June the Comte d'Antraigues was arrested at Trieste with papers implicating Pichegru. Bonaparte at once forwarded them to Barras, after expunging a passage which might have been used against himself. This brought matters to a head. On September 4th the Jacobin Directors helped by Bonaparte's nominee, General Augereau, who was put in command of the troops in Paris, carried through the *coup détat* of the 15th Fructidor. Strengthened by the exclusion of Barthélemy and Carnot, the new Directory assumed almost dictatorial powers. Its control was re-established on an alliance with the army. It was the first unashamedly military *coup* since 1789, and an omen of what was to follow two years later. Any hopes that the Austrian negotiators at Leoben had of extracting favourable terms from a government weakened by internal discord were disappointed.[7]

At Milan, meanwhile, Bonaparte was making the most of the personal prestige he had won by his twelve months' victorious campaign—for April 12th was the anniversary of his opening battle at Montenotte. On May 5th he came into residence (the royal phrase is not inappropriate) at the palace of Mombello, belonging to the Crivelli family, outside Milan. There Joséphine queened it—and none could do so more acceptably—over a Republican court, wearing a cameo necklace presented to her by the Pope, and surrounded by the leading poets and artists of the country, whilst Bonaparte himself discussed geometry with Mascheroni, patronized the Observatory at Verona, accepted the dedication of Monti's *Prometeo*, and held long conversations with Melzi about the political future of Italy. All this, he knew, would be reported in Paris by French visitors. To counteract any jealousy that might arise there, he was careful to keep the army of Italy strong and contented. The veterans of 1796 were picked out for promotion, and a *corps d'élite* was specially attached to the general's person. Inscribed swords were presented to the hundred bravest men in the ranks, selected by the vote of their comrades. The Grand Army and the Imperial Guard were already in the making.

But Bonaparte's Jacobinism was hardly suspect. From Milan, almost from Mombello, he published two papers: *Le courrier de l'armée d'Italie*, nominally edited by *une société de Français républicains*, but in fact by Jullien, a young Robespierrist, implicated in the Babeuf plot, which spread ultra-republican sentiments under the badge of the *fasces* and the *bonnet rouge*; and *France vue de l'armée d'Italie*, a 'political administrative and literary' journal, republican too in its sentiments, but anti-terrorist, edited by Regnaud de Saint-Jean d'Angely, as moderate a Jacobin as Jullien was an extremist. The relative popularity of the two papers can be judged by the fact that the first ran to 248 numbers, the second only to 18: but Bonaparte could quote whichever he pleased.

He was no longer supervised by a *Commissaire aux armées*. Garrau and Clarke, instructed to report on his conduct, gave reassuring accounts of his republican sentiments. He had missed no opportunity for assuring the

Directors of his loyalty to the government, or for reminding them of the amount of 'reparations' (as they would be called nowadays) which he had levied from the Italian states—a letter of May 26th puts the total at over 12 million francs, or some £600,000.

On the anniversary of the Fall of the Bastille, which was celebrated with an elaborate fête, Bonaparte told his troops: 'Soldiers! You see before you the names of your brothers in arms who died on the field of honour for the liberty of their country. They have set you an example. You owe your whole duty to the Republic, to the happiness of thirty million Frenchmen, and to the glorious name which has received fresh distinction from your victories. I know that you are deeply moved by the ills that threaten the Fatherland. But it is not in any real danger. The men who secured its victory over allied Europe are still there. Mountains separate us from France: but you would cross them with all the swiftness of an eagle to uphold the constitution, defend liberty, and protect the government and the republic. The government watches over the deposit of law committed to its charge. The moment when the royalists show themselves will be their last. Do not be disturbed. Let us swear by the shades of the heroes who died at our side for liberty, let us swear on our new banners, "Total war against the enemies of the Republic and of the Constitution of the Year III." ' Nor could there be any doubt that such were their sentiments.

The earnest of this loyalty, and of a promise which was almost a threat, was the mission of Augereau, which saved the Directory on September 4th. Staunch Jacobins such as Thibaudeau (who presented a report to the Five Hundred on August 21st), might object to the intervention of the army in political matters. But after that service it was unlikely that the Directors would press any doubts they had with regard to Bonaparte's peace policy. That the government and the higher command did not see eye to eye about the future of Italy had long been obvious. As time went on, differences of opinion appeared within the Directory itself. The anti-Catholic Reubell was for destroying the Pope: La Revellière already dreamed of a united Italy: Barras hesitated to give up such valuable conquests. Bonaparte took advantage of these disagreements to negotiate the preliminary terms of Leoben without consulting Paris; whilst Clarke, the accredited diplomatist of the Directors, tactfully stayed at Turin.

Clarke's mission dated originally from November 15th, 1796, when he had been commissioned by the Directors, at Carnot's instigation, to follow up certain proposals made by French agents at Vienna, and to appeal directly to the Emperor for a general armistice. He was an Irishman, of more charm than intelligence, who had come to the front in the service of the Duc d'Orléans. The programme he was instructed to carry out was of course contrary to Bonaparte's republicanizing policy in north Italy, and was compromised by Bonaparte's promises to the King of Sardinia. His mission at first prospered at Turin, where he presented letters of recommendation from the old anti-republican Choiseul; but at Milan he was suspected and snubbed by Bonaparte; and the refusal of Thugut to give him any facilities soon brought his mission to a standstill. Meanwhile Bonaparte was, as usual, altering the whole outlook by military means. When Clarke next set out for Italy (February 3rd, 1797) he brought proposals more acceptable to the victor of Arcola and Rivoli, and was instructed, in a significant afterthought, to co-operate fully with the general in his negotiations, and 'neither to propose nor make any moves until they have been found to be consistent with the interests of the republic and the safety of its army.'

On April 8th, the day after signing an armistice with the Archduke Charles, Bonaparte outlined the terms he intended to impose. 'If the Emperor surrenders to us his possessions on the left bank of the Rhine, and recognizes the Rhine as the frontier of the Republic; if he cedes to the Cispadane Republic the Duchy of Modena and Carrara; if he hands over Mayence to us unimpaired in exchange for Mantua; then I think we shall have made a much more advantageous peace than that envisaged in the instructions I have received from General Clarke.'

Ten days later, after signing the peace terms at Leoben, he had to excuse the granting of less severe terms, for now the Rhine frontier settlement remained vague, and Austria was compensated for the loss of Lombardy (west of the Oglio) by the possession of Venice, with its territories on the mainland of Italy (east of the Oglio) and in the Adriatic; and he did so by alleging the precariousness of his military position, and the necessity of acting without Clarke. 'If I had insisted, at the opening of the campaign, on advancing to Turin, I should never have crossed the Po: if I had insisted on advancing to Rome, I should have lost Milan: if I had not insisted on marching on Vienna, it might have been fatal to the Republic. The one and only plan for destroying the Emperor was the one I have carried out, and that with only 6000 cavalry and 20,000 infantry': another such force might have crossed the Rhine, and made his victory complete. (The irony of the situation was that Moreau in fact crossed the Rhine two days after the signing of the terms at Leoben, and Bonaparte did not hear of it till too late.) After waiting ten days for Clarke (he says), he had taken the responsibility of signing the terms himself. 'You gave me full plenary powers (*plein pouvoir*) over all diplomatic [*but he surely means 'military'?*] operations; and, as things were, the preliminaries of peace, even with the Emperor, had become a military operation.' Three days later he wrote again. 'The House of Austria (he said) has immense resources. It has used English gold to make war, and its people are attached to their government. By granting it favourable terms we make ourselves independent of the King of Prussia, and in a position to hold the balance between the two Powers.'

A week later he urged another consideration: the Leoben settlement was the only way to get a free hand to deal with Venice—'that cruel and bloodthirsty state.'

13

Bonaparte's treatment of Venice was, in fact, the crux of the whole situation. During his eastward advance from the Isonzo he had been careful to do nothing to offend the government of the Doge, which might endanger his southern flank: the quarrels and accusations of the previous winter were temporarily forgotten. But the wealth and weakness of the Venetian republic had from the first marked it out for victimization. The two million inhabitants of its territories enjoyed an annual revenue of over a million and a half sterling. Its bank was the financial centre of Italy. Its luxury products were in demand all over the Western world, and were carried by its ships to all the ports of the Levant: Viennese coinage was current throughout the nearer East. Its 'republic' was in reality a decadent oligarchy, unlikely to win much sympathy from French Jacobins. The possession of Venice was, therefore, an obvious and easy bribe with which to induce Austria to surrender its claims to Lombardy and the west bank of the Rhine: the more so as the Emperor had already, in January 1795, revealed to Catherine of Russia his desire to regain 'the territories usurped by the Venetian Republic' at the head of the Adriatic.

The first suggestion of such a transaction came from Clarke at Turin, in the month that the French advance on Vienna began, and concerned only the cession of Venetian Croatia; but this was some justification for the larger concessions that Bonaparte proposed at Leoben at the end of his five weeks' campaign. No sooner was the armistice of April 9th arranged than he sent Junot to Venice with letters full of accusations and threats. The Venetian envoys sent to Gratz were received with menace of a revenge more cruel than that of Attila and his Huns.

Just at this moment two incidents occurred which gave Bonaparte a convenient text for his accusations: a French ship was fired upon and boarded by the Venetians, and in a clash between rival forces at Verona a number of Frenchmen (perhaps as many as 400) were killed. The second incident came at such a convenient moment for Bonaparte that it was said to have been instigated by his agents. He certainly lost no time in making it an excuse for marching upon Venice, demanding the dismissal of the English ambassador, and refusing to treat with the Venetian envoys until the crime of Venice had been avenged. To the Directory he wrote on April 30th: 'If French blood is to be respected in Europe, if you have no wish to be cheated, a terrible example must be made of Venice. Blood for blood (*il nous faut de sang*). The Venetian admiral who presided over this assassination must be publicly brought to trial.'

In face of the French advance the old Doge Manin—he was to be the last of his succession—could do no more than arrest prominent Franco-phobes, and attempt to bribe Barras: Vienna remained ominously silent. On May 12th he agreed to accept a provisional government nominated by Bonaparte. During the night of the 15th Baraguay d'Hilliers entered the port with vessels provided by the Venetians themselves, and took possession of the city. A tree of Liberty was planted in front of St. Mark's, a copy of the Rights of Man was placed under the paw of the Venetian lion, and the colonnade of the Piazetta was covered with inscriptions in honour of Bonaparte.

The terms of surrender were dispatched to the Directory next day, with a covering letter in which Bonaparte explained their relative moderation by the need of keeping Venice 'in play' until it could be used in the final terms of peace with Austria. And so it was. So long as anything might be gained from the difficulties of the Directory, and the uncertainty whether Bonaparte's policy would be supported in Paris, the Austrian envoys did their best to spin out the negotiations. 'It would be impossible for them to make fun of us more shamelessly,' wrote Bonaparte to the Directors on July 28th; he complained to the Emperor the same day that ever since the arrival of Merveldt at Mombello negotiations had slowed down, and that still, four months after their initiation, the Austrian representatives had not received plenary powers. A fortnight later, in a confidential letter to Talleyrand, he said that the only way to shake the Austrian court out of its dilatory tactics was to threaten another advance on Vienna; and he mentioned rumours (to the Directory, August 16th) that the Imperial armies were themselves on the move.

But the news of Fructidor (September 4th) and of the breaking off of the Anglo-French peace negotiations (September 19th) convinced even Thugut that it was no use standing out for better terms. With Cobenzl representing this new mood, and Bonaparte determined to carry through his plan, in face of a last-minute attempt by Barras to prevent the sacrifice of Italian territory, peace was signed at Campo Formio, midway between the headquarters of the rival plenipotentiaries, on October 17th—just six months after the preliminaries of Leoben. In return for the cession of his territories on the left bank of the Rhine—the princes so expropriated were to be compensated at a Congress to be held at Rastadt—the Emperor re-ceived Salzburg, Venice and the Venetian lands between the Lago di Garda and the Po, Istria, Dalmatia, and the Bocche di Cattaro. The rest of the Venetian land territory went, with Modena, Ferrara, Bologna and Romagna, to the Cisalpine Republic. France took the Ionian Islands and the Albanian possessions of Venice.

During the three months that elapsed between this treaty and the entry of the Austrian troops (January 18th, 1798) their French masters robbed the Venetian Republic of everything of value they could carry away. They stripped the gilt fittings off the ceremonial barge in which the Doge every year celebrated the wedding of his city with the Adriatic, and they took down the bronze horses from Byzantium which stood over the western porch of St. Mark's. But they stand there once more today, facing three great Italian flags, as though defying any foreign soldier to set foot in Venice again.

IV

MALTA

(1797-1798)

VENICE! Perhaps, after Rome, there was no city in Europe which meant so much to the eighteenth century: Venice the bride of the sea; Venice the meeting-place of West and East; Venice a treasury of art and architecture; Venice a home of music and drama; Venice a resort of luxury, fashion and frivolity. But to the realistic view of the French Republic in 1797 it was a government, a port, an arsenal and a fleet to be made use of, if not by persuasion, then by force; and to one mind at least, a mind trained in the combined operations of the Riviera coast-line, it was an open door to the Adriatic and the eastern Mediterranean.

It would be interesting to know when Bonaparte first thought of Venice in this way. During the early months of the Italian campaign it appears in his correspondence only as a factor to be allowed for in strategy, as a possible danger to an invader pressing eastwards beyond the Adige. The first mention of its fleet is as an obstacle to an attempt to coerce its government from the mainland. During and after the advance to Leoben it is still thought of as a strategic danger-point; and during the peace negotiations as a pawn in the diplomatic game. But it is soon clear that, unless or until Venice is handed over to Austria in exchange for the Rhine frontier, its peculiar resources are to be used for the benefit of its French conquerors. Its port and fleet and arsenal are to be the means by which French naval power occupies the islands of the Adriatic, seizes Malta, and prepares an expedition for the conquest of Egypt. Whatever Bonaparte's complaints about the dilatoriness of the Austrian negotiators, these plans must have consoled him during the six months between Leoben and Campo Formio. The terms of peace for which he was working would indeed bring them to an end, unless Venetian resources in ships and supplies could be transferred from Venice to Toulon, from the Adriatic to the western Mediterranean. This, therefore, was the secondary aim he had in view.

Towards the end of May 1797 the great design appears almost suddenly, almost complete, in Bonaparte's correspondence. On the 26th he writes to the Directors: 'The island of Malta is of outstanding importance for us. The Grand Master is dying. His successor is apparently a German; but it would only cost 5 or 600,000 *francs* to secure the succession of a Spaniard. Could it not be hinted to the Prince of the Peace [*Godoy, with whom the Franco-Spanish treaty had been concluded in August* 1796] that he might concern himself with this all-important matter? The 37,000 inhabitants of La Valetta are strongly Francophil. There are no English in the Mediterranean now. Why should not our fleet, or that of Spain, before sailing into the Atlantic, touch at La Valetta, and occupy it? The Knights only number 500, and the regiment of the Order has no more than 600 men. If we miss this opportunity Malta will fall into the hands of the King of Naples. It is a small island, but of inestimable value for us.'

The same day Bonaparte gives General Gentili instructions to fit out an expeditionary force for the Adriatic. Baraguay d'Hilliers will put at his disposal two battalions of infantry, with artillery and ammunition. He will find at Venice five frigates under Bourde, and transports, too, if needed. He must start as promptly and secretly as possible, sail to Corfu, and seize all the Venetian establishments in the Levant, taking care to act as an ally of the Venetian Republic, and in full accord with the commissioners sent by the new government. Besides taking with him two or three Venetian frigates and 600 Venetian rank and file, he is to seize, either at sea or at Corfu, any Venetian ships of war that do not join him of their own accord. If the natives show signs of independence, he is to flatter their opinions, not forgetting in his proclamations to speak of ancient Greece, Athens and Sparta; and he will have some Corsican officials with him (a Napoleonic touch) who understand how to manage islanders, and know the local languages.

Another dispatch to the Directors (May 27th) excuses this high-handed treatment of a sister republic. 'Venice (he declares) has been decadent ever since the discovery of the Cape of Good Hope and the rise of Trieste and Ancona: it can hardly survive the blows we have given it. Its people are stupid, lazy, and quite unfitted for liberty. It has no mainland, and no water supply. It naturally belongs to those whom we make owners of the mainland. We have only to seize all its means of defence, with Corfu and Ancona, which is becoming stronger every day, and which we can hold until the negotiations at Rome enable us to keep it.' The Venetians are thought to be sufficiently rewarded (July 4th) by the removal of the embargo temporarily placed on their port, and by the privilege of using their dockyard for the construction of five French ships (July 7th) at their own expense.

Bonaparte's account of the expedition to Corfu is given in a dispatch to the Directory dated from Milan, August 1st. 'After a successful fortnight's voyage (he writes) the fleet which left Venice anchored in the roads at Corfu. Four Venetian warships which happened to be there joined forces with our fleet [*this way of putting it may be read in the light of Gentili's Instructions already quoted*]. On the 10th *messidor* our troops disembarked, and occupied the Corfu forts, in which they found 600 pieces of artillery, mostly of bronze. A huge crowd gathered on the shore to greet our troops with such cries of eagerness and enthusiasm as animate people who are recovering their freedom. At the head of the crowd was the "pope" or religious chief of the district, an educated man of great age. He advanced towards General Gentili, and said: Frenchmen! you will find in this island a people ignorant of those arts and sciences which distinguish other nations. But do not despise them on that account: they can still become again what they once were. Read this book, and learn to appreciate them. The general opened with curiosity the book which the "pope" presented to him, and was not a little surprised to find that it was the *Odyssey* of Homer. [*Again, in view of Gentili's Instructions, one cannot help wondering whether this incident was entirely spontaneous.*]

'The islands of Zante, Cephalonia and Santa Maura (the dispatch continues) have the same aspirations, and express the same wish and feeling for freedom. Every village has its tree of liberty [*planted by the French?*]. Every commune is ruled by a municipal body; and these people hope that, under the protection of the Great Nation, they will recover the arts, the sciences, and the commerce that they have lost under the tyranny of oligarchs.' And so it goes on.

But Bonaparte's real thoughts were not for the country of the Princess Nausicaa, or the ruins of Ulysses' palace, on which citizen Arnauld had planted the republican tricolor, but for the commercial and strategical importance of this outpost in the Adriatic. 'The islands of Corfu, Zante, and Cephalonia,' he wrote again to the Directors on August 16th, 'matter more to us than all the rest of Italy put together. I believe that, if we had to choose, it would be better to restore Italy to the Emperor, and to keep the four islands. They are vital to the wealth and prosperity of our commerce. The Turkish empire is breaking up every day. If we held these islands we should be in a position either to bolster it up as long as possible, or to take what part of it we want. It will not be long [*here his imagination takes another jump*] before we realize that, if we are effectively to destroy England, we must get hold of Egypt.' (It is worth recording that, ten years before, W. A. Miles had urged on Pitt 'the importance of having an establishment in Egypt, and maintaining the free navigation of the Black Sea.')

To Talleyrand, Minister of Foreign Affairs, he repeated these ideas a month later (September 13th). He was no doubt encouraged to do so by hearing of (though he does not seem to have read it) Talleyrand's address to the *Institut* on July 3rd, in which he had urged the advisability of finding new colonies in the Levant to compensate for the loss of trade with America. But Talleyrand envisaged this policy as following on a general pacification. It was Bonaparte's ambition to initiate it at once, and to make the Levant a fresh front against England. 'We must never give up Corfu and the islands,' he insists again: 'they will provide us with huge commercial opportunities, and they will be of intense concern to us in all future movements in Europe.

'Why should we not (he continues) seize the island of Malta? It would be easy enough for Admiral Brueys to anchor there and occupy it. The town of Valetta has no defenders except 400 Knights and 500 soldiers [*notice the optimistic reduction of numbers since May 26th*]. The inhabitants, more than 100,000 of them [37,000 *before*] are strongly Francophil, and disgusted with the Knights, who can't support themselves, and are dying of hunger. I have made a point of confiscating all their property in Italy. With the island of Saint-Pierre, which the King of Sardinia has ceded to us, with Malta, Corfu, etc., we shall be masters of the whole Mediterranean.

'Supposing (he goes on) that by terms of peace with England we had to give up the Cape of Good Hope, we should then have to seize Egypt. Egypt has never belonged to a European nation: for some centuries only the Venetians have had a partial and precarious hold on the country. It would be possible, starting from here [*he means Venice*] with 25,000 men, and a convoy of eight or ten ships of the line or frigates, to occupy the country. Egypt does not belong to the Turkish Sultan; but Talleyrand had better find out how he would react to the expedition. With armies like ours, to which all religions are the same, Mohammedans, Copts, Arabs, idolaters, etc.—none of it concerns us; we should respect one as much as another.'

Talleyrand's reply to this letter, dated September 23rd, said that the Directors approved of the plan for seizing Malta, and that he would write at greater length about the Egyptian suggestion [this letter is not extant]: but for the moment he confined himself to saying that 'if one were to conquer Egypt, it would have to be for the Porte, in order to outwit the Russian and English intrigues which are constantly cropping up again in that unhappy country. In return for such an important service the Turks could easily be induced to grant us all the influence and commercial privileges we might desire. As a colony Egypt would replace the Antilles;

as a route, it would secure us the commerce of the Indies.' The Minister of Marine (Pléville le Pelley) disapproved of the idea, but relented so far as to send Monge two bundles of maps and papers about Egypt.

2

As the impulse which carried Bonaparte's hopes and ambitions within sight of Vienna had been interrupted twice by orders to march south upon Rome and Naples, so the urge which he felt at Venice for the conquest of Malta and Egypt was overruled by events which diverted his energies, for six months, to enterprises nearer home.

On November 5th, 1797, he heard that he had been appointed Commander-in-Chief of the army of England, and plenipotentiary of the French Republic for the negotiations at Rastadt; and on November 19th he left Turin for Rastadt and Paris. It would not be till May 4th, 1798, that he could sail from Toulon for Malta and Alexandria. The intervening six months were spent on the diplomatic mission to Rastadt (November 20th-December 2nd), a triumphal reception at Paris (December 5th-February 7th, 1798), and a visit of inspection to the Channel ports (February 8th-19th). The period from February 23rd, when he presented to the Directors his report against the invasion of England, to May 4th, really belongs to the Malta-Egypt expedition, to the preparation of which all Bonaparte's energies were then devoted.

The journey to Rastadt took a week. Bonaparte enjoyed travelling, and there was no need to hurry. At Geneva he nearly encountered his old patron and (officially since the *coup d'état* of Fructidor) new enemy, Carnot, who had taken refuge at Nyon. At the old walled town of Morat he went, like any modern tourist, to see the bones of the Burgundians who fell in the battle of 1476, and declared that Charles the Bold was mad to have been beaten. He dined at the famous 'Three Kings' at Basle overlooking the Rhine. He arrived at Rastadt on the evening of November 26th.

He did not think much of the business which had brought him there: to arrange for the simultaneous evacuation of Mayence by the Austrians and of Venice by the French. But he took the opportunity to display his knowledge of German history, and to administer a snub to the Swedish representative, Count Axel Fersen, the adviser, and (most people believed) the lover of Marie-Antoinette, who had been chiefly responsible for the Flight to Varennes in 1791. 'The French Republic (he informed him) will not suffer it that men who are only too well known for their relations with the late French court, men whose names may still be on the list of *émigrés*, should come and outface the ministers of the greatest people on earth. The French nation puts its self-respect even before its political interests.' And he showed him to the door.

On November 30th Bonaparte received the hoped-for recall to Paris. The next day the evacuation agreement was signed, and he set out again. In the evening of December 5th he drove into Paris: not, as at Rastadt, in a coach drawn by eight horses and with a mounted escort, but like any civilian in a *voiture de poste*. Joséphine was not at the rue de Chantereine —she did not arrive till the end of the month; and he must have missed her companionship in the round of business and social engagements that now took up all his time: December 6th, interview with Talleyrand at the Foreign Ministry, and with the Directors at the Luxembourg; 10th, official reception at the Luxembourg and dinner at Talleyrand's; 11th, dinner with the new Director, François de Neufchâteau, to meet the intellectuals—Sieyès, M. J. Chénier, and Laplace; 14th-23rd, work at the Ministry of Marine on the English invasion project; 24th, dinner for 800 guests at the Muséum; 26th, his first appearance as a member at the *Institut*. On December 30th, the evening of Joséphine's arrival, they visited the Théâtre des Arts; on January 3rd, 'all Paris' was at a magnificent fête given by Talleyrand; and on the 21st, as a member of the *Institut*, he attended a service at Saint-Sulpice on the anniversary of the death of Louis XVI.

Paris had known Bonaparte as a schoolboy, as a penniless careerist, and as a suppressor of public riot: it now fêted him as a national hero. He could have no doubt that the capital was at his feet: but he was shrewd enough to keep his head and to calculate his chances. He had in his pocket the letter of July 19th in which the Directors expressed their full approval of his 'political and military' conduct of affairs in Italy, with special reference to Genoa and Venice: but this had been signed by Carnot, and Carnot was now in exile. He hardly knew where he stood with the Directors of Fructidor, though it was the fear of his own army which had put them into power.

When, in the Council of the Five Hundred, Malibran proposed that the Faubourg Saint-Marceau (*nom fanatique et ridicule*) should be renamed Faubourg d'Italie, that there should be erected a monument to the army of Italy, and that Bonaparte should be granted a bonus of £15,000 and a pension of £2500, there was *une très-vive agitation*, and the House proceeded to the order of the day. When he was elected to the First Class of the *Institut* by 305 votes out of 312, and sat with Arnault between Monge and Berthollet, as a *Mécanicien*, Lebrun celebrated the occasion in verse:

> *Collègues, amans de la victoire,*
> *Bonaparte en est le soutien:*
> *Pour vôtre mécanicien*
> *Prenez celui de la victoire.*

But Bonaparte knew that they were jealous of him. Paris soon tires of its heroes. Not all the Austrian flags hung in the Invalides by Bonaparte's victorious generals; not all the famous pictures and statuary displayed in the Louvre; not all the news of peace terms extracted from a humiliated enemy, could long postpone the inevitable *ennui*.

3

Bonaparte was quick to feel the change of atmosphere, and would welcome any opportunity of fresh employment in the field. In his first speech at the *Institut*, on December 23rd, he had declared that 'the real conquests, the only kind which leave no regrets behind them, are those made over ignorance. A nation's most honourable and useful occupation is to contribute to the spread of humane ideas. Henceforth the true power of the French republic should consist in the appropriation of every new idea in the world.' It must have occurred to his hearers that Egypt was a more favourable field for experiments in republican science and culture than England or Ireland; and the plans upon which Bonaparte had been working for the past fortnight implied the mobilizing of an expeditionary force in the Mediterranean which might as easily be directed towards the east as the west. Pléville le Pelley, Minister of Marine, had reported on December 11th that a large enough fleet could be collected at Brest to secure command of the Channel, and a safe crossing: but he was less sure about transports; and it was to report on this side of the problem that Bonaparte was dispatched to inspect the Channel ports (February 12th).

How far his mind was already made up is open to question. But he must have drawn unfavourable conclusions from Hoche's failure to land at Bantry Bay in 1796, and he cannot have been impressed by his three short interviews with Wolfe Tone in the third week of December 1797. Was it without his knowledge that, as soon as he had started for the Channel, Talleyrand produced his report in favour of the Egyptian expedition? However this may be, the impression left by his flying visits to Etaples, Boulogne, Ambleteuse, Calais and Dunkirk, and his short round by Nieuport and Ostend, is that he was looking for evidence of the insufficiency of the ports and the preparations. His summary verdict may very well have been that described by Bourrienne, who says that he asked him on the way back: 'Well, General, what do you think of it all? Are you satisfied?'—and he replied, with a shake of the head, 'It would be too much of a toss-up (*un coup de trop chanceux*): I shan't risk it.' To Marmont he remarked, 'Nothing can be done with these fellows: they haven't the means to carry out the plan. We should need a whole fleet of transports; and already the English have more ships than we have. The indispensable preparations are beyond our means.'

Ireland might be the British Vendée; but Bonaparte had no desire for a second Quiberon. He thought he understood naval affairs as well as military. He shared the common French view that there was no great difference between *l'armée de mer* and *l'armée de terre*. He had some not very happy memories of 'combined tactics' in Corsican waters. He believed that a direct attack in force on London, the heart of British wealth and government, was the most likely road to victory over France's last and most stubborn opponent. Capitals always drew him on. But he had no illusions as to the difficulty of such an expedition. The report that he presented to the Directors after his inspection of the Channel coast is so important in itself, and of such interest, that it deserves more attention than is usually given to it.

'Whatever efforts we make (he wrote), we shall not acquire supremacy at sea for a number of years yet. A landing in England without command of the sea would be the most audacious and difficult operation ever carried out. It could only be done either by a surprise crossing, or by avoiding the British fleet blockading Brest and the Texel, or by a night landing in small craft (which would take six to seven hours) at some point on the coast of Kent or Sussex. This last would need long nights, and would be impossible after April. The development of *nôtre marine* is four months behind that of England: a few ships at Brest and Dunkirk, neither ready nor able to put to sea; some armed sloops (*chaloupes canonnières*) at Brest, L'Orient and Cherbourg, but no chance of concentrating them. The English expedition seems therefore to be impossible before next year; and then it will probably be held up by commitments on the continent. The real opportunity for such an expedition has been lost, perhaps for ever.'

Still, he admits, if by March we could mobilize and arm all our available vessels from Bordeaux to Antwerp, and concentrate them at Havre or Dunkirk, 'the expedition might still be possible.' This would involve a number of new measures and appointments, an expenditure on the navy alone of £40,000 a week (with another £15,000 for the army); it would mean speeding up the dockyards, 'pressing' sailors, and confiscating British and neutral ships. It would also require the exclusion of foreign, and especially British and American ships from our harbours, and the drafting of troops from Switzerland, Lyon and Nîmes for the army of invasion.

If all this is beyond our means (and Bonaparte evidently thinks it is), then 'we must give up any idea of an English expedition, content ourselves with keeping up the appearance of it, and concentrate our attention and all our means on the Rhine, so as to deprive England of Hanover and Hamburg. It is obvious that, to accomplish both these aims, we must not keep a large army at a distance from Germany. Alternatively (he goes on) we might well make an expedition into the Levant, to threaten *le commerce des Indes*.

'If none of these operations is feasible (he ends), I see nothing for it but to make peace with England. I am convinced that she would accept today the proposals turned down by Malmesbury. If so, we could derive great advantages from our negotiations at Rastadt: and if peace were concluded whilst the Congress is still sitting, we should *ipso facto* find ourselves able to stiffen our demands on the German Empire.'

Bonaparte was too shrewd to commit himself completely against the English invasion and in favour of an expedition to Egypt; and for some days, whilst the decision was still *sub judice*, the preparations for the invasion went on. They had in fact gone so far that at the meetings of the Directors on February 24th and 25th the English plan was still accepted, and resolutions were taken upon it consequential on the difficulties raised in Bonaparte's report. But on March 2nd came a gloomy message from the interim Minister of Marine, Lambrechts, more than confirming Bonaparte's account of the backwardness of the naval preparations in the north; and within a week opinion swung round in favour of the alternative scheme. Contemporary gossip, echoed in Barras's *Memoirs*, said that some of the Directors were attracted by the idea of keeping the army as far as possible away from the capital, or that La Revellière viewed Bonaparte as a missionary of his favourite cult, Theophilanthropy. But surely Protestant London was a more likely mission-field than Mohammedan Cairo?

No. The ruling considerations were practical enough. The most effective naval and military forces of the Republic were in the south; Toulon and Marseille were better bases than Brest and Cherbourg; Venice could provide ships as well as Antwerp; and above all the Mediterranean, unlike the Channel, was for the moment free of British ships: even if they returned there, it gave more space in which to move. Finally it was estimated that, whereas it would require over 42,000 infantry and 4500 cavalry to invade England, Egypt could be conquered by a force half that size.

So on April 28th Berthier was instructed to countermand the drafting of troops from the army of Italy to that of England; and on March 5th Bonaparte presented to the Directory, evidently by request, a Note estimating the forces that would be required to seize Malta and Egypt, and the probable expense of the expedition. He placed this at the moderate figure of £250,000, excluding the cost of preparations. From that moment the Egyptian expedition held the field; and the stepping-stone to Egypt was Malta.[1]

4

The case for the seizure of Malta had been in the minds of the Directors for at least six months before the decision of March 1798, and had only been temporarily put aside during the preparations for the English invasion.

The Revolution in France had drastically altered relations with the

Knights of Malta, the nominal but in fact impotent rulers of the island. The law of July 30th, 1791, had suppressed all Orders of Chivalry in France; but, in deference to the long-standing arrangement by which the Knights of Malta received an annual subsidy from France towards the up-keep of the port and hospital at Valetta (of so much importance to French trade with the Levant), there was no interference with their rights. But a year later (September 19th, 1792), all property in France belonging to the Order was sequestrated, and the lands and buildings sold; the proceeds going to provide pensions for their previous owners.

As early as August 1790 delegates of the principal French ports and manufacturing towns had petitioned the Assembly to annex the island. Caruson, sent on a mission there in 1796, reported in favour of exploiting the financial difficulties of the Knights, and acquiring so valuable a commercial centre. So long as Austria held Venice it had an opportunity of seizing Malta; and it seemed to be the first move in this direction when, on the death of the Grand Master of the Order in July 1797, he was replaced by Hompesch, the Austrian nominee. This was the occasion on which Bonaparte first urged the importance of the Ionian Isles as a stepping-stone to the Levant.

Now it was part of his contention, in the report of March 5th, that the forces necessary for the invasion of Malta and Egypt were already available in Italy or the south of France, and need not be drawn from the army of England: the British Admiralty might still think the expedition was intended for the Channel, and might leave the Mediterranean unguarded east of Gibraltar—as in fact they did until the very time of Bonaparte's sailing. He reckoned that, between them, Civita Vecchia, Genoa, Corsica, Marseille, Nice and Antibes could supply 24,600 infantry and 2800 cavalry, approximately the 20-25,000 infantry and 2-3000 cavalry that he had estimated would suffice for the expedition. The necessary artillery, put at 60 field and 40 siege guns, could be supplied from the same depots, together with 3-500 cannon-balls each; and every soldier would have what was thought enough in those days—100 rounds of ammunition. The ships and transports had still to be manned: gunners, sappers, bridge-builders and so forth would swell the total.

When the expedition at last got under way, it consisted, according to an official return made to Bonaparte on May 13th, of 13 ships of the line (*vaisseaux*), 6 frigates, 1 corvette, 2 more *vaisseaux* and 7 frigates acting as armed transports (*armées en flûte*), and 26 small craft (*bâtimens légers*): the crews of all these vessels numbered 3488 men. The convoy consisted of between 280 and 309 ships of all sizes, with crews totalling 3000 men. The members of the landing force included (according to the pay-sheet) *État-major général*, 143 persons; *État-major d'Artillerie*, 67; *Corps de génie*, 66; *Commissaires des guerres*, 26; *Officiers de santé*, 168;

Trésorerie de l'armée, 41; *Administrations*, 445; *Savants, artistes*, etc., 167; *Infanterie légère*, 5403; *Infanterie de bataille*, 19,669; *Guides*, 480; *Troupes à cheval*, 2810; *Artillerie et génie*, 3245; *Officiers de corps (au complet)*, 2270. This gives a landing force of 35,000: but to these there still remained to be added a body of some 1500 *Conducteurs et canonniers d'artillerie*; together with the crews of the war-ships (3488) and of the transports (3000): so that the grand total cannot have been less than 43,000—nearly double the number estimated in Bonaparte's report of March 5th, little smaller than the force required for the invasion of England.

Bonaparte had been given (March 5th) practically *carte blanche* in planning the expedition. He spent the intervening eight weeks, as his correspondence shows, in elaborate and extensive preparations. He was in supreme command both of the army and of the fleet, with Brueys as nominal admiral, Berthier as chief of staff, Caffarelli in command of the engineers, Dommartin of the artillery; with Desaix, Kléber, Menou and four other divisional generals; Lannes, Murat, Davout and ten other brigadiers; and Junot, Eugène Beauharnais and Louis Bonaparte on the staff. A letter to Brueys (April 22nd) shows Bonaparte's complete confidence in his own ability to issue orders for the disposition of the fleet and convoy, the duties of the frigates, and the formation to be adopted in the event of a naval engagement with the British fleet. 'This plan of mine,' he ends, 'is perhaps contrary to that generally adopted, but the benefits I see in it are so great that I am sure it will be to our advantage.'

But Bonaparte had not forgotten that this was to be something more than an operation of war. Was he not a member of the *Institut* as well as a general? Egypt was to be conquered, but it was also to be civilized. If it would be exploited as a colony, it would also be explored as a museum of antiquities. He would bring back to Paris the wealth of the East, as he had already sent back the wealth of the South—statues, inscriptions, manuscripts. So he would take with him men of learning and science, a *Commission des Sciences et des Arts*: Monge, who had experience of this work in Italy, and who would bring with him Vatican experts in Propaganda, with their types and presses in Greek, Arabic and Syriac; Berthollet the chemist; Fourier the geometrician, with his best pupils from the *École polytechnique*; Dolomieu the mineralogist; and many others—astronomers, surveyors, naturalists, antiquarians, engineers, orientalists, and even aerostats: for if there were not opportunities in Egypt for their special studies they could always make themselves useful by designing forts, constructing bakeries, or manufacturing gunpowder. Not content with these representatives of science, Bonaparte included in his travelling Academy a poet, a composer, and a singer, with Arnault to stand for literature. Thus no less than 167 intellectuals landed with the army at Alexandria; and it might well be argued that their part of the work done, the *Description de l'Égypte* was the most valuable result of the expedition.

For himself, Bonaparte ordered the first of those portable libraries, specially printed and bound, which he took with him on all his long campaigns (a specimen is preserved in the Royal Library at Windsor). This one, purchased for him by J. B. Say, included sections on sciences and arts, geography and travel, history (the largest number), poetry, novels, politics and ethics (represented by the Old and New Testaments, the Koran, the Vedas and Montesquieu's *L'Esprit des Lois*). The choice had no special reference, except perhaps the Koran, to the circumstances of Egypt: it represented personal taste, and was much the same when he went to Spain in 1808. The maps he took with him included (significantly enough) not only Egypt, but also Bengal (Rennel's atlas), and the valley of the Ganges.

The destination of the French armada was a secret well kept on the French side of the Channel, and not discovered by the British until Bonaparte was nearly at Malta. The *Moniteur*, which records every function that Bonaparte attended in December and January, is singularly silent about his movements in March and April. A *communiqué* issued to the press by the Directors on March 31st said that he was ordered to Brest to take command of the expedition against England. On the same day the Minister of War was asked to present a plan for an 'army of Portugal'— a scheme with which the government had been playing since the beginning of the year. On April 2nd both the *Moniteur* and the *Surveillant* hinted that the Toulon fleet was destined for Egypt, with the consent of the *Grand Seigneur* (the Sultan of Turkey); and the *Surveillant* went so far as to add that Egypt might be the base for an attack on the English in India. But as late as May 7th the *Publiciste* affirmed that the French and Venetian fleets were going jointly to raise the blockade of Cadiz, and then to invade Ireland or England.

British opinion, preoccupied with the troubles in Ireland, was ready enough to be misled; and the Admiralty, with its Mediterranean fleet concentrated off Cadiz, thought it sufficient up to the middle of April to close the exit of the Mediterranean by stationing a few ships at Gibraltar. But about April 20th, in view of Austrian apprehensions for the safety of Naples, and growing suspicions as to the aim of the mobilization at Toulon, they ordered Nelson, who had just joined St. Vincent off Cadiz (May 2nd), to enter the Mediterranean with a small force, and to see where the French fleet might be going.

After a month's aggravating delay, due first to a sudden crisis at Vienna, which might have meant another visit to Rastadt, and then to the persistence of contrary winds, the armada at last sailed on May 19th.

It was perhaps, as General Royer remarked, the greatest fleet seen in the Mediterranean since the days of the Crusades. Nature herself might seem to pause, astonished at the sight. The 300 vessels of the convoy, largely manned by landlubbers, and unskilfully handled by officers who did not know their trade, their decks crammed with guns, horses and sea-sick soldiers, huddled along like a flock of sheep, shepherded by *l'Orient* and her consorts, which sailed up and down, to and fro, now before and now behind, trying to enforce some kind of formation into a fleet which covered four square miles of sea. Bonaparte knew well (Brueys had warned him a month ago) what might happen if this amateur armada met the homogeneous and experienced British fleet, and had, on his advice, removed the tricolor badges and caps of liberty displayed by his exuberant crews; else how could they hope to escape by hoisting neutral colours?

The routine and the incidents of the voyage can be recovered from Bonaparte's letters and orders, and from the journals of Laugier, Theriotte, Blanquer, Reynier, Damas, and others to whom it was a new and exciting experience. Bonaparte himself had expected to be seasick throughout the voyage, and was agreeably surprised to be able to report, after a few days at sea, *Au large, je n'ai pas été malade.* In their cramped quarters, with time heavy on their hands, the officers quarrelled with each other, and vented their ill temper on the civilians. Some of these at least could keep up their spirits with the thought of what lay ahead. 'Here am I,' wrote Monge on May 25th, 'transformed into an Argonaut! This is one of our new Jason's miracles. He is beating the seas, not for the mere acquisition of a fleece whose gold would not much increase its value, but to bear the torch of reason into a land where it has not been seen for centuries, to enlarge the realm of philosophy, and to carry the national glory further afield.'

5

The forces of Nature, and what men are pleased to call Chance, were to play a large part in the drama that opened on May 4th, 1798: a more decisive part than they do in modern warfare, since both sides were at the mercy of wind and weather, and neither knew what might be going on beyond the visible horizon (which at sea level is less than three miles away); and a part which bore more heavily on a force pursuing than on a force pursued.

On May 4th Nelson arrived at Gibraltar on the *Vanguard*, and there joined *Orion*, *Alexander*, four frigates (*Caroline*, *Emerald*, *Flora* and *Terpsichore*) and *Bonne Citoyenne* (sloop). On the 7th he detached *Caroline* and *Flora* with orders to look in at Minorca and Barcelona, and remain ten days between S. Sebastian and Toulon, in case the French fleet sailed towards Gibraltar. They were then to return to Gibraltar. On the 8th Nelson himself with the rest of the squadron sailed for Toulon. Within ten days the wind which kept Bonaparte in harbour carried him to Cape Sicie, where on May 17th the *Terpsichore* captured *Le Pierre*, a French corvette coming out of Toulon, and learnt that the French armada was still there. On the 18th Bonaparte wrote that *citoyen* Chasse of *Le Félix* had reported a British fleet of thirty sail off Minorca on May 4th; and a similar account came from four Spanish frigates arriving on the same day. He inferred 'there are several English flotillas in the lower Mediterranean, but it doesn't seem likely that they are in a position to trouble us.' He had no idea that Nelson was so near.

At this moment a change of wind from south-east to north-west altered history. Bonaparte slipped out of harbour on the 19th, before Nelson discovered that he had gone. On the evening of the 20th it freshened to 'a strong gale,' which 'being fair for the enemy' under the shelter of Corsica, carried his armada safely down the east coast of the island, whilst Nelson's squadron, further west, was caught in 'a gale which blew with uncommon violence on the 21st,' and had to run south to avoid shipwreck on the west coast: *Vanguard* first lost all her top-masts, and then her foremast: *Alexander* and *Orion* lost their main-topsails: the frigates with them parted company, and were not seen again: and on the 23rd *Vanguard* was with great difficulty towed by *Alexander* into the little bay and port of San Pietro at the south-western extremity of Sardinia. Here with amazing speed the flagship rigged a jury-mast, and on the 27th Nelson sailed north again to resume his watch on Toulon. He little knew that Bonaparte's fleet was by now off the north-eastern end of Sardinia, and was sailing south along the east coast whilst he was sailing north along the west side of the island.

By now a larger squadron under Troubridge was coming up to his assistance. On May 30th, whilst his three ships were limping back towards Toulon, and his frigates, having parted company in the storm, turned back to Gibraltar under the impression that the *Vanguard* would have to refit there, too, Troubridge in the *Culloden*, with *Bellerophon, Minotaur, Defence, Goliath, Majestic, Swiftsure, Theseus, Audacious* and *Leander,* sailed from Gibraltar towards Toulon. He hoped either to join Nelson there, or to meet him on the way—for *Alcmene* had been sent on ten days before, instructing him to return to Gibralta, and Troubridge did not know that owing to the storm the message never reached him. On June 5th the *Mutine* (brig), sent ahead by Troubridge, spoke to Nelson's squadron and told him that Troubridge was on his way. The two squadrons sighted one another on the 7th, and joined the same night.

Nelson had by now received news from a Marseille vessel (May 28th) that Bonaparte had left Toulon on May 19th. As Troubridge had seen nothing of him, it was clear that he must have sailed towards Sicily and Malta; and the combined fleet, now under Nelson's command, set off in pursuit. Its force of thirteen ships of 74 guns and one of 50 had every hope of destroying Bonaparte's thirteen (one of 120 guns, three of 80, and six of 74) if only it could overtake them. But the British fleet was now without frigates, an unforeseen handicap, especially in pursuit: it was neither safe nor profitable to detach the slower sailing ships of the line for scouting purposes. All that Nelson could do was to sail more or less blind-fold down the Italian coast, exploring possible hiding-places, and hoping for news from passing vessels.

Off Civita Vecchia on June 14th he heard from a Tunisian vessel that the French had been seen off Trapani at the north end of Sicily on the 4th sailing east. He hoped he might catch them landing there: if not, he thinks they must be heading for Alexandria, to dispatch troops to India: 'but, be they bound for the Antipodes,' he will bring them to action. On the 18th he heard from Troubridge, who had been sent into Naples for news, that they had sailed for Malta, and he started in hot pursuit, sending on word to the Grand Master that he hoped to be in time to prevent their landing: but on the 23rd he got fresh news that they had taken Malta on the 15th (really the 11th-12th), and had sailed again with a north-west wind on the 18th.

Meanwhile Bonaparte, favoured by Nature and Fortune, had turned an optimistic eye on the risk he was running. On May 23rd, his fifth day at sea, whilst the crippled *Vanguard* was being towed into San Pietro, he wrote home: 'They say there are some English ships cruising off Sicily; but I don't think they are strong enough to upset our operations.' Yet on the 27th, the day on which Nelson left San Pietro again for Toulon, he refused to detach any of his capital ships to meet a convoy from Civita Vecchia; for, 'if, 24 hours later, we signalled 10 English ships of the line, I should only have 9 instead of 13'; and the next day, reporting the capture of the crew of an English brig, driven ashore and burnt on the Sardinian coast, he believed there was a British fleet in the neighbourhood, but 'I think it has no more than 5 or 6 ships of the line at most.' He may have had an inkling of Nelson's presence, but he knew as little of Troubridge's whereabouts as either Nelson or Troubridge did of his.[2]

6

The capture of Malta was accomplished in thirty hours. In size, shape and conformation not unlike the Isle of Wight, it was vulnerable only on its northern coast, where its valleys, running down from the 800-ft. southern heights, opened into a series of rocky bays, which could be entered by boats from ships lying close off shore. For many centuries this weakness had been exploited by a succession of invaders—Phoenicians,

Greeks, Carthaginians, Romans, Vandals, Goths. Malta became part of the Byzantine Empire in the sixth century, and passed to the Moors in the ninth. They were expelled by Count Roger of Sicily in the tenth century, and, after a period of Hohenstaufen ownership, under a marriage contract, it fell to Peter of Aragon, and became one of the jewels of the Spanish crown. It was Charles V of Spain who in 1530 gave it to the Knights of St. John, when the Turks expelled them from Rhodes. Since then its fortifications had made it impregnable, and until latterly it might have been thought that an eighteenth-century invader would meet with no more success than the Turks in 1565. In particular, its capital, Valetta, with its deeply indented harbour, like the jaws of some beast of prey, each rocky headland crowned with a fort and bristling with guns, was regarded as 'next to Gibraltar, the strongest position in Europe.'

But the reports of French agents as to the weakness of the garrison and the divided sympathies of the Knights and the people had not been exaggerated. In an apologia put out after the event on behalf of the Grand Master it was asserted that the French fleet was sighted on June 6th (the convoy was three days ahead of the main fleet), and that all proper steps for defence had been taken by the 9th. In any case Hompesch had received warning of the attack from his plenipotentiary at Rastadt, who had learnt the destiny of the fleet from Treilhard, one of the French representatives there, about June 4th. Yet when the assault came, practically no resistance was offered. Hompesch cried, Treachery!; but incompetence might have been a better word.

The operation was described by Berthier, Bonaparte's infallible Chief of Staff, within a few hours of its conclusion. Gozo, the northern island, was sighted by the French on June 9th. During the day Bonaparte asked to be allowed to water his ships at Valetta: they could not otherwise continue their voyage. Hompesch, according to his own account, agreed to admit four ships of the line at a time, as allowed by the arrangement that then stood for International Law: according to Bonaparte he would only admit four transports, which would have meant an intolerable delay. Anyhow it gave the French commander a *casus belli*, and he ordered the assault. At 2 a.m. on June 10th the French left their convoy lying east of Gozo, and approached the shore of the main island. Reynier landed on Gozo (corresponding to Lymington), Baraguey d'Hilliers at the north-west corner of Malta (Yarmouth), Vauvois half way from there to Valetta (Newtown River), Desaix at the south-east corner (Bembridge), and Bonaparte himself at the entrance to Valetta harbour (Cowes). At 9 a.m. the next day the garrison asked for an armistice: at midnight their representatives, headed by a French member of the Order, were aboard *l'Orient*: at 3 a.m. on the 12th the capitulation was signed. Next day the French fleet anchored in Valetta harbour.

The character of the opposition can be gathered from the estimate of losses—3 killed and 5 or 6 wounded on the French side; the Maltese casualties equally light, and 700-800 prisoners taken. When the garrisons were rounded up two days later they numbered no more than 30 officers and 900 men. With them there fell into French hands two ships of the line, a frigate and several smaller vessels, some disarmed frigates, 1500 guns (mounted), 30,000 muskets, and immense stores of powder and provisions. It hardly needs the detailed narratives of Desaix's attack (by Savary), of Vaubois's (by Sulkowski), and of Reynier's (by himself) to embroider the plain facts. It would not be true to say that there was no resistance: Bonaparte's own account speaks of 'a lively but extremely inaccurate cannonade' during the night of the 10th, and even of an attempted sortie by the garrison; but there was no heart in the defence. Seldom in the history of war has so strong a position yielded so easily.

7

Bonaparte could not afford to stay at Malta longer than was necessary to water and provision his fleet. That would take six days. In six days, therefore, he must reconstruct the government and reorganize the defence of France's new possession. For the first time he was in a position to carry out his political ideas without a shadow of interference by the Directory, and with complete mastery of the whole field. His acts during these six days stand half way between his partial escape from government control in Italy and his more leisurely and remote emancipation in Egypt. This intermediate stage in his development is of greater interest than one would suppose from the little attention paid to it by historians. The *ordres* that he issued, almost at the rate of ten a day, dealing with the political, economic, religious and educational reorganization of the first French republican colony, not only show his energy of mind and fertility of ideas, but also contain anticipations of the work of the Consulate and Empire.

Bonaparte was a Mediterranean islander. As a Corsican he thought he knew how to manage the proud and indigent aristocracy of Malta, its idle and superstitious natives: Hompesch was a lesser Paoli. He would reduce Malta, as he had not been able to reduce Corsica, to the status of a *département* of the French Republic. The sins of the Knights were many, as he reminded them in the *Exposé de la conduite de Malte* with which he justified his seizure of their island. They had encouraged royalist *émigrés*; they had defied the law abolishing *commanderies*; they had allowed Spanish and English ships facilities denied to the French; they had persecuted and imprisoned partisans of the Revolution. All members of the Order, therefore, under sixty, beginning with the Grand Master, were to be expelled within a week; exception made only of fifteen French and two Tuscan citizens who had given information or funds in support of Bonaparte's plans for the invasion of England; together with a few more who were unprofessed and married members of the Order, or who were engaged in certain useful trades or professions. Those under twenty-six he proposed to take with him to Egypt. But, like the French religious orders during the Revolution, these exiles were not to be left unprovided for, but pensioned out of the proceeds of their confiscated property. With them were expelled, within forty-eight hours, all subjects of nations at war with France, especially Russians and Portuguese; and a seal was to be set on all English, Russian and Portuguese goods. Turks, considered as undesirables, but nominal allies, were to be repatriated, and any persons found in prison for their opinions were at once released.

The national revolution was emphasized in Malta, as it had been in France, by the abolition of all armorial bearings, uniforms, liveries and titles of nobility; and in every church the arms of the French Republic replaced those of the Order. No natives might adopt French dress except as a special reward for French sympathies or gallant actions: but every-one must sport a tricolor cockade. Finally it was stated, in language reminiscent of the Declaration of Rights, that *Tous les habitants de Malte sont désormais égaux en droits. Leur talents, leur mérite, leur patriotisme, leur attachement à la République Française établissent seuls entre eux la différence.* In other words, they must all pay taxes, and none of them might carry arms. The point about patriotism was emphasized by an order that any Greeks having relations with Russia should be condemned to death, and that any Greek ships caught sailing under the Russian flag should be sunk.

The islands were divided in the French fashion into *cantons* of not less than 3000 inhabitants, and their government was entrusted to a *Commission de gouvernement* with civil, judicial and administrative functions. Its effective body was a *bureau* of three members *en activité constante de service*: its *conseil* of nine members only met every ten days to hear what the *bureau* had done. But the *bureau* itself could do nothing except on a proposal from or after consultation with the *commissaire*, and all its acts had to be counter-signed by him, and by the *général de division*, the Commander-in-Chief of the garrison. It was in fact a military despotism: for the Commander-in-Chief, not the *commissaire*, was instructed to make a tour of inspection once a month in Malta, and once every two months in Gozo, 'in order to see the inhabitants, and talk to them, to make sure that the commandants are guilty of no offences against individuals, and to suppress any abuses.' Both the policing and the garrisoning of the islands were under his control.

For these purposes he could command not only the 3000 men whom Bonaparte left behind as garrison (consoled by white cotton uniforms with red and blue facings, as well as the use of new barracks and the best hospital), but also two battalions of a National Guard, each 900 strong, to be raised from the rich Maltese families, the merchants, and those who valued public order, who were to act as armed police; the old *corps de chasseurs*; two companies of veteran soldiers of the Order (two more were to be deported, whether they liked it or not, to garrison Corfu, for Bonaparte did not want too many ex-soldiers at Malta); four companies of the old gunners of the forts (but under French officers); and a company of 30 rich young men, aged 15 to 30, similar to the *guides* of the army. As compensation for the loss of 3000 French soldiers left behind, Bonaparte forcibly incorporated 470 men of the old Maltese garrison into his expeditionary force. Their wives and children were allowed to accompany them. Boys old enough to serve became *mousses* (powder-monkeys).

As soon as possible new taxes were to be imposed—customs duties, taxes on wine, tobacco and salt, payments for stamps, registration, house-letting, domestic servants—to bring in £36,000 a year, of which all but £6000 was to go to the army. Street lighting and cleansing, upkeep of roads, water supply, quarantine establishment and so forth would be met by special charges. Everything would be reorganized, from the post and hospitals to the *Mont de Piété* (state pawn-shop) and *l'établissement dit de l'université*, which (in spite of its name) controlled the grain supply of the island. Bonaparte thought of everything. Nothing, as Wellington once remarked, was too small for his proboscis.

He even remembered religion and education. The Francophil bishop, whom he congratulated on his truly Christian and patriotic behaviour, was specially exempted from an order of banishment within ten days issued to all foreign priests: their benefices were given to native clergy, and any surplus revenue would go to the poor. Only one convent of each religious Order was to be allowed: all private foundations were closed down. But the Jews might establish a synagogue. Marriage questions went to the civil courts. No question might be referred to any foreign prince, or to the Pope. The clergy must administer the sacraments free of charge. Bonaparte (with the Civil Constitution of 1790 in mind) was envisaging a national church in partnership with the secular government.

As for education, two of the last *Ordres* he issued before sailing for Egypt set up (on paper) an *École centrale* in place of the old University, with chairs in arithmetic and stereometry, algebra and stereotomy, geometry and astronomy, mechanics and physics, navigation, chemistry and oriental languages; with a library (the librarian also taught geography), a museum of natural history, a botanical garden, and an observatory; and courses in anatomy and midwifery at the Malta hospital; as well as fifteen *Écoles primaires,* in which the children would learn reading and writing in French, the elements of ciphering and navigation, and 'the principles of morality and of the French constitution.'

Bonaparte's programme included one more provision based on the experience of his own military education: sixty Maltese boys from well-to-do families were to be sent to Paris to be trained there in the Colleges of the Republic, at the charge of their parents (£40 a year, plus travelling expenses).

There is another reason, besides the inherent interest of these measures, for fixing attention on Bonaparte's short stay at Malta. Every sailor, and perhaps every soldier too, has a special affection for his first independent command. It must have been with special indignation that Bonaparte heard of the recapture of Malta by the British two years later; and his personal as well as political attachment to the island added to the pertinacity with which he resented our clinging to it during the negotiations of 1803. Perhaps, if he had proceeded straight to Egypt in 1798, the Peace of Amiens would never have broken down.[3]

8

On June 19th, whilst Bonaparte's armada was setting sail from Malta, Nelson was hurrying south from Naples, and Saumarez of the *Orion* was enjoying 'a delightful view of Mount Stromboli' in eruption, together with the 'sulphurous vapour' carried by 'a pleasant breeze which will soon waft us through the straits of Messina.' And so it did. Next day they passed the straits, and saw Etna too 'disgorging columns of smoke.' But then they were delayed by contrary winds, and were not off the south-east point of Sicily till the 22nd. At this moment Bonaparte, having also been delayed off Malta, crept ahead, and must have crossed during the afternoon of the 21st the course followed by Nelson during the evening of the 22nd. It was a close thing. 'We saw three French frigates this morning,' writes Saumarez on the 22nd, 'but they were not considered of sufficient importance to run the risk of separating the squadron in chasing them.' If Nelson had had frigates of his own, they would no doubt have been sent in pursuit, and could hardly have missed sighting the French armada.

From that point onwards, still uncertain where the French might be, Nelson took an unusual (because uncharted) and more southerly course than Bonaparte, and reached Alexandria in seven days, on June 28th: Bonaparte, following the orthodox course some fifty miles further north and hampered by his convoy, took nine days, and reached Alexandria on the 30th: by that time Nelson, finding the harbour at Alexandria empty, was well away to the north-east. Nature and Chance had saved the French again; but only for a time.

V

EGYPT

(1798-1799)

I

THERE CAN BE little doubt that, ever since he saw the Adriatic, Bonaparte's mind had been set on an expedition to Egypt. The occupation of Corfu, enthusiastically described in his letter of August 1st, 1797, had been the first stage in an imaginary journey to Malta, to Egypt, to Mesopotamia, to India. This dream coloured his occupation of Venice, and his naval preparations in the Mediterranean. It crept into his plan for the mobilization of the fleet on December 14th—for could not such an armada be as easily directed east as west? It formed the shortest but the most important paragraph in his Report of February 23rd; it was the one way of attacking England against which no objection was urged. All who were in his confidence must have known that it already obsessed his mind, and that nothing else would so engage his energy and ambition. The Directors had no need, as has sometimes been urged, to tempt him to leave the country: he was burning to go.

In 1672 the philosopher-statesman Leibniz had presented to Louis XIV a *Projet d'expédition d'Égypte* which he hoped might distract that monarch from his designs upon the continent of Europe. This work is not without significance, since it foreshadows many of the reasons which influenced Bonaparte and the Directors a century and a quarter later. It stresses the historical links between France and Egypt, since the time of the Crusades; the right and glory of its conquest; its easiness, in view of the poor defences of the country, and the decadence of its suzerain, the Turkish Sultan—weak in military and naval forces, distracted by palace plots at home and by Christian dissidents abroad. It calls attention to the natural wealth of the country, and its strategic position across the flow of Dutch trade with the East Indies. 'What could be more just (it ends) than a holy war undertaken for the good of humanity, the benefit of Christendom, the deliverance of the oppressed, and for the sepulchre of God? But there are more worldly inducements. 'Amongst all the regions of the known world,' Leibniz asserted, 'China alone excepted, Egypt stands first. It is crammed with such an abundance of good things that it could scarcely contain any more. There is first the most important isthmus in the world—that separating its greatest seas, the Ocean and the Mediterranean; a place that cannot be avoided without circling all the sinuosities of Africa; the connecting point, the obstacle, the key, the only possible door between two areas of the world, Asia and Africa; the meeting-point and marketing-place of India on one side, and Europe on the other—it is the Panama of the East. Egypt is the jewel of the Orient. By its populousness and its wonderful fertility it flowers alone in the midst of deserts.'

Leibniz spoke from hearsay. Later travellers had added more direct evidence. Nicolas Savary dated the first of his *Letters on Egypt* 'Alexandria, 24th July, 1777.' He had then been three years in the country. His book is an encyclopaedia of information—historical, geographical, cultural, archaeological—written in a romantic vein, and laying stress on the richness of the country's vegetation and the abundance of its resources. 'Did but art give the smallest aid to nature, delicious gardens might be formed at small expense; for this happy climate unites a fruitful soil, abundant waters, the most odoriferous shrubs, and the purest sky.' Moreover, 'if Egypt fell into the hands of an enlightened people,' it would not be difficult to divert a branch of the Nile into the Red Sea; and such a canal would enable 'the stuffs of Bengal, the perfumes of Yemen and the gold dust of Abyssinia' to be exchanged at the port of Cosseir for 'the grain, the linens and the various productions of Egypt.' 'This beautiful country, in the hands of a nation friendly to the arts, would once more become the centre of the commerce of the world . . . Alexandria would revive from her ashes'; and 'an observatory placed under this serene sky would add still further to the progress of astronomy.' 'I hope,' he ended, 'that some European, influenced with the love of glory, and wealthier or more favoured than me, will immortalize himself by collecting the information and the manuscripts I have mentioned; and, above all, by procuring for enlightened nations the unknown history of the people of Yemen, of Mecca, of Medina, and of the interior parts of Arabia.'

Bonaparte had discussed Savary's book with Desaix at Passeriano in December 1797, and there can be little doubt that it influenced the planning of his expedition. An optimist where his ambition and imagination were engaged, he preferred to think that Egypt was in truth a land of milk and honey.

But it is to be noticed that when he came back from Egypt it was not Savary whom he frequented and quoted, but Volney, an old Corsican acquaintance, the author of *Travels through Syria and Egypt in* 1783-5—a more critical and philosophical work, based on thirty-six years' residence in Egypt, as against Savary's three, and pouring cold water on that writer's ideas of French exploitation. He had come by hard experience to prefer truth to fairy-tales. Berthier, too, in the preface to his *Relation* of the Egyptian campaigns, says that Volney was the best authority, the only guide who never deceived them.[1]

2

When the armada set sail from Malta few besides Bonaparte himself knew what was its destination. When the sailing directions were signalled, all kinds of guesses were made. But it soon became clear that the expedition was to land on a hostile shore. Elaborate directions were issued for the rearrangement of ships and men, so that each part of the convoy might form a separate unit. A *revue générale* was held, to see that everything was in order. And on June 22nd Bonaparte issued a *Proclamation à l'armée de terre* which not only made it clear that Egypt was the objective of the expedition, but instructed the troops in their conduct towards the people of an 'allied' power.

'Soldiers! (it began) you are about to undertake a conquest whose effects upon the civilization and commerce of the world are incalculable. You are going to strike a blow against England more effective and more deeply felt than any other; a preliminary to her death-blow. We shall have tiring marches to make, and plenty of fighting: but we shall succeed in every enterprise, for fate is on our side. The Mameluke Beys, who encourage only English commerce, who have heaped every outrage on our merchants, and who tyrannize over the unhappy dwellers of the Nile—within a few days of our arrival they will be no more.'

Then followed orders as to the proper treatment of the natives. 'They are Mahometans. The first article of their creed is "There is no God but God, and Mahomet is his prophet." Do not contradict them. Deal with them as you dealt with Jews and with Italians. Respect their *muftis* and their *imams*, as you respected rabbis and bishops. Show the same tolerance towards the ceremonies prescribed by the Alcoran as you showed towards convents and synagogues, the worship of Moses and the worship of Christ. The Roman legions protected all religions. You will find in this country different customs from those of Europe: you must get accustomed to them. The people you are going amongst do not treat women as we do: but in every country rape is a crime. Loot benefits only a few: it gives us a bad name, it squanders our resources, and it makes enemies of people whom we need to have as friends. The first city we shall see was built by Alexander. We shall find at every step of our march memories fit to move all Frenchmen to imitate his exploits.'

Bonaparte called himself, at the head of this proclamation, 'Member of the National Institute, and General in command of the Army of Egypt.'

But if he generally remembered that he came to civilize, he never forgot that he had first to conquer. To the Pacha of Egypt, the Sultan's Viceroy, he wrote explaining the meaning of the invasion. The Directory, he said, had frequently asked the Sublime Porte to punish the Beys of Egypt for their ill-treatment of French merchants, but without result. 'The French Republic has therefore decided to send a powerful army to put an end to the brigandage of the Beys,' as it did before in Tunis and Algiers. 'You (he uses the intimate *toi*) who ought to control the Beys, whilst in effect they hold you at Cairo without authority or power—you ought to view my arrival with pleasure. No doubt you already know that I come with no hostile intention against the Alcoran or the Sultan. You know that the French nation is his one and only ally in Europe. Come and meet me then, and join with me in cursing the impious race of the Beys.'

Nevertheless Bonaparte must have had some doubts as to whether the Sultan or his representatives, who had not been consulted about it, would welcome an invasion of his territory, however altruistic, however humanitarian, by a 'unilateral' ally. But this, he considered, was Talleyrand's affair. In a report to the Directors on January 27th the Minister had written: 'Why should we sacrifice our interests any longer to a power whose friendship is a matter of words (*équivoque*), and which is on the edge of disaster? Egypt means nothing to Turkey: she has no shadow of authority there.' Again on February 13th he repeated the same argument in greater detail: the Pacha of Egypt was the slave of the Beys: the Porte derived no revenue from the country: its suzerainty was a mere form, since the Beys exercised all rights over the territory. In short, the Sultan could raise no valid objection to a French intervention in Egypt—an intervention based on such grounds as Bonaparte alleged in his proclamation of June 22nd.

But this reasonable attitude must be explained to the Sublime Porte. 'I think,' Talleyrand ended, 'that an invasion of Egypt should be combined with the dispatch to Constantinople of a negotiator who has to the full the subtlety and firmness appropriate to the circumstances, and who carries instructions drawn up by a man of experience. I do not think these negotiations need be fruitless: I have in my mind arguments which may prove successful, and I will present them, when the time comes, to the Directory.' As for the other Powers, Talleyrand supposed that England, under the threat of invasion, would be unable to do anything; and that Russia, Prussia and Austria would hardly be in a position to object to a minor piece of brigandage so similar to the partition of Poland.

The charms by which Talleyrand hoped to win the ear of the Sultan were explained in a *Projet de Mémoire pour servir d'instructions au ministre plénipotentiaire de la République auprès de la Porte ottomane* on March 16th. The partitioning of Turkey was to compensate France for its exclusion from the share-out of Polish territory in 1772, 1793 and 1795. The temporary loss of Egypt would benefit the Sultan, by ridding the Levant of English ships and English trade—'temporary,' because (this was the essence of his scheme) 'the Directory is and always will be determined to restore Egypt to the *Grand Seigneur* in the form that he possesses it today'; and Talleyrand found precedents for this procedure in the treaties by which the Porte had ceded the Crimea to Russia and part of Bosnia to Austria.

As soon as Bonaparte had left Paris for Toulon, Talleyrand informed Ruffin, the French *chargé d'affaires* at Constantinople, of the destination of the armada and of the policy behind the expedition; and warned him to expect the arrival of an ambassador about the middle of July. This was not at all what Bonaparte had expected. It had been understood that Talleyrand himself would be the ambassador, and that he would start for Turkey soon after Bonaparte had started for Egypt. True, the vessel that was to carry him there was not ready as soon as it might have been, and the news of the fall of Malta, which was to be the signal that all was well, was late in reaching him, owing to the capture of the French vessel that carried it. But Bonaparte's letters during the summer are full of questions as to Talleyrand's part in the affair. He may have suspected cowardice, if not treachery.

The truth seems to be that Talleyrand could not be spared from Paris owing to the sudden danger of a rupture with the United States over the 'XYZ' affair. It is not so clear why Descorches (nominated as ambassador in September) never even started for Constantinople.

Meanwhile Ruffin was instructed (July 26th, August 3rd) to play for time, and to explain to the Porte that the French occupation of Egypt was not a permanent annexation, but only a temporary means towards securing predominance in the Mediterranean, which was to the Directory as 'naturally' a French lake as the Alps and Pyrenees were to Danton the 'natural' frontiers of France. Soon after receiving these instructions (September 2nd) the unhappy Ruffin was thrown into prison with all his staff, and remained there for three years, meditating, no doubt, on the unreasonable resentment of the *Grand Seigneur*, and the clever way in which the Foreign Minister had escaped the consequences of his own acts.[2]

3

Few Europeans approach the North African coast for the first time without excitement and emotion. The brilliance of the sky, the exhilarating dryness of the air, the sharp contrasts of sunlight and shadow, the rare green of the date-palms, standing out against the dull gold of the desert— all are strange to Western experience; but behind the newness is a suggestion of a world incredibly old, mysterious and rather terrifying. To a

modern traveller, walking down the gangway from his liner, this impact
is softened by the quays, the streets, the hotels and all the paraphernalia of
a modern seaport. Alexandria has become an oriental Marseilles. But
when Bonaparte and his company landed on the open shore west of the
harbour the modern town was not in existence, and little was left of the
great city of Alexander's successors which had stood there two thousand
years before—of the libraries, the museums and the lecture-rooms where
Greek savants had founded mathematics and the natural sciences,
where Christian philosophers had disputed with Neo-Platonists, and where
Athanasius had overcome the Arians.

For a thousand years the country had been under Moslem and Turkish
misrule. Cairo had become the capital, and Damietta the port of Egypt.
'This city,' wrote the *commissaire* Jaubert within a week of the landing,
'has nothing of the ancient Alexandria but the name. The ruins of its
former circuit announce that it was once a most extensive place'; its population, once reckoned at from 300,000 to 600,000, was now no more than
5000. 'It is a mere heap of ruins, where you see a paltry hovel of mud and
straw stuck against the magnificent fragments of a granite column'—
such as Pompey's column, so-called, really a sailors' landmark, and the two
'Cleopatra's Needles' which now stand in London and New York. The
French invaders might well doubt whether this was the earthly Paradise
described by Savary, and not rather the land of disillusion and despair
against which Volney had warned them in vain.

They landed by night at Marabout, the extreme west end of the bay,
where a promontory and islands gave some shelter from the north-west
wind. They had to row six or seven miles in open boats in a rough sea—a
difficult and dangerous operation, says Berthier, the most exact of reporters. Bonaparte was the first on shore, at 1 a.m. The men formed up
on the beach, about 4300 of them, without horses or guns, and marched
through the night five or six miles across the desert in three columns led
by their generals, one of whom was Caffarelli with his wooden leg. At
dawn they were in front of the walls of the old city. They parleyed, but
were met with shots and shouts of defiance. Bonaparte ordered the assault:
the walls were scaled, and the troops drew up inside the city. By midday
Alexandria had fallen for the loss of six officers and fifteen men killed and
twenty wounded.

Many of the inhabitants fled on the approach of the invaders: those who
remained expected nothing better than to have their throats cut and their
women raped by the French soldiery. Bonaparte's first act was, therefore,
to post up in the town, a Proclamation in the native tongue—the first
product of his Arabic press.

Peoples of Egypt (it ran), they will tell you that I have come to destroy
your religion: do not believe them. Answer that I come to restore your

rights, to punish the usurpers, and that I respect, more than ever the Mamelukes did, God, His Prophet, and the Alcoran. Tell them that all men are equal in God's eyes, and that the only difference between them consists in their talents and their virtues. What wisdom, or talents, or virtues have the Mamelukes, that they should enjoy a monopoly of everything that makes life pleasant and agreeable? Is there a good piece of land? It belongs to the Mamelukes. Is there a beautiful slave-girl, a handsome horse, a fine house? They belong to the Mamelukes. If Egypt belongs to them, let them produce God's deed of sale. No: God is just, and has compassion on the people. . . .

'Cadis, cheiks, imams, tchorbadjis: tell the people that we are the friends of all true Moslems. Have we not destroyed the Pope, who preached war against the Moslems? Have we not destroyed the Knights of Malta, because those madmen believed it was God's will that they should make war on the Moslems? Have we not been all through the centuries friends of the Grand Seigneur (may God fulfil his desires!), and enemies of his enemies? The Mamelukes, on the contrary, have always been rebels against the authority of the Grand Seigneur, and still refuse to recognize him, doing only what seems right in their own eyes.

'Thrice blessed those who take our part! They will benefit in property and in position. Blessed even those who remain neutral! They will have time to get to know us, and will come round to our side. But cursed, nay thrice cursed are those who take arms for the Mamelukes, and fight against us! There is no hope for them: they are doomed to destruction.'

It may be doubted what the fellahin made of this manifesto of communism and civil war, or whether their cadis, cheiks, imams, and tchorbadjis really believed that Bonaparte's mixed forces of Frenchmen, Italians and Maltese came as enemies of the Pope and champions of Islam. But they could at least understand the warning contained in the five Articles that stood at the foot of Bonaparte's republican poster, warning the natives what treatment they might expect if they did not welcome the invader. All villages on the line of march (said these Articles), must hoist the tricolor and send deputations to the French army. Any which take arms against the invader will be burnt down. All which submit must hoist the French flag alongside that of 'our ally' the Sultan. The cheiks must seal (for French use) all property of the Mamelukes. They may retain their posts; and prayers may be offered as usual: but 'Everyone must thank God for the destruction of the Mamelukes, and cry: "Glory to the Sultan! Glory to his ally, the French army! A curse on the Mamelukes! Happiness to the Peoples."'

During the week that Bonaparte spent at Alexandria he did everything he could to make his regime respected by the people, and prized by their local rulers. All the inhabitants were disarmed, and ordered to wear the tricolor; but the *muftis, imams,* and *cheiks* were allowed to wear tricolor shawls, and the French sentries were instructed to salute them when they passed. Property belonging to the Mamelukes or to foreigners was confiscated; and the foreign consuls' houses were taken over by the army: but native property was respected, troops were forbidden to enter the mosques, and pillagers were shot. The parting orders to Kléber, who was left in charge during the march up country, were 'to remain on good terms with the Arabs, and to pay the greatest respect to the *muftis* and principal *cheiks* of the country.'

'You must accustom these people by degrees (Bonaparte wrote), to our ways and ideas; meanwhile, you must leave them plenty of latitude in their own affairs, and be particularly careful not to interfere with their administration of justice, which deals with divine laws and is all based on the *Koran.*' He may not have believed what he wrote home to the Directors in his first Report: 'This nation is all that travellers and story-tellers have said—a calm, proud, and courageous people': but he realized from the first that he could best control them through their own native authorities under the general supervision of French officers or civilians.

4

A week after his landing at Alexandria Bonaparte began his march on Cairo. Cairo, Alexandria, and Rosetta are the corners of an equilateral triangle of which each side is about 120 miles long: Alexandria, thirty-five miles west of the western mouth of the Nile, Rosetta at its eastern mouth, and Cairo at the point where the river splits into its two branches. From Alexandria, which lies on a spit of sand enclosing the lagoon called Lake Mariut, rather as the Chesil Bank encloses East and West Fleet, an old canal led past Damanhour into the western branch of the Nile at El-Ramanieh. The natural line of march was along this canal. Once the troops on land had reached the river bank, they could be accompanied and supplied by vessels of light draught coming up the east branch from Rosetta: this was the duty entrusted, after Menou had captured Rosetta, to *Contre-amiral* Perrée of the *Cerf.* It was by the same route that General Hutchinson advanced in 1801; and it is the route followed by the modern railway.

It took Bonaparte's army of some 25,000 men (allowing for 6000 or so left behind to garrison lower Egypt) a fortnight to reach Cairo. Ten miles a day was good marching in a country as bare as a man's hand, and as hot as a furnace, where the only drinking-place was an occasional well of brackish water. French troops always marched light, and relied on the land to supply their needs. The complaints which can still be read in the letters of French officers, captured by the British fleet and printed in London, are the best commentary on this terrible march. 'You can have no idea,' writes Damas to Kléber, 'of the fatiguing marches we made to get to Cairo; never halting till 3 or 4 o'clock in the afternoon, after broiling in the sun all day; the greatest part of the time without food; obliged to glean what the divisions which preceded us had left in those detestable villages, which they had frequently pillaged; and harassed during the whole march by those hordes of robbers called Bedouins, who killed not only our men, but our officers, at 25 paces from the main body.' Guillot, thrown from his horse, 'was obliged to walk barefoot for 19 days on the burning sand and gravel of the desert . . . not having a bit of bread to eat, nor a drop of water to moisten his mouth: all the comfort I had (he wrote home to his mother) was in cursing and damning the trade of war, more than a hundred times a day.' Some of the men, wrote General Royer, were so tired that they threw away their packs; some died of thirst, others of hunger or heat; some 'seeing the sufferings of their comrades, blew out their own brains; others threw themselves into the Nile, and perished in the water.'[3]

There was no organized opposition; only two skirmishes near El-Ramanieh and Chabrakhyt, when the flotilla got ahead of the troops, and ran into trouble. But when on the 20th the army at last came in sight of the pyramids of Gizeh, and of the Mameluke host, even the unimaginative Berthier was struck by the spectacle. 'The Mameluke cavalry,' he says, 'was covered with glittering armour. Behind them we could see on their left the famous pyramids, whose indestructible bulk had outlived so many empires, and defied for thirty centuries the attacks of time. On their right were the Nile, and Cairo, the Mokattam, and the fields of ancient Memphis. . . .'

The next day 6000 brave men, well armed, finely mounted and supported (but uselessly) by twice as many men on foot, charged heroically against the French squares, and were mown down by musketry fire. It was not a battle, but a massacre like Kitchener's victory at Omdurman just a century later. The French losses were ten men killed and thirty wounded; but French historians, following Bonaparte's own exaggerations, have multiplied the numbers of the Mamelukes by more than ten, and put into his mouth a legendary speech to his troops referring to the pyramids: 'Soldiers, forty centuries are looking down upon you.'

The evening of the battle was spent stripping the dead horses of their harness, and the dead Mamelukes of purses filled with gold. Next day, at Gizeh, Bonaparte received the surrender of Cairo, which offered no resistance; and on July 24th he made a triumphant entry into the city.

But victory was embittered by news from France, which caused the ill-temper reported the same day by Eugène Beauharnais to his mother Joséphine. Bonaparte had heard rumours that she had been unfaithful to him. He wrote next day to his brother Joseph: 'I may be in France again in two months. Please look after my interests. There is plenty to worry me at home. Your friendship means a lot to me: were I to lose it, and to see you betraying me, I should become a complete misanthrope. It is a melancholy business when all the affections of one's heart are wrapped up in a single person. I want you to arrange to have a country place ready for me when I return, either in Burgundy, or near Paris. I am counting on spending the winter there, and seeing no one. I am sick of society. I need solitude, isolation. My feelings are dried up, and I am bored with public display. At 29 I am tired of glory; it has lost its charm, and there is nothing left for me but complete egotism.'

This might seem a strange outbreak for such a man at such a moment. That Bonaparte had always hoped, after a summer campaign, to leave Egypt under a government and a garrison, and return home, cannot be doubted; nor that he was still in love with his wife. But it was no more than a passing mood of depression, like that he had expressed, also to Joseph, three years before (August 12th, 1795), which made him speak of renouncing his career. It did not last long. He found life far too absorbing and power far too sweet.[4]

5

It was a matter of urgent importance to settle the government of the capital and of the country. This was Bonaparte's occupation, day in and day out, for six months (save six weeks) from July 24th, 1798, to February 10th, 1799. His correspondence for this period is the record of a great achievement: more than a conquest, more than the founding of a colony: a work less like that of Kitchener than of Cromer: for Bonaparte laid the foundations of modern Egypt, and proved himself not merely a leader or an organizer, but a statesman.

In striking direct at the capital of Egypt, Bonaparte had followed the intuition, at once military and political, which led him in later years to Vienna and Berlin, Madrid and Moscow. To hold Egypt with his small army he must follow the plan that he had found successful in Italy: destroy any central government that might organize resistance, exploit its subservient or rival local authorities, placate the religious leaders, and terrorize the common people.

Cairo, the first city of Egypt, produced no better impression on its conquerors than Alexandria. 'We are arrived at length,' wrote Damas to Kléber on July 27th, 'at the spot so much and so eagerly desired! How different it is from what the most cool and temperate imagination had figured it to be! This wretched travesty of a town (*l'horrible villasse*) is inhabited by a lazy set of wretches who squat all day before their filthy huts, smoking and taking coffee, or eating pumpkins and drinking water. It is easy to lose oneself for a whole day in the stinking and narrow streets of this illustrious capital.' Yet Cairo contained the Citadel, the guarantee of Mameluke power, and the mosques, the centres of law and worship throughout the land. From Cairo rumour would carry on camel-back to every quarter of the country—yes, and into the whole Moslem world— news of the downfall of the dreaded Mamelukes.

Bonaparte's first act, on July 22nd, after receiving from the terrified *cheiks* the surrender of the capital, was to publish a Proclamation, in which he said: 'Let all who are afraid be calm. Let all who have fled return to their homes. Let the day's prayers be said as usual. I wish it to be so always. Have no fears for your families, your houses, or your property; least of all for the religion of the Prophet, which I love (*que j'aime*).' To the Pacha of Cairo he explained: 'The intention of the French Republic in occupying Egypt was to drive away the Mamelukes, who were both rebels against the Porte and open enemies of the French government. Now that it is mistress of the country its intention is to maintain the Pacha of the Grand Seigneur in his revenues and his functions. I beg you to assure the Porte that it will suffer no kind of loss, and that I shall see to it that it still collects the same taxes as it has done hithero.' The Pacha (Abou Bekir) did not wait to receive this reassurance; he had fled to the north with Ibrahim: but the Proclamation, followed by an announcement that the preservation of order in the city would be placed in the hands of a native *Divan*, had a tranquillizing effect, which was soon felt also in Alexandria and Rosetta, where Kléber and Menou were faced with a similar situation.

The Cairo *Divan* consisted of nine *cheiks*, who were to meet every day, and deal with the policing, provisioning and sanitation of the city. They were warned to do nothing 'against the interests of the army'; and their meetings were attended by a French *commissaire*, whose business it was to 'try to get to know the different characters of its members, and the amount of confidence that could be placed in each of them.' Tallien, who received these instructions when he succeeded Beauvoisins as *commissaire* on August 30th, can hardly have found his experience of excitable Jacobin *comités* much help towards understanding the 'nine bearded automata, in Turkish dress and splendid turbans,' whose costumes 'put General Royer in mind of the figures of the twelve apostles in his father's cabinet.' As soon as they were constituted, these elders were asked to advise Bonaparte as to the setting up of provincial *Divans*, the law of inheritance, the constitution of courts of civil and criminal justice, and measures for safeguarding property and collecting taxes. But Bonaparte did not wait for their advice. An *Ordre* was issued the same day setting up provincial *Divans* of seven members, with similar functions. They too had under them an *Aga* (chief constable) and a body of Turkish police (*Janissaries*) armed with muskets or clubs; and educated Copts, with the ominous title of *Intendants*, to levy taxation: Bonaparte preferred to delegate both these unpopular duties to an alien race; always, of course, under French supervision.

'The Turks,' as Bonaparte instructed Menou, 'must let their conduct be ruled by extreme severity. Here in Cairo I have heads cut off at the rate of 5 or 6 a day. Hitherto we have had to treat the people tactfully, in order to destroy the reputation for terrorism which preceded our arrival. But now we must make sure that the natives obey us; and for them obedience means fear.' This would always be his policy. When Koraïm, the Sheriff of Alexandria, betrayed his trust, and failed to pay the fine imposed upon him, Bonaparte had him brought to Cairo, and executed in the square outside the citadel: his head was paraded through the streets with an inscription saying he was a rebel against the French Republic, and a Mameluke spy.

Two months after the institution of the *Divans*, Bonaparte crowned his constitutional edifice with an *Assemblée de tous les notables des quatorze provinces de l'Égypte*, renamed a month later *Divan Général*. This body was probably modelled on the *Notables* convened by Calonne and Necker on the eve of the Revolution. Like them they were nominated, not elected: then by the crown, now by the generals commanding in the provinces, who were instructed to choose persons 'of the greatest influence over the people, the most distinguished by their enlightenment, their talents, and the way in which they accepted the French regime.' Special care was to be taken to exclude any who had openly opposed the new government: indeed the names of any such were to be reported to Bonaparte.

The nominees included three *hommes de loi*, three *négociants* and three *fellahs*, *cheiks-el-beled* and *chefs d'Arabes*: making in all a total of 189; not dissimilar to the 142 members of the *Notables* of 1787. Their functions were occasional and purely consultative. Bonaparte's intention, as he told Monge and Berthollet when he appointed them *commissaires*, was that membership of the *Divan* 'should accustom the Egyptian *Notables* to the ideas of assembly and government': they were to be told that he had summoned them 'to ask their advice, and to know what ought to be done for the happiness of the people—what they themselves would do, if they had the right that we have earned by conquest.'

Such partial concessions to the appearance of self-government are remarkable enough at the time and in the circumstances; but they were without any real effect upon the autocratic and military system which was the only method of government that Bonaparte could understand. Thus it would be a mistake to suppose that in any real sense he decentralized his authority. He was the sole initiator and enforcer of the new regime. He issued, over the heads of his *sheiks*, his *agas* and his *intendants*, a constant series of *ordres* and *arrêtés*, setting up institutions which he confidently hoped, as so many empire-builders have done before and since, would transform a primitive people into a modern state.[5]

Cairo had its own mint, which turned the jewellery and plate of the Mamelukes and rich merchants into *louis*, *écus* and *livres*. It possessed a *commission de santé*, and a *bureau de santé et salubrité*, with power to impose the death penalty for serious offences against the anti-plague regulations. A postal service was set up, with the same charges as in France (it cost half a *franc* to send a letter from Cairo to Alexandria), and after the Cairo revolt three companies of Greeks were enrolled to protect the *diligences*. An *arrêté* of September 10th set up *tribunaux de commerce* modelled on the one judicial institution of the old regime in France which had survived the Revolution of 1789. Lazarettos were organized at Cairo, Alexandria, Damietta and Rosetta. A *bureau d'enregistrement* was set up in every provincial capital, where, for appropriate fees (one and a half *francs* for a passport, five for a divorce, twenty-one for a will), all legal documents had to be stamped, all titles to property registered, and all businesses licensed—a merchant might have to pay the equivalent of £60, a manufacturer £35, a shop-keeper or inn-keeper £25, and even a boatman or hirer of camels and donkeys from £2 to £10 for the right to ply his trade.

Cairo had its own National Guard, ten companies strong, composed, like those of the Revolution, of European residents, stiffened with non-militant members of the army establishment. A tax was levied on all house property in the city, after a summary inspection by six architects; and the rates, collected by Copt *écrivains*, ranged from two and a half to ninety *francs*. A *commission administrative* requisitioned Mameluke property—not even the *harems* were exempt from their investigation—and whatever might be wanted from the bazaars; as well as recovering arrears of taxes from the provinces. There was to be a hospital with 300-400 beds for the poor of Cairo. An *inspecteur général des domaines* was to investigate and improve the state of agriculture on land declared national, and entrusted to certificated tenants. A *conseil des finances* was to report to the *administrateur des finances* on means for improving the coinage, and paying the troops better, 'without sensibly reducing the revenue of the Republic': any government might be glad to know its findings. A *conseil d'administration des hôpitaux* was organized, and military cemeteries set apart at six places, with Turkish grave-diggers.

The difficulty of organizing life in Egypt on lines that would seem rational to an eighteenth-century *philosophe* were increased by the chaotic weights, measures, and currency that were found there. How was the new decimal system, the pride of republican progress, to be reconciled with three linear measures—one of them confined to the measurement of the height of the Nile; with the measurement of distances between place and place by the number of hours it took a loaded camel to get there (citizen Jacotin calculated that a caravan averaged three-quarters of a *lieu*, or about two miles an hour); with land-areas measured in three different *fedans*, representing the productive value of the ground, and varying from forty-five to eighty-one *ares* (i.e. about one-two acres)? How could a decimal system be used in markets where the only uniform unit of weight was the *drachma*, equivalent to three *grammes* (=three cubic *centimètres*), and most commodities were reckoned in *rottles* which varied according to the thing weighed; whilst, for money, there were in circulation twelve gold coins and eighteen silver from all over the Levant, as well as the *para* or *médin* in which the poor man reckoned all his values, and the *talari* (150 *paras*) in which it was convenient to tax the well-to-do. No wonder Bonaparte employed native *intendants* to collect his taxes. Frenchmen of the Revolutionary era must have thought themselves back in the Middle Ages.[6]

6

Himself a child of the eighteenth century, Bonaparte knew as well as any *philosophe* that popular religion was a force to be feared, and therefore courted. The change of policy from kindness to intimidation which he laid down for his police was combined with an increasing outward respect for the beliefs and institutions, the professors and priests of Mohammedanism. He saw that Islam was not like the Catholic church, which concealed beneath an appearance of uniformity an explosive individualism, but rather a rule of life, a code of cleanliness and hospitality and trust in Providence enforced with military precision upon an army moving and camping in the desert. Volney had predicted that any conqueror of Egypt would have three wars upon his hands: one against England, one against Turkey, and one against the Moslem population. Bonaparte, like Kitchener or Allenby, would be forced to tolerate what he could not afford to defy.

But he brought to the business a personal sympathy which few Englishmen could profess, and the beginnings of that easy adaptation to the African mind and manners which has marked French colonial enterprise ever since. He never wavered from the behaviour prescribed to his troops in the Proclamation of June 22nd, and promised to the people in those of July 2nd and 22nd. He had claimed to be an enemy of the Pope, and of the Catholic Order of Malta: he had professed himself an admirer of 'Allah, his Prophet, and the Koran,' though he had few illusions as to the real thoughts about him and his army of infidels in the minds of the silent dignified *sheiks*, the fanatical *imams*, or the learned *mullahs*. He knew that Islam resembled Judaism in so far as it was a code of law based upon the interpretation of an inspired book. He saw, as any modern traveller might see, the young scholars squatting on the ground in the cloisters of El-Azhar as their teachers expounded the text of the Koran. They were the future missionaries of Islam. The destiny of French rule in the Near East would depend on what they taught about the foreign invader.

Could Bonaparte induce the *mullahs* to find predictions of his regime amongst the inspired words of the Prophet? Would they accept their invaders, upon any reasonable conditions, as proselytes, or even as true believers? He encouraged the *muftis* of the four Mohammedan sects to frequent his quarters and to discuss theology with him: he was quick to acquire a smattering of the Koran. Would they grant him a *fetwa*, an order to the Egyptian people to take an oath of allegiance to his regime? Certainly, was the reply, if he and his army would accept the conditions of the faith: circumcision, and abstention from wine-drinking. After long negotiations, and a reference to the Moslem headquarters at Mecca, a modified *fetwa* was published: the two conditions were waived; and Bonaparte's orthodoxy was proclaimed from the minarets of every mosque in the land. But it can hardly be doubted that to the mass of the people he still remained a heretic, and his troops an army of infidels.

Bonaparte did all he could to exploit the ground gained by this official recognition. He offered the protection of French troops for the annual pilgrimage to Mecca. He wrote to the French consul at Tripoli, to the Sheriff of Mecca (this letter was also to be circularized in the Levant), to the Sheriff of Syria, and to the Pacha of Aleppo, explaining his presence in Egypt, and assuring them that he had the support of the representatives of Islam. 'We Frenchmen,' he informed the Pacha, 'are no longer the infidels who in a barbarous age came to fight against your faith: we realize how sublime it is: we profess it ourselves: and the moment has come for all Frenchmen to be regenerated and to become believers like yourselves.'

How far the successor of St. Louis went in his personal behaviour towards professing Mohammedanism it is hardly fair to judge from Parisian gossip and English caricatures. But it is certain that the anniversary feast of the birth of the Prophet (August 19th-22nd) was celebrated by the French army at Cairo, Alexandria and Rosetta with honours—military parades, gunfire, illuminations, fireworks (the first ever seen in Egypt) and torch-light processions—similar to those of the 1st Vendémiaire (September 22nd), 'the anniversay of the founding of the Republic.' Bonaparte saw nothing amiss in honouring Mahomet with the singing of the *Marseillaise*, or crowning triumphal arches with the crescent and the cap of liberty, the Koran and the Rights of Man. East was West, and West was East. *Le bon Dieu* was Allah, and Bonaparte was his Prophet.[7]

7

Bonaparte, whilst in Egypt, always signed himself first as 'Member of the *Institut*,' and secondly as 'Commander-in-Chief.' He never lost sight of the scientific and archaeological aims of his expedition, and had no intention of leaving his train of *savants* unemployed. They had an unhappy experience at Alexandria, where they landed by boat, and spent five days without food or lodging, after a large part of their equipment had been wrecked and lost at the entrance to the harbour. One party remained at Alexandria, and another went to Rosetta, whilst Monge and Berthollet boarded the flotilla to Cairo, and came under fire in the action at Chabrakhyt. Very soon two presses were at work: that of Marcel, at Alexandria, printed in French, Greek and Arabic; that of Marc Aurel, at Cairo, only in French. It was not until January 1799, that Marcel's press was installed at Cairo, and the two amalgamated as *l'Imprimerie Nationale*. It was the main business of the Cairo press, apart from public notices, to print every five days a paper called *le Courrier de l'Égypte*, and every ten days *la Décade égyptienne*, described as *journal littéraire et d'économie politique*, the official organ of the *Institut*.

The *Institut d'Égypte* was founded by an *arrêté* of August 22nd. Its principal objects were defined as 'the progress and propagation of enlightenment in Egypt; research, study, and publication of facts about the country—natural, industrial, and historical; and the giving of advice on various questions about which it is consulted by the government.' It had four sections of twelve members—mathematics, physics, political economy, and literature and arts. It was to meet twice every ten days, from 7 to 9 a.m. The duties of its officers were elaborately defined. Salaries were on ten scales, ranging from £2 10s. to £25 a month. It was to hear papers read, and publish them, along with its reports. Its utilitarian purpose was brought home to its members at its first session, when Bonaparte proposed six questions for its consideration: (1) improvements in the army bakeries? (2) a local substitute for hops in brewing beer? (3) a means of cleaning and freshening Nile water? (4) whether water-mills or wind-mills are best at Cairo? (5) local materials for making gun-powder? and (6) as a concession to higher interests, improvements in Egyptian law, justice and education?

But in fact its members were soon engaged in all manner of learned research. A volume entitled (in the English translation published in London in 1800) *Memoirs relative to Egypt, written in that country during the campaigns of General Bonaparte by the learned and scientific men who accompanied the French expedition*, contains, amongst its thirty-eight papers, a 'Memoir relative to the optical phenomenon known by the name of Mirage,' by citizen Gaspard Monge; 'Observations on the Wing of the

Ostrich,' by citizen Geoffroy; 'Observations on the Colours of the Sea,' by citizen Costaz; and 'Analysis of the Slime of the Nile,' by citizen Regnault; as well as an 'Arabian Ode on the Conquest of Egypt,' transcribed and translated by citizen J. J. Marcel, which runs thus: 'The chief who marches at their head is impetuous and terrible; his name terrifies kings; princes bow their haughty heads before the invincible Bonaparte, the lion of battles; his courage sways irrevocable destiny, and the heavens of glory are prostrate before him.' The volume also includes geographical surveys, with maps, of Lake Menzaleh and the valley of the Natron Lakes, and a number of papers of medical, agricultural, and archaeological importance. For the members of the *Institut* did not merely sit and meditate in the fine building that Bonaparte allotted them in Cairo, but travelled all over the country, from the Delta to the first cataract, studying its monuments, and collecting the material which formed the magnificent *Description de l'Égypte* published in nine volumes in 1809-28.

Bonaparte, whose name appears amongst the twelve members of the Mathematical section of the *Institut*, made his own contribution to its researches by spending a fortnight (December 29th-January 6th) on a desert journey to investigate Suez, the Fountains of Moses, and the remains of the ancient canal joining the Red Sea to the Mediterranean: for to recreate this means of communication between West and East was one of the main objects of the occupation of Egypt. He took seven other *savants* with him, and a carriage drawn by six horses—the first of its kind ever seen in the desert; but himself rode on horse-back. Their visit to the Fountains of Moses nearly ended fatally, for their guides misled them, the riders were caught, like Pharaoh and his host, in the rising tide of the Red Sea, and had to swim for their lives. They nearly lost themselves, again, after following the course of the old canal too late at night, and were fortunate to get back safe to camp.

The sequel to this expedition was a survey of the isthmus of Suez, carried out under great difficulties by the engineer Le Père, which established the fact that there was no insuperable obstacle to the southern half of the canal constructed by de Lesseps seventy years later.

Of less practical but more archaeological and artistic value was the exploration of the Nile Valley southwards by Vivant-Denon as far as the first cataract. Dendera, Thebes, and Karnak revealed beauties hardly dreamed of by earlier travellers. The science of Egyptology was born; and citizen Bouchard's discovery of the Rosetta stone baptized it with the name of Bonaparte. It is not without justice that there can still be read on the gate of the temple of Philae, when it is not submerged beneath the water of the Assouan dam, the proud inscription engraved by Casteix recording the arrival there of a French army under Desaix on March 3rd, 1799. War and culture had for once marched hand in hand.[8]

8

It was on his arrival at Belbeis late on August 13th, 1798, that Bonaparte heard of the destruction of his fleet by Nelson in Aboukir Bay during the night of August 1st-2nd. This disaster, though he did not like to admit it, altered the whole outlook of his expedition.

His first preoccupation, on landing at Alexandria, had been to provide for the security of his *armée de terre*: his second thoughts had been given to the fate of his *armée de mer*, which, now that a superior British fleet was at large in the Mediterranean, had become less an asset than a liability. He still looked to it, but dubiously, to keep up communications with Malta, Corfu and Toulon. This could best be done by fast-sailing frigates: what was to happen to the thirteen ships of the line, which either could not enter the harbour at Alexandria, or, if they did succeed in forcing an entrance, would be trapped by the first British ship that found them there?

About twenty miles east of Alexandria Bonaparte's maps showed him a bay almost exactly like that of Alexandria, but more than twice as large, with Rosetta similarly placed on the neck of its eastern promontory, and at its western end the smaller promontory of Aboukir, with outlying islands and reefs, which gave some shelter from the prevailing north-western wind, as Marabout had done for his landing on July 1st. Here there was a good anchorage about three miles off shore, with the possibility of getting supplies from Rosetta across the bay, and of keeping up communications with Cairo by the western branch of the Nile. Here, therefore, Brueys proceeded to lay up his ships, anchoring them 500 feet apart in a curved line from south-west to north-east, and so near to the western shallows that he supposed an enemy fleet would be forced to attack him on his open flank, ship to ship; in which event he hoped that the additional gun-power gained by moving some of his guns from the landward to the seaward side would give him an advantage he could not hope for in a running fight at sea. He was, however, short of men, and short of food; and when the British fleet came in sight he had hurriedly to recall working parties which had gone ashore to dig for water.

At 2 p.m. on August 1st, a fine day with a stiff breeze blowing from north-west, the mast-heads of Nelson's fleet came in sight over the western islands. Every minute they drew nearer, and by 5 o'clock it was certain that Nelson meant to attack. He had failed to realize, when he had been off Alexandria a month before, that the French were still behind him; instead of waiting for them there he had spent the intervening weeks scouring the Mediterranean from Cyprus to Sicily. Now at last his hour had come: he would not even wait for all his ships to catch up: he would strike at once: it was 'Westminster Abbey or a peerage.'

By the bold initiative of her captain, the *Goliath,* which led the line, steered inside the French left, through the narrow gap between it and the shallows (arguing that where a French ship could swing, a British ship could sail), and was followed by *Zealous, Orion,* and *Theseus. Audacious,* breaking through the French line, reached a similar position on the 'blind side' of the enemy. Nelson himself in *Vanguard* led outside the French line, and was followed by the rest. The first nine French ships thus found themselves attacked by thirteen, and on both sides. Superior gunnery did the rest. As evening turned to night, watchers on the shore at Rosetta, climbing onto towers and housetops, anxiously looked westwards, hearing gunfire and seeing a glow in the sky, as the French flag-ship, *l'Orient,* took fire, and finally blew up: though they could not tell whether she was friend or foe, and had no notion how the fight was going.

When the last French ship had surrendered or escaped—which was not till near midday on August 2nd—it was found that all but two of Bonaparte's capital ships, and two frigates, had been captured or destroyed. The British casualties were 218 killed and 678 wounded: light losses, one might think; the *Theseus* fought for twelve hours, and was pierced by eighty large shot, yet had only six men killed and thirty-one wounded. The French casualties were never accurately determined. Bonaparte's own summary gives the figures as 600 killed or drowned, and 800 (of whom 150 seriously) wounded.

Bonaparte was never inclined to blame himself if others could be found fault with, or to allow them credit if he could take it himself. In his account of the battle written to the Directory on August 19th he says that on the day before he left Alexandria (July 6th) he instructed Brueys to bring his fleet into Alexandria harbour within twenty-four hours; but, if this could not be done, to discharge at once all the artillery and other effects of the land army, and to sail for Corfu. But Brueys did not think he could discharge his cargo where he was, and moved to Aboukir Bay. 'So I left Alexandria (writes Bonaparte) firmly believing that within three days the fleet would either have entered the harbour of Alexandria or have sailed for Corfu.' Up till July 27th (he says) he heard no more. Then he was astonished to get several letters from the admiral showing that he was still at Aboukir. 'I wrote at once to impress upon him that he should not lose an hour in either entering Alexandria or going to Corfu.'

So Bonaparte exculpated himself at the expense of one who could never answer back. But the answer is in Bonaparte's own letters. On July 3rd he had written to Brueys: 'In the present situation of the army it is indispensable to arrange matters so that the fleet can manœuvre as events may require, and to put itself out of reach of (*se trouver à l'abri de*), the superior force that the English may have in these seas . . . The Admiral will inform Bonaparte tomorrow whether there is anchorage for the fleet at

Alexandria, or whether it can defend itself, anchored in line in the Aboukir roads, against a superior enemy fleet.' If neither of these courses is possible the fleet must sail for Corfu: or if the enemy appears in superior force, this must at once be done.

From this it is clear that in anchoring at Aboukir, in the belief that he could defend himself there, Brueys was in fact following one of Bonaparte's own suggestions—the third alternative to entering Alexandria or sailing to Corfu—and that it was this which led to the disaster. It is very difficult, taking the correspondence as a whole, to accept Bonaparte's version of the affair. The historian, too, like any detective, grows suspicious when he finds that so many of the original documents dealing with the Egyptian campaign were destroyed by the suspect's own orders, and that he has to be content with copies.

However this controversy may ultimately be decided, there can be no question that Bonaparte showed little generosity towards the memory of the man whom he held responsible for such a blow to his designs. Though in an affecting letter to Mme Brueys (August 19th) he speaks of the 'honourable death' of his 'friend,' there is not a word of excuse. Ganteaume is congratulated on having been saved for future revenge, and Villeneuve on having tried to dissuade Brueys from fighting as he did. A street in Cairo is named after Commodore du Petit-Thouars of the *Tonnant*; and a ship after Thevenard, Captain of the *Aquilon*. But Brueys's name disappears, with the stigma of failure, as Dupont's did after Baylen, into the growing legend of Bonaparte's invincibility.

Soon the *situation horrible* of August 15th has become *cette affaire*: the number of casualties, at first *pas considérable*, becomes *peu de morts et fort peu de blessés*; and Bonaparte's optimistic mind is not only building a new fleet, but speculating: 'If the English continue to dominate the Mediterranean they will force us to even greater exploits than we had intended' (August 21st) in Syria, Turkey, India? . . .

Yet Bonaparte cannot keep his mind off the subject. 'It's no use pretending,' he writes to Kléber on September 9th, 'that our generals [i.e. *admirals*] rather than our fleet were beaten on the 14th. The English had the same number of ships as we had, yet they were three or four to one. I can see nothing here but bad tactics (*une fausse combinaison*). It gives me a favourable impression of Admiral Nelson, but not a proportionably unfavourable one of our own fleet. I am still strongly convinced that if the English had really wanted to attack us during the voyage we should have beaten them handsomely.[9]

9

Bonaparte professed to make light of the blockade which the destruction of his fleet enabled the British to impose on the Egyptian coast. 'It will have no result,' he wrote to Kléber (September 17th); 'the equinoctial gales will see to that.' What matter if a *commissaire* or two were captured? It was not worth parleying with the enemy about them, and pandering to British pride. All the same it was a serious reminder of the importance of sea power, when he could not count on his dispatches to the Directory (though sent in facsimile via Malta, Tripoli, Ancona and Constantinople), ever reaching them; and when the cargoes of food and timber from Corfu were seized *en route*, so that he could not develop the coastal trade with the ports of the Aegean on which he counted for the prosperity of France's new colony. Writing home on September 8th he adds a postscript to say that a courrier named Lesimple has just arrived from France, but that his ship was sunk off Alexandria, and he lost all his dispatches except one letter from the Directors: it is the first he has received from them since he left France.

After that he heard no more from Europe for five months. During this period his anxiety to get news appears constantly in his correspondence. One messenger after another is sent off: Mailly on September 12th, Louis Bonaparte on October 23rd, a courrier to Constantinople on November 9th, Guibert to the British fleet at Rosetta on November 16th, Sucy sent home on sick leave on November 25th, Arnaud to Derne on December 9th, Beauchamp to Constantinople on December 11th, Fourès on a secret mission to Malta and Paris on December 18th—he was captured by the British on his first day at sea; his wife remained behind as Bonaparte's mistress—Croizier to Corfu on the same day, another party of officers on sick leave on February 5th.

The instructions to Guibert are worth noting. He is to go on board the English admiral's ship, taking copies of the Egyptian papers, and to try to get European papers in return. He is to say that Bonaparte gets plenty of news from Corfu and Constantinople, and that he sends officers to France every day. He is to say that Bonaparte is at Suez, where numbers of ships are arriving from Mauritius. He is to end by offering to water the British ships—as Bonaparte supplied Wurmser with medical and other necessities during the siege of Mantua—if the admiral will send a *parlementaire* to Cairo. (But almost on the same day Bonaparte is writing to General Menou blaming him for not capturing some British boat's crews which had come ashore for water at Goghaz.) These pretences are transparent, and his real feelings are plain.

Why is he so anxious for news? He wants to know what is happening at Rastadt, where he thinks the seizure of Egypt and the threat to India will bring peace nearer. He wants to know whether Talleyrand or any other ambassador is yet at Constantinople, and whether or not he is at war with the Porte. He wants reinforcements to be sent from Toulon: is anything being done about it? But most of all he is anxious about his own

career. The Egyptian expedition had been designed as a summer campaign. He had promised the Directors to return to France in October,
leaving behind him, no doubt, a sufficient force to garrison the new
colony. He would then be available to resume command of the army of
invasion against England, as he had undertaken to do.

But now (he writes on September 8th) his return must be delayed for
several months. Evidently the most he can now hope for is that a fast
ship, carrying himself and a few others, may slip through the blockade
during the dark winter nights. The army and the *Institut* will be stranded
in Egypt, without hope of return, so long as the British maintain their
blockade in the Mediterranean. His personal intentions are clear enough
from a sentence in his letter of December 18th to the Directors: 'We are
waiting for news from France and Europe, like thirsty men waiting for
water (*c'est un besoin vif pour nos âmes*); for if the national prestige had
need of us, nothing would console us for not being on the spot (*si la
gloire nationale avait besoin de nous, nous serions inconsolables de n'y pas
être*).'

Meanwhile the situation in Egypt had changed. The Cairo revolt (October 21st) had been repressed, and the return of 'representative government' was marked by the restoration of the *Grand Divan* on December
21st. Renewed activity by Turkish and Russian ships off Rosetta, and the
appointment of the Francophobe Ahmed (Djezzar) Pacha as Governor
of all Syria, showed that there was danger of an attack on Egypt by land.
Bonaparte had already been making preparations—mapping Lake
Manzaleh, exploring the Isthmus of Suez, establishing outposts, recruiting
dromedary corps, and so on—for a counter-move across the Syrian border.
If he had received news, even at this late hour, that he was needed at
home, he might have called off the Syrian expedition. But on February
5th, 1799, he at last received letters brought by a Ragusan wine-ship which
slipped through the blockade, and heard from two Frenchmen on board
that when they left Trieste on October 24th the Congress of Rastadt was
still talking, that Descorches was on his way as ambassador to Constantinople (this was not true), and that the Turkish ambassador was still in
Paris. There was no change in the government except the addition of
Treilhard to the Directory, and the credit of the *Corps législatif* stood
higher than it had done five months before. The army was being reinforced by 200,000 men of eighteen to thirty with the strange new name of
conscrits. Jourdan was in command in Italy and Joubert on the Rhine.
Though all Europe was arming, no power threatened war.

This news was reassuring. There was no reason why Bonaparte should
not go ahead with his invasion of Syria, and postpone his return to France
until the time was more ready for his intervention. 'I am off this very

minute,' he wrote to the Directors on February 10th: 'It is likely enough that when you read this letter I shall be standing on the ruins of the city of Solomon.' He gave, as the three aims of his expedition: first, to secure the conquest of Egypt by establishing a strong post beyond the desert, and so preventing any junction between one army coming overland and another landing in Egypt: secondly, to force the Porte to declare itself, and so help on the negotiations at Constantinople: and thirdly, to deprive the English blockading squadron of the supplies it gets from Syria. But he still puts in a qualifying clause. 'If,' he writes, 'during March confirmation comes of Hamelin's (the French passenger's) report, and France is at war with the Kings, then I shall come home at once (*je passerai en France*).' [10]

10

The invasion of Syria was preceded by a barrage of letters in terms calculated either to intimidate or to placate the Moslem rulers of the Levant. Already, when there was some fear that the news of the destruction of his fleet might encourage Arab and Turkish opposition, Bonaparte had made diplomatic overtures to the Grand Vizier at Constantinople, and had dispatched Beauvoisin and Mailly to interview the Pachas of Sidon and Acre, and of Aleppo. Now he wrote to the Commandant at Jaffa, the *cheiks, ulemas* and inhabitants of the provinces of Gaza, Ramleh and Jaffa, to the *cheiks, ulemas* and Commandant of Jerusalem—his favourite wife was an *ancienne couturière française*, who had written, offering to help Bonaparte—and to the *mullah* Murad-Radeh at Damascus, saying that he was entering Palestine only to drive out the troops of Djezzar-Pacha, which had violated Egyptian territory, and to secure them justice and religious toleration: but he thought it effective to add: 'I am as terrible as the fire from heaven against my enemies, but mild and merciful towards the people, and those who would be my friends.' To Djezzar-Pacha himself he remarked, scornfully: 'What reason could I have to deprive an old man whom I do not even know of the last few years of his life; or to add a few leagues more to the country I have already conquered?'

At first it seemed as though nothing could stop him. He left Cairo on February 10th and led a force of 10,000 men into the desert. On the 20th he captured the frontier post of El-Arish. On the 25th he occupied Gaza, after a terrible march across the desert: 'Here we are up to our knees in mud and water,' he writes to General Dugua; 'the weather is as cold as it is at Paris at this time of the year; you are lucky to be enjoying the sunshine of Cairo.' And to Desaix: 'We have crossed seventy leagues of desert, and it has been excessively fatiguing: brackish water, often not even that; we have had to eat dogs, donkeys and camels. For the last three days there has been a horrible wind and torrents of rain.' But five days later they were at Ramleh; on March 7th they took Jaffa, and after a week's stay marched on Haifa and Acre, which was reached on March 20th. Here for the first time, and finally, he was halted: two months passed in fruitless attempts on the town; and on May 17th, after the seventh assault, he struck camp, and marched back the way he had come.

He had boasted to the Directors on March 13th: 'The army of the Republic is mistress of the whole of Palestine.' How was he to explain the two months' halt and failure at Acre, which if taken would have been of little account, but untaken became the crux of the campaign? His correspondence gives three explanations, and they are inconsistent with one another. To the Directors, on May 10th, he wrote: 'Today we are masters of the chief points in the defences of the town (*rempart*) . . . It only remained to make our way (*cheminer*) into the town itself. This would have meant siege operations (*ouvrir la tranchée*) against every house in the place, and losing more men than I care to do.' To General Desaix, on the 16th, he said: 'I have occupied the chief points in the circumvallation (*enceinte*) of Acre. We did not think it the moment (*à propos*) to assault the second line of defence (*enceinte*): it would have meant too much waste of time and lives.' The Cairo *Divan* was informed on the same day: 'Not one stone of the town has been left upon another. All the inhabitants have evacuated the town by sea.' Finally, in a second report to the Directors, on May 26th, he says that spies, deserters and prisoners had all reported that plague raged in the town, with more than sixty deaths a day: if his soldiers had entered it, and had begun pillaging, they would all have caught the infection.

The real facts are not difficult to reconstruct. Bonaparte's small army of 10,000 was already weakened by lack of food (they had had no bread since they left Cairo) and by disease. The easy capture of El-Arish, Gaza and Jaffa had led the French command to underrate the defences of Acre, which was not only surrounded on three sides by the sea, but had been strengthened with all the resources of the art of fortification—wall and ditch, *escarpe et contre-escarpe*—by Phélippeaux, a young French engineer, a contemporary of Bonaparte himself at the *École Militaire*, and now serving with the British naval commander, Sir Sidney Smith. Smith, too, with two ships of the line, *Theseus* and *Tigre*, and *Alliance* (frigate) had arrived off the port in time to capture most of Bonaparte's siege train on its way by sea to Jaffa. These guns and gun-boats were employed against the besiegers, and backed by landing-parties of marines, who joined at critical moments in the sorties or counter-attacks of the defenders. The first assault came on March 28th: others followed on April 1st, 24th, 25th and May 1st, 7th, 8th and 10th. These last were helped by a few heavy guns at last landed at Jaffa.

On May 7th about thirty Turkish sail were sighted, coming from the direction of Rhodes to reinforce the defence: this determined the final assault. The crucial fight for the possession of the breach in the walls effected on May 10th is vividly described in the dispatches of Sir Sidney Smith to Lord Nelson: the attacking column raked by 'a French brass eighteen pounder, in the Lighthouse Castle, manned from the *Theseus*, under the direction of Mr. Scroder, Master's Mate, and the last mounted twenty-four pounder in the north Ravelin, manned from the *Tigre*, under the direction of Mr. Jones, Midshipman,' whilst 'the *Tigre's* two 68-pound carronades, mounted in two *germes* lying in the Mole, and worked under the direction of Mr. Bray, Carpenter of the *Tigre* (one of the bravest and most intelligent men I ever worked with), threw shells into the centre of this column with evident effect': the 'French standard' nevertheless seen at daylight, 'on the outer angle of the Tower': the boats' crews landed at the Mole, and led up to the breach armed with pikes: the Turks hurling down stones on the heads of the French: Djezzar-Pacha (the old man whose declining years Bonaparte had hesitated to shorten), quitting his station, 'where according to the ancient Turkish custom, he was sitting to reward such as should bring him the heads of the enemy, and distributing musket-cartridges with his own hand,' to join in the fight: the 'group of French generals and *aides-du-camp* . . . seen assembled on Richard Cœur de Lion's Mount, with Bonaparte distinguishable in the centre of a semi-circle; his gesticulations indicating a renewal of attack': and the final scene in the garden of the Pacha's *seraglio*, a little before sunset, where 'in a very few minutes the bravest and most advanced' of the attacking force 'lay headless corpses, the sabre, with the addition of a dagger in the other hand, proving more than a match for the bayonet.'

'Bonaparte,' the dispatch ends, 'will no doubt renew the attack; indeed the town is not, nor ever has been, defensible according to the rules of art; but according to every other rule it must and shall be defended—not that it is itself worth defending, but we feel that it is by this breach Bonaparte means to march to further conquests. 'Tis on the issue of this conflict that depends the opinion of the multitude of spectators on the surrounding hills, who wait only to see how it ends to join the victor; and with such a reinforcement for the execution of his known projects, Constantinople, and even Vienna, must feel the shock.'

But the attack was not renewed. Bonaparte had met his first defeat on land; and he owed it, as he owed the destruction of his fleet nine months before, to one of those 'imponderables' that he never quite learnt to take into account—the spirit of the British navy.

Whilst it is legitimate to emphasize Bonaparte's failure at Acre, it must not be forgotten that during a pause in the siege operations (April 15th-18th), he had hurried north, to help Kléber throw back a Turkish army which was marching to the relief of the town, and would, if unchecked, have proceeded to the invasion of Egypt. The battle of Mt. Tabor (April 16th) was a brilliant and decisive affair, which put an end to the threat of invasion by land, and provided some justification for the abandonment of the siege of Acre.

Two incidents during the Syrian campaign have been much debated, and claim consideration by any biographer of Bonaparte. He was, in the ordinary way, a merciful man, and shared the humanitarian ideas of 1789. He had forbidden the use of torture (by beating) to extract information from his subjects in Egypt as 'contrary to reason and humanity.' 'The wretched victims,' he had written to Berthier, 'only say what first comes into their heads, or what they see that they are wanted to say.' But it is established that after the storming of Jaffa he not only allowed his troops to massacre the townspeople, but also ordered their 3000 prisoners to be put to death, rather than weaken his forces by providing them with food and an escort. Again, during the advance he did not hesitate to visit his plague-stricken soldiers in the Jaffa hospital; but on the retreat there is little doubt that, unable to carry a number of incurably sick men with him, and unwilling to leave them to the vengeance of the enemy, he gave orders that they should be given a fatal dose of opium.[11]

II

There was one good reason why Bonaparte should return to Egypt, whether or not he was victorious at Acre. He had received on March 25th a letter written by Talleyrand for the directors on November 4th, 1798, telling him that Russia and Turkey had declared war on France, to be followed soon by Naples and Austria, and that a Russian army had already invaded Italy. This was the signal for his return to France. But he could not go yet. Although he had defeated one Turkish army at Mt. Tabor, he felt sure that his retreat from Palestine would be followed by an invasion of Egypt; for the ships seen off Acre, two of which had been taken by Pérée soon afterwards, belonged to an expeditionary force of 20,000 men mobilized at Rhodes. 'Egypt calls me,' he had written to the Directors on May 10th: 'Having reduced Acre to a pile of stones, I shall recross the desert, and be ready to receive the European [*i.e. Russian*] or Turkish army which is likely to land in Egypt in Messidor or Thermidor': and in his Proclamation to the army, on May 17th: 'We are returning to Egypt: the season for invasions recalls me there.'

The retreat across the desert cost the remnants of his army another fortnight's painful marching. Bonaparte, to the Directors, had put his losses at 500 killed and 1000 wounded, but in fact 700 men had already died of the plague, and 2000 sick had been sent home from Jaffa; it is doubtful whether more than half the total of 10,000 returned alive. It was thought wise to herald his return by an 'inspired' proclamation put out by the *Divan* of Cairo in which 'Sultan Bonaparte' (as though he had defeated and dethroned Selim) was said to have 'returned to Egypt, first to keep his promise that he would be back there within four months (for his promises are sacred trusts): and secondly to drive away, like mists before the sun, those wicked men, the Arabs and Mamelukes, who have been sowing trouble and sedition in some of the provinces. He loves Cairo (the proclamation continued) and Egypt, its river, its produce, and its splendours: it is his wish that our country may prosper till the Last Judgement.'

On the morning of July 15th news came of the expected arrival of the Turkish expeditionary force off Aboukir Bay. Their ships anchored where Brueys's had done, several miles off shore; their men landed on the promontory at the west end of the bay, and occupied the fort which had failed to prevent Nelson's attack on the French fleet. Within three days Bonaparte was at El-Ramanieh, where he concentrated some 10,000 men and advanced to the attack. The Turks waited for him, apparently thinking their entrenched position, backing on the sea, would be a second Acre.

We owe to that strange painter, Benjamin Robert Haydon, whose *Autobiography* covers exactly the period of Napoleon's public career, a word-picture of Bonaparte at this moment, which he had from the French artist Rigaut, a member of the Egyptian expedition.

'Rigo said that the night before the battle of Aboukir he lay on the ground in the same tent with Buonaparte . . . Rigo said he was never near Buonaparte but he was attracted by his physiognomy: there was something in his face so acute, so thoughtful, so terrible, that it always impressed him, and that this night, when all the rest were buried in sleep, he could not avoid watching him. In a little time he observed Napoleon take the compasses and a chart of Aboukir and the Mediterranean and measure, and then take a ruler and draw lines. He then arose, went to the door of his tent and looked towards the horizon; then returned to his tent and looked at his watch; after a moment he took a knife, and cut the table in all ways like a boy. He then rested his head on his hand, looked again at his watch for some time, went again to the door of his tent, and again returned to his seat. There was something peculiarly awful in the circumstances—the time of night—his generals soundly sleeping—Buonaparte's strong features lighted up by a lamp—the feeling that the Turks were encamped near them, and that before long a dreadful battle would be fought. Rigo said that his feelings were so alive that he could not have slept . . . In a short time Napoleon called them all up, ordered his horse, and asked how long before daybreak.' [12]

It was not a bloodless victory: the infantry were at first repulsed and the cavalry had to come to the rescue: Berthier admits that the French lost 150 killed and 750 wounded. But it was complete: of the Turkish force 2000 were killed on the field, 200, with their commander, Mustapha, captured, and no less than 10,000 shot or drowned as they vainly attempted to swim to their ships. Another 1800 were found killed and 300 wounded in the fort, where a remnant of 2000 surrendered next day. These figures are Berthier's, and therefore unlikely to be exaggerated: they amount to the total annihilation of an army of 16,300 men. Perhaps Bonaparte, who had told his men that they were fighting against six times their number, was not displeased that Kléber came up too late to join in the battle. He might very well have waited for him. But he remembered that Mt. Tabor had really been Kléber's victory; and he preferred to beat the second Turkish army alone—particularly on the spot where Nelson had annihilated his fleet nearly a year ago.

12

Now that both counter-invasions had been defeated, nothing but the British blockade stood between Bonaparte and Paris. If he needed a final omen to determine his decision, it was supplied by the man whom he had already begun to regard with a superstitious eye—Sir Sidney Smith. For it was from the British admiral that his *aide-de-camp* Merlin procured copies of the *Gazette de Francfort* and the *Courrier français de Londres* for June 6th and 10th, containing news of Joubert's defeat in Italy and Jourdan's on the Rhine. Smith also told him that Nelson had intercepted another letter from the Directors, dated May 26th, 1799, ordering him to return to France. A third letter in the same sense, dated September 20th, he did not receive until after his landing.

His mind was at once made up. He spent only a week at Cairo after his return from Aboukir. He arranged with Ganteaume for two newly built and fast frigates, *Muiron* and *Carrère*, and two fast *avisos*, *Indépendant* and *Revanche*, to be got ready for him. He would sail as soon as the British blockading squadron was out of the way. On the evening of August 17th, he heard from Ganteaume that it had sailed for Cyprus, leaving only a brig behind. Within three hours his companions had their sailing orders. Next morning fifteen of them started down the Nile. At midnight on the 22nd they were on board. The flotilla sailed next day.

On the *Muiron* were Bonaparte, Ganteaume (in command of 'the fleet'), Berthier, Andréossi, Bourrienne, Eugène, Monge, Berthollet; on the *Carrère*, Dumanoir (in command), Lannes, Murat, Marmont, Denon, Parseval. The total company was not less than 400. What a risk to take! What a prize, had they been intercepted!

Before sailing Bonaparte wrote a batch of letters (they are all dated the 22nd) explaining his decision. To Menou he simply said: 'I am off tonight for France'; to Junot: 'When you get this letter I shall be far from Egypt.' But to Pouissielgue he explained: 'Important events which happened in Europe between March 15th and June 15th have made it an imperative duty for me to return there as quickly as possible. I have hope, with a little luck, to arrive there before the fall of Mantua.' To Dugua he said: 'When you read this I shall be in the midst of the vast ocean. The circumstances in which France is placed have made it an imperative duty [*the same phrase again*] to return there. Besides, it is the only way to secure the welfare of our establishment here, and of every member of the army.' During the winter, he promises, ships will bring reinforcements to Egypt, and Dugua will be able to return to his place in the Legislative Body.

To Kléber, whom he left in command of the army of occupation, he explained that he had ante-dated his start because the British squadron had temporarily left Alexandria. He enclosed papers with the news. 'We have lost Italy: Mantua, Turin, Tortona are besieged: I have reason to hope that Mantua may hold out till the end of November. I am in good hope, if fortune smiles on me, of arriving in Europe before the beginning of October.' Kléber may expect reinforcements: but if they do not come by May, and if there are more than 1500 deaths from the plague, he is to sue for terms from the Porte, even if it means the evacuation of Egypt. Finally, to the *Divan*, which he still seems to have thought more gullible than it really was, he wrote: 'Having been informed that my fleet was ready, and that a formidable army was on board . . . I have taken the decision to place myself at the head of my fleet.' They are to trust Kléber as they trusted himself, and to see that when he returns 'in two or three months' time' he will 'have cause to be satisfied with the people of Egypt.'

VI

PARIS

(1799)

I

A NORTH-WEST WIND had blown Bonaparte from France to Egypt in six weeks. For three weeks after leaving Alexandria the same wind forced him (luckily enough) to take the southern route along the African shore, out of the way of British shipping: then in another three weeks a south-eastern wind blew him back to France. Fortune smiled, as he had begged and expected her to do. He once more slipped through the net of the British blockade. Sidney Smith was refitting at Corfu: Nelson was being fêted and flattered at the Neapolitan court. But English frigates were always on the move in the narrow seas between Malta, Palermo and Naples; and the autumn nights were too short to give much protection: yet Bonaparte and his 400 never sighted a British sail till their last night at sea, and landed safely at Fréjus, after five days' (wind-bound) stay at Ajaccio, on October 9th. It was from the same beach that he was to embark for his exile at Elba, fifteen years later, taking this landing as a good omen: for the people of the coast, who had seen the armada sail away eighteen months before, welcomed him so enthusiastically that the quarantine officers could not do their work. Six hours later he was on his way to Paris.[1]

'Bonaparte,' says one who saw him at this time, 'was looking very thin and yellow, his complexion tanned, his eyes sunken, his figure well-shaped, but a little too thin. His forehead [for the portrait spares no detail] was high and prominent. He had not much hair, especially on the temples, but it was very fine and soft, of an auburn tint. His fine blue eyes were incredibly expressive of every emotion; sometimes kind and caressing, sometimes serious and hard. He had a beautiful mouth; the lips symmetrical and rather thin, especially when he was in a bad temper: the teeth, though not very regular, white and good—he never had any trouble with them: his nose of a perfect Greek shape, and his sense of

146

smell extremely keen. He had a very strong head, twenty-two inches round, rather more long than broad, and consequently a little flattened at the temples, extremely sensitive; very small ears, well shaped and well placed; a rather short neck; narrow shoulders, a broad chest with very little hair on it, a shapely thigh and leg, small feet, and well-spaced toes without any corns or callouses. His arms were well-shaped, his hands admirable.' This witness gives his height as five feet, two inches, three *lignes*. He was dressed, when he arrived in Paris, in a civilian's round hat, and an olive-green riding-coat, with a Turkish scimitar belted round his waist.[2]

Bonaparte had avoided Malta on his way home. No doubt there might be British ships lurking off Valetta. But Malta belonged to an episode that he had for the moment put behind him, and its future would depend upon what happened in France. Corsica was different. He could not resist its scented shore, the home and speech of his childhood, and the embraces of his old nurse Camilla Ilari. He thought of his visit there not as the end of an Egyptian adventure, but as the beginning of a European one. When he left Ajaccio for Fréjus he was once more the young soldier of fortune offering his sword and his wits in the service of an adopted country.

But, like others of his generation who had burnt their fingers in the fire of revolution, he had developed an extra sense of self-sufficiency and self-preservation. His companions on the *Muiron* reported that they had discussed what was to be done if they met a superior British force, and that Bonaparte had said he would sooner blow up the ship than be taken prisoner. If he said so, it was not his real mind, but the theatrical pose of his generation (which Nelson shared too), expressed in the Italian rhetoric that his reporters so often misunderstood. He was no Richard Grenville, to

Fall into the hands of God, not into the hands of Spain.

As he approached the shores of France he was thinking of the future to which Fortune was leading him: France's need of him, and his need of France. Italy and Egypt were behind him, as Corsica was within him. But they had shaped his native character and his ideas to new uses. He believed himself destined, and knew himself fit, to remodel the French state, and to carry the revolutionary tricolor round the world. Bonaparte was great and dangerous, because he united reason with passion: the rationalism which is the natural religion of Frenchmen with an ambitious imagination which turned it from criticism to construction: the insularity of a Corsican with the internationalism of a soldier of fortune.

Bonaparte reached Paris on the morning of October 16th, after a week's travel by Aix, Avignon, Valence, Lyon, Chalons and Nevers. His mother was there to greet him, but not Joséphine, who, hearing of his landing on the night of October 10th, had set out to meet him, but took the more easterly route by Auxerre, and just missed him at Lyon. She was back on the 18th: he forgave her M. Charles; she forgave his Mme Fourés; and they were reconciled. Passion had changed into an affection as deep and lasting as either of them were capable of feeling. To her he stood for an establishment, worldly success, and hero-worship: for him she provided the social graces of a hostess and the charms of a mistress.

The return from Egypt was very different from the return from Italy two years before. There were no public receptions, and only one banquet —a subscription dinner for 700 given by the two Councils to Bonaparte and Moreau on November 6th. Instead, a steady round of visits and private talks: with the Directors, at the Luxembourg; with Talleyrand, at the Foreign Office; with brother Joseph at his grand country house at Mortefontaine; with Fouché and Jourdan; with Moreau and Bernadotte, who asked thirty friends to meet him at dinner; and frequently, preferably at night time, with Sieyès. But the news of his arrival had spread to every corner of Paris. His health was drunk in the *cabarets*. Songs in his honour were sung in the streets. Crowds gathered to see him ride to the Luxembourg, or stood outside his house, or cheered him at the opera. The *Messenger* was not far wrong when it said, 'Every one waits for Bonaparte impatiently, because to everyone he brings new hope.'

The first letter he wrote when he landed had asked the commandant at Toulon to send out to Kléber copies of the *Moniteur* and other papers for the last six months: and his first preoccupation must have been to find out what had been happening since he left France, and what was the state of public opinion in Paris. If he looked through the papers, as the historian can look through them in Aulard's collection of contemporary documents, he would have been amused, first, by the speculations—some of them genuine, and some of them intentionally misleading, about the destination of his expedition: he would even have read a detailed description of how he had captured Gibraltar. Then he would have found, during the seventeen months of his absence, an almost complete ignorance of what was going on in Egypt or Syria, punctuated by occasional official *communiqués*, announcing the capture of Malta, the loss of the fleet at Aboukir Bay, or the fighting at Acre (this in some detail, from the *Court Gazette* of Vienna); and, along with these scraps of news, a constant crop of rumours—rumours of defeat and disaster in the Opposition papers, and counter-rumours of victory in the government press.

Often there was a more personal tone: the *Nouvelliste politique* would object to the *Conservateur* describing Bonaparte as 'the French Caesar,' and say that people would soon be regretting Robespierre under a worse tyranny; the *Journal des Francs*, going one better than the *Conservateur*,

would speak of him as the conqueror of India, China, and Asia, 'mount-
ing the throne of the universe': and the royalist press would retort with
the rumour that he had been killed 'along with his 40,000 *déportés*'; for it
was a favourite theme of the Opposition that the Directors had hoped to
get rid of him and his army by sending them to Egypt. But during the
last few months the papers had settled down into a dull indifference—the
very atmosphere best suited for the project that Bonaparte had in mind.[3]

He knew France well enough to be able to fill in much of the background of public opinion; and he made it his business to talk with everyone who could tell him what was going on behind the political scenes—
the parties, the personalities, the jealousies, the intrigues. Within less
than a month of his return to Paris he had the whole intricate affair in
his head, and was ready with the plan of a *coup d'état*.

France had been at war ever since the proclamation of the Republic,
seven years ago; and war, though it had its *panaches*, was really incompatible with the republican way of life—with liberty, equality, fraternity;
with the rights of man; with economic prosperity, and social security, and
a peaceful domesticity—just that civilization which was the soul of France,
and to which new meaning seemed to have been given by the ideas and
achievements of the Revolution. True, the military disasters which had
brought Bonaparte hurrying home were retrieved by Brune's victory over
the Anglo-Russian forces in Holland, and by Masséna's defeat of the Russians at Zürich (September 23rd and 26th): but these victories did not
seem to bring any nearer the peace that all desired.

If France was tired of the war, it was also tired of the Directory, which
it suspected of exploiting the war in its own interests. Ever since the *coup
d'état* of Fructidor, when the support of Bonaparte's Italian army, represented in Paris by Augereau and his troops, had enabled the Directors to
constitute themselves, as the Committee of Public Safety had done six
years before, into a group dictatorship, this opposition had been growing
more acute; and so had the government's reaction against it. The new
dictatorship, unlike the old, was not based on popular consent; it had
been imposed on Paris by force. At the elections in the spring of 1798, held
just as Bonaparte was starting for Egypt, a Jacobin majority was only
kept out of power by quashing the votes of the electorate, and the resentment of the country was little appeased by the financial, educational and
administrative reforms afterwards introduced by Ramel and de
Neufchâteau.

When, to carry out the aggressive policy of the Directory in Switzerland
and Italy, and to meet the consequent threat of war from the Second Coalition, recourse was had to the *loi Jourdan*, calling 200,000 young men to
the colours with the new name (which had so startled Bonaparte) of
conscrits; when nevertheless, in the summer of 1799, Jourdan was driven

back on to the Rhine, and a series of the Republic's best generals defeated by Survorov in Italy, discontent grew intense. Following a defeat of the government nominees at the spring elections of 1799, the two Councils carried through a counter *coup d'état* of their own, which (as Bonaparte had heard) left the Legislature in a stronger position than it had hitherto held *vis-à-vis* a new and weakened body of Directors: a situation which encouraged both Jacobins and Royalists to make fresh efforts to upset the constitution.

2

At this point in his review of the situation Bonaparte found himself almost necessarily drawn into consultation with three men who, like himself, had with some difficulty survived the Revolution, had served, with increasing doubts, under the Directory, and were now convinced of the need of a new constitution. The French kings of the old regime, surrounded by intriguing relations, and ignorant of worldly affairs, were accustomed to entrust their policy to foreign ecclesiastics, better educated than themselves, without family encumbrances, and trained in the subtle diplomacy of Rome. By a curious chance the three men upon whom Bonaparte relied to make him master of the state were all ex-ecclesiastics: Fouché, Talleyrand, and Sieyès.

Fouché had been educated in the Oratoires of Nantes and Paris. Though he never took major Orders, he spent his twenties in clerical dress and tonsure, teaching science to young revolutionists. Chance took him in 1788 to Arras, where he met Robespierre, courted his sister Charlotte, and lent him his coach fare when he was called as a deputy to Versailles in 1789. Next year he was back at Nantes; in 1792 he appeared in Paris as a married man, and deputy for Loire-Inférieure in the National Convention. A Jacobin of the Left, he never lost the Oratorian touch, and revealed a monastic austerity, a casuistry and a scientific sureness in all he undertook. Most of his time as a deputy was spent on missions in the provinces. At Nantes, Troyes, Dijon, Nevers and Moulins he acquired the reputation of a bitter anti-clerical; at Lyon that of a bloodthirsty terrorist.

The double role displeased his patron Robespierre, whose designs upon him he only just succeeded in anticipating at Thermidor. In the reaction after the fall of Robespierre he could not shift all the blame for his misdeeds onto a Carrier or a Collot d'Herbois, and his arrest was decreed. But it was never carried out. From 1795 to 1798 he lived in retreat, or begging jobs from the Directors; till his support of the *coup d'état* of Fructidor brought him once more into power as Minister of the Republic at Milan and in Holland. Finally, just as Bonaparte was leaving Fréjus, he set off for Paris, with his nomination as Minister of Police in his pocket.

Fouché's political programme was that of a policeman and a regicide. A royalist restoration would mean for him, as for so many others, exile, if not execution: so the royalists must be kept down, and not less the Jacobins, whose reapperances had always occasioned royalist reactions: but best of all (he reckoned) would be a military dictatorship, with the army at the call of the government, and both at the back of the police. On August 3rd, whilst Bonaparte was returning to Cairo from his victory over the Turks, Fouché had startled all Paris by a Proclamation in which he published his intention to 'restore peace at home, to put an end to the murder or oppression of republicans, to confound the plots of traitors, and to deprive foreign intriguers of any hope of accomplices.' His subsequent measures against the Popular Societies, the Jacobin Club, the press, and the royalists in the Vendée showed that he would do what he said. Evidently Bonaparte would find him indispensable.[4]

Talleyrand, fifteen years older than Bonaparte, and five older than Fouché, had more knowledge than either of the 'Victorian age' of France which to the new generation seemed as far away as the Middle Ages. By birth an aristocrat, by temperament and preference a layman, and by accident an ecclesiastic, he had as a young man received the blessing of Voltaire, corresponded with Mirabeau, became an Orleanist and a Freemason, and played a big part in the Constituent Assembly as deputy for the clergy of Autun. A close acquaintance with church business and a good head for finance qualified him to carry through the Civil Constitution of 1790; and the accident that he was a bishop made him the natural person to sing mass for the nation at the Federal Fête of 1791, and to lay hands on the first bishops consecrated in defiance of the Pope. But nature had made him no more a Jacobin or a republican than a priest, and he was glad to secure a diplomatic appointment in London in 1792, and to watch the guillotine at work from the other side of the Channel. In March 1794 he sailed under an expulsion order to the United States; but was back amongst the French émigrés in Hamburg in July, and in Paris in September 1796.

Talleyrand had been too long abroad, and had kept too much strange company, to be easily acceptable either to the Directors or to the Paris police. A letter which he published by way of apologia proved only, said his old patron J. Chénier, that 'after being an anarchist, an Orleanist, and only not a Robespierrist because Robespierre had no use for him, he has become a Directorist, with a view to attaching himself to whatever party is next in power.' This was not far from the truth. Talleyrand needed money, to enjoy the society of fashionable women; he needed power, to revenge himself on life, which had afflicted him with lameness; and was confident that he could manage the foreign affairs of the country better than Delacroix. Helped by Mme de Staël, he laid siege to Barras, the one Director (and the most influential) who showed some partiality for him, and on July 18th, 1797, was appointed Minister of Foreign Affairs. He now had one of the finest houses in Paris, with a carriage and £5000 a year, and endless opportunities of acquiring more: he founded a vast fortune by speculating on the *coup d'état* of Brumaire, and according to one estimate his diplomatic earnings during the two years before the Life Consulate amounted to £682,500.

But he was still looking out for the next party to be in power; and soon followed and flattered the rising fortunes of Bonaparte. Bonaparte, for his part, was quick to congratulate him on his appointment as Minister, and confided to him his private opinion of the Austrian negotiators at Campo Formio (September 6th), and his views on political science (September 19th). Their relations after Bonaparte's return from Italy have already been noticed; so has Talleyrand's failure to carry out his part in the Egyptian expedition. Perhaps Bonaparte would not have forgiven him for this, had he not already been punished for it. He was blamed for the disasters of the summer of 1799, whether rumoured or real; he became involved in an unfortunate law-suit; he was suspected by the Directors of resenting their supervision, and coveting their succession; and on the same day as Fouché became Minister of Police he resigned the Ministry of Foreign Affairs. But the moment was well chosen. His friendship with both men made him the natural intermediary between Bonaparte and Sieyès, and one of the First Consul's earliest acts was to reinstate him in the *Hôtel des Relations Extérieures*.[5]

Through Talleyrand Bonaparte kept in touch with the *Cercle Constitutionnel* or *Club de Salm*, which had been founded by supporters of the Directory, in opposition to the *Club de Clichy*, during the elections of 1797, and which soon became the source of various plans for the reform of the Constitution. The principal authors of these plans seem to have been Benjamin Constant and his mistress Mme de Staël, the comte de Laraguais, and Henri de Saint-Simon: but they were also known to Barras, to Sieyès and to Bonaparte. Otherwise he would hardly have written to Talleyrand, with the intention that it should be shown to Sieyès, a letter of September 19th, 1797, in which he expressed his views about the reform of the constitution; neither would he have ventured, in his speech before the Directors on December 10th the same year, to say that the Peace of Campo Formio initiated 'the era of representative governments,' and that 'when the happiness of the French people rests on the basis of better organic laws, the whole of Europe will be freed.' The details of reform envisaged by this group were not always the same. Mme de Staël and Constant believed in government by what we should call a reformed House of Lords. Laraguais seems to have cast his patron Barras for the part of 'perpetual President.' But all, not least Bonaparte, wished to strengthen the executive, and to reduce the functions of the legislature: it had outlived its work, and become a danger to the republic of its own making.

So thought the amateurs; but there was, they all agreed, a Professor of Comparative Constitutions, who alone was competent to put their ideas into shape. Sieyès, like Talleyrand an unwilling priest and an unbeliever, yet had none of the other's worldly tastes or social aptitudes, and passed through the scenes of the revolution as a critic goes the round of the theatres, learning the secrets of good writing and acting, but having no ambition either to write or to act. It remains a puzzle why and how he produced the most successful political pamphlet of 1789. His career in the Constituent Assembly, and during the republican regime, became more and more that of an 'elder statesman' who must be consulted by each party in power, but who gives his support to none; or of a professor of philosophy whose sayings are reverently quoted by his pupils, but who commits nothing to the press. He hated the Constitution of 1793, and kept out of sight during the Jacobin dictatorship. He disliked the Constitution of 1795, though it approximated to a formula of his own which he had hoped would prevent any recurrence of the Jacobin dictatorship—disliked it particularly because it did not include the *Jury constitutionnaire* which was to his mind the essential ingredient of his recipe. He regarded the *coup d'état* of Fructidor as only the first step towards the setting up of a new—and this time perfect—constitution.

But each political *coup* during the revolution had involved a franker appeal to force than the one preceding it—July 14th, October 6th, August 10th, June 2nd, Thermidor, Vendémiaire, Fructidor—the line seemed to go on to the crack of doom. Like Lenin, and at much the same age, he realized that a revolution could not be carried through without shooting; and he was looking round for a soldier to do this for him. His choice of Bonaparte was inevitable rather than natural; the two men had little in common, and their ideas of how the affair was to end were quite different. Sieyès wanted a constitution under which no power in the state should predominate—a perfect division of political labour: Bonaparte was determined that one man should rule. But it would be dangerous to say so; and in all their conversations about ends he kept his own counsel about means. He admitted to Reubell three years later that he thought the Directors had missed a good chance of 'consolidating the government' after Fructidor: he was determined not to let a second chance go by. What had been done in Holland, in Switzerland, and in the Italian republics could be done in France. The new wine of centralized power could no longer be contained in the old bottles of representative government. New receptacles must be created for it.[6]

3

Whatever secrecy surrounded the preparations for the *coup d'état* of 18th-19th Brumaire, little controversy exists as to the way in which it was carried out; although some accounts of the events of November 9th-10th, 1799, are extremely confused and obscure. The conspirators made the mistake of trying to bring about an unconstitutional change constitutionally, and therefore risked failure by doing in two days what might have been done in one. They did not care how they got rid of such Directors as were not in the plot: but they wished the Legislature to get rid of itself. To do this, the Council of Ancients had to be frightened by the rumour of a Jacobin rising to remove their next session from Paris to Saint-Cloud, and to put themselves under the protection of Bonaparte and the troops of the Department of the Seine.

Both these parts of the plan were successfully carried out on November 9th. When the Ancients met, Cornet, the President of their *Commission des inspecteurs*, announced in vague terms the discovery of a conspiracy. Regnier, who was in the chair, proposed the move to Saint-Cloud, and the deputies, many of whom were aware of what was going on, agreed. Bonaparte appeared, and made a speech, the gist of which was: 'The Republic was at its last gasp: your decree has saved its life. Don't be discouraged by past precedents. There is nothing in history like the end of the eighteenth century, and nothing at the end of the eighteenth century analogous to this moment. What we want is a republic founded on true liberty, social liberty and national representation; and we are going to have it. That I swear, in my name, and in that of my comrades in arms.' This was not the oath of loyalty he had been summoned to take; but it was accepted in lieu of it. Moreau was sent to guard the Luxembourg. There the Directors were required to sign the decree of the Ancients. Barras preferred to resign: Gohier and Moulin added their signatures to those of Sieyès and Ducos.

But next day, at Saint-Cloud, things began to go wrong. The Ancients, meeting in the *Galérie de Mars* at two p.m., listened to another harangue by Bonaparte which the histories usually describe as 'incoherent,' but which, in the official version printed in the *Journal Militaire*, is an instructive personal version of the *coup d'état*. 'Yesterday,' he is represented as saying, 'I was staying quietly in Paris, when I was summoned by you to provide military support for the transference of your session to Saint-Cloud. Now I am attacked as a second Caesar or Cromwell. They talk of a military government. But I am only acting through and for you. The Republic has abdicated. Four of the Directors have resigned, and the fifth is under police protection. The Five Hundred are at sixes and sevens. Everything depends on the Ancients. Let us join in saving liberty, in saving equality!' (*A voice*: 'What about the Constitution?') 'The Constitution! You yourselves destroyed it on 18 *fructidor*, on 22 *floréal*, on 30 *prairial*: nobody has any respect for it now.' As for himself, he will speak frankly. Ever since his return he has been approached by one party after another, each calling themselves the only true patriots, to help them to get rid of their political enemies. But 'I am not an intriguer: you know me well enough for that: and I think I have given sufficient pledges of my devotion to my country.' He will stand by the principles of the constitution: when those are restored, he declares that he will be 'nothing more in the Republic than the arm to support what you have established.'

The last part of the speech was by no means so conciliatory as this official version made out. 'If I am a traitor (he is reported as saying) it is for each of you to be a Brutus. But if anyone calls for my outlawry, then the thunderbolt of war shall crush him to the earth. Remember that I march hand in hand with the god of fortune and the god of war.' As he was withdrawing there were cries of 'The General Committee!'—There was no need of it, he replied: it was for the Ancients themselves to decide the issue: he left it to them.

From the Ancients Bonaparte went on to the meeting of the Five Hundred in the Orangery, accompanied by four men of the *Garde du Corps Législatif*. Here he was greeted with cries of *à bas le dictateur!* and the terrible threat of outlawry, *hors la loi!* There followed a fracas in which two of the guardsmen stood between Bonaparte and the legendary stilettos of the deputies, and he was forced out of the hall. His brother Lucien, in the chair, could not control the deputies, who were proceeding, on Augereau's motion, to a decree of outlawry, when the guards, appealed to by Lucien to save their general, marched into the Hall, and drove out the Council.

When this 'purge' was reported to the Ancients, they voted the suppression of the Directory, the creation of an executive commission of three, and the transformation of the legislature into two Standing Committees of twenty-five. At nine p.m. a 'rump' of the Five Hundred, Lucien presiding, confirmed this action, and named Sieyès, Ducos, and Bonaparte as provisional Consuls of the French Republic. Before midnight the three took an oath of loyalty to the 'Republic, one and indivisible, liberty, equality and the representative system.' It was almost, Lucien thought, a second Tennis Court Oath. But with what a difference!

4

It had been stipulated in the Law of the 19th Brumaire that the two committees which now represented the French people should 'prepare the changes to be introduced into the organic provisions of the constitution, whose faults and inconveniences had been proved by experience.' But in fact they could only wait for the proposals that they knew would be laid before them by the new Consuls and their advisers. There can be no question that these proposals, in their original form, came from Sieyès: but, as he disliked putting his ideas on paper, and preferred to carry his constitution in his head, it has been endlessly debated by historians which of the rival versions given in Daunou's *Tableau figuratif*, in the *Théorie constitutionnelle* of Boulay de la Meurthe, and in Roederer's *Organisation d'un gouvernement représentatif* most closely reproduce his views.[7]

This, however, is a matter of little importance, compared with the reception of Sieyès's proposals by Bonaparte. If the 'elder statesman' imagined that he would be able to outwit a mere soldier, he was sadly mistaken. Bonaparte soon heard from Roederer and Boulay the outlines of Sieyès's plan, and raised important objections. During the second half of November Sieyès had three meetings at his house, at which he redrafted his proposals. On December 1st Talleyrand arranged an interview between him and Bonaparte; but they were hopelessly at variance, and strong words passed. A bigger meeting on December 4th, at which the Consuls met certain members of the two committees, sat until two a.m. on the 5th, and then empowered Daunou to draft the document in final form as a whole. On December 12th, in another night sitting in Bonaparte's rooms, Daunou read out his draft, article by article, and the two committees finally adopted it.

It was a complete victory for Bonaparte, who allowed Sieyès the humiliating consolation of nominating him as First Consul, with Cambacérès and Lebrun as his colleagues. They were thereupon appointed by acclamation to take office as soon as the Constitution came into force. Three days later (December 15th) the three provisional Consuls (as they remained meanwhile) addressed a Proclamation to the nation stating that the new constitution was 'based upon the true principles of representative government, and on the sacred rights of property, equality and liberty. The powers it sets up (they said) will be strong and lasting. Citizens, the Revolution is stabilized on the principles which began it. The Revolution is over.'

What, then, had been the point so much at issue? Why had it taken five weeks to 'save the Republic'? How could Sieyès and Bonaparte both sign a document to which they attached completely different meanings? The essentials of Sieyès's plan were (1) two legislative bodies, a *Tribunat* and a *Corps législatif*, (2) a *Sénat Conservateur* (its original name was *Collège des Conservateurs*) representing the 'Jury' that had been rejected in framing the last constitution, and (3) an executive consisting of a Great Elector (a term Sieyès had picked up at Berlin) and two Consuls. There was little dispute as regards the legislature, and not much as to the powers of the Senate; the only real issue came over the description of the first Consul as 'Great Elector,' and it was a personal one.

Sieyès hoped, by inducing Bonaparte to accept a nominal headship of the state, to confine him to the appointment of ministers, generals and ambassadors, and to the supervision of their work, whether in peace or in war, whilst himself being always liable to be called to account for misconduct by the Senate. Bonaparte's natural masterfulness, and his experience of autocratic powers in Italy and Egypt, would not tolerate such a position: there must be in the long run (he held) a single person with direct control over the whole state, both in peace and war. The issue at last lay between Sieyès's formula, which gave the second and third Consuls *voix délibérative* (a right to one of three equal votes) and Bonaparte's formula, which gave them only *voix consultative* (the right to express their opinion). The second formula won the day. The second and third Consuls were to sign their names to anything decided after the first Consul had consulted them; but his decision was final (*la décision du Premier Consul suffit*). Thus, by a stroke of the pen, a constitution designed to spread responsibility as widely as possible became one in which it was all concentrated in a single pair of hands. The carefully balanced checks and counter-checks of Sieyès's 'perfect distribution of political labour' only served to increase the centralized power of a first Consul who was in fact an autocrat. Sieyès signed the new constitution as executor of the will of the deceased republic; Bonaparte signed it as Heir Presumptive of a Life Consulship, if not of an Empire.

The *Brumairiens*, as French historians call them—Sieyès and his friends, who were responsible for altering the government of the country —acted, as every party in power since Thermidor had acted, under the double fear either of a Jacobin or of a royalist *revanche*: they knew that their property, their citizenship, and perhaps their lives would be in danger in the event of another Reign of Terror—whether 'red' or 'white.' The natural way to avoid this fate was a constitution *à la Sieyès* which would prevent the capture of political power by either party. But the army and the people saw another solution: not a constitution, which would end like those which had gone before it, but a man: a man who was, as Regnier declared, 'a hero whom France holds dear, not so much for the number of his victories as for the desire he has so patently expressed to become the peace-maker of the world: a man who will know how to rule as he has known how to fight and to win.'

The *Brumairiens* did not like this solution, but they feared a Corsican less than a Frenchman, and a soldier less than a politician. The convinced and conscientious revolutionists—the men of 1789, the Jacobins of 1792— might be against Bonaparte; but he had behind him 'the anonymous Revolution'—the mass of the people. Most Parisians regarded the events of 1799 with indifference, but welcomed the First Consul with something like the enthusiasm of 1789 and 1792. The 95 Articles of the Constitution meant nothing to them. But, as again fifty years later, they knew a name, and that was enough. It was, according to Las Cases, Sieyès who summed up the situation: 'Gentlemen, you have got a master—a man who knows everything, wants everything, and can do everything.'

5

During the seven weeks that had passed between the *coup d'état* of Brumaire and the publication of the constitution of the Year VIII, Bonaparte was well aware that the new government was on trial, and carefully veiled the coming dictatorship. He presided over the Council of Consuls every third day. He dressed as a civilian. Though he exploited the legendary daggers of the Five Hundred, it was to discredit the Jacobins rather than to glorify himself. Talleyrand, not Bonaparte, made a fortune out of the favourable movements on the *Bourse*. Royalist and Catholic suggestions that the new regime was anti-republican were snubbed. Protests against the events of Brumaire by departmental authorities and provincial Jacobin clubs were met by sending twenty-four deputies round the country to spread, 'with the utmost mildness and moderation,' the official version of what had occurred. Many moderate politicians agreed with Miot de Melito in disliking what had been done, but in trusting the men who had done it. Even extreme Jacobins were impressed by the terms in which the regicide and terrorist Barère compared Bonaparte to Curtius and Solon. For seven weeks Bonaparte put himself in tune with the modest note of the *Brumairien* apologias; made himself all things to all men, so that he might win all to the support of the new regime; set himself to become the one uniting and indispensable figure in the state.[8]

Although during this time he was First Consul only every third day (for the three took turns in alphabetical order), it could not be doubted that he initiated most of the consular business: an *Ordre du jour* (November 11th) thanking the troops, a proclamation *Aux Français* (November 12th) announcing the constitution: *arrêtés*, improving the conditions of life of old soldiers at the Invalides, and even suggesting that they should be housed in the palace of Versailles: and messages to the committee representing the Five Hundred, proposing an amnesty for political offenders, and the celebration of two national fêtes (and two only)—July 14th, for the 'triumph of liberty,' and Vendémiaire 1 (September 22nd) for the 'foundation of the Republic.'

It was soon known that Bonaparte had not forgotten his comrades in Egypt. Not only was the army of the Orient thanked in a public proclamation, but Berthier, now Minister of War, was instructed to send off to Alexandria a frigate with a Bonapartist name (*le Lodi*) and other vessels, carrying surgeons, doctors, arms, ammunition, and a company of actors, including female dancers; whilst funds were set aside for the pay of soldiers returning home, allowances to the families of men abroad, and pensions for the widows of officers killed on service.

Nor were individuals forgotten. Those Knights of Malta who had been allowed to stay on the island as a reward for their Francophil opinions were assured of French citizenship. Friendly letters were written to Jourdan the victor of Fleurus and to Beytz the diplomatist of Campo Formio, who had both expressed dislike of the *coup d'état* of Brumaire. When Sieyès retired from his provisional Consulship he was compensated with a fine national estate. Everything was being done to make the new regime popular with all parties, and to win the co-operation of all classes in the country. As Bonaparte said in his letter to Beytz, 'I want you all to rally round the mass of the people. The simple title of French citizen is worth far more than that of *royaliste, clichien, jacobin, feuillant,* or any of those thousand and one denominations which have sprung, during the past ten years, from the spirit of faction, and which are hurling the nation into an abyss from which the time has at last come to rescue it, once and for all. This is the aim of all my efforts. It is that upon which is centred from this moment the regard of all thoughtful men, the esteem of the people, and the hope of glory.' And in his proclamation *Aux Français* he said:

'To make the Republic loved by its own citizens, respected abroad, and feared by its enemies—such are the duties we have assumed in accepting the First Consulship. Its citizens will love it if the laws and the authoritative acts of Government are always marked by the spirit of order, justice and moderation.' [9]

A good constitution does not necessarily mean a well-governed people. Everything depends upon how it is regarded, how it is interpreted, how it is applied. The old Diceian difference between a 'fixed' and a 'fluid' constitution turns less upon the possibility of changing the constitution, than upon the way it is worked. The constitutions of 1791 and 1795 had been designed and used to keep a party or class in power: and they had failed because they had not bent, but broken, under the double stress of a government and a people unused to compromise and accustomed to revolutionary change. France now had a constitution based on the political disillusionment of ten years—ten years by the calendar, but they felt more like fifty. It was tired of revolution; and it had at its head a man who belonged to no party but that of the country, and served no end but his own ambitions; who was as determined as ever the Jacobins or the Directors had been to remain in power; but who intended to do it by the collaboration of all parties in the state, and by interpreting the constitution instead of altering it.

The coinage of a country is the face it shows to the world. By refusing to put his head on any coin until the Year XI (1802-03) Bonaparte disclaimed personal dictatorship. By retaining on the reverse of his currency, from 1799 to 1809, the inscription *République Française* he asserted the continuity of his government, whether as Consul or Emperor, with the national sovereignty, exercised by popular representation, which was the first article of the revolutionary faith. There was considerable discussion in the *Institut* (whose *zième classe* represented the old Académie des Inscriptions) as to what further emblem and inscription should appear on the coinage: a republican cock, a lion, an elephant, or an eagle? Royalists who could not expect the *fleur de lys* to remain were gratified when the choice of the motto *Dieu protège la France* showed that the Consuls at least recognized the Deity.

6

What in fact did the sovereignty of the people amount to, under the constitution of the Year VIII? No exact enumeration of the French people existed at this time; but in the *Dictionnaire géographique et méthodique* published in the Year III (1794-95), by which time the Republic included the new departments of Mont Blanc, Alpes maritimes, and Mont Terrible, the population is given as 27,613,814: it would be safe to say that by 1799 it amounted to 30 millions. In 1794-95 the number of 'active citizens,' i.e. those entitled to vote in municipal or national elections was 4,328,011. This figure, which had been much the same under the constitution of 1791, has generally been taken to represent about two-thirds of the adult population. But in the paper constitution of 1793, and now in that of 1799, 'universal suffrage' took the place of this limited vote, and it must be supposed that the number of 'Frenchmen of the age of 21 with a year's domicile' who were inscribed on the civic register of their *arrondissement communal* was more like 6 million.

Very well. But how did they exercise their vote? Suppose a *commune* of 1000 voters. They could elect 100 of their number on to a *liste communale*, and from these the local J.P.s (*juges de la paix*) and other officials were chosen. There the direct power of the vote ended. The 100 in their turn selected ten of themselves to form a *liste départmentale*—from which departmental officers were taken. Finally these ten selected one to a *liste nationale* of persons 'fit for public national functions.' Once made up, these lists could only be altered, by filling up vacancies, every three years. The total numbers so elected would be: on the *liste communale*, about 600,000, on the *liste départmentale*, 60,000, on the *liste nationale*, 6000. Aulard has every right to call this electoral system *dérisoire*, and to say that under an appearance of democracy it really shut out the people from political power.[10]

Yet it does not follow that Frenchmen resented this, as a modern electorate would. An electoral consciousness is of slow growth, and effective control of the government by the people cannot be gained without a long apprenticeship in gradually effective Opposition. The disrepute into which elections had fallen during the Revolution gave the *Brumairiens* some excuse for their summary treatment of the right of franchise. Indeed few people still thought in terms of 'rights': there was no Declaration of Rights at the head of the new Constitution. It was thought more important that there should be elected assemblies than that they should be elected in any special way: and indirect election had long come to be accepted as the normal method.

The deputies to the two legislative assemblies—the *Tribunat* and the *Corps législatif*—were chosen from the 'national list' (composed as above) by the *Sénat Conservateur*. This was a body of sixty distinguished men (increasing in ten years to eighty) at least forty years old, the majority selected by the Consuls, the rest co-opted from nominees of the leglislature or of the First Consul, and holding office for life. The Senate had other important elections to make—the Consuls, the judges in courts of appeal, and the heads of the finance department (*commissaires à la comptabilité*): it had also the power to annul unconstitutional acts of government reported to it by the Legislature. For it was, in Sieyès mind, to be like the American Senate and Supreme Court in one—the ballast of the ship of state: but Bonaparte soon made it a means of circumventing the legislature, and an instrument of his personal power. It became (to use another metaphor) the lock on the door of the constitution, and he held the key. In course of time, to keep it well-oiled, he not only provided individual Senators with valuable estates (*Sénatoreries*), but also endowed the Senate as a whole with property in Tuscany bringing in £5000 a year.

The twenty-nine 'foundation members' of the Senate, indeed, were mainly nominees of Sieyès and Ducos, the outgoing Consuls, and opposed to Bonaparte: ex-deputies of the Revolutionary assemblies, or of the Ancients and the Five Hundred. That was, no doubt, why they were particularly exhorted to lay aside the spirit of faction. But Bonaparte had his list too: his supporters during Brumaire, his learned companions in Egypt, a group of generals, and so forth (it was now shown why he had not returned from Egypt alone); and it was not long before the party of Sieyès lost ground, especially after its leader's retirement to the national estate with which Bonaparte bought off his opposition. The Senate received its *coup de grace* (in the way that Bonaparte won his greatest political victories) at the battle of Marengo. It soon became (at least in theory) what a 'reformed' House of Lords might be in the British constitution: a constitutional Court of Appeal composed of elderly and distinguished representatives of all branches of public life; standing for continuity, vested interests and the *status quo*. But it soon lost all initiative, and became (elections apart) a Commissioner of Oaths for witnessing whatever signature was put before it. If it obstructed the Life Consulate in 1802, it took the lead in promoting the Empire in 1804, and in destroying it in 1814. It was a weather-cock pointing to the wind of power.

Legislation, by the constitution of the Year VIII, was entrusted to two Houses: a *Tribunat* of 100 members, aged at least twenty-five; and a *Corps législatif* of 300, aged at least thirty. Of the latter one at least had to come from each Department; but all 400 were chosen by the Senate, after a long and complicated procedure, from the *liste nationale*. That the age qualification should have been put so low (the average age of deputies during the Revolution was a little over forty) indicates both the early maturity common in the eighteenth century, and the legislators' wish to muzzle would-be politicians at the 'dangerous age' by putting them into parliament. The younger and abler members of the *Tribunat*—largely writers and orators—could indeed discuss proposals for legislation sent to them by the *Conseil d'état* (they could not initiate any) and propose (without amendment) their acceptance or rejection: but the *Corps législatif* during its four months' sessions could only listen to speeches by representatives of the *Conseil* or *Tribunat* introducing these measures, and record in secret, without discussion, the final decision of the legislature. It may be a good plan to separate speechmaking from voting (it is the legislative practice at Cambridge); but little interest could be taken in the proceedings of the *Corps législatif* either by the deputies or by the limited public admitted to their sessions, when the speakers were not allowed to vote or the voters to speak, and none of them directly represented the people.

It was impossible for the Senate, with the *liste nationale* before it, to avoid nominating to the legislature the only experienced politicians in the country—those who had been members of the revolutionary assemblies, or of the Councils of the Directory. There were in fact 57 of the former and 330 of the latter included in the three bodies—387 out of 460: consequently Bonaparte had to expect opposition in the legislature. But the position and prestige of the *Tribunat* and *Corps législatif* were so weak that he had little difficulty in countering them: soon both Houses found themselves shouldered out of employment, and the government of the country was carried on through acts of the Senate (*Senatus-consultes*) or by orders given direct to the Ministers. The work of Parliament was done by the Privy Council.

The revolutionary constitutions had been careful to distinguish between *lois* and *décrets*: matters of greater importance put through the legislative machine, and matters of lesser importance or greater urgency that could be dealt with by a simple vote of the assembly. There was no such provision in the constitution of Brumaire. Bonaparte could therefore make use of the *Conseil d'état* to 'legislate by Order in Council,' if he feared opposition in the legislature, or had some urgent plan to put through in a hurry: and to a man of his temperament almost anything might seem a matter of urgency.

He would have preferred to dispense altogether with a legislative assembly. 'France,' he told Gourgaud at St. Helena, 'needs no constitution; it is essentially a monarchical country. To have an assembly is a sure way to start a revolution; it immediately splits into two parties, with the resulting feuds and passions.'

The *Conseil d'état* was a revival, under the one of its names that might least offend republican ears, of the *Conseil du Roi* of the French monarchy. That, not unlike Britain's Privy Council, consisted of a general body, which tended to become honorary and inactive, and a number of sectional committees, amongst which the business of government was split up: e.g. the Judicial Committee of the Privy Council, the only one which still survives. Sieyès seems at first to have contemplated two *conseils*, one attached to each of his two Consuls, with executive as well as legislative powers. Bonaparte fastened on the idea of a single *conseil* attached to the First Consul, so long as its functions were purely consultative, and the ultimate decisions were left to himself. It would enable him to choose a body of experts whom he could consult on the various matters of state; who could dispatch public business quickly and efficiently; and through whom he could keep a firm hold on the legislature, the judiciary, and the administration. And it was so.

The Council generally found it best to agree with the First Consul: but there were occasions when they voted him down. One of them, Thibaudeau, a sound Jacobin, and of independent mind, so much admired Bonaparte's interventions in debate that he made notes of his speeches. Another, Chaptal, wrote: 'We met in the First Consul's rooms almost every evening, and deliberated from 10 till 4 or 5 a.m. It was in these conferences that I came to know the great man to whom we had just entrusted the reins of government. Though still young, and with little experience of administrative detail, he brought to our discussions an astonishing clarity, exactness, power of argument, and width of view. An untiring worker, and full of resource, he collected and co-ordinated facts and opinions relating to every part of a huge system of administration with unrivalled sagacity . . . Though he worked as much as twenty hours out of the twenty-four, he never showed signs of mental or physical fatigue.'

The constitution of the Year VIII was more than usually sketchy on the subject of the *Conseil*. It only said (Article 52) that 'Under the direction of the Consuls a State Council is empowered to draft proposals of laws and of rules for public administration, and to deal with difficulties arising out of administrative matters'; and (Article 75) to authorize judicial proceedings against 'Government agents, excepting Ministers, on matters concerning their duties.' But a Consular *arrêté* of December 25th added (Article 11), 'The State Council interprets (*développe*) the meaning of the laws when questions which come before the Consuls are referred to it.' It would not be long before these meagre but vague instructions were stretched to cover the whole business of government.

Another *arrêté* of December 25th named twenty-nine members of the *Conseil*, and divided them into five sections, dealing with War, the Navy, Finance, Legislation, and Internal Affairs. They were men of varied political views, extreme Jacobins and Royalists alone being excluded (only one was a regicide). They had been chosen with less regard to party services or public repute than to their competence and keenness for the work Bonaparte intended them to do—the reconstruction of the state. They must all be men of experience, and men of ideas. Ten of the twenty-nine were lawyers as well as politicians; thirteen had held important posts in the administration; four had risen high in the army or navy— Brune was a general with liberal opinions, almost a Jacobin; nine were men of learning or technical skill. It is worth noticing, too, that seven of the original twenty-nine were still members of the *Conseil* when it came to an end fifteen years later; and that of the 112 whose names appear on the register during that time thirty served for five to nine years, and thirty-five for ten to fifteen: this secured a continuity of policy that could not have been hoped for in a body automatically changing from year to year.

Soon (by an *arrêté* of January 12th), Bonaparte was arranging the work of the Council, in its various sections. The *Conseil général des Finances* was to meet on the first day of every ten-day week (*décade*), the *Conseil d'administration de la guerre* on the fourth, that of *la marine* on the sixth, that of *justice* on the eighth; that of *relations extérieures* on the eighteenth of every month, that of *l'intérieure et police général* on the twenty-eighth. The *secrétaire d'état* kept the minutes of all these *conseils*, and summoned to their meetings, the day before, such persons as the Consuls might determine. But the Minister of Finance had the right to be present at them all, if he wished, and Ministers might bring with them the divisional heads of their departments.

The amount of work done by the *Conseil d'état* during its fifteen years was remarkable: though its archives were destroyed in the fire of 1871, one has only to look at the *Bulletin des Lois,* and at the five parts of the *Code Napoléon*, or to consider what is implied in the 58,435 separate items on the agenda of the Council between 1800 and 1813, to realize the immensity of its work. Molé was not flattering Bonaparte's regime when he described it as 'a government in whose eyes fitness and ability outweighed all other qualifications; a government which attracted to its service everything that could add to its activity and its prestige.'[11]

It might be expected that the ten Ministries (Foreign Affairs, Finance, War, Administration of War, Navy and Colonies, Public Treasury, Justice, Home Affairs, Police and State Secretariate) would be independent of the Council of State. But in fact Bonaparte was careful to subordinate them to it, and through it to himself. He appointed and dismissed Ministers at will. He had already subdivided the functions of the old Ministries by separating War from Administration of War, Finance from Public Treasury, and Home Affairs from Police. He soon went a step further, and set up 'satellite' Ministries under the direction of members of the State Council, who had, if they wished, direct access to him over the head of the original Minister. Thus to the Ministry of the Interior were attached special Departments dealing with Religion, Education, Roads and Bridges, Museums and the Post Office; and to Finance others dealing with the Public Debt, Sinking Fund, Customs, National Property (*domaines*), and *Octrois* (later *Droits Réunis*).

Some of these 'satellite' departments achieved the importance and independence of real Ministries: it depended partly upon the importance of their functions, and partly upon the personality of their Directors. Fouché, the one Minister who survived Brumaire, and Talleyrand, who was irreplaceable, stood apart. Berthier at the War Office, Gaudin at the Treasury, and Maret at the State Secretariate were men whom Bonaparte could trust to carry out his orders without adding ideas of their own. When his brother Lucien, rewarded with the Home Office for his services at Brumaire, showed signs of presuming on his relationship, he was replaced by Chaptal. The administration of the *Concordat* (Church settlement) under Portalis became so important that the *Direction générale des cultes* was within two years erected into an independent Ministry. But this multiplication of Ministries, actual or potential, did not mean, as it would under Parliamentary government, a multiplication of responsibilities, but merely a delegation of Bonaparte's supreme power. To make certain of this, and to prevent the caballing of Ministers, Bonaparte never convened them as a Cabinet, but conferred with them separately about the affairs of their departments.

7

The successful functioning of a central government depends upon the efficiency of local administration. Bonaparte was well aware of this. He remembered, as all Frenchmen of his generation did, the system of military *gouvernements*, administrative *généralités*, and feudal *bailliages* upon which the Bourbon regime had been erected. He was proud, as all republican-minded Frenchmen were, of the new departmental system by which the Revolution had broken up the old provincialism, to create a French nation, and French citizenship. But he also knew that each successive constitution since 1789 had tried to subdivide the *départements* in such a way as to favour the electoral chances of the party in power.

Under the old system nothing intervened between the royal power, represented by the *Intendants* of thirty-six *généralités*, and the *maires* of 40,000 *communes* or *municipalités*. The Constitution of 1791 had filled the gap by combining the 40,000 *communes* into approximately 4000 *cantons*, and the 4000 *cantons* into 550 *districts*. These intermediate units could be trusted to produce electors and administrators representing the interests of the middle class, and to exclude the mass of the town and country 'workers.' The paper constitution of Condorcet, which was to have secured the dominance of the Girondin party, carried this notion further by regrouping the *communes* into *grandes communes*, which, it was hoped, would disorganize their voting power. The Jacobin reply to this, in the Constitution of 1793, was to return to the 40,000 *communes*, and to make them the primary electoral constituencies. Finally the Girondinesque Constitution of the Year III had restored Condorcet's plan in the form of 400 *arrondissements* and 5000 *cantons*.

Bonaparte was a good Jacobin. He believed in centralized control. But he saw more clearly than had been possible for the men of 1793 that this could best be secured by returning to the pattern of pre-revolutionary France. In December 1799, he dictated to Lucien a Note in which he declared his intention to base the local government of the new regime on the *communes*. 'If one is to regenerate a nation,' he said, 'it is much simpler to deal with its inhabitants a thousand at a time than to pursue the romantic ideal of individual welfare. Each local body in France represents a thousand inhabitants. If you work for the prosperity of 36,000 communities you will be working for that of 36 million inhabitants. Before the Revolution every village belonged to its landlord and to its priest. But since 1790 each municipality has become a real person, under the protection of common law, with the right of possessing, acquiring, and buying property, and of performing, for the benefit of the municipal family, every act contemplated in our codes. In that lay the germ of French prosperity.' Unhappily, during the Revolution, 'these 36,000 local bodies have been, like 36,000 orphan girls, neglected or defrauded by the municipal trustees of the Convention or of the Directory . . . and this looting is still going on under the slack municipal system of the Year III.' It is necessary, therefore, he concludes, to reorganize the finances of the municipalities, to restore them to solvency, and to make them healthy members of a healthy state.[12]

Two months later the Local Government Act of the 28th *pluviôse* (February 17th, 1800) carried out this idea. The 5000 *cantons* of the Directory were suppressed, and nothing intervened between the 400 *arrondissements* and the 40,000 *communes*. The former were too few and the latter too many to embarrass a centralized government. There would be no possibility of independence. At the head of each *département* (there were now 98 of them, and there would soon be 102) was a *préfet* (a name recalling the provincial governors of the Roman Empire) appointed by the First Consul, and personally responsible to him. True, the *préfet* had a *conseil*; but its members, too, were nominated by Bonaparte. Over each of the 400 *arrondissements* was set a *souspréfet* also nominated by the First Consul; and, as an extra precaution, the capital town of his *arrondissement* was transferred to the jurisdiction of the *préfet*. Each of the 40,000 *communes* had its *maire*; but he was appointed, where the population exceeded 5000, by the First Consul, or, where it was less, by the *préfet*; and it was the *préfet* too who nominated the municipal *conseil*.

The mayor and his council had plenty to do: that was essential to Bonaparte's plan: the more parochial their interests, the less danger of political action. They had to keep order, to assess (but not to levy) taxation, to register births and deaths, to collect *octrois*, and to keep the municipal accounts. But always they were under the eye of the prefect and sub-prefect, always they were liable to a reprimand from the Tuileries. For though it is arguable that 102 prefects were individually less powerful than thirty-five Intendants, and had less prestige than the sixty archbishops and bishops amongst whose dioceses their departments were distributed, it cannot be doubted that the central control of Bonaparte exercised through this bureaucracy was far more searching and efficient than that of Louis XIV and his successors. If a letter was written, it was answered. If a law was passed, it was carried out. If a fault was committed, it was noticed and punished. The inhabitants of Clohars-Carnoet or Castelnau de Magnoac felt for the first time that their affairs were known in Paris, and their interests borne in mind by the government. It did not irk them that they had no say in the choice of their rulers: they had few pleasant memories of the departmental and district directors they had so elaborately elected during the last ten years. They liked best a monarchial government, provided it was strong and just.

That, on the whole, the new system provided. The Prefects were ex-members of the Revolutionary assemblies, lawyers, magistrates, men of affairs; some had served in the army or in the church; a few were ex-aristocrats and *émigrés*. Their average age was that of deputies in the Convention, forty or a few years older. They were chosen for their proved experience, their capacity for hard work, and their loyalty to the new government. If the taxes were now more efficiently collected, and if it was more difficult to evade conscription, there could be put against this better roads and bridges, safer travel, and prompter punishment of crime.

France had waited long for a good system of local government: it has never found occasion since to alter the essentials of that which it was given under the constitution of 1799. The departments, the prefects, the mayors remain as they were set up by Bonaparte a century and a half ago.[13]

8

No government, central or local, could do without cash. Bonaparte, brought up in a provincial and almost primitive society, accustomed to think of a few thousand francs as a fortune and an acre or two as an estate, knew next to nothing of high finance. But he had experienced poverty and could understand bankruptcy—bankruptcy such as that of the state of which he took charge at Brumaire, when there was less than £8000 in the Treasury to pay the army, the officials, and the interest on the national debt. Credit—though the funds showed a rapid rise— would take too long to establish. It was not the moment for another war of loot. More prosaic steps must be taken to pay the way of the government. These, under the advice of Gaudin and Mollien, took two forms.

The traditional skill of the French peasant in evading the payment of taxes had defeated the *collecteurs* of every regime from the Bourbons to the Directory; nor was this much to be wondered at, when there was no just and agreed basis of assessment. Bonaparte at once took the business in hand, and soon had two sets of officials at work, one for assessing and the other for collecting the taxes, in every *département, arrondissement* and *commune* of the country: all of them subject to the control of *inspecteurs généraux du trésor*, a *receveur général* and a *cour de comptes*.

The development of banking, haunted for nearly a century by the spectre of 'Law's system,' and discouraged by the French peasant's preference for hiding his money under his own roof, had produced, by the end of the Revolution, a small number of private banks with limited capital, specialized functions, and little security: a *caisse des comptes courants*, a *caisse d'escompte du commerce*, a *comptoir commercial*, a *banque territoriale*, and so forth. These suited their own clients, who distrusted government control over their borrowing and investments. But in 1799 these banks proposed to charge the government 16 per cent interest on loans: it was impossible to conduct the affairs of the Treasury without something like a national bank, supervised by the government. The group of bankers concerned in the *caisse des comptes courants* was accordingly persuaded or coerced into taking over the assets of the

Treasury and becoming a *Banque de France*. This would act as middle-man between the collecting and spending departments of the state; by its control of the money market it would reduce the rate of interest on loans; and it would in time be given a monopoly of the issuing of notes.

With the resumption of war in 1803, and particularly with the subjection of Spain, Austria, Prussia and the states of western Germany to all kinds of contributions, this financial structure was extended and elaborated: but it remained throughout Napoleon's regime essentially a hand-to-mouth system, a complex of cash transactions, carried on without loans, because subsisting without credit: an exact antithesis of the financial system which Britain preferred, and which in the end proved its superiority—if anything in economics can be proved. [14]

9

Under Article 95 of the law of the 22nd Brumaire the new Constitution had to be 'submitted to the acceptance of the French people.' In 1793 and 1795 the national will had been ascertained by convoking the 'primary assemblies,' i.e. those qualified to vote in the parliamentary constituencies. But the Constitution of 1793 had been solemnly proclaimed before the votes were counted, and that of the Year III had been seriously modified by decrees which received only one-sixth of the votes given for the Constitution itself: even that had received 750,000 less votes than the Constitution of 1793.

This time there was to be no mistake about the unanimity of the nation. No primary assemblies would be convoked. No opportunity would be given for making speeches, or organizing opposition. In every commune lists would be made of individuals voting by name either for (*oui*) or against (*non*) the constitution; and everywhere except in Paris the lists would be open for a month. Meanwhile public opinion would be influenced by the fact that the constitution was already in operation, that the *rentes* had risen in the week following the 18th Brumaire from 11.38 to 20 *francs*, that peace was being restored in the hitherto endless revolt of the Vendée, and that a partial amnesty had been granted to the *émigrés*.

These demonstrations of good government, added to so much other evidence of Bonaparte's efficient and conciliatory policy, were not unnaturally reflected in the result of the *plébiscite*, which was officially given (February 7th, 1800) as FOR, 3,011,007 and AGAINST, 1562. It is likely enough that the figures were 'cooked'; and the subsequent history of *plébiscites* shows how easily they can be used to produce an effect of unanimity; so that they have latterly become the favourite propaganda of dictators. But there can be little doubt that Bonaparte had behind him, at this moment, the substantial will of the French people.

During the six months that he spent in Paris, until the coming of the spring made it possible to open a new campaign, Bonaparte worked harder than ever he had worked before. At first he and Joséphine lived in ground floor rooms in the Petit Luxembourg; but soon he bought a country house, Malmaison, and spent his week-ends away from the noise of the capital. On February 19th he took up his official residence at the Tuileries, driving there in state with the other Consuls, and afterwards reviewing the troops in the courtyard from which Louis XVI had been attacked by the people of Paris in August 1792. It was a gesture that could not be misunderstood.

It is said that whilst one fellow-Consul, Lebrun, chose apartments in the south wing called the Pavillon de Flore, the other, Cambacérès, preferred to lodge outside: Bonaparte, he remarked, would soon need the whole palace for himself. At present he was content with a bedroom, bathroom, study, dining-room, an audience chamber and a large ante-room; and with a staff of ten senior attendants (*intendant, chef*, librarian, coachman, *valets-de-chambre*, and his Mameluk, Rustan) and fifteen subordinates—all under the direction of his secretary, Bourrienne.

Here he attended the almost daily meetings of the *Conseil*, or of its committees. Here he entertained, on the second and seventeenth days of each month, the Diplomatic Corps—on the second of each *décade* Senators and Generals; on the fourth members of the *Corps législatif*; on the sixth, those of the *Tribunat* and the Court of Appeal. The three Consuls met for consultation every day. At 10 p.m. Bonaparte expected to receive reports on their day's work and correspondence from the Ministers of War, Home Affairs, and Police. Long hours were spent in personal interviews, or in dictating letters to his secretary. There might one day be a dinner for eighty, including seven ladies; another day, *déjeuner* for twenty: if Bonaparte were in a bad humour he would be finished in eighteen minutes, eating mushrooms, and a lot of pastry, and drinking a little wine. On other days there might be a ball at Lucien's; a presentation of flags at the Invalides; a review of the *Garde consulaire*; a diplomatic dinner; a meeting of the *Institut*; or a visit to the Opera. There was, at all these functions, little of the formality of the pre-revolutionary Court, and less of its manners. Bonaparte himself, so long as he was Consul, cared little how he dressed: he and his generals were more accustomed to camp life than to the niceties of the drawing-room. His ministers and their ladies had lived through ten years of revolution and six of war. Few, save Talleyrand, remembered or regretted the *douceur de vivre* of the old regime.[15]

France, it is commonly said, was ready enough to surrender the *liberté* which was its second desire in 1789 for the *égalité* which was its first; and Bonaparte knew it. But in fact circumstances proved too strong for any government policy. 'Since Brumaire,' wrote a royalist correspondent in October 1803, 'everything has changed. The luxury of the rich finds more and more openings. The *émigré* families which have recovered part of their property will no more admit than they did in the old days that an actor is their social equal. The families that have come to the top since the Revolution are doing their best to destroy the equality to which they owe their rise. Those who once had a title want to get it back, and those who had not, wish to secure one. The contractors and bankers of the Revolution are almost as purse-proud as the tax-farmers of the age of Law.'

The new manners corresponded to the new alignment of classes. 'All these upstarts (says the same writer), these heirs of a criminal revolution, don't yet know how to comport themselves. They have no idea when to be polite, or familiar, or reserved, or respectful, or affable. Their manners are always out of scale, either boorish or overbearing; and their unsureness of themselves upsets all one's relations with them.' This has always been the complaint of the *nouveaux pauvres* against the *nouveaux riches*. Now, in 1803, it marked the beginning of a new order of society, the result of an economic and social revolution which was substituting plutocracy for aristocracy, a multitude of underpaid officials for a few provincial dictators, and a nation of small proprietors and *rentiers*, still Catholic and conservative at heart, for an ordered hierarchy of social classes. It was this new France which raised Bonaparte to power—and destroyed him.[16]

VII

AMIENS

(1800-1802)

Two THOUGHTS were in the minds of the *Brumairiens* when they over-threw the Directory, and in the minds of the French people when they accepted the constitution of the Year VIII—union and peace. It was be-cause Bonaparte shared this desire, and showed the will to accomplish it, that he was acclaimed as the head of the State. He was a realist. His whole temperament and training—all he had learnt in Corsican ven-dettas, Parisian revolutions, the civil and ecclesiastical feuds of Italy, the clash of Eastern and Western ideas in Egypt, with his soldier's habit of identifying order with discipline, and backing every request with an appeal to force—made it clear to him from the first that peace could only be won by the sword. His motto was on the new coinage—*Union et Force.*

First, pacification on the Home Front. During the whole period of the revolutionary war the western departments of France, and sometimes the southern too, had been in a state of rebellion against the government of Paris, backed by royalist refugees, and blessed by bishops who had refused to accept the church settlement of 1790. On December 28th, after fruitless negotiations with the royalist d'Andigné, Bonaparte issued a proclamation to the inhabitants of the Departments of the West calling their attention to the achievements of the new government, especially its abolition of the Forced Loan and the Law of Hostages, and its clem-ency to the *émigrés*; guaranteeing liberty of worship, and promising pardon to those who submitted. But in the same breath punishment was threatened to all who, 'after the Declaration, still resisted the national sovereignty.'

Little time was given for repentance. The very next day General Hédouville received instructions to use the 'army of England' against the western rebels, with the advice: 'If it comes to fighting, be active and severe: it is the only way to shorten a war, and to make it less deplorable for mankind.' A fortnight later operations began under Brune, heralded by a threat to execute villagers carrying arms, or preaching rebellion. Fighting, marked at times with the ferocity customary in civil war in the west, went on for three months, till, on April 18th, Brune was freed to succeed Berthier on the Italian front, and his successor, Bernadotte, was advised (May 1st) that he had now no serious opposition to deal with, but must conciliate the priests, and exercise moderation.

The brigandage which was rife, particularly in the south, was dealt with by reorganizing the *gendarmerie* in brigades of 100 men (5200 in all) attached to departmental *maisons de détention*, with orders to escort *diligences*, clear the roads and woodlands, and lay ambushes for the brigands.[1]

2

The more difficult affair of the peace abroad was approached in the same realistic spirit. The campaign was opened on the very day that Bonaparte became First Consul by personal letters to the King of Great Britain and Ireland, and to the Emperor, announcing his accession to power, and asking, in rather rhetorical terms, why an end should not be put to the fighting which had been going on for six years. 'Why should the two most enlightened nations in Europe (he wrote to George III), both more powerful than safety or independence demand, go on sacrificing their trade, their prosperity and their domestic happiness to false ideas of greatness?' Such ideas, he told the Emperor, were utterly alien to his own mind: his one wish was to prevent further bloodshed.

But on the same day he issued a proclamation 'To the soldiers of France' in which he said: 'It is no longer a question of defending your frontiers, but of invading enemy states.' Within the next few weeks plans were afoot for naval expeditions to the west coast of Africa, to Malta and Egypt, to the whaling grounds of the Arctic, and to the West Indies, with the intention of destroying British shipping and distracting British attention from the real seat of war. At one moment Bonaparte seems to have thought of reviving the plans for the invasion of Ireland: Talleyrand at least was instructed to get into touch with any Irish agents there might be in Paris.

On March 1st Lucien Bonaparte is told to commission Lebrun and Rouget de l'Isle to write a *Hymne aux Combats* to the tune of the *Marseillaise* or *Chant du départ*, suitable to all the circumstances of war, and with the moral, *La paix vient après la victoire*. The Prefects (March 8th) are instructed to recommend their people to trust the government, and to exhort the youth of the countryside to join in a patriotic crusade. France only desires peace, said the Proclamation of March 8th: it is the *horrible politique* of England that aims at dismembering and ruining France: and this can only be met by 'money, steel, and soldiers.'[2]

But though England was the ultimate enemy, Austria was still the traditional and only tangible foe on the continent—Austria which, in spite of Talleyrand's appeals to Thugut, refused to desert the second Coalition and to make peace on the basis of the terms of Campo Formio. Austria, therefore, would be attacked on the traditional front, stretching from the middle Rhine through the Swiss and Maritime Alps to the Gulf of Genoa: but with one important innovation. At Dijon, behind the centre of this line, would be massed an 'army of reserve' of 40,000-60,000 men, equally ready for defence or offence, and in a position from which it could reinforce either the army of the Rhine or the army of Italy. So public opinion was instructed.

But in fact it was not at all an army of reserve, but an army of invasion. It was to wait at Dijon just so long as it might take Moreau to drive back the Austrian right, and establish himself beyond the Rhine. It would then cross the Alps into Italy, and annihilate the Austrian left. The moment and means of this move must depend on several factors: the speed of Moreau's advance, the melting of the Alpine snows, the choice of the best pass, the possibility of feeding an army accustomed to live on the land, and the positions occupied by Mélas and Masséna in Italy. It was Bonaparte's plan, and only Bonaparte could settle these crucial questions. Meanwhile, since, under the new Constitution, no Consul could command in the field, he put at the head of the army of reserve Berthier, the Minister of War, a man long accustomed, as Chief of Staff, to carry out his orders; with the assurance that he would soon follow him to the front.

In fact Bonaparte's doubts were settled, in the third week of April, by the bad news that came from Italy. The force optimistically called the army of Italy—remnants of the troops defeated during the previous summer, regrouped under Masséna's command, and numbering some 39,000 men—was concentrated in the Genoese Riviera; but it could make no headway against Austrian forces under Mélas more than twice as strong, and was now (April 24th) blockaded in Genoa, with no more than a month's provisions in hand.

Bonaparte lost no time in ordering the necessary movements. Berthier was to march at once to Geneva, without waiting for Moreau to cross the Rhine, and to penetrate into Italy at full speed by the Great St. Bernard. This was now preferable to the St. Gothard (which he had originally chosen), as leading more directly to a point (Aosta) from which the army could turn either towards Genoa or Milan; and the distance to be covered without provisions was only four days' march, with the hospitable monks of St. Bernard as a half-way house; at Aosta they would be in a rich country well suited to the needs of a hungry army. Lacourbe, with a force of 25,000 men detached from Moreau's right, was to cross by the St. Gothard. On the Rhine front Moreau was to speed up his advance—he was in fact already on the move. At the moment Bonaparte left for the front on May 5th he had news of the first victory on the Rhine. *Gloire et trois fois gloire!* he wrote to the victor; and took it for a good omen.[3]

Bonaparte is always worth following on his journeys. He is then most natural, most romantic, most boyish. Although he could not technically command the army of reserve, he was determined to be with it, and to see that Berthier won the victory that would satisfy the prayers of the French people and establish his own regime. He left Paris on the afternoon of May 6th, and arrived at Geneva at 3 a.m. on the 9th. The first night out, at Avallon, he heard from an envoy of Masséna that the troops at Genoa were already suffering privations: they would hold out for another month. At Dijon next day he held a review. At Auxonne, his old garrison station, he visited places he had not seen since he was a young lieutenant, met his former music master, and promised a pension to a veteran of Valmy. At Dôle he inspected a canon-foundry, and conversed with one of his teachers at Brienne. At Morez, the same night, he showed himself to an enthusiastic crowd. 'Are you going to give us peace?' they cried: 'Yes, I am,' he replied with a smile (though looking pale and tired) which they never forgot. At Geneva, where he stayed three nights with de Saussure (and heard, no doubt, the story of his ascent of Mont Blanc), he studied maps of the St. Bernard, arranged the time-table of the march, and made the necessary appointments—Lannes to lead the advance guard, Murat to command the cavalry. He had an interview with Necker, who lived at Coppet near by; Necker said afterwards 'All his tastes are those of a hero': but Bonaparte thought him 'a regular don (*régent de collège*), with a heavy and pompous manner.'

From Geneva he drove to Lausanne, where he spent four nights, and held more reviews: he heard again from Masséna, and sent back a message to say 'Very soon Italy will be conquered and Genoa relieved.' His own delays, at which he doubtless chafed, were due to the inevitable difficulties of the army. Hearing that Lannes had reached the summit of the St. Bernard on May 16th he pushed on to Martigny, where the real climb began—fifty miles to Aosta, and ten of them a mountain track. Here he put up for three nights at the Bernadine monastery, but excused himself from hearing mass. He wrote to Joséphine that the weather was cloudy, and refused leave to a number of wives who wanted to accompany their husbands on the march: '*La citoyenne Bonaparte* has stayed in Paris: you can do the same.'

He was worrying about the news: the advance beyond Aosta was held up by the fort at Bard. So next morning he set off on horseback as far as St. Pierre, and then mounted a mule, led by the young guide named Dorsaz whose narrative has added some lively details to a half legendary journey. We are told what he had for dinner with the prior of St. Bernard, how he turned over a copy of Livy in the monastic library, looking for the account of Hannibal's crossing of the Alps, and how, exasperated at the zigzag descent, he sat down and slid *sur le derrière*, and took to a horse again at the bottom of the pass. He reached Aosta on the 21st.

Bonaparte's own language romanticizes the whole affair. 'We are struggling (he writes to the Consuls, from his monastery at Martigny), against ice, snow, whirlwinds, and avalanches. The St. Bernard, astonished to see such a multitude struggling across it, is putting obstacles in our path.' There are some highly coloured passages, too, in Berthier's *Report* of May 28th, which are probably by the same hand. 'The First Consul,' says the *Bulletin* of May 24th, 'came down from the summit of the St. Bernard balancing himself on snow, crossing precipices, and sliding over frozen torrents.'[4]

3

The Marengo campaign has been so overlaid with legends that the historian is almost afraid to credit Bonaparte with his most fortunate victory. It is not true (as Bourrienne says) that he put a pin in the map, three months beforehand, to mark the place where he would defeat the Austrians. It is not true that he led his troops on a prancing steed (as David painted him), over the St. Bernard: his mule was several days behind the advance-guard of Berthier's army. It is not true that he slept by the road-side at Albaredo, whilst the troops stole silently by for fear of waking their general. Desaix's dying words on the battle-field are a fiction.

What historians would like to know, and what they have never satisfactorily decided, is the real intention of Bonaparte's plans and movements during the three weeks preceding the battle of Marengo. The sole motive for urgency since April 24th, indeed since April 11th, had been the desperate position of Masséna at Genoa. Bonaparte had played with the idea that he might break out towards Acqui or Parma; but he must have known that his starving troops were in no state to do so. He heard from him on April 30th that he was surrounded (*absolument cerné*), and sent back a message on May 5th that he was expected, whatever happened, to make his provisions last till June 4th. He wrote to Desaix on May 14th, 'I am going down into Italy with 30,000 men to relieve (*dégager*) Masséa, and drive out Mélas': when he gets to Ivera there may be news obliging him to march straight on Genoa: when Masséna is relieved (*débloqué*), St. Hilaire at Marseille must have troops close at hand to join in the pursuit of Mélas. Five days later, at Martigny,

he is still uncertain whether, from Ivera, he will march on Genoa or
Milan.

But once at Ivrea (May 26th) nothing more is heard of the relief of
Genoa. Unless the Austrians, hearing of his arrival in Italy, decide to
raise the siege, Masséna may starve, and surrender. He is no longer a
hero to be rescued at the cost of compromising Bonaparte's whole design:
he has become the bait of the trap into which Mélas is to be enticed. The
longer Masséna holds the Austrians in the western Alps, the more certainly can Bonaparte block their retreat to the east. So for three weeks,
with his base at Milan, he builds up his army on both banks of the Po
between Pavia and Piacenza, whilst Masséna's garrison is starved into
surrender. He ought to have allowed the civilians to starve (Napoleon
said at St. Helena), rather than the soldiers to surrender: Masséna was
too humane for 'total warfare.' If, by an irony of fortune, surrender
came on the very day that Mélas had ordered Ott to raise the siege (as
he learnt from intercepted dispatches), and another twelve hours' delay
would have prevented it, Bonaparte had not made a single move westwards that might hurry the Austrian retreat; though he pretended, in
his letters to the Consuls in Paris, that his junction with Masséna's forces
would soon come about (June 5th, the very day of the surrender), and
that his army was within three days forced march of Genoa when Mélas
called off the besiegers.

Meanwhile Mélas's failure to retreat was playing into Bonaparte's hands.
On May 16th Suchet reported that he had launched an attack on the Col
di Tenda and Borghetto—an attack that Bonaparte attributed to news of
Berthier's move to Geneva, and urged as an additional reason for speeding up his march. This would, Bonaparte thought, put off any fear of an
Austrian appearance in the Milanese till May 26th-27th. On May 19th
Mélas was reported at Nice, still unsuspicious (*ne se doutant de rien*); but
on the 25th he moved hurriedly to Turin; Bonaparte estimated his total
force at 54,000 or 62,000. 'In ten days it will all be over,' he writes on the
27th. But Mélas is still at Turin on May 30th: and Ott still before Genoa
on June 2nd.

By June 7th the French army had massed 'astride the Po' at Stradella
and St. Giovanni, ready to transfer its forces to whichever bank Mélas
chose for his retreat: he could not now avoid a pitched battle: he was
'absolutely cut off.' On June 9th the Austrian right, under Ott, was defeated by Lannes at Montebello. Probably Bonaparte, hearing at this
moment of the fall of Genoa, thought Mélas would try to break away
in that direction; anyhow he believed that he could not cross the Bormida, which meandered northwards between the two main armies immediately west of Alexandria, so he detached Desaix across the Po to
bar the route southwards.

But at dawn on the 14th Mélas suddenly threw 30,000 men and 100 guns across the Bormida, and found Bonaparte, with his forces scattered, unable to oppose to them more than 22,000 men and 14 guns. At this point the official correspondence suddenly fails; and there can be little doubt that Bonaparte suppressed documents which might have betrayed the confusion into which his plans were thrown, and his nearness to defeat. After a *Bulletin* of June 10th and a letter to Petiet, a *conseiller d'état* at Milan, describing the victory of Montebello, there is only a solitary message to Lannes on the 13th, telling him to attack and defeat 'whatever enemy he has in front of him.' The next document preserved is another letter to Petiet on the 15th, saying, 'I expect you have heard from Headquarters the result of the affair of Montebello and the battle of Marengo, which has decided the fate of Italy and of M. Mélas's army.'

To fill the gap, we have only the *Bulletin* of June 15th, giving an 'official' account of the battle whose untruthfulness has been exposed by many historians. It admits that the initial attack across the Bormida was a surprise (*L'essential est qu'on ne se laisse pas surprendre*, Bonaparte had written to Berthier a week earlier). It says that during the morning the French, outnumbered two to one, four times retreated and four times regained the ground lost; that the Guard stood like a granite redoubt against repeated cavalry charges and heavy artillery fire, and held up the enemy left, till the French right broke and retreated, and 'the battle appeared to be lost.' Yet the Austrians 'were allowed to advance' as far as St. Juliano, where 'Desaix's division was in the battle line' (as though by a prearranged plan: it had in fact been hurriedly recalled from its mistaken march towards Genoa two hours after the fighting began and did not come into action until 2 or 3 p.m.). Thereupon (not Desaix's leadership, but), 'the presence of the First Consul revived the *morale* of the troops: "Children," he said to them, "remember that it is my habit to sleep on the battle-field"'; and with cries of *Viva la République! Viva le Premier Consul!* they charged on the enemy, Desaix at their head; Kellermann delivered a cavalry blow at the right moment; the whole army joined in, and the enemy fled in panic.

The elements of fiction in this account have their climax in the description of the death of Desaix, from whom and from Kellermann Bonaparte had stolen the credit of victory, and who was in fact killed outright. 'He only had time to say to young Lebrun, who was with him, "Go and tell the First Consul that I die regretting having done too little to live to posterity."' When they came to report his death to the First Consul, in the thick of the fighting, only one sentence escaped him: 'Why cannot I weep for him?' Such theatrical self-display does not necessarily mean that Bonaparte was a hypocrite, but rather that he was still so uncertain of his position as head of the state, that he would take every opportunity, even at the expense of truth and generosity, to build up the legend of his invincibility and of his human-kindness. So do most dictators.[5]

Another sign of this anxiety was the frequency with which Bonaparte reminded his fellow-Consuls that he would soon be back in Paris. He did not trust them out of his sight. He was afraid of the people of the capital. He wrote to the Consuls on May 24th, 'I hope to be back in Paris in a fortnight'; on the 27th, 'I shall be in Paris at the end of Prairial' (June 19th); and on June 5th, 'You can announce that I shall be in Paris by June 14th-15th.'

As things turned out, June 14th was the date of the decisive battle. Now there is less hurry, and July 14th, the annual fête in honour of the Fall of the Bastille, can coincide with the triumphal return of the victor of Marengo. Lucien is to get someone to compose a cantata in the Italian style celebrating 'the liberation of the Cisalpine Republic and Liguria, and the glory of our arms,' and it is to be sung by a famous *prima donna* —Billington, or Grassini; the celebrations are to end with a display of fireworks. But Bonaparte is still cautious. 'I shall arrive in Paris,' he tells Lucien, 'unannounced. I do not wish to have any triumphal arches or any sort of ceremony. I have too good an opinion of myself to attach much importance to trifles of that kind. The only triumph I care for is public approval.'[6]

Bonaparte left Milan on June 25th and was back in Paris in less than a week, travelling by the Mt. Cenis, Lyon, Dijon and Nemours. The return of the Guard was so timed that they arrived on the very morning of the fête of the Bastille, which was celebrated at the Invalides and on the Champs de Mars with unprecedented enthusiasm. In the evening, at a banquet in the Tuileries, Bonaparte toasted 'the French people, the sovereign ruler of us all.'

4

The tactical aim of the campaign of Marengo had been to relieve Genoa and to drive the Austrians out of Lombardy. Its strategical aim had been to compel the Emperor to make peace. Satisfied that he had done all he could towards the first end, Bonaparte now addressed to the Emperor, two days after the defeat of Mélas army, a long letter (dated as from Marengo), which he hoped might secure the second. He sent no such appeal to George III; he remembered too well how coldly his letter six months earlier had been received, and how Fox had only been able to collect 64 votes out of 329 in the House of Commons in favour of peace (February 3rd, 1800). But he seems to have thought Francis still open to reason or to sentiment. The letter of June 16th contains plenty of both, expressed in the rhetorical style which Bonaparte had by now made his own. As he said naïvely but truly enough to Talleyrand, when enclosing a copy, 'It differs from the style and form usual in such communications; but I have a feeling that everything going on around us has something new about it.'

The document was partly an attempt to work on the Emperor's humane feelings: 'From the battle-field of Marengo, surrounded by suffering men, I implore Your Majesty to hear the cry of humanity, and not to allow the offspring of two brave and powerful nations to slaughter one another for the sake of interests of which they know nothing.' It was partly an argument: 'What reasons can they allege who, in Your Majesty's study [*this means Thugut*], counsel the continuance of the war? The interests of religion, and of the church? . . . The character of the French Government, which is not hereditary, but elective? . . . The interests of the German Confederation? . . . The extension of Your Majesty's territory in Italy? . . . The balance of power in Europe? . . . The destruction of revolutionary principles?' Each possible motive is refuted in turn.

The letter ends by urging the Emperor to transform the terms of Campo Formio, and of the armistice just concluded, into a permanent peace. 'I beg Your Majesty to read this letter with the feelings which prompted me to write it, and to believe that, next to the happiness and interests of the French people, nothing concerns me more than the prosperity of that nation of soldiers whose courage and military prowess I have admired for the last six years.' The insincerity of the last paragraph need not be allowed to spoil a genuine attempt to get by words of persuasion what Bonaparte may all the same have anticipated he could only secure by force of arms.

The Emperor did indeed seriously consider coming to terms, especially when, a month after Marengo, Moreau occupied Munich and imposed the armistice of Parsdorf (July 15th). He would be well out of the Italian affair if he could write off his losses on the lines of Campo Formio. True, the last promise of subsidies from England had stipulated that Austria should make no separate treaty before February 1801: but it might well be possible to prolong negotiations until that date, and so to prevent the French from attacking again during the autumn or winter. Accordingly the Comte de St. Julien was sent to Paris with an ambiguous letter and uncertain powers, and was allowed to sign preliminaries by which France gained the left bank of the Rhine. But he was at once disowned by Thugut, who insisted that England, Austria's ally, must be represented at the conference, and suggested that this should be held at Lunéville.

Bonaparte and Talleyrand had no illusions about Austrian diplomacy. The army of Marengo was told ten days after the battle that it might soon be engaged in another campaign, and preparations were pushed on for the invasion of Germany. Steps were taken to isolate Austria by making friendly overtures to Russia and Turkey, to the King of Prussia and to the King of Spain. When the Emperor refused to ratify St. Julien's signature, Bonaparte wrote to Carnot that he was merely trying to 'tide over the winter,' and instructed Moreau to reopen hostilities. A statement was put out to all 'public functionaries' describing the situation, and saying that, unless within twenty-four hours the Emperor agreed to treat separately, 'the troops of the Republic would fear neither snow nor the rigour of the seasons, but would prosecute the war during winter to the bitter end.'

The Emperor answered this threat by sending his most trusted negotiator, Cobenzl, who had carried through the second and third partitions of Poland, to meet the French plenipotentiary, Joseph Bonaparte, and allowed him to go on from Lunéville to Paris for a volcanic interview with the First Consul (October 28th); the rendezvous shifted back to Lunéville on November 5th. The talks covered three topics: the compensation, at the expense of the ecclesiastical states on the right bank of the Rhine, of the secular princes on the left bank whose lands would be transferred to France; the line of demarcation in north Italy; and the provision of territory in central Italy for the Duke of Parma, the brother-in-law of the King of Spain, in return for his cession to France of Louisiana under the treaty of San Ildefonso (October 1st).

When the negotiations had dragged on for another month Bonaparte lost patience, and on November 28th five French armies advanced to the attack on a front which now stretched from the Danube to the Arno. Bonaparate was counting on fresh victories for himself in Italy when on December 3rd Moreau utterly defeated the Austrians at Hohenlinden, west of the Inn, and pushed on his cavalry to within fifty miles of Vienna. Before the month was out the Emperor accepted the armistice of Steyer. Two months later (February 9th, 1801) Cobenzl signed the treaty of Lunéville. France received the left bank of the Rhine from Switzerland to Holland. In Italy the Emperor kept Venice and the Dalmatian coast, Istria and the islands previously Venetian, with eastern Lombardy up to the Adige. The Swiss, Dutch, Cisalpine and Ligurian Republics were recognized. Tuscany went to the Duke of Parma, and its Duke was compensated with Austrian territory at Salzburg and Berchtoldsgaden.

Thus ended negotiations which illumined and justified Bonaparte's control of foreign policy. The Ministry of Foreign Affairs was still, in spite of constant changes of personnel during the last ten years, the most old-fashioned and traditional of them all; Talleyrand and his 'permanent secretary,' d'Hauterive, were the most independent of the First Consul's advisers. Yet it was the First Consul who dictated their policy, and General Bonaparte who enforced it. His insistence upon the line of the Rhine and the Adige; his refusal to include England in the negotiations unless she first agreed to a naval armistice; his threat to break off the conversations and to resort to force of arms—a threat actually enforced on the second occasion of delay—and his tempting offers to Spain, Russia, and Prussia, in order to isolate Austria and England—all were characteristic of the 'New Diplomacy'—a diplomacy which in its territorial claims still followed the old classical pattern of Louis XIV and the Committee of Public Safety, but which gave new force to the Latin motto on the Bourbon guns—*Ratio Ultima Regum*. War had been a running commentary on the Old Diplomacy: it was the final argument of the New. Louis XIV's negotiators had waited to see which way the fighting might go: Bonaparte provided his negotiators with the necessary victory.[7]

5

England now stood out as the one opponent in Bonaparte's war to end war; and the depth of his resentment against his most stubborn enemy can be seen in the invective he allowed himself in the *Bulletin* of June 18th: 'Whatever the court of London may do, there will be no civil war in France. Belgium shall form part of the territory of our great people. Holland and Spain, with the same interests and passions at heart, will redouble their efforts against the tyrant of the seas. The Englishman, isolated in his island for six months of the year, will have to wait till the Elbe is free of ice to get news of the continent. England, by its arrogance, its venality, and its corruption, will earn, as Austria and Russia have done, the hatred and contempt of every Frenchman.'

During the year that had still to run between the treaties of Leoben and Amiens the superficial successes were still England's; but below the surface the tide was flowing towards a French peace. The capture of Malta (September 5th), was for a time offset by the refusal to hand it back to the Knights, now represented by Tsar Paul of Russia, and by his consequent revival of Catherine's League of Armed Neutrality, through which Prussia and the Scandinavian powers threatened to exclude Britain from the Baltic. But on March 23rd, 1801, Paul was assassinated, and his Anglophobe policy reversed by his successor, Alexander I. On April 2nd, Parker destroyed the Danish fleet at Copenhagen. The Armed Neutrality was disarmed in a week.

In Egypt, which Bonaparte still hoped to hold either by arms or diplomacy, the convention of El Arish between Kléber and Sir Sidney Smith (February 24th, 1800) was repudiated by both governments, and for a few weeks the French army seemed to have re-established its position, defeating another Turkish invasion at Heliopolis (March 20th), and recovering Cairo. But Kléber was assassinated (June 14th), and his successor Menou, defeated by a British expeditionary force under Abercrombie (March 21st, 1801), capitulated. This disastrous end to an enterprise so near his heart, whilst he was still celebrating the achievements of the army in Egypt, and attempting to send it officers, ammunition and actors, was a blow to Bonaparte's pride rather than to his power; for Egypt had long been a liability: and its loss removed the last obstacle to peace.

At the time of Marengo Pitt had doubted the extent of Bonaparte's victory. In his later speeches (November 11th, 27th, 1800, February 2nd, 1801), he had admitted the growing difficulties of the situation at home —'I fear it is clear (wrote Crabb Robinson on January 2nd), that the Sun of England's Glory is set'—whilst refusing the inquiry into the State of the Nation called for by the Opposition; but he had hinted at the possibility of a 'safe and honourable peace.' On March 14th Pitt resigned; but on November 3rd he spoke again in Parliament in support of Addington's peace policy, emphasizing (oddly, to our minds), the relative unimportance of the Mediterranean compared with the Indies, and speaking as though Malta and Minorca might well be sacrificed if we kept Trinidad and Ceylon. He denied that the restoration of the Bourbons had ever been made a *sine qua non* of a settlement, though he regretted that it could not be so. France had at least been rid of Jacobinism, and the world taught that revolutions ended in military dictatorships. But England had fought for security, and he hoped, even believed, that this had now been won. What France had gained in territory it had lost 'in population, in commerce, in capital, and in habits of industry'; whereas English wealth and maritime power, still unimpaired, had 'added strength to our security and lustre to our national character.' If the French shared this point of view—and he saw signs of it—'we had every prospect of enjoying a long peace.' The preliminaries, which had been signed in London on October 1st, and ratified on October 10th, became, on March 25th, 1802, the Peace of Amiens.

The news of peace was received in England with 'demonstrations of joy risen almost to madness,' wrote Crabb Robinson on October 20th; 'among the transparencies exhibited in London Bonaparte's portrait was shown with this inscription "The Saviour of the World." ' [8]

6

So half Bonaparte's programme—peace abroad—was achieved. The other half—peace at home—could not be accomplished by the signature of a document. It must be the gradual work of a regime that strove to conciliate political parties, to further commercial interests, to reorganize local administration, to educate and direct public opinion; subjecting every branch of government to central and personal control, and always backing persuasion by force. Bonaparte's system of rule did not materially change between 1800 and 1814, whether he was First Consul, Consul for Life, or Emperor; but it was growing all the time; and it will be best studied in its later stages.

One cause of national disunion, however, was so serious that it had to be dealt with at once, and yet of such a kind that it might almost be abolished by a stroke of the pen. This was the church question. Everyone was aware of it. Every party held opinions about it. Bonaparte himself, brought up amongst a Catholic peasantry, educated in schools supervised by Catholic priests, studying books which debated the reasons for and against (principally against) orthodoxy, and breathing every day the sceptical atmosphere of the *Institut* and the camp, knew well that, however much western European society may quarrel with the creed and cult of the church, it cannot escape from the influence of Christian thought and conduct embedded in its institutions and ideas.

Least of all could France—a country which (until the last ten years) had never known any but Catholic kings and bishops in obedience to Rome; a country which had passed through no Reformation, the vast majority of whose people had never known any Christianity but that of the priest and the mass, and whose whole culture and life resembled its soaring cathedrals, full of holy images, of lights and altars and coloured glass, but with worldly scenes and faces of devils looking down from groined roofs and gargoyles; and all set in the market square and amidst jostling house-fronts—least of all could France forget that it was a Catholic country. To be a Frenchman was to be baptized and shriven and buried a Catholic: the few Protestants were almost foreigners; almost as alien as Jews and Turks, as likely to be damned as heretics and infidels. The church, too, was not merely a calendar of dioceses, parishes, and congregations: it was a rich and powerful corporation, owning vast properties in houses and estates, exercising jurisdictions, registering and regulating the married life of the people, educating their children, tending their sick and poor, and even, on occasion, championing their liberties against the rival authorities of king and landlord.

The Revolution had superficially changed all this. In 1764 the Jesuit Order had been expelled from court and school. Louis XVI had given Protestants civil rights, and freedom of worship; their children were no longer illegitimate; they could vote as well as pay taxes; they could hold public office; they could meet for worship in their own 'temples.' In August 1789, the church lost that part of its revenue which came from tithes and payments for services. In November its property was nationalized and put up for sale. In February 1790, all religious Orders were dissolved. From July, by the settlement called the Civil Constitution of the Clergy, all bishops and clergy were elected by the people and paid by the state. As a consequence they were required to take an oath of fidelity to the nation, the law, and the king, and of readiness to support the Civil Constitution.

Upon this issue the bishops and clergy split up into two bodies, the 'Constitutionals' who accepted service under the state, and the 'Refractory' or 'Non-jurors,' who refused it. This soon came to mean a schism which divided diocese from diocese, and set up parties in every parish. The non-jurors, more and more identified with political opposition to the Revolution, came under a series of penal laws, and either emigrated or were interned. There were not enough Constitutionals to fill the places they left vacant. Many churches were closed, the sacraments not administered, the bells not rung, or taken down to be turned into cannon or coins.

At last, under the pressure of war at home and abroad, of Papal denunciation and political anti-clericalism, the situation was so exacerbated that in February 1795 the Convention passed the law of *ventôse*, Year III, under which the State no longer recognized or subsidized any religious body—in other words, 'disestablished' the Catholic church—and only exercised police supervision over the public and political activities of rival religious cults. This law ruled the church question until Bonaparte's Concordat of 1801.

But under the Directory the settlement of 1795 was frequently modified both in law and in practice. Already in May 1795, the Convention had offered the non-jurors the return of their churches if they took an oath of obedience to the laws of the Republic (the oath was re-worded in September); and this further sub-divided them into a 'Paris' group, who agreed to this condition, and a 'Lyon' group, who refused it. In December 1796, the penal laws of 1792-93 against the non-jurors were repealed; but after the *coup d'état* of *fructidor* (September 5th, 1797) they were reinforced, with the penalty of deportation. The Directors were, in fact, practising towards the clergy the same see-saw policy (*la bascule*) which they found so helpful in dealing with the political extremists: if the royalists won an election, or subsidized a revolt, the non-juror priests suffered; if the Jacobins did so, they were more leniently treated. The only positive policy which the government superimposed upon this negative rule-of-thumb was the encouragement it gave to the intellectualist cult of Theophilanthropy, and to the municipal observance of the *décadi* (the 'tenth day,' which the Republican Calendar had substituted for Sunday) with readings of the law, singing of the *Marseillaise*, and patriotic exhortations: and this, so far as it went, took the place of the *Culte de l'Être Suprême* that had been inaugurated by the Committee of Public Safety in 1794.

The result of all these changes was that by 1799 the Catholic religion, instead of being a steadying and unifying influence in the life of the country, had become a source of disunion, and a cause of offence. So much, no doubt, was known to Bonaparte: he would not know a tithe of what the modern historian can learn about the state of the country parishes, the sufferings of the clergy, or the progress of 'de-Christianization' in the towns, from the study of such contemporary documents as Grégoire's *Annales de la Religion*, or the *Livre de compte de l'Abbé Glaize*, and the researches of writers too often anxious to prove a case for or against the church.

But no Parisian, at least, can have been ignorant of what had been going on at Nôtre Dame, the centre of the national religion, between 1795 and 1799. The cathedral had for some five months during the Jacobin Terror shared the prohibition of public worship in such of the Paris churches as had not already been sequestrated or closed. On August 11th, 1795, six months after the Law of *ventôse*, Year III, the twenty-three keys of the cathedral were formally handed over to a part-clerical and part-lay *Société catholique*, which now made itself responsible for restoring religious worship there. They found the nave and crypt encumbered with 1500 wine-barrels which were on their way to the military hospitals, the windows without glass, the doors closed with planks, and much of the interior so plundered and dilapidated that it was difficult to find space for a congregation. Gifts of pulpits, confessionals, altar vessels and linen, and so forth, were gladly welcomed. The Society engaged priests, singers and musicians, drew up rules for the conduct of services, and put up notices warning people that they must take off their hats, or stay outside. This was the more necessary because the cathedral might still be requisitioned by the city authorities for secular functions, such as the taking of the oath of hatred to royalty in January 1797.

Protestant services were also carried on there; and in February 1798, the *Société théophilanthropique* demanded the use of the cathedral for its devotions. The Committee, rather than offend the government, surrendered the choir and the nave, the organ and the high altar, and put up a new altar for Catholic worship on the north transept. However, after May 1798, the Theophilanthropists did not reappear, and the Catholics returned to the body of the building, though still under the necessity of giving it up, every *décadi*, stripped of its ecclesiastical emblems, to the Municipality, for meetings of electors, and civil marriages.

When the signing of the Concordat was celebrated in Nôtre Dame on Easter Day, 1802, the cathedral of Paris had already been in Catholic use for four years, and the 'national altars' that Bonaparte claimed to be setting up had long ago been restored by the zeal of the *Société catholique*. Nor did Paris stand alone: similar societies were taking over, restoring, and maintaining the cathedrals and churches—perhaps to the number of 30,000—all over the country.[9]

Nevertheless three things remained to be done which could only be done by the state. The divisions between and within the different bodies of Christians—Constitutionals, Non-jurors, and Protestants, not to mention the Decadists and the Theophilanthropists, had to be settled: relations had to be re-established, if possible, between Catholic France and the Papacy: and the finances of the church had to be set on a permanent basis.

7

As for the first problem, Bonaparte would unhesitatingly set aside as impracticable the idea that Protestantism might be declared the national religion. However patriotic and amenable they had shown themselves during the revolution, the Protestants remained a small and almost foreign minority: their modern representatives in southern Ireland might as reasonably hope to become the established church of Eire.

But no less an authority than Aulard, who founded the modern study of the Revolution, always maintained that the separation of church and state, under the law of 1795, had by 1799 produced 'a rich and varied flowering of religious life,' that cults 'new and rational, old and mystical' existed side by side, 'without coming to blows or civil war,' and 'without harbouring any serious grievances against the state.' Bonaparte, he thought, destroyed this system, just when it was beginning to work well, in the interests of a Catholic monopoly, because he wanted to have under his hand the ecclesiastical as well as the political control of the nation. 'He suppressed the regime of Separation, and made the Concordat, simply because he wished to be Emperor.'

Such a view deserves respect. It gains some support from the opposition to the Concordat amongst the intellectuals of the *Institut*, the confirmed anticlericals, and the Jacobins, not least in the army, who could never forgive the clerical support given to royalism and counter-revolution. It finds some support, too, in the subsequent history of the Church of the Concordat, and in the fact that, when France finally settled down under the Third Republic, it returned to the regime of separation that Bonaparte had abolished a hundred years before. Nevertheless, it must be rememberd that, if there was not civil war in 1799, neither was there civil peace; and that the uneasy co-existence of Catholics and Protestants, Decadists and Theophilanthropists under the roof of Nôtre Dame was unlikely to extend into the 40,000 *communes* of an illiterate and intolerant peasantry, accustomed to identify religion with the Pope, the priest and the mass.

If Bonaparte wished to make peace with the Papacy, the traditional form of such an arrangement was a Concordat; the traditional occasion a French victory on Italian soil. What Francis I had done after Marignano, Bonaparte would do after Marengo. The motive was still the same as it had been in 1515, and indeed as it had been in the abortive negotiations between the Constituent Assembly and the Papacy in

1789-91: to unite Catholic France, whether monarchial, revolutionary, or republican—for Bonaparte still insisted that he was the First Magistrate of a republic—to the Head and body of the Catholic church. 'My policy,' he told the *Conseil d'état* on August 16th the same year (if we are to believe Roederer), 'is to govern men as the great majority wish to be governed. That, I believe, is the way to recognize the sovereignty of the people. It was as a Catholic that I won the war in the Vendée, as a Moslem that I established myself in Egypt, and as an Ultramontane that I won the confidence of the Italians. If I were governing Jews, I should rebuild the temple of Solomon.' So, as he was governing Frenchmen, the great majority of whom were Catholics, he would negotiate a fresh Concordat with the Papacy, and 'rebuild the altars,' even if they were not entirely destroyed, of an orderly, uniform, and solvent church.[10]

8

Bonaparte's approach to the Vatican was eased by the death in exile of Pope Pius VI on August 29th, 1799, and the election as his successor of Cardinal Chiaramonti, on March 14th, 1800, under the name of Pius VII. A professed Benedictine, the new Pope was no diplomat or politician, but remained all his life a monk in a tiara. His piety and simplicity seemed likely to make him pliable to the demands of the French government; and his Christmas homily, 'Be good Christians, and you will be good democrats,' sounded to Bonaparte like good Jacobinism. But where his conscience was engaged he could not be bullied or cajoled. He would be 'small in small matters, but great in great.'

Within a few days of his entry into Rome (July 3rd), Pius received a letter from Martiniana, the archbishop of Vercelli, reporting a conversation with Bonaparte on June 25th on his way back from Marengo to Paris. In this the victorious general had sketched the outlines of a settlement between the Papacy and the French government which he wished to be submitted to the Pope: all the French bishops to give up their sees, so that the better might be reappointed, and the worse removed; the number of dioceses to be reduced; the Pope to surrender any claim to church property sequestrated during the Revolution; and the State to make itself responsible for the payment of the clergy. The negotiations so begun lasted a whole year, and it was not till midnight on July 15th, 1801, the anniversary of the armistice of Marengo, that the text of the Concordat was finally signed. The length and complexity of the negotiations can be judged from the 1279 pieces contained in Boulay de la Meurthe's *Documents sur la négociation du Concordat.*

But no one, except perhaps Bonaparte, expected that it would be an easy matter to turn the conversation of Vercelli into a signed agreement acceptable to habits of mind and theories of church and state so far apart as those of Rome and Paris: 'A business arrangement (as a royalist writer called it), between Christians and philosophers, made in the name of a government that was neither philosophic nor Christian.' The issue was fought out over no less than ten successive drafts before the final text was agreed upon.

The main points of difference were five. First, the Pope agreed unwillingly to request the resignation of the 'refractory' bishops; for a long time he refused to recognize the status of the 'constitutional' bishops, even by asking them to resign; in the end he compromised by issuing two different Bulls, one to the 'bishops in communion with the Holy See,' and another to those who 'occupied sees without institution by the Holy See.' Secondly, Bonaparte insisted that the Pope's resignation of the church property nationalized and alienated during the Revolution should be 'immutable,' whilst the Pope refused to recognize the rights of the new owners: a formula was at last found by the ingenious Consalvi to bridge this gulf. Thirdly, the Pope wanted Bonaparte to pay the newly instituted bishops and clergy from endowments (*dotation*); but he insisted that it must be by salaries (*traitement*), which would put them more under the control of the state; and he got his way. Fourthly, the Pope was insistent that the Concordat should describe Catholicism as the established religion (*religion d'état*), or at least the 'dominant' religion of France: in the end it was described as 'the religion of the great majority of the citizens'; and the Pope was consoled by a clause which anticipated 'the establishment of Catholic worship' and recognized 'the special profession' made of it 'by the government in the persons of the Consuls.' The fifth and most crucial issue was the clause expressing the relation between the secular and spiritual controls. In the final draft it ran thus: 'The Catholic religion shall be freely practised in France. The government removes all obstacles that might oppose it. Its worship shall be public, so long as it conforms to such police regulations as are required by public peace.'

Minor matters were settled more easily: the reduction in numbers and the rearrangement of dioceses and parishes: bishops to be nominated by the First Consul and instituted by the Pope; an oath of fidelity to be taken to the government (not to the Constitution); the bishops to nominate the clergy; the government to hand over to the bishops all churches still available for use. Bonaparte even ordered Duroc to construct in the Tuileries, opening out of his bedroom and study, and in place of the present bathroom, a small private chapel, where 'Consular Mass' might be said, and where the bishops could take the oath.

The Concordat was signed by the Pope on August 15th, by Bonaparte on September 8th, and the ratifications exchanged on the 10th. But this was not the end. Bonaparte, who had at various times hoped to publish it on August 15th (the Feast of the Assumption, and his own birthday), on the anniversary of the 18th Brumaire, or on Christmas Day, postponed his triumph until he could make it more complete by embodying the Concordat in a *loi des cultes* passed by the *Corps législatif* (April 8th, 1802) and by tacking on to it a series of so-called Organic Articles, by which the 'police regulations' mentioned in the agreed text as possibly 're-quired by public peace' were transformed into an operative system of state control. To this the Pope would certainly not have agreed, and he never ceased to protest against it.

The 17 Articles of the Concordat represented the essentials of a working agreement between the Republic and the Papacy. The 77 Organic Articles stood for Bonaparte's resolve to close every possible door between the French bishops and the Pope, and in every practicable way to subordinate the church to the state. The new Gallicanism would leave no loopholes for Ultramontanism.

In future no Papal bull, or any such document (seven different terms were used to prevent evasion) could be published or implemented in France without leave of the government. No Papal representative (five terms used) could act in any way on French soil without such permission. No decrees of church synods or councils outside France could be published in the country, nor could the French church itself hold any such gatherings, without the consent of the government. Ecclesiastical abuses of any kind were to be referred to the Council of State.

The bishop's control of his diocese was also limited in various ways. He could have no diocesan establishments except a Chapter and a Seminary. He could not appoint a *curé* or a member of his Chapter without the approval of the First Consul. He could not be absent from his diocese without leave. He had to visit every parish in his diocese every five years. He could not authorize the use of a private chapel, or services outside a church, without government consent; and he must consult the prefect about the ringing of church bells or the holding of special services ordered by the government.

After all these limitations, it comes almost as a surprise that, though all clergy were now compelled to wear clerical dress (which had been forbidden during the Revolution)—they must be *habillés à la française et en noir*: bishops were allowed to wear a pectoral cross and purple stockings, and might style themselves either *citoyen* or *monsieur*. Bonaparte had even arranged with Portalis for a cheap supply of mitres, croziers and crosses at the expense of the state.

Curés, like bishops, must take the oath of allegiance to the state, must reside in their parishes, must obey their bishops, cannot work outside the diocesan system, or transfer to another diocese without permission, cannot use any but the standardized liturgy, or celebrate any festival not in the Revolutionary calendar, or dress as a bishop (even if they were exbishops, *démissionaires*); they must pray for the Republic and Consuls at every parish mass, can give out no notices in church except about services or when ordered by the government to do so, and must pronounce the blessing of the church (*bénédiction nuptiale*) over couples who have been married in a civil ceremony. There was to be no indiscipline in the Church of France.

The proclamation accompanying the publication of the Concordat (April 17th) was in Bonaparte's most rhetorical style: he was more than ever in love with his Italian grandiloquence, and supposed that Frenchmen must like it too. 'An insane policy [he means the regime of separation of church and state] has tried to crush religious disagreement beneath the *débris* of our altars, the very ruins of religion. Its mere word put an end to those pious ceremonies at which our citizens called each other by the kindly name of "brother," and acknowledged their equality under the hand of the Creator. The dying man in his lonely agony heard no more the voice of consolation which summons Christians to a better life. God himself seemed exiled from the world of nature . . . To bring this disorder to an end it was necessary to place religion once more on its proper base, and that could only be done by means which religion itself approved . . . The Head of the church has, in his wisdom, and in the interests of the church, considered proposals dictated by the interests of the state. He has made his voice heard by the pastors of the church. What he approved the government has agreed to, and the legislature has made a law of the Republic. Thus there is an end to all elements of discord.'

There follows an exhortation to the clergy which leaves no doubt as to the political aims of the whole transaction. 'Ministers of the religion of peace! See that this religion attaches you to the interests of the country. See that your teaching and your example shape young citizens in love of our institutions, in respect and affection for the authorities which have been created to guide and protect them. See that they learn from you that the God of peace is also the God of war, and that He fights on the side of those who defend the independence and liberty of France.' [11]

9

The application of the Concordat raised difficult problems both for the French government and for the Papacy. Caprara, as Papal legate *a latere*, was overwhelmed with petitions from secular clergy and members of Religious Orders who had in one way or another broken their ecclesiastical vows during the Revolution, and now wished to retain or recover their status. Many of them—it was said they numbered 7000—had made civil marriages: could they be regularized by the church? Some married men had been ordained and held cures: might they keep their wives and their livings? Could an ex-Chouan who had fought and taken life receive Holy Orders? Might a married priest now living apart from his wife retain his benefice? All kinds of problems arose with respect to ex-priests who had become officers in the army, government officials, or members of the professional classes. Caprara dealt with each case on its merits, and kept a register of the petitions and of his answers to them. It can still be read amongst the *Archives nationales*—a strange record of human nature torn between the claims of religion and of the secular life.

On the other hand, it is only necessary to look through Bonaparte's correspondence during the early months of 1802 to realize how many questions of church discipline were raised for the secular government by the application of the Concordat, and how many reasons could be alleged for strengthening the hands of the state to deal with them. The bishop of Nancy is found demanding retractions from ex-constitutional clergy. He has no right to do so. Ex-constitutionals, whether bishops or clergy, are by their simple acceptance of the Concordat in full communion with the church. It would be politically and morally disastrous to ask more. The bishop of Angers has dismissed an ex-constitutional *curé* after forty-three years' service: he had no right to do it without government consent. Bonaparte hears this practice is going on everywhere: Portalis must report. The bishops of Rennes and Clermont are persecuting constitutional priests. 'Tell them that I want constitutionals fully represented; that the French people and the Pope want unity, and no persecution. See that it doesn't happen again.' The bishop of Quimper is associating with 'bad priests': censure both parties. At Nancy a *commissaire de police* has tried to stop a funeral procession, and torn a pall off a coffin. This is illegal. The Minister of Justice must deal with him. The prefect of La Meurthe has no right to close a synagogue. Portalis must tell him so. So it goes on.[12]

Clearly enough, some of the non-juror bishops were trying to pack the parishes with men of their own party, and it was not going to be easy to enforce a spiritual amnesty between those who had been on opposite sides in the quarrels of the last ten years about Jacobinism, clerical marriage and the civil oath, especially when, in most country districts at least, the 'refractory' *curé* was regarded as a 'good priest' and the 'constitutional' as a 'bad priest' *sans phrase*.

Very instructive in this and other respects is Bonaparte's letter of advice to his uncle Fesch when he is appointed to the archbishopric of Lyon (November 2nd, 1802). 'Be careful what you do (he writes), but appoint as many constitutional priests as possible, and make certain of support from this party. You must face the fact that whilst this controversy about constitutionals and non-constitutionals is for most of the priests a matter of religion, their leaders regard it purely as a political question . . . What I should really like as your first move, would be for you to give your hand to one of the most consistent members of the refractory party— provided he is not too much of an extremist—and also to one of the most consistent members of the constitutional party, and to bless them and embrace them both at once, telling them that union and brotherhood are the foundation of all religion. Some striking gesture of this kind would have good results for religion, and benefit the state . . . As for the mere talkers [*about dangers of schism*] you should reply that trying to humiliate one's neighbour means raking up memories of the time when he was an enemy, and thereby violating the first principle of the law. The Archbishops and bishops of 1802 are not the Archbishops and bishops of 1789: they are those who come nearest to the Early Church.'

Fesch was Bonaparte's own uncle, whom he had snatched from a comfortable and worldly life in Paris, after a rapid reconversion to orthodoxy and an easy form of penance and absolution, to be promoted in a few weeks to the archbishopric of Lyon. It was a diocese in which constitutional priests predominated, but had been unfairly treated by the outgoing archbishop. Hence Bonaparte's letter, backed by a speech to representatives of the clergy of Lyon. Outwardly the new archbishop carried out his nephew's instructions, and soon pacified the diocese. Yet his own leanings were towards the non-jurors; he enjoyed ritualistic functions; and his tenure of the see culminated in a magnificent funeral mass for the body of General Leclerc (which Pauline Bonaparte, his widow, was conveying from Toulon to Paris), with a sermon extolling the First Consul's services to Catholicism. Nevertheless Fesch's six months' archiepiscopate saw the beginning of a process by which the control of the French church gradually slipped out of the hands of the state (however pertinacious Bonaparte's attempts to retain it) into those of the Papacy.

This development can be seen even more clearly in the eight years' rule of Champion de Cicé in the diocese of Aix. The political reasons which led Bonaparte (following the Constituent Assembly) to identify the new dioceses with the departments, and (by a further refinement) to allot several politically peaceful areas to a single diocese, had made the archbishop of Aix the spiritual ruler of three departments; so that he had little to fear from the prefects and their subordinates, even supposing they had been (which Bonaparte's nominees seldom were) anticlericals. He had behind him a long experience of administration, and enjoyed a prestige both royal and revolutionary. Had he not been bishop of Rhodez and archbishop of Bordeaux before the Revolution, and *garde des sceaux* in Louis XVI's ministry of 1789?

Returning to the Midi, where he had spent his first episcopate, he knew how to win the hearts of the southerners, and to reconcile the quarrels of clericals and anti-clericals, jurors and non-jurors, supporters and opponents of the Concordat, which were distracting the prefects and the police. He began with a fine gesture, fixing his enthronement for July 14th, the national festival. In his first Charge, naming himself Archbishop of Aix and Arles 'by the grace of God and the authority of the Holy See,' he asked for the co-operation of the civil authorities. On July 15th, at Marseille, he stayed with the Prefect Delacroix, met the local officials, and celebrated a Cardinal's mass, with a *Te Deum* and the new prayers for the Republic and Consuls. At Arles, whose mayor was hostile, and in the department of Var, where the Prefect Fauchet was suspicious of him, he produced an equally good impression, going by sea to 'terrorist and atheistical' Toulon, and in ten days reconciling it to the *église concordataire*. On this basis he built his policy of exploiting the state for the benefit of the church. He missed no opportunity—the funeral of Leclerc, the Life Consulship, the Peace of Amiens, the burial of Pius VI—to carry out the orders of the government, and to extol the benefits of the Consular regime.

But in the appointment of his clergy—middle-aged men, mostly of local origin, pensioners of the Constituent Assembly, but of all parties in the church—in the financial reorganization of the diocese, and in his insistence on the right of public services, processions, bell-ringing, festivals, and sacramental marriage preceded by the 'calling of banns,' he gradually built up a Catholic tradition which Portalis welcomed and with which Bonaparte could find no fault. The First Consul's approval of the archbishop's regime was proved by his dismissal of Delacroix, the only Prefect who tried to obstruct it, and the appointment in his place of Thibaudeau, who, as the crown of his ability, knew when to let well enough alone.

It would be rash to assume that in all the sixty dioceses of the *église concordataire* things went as smoothly as in that of Aix. Some bishops tipped the delicate balance between church and state towards Paris, others towards Rome. Sometimes special conditions settled the issue. If at Marseille, which suffered all through this period from the British blockade, it needed all de Cicé's tact to establish the Concordat, at Strasbourg the appointment of a 'Constitutional' bishop coincided with the pulling down of the immense *bonnet rouge* which had decorated the cathedral spire ever since the Terror, and was followed by a period of religious peace and economic prosperity, due to the passage of Napoleon's armies to and fro across the Rhine. But there can be little question that upon the whole the 'episcopal Gallicanism' which de Cicé established in three important departments of the Midi—a system of Catholic worship and clerical discipline free from serious interference either by Pope or Consul —was, within five or six years of the signing of the Concordat, becoming the pattern of church life throughout France. Napoleon had on the whole succeeded in what he described at St. Helena as the most difficult enterprise of his career.[18]

10

Hardly less important than the Concordat, as a means of unifying the nation and establishing the Consular and Imperial regime, was the *Code Civil*. Both were revisions of the work of reason in the light of experience. The Concordat republicanized the Articles of Bossuet: the Code republicanized the *Ordonnances* of Colbert. Both preserved the essential pattern of the Revolution: both reframed it in the *cadres* of the *ancien régime*. Both recognized and exploited the need that most Frenchmen feel for a power which will control and an authority which will decide. 'France,' said Renan, 'which finds it obvious that a law issuing from Paris should at once apply to the Breton peasant, the Alsatian artisan, and the nomad shepherd of the Landes, would think it equally natural that there should be at Rome an infallible authority to regulate the conscience of the world.' The influence of a Code in establishing his regime, Bonaparte reckoned, would be as subtle and far reaching as that of a Concordat; setting up models of social conduct, defined in print and enforced by the magistrate, alongside the Christian virtues and Catholic duties inculcated by the priest; models to which the public conscience would gradually and unconsciously assimilate itself: for it is untrue (he would hold) that people cannot be made better by Act of Parliament. In any case something must be done to systematize the huge mass of legislation left behind by the Revolution—the 14,400 decrees on which Merlin and Cambacérès had based the 797 articles of their draft Code of 1793; so that the courts might know what laws they were to administer, whilst litigants and criminals might rely upon being treated with equal and calculable justice.

The first we hear of the Code is an *arrêté* of August 12th, 1800, instructing the Minister of Justice to summon three distinguished lawyers—Tronchet, Bigot de Préameneu, and Portalis—with Maleville as Secretary, to *tenir des conférences sur le rédaction du code civil*. Tronchet and Bigot represented the *droit coutumier*, Portalis and Maleville the *droit écrit*, the two traditional forms of French law, which had to be combined in the new Code. They were to take as their starting-point four projects for a civil code drawn up by the Convention and the Directory. They were to fix the plan of a code, and to discuss its underlying principles. They must present the result to the Consuls within five months, and sit with the *Conseil d'état* to discuss it. Similar committees were set up to draft a criminal code (March 28th, 1801), a commercial code (August 3rd, 1801), a rural code (August 10th), and a code of civil procedure (March 24th, 1802).

The draft of the civil code, after being submitted to the *Tribunal de*

Cassation, was discussed by the *Conseil d'état* from July to December, and each *titre* embodied in a *loi du code* submitted to the *Tribunat* and *Corps législatif*. There it met with so much opposition that it was withdrawn for more than a year; and was not finally passed, as a whole, until March 24th, 1804.

The title *Code Napoléon*, which was prefixed in 1807, has been too easily taken to mean that Bonaparte inspired the whole, or that it was a new creation of the Consular regime. It was in fact, like the revolutionary armies, an *amalgame*, in which the new recruits—the laws and decrees of the Revolution—were stiffened by the presence of a proportion of veteran principles drawn from the royal *Ordonnances*, and, through them from the underlying rules of Roman jurisprudence.

The *Code Napoléon* (i.e. the Civil Code), as printed in 1810 contained less than 120,000 words, and could be carried in the pocket. Its 2281 Articles, numbered consecutively, were grouped into 3 *Livres*, containing 11, 4, and 20 *Titres*; and a 60-page *Table des matières* enabled the reader to turn up any point in a moment. A French citizen had no right to claim ignorance of the law. Three other advantages may be noted. Administrative details are embodied in the law—for instance, in the *Dispositions générales* concerning the *état civil* (Liv. I, Tit. II, Cap. I) there are careful definitions of controversial terms—e.g. the different kinds of *immeubles* and *meubles* under the head of property (Liv. II, Tit. I, Cap. I): and penalties are prescribed for officials who fail in their duty of carrying out the terms of the law—e.g. in regard to marriage (Liv. I, Tit. V, Cap. I). Many of the difficulties of case-made law, administrative interpretation, and expensive litigation are thus set aside. Even the possibility that, in a country the size of France, there might be disputes about the date of reception of the Code is met by adding a *Tableau des distances de Paris aux chefs-lieux des départements*, reckoned in *kilomètres*, *myriamètres* and *lieues anciens*: it being ruled (Tit. Préliminaire, Art. I) that the Code come into effect within one day after promulgation, plus an extra day for each twenty *lieues distance* from Paris (the *résidence impériale*) to the departmental capital: a good example of Bonaparte's attention to detail.

The most superficial reading of the Code reveals certain characteristics, which were not so much due to Bonaparte himself (however talkative during his attendance at the discussions of the lawyers who drew it up) as to his concurrence with the point of view of his advisers, and with the development of public opinion between 1799 and 1802 (while the Code was still preparing) which accepted the main results of the Revolution, but reacted against some of its extremer manifestations. But it is worth noting that, of the 55 (out of a total of 106) meetings that Bonaparte attended, 35 coincided with the discussion (July 1801-January 1802) of civil rights, marriage, paternity, divorce and adoption; and on these questions the Code took a line that might be called Napoleonic.

Thus the serious penalties attached to *mort civile* were reminiscent of a time of foreign and civil war. The precautions safeguarding marriage, e.g. the demand for birth certificates (Bonaparte had not forgotten the laxity which allowed Joséphine and himself to misrepresent their ages), and the requirement of parental or family approval—were a criticism of the easy-going 'republican marriages' of the last ten years. The law which allowed divorce to either party for adultery, cruelty (*excès, sévices, ou injures graves*), or crime (*condamnation à une peine infamante*), but put immense obstacles in the way of divorce *par consentement mutuel*, was an attempt to accept but limit the new rights given to women by the Revolution, and a protest against the growing popularity of divorce; for in Paris during 1799-1800 one marriage in every five ended in divorce.

The insistence on the control of children by their parents—the recourse to one month's imprisonment below the age of 16, or to 6 months after 16; the right to enjoy children's property up to the age of 18; the power of preventing a son's marriage till the age of 26, and of a daughter's till 21; and the recognition of the *acte respectueux*, by which sons or daughters intending to marry, up to the ages of 30 or 25, had to ask their parents' consent three times at a month's interval: all these provisions showed a return towards the social discipline of pre-revolutionary France.

As to the law of property, there was little desire to undo the formidable revolution of the last ten years. The only *servitudes* left were certain charges on inherited property; the only *privilège* mentioned in the Code is *un droit que la qualité de la créance donne à un créancier d'être préferé aux autres créanciers*. At the same time property is defined as *le droit de jouir et disposer des choses de la manière la plus absolue*, limited only by law and government regulation: and the equalitarian subdivision of an inherited estate amongst all members of the family is limited by the right of the testator to settle a portion of his property by will.

In these and in other respects the Code was a child of its age, an embodiment for all time of the great social revolution from which it sprang. The Prussian *Allgemeines Landrecht*, drawn up ten years before, belonged to the old world: the *code civil* belongs to the new. It not only permeated French society: it followed the French banners across Europe —into Belgium, Holland and Luxembourg, into Bavaria, Baden, Westphalia and Switzerland: Junot was bidden to translate it into Portuguese, and Murat into Spanish, for use in the Peninsula; its influence has been felt in the legislation of Italy, Rumania, and Egypt, it has travelled overseas to Canada, Louisiana, Bolivia, Haiti, Japan.[14]

II

On Easter Sunday (April 18th, 1802), within ten days of the passing of the *Loi des cultes,* and the morning after the ratification of the Treaty of Amiens, Bonaparte drove in state from the Tuileries to Nôtre Dame, accompanied by a colourful procession of generals, officials and diplomatic representatives, and there heard Pontifical High Mass performed by the choir of the *Conservatoire* and 150 musicians under the direction of Méhul and Cherubini, with a *Te Deum* in honour of the pacification of Europe and of the Catholic church. The procession had little of the theatrical perfection of David's revolutionary pageants; but neither had it their artificiality. Those who filled the hired cabs and dilapidated state coaches were the men who had won Bonaparte's battles and were constructing Bonaparte's state—generals fresh from the front, officials torn from their desks. They had not the look or the gestures of the old royalty, and many of them scoffed at the old religion: but they were doing the work of both. The First Consul was received at the great west door as any Bourbon might have been, by the nonogenarian Archbishop of Paris. A sermon was delivered by the bishop who had preached at Louis XVI's coronation. At the moment of the Elevation, according to old custom, a fanfare was sounded, and the troops in the cathedral presented arms.

It was—look at it as you will—one of the great moments, indeed the greatest, in Napoleon's career. The young Corsican was still four months short of his thirty-third birthday. Seven years ago he had been almost unknown outside a small professional circle. In the last six years he had fought three spectacular campaigns, and by his victories forced himself upon France, and France upon Europe. Here and now, in the building which for more than six centuries had symbolized the union of the French monarchy and the Catholic church, and beneath whose roof had echoed the prayers and praises of twenty-five generations of Parisians, he stood as the consummater of a nation's revolution, and the architect of its regeneration. He had unified France; he had pacified Europe; he had reunited the church. He had plans on foot for the codification of the laws, for the administration of the provinces, for the education of the people. Great parts of the world beyond the Alps and the ocean were to enjoy constitutions modelled on that of the French Republic. Paris was to be embellished by the skill of its architects and the plunder of Florence and Rome. Foreigners were invited to see for themselves how France had recovered from the poison of Jacobinism without recourse to the antidote of Royalism. The French Republic stood four-square to any wind that might blow.

It was an astonishing achievement that Paris celebrated on Easter Day, 1802. How fortunate that man cannot foretell the future—that no one in Nôtre Dame could envisage 1812, 1814, 1815!

There exists in the British Museum a letter, in Bonaparte's hand, dated August 28th, 1798, and captured by a British frigate off Alexandria, at the end of which he speaks boastfully of his position in Egypt. Below the hurried and almost illegible signature 'Bonaparte' are three words written in Nelson's painfully acquired left hand: 'Mark the end. Nelson.' Were they a comment ... or a prophecy? [15]

VIII

FRANCE

(1802-1804)

PHILOSOPHERS may debate the reality of time. Historians must assume it. The science which investigates human happenings and the art which arranges them into a narrative demand a before and an after. Nor is anything gained for history, or the philosopher in any way appeased, if a vague flux of duration is substituted for the years, months, hours and minutes of the clock and the calendar. For history everything has a beginning, a middle and an end. The course of events really turns on what happened in a particular moment of time and at a particular point of space.

The historian is therefore right in fixing in space and time the point at which a kingdom or a career ceased to rise and began to fall. Suppose an accumulation of acts, some making for survival, some for destruction, suppose even that they overlap in time, so that the spectator on the shore of history cannot be sure whether the tide is yet on the turn: still, if he is observant enough, he will record one wave which is the highest of them all, and one which marks the first failure to reach that level.

Where should this moment be fixed in the career of Napoleon Bonaparte? A military historian, looking for a point at which victory gave place to defeat, might find it between Jena (or perhaps Wagram) and Moscow. A naval historian might prefer Trafalgar. A political historian, looking at the balance of power on the continent, might find the turning-point at Tilsit. A historian who envisaged the Napoleonic period as a struggle between France and Great Britain for the control of European and overseas trade would prefer to take the moment when the challenge was thrown down and taken up at the breach of the Peace of Amiens. A Frenchman, asking himself at what point Bonaparte's system of government ceased to secure the blessings of the Revolution and began to return to the practices of the Bourbon monarchy, might choose the moment at which the First Consul crowned himself Emperor of the French. But he would be as likely to argue that this act had been implicit in the assumption of Life Consulship two years before, and that it made little difference to the character of the government, or to the working out of the laws and institutions which had been inaugurated at Brumaire.

The concurrence of these lines of argument points to the year 1802 as the turning-point—the year of the Treaty of Amiens, of the Concordat, and of the Consulship for life. Each was a climax, a settlement: of the war in Europe, of the crucial issue of the Revolution, of Bonaparte's own rise to power. Each enclosed germs of decay: a treaty which was only a truce, a pacification which inaugurated a new struggle, the climbing of a mountain shoulder which revealed the true summit at last within reach. If an exact moment is needed, let it then be that of the Elevation in the mass of Easter Day, April 18th, 1802, when the material might of the Napoleonic republic did homage to the central miracle of the Catholic faith.

The historian who finds the turning-point of Bonaparte's career in 1802 need not prove that there were no respects in which he grew more admirable, or France more prosperous, in the years that followed. Such a thesis would be absurd. What he means is that, in the long verdict of history, plans begun then, institutions founded, tendencies encouraged, already held in them the germs of failure; and that before the rise was ended the fall had begun.

The main test of a ruler's greatness, and measure of his success, must be looked for, not abroad, but at home; not in the extent of the countries under his control, nor in victories won far away, but in the streets of his capital, and in the villages of his countryside. If the heart is sound, the body will be healthy. Brought up under a revolution which took its orders from Paris; owing to the favour of the sovereign people a career which its whims might at any moment have destroyed; balancing, in Italy, his personal prestige against the policy of the home government; anxious in Egypt for the moment when he might return from exile, and make a bid for political power; and all his life turning his eyes back—from Rome, from Vienna, from Madrid, from Berlin, from Moscow—to the one country and capital he could not intimidate or compel: Bonaparte was the last man in the world to forget this first condition of good government.

It is therefore natural to begin the history of the years 1802-15 by inquiring into the state of France under the Consulate and Empire, with particular attention to the way in which the laws and institutions of 1802 developed during the succeeding years: for here, if anywhere, should be found the evidences of health or the symptoms of disease. The historian must adopt the motto of Napoleon's imperial policy: 'France first.'

2

It was traditional and natural that France should be ruled from Paris. It is therefore worth while to inquire how much time, during the different parts of his career, Bonaparte spent in or near the capital.

Since his return from Egypt, twenty-one months ago, he had been away less than three months—from May 6th to July 2nd, 1800, on the Marengo campaign, and from January 8th to 31st, at Lyon. All the rest of the time since Brumaire he had been working incessantly at the reorganization of the government, the settlement of the country, and the establishment of peace. Now, from Easter Day, 1802, till the rupture of the Peace of Amiens, in the third week of May 1803, he was constantly in and out of Paris, which he visited during the summer months from Malmaison, and during the autumn and winter from Saint-Cloud. On June 24th he went for a fifty-day tour in north France and the Netherlands; from November 4th to 17th and December 31st to January 5th, 1804, he was at Boulogne; and on July 18th he set out on another tour to the Channel ports and the lower Rhine that lasted three months. But it was not until April 2nd, 1805, that he again left the capital. In other words, from Brumaire to the time of this journey to Italy he had spent only 259 out of 1723 days away from Paris—not much more than one day in seven. Afterwards it was very different. Though the longest absences were generally followed by substantial spells in Paris, the total time spent abroad up to the time of his abdication in 1814 was 1420 days out of 3160, or more than one in three.[1]

The impression given by most histories that Bonaparte was constantly away from Paris, travelling and fighting up and down Europe is not even true of the second part of his dictatorship. It is a complete misunderstanding of the first part. It was only by staying at home and sitting at his desk for those five and a half years that he was able to accomplish the work upon which, far more than his military campaigns, his fame deserves to rest. Hence the historical importance of Napoleon's Correspondence, and the interest of his methods of work.

None of the Bonaparte family wrote legibly, Napoleon least of all. His own explanation was that his thoughts ran too fast for his pen. He was in fact accustomed to express himself in talk, not writing. He soon took to dictation, and the vast majority of his letters and memoranda are in this form, signed with a vigorous but increasingly hurried 'Napol,' 'Nap,' 'Np,' or 'N.' Such private letters as he still wrote in his own hand, for instance those to Joséphine, gave infinite trouble to their recipients, and are undecipherable except by experts.

Between 1797 and 1814 Napoleon employed three principal secretaries: Bourrienne, Méneval, and Fain. All of them wrote memoirs, and leave us in no doubt as to how the Emperor's correspondence was done. In Paris, whether in the early years at the Luxembourg or the Tuileries, or afterwards also at his country homes, Malmaison or Saint-Cloud, every hour of the day, from ten to five, was taken up with reading documents, dictating or correcting letters, giving interviews, or attending meetings or functions. Sometimes, when there was a special press of business, Napoleon would be at work by himself from two a.m., and would summon his secretary to begin his correspondence at any time between four and seven. Hour after hour the secretary sits there, 'as silent as a piece of furniture, answering if the Emperor asks a question, writing if he says, "Write," and in the intervals addressing old letters or making fair copies of new ones.'

Napoleon's Italian eloquence was generally disciplined, in dictation, by a wonderfully clear mind and a methodical arrangement of matter: only occasionally, when addressing his recalcitrant brothers, or riding his hobby horse against the Pope, he would loose a stream of rhetoric, which the bewildered secretary had to reconstruct afterwards from hurried jottings and extemporized shorthand.

When Napoleon left Paris, or when he went to the front, his secretaries and his portfolios went with him. In the field, wherever he might be, his blue and white tent was pitched, with its two compartments—a study and a bedroom. The papers and books were unpacked, the maps were spread out, and, the moment fighting was over, dictation would begin again. However far it was to Paris, the Emperor's dispatches must come and go every day. Whilst he travels in his yellow *voiture de poste* or green-upholstered *berline* from place to place, Berthier, his Chief of Staff, is by his side; and, as they jolt along, Napoleon goes through his order-books and muster-rolls, makes his decisions and dictates his commands.

How many documents did Napoleon write or dictate? The Committee of editors in 1854 estimated them at 64,600: others have put the figure a good deal higher: many supplementary collections have appeared during the last hundred years, so that there are now some 41,000 in print. But perhaps as many again have been lost, or not yet published. Suppose the total to have been 80,000. That would mean that he dictated fifteen letters, orders, etc., a day during the fifteen years of his rule. Sometimes, we discover, there were more, sometimes less. When Eugène became Viceroy of Italy in 1805 he received twenty-one letters, many of them long and important documents, in a single week. Decrès once received five in a day. But at the time of the Emperor's marriage to Marie-Louise he only wrote eleven letters in fourteen days.

In 1854 Napoleon III set up a Commission to collect and publish the correspondence of the founder of his dynasty: and during the next ten years fifteen volumes were printed, containing 13,094 documents dating from 1793 to August 1807; but many were omitted for reasons that seemed good to the editors. In 1864, when he was none too happy upon his throne, he began to fear that the Commission was publishing documents that might discredit his dynasty; so he set up a new Commission, under Prince Jérôme Napoleon, to carry out the remainder of the work on more edifying lines: that is, they were 'to publish what the Emperor would have published, if, surveying himself, and anticipating the verdict of history, he had wanted to display his person and system to posterity.' Naturally, then, the remaining volumes of the series have to be treated with even more reserve than their predecessors; and have to be supplemented by the later publications in which Du Casse, Lecestre, and other editors have collected documents which were omitted by the Commission, or have since come to light. But the official Correspondence still remains the one indispensable authority for any biographer of Napoleon.[2]

The dictating of letters, as most men in public life discover, is the least exacting part of the day's work. The private interviews, the committee meetings, and the public engagements take up more time, and use up more energy. Some impression can be drawn from contemporary memoirs and from the press as to Bonaparte's public engagements and court functions. In addition to the almost daily meetings of the Consuls, and those of the Council of State and its various subdivisions, of which some account has already been given, a Court Gazette would record during the summer of 1802 such events as the following. May 3rd, reception of bishops; May 7th, reception of General Menou; May 9th, taking of the oath by nine recently appointed bishops; May 12th, a review, luncheon with the officers, and in the evening a performance at Malmaison of Paisiello's *La Serva Padrona* by an Italian company; June 4th, a review; June 26th, a visit to the Sèvres china factory; June 30th, a performance of the *Barbier de Seville* at Malmaison, with Hortense as *Rosina*; July 11th, an excursion by water at Mortefontaine, when the boat capsized, and Bonaparte was in danger of drowning; July 14th, a review, and presentation of colours; July 17th, reception of the Chapter of Nôtre Dame; August 8th, visit to the Jardin des Plantes with Joséphine; August 10th, visit to the Théâtre Français; August 15th, fête in honour of the Life Consulship, with a concert (300 players), a *Te Deum* at Nôtre Dame, and a family dinner and theatricals at Malmaison; August 19th, another visit to the Théâtre Français; August 21st, swearing in of senators at the Luxembourg; August 27th, dinner for 200 at the Tuileries; September 1st, reception of Corsican envoys; September 2nd, review, reception of diplomats, dinner for 200; September 12th, trip by river from Paris to Saint-Cloud; September 22nd, visit to the Exhibition of National Industries at the Louvre, to a show of pictures by Isabey at the Salon, and in the evening to the Opera; September 24th, distribution of prizes in connection with the Exhibition; September 26th, first official Sunday mass at Saint-Cloud; October 7th, diplomatic reception and state dinner at the Tuileries (the same, in future, on the 15th of every month) . . . And so it goes on.[8]

3

Within less than four months from Easter Day, 1802, Bonaparte became First Consul for life, with the right to choose his successor (August 2nd, 1802): within two years (May 18th, 1804) he became Napoleon Bonaparte, Emperor of the French, with the Imperial title hereditary in his family.

In another country, with a different national character, a less recent revolution, and a longer experience of representative government, this might never have happened. Even in France, a traditionally monarchical country, even after a social revolution which had destroyed the old obstacles to despotism, even in face of a disillusioned and weakened legislature, it would never have been possible unless Bonaparte had been supremely self-confident, and sure of the support of the mass of the people. With this confidence and this surety he cleverly took advantage of the political situation to enforce a settlement which was from the first its logical outcome.

As First Consul he already ruled alone. True, he met the second and third Consuls daily, consulted their opinion, and had them at his side at the greater functions of state. When he was away from Paris on his Normandy tour in November 1802, he wrote to Cambacérès almost every day, giving an account of his doings. But nobody supposed that the policy pursued was not his policy, or the decisions taken not his decisions. The two transitions from Consul to Life Consul and from Life Consul to Emperor were less the initiation of a new system of government than the recognition of one already in being. The constitutional changes that followed merely carried a step further principles inherent in the *coup d'état* of Brumaire; the creation of an Imperial family and of a royal court was already implicit in the chapel, the theatre and the ante-rooms of the Tuileries.

The care which Bonaparte took to magnify the victory of Marengo and to cry down that of Hohenlinden was evidence of how much he stood to win or lose on a single throw—not merely his reputation as a soldier, but his prestige as First Consul, and the whole future of the new regime. It was a risk to leave Paris so soon after the *coup d'état*. The country held its breath whilst he was away. The news of Marengo was greeted with more than a sigh of relief: with rejoicings rather like those of a crowd come to watch the execution of a popular favourite when he is reprieved at the scaffold. Bonaparte had gambled with the fate of the nation, and had won.

For France was still full of dissension, disloyalty, and downright anarchy.

It was not till after Marengo that 'Louis XVIII,' the hope of the royalists, retired from Mitau to Warsaw, and from Warsaw to London, pursued by Bonaparte's malediction: 'You need not think of returning to France: you would have to step over a hundred thousand dead Frenchmen.' It was not till after Marengo that Talleyrand, Fouché, Roederer and other leading Brumairians decided to put their hankerings after royalism at the service of a First Consul who might become an Emperor. It was the popular enthusiasm roused by Marengo that enabled Bonaparte to overawe the legislature, and to carry through by a *sénatus-consulte* the proscription that followed the Opera Plot of December 24th, 1800: the shooting, guillotining, or deportation of more than a hundred Jacobins. It was after Marengo that, at last, military operations, backed by special courts which judged without juries and without appeal, got the measure of the *chouans*, *chauffeurs* and brigands of the western departments, and 'Georges' (Cadoudal), whose name had become almost an obsession to Bonaparte, fled into refuge across the Channel.

When the victory of Marengo was followed by the Peace of Amiens, Bonaparte stood on the watershed of his career. It might be thought, and was hoped by many of those who had hitherto supported him, that with peace at home and abroad there would come at last some measure of that Liberty which for ten years had evaded the grasp of the Revolution. It might be urged that no change in his constitutional status could give the First Consul more real influence, compatible with 'representative republicanism,' than he already possessed; and that to concentrate in his person fresh privileges and a longer spell of office was to invite more plots and quick disaster.

Bonaparte thought otherwise. He had never believed in parliamentary government. A state should be governed, like an army, by a strong and centralized executive. Liberty was the fruit of discipline; and the remedy for indiscipline was less liberty. Civil mutiny was the worst of all crimes, punishable by civil death. Continuity of control was essential: if the general in command is struck down, there must be someone designated and trained to take his place. And to reinforce this military analogy there was growing in Bonaparte's mind a fondness for the old monarchical way of government, with its throne, its court, its royal succession; for a tradition as deeply planted in the French mind as that of the Catholic church; for a regime in which he would play the part both of Emperor and of Pope.

The obstructive tactics of the legislature in face of the Concordat, the Code, and the Legion of Honour determined the next step towards autocracy. Early in 1802 the State Council decided that the time had come to carry out the constitutional replacement of one-fifth of the members of the Tribunate. The opportunity was taken to exclude the most troublesome representatives of the Opposition. Not only so. The Tribunate was subdivided into three sections, only one of which considered legislation proposed by the State Council, and that after it had been discussed in private between the sectional *rapporteur* and chosen representatives of the Council, under the eye of the First Consul: thus all effective opposition in either body was scotched.

The army still grumbled; but the disaffected generals could be dealt with by military discipline. The *complotte des libelles* of 1801 was easily suppressed. Bernadotte, the most implicated, was sent to an eastern command, Lannes to Lisbon, Brune to Constantinople; and several officers found themselves little better off than the *déportés* of the Opera Plot.

The wave of enthusiasm which greeted the pacification of Amiens did what more was required. The congratulations of the Legislature carried with them a desire to mark in some way the gratitude of the nation to the First Consul. Bonaparte's friends knew what he wanted. Brumaire was not to be just another of the *jours* of the Revolution, a mere date in the republican calendar. The constitution of the Year VIII was not to disappear, as its predecessors had done, in another reaction. It was to be transformed into something to which Jacobinism had more than once looked forward, and royalism had always looked back: an autocracy, a civil despotism backed by the army, the life-rule of a strong man. Thus both Jacobinism and royalism would be discredited by being overpassed; and the mass of the people would be secured in their new Conservatism—the Conservatism (than which there is none profounder) of small landowners and petty capitalists.

It was not difficult to find a way of doing this by exploiting the silences of the Constitution of the Year VIII. The Tribunate would not decide what form the national gratitude should take. The Senate shrank from proposing more than Bonaparte's re-election as First Consul for ten years. A group of Senators, including the Consuls and their chief supporters, over-riding the Legislature, proposed a *plébiscite*, an appeal to the nation. Thirty-five and a half million Frenchmen voted that Bonaparte should be Consul for life, and only eight thousand said 'No.' Amongst the majority one is surprised to find the name of Jeremy Bentham, who voted in virtue of the French citizenship given him in 1792. In the Tribunate Carnot was against it: Lafayette wrote from the country—it was the voice of 1789— that he could not consent without better security for political liberty. But though there was no privacy about the voting, and dissentients might fear victimization, there can be no question that the almost unanimous voice of 1802 was for 'Bonaparte and the Peace.'

A *sénatus-consulte* of August 4th, 1802, drafted by the Consuls and four members of the State Council, gave constitutional shape to the will of the people. All three Consuls were now to hold their positions for life: but the second and third were nominated by the First, and he had the right (which it had been thought unwise to mention in the *plébliscite*) to designate his successor. A new *Conseil privé*, consisting of the Consuls, two Ministers, two Senators, two State Councillors, and two Grand Officers of the Legion of Honour, now drafted *sénatus-consultes*, and sanctioned the First Consul's declarations of peace and war. The First Consul nominated the majority of the Senators, and could employ them in important offices of state. The *Corps législatif* (deprived of regular meetings) and the Tribunate (reduced to fifty members) ceased to exercise any legislative functions. The role of the State Council, now displaced by the *Conseil privé*, was no more than honorary. A new system of popular election took the place of that set up under the Constitution of the Year VIII, which had proved unworkable. Colleges of electors, appointed for life, reinforced the middle-class control over representation. Meanwhile more and more appointments—of electors, chairmen, magistrates, senators and public servants of all kinds—fell into Bonaparte's hands, and transformed a nominally democratic government into an oligarchy of officials and experts appointed and dismissed by a single guiding will. This, at the beginning of the nineteenth century, was a new theory of government. It set the pattern for much that happened in later years, and has become a model for industrial as well as for political dictatorships.[4]

4

Bonaparte left no doubt in the public mind that the Life Consulship was only a stage towards something more. In his Allocution to the Senate on August 3rd, thanking them for his new honour, he ended: 'The desire of the Senate has carried out the wish of the People: and thus it has associated itself, more closely than before, with all that remains to be done (*tout ce que reste à faire*) for the happiness of the country.' But he would not be hurried, and when his brother Lucien published a pamphlet entitled *Parallèle entre César, Cromwell, Monk, et Bonaparte*, he was promptly exiled to the embassy at Madrid.

However, within two years the pattern of events which had led to Brumaire and the Life Consulship recurred, and made possible the transition to the Empire. The breakdown of the Peace of Amiens, which Bonaparte was able without much injustice to attribute to British hostility towards himself, and to a desire to humble the French Republic, focused national loyalty and hope, almost as Marengo had done, upon the Tuileries. A fresh plot, in which 'Georges' reappeared for the last time, and Moreau and Pichegru compromised the higher command, was dramatically scotched by the kidnapping and summary execution of a foreign Prince, the Duc d'Enghien, who was suspected of being the rallying-point of the conspiracy. Eight of those implicated were put to death. Pichegru committed suicide in prison. The execution of d'Enghien brought

Bonaparte more discredit outside France than any other single act of his career, and the degree of his responsibility for it has been debated beyond reason. For at least he ordered the trial and allowed the execution, reckoning that it would be a deterrent to all royal instigators or figure-heads of plots against his regime. It is perhaps significant that the official correspondence contains only two letters on the subject.

The fear of a retaliatory attempt at assassination was now made a fresh argument for legitimizing the succession. There was no power of opposition left in the legislature. A *sénatus-consulte* of May 18th, 1804, declared that the government of the Republic was entrusted to an Emperor, to be called 'The Emperor of the French,' that 'Napoleon Bonaparte, at present First Consul of the Republic, is Emperor of the French,' and that 'the Imperial dignity is hereditary.' This last clause (only) was submitted to a *plébiscite*, of which the result was officially given (after adding 450,000 hypothetical votes to the 'Yeas' for the army and navy) as 3,572,329 for and 2579 against the proposal. So Bonaparte became *Napoléon, Empereur des Français*, and the potential founder of a fourth French dynasty.

As before, the breaches in the Constitution by which Bonaparte had forced his way to power were now declared to be a right of way. The name *République Française*, retained in the *sénatus-consulte* of May 18th, remained for four more years on the reverse of the coinage; but the obverse now read *Napoléon Empereur*. Napoleon was Emperor 'by the grace of God and the constitutions of the Republic.' The senators, who had been the agents of each step in Bonaparte's advance to power, were in future to be nominated by himself, and were chosen almost entirely from senior officials, ex-ministers, generals, nobles and big landlords, with a few bishops; but no literary men, scientists, or men of business were included. The sub-division of the Tribunate reduced that body to the same silence and importance as the *Corps législatif*. The Emperor soon ceased to consult either of them, and legislated by *sénatus-consultes* (submitted by the *Conseil* to the senate) or by *décrets* drafted and executed within the closed circle of the *Conseil* itself.

It may be asked, why did Bonaparte choose the title of *Empereur*, not that of *Roi*? There were good reasons in French history and in his own mind; and a few acute observers knew what they must be. He was disconcerted when, some months before the declaration of the Life Consulship, Jacques Necker, the old Finance Minister of Louis XVI, now living in retirement in Switzerland, published a book in which he shrewdly criticized the Constitution of the Year VIII, spoke of Bonaparte 'springing fully armed from the head of the legislature,' and foretold, by two years, the coming of the Empire. The Bourbon monarchy, he said, could not be revived, because the aristocracy upon which it rested had been destroyed. A limited monarchy of the English type was inconsistent with

the constitutional pattern of Brumaire. 'There is one means equally foreign to republicanism and to a limited monarchy, which can yet serve as
the basis and support of a hereditary government; the very means that
initiated and perpetuated the Empire in the great families of Rome—the
Julians, the Claudians, the Flavians—and which ended too by destroying
their authority: and that is the force of arms—the Praetorian Guard, and
the armies of the East and of the West. May God save France from such
a destiny!'[5]

This prophecy lost Necker a debt of £100,000 which he was claiming
from the government, and led to his daughter's expulsion from Paris. But
Madame de Staël had her revenge. The wife of the Swedish ambassador,
mistress of Louis XVI's minister of war in 1791-92, and the confidante of
many of the leaders of the Revolution, she knew Bonaparte's background
as few knew it. She was, besides, the cleverest Frenchwoman of her time.
She occupied part of her exile in writing down her impressions of Bonaparte; nor are they so hostile as to be unworthy of credit.

When he first made his mark, at Vendémiaire, it was unkindly suggested that he had been ready to fight for whichever side—Convention or
People—offered better terms. This she is certain was untrue; for he
always had a flair for being on the winning side. Nor was he handicapped by another common failing. She describes a conversation with
General Augereau. 'I asked him (this was in 1796) whether it was true
that Bonaparte aimed at making himself King. Surely not, he replied;
the young man is too well brought up for that.' A French Republican was
trained to despise royalty. But Bonaparte was not a Frenchman: he had *not*
been well brought up: he would need other reasons for refusing a crown.

Madame de Staël was (she admits) affected, even in those early days,
by something mesmeric in Bonaparte's personality. The ordinary epithets
—*bon, violent, doux, cruel*—did not apply to him. He could be charming
if he tried: but his nature was without love or hate. 'Himself is the only
man he recognizes: all other beings are mere cyphers.' He is a heartless
realist; and no consideration will turn him from the pursuit of self-
interest. When, to finance the expedition to Egypt, Bonaparte favoured
an invasion of Switzerland, to seize the treasury at Berne, Madame de
Staël spent nearly an hour pleading with him; but 'all the eloquence of
Demosthenes and Cicero would not have induced him to sacrifice an
atom of his private interest,' and he diverted the conversation to art and
a country life. On such subjects he could be agreeable, but never natural:
'the only attitude that comes naturally to him is that of a man giving
orders (*C'est un homme qui ne saurait être naturel que dans le comman-
dement*).'

This was the man in whose person the Empire was designed to secure
the succession, to guarantee republicans against a return of the Bourbons,

and to provide royalists with a synthetic throne. It was the embodiment of a dynastic ambition, the outline of a regime which could hardly be maintained by peace, or confined within the frontiers of a single country, but must stand or fall by the military fortunes of an ambitious and unscrupulous dictator.[6]

5

By this time few people in France knew or cared what changes were made in the Constitution: but they were increasingly conscious of the transformation of government and society from a republican to an imperial fashion of thought and conduct. They did not generally, as good Frenchmen, question the evolution of the Empire, any more than, as good Catholics, they questioned the development of the dogmas of the church. Their patriotism was as intuitive and logical as their religion. Bonaparte had counted on this feeling. He set himself to foster it, by surrounding and illustrating the imperial presence with symbols and sacraments calculated to reward and reassure the faithful.

Senators whom Bonaparte wished to reward for special services received a mansion and a life interest in national domains worth from £1000 to £1250 a year, on condition of three months' annual residence, and occasional reports on the state of public opinion in their district. Clergy who showed most attachment to 'the Concordat, religion and the government' were rewarded with grants of £7 10s. from the Ministry of Worship. It was originally intended that each of the 350 members of the fifteen cohorts of the Legion of Honour—soldiers and civilians selected by the Emperor—should receive a stipend, in return for an undertaking 'to devote himself to the service of the Republic, to oppose any attempt to restore feudalism, and to co-operate in the maintenance of liberty and equality': but in the event the undertaking was enforced, whilst the stipend was replaced by a star attached to a red ribbon, which a British cartoonist represented Bonaparte as cutting out of the republican *bonnet rouge*.[7] With the creation of the Empire, and its need of a court, new titles appeared every day, and a decree in more than 250 articles was needed to settle questions of precedence between the *grandes dignités de l'Empire* (*grand électeur, archi-chancelier, archi-trésorier, connétable, grand amiral*), the *grands officiers*, both military (*maréchaux, inspecteurs, colonels généraux*) and civil (*grand aumonier, grand maréchal du palais, grand chambellan, grand écuyer, grand veneur, grand maître des cérémonies*), and the lesser dignitaries (*préfets de palais, chambellans, écuyers* and the rest).

Some of these titles carried important estates. At first they went only to the Emperor's relations by blood or marriage; but soon to generals and statesmen: Parma to Cambacérès, Piacenza to Lebrun, Massa to Regnier; twelve Venetian duchies to Soult, Bessières, Duroc, Champagny, Victor, Moncey, Mortier, Clarke, Maret, Caulaincourt, Arrhigi, Savary; Bene-

vento to Talleyrand and Pontecorvo to Bernadotte (both with the titles
of Prince and Duke); and other Italian, Spanish and Portuguese duchies
to Oudinot, Macdonald, Gaudin, Fouché, Suchet and Junot. Finally (by
décret of March 1st, 1808) all *grands dignitaires* were entitled *Princes*, all
ministers *Senators*; life members of the council, *présidents* of the *Corps
législatif* and archbishops became *Comtes*; all presidents of electoral colleges, *premiers présidents* and *procureurs* of the courts, bishops, and
mayors of *bonnes villes* became *Barons*; and members of the Legion of
Honour, *Chevaliers*. Moreover these titles, if supported by a sufficient
income, varying from £10,000 for *princes* to £150 for *chevaliers*, became
hereditary. Thus by a stroke of the pen Napoleon created a new peerage,
to any rank of which he could add at will—as he did when, after the
campaign of 1809, he raised Berthier, Masséna and Davout to the dignity
of *Prince*. In all, he created thirty-one Dukes, 452 Counts, 1500 Barons
and 1474 Chevaliers.

Monetary exactions in time of war were now pooled, and distributed at
Napoleon's pleasure: small pensions of from £25 to £500 to men and
officers of lower rank, larger sums to generals, ministers, and members
of the new nobility. More than 5000 of these received grants in cash or
estates sufficient to buy a house in Paris and to live in some style: Berthier,
for instance, got as much as £70,000, and some thirty military or civil
dignitaries received from £2500 to £5000 each. The new nobility was
also a new plutocracy.[8]

Statesmen, generals and high officials were not the only beneficiaries of
the new regime. Bonaparte's benevolent despotism must be felt by every
class, and in every corner of the country. How this was done may best be
judged by taking a cross-section of his correspondence during the two
years from the spring of 1801 to the spring of 1803.

The interests of the middle-class business men, traders and shop-keepers
were considered in the attention paid to the maintenance of order: the
reform of the *gendarmerie*, the safe-guarding of the *diligence* service, the
building and repair of roads, and the construction of canals—this is, for
instance, the largest item in the estimate of expenditure under the head
of *ponts et chaussées* for the Year XII. Both in Paris, and when he is on
tour in the provinces, Bonaparte makes a point of visiting factories, and
encouraging local industries. He orders furniture for his study at the
Tuileries from the cabinet-makers of Beauvais. He plans an annual exhibition of the products of French industry, and distributes prizes for the
best exhibits. The national forests are not forgotten. He even starts a
scheme for developing coral-fisheries off the coasts of Tunis and Algiers.

A member of the *Institut*, he is interested by inclination as well as
policy in art, literature and science. He commissions pictures of his victories, acquires the Théâtre Français for dramatic productions approved

by the government, and draws up a list of the ten best painters, sculptors, composers, singers, architects, and 'artists of other kinds whose talents deserve public attention.' He is prepared to spend £500 on Fulton's *Nautilus*, the first submarine; and Fulton's steam-boat was seen on the Seine in 1803: but these experiments were not followed up. He orders the publication of the scientific and learned results of the Egyptian expedition. He interests himself in the appointment of a professor of Latin at the Collège de France. He instructs the Minister of the Interior to offer a prize of £150 for experiments in *le fluide galvanique*, and £300 to any-one advancing scientific knowledge as much as Franklin or Volta have done. He has been reading Lalande's *Mécanique céleste* (which the astronomer had dedicated to him), and regrets that the force of circum-stances has diverted him from a scientific career. He invites the professor of mineralogy at the *Muséum d'Histoire naturelle* to write a school text-book. He instructs the Minister of the Interior to continue Garat's stipend, as the 'founder of the French school' of singing. The *Institut* was ordered to draw up a *tableau général* showing French progress in science and literature since 1789, and to make a further report every five years. When Vestris, the dancer, asked leave to take up an engagement in London worth 1300 guineas, on the ground that he could not otherwise pay his debts, Bonaparte refused it, but called for a report on his debts, and prom-ised him a pension on his retirement.[9]

Bonaparte was well aware of the good impression produced by a Civil List. Mlle de Vicq, whose father had built the Saint-Quentin canal, fell into sickness and destitution: she was offered a pension, and apartments at Versailles. Places in the Prytanée, with provision for free education, were granted to a grandson of Buffon, the naturalist, to a son of the revolutionary Desmoulins, to a young soldier of fifteen who had lost a leg in battle, and to ten boys from the island of Elba. Even Charlotte Robespierre, the sister of Maximilien and Augustin, was given £30, and an allowance of £7 10s. a month.

Meanwhile the Paris crowd was gratified and entertained by a presen-tation of flags captured in Italy, with an oration in praise of Moreau, Masséna and Berthier; and July 14th was celebrated with a parade of troops, followed by a display of fireworks. The bronze horses from St. Mark's at Venice were erected on pedestals in the *grande grille* of the Tuileries; the Quai d'Orsay was rebuilt, and the rue de Rivoli constructed. Hymns were commissioned for a fête in honour of Joan of Arc. Even more to the public taste was the attention paid to the old problem of providing cheap bread for the Paris poor, and work for the unemployed, on canals, quays, demolitions, road-making and so on; and to the proper management of the Enfants-Trouvés and the Invalides, in which so many poor Parisians began or ended their existence.[10]

6

Nobody was more aware than Bonaparte of the necessity of backing bribery with compulsion. He was in a position to put into practice the maxim which Robespierre had enunciated as a theory of government: 'The mainspring of government in times of peace is virtue: in times of revolution it is virtue and intimidation—virtue, without which intimidation is disastrous, and intimidation, without which virtue is impotent.' But he did not in fact believe the people, as Robespierre claimed, to be virtuous; nor did he distinguish between the people and the people's enemies. The clear-cut distinctions of 1794 were now blurred. All classes—rich and poor, propertied and proletariat, old nobility and *nouveaux riches*, Jacobins and royalists—were equal and prostrate beneath the Imperial bureaucracy. One formula must suffice for them all.

This formula was found in the police—*police* in the continental sense of the whole body of rules for the maintenance of public order and security, together with the agents necessary for administering them. The basis of this structure was the Code Napoléon: then came the judicial system, with its hierachy of courts and judges: then the police, in our sense of the word, and the prisons: then the Censorship: and menacingly, alongside of all this, military courts, special tribunals, arbitrary imprisonment and deportation. It is important to inquire how heavy a burden this system laid upon the country.

In dealing with the courts Bonaparte did little more than re-enact (Law of 27 *ventôse An* VIII) a system which was one of the best creations of the Revolution and which has remained substantially unaltered ever since. He concentrated, as usual, upon controlling the persons who carried it out. The revolutionary method appointing judges by popular election had hardly outlived the Directory. As Consul for life, Bonaparte selected J.P.s (*juges de paix*) from lists sent in by the cantonal assemblies, and nominated judges of appeal to the senate. Though judges were nominally appointed for life, they were put on probation for the first five years, and subjected to a series of 'purges,' to make sure that only efficient and loyal men survived. At the same time the jury system—a thoroughly foreign institution which had never thrived on French soil, and which Bonaparte disliked as an intrusion of amateurism into professional affairs—was reduced to a minimum.

Unfortunately the criminal courts were disfigured by the restoration under the penal code of such punishments as public decapitation and exposure of the body, cutting off the right hand of parricides, branding, the pillory, and life sentences to hard labour.

When Sir Samuel Romilly visited Paris in 1802 he made a point of attending the courts. He found the *Tribunal criminel* sitting under busts of Brutus and Rousseau (those of Marat and Le Peletier had been removed), without a jury; a main feature of the procedure was the public examination of the prisoner by the judges. He witnessed an execution of a murderer by guillotine in the Place de Grève, the victim wearing the *chemise rouge* of a parricide, amidst a great crowd of spectators, principally women.

The various kinds of prison—*maisons de correction, maisons de force, bagnes*—were filled not only through the courts, but also by a revival of the *lettres de cachet* system, which the Revolution had mercifully destroyed: an order signed by the *grand juge* and *ministre de police* was enough to put anyone in prison.

An English reader may naturally inquire whether, as an offset to this surrender of public liberties under the Napoleonic regime, the individual citizen had any security against such arbitrary arrest and imprisonment. The answer is that the only equivalent to our *Habeas Corpus* Act was Article 46 of the Constitution of the Year VIII. This said that if the government were informed of any conspiracy against the state it could arrest suspected persons, but that if they were not either released or brought to trial within ten days, this 'constituted the crime of arbitrary detention on the part of the minister signing the warrant of arrest.' What then? During the Revolution there had always been the 'open eye' of the Cordeliers Club or some Popular Society to take up such cases; and the National Assembly might be moved by any deputy to intervene. But now the assemblies were impotent; there were no popular clubs or societies; and the only remedy lay with two committees of the Senate, one dealing with liberty of press, and the other with liberty of the individual.

How did this *Commission de la liberté individuelle* set about its vital task? When a case of detention for more than ten days was reported to it, it invited the minister responsible either to release the prisoner or to put him on trial. It repeated its invitation twice more, at intervals of a month. If still nothing was done, it convoked the Senate and reported 'that there was a strong presumption that so-and-so is being detained arbitrarily.' Thereupon the *Corps législatif* denounced the minister to the *Haute-Cour* of justice. This procedure was claimed by its authors to be a triumph of Holy Liberty. But in fact, during the ten years of its existence the committee never declared a single person to be arbitrarily imprisoned, and never reported a minister to the Senate; the *Haute-Cour* nevet met. The principle adopted for dealing with complaints was that 'the Committee will always regard itself as a sentinel set by the constitution to safeguard individual liberty against any really arbitrary attempt (*toute entreprise véritablement arbitraire*), but it will never forget that a state cannot be maintained except by the firm, just, and considered action of its government.'

Of 116 prisoners dealt with during 1804-05, the minister appealed to released forty-four; seventeen were said to be outside the jurisdiction of the committee; thirty-three were adjourned for further information; and twenty-one were still under discussion at the end of the year. Once, and once only, the committee appealed to Napoleon himself; and the Emperor, writing from Warsaw, authorized the release of a government contractor who had been wrongfully arrested six months before. There was, too, the instance of Mme Chaumette, a paper-seller, who had spent three and a half years in prison without ever having been brought to trial: she was apparently the widow of the notorious Jacobin guillotined in 1794, and therefore suspect. After four years she at last obtained her release. It must be added that release more often than not meant banishment, under police supervision, to some place outside the control of the committee. Such was *Habeas Corpus* as understood by the Imperial regime.

Statistics of the number of prisoners are not easy to obtain. The official version (Montalivet, 1813) was that the number of criminal charges diminished, between 1801 and 1811, from 8500 to 6000, the number of convictions from 8000 to 5500, and the number of death sentences from 882 to 392. During the same period, according to Montvéran, the number of executions in England, with a population less than half that of France, went up from 3400 to 6400. But the number of convict prisons (*bagnes*) grew from three to nine, and the convicts in them from 5416 in 1792-1801 to 10,342 in 1802-1810, 14,539 in 1811, 14,979 in 1812, 16,213 in 1813 and 16,305 in 1814. The number of state prisoners in the Temple at Vincennes, Mont Saint-Michel, and elsewhere by 1814 has been put at over 2500.

Probably the police system, however arbitrary, however brutal, weighed less heavily on the country than the supervision exercised through a dozen different channels over private conduct and opinion. The first punished the licence of the few: the second prevented the liberty of the many. It was no longer a crime to be a priest, an aristocrat, or an *émigré*; no decent citizen went in fear of denunciation or arrest. But no one was sure that his conduct was not being reported to Fouché by some *commissaire de police*, or his letters opened in the post, or his character taken away by one of the Emperor's private correspondents. There were spies everywhere. It was Bonaparte's aim to know what everyone of consequence was thinking and doing—to have all their names on his lists, to be able to put his finger on them quickly and silently in case of need. The atmosphere of Paris society was like that of a school managed by an efficient and unimaginative headmaster. He liked to play off one authority against another, to check the reports of the prefects by those of senators in their *arrondissements*, or of *conseillers* employed on special missions. He was constantly exchanging information about the movements of suspected persons with Fouché and his subordinates at Rome, Florence,

Turin, and Amsterdam. He would collate information received from the Foreign Office, the Home Office, the Treasury, and the War Office; or play off the *gendarmerie* against the Paris police. He knew less than he supposed, or than his victims suspected: but it was enough to make life uneasy and insecure.[11]

Literary men, editors, and theatrical managers were subject to a continual and harassing censorship. The most dangerous and the most intangible enemy of any regime in France, since the Revolution sanctified liberty of expression, had been public opinion. This did not express itself, as it would now, through meetings and petitions organized by political parties, or in daily papers with huge circulations representing widely held points of view, or trading upon the non-political interests of the many to propagate the views of the few. France, which had practically no papers before 1789, had since then produced a rich crop of small ephemeral journals, the work of individual editors or of groups of writers and printers anxious to publicize their views. Some sixty papers appeared for the first time in 1789, another forty or so in 1790, another two dozen in 1791, at least as many again in 1792, another dozen (it was by now becoming dangerous for the Opposition) in 1793, and even a final crop (most of which were short-lived) in 1794. Only a few of these, patronized by the government of the day, enjoyed large circulations. The semi-official *Moniteur* alone achieved the size of a modern paper: the rest were in *octavo* or *duodecimo*, seldom ran to more than four pages and appeared only once or twice a week. They were the more dangerous because they were cheap; the cost of an annual subscription to a daily paper was from 36s. to 48s., whereas that of a daily paper in London was £8 10s. a year. They were without exception partisan, often bitterly personal, libellous, scurrilous. No government could afford to leave them alone. The old remedy was to break up the presses and confiscate the type of Opposition papers; or in extreme cases, such as that of Desmoulins and the *Vieux Cordelier*, to arrest and guillotine the editor.

Bonaparte, who had suffered from the attacks of the Opposition press during his campaign in Italy, was not likely to put up with the slanders or indiscretions of irresponsible journalists. In the matter of military or naval news they were not unwilling to conform to government orders. They had helped to mystify the British Admiralty as to the destination of the Egyptian expedition. They accepted Fouché's warning not to report the fleet movements in the spring of 1801. But the printing of news, whether home or foreign, was the least alarming function of these papers. The problem was to restrain their expressions of opinion. No formal censorship had been set up during the Revolution, and Bonaparte did not wish to affront a ten years' tradition in favour of liberty of libel. It was easier and more effective to limit the number of papers, and to supervise them. When he became First Consul there were still seventy-three political journals in Paris. By an *arrêté* of January 17th, 1800, he arbitrarily suppressed sixty of them, and prohibited the publication of any more. By the end of the year only nine remained. During the next twelve months the number of subscribers to such papers decreased from 50,000 to 35,000. At the same time the non-political journals, encouraged by the government, increased from twenty-two to thirty-eight, and their subscribers from 4000 to 7000.

As for the *Moniteur*, Napoleon did not directly subsidize it, but he followed the practice of the revolutionary governments in ordering copies for circulation to the armies in the field, or for propaganda purposes in foreign parts. Its political articles were contributed by himself (as for instance an article in April 1801, giving his version of the Copenhagen affair, and accusing England of being responsible for the assassination of Tsar Paul), or by his Foreign Minister: many of its articles on Home Affairs came from the Minister of that department; and official communications of various kinds appeared in other columns: only under the head of literature, poetry and drama, was the editor relatively free from government supervision.

Napoleon's correspondence shows how his supervision of these tolerated papers was carried out. Fouché is told (July 1801) to prevent the papers from publishing reports of English origin damaging to French trade; or to deal with an undesirable article in the *Journal des Défenseurs* suggesting that the government discriminated between the clergy on theological grounds. Early in June 1803, the Minister of Justice is instructed to censure two editors for reproducing British propaganda from German papers. In 1806, finding that the various church papers showed differences of opinion (did they ever fail to do so?), Napoleon decided to combine them all into a single paper, to be sent to all their subscribers: it would be called the *Journal des curés*, and its editors would be appointed by the Cardinal-archbishop of Paris. But soon even this paper fell under the accusation of Ultramontanism. Again, in 1807, Fouché received from the Emperor a long criticism and complaint of the *Courrier* and the *Journal des Débats*. Three years later the provincial press was limited to one paper a department, and it was ruled that from next year onwards only four papers should appear in Paris, and those under police supervision. The rest were confiscated and suppressed.

An interesting *Memorial respecting the present state of the British Press* issued in 1812 pointed out that whilst England had led France in the invention of Colonel Congreve's rockets and Colonel Shrapnell's spherical case-shot, 'there is just one circumstance in which the little Corsican usurper has got the start of us,' viz. the use of the Press. 'It is a mortifying truth that he has done more mischief by means of the *Moniteur of Paris* than he has ever effected by the united efforts of the cannon and the sword.' The writer urged that, without interfering with the liberty of the London press, especially the eighteen Sunday papers, to print libellous and scandalous matter, and to misrepresent the policy and position of the country, a ministerial paper should be published, to inform the public of the true state of affairs.

It was no doubt to take advantage of this feeling that Lewis Goldsmith, whom Talleyrand had employed for some years to edit from Paris an anti-British paper, the *Argus*, for foreign consumption (it was distributed, for instance, in the West Indies, and amongst Britishers interned at Verdun), when he was dismissed, returned to England and began to publish in 1811 the *Anti-Gallican*, afterwards called the *British Monitor*. But the author of the mendacious *Crimes of the Cabinets* (1801) attacking the British 'plans of aggression for the annihilation of the liberties of France' had some difficulty in explaining how he came to write, ten years later, his scurrilous *Secret History of the Cabinet of Bonaparte*, and was distrusted on both sides of the Channel.

It was not enough to censor the daily press. Any publication might endanger Napoleon's regime. Hitherto he had relied on information supplied by the Minister of Police, and by his 'Librarian' Ripault, who had orders to read and analyse all the books, papers, plays, lectures and posters that appeared in Paris, and to send in daily or weekly reports. Or he had required individual publishers to submit two copies of every book, before publication, to the *bureau central de la police*. The only possible step left was to set up a regular censorship. This he did by appointing in February 1810, a *directeur de l'imprimerie* and a distinguished body of *censeurs impériaux*, by closing down 97 out of the 157 presses in Paris, and by requiring publishers to take out a licence and subscribe to an oath. The senatorial committee that protected the liberty of the press now had nothing to do, for there was no more liberty to protect.[12]

What did all this mean for individual writers? In February 1803, Madame de Staël, who had been forbidden to visit Paris since the publication of her father's book the year before, was reported to be at Melun. Bonaparte wrote to the Minister of Justice telling him to send a police officer to 'have her taken back at once over the frontier, and sent either to the country of her late husband (Sweden), or to her father's home (Switzerland). This foreign intriguer (he said) must not remain in France, where her family have done so much harm.' When Sales wrote an 'anti-revolutionary pamphlet' Cambacérès was told to see if he could not get him turned out of the *Institut*. Lalande, in 1805, reprinted Maréchal's *Dictionnaire des athées*: he was forbidden to publish anything again. The *Mercure* was suppressed for an article Chateaubriand wrote in it in 1807

—though it was he who had done more than anyone to publicize the Concordat by his *Génie du christianisme* five years before.

Dramatists were no freer than other writers. Bonaparte held the same
view of the educative value of the stage as his old patron Robespierre, and
was as nervous as any Jacobin lest anti-government sentiments might raise
a laugh or a cheer in audiences always ready to find political and topical
references in the play of the moment. Fouché, the strange confidant of so
many of Bonaparte's literary prejudices, was told that no references should
be allowed to historical events that might reflect on the present regime.
Henri IV is a dangerous subject, and should be vetoed. Couldn't the
author (Raynouard) write instead a tragedy showing the succession to
the French throne of 'a saviour of the nation'—someone like the *Saul* of
Handel's oratorio—'a great man succeeding a degenerate king?' He
insists on the suppression of a couplet in the *Tableau des Sabines* referring to himself, and censures the mayor of Bordeaux for allowing a reference on the local stage to 'Louis king of Tuscany.' He objects to the
staging of any sacred subject, such as an opera introducing the death of
Abel: mythological or historical ballets may be given, but nothing alle-
gorical: the 'Rape of the Sabine Women' is the kind of thing wanted, but
he would prefer something 'more appropriate to modern conditions.'

In the later years of the Empire the Baron de Pommereul and his
assistants at the hôtel Carnavalet reviewed the French classics with an
inquisitorial eye. Voltaire's *Mérope* was censored because it showed a
queen in mourning for the absence of her two sons—it might be taken
for France praying for the restoration of the Comtes de Provence and
d'Artois? and the *Athalie* of Racine because it contained in the line

Le sang de nos rois crie, et n'est point écouté

—a possible reminder of the execution of the Duc d'Enghien.

One way or another, Napoleon might flatter himself that his literary
men were as well drilled as his clergy or his armies. But it never seems to
have occurred to him—though himself a great reader and once ambitious
to be an author—that such a system was not likely to produce good literature. If it did not (he thought) it was because it was not properly administered. 'People complain,' he wrote to Cambacérès, 'that we have no
literature. It is the fault of the Home Minister'; he 'ought to set about
getting some decent stuff written.'

Artists and architects were less subject to censorship than writers or
publishers only because they could not so easily offend. Most governments
and all dictators need buildings, statues and pictures to advertise their
fame: it is an unlikely accident if their taste is good, or if they allow any
creative freedom to the artist. Napoleon's requirements for buildings or

monuments were that they should be big, lasting, quickly erected and cheap. For materials he preferred granite and metal. Though he admired Fontainebleau and Nôtre Dame, the designs he preferred were plain and geometrical. He would have liked the Albert Hall, the Nelson Column (but with elephants instead of lions), and the entrance gate to Euston Station. If architects met his tastes, he was prepared to spend sums of almost Bourbon dimensions upon imperial arches, pillars and palaces; some £5 millions between 1804 and 1813 in Paris, and £7 millions in the provinces.

Painters and sculptors too profited by the Emperor's patronage, and had little scruple in producing works likely to attract his favour. One of his first acts after Brumaire (February 1800) was to order for the Tuileries statues of Demosthenes, Alexander, Hannibal, Scipio, Brutus, Cicero, Cato, Caesar, Gustavus Adolphus, Marlborough, Washington, Frederick the Great, Mirabeau, and nine other patron saints of the new regime. Thereafter he spent on an average £16,000 a year on pictures and sculpture. A series of statues commissioned for the Salon of 1806 worked out at £700 each, and sixteen pictures ordered at the same time were priced at £400 each. In both cases it was ruled that any artist failing to send in his work by a fixed date would be disqualified for any future commission. But though his motives and his taste were questionable, it cannot be denied that the Emperor's patronage kept the artists of the age alive, and gave its name to a style which left its mark on the history of art.[18]

7

Napoleon's censorship of press and stage was the negative side of his plan to control public opinion. Its positive side was his educational system. Nothing, in any country, and at any time, is a better test of the character of a government than its educational policy; and nothing in the Napoleonic regime is more characteristic.

The revolutionary Assemblies had held high ideas of their duty to educate the people, but had done very little about it. They inherited from the monarchy the notion that public education was best left to the church, which through its curés and schoolmasters taught reading and writing and perhaps a little Latin to a bright boy here and there, and through its bishops might pay for his further education at some collège in a neighbouring cathedral city, and ultimately send him to a University. Others, of course, went through the same course at their parents' expense. Most of the lower and middle-class leaders of the Revolution had passed through these semi-clerical schools and colleges, and some of them had taken minor orders, before deciding for a more congenial career in journalism or at the bar.

The disendownment of the church under the Revolution, and the requirement that clerical teachers as well as parochial clergy should take the oath demanded under the Civil Constitution of the Clergy, practically destroyed this means of education. The revolutionary Assemblies had intended to put a national system in its place, providing both for primary and secondary education at the public cost. But although more than one Education Bill was introduced and discussed, nothing was done, until, during the last days of its existence, the Convention set up *écoles centrales*—County secondary schools (as we should call them), with a liberal curriculum and picked teachers—in the main provincial centres (there was to be one for each department): but the primary schools envisaged at the same time (October 25th, 1795) never came into existence.

Bonaparte and his *Brumairien* friends did not like these county schools. Their teaching did not include the classics, or the Catholic faith: it was too liberal, too detached from political and civil utilities—in a word, too academic, or, to use the fashionable reproach for revolutionary high-thinking, it smacked of *idéologie*. Yet Fourcroy, the author of the system that replaced them, had to admit that they were 'the refuge of all the men most skilled in useful knowledge,' and 'one of the most remarkable achievements of the republican regime.' Bonaparte himself, whose self-education had been liberal enough, yet remembered with a gratitude that increased with years what he owed to the more specialized and disciplined teaching of the *écoles militaires*. He did not believe in education for education's sake, but in education for the service of the state. The state needed not only soldiers but also administrators, magistrates, experts in every branch of civil life. He would have schools organized to produce a perfect personnel for the public services, schools in which military and religious discipline would be nicely blended, and the classical basis of the old eighteenth-century culture correct the revolutionary fondness for 'national' French.

On the ruins of the old college of Saint-Louis le Grand, where Robespierre and his friends Fréron and Desmoulins had learnt Roman republicanism and Voltairian anti-clericalism, the Directory had preserved the *Prytanée*, in which *professeurs* still instructed *boursiers* and *internes* in the old liberal sciences. Bonaparte's first essay in educational reform (March 22nd, 1800, July 6th, 1801) was to reorganize the *Prytanée* as one of a group of State-supported boarding schools, competing with and ousting the *écoles centrales*, which were finally closed in 1803-04.

Whether he went to Paris, Fontainebleau, or Saint-Cyr, or to the affiliated schools at Brussels, Compiègne, or Lyon, the boy of eleven or twelve now found himself dressed in a blue uniform with metal buttons, drilled twice a week, marched from class-room to chapel and counter-marched from chapel to class-room, and forced to obey a code of rules less like those of a school than of a barracks. Many of these boys were sons of officers who had distinguished themselves in the French service, and so got their education free. It was a charity that Bonaparte liked to exercise. It earned him easy gratitude, and provided cheap recruits for the public services.

In 1802-03 the *Prytanées* were supplemented by the *Lycées*, and by the *écoles secondaires*. The forty-five *Lycées* (of which only thirty-nine actually came into existence) set up under the *loi Fourcroy* of May 1st, 1802, carried Bonaparte's idea of a military-religious education a step further. They contained, by the spring of 1805, more than 3000 state scholars (*élèves nationaux*). Like some modern Catholic public schools, they were under dual management: lay *administrateurs* (who mere married) supervised discipline, whilst *professeurs* (who were bachelors, and therefore might include clergy, and could be secured for lower salaries) were responsible for the teaching. In a long letter to the Minister for Home Affairs on June 11th, 1801, Bonaparte explained his ideas of Secondary Education. Boys under twelve, divided into classes of twenty-five, were to learn reading, writing and arithmetic, with the elements of grammar; elementary Latin; drawing, dancing, and the use of arms; with some natural history, geography, and ancient history. Boys over twelve would be divided into a civil and a military side: the first would go through a full course of classics, rhetoric, and philosophy; the second would study mathematics, astronomy, fortification, planning, etc.—even the principles of physics and chemistry, how to serve a gun, and so forth.

The *Prytanées* and *Lycées* were by no means the only secondary schools recognized by the Napoleonic government. The *écoles secondaires* allowed for in Fourcroy's scheme soon numbered 700, some supported by the *communes*, and some by private enterprise. Napoleon himself, when dealing with a demand for higher fees, to make the *Lycées* pay their way, remarked (February 16th, 1805), 'There are plenty of excellent secondary schools which give a full education for no more than £20 a year.' In fact the prefects' returns for 1805 show that there were by then 1083 secondary schools in the country, with attendances ranging from 200 at Rennes or 450 at Orleans to over 2000 at Lyon.

On the other hand, the primary schools that Fourcroy also visualized in his scheme of education, but which he left to local enterprise, never progressed much beyond the point they had reached under the old regime. Here and there an energetic prefect or bishop might organize such a school. But in more than one department half the *communes* had no teacher, and there was no money to pay for their training. The country people as a whole remained uneducated and illiterate.

Yet an uneducated people is not necessarily an unintelligent one. The Revolution had destroyed the schools, but it had inaugurated an informal and indirect education through its appeal to popular support—its papers, its posters, its laws, its elections, its meetings and speeches, even the singing of the *Marseillaise*. By breaking down local and provincial boundaries it had created a French nation, and popularized the French language. So it went on. Not all Napoleon's insistence on the value of Latin, which he perhaps thought the proper language for the new Empire of Charlemagne (he ordered a Latin oration to be pronounced in honour of his marriage to Marie-Louise) could obliterate the impression made on the public mind by the constant use of French in his laws, his proclamations, and the thousand and one documents issuing from his ministerial departments. This was not a literary or academic education; but it did something to open and enlighten 30 million minds—perhaps a little more than was intended or appreciated by the head of a dictatorial regime.[14]

8

His experience of the *Prytanées* and *Lycées* soon led Napoleon to a fresh step in the standardization of education. Early in 1805 he dictated a Note outlining an Order of Teachers modelled on that of Ignatius Loyola. His tidy military mind envisaged 'a teaching Corporation of all the *proviseurs, censeurs,* and *professeurs* in the Empire under chiefs like the Generals and Provincials of the Jesuits': a hierarchy, with promotion from lower to higher, and the Emperor's approval and patronage as the first prize of the profession. 'Everyone knows how important the Jesuits were. It would not be long before the same prestige attached to the Corporation of Teachers, if people saw a man whose education had begun in the *Lycée* picked out for his talents to be himself a teacher, promoted from stage to stage, and finding himself, before the end of his career, in the front ranks of state officials.' Then he warms to his subject. 'Of all political questions this is perhaps the most important. There will be no stability in the state until there is a body of teachers with fixed principles. Till children are taught whether they ought to be Republicans or Monarchists, Catholics or Unbelievers, and so on, there may indeed be a state, but it cannot become a nation.'

So there came into existence, by the law of May 10th, 1806, and the decree of March 17th, 1808, 'under the title of Imperial University, a body with sole responsibility for public teaching and education throughout the Empire.' It was more powerful than a Board of Education, and better disciplined than a National Union of Teachers. Every college and secondary school in the country existed by its leave and worked under its eye: every teacher took an oath to obey his superiors and to keep the rules of his profession—as, for instance, to report where he was spending his vacations, and not to visit Paris without leave of the Grand Master of the Order; if he broke the rules he was liable to imprisonment. The only promotion was from the worse paid position of teacher to the better paid one of manager. But the teacher had little hope of rising to the summit of the hierarchy, where (in Paris alone) a Grand Master, a Chancellor, a Treasurer, thirty Councillors and ten Inspectors drawn from the official hierarchy, with as many subordinates, enjoyed salaries ranging ·from £300 to £5000 a year.

This University was Napoleon's Board of Education. During the six years that most boys spent on their education, between the extreme ages of nine and eighteen, they followed the course prescribed by the University—two years of grammar, two of humanities, one of rhetoric, and one of higher mathematics; they competed for University prizes; they received University degrees. If they did not all turn out alike, it was because it proved impossible to enforce complete uniformity on the communal and private secondary schools; because the system never included the education of children under nine; and because Napoleon, who standardized everything else, never succeeded in standardizing human nature. Nevertheless, the Imperial University was an all-important part of Napoleon's France, and has left its mark on a national education whose boast it long remained that the Minister of Education in Paris could tell at any moment of the day what every child in the country was being taught. Jacobins might object that this system was more in line with the old regime than with the new, that it had reimposed upon the schools the dead hand of Catholicism, and that, like other Napoleonic institutions, it substituted for a larger number of ill-paid officials a smaller number of highly paid. Such, they were to learn, is the dictatorial way of life.[15]

As for Napoleon's views on the education of girls, without which this survey would be incomplete, they cannot be better explained than by quoting a Note he dictated from Finkenstein in Poland the day after the battle of Friedland (May 15th, 1807): for he prided himself on being able to concentrate his mind on any subject, however remote.

'What are the girls brought up at Écouen going to be taught? You must begin with religion in all its strictness. Don't allow any compromise on this point. Religion is an all-important matter in a public school for girls. It is the mother's surest safeguard, and the husband's. What we ask of education is not that girls should think, but that they should believe . . . In the *lycées* I only prescribed the necessary minimum. At Écouen things must be entirely different. Nearly all the exact knowledge taught there must be that of the Gospel. I want the place to produce, not women of charm, but women of virtue: they must be attractive because they have high principles and warm hearts, not because they are witty or amusing . . . Every day the pupils must have regular prayers, hear mass, and learn the catechism.

'In addition the girls must be taught writing, arithmetic, and elementary French, so that they may know how to spell; and they ought to learn a little history and geography: but care must be taken not to let them see any Latin, or other foreign languages. The elder girls can be taught a little botany, and be taken through an easy course of physics or natural history. But that too has certain embarrassments. The teaching of physics must be limited to what is necessary to prevent gross ignorance and silly superstition, and must confine itself to facts, and not indulge in reasoning which directly or indirectly touches on first causes. . . .

'But the main thing is to keep them all occupied, for three-quarters of the year, working with their hands. They must learn to make stockings, shirts, and embroidery, and to do all kinds of women's work . . . I should like every girl who leaves Écouen, and finds herself at the head of a small household, to know how to make her own frocks, mend her husband's things, make clothes for her babies, provide her little family with such occasional delicacies as can be afforded by a provincial house-keeper, nurse her husband and children when they are ill, and know in these matters, because she has been taught it beforehand, what invalids have learnt by experience. . . .

'Dancing is necessary for the health of the pupils; but it must be a cheerful sort of dancing, not the kind they indulge in at the Opera. They may have music, too, but only singing. . . .

'With the exception of the Headmaster, all men must be excluded from the school. No man must ever enter within its walls, under any pretext whatsoever. Even the gardening must be done by women. My intention is that in this respect the establishment should be as strictly ruled as a convent. The Headmistress herself must not be allowed to receive men, except in the parlour; and if it is impossible to exclude a girl's relations in cases of serious illness, at least they must only be admitted by special permission of the Grand Chancellor of the Legion of Honour . . . I need hardly say that the only women employed in the school must be elderly spinsters, or widows without children; that they must be entirely under the control of the Headmistress; and that they must never receive men, or go outside the walls of the school. It would no doubt be equally super-fluous to remark that nothing is worse than the idea of letting young girls appear on the stage, or stimulating rivalry among them by allowing them to take places in form. Competition should be banned: we don't want to rouse their passions, or to give play to the vanity which is one of the liveliest instincts of their sex.' [16]

One last matter by which any government may well be judged is its treatment of the Jews. There were, it was estimated in 1806, 64,000 Jews in France of whom 26,000 lived in the two departments of Haut and Bas Rhin. Relieved of their religious and civil disabilities since 1791, and surviving a recurrence of anti-semitism during the Terror, they had under the Directory and Consulate more and more assimilated themselves to Frenchmen, and played a part in business and affairs. But they were still a society and a church apart; and in 1805 Napoleon had to make up his mind whether, as proposed by his Minister of Religion, they should be included along with Catholics and Protestants in the settlement of the Concordat.

Napoleon liked to identify the 'charity' of the New Testament with Catholicism, and the 'cruelty' of the Old Testament with Judaism. He shared the common Catholic dislike of Jews, and exaggerated the extent to which, long driven out of other trades, they had given themselves to money-lending. When the matter was discussed by the *Conseil d'état* in April 1806, he insisted that it was dangerous, especially in the frontier departments of Alsace, to allow all the rights of French citizenship to a people who were not merely a sect, but a foreign nation, and capable of any crime.

But on second thoughts, and in view of the opposition of the *Conseil d'état*, he accepted the decree of May 30th, which arranged for the summoning of a Jewish assembly to regulate their affairs. On July 26th, 1806, seventy-four deputies of the Jewish communities, chosen by the prefects, met in St. John's chapel, by the Hôtel de Ville of Paris. They were faced by a *questionnaire* in twelve heads, dealing with the relations between Jews and Christians, their obligations as French citizens, the organization of their community, and the practice of usury. The deputies having returned tactful answers to these rather provocative questions, Napoleon once more intervened. Why should not the whole question be settled by convoking at Paris a meeting of the Grand Sanhedrin, the Jews' Parliament, their final authority in civil, religious and political affairs? Why should not this body, in return for Napoleon's guarantee of Jewish civil and religious liberties, draw up under his guidance (another Moses) a new Law, an addition to the Old Testament and the Talmud, regulating the French-Jewish community?

No sooner said than done. The Synagogues were circularized; and on February 9th, 1807, the opening session was attended by forty-five rabbis and twenty-six laymen drawn from twenty-eight departments. But now, instead of a *questionnaire* they received a body of Instructions from the Emperor, which he had drawn up in the depths of Poland (they were dated, 'Posen, November 29th') and in which he laid down rules for the relations between Jews and Christians, and for the government of the Jewish community, together with various limitations to their freedom of business, especially money-lending. But the two essential provisions, no doubt, in his mind, were the obligation of the Jews to pay taxes, and to provide recruits for the army.

The Sanhedrin could do nothing but give solemn form to these regulations, and on March 9th it was dissolved. Its work was not epoch-making, neither was it ineffective. The Jewish community continued to assimilate itself to its surroundings a little more rapidly than before.[17]

When the Peace of Amiens ended the nine years of war that had prevented Englishmen from crossing the Channel, some thousands of that inquisitive race took the opportunity to visit Paris. A seven-weeks' stay, including hotels, restaurants and sight-seeing, cost £30. They found the French people cheerful, friendly, and of course talkative. Dancing seemed to be more than ever their favourite amusement. The Palais-Royal, renamed *Maison Égalité*, was still the centre of popular entertainment. But the seven hundred coffee houses where the revolutionists had disputed and caballed were now supplemented by luxurious eating-houses with elaborate bills of fare: at Versailles even the Petit Trianon had become a restaurant. The streets were better kept and lighted than in the old days: there were fewer private carriages, but more public vehicles. At night-time coaches and cabs had to carry bells and lamps. The police were more efficient than they used to be. Picture galleries, libraries and museums were open to the public, and full of interesting exhibits, mostly looted from Italy during the war of 1796-97. In the Musée des Monuments Français one might see tombs of French kings taken from Saint-Denis, and other relics of the pre-revolutionary church.

There were living relics, too, of the old regime—surviving members of the *noblesse*, or returned *émigrés*, who lamented the old society and refused to recognize the new—whether the official aristocracy created by the Consular government, or the *nouveaux riches* who owed their money and position to exploiting the revolution and the war. And there were Jacobins too—terrorists and anti-clericals who had lost their political fanaticism, but who could not forgive Bonaparte for becoming a dictator and re-establishing the church. It seemed to staid Englishmen an artificial, uneasy, rather hectic and vulgar atmosphere. But, as in Italy under Mussolini, what had been lost in 'old-world' glamour had been gained in efficiency, comfort and cleanliness. With his patronage of science and his insistence on hard work and 'value for money,' Bonaparte had substituted a reality of tangible value for the too expensive dreams of the revolutionists. This might not be Utopia; but neither was it Cloud-cuckoo-land. It was a Welfare Dictatorship.[18]

9

Six days after the Tribunate had accepted the proposal that the First Consul should become the Emperor of the French, and eight days before the Senate had confirmed it, Bonaparte asked Caprara to sound the Pope as to the possibility of his coming to Paris (or it might be Aix-la-Chapelle) to officiate at his coronation. After three months' difficult negotiations Pius consented.

The idea had been in Bonaparte's mind for some time. He had taken the opportunity, early in 1803, of the Pope's courtesy to Joséphine to ingratiate himself, hoping to efface the bad impression left by the business of the Organic Articles. On January 22nd, 1803, when sending to Paris the cardinals' hats promised to certain French bishops, Pius had written a personal letter to 'his dear daughter in Christ, Victoria Bonaparte,' and she had replied, sending him a rochet that 'she had had made for him' and for which Bonaparte had paid £350. The letter of thanks was addressed a little more accurately to 'Joséphine-Victoria': under whatever name, she might (the Pope seems to have thought) influence Bonaparte towards piety and the interests of Rome.

It was apparently not long after this exchange of compliments that Bonaparte thought for the first time of claiming the succession of Charlemagne—Charlemagne, who had been crowned at Rome, a thousand years before, 'Emperor of the Romans.' For on April 29th, 1803, he ordered a statue of Charlemagne to be erected in the Place de la Concorde or Place Vendôme; and on October 1st elaborated this idea into a column in the Place Vendôme modelled on Trajan's column at Rome, with a statue of Charlemagne on the top. It so happened that at the moment two such statues were available, which had been brought to Paris from Aix and Ghent. But when it was ultimately erected, the figure proved to be that of Napoleon in classical dress, as a Roman emperor.[19]

The assumption of the Imperial title had already been celebrated with a series of secular functions, culminating in a ceremonial distribution of crosses of the Legion of Honour at the Invalides, followed by Mass and a *Te Deum*—elaborate enough, but lacking just that flavour of antiquity and universality that only a Papal coronation could supply.

Bonaparte's ulterior motives were obvious. A papal coronation would give the new throne a prestige at home and abroad resembling that of the Bourbons, which it had displaced, and rivalling that of the Habsburgs, which it hoped to humiliate. 'Emperor of the French' was at present no more than a title conferred by 'Act of Parliament': it would become a reality, an object of national homage and popular faith, if its holder were anointed and crowned by the head of the Universal Church. All Europe would know that the Papacy, which had anathematized the Revolution, gave its blessing to the Empire founded upon it.

There were, it is true, several objections. One was that the Comte de Provence, as 'Louis XVIII,' still claimed to be the only successor to the French throne, and commanded the allegiance, though no longer of the mass of the people, yet of a small and fanatical body of aristocrats and Ultramontanes, organized as *Chevaliers de la foi* into *bannières* up and down the country, and pledged to work for the overthrow of the 'Usurper.'

Soon after Brumaire (December 19th, 1799) Louis had drafted a long letter to 'General Bonaparte' saying that his eyes had followed 'the victor of Lodi, Castiglione and Arcola, the conqueror of Italy and Egypt,' and saw in him 'the saviour of France': 'General (he ended), you have to chose between two roles; you must be either Caesar or Monk.' In short, be Monk, put me on the throne, and you will earn 'the gratitude of your King and of all future generations of Frenchmen.' The reply was that Louis would return to France only over the dead bodies of a hundred thousand Frenchmen. Now, after nearly four years, the prestige of the Bourbon monarchy seemed to have sunk so low that it might accompany the Habsburg empire into oblivion.

Early in 1804 Bonaparte thought it worth while to approach the Comte de Provence indirectly through diplomatic channels, and to ask the King of Prussia to suggest his abdication. But when nothing came of this move he thought little of it. The Bourbons, as was apparent enough ten years later, were rapidly losing ground in the country, and the attempts of the *Chevaliers* to exploit feeling against the Emperor remained ineffective.[20]

Again, France was a Republic, and Bonaparte held his throne by the will of the people, not by leave of the church. But he was confident that he had the French church under his hand, and could override Jacobin protests. If the Pope tried to make conditions, or to exploit the situation in the interests of Ultramontanism, he would know how to deal with him, as he had done in the matter of the Concordat.

As for Pius VII, he was not hostile to the proposal of a papal coronation: he was grateful, and remained so all his life, in spite of what he suffered at Napoleon's hands, for the Concordat. But he was embarrassed by it. He knew very well how bitter would be the protests and misrepresentations of 'Louis XVIII' and the royalists, the Austrian court and the recalcitrant bishops in exile—more bitter than ever since the execution of the Duc d'Enghien. Certainly these considerations could not be allowed to outweigh the religious advantages of friendship with the victor of Marengo. But no Pope had crowned a French monarch at Paris since the doubtful days of Pepin le Bref, more than a thousand years ago; and even in the long annals of the Papacy that could hardly be accounted a precedent. Should the head of the church visit with his approval the country which had annexed Avignon and the Legations, and the city which had desecrated its churches, massacred its priests, burnt his predecessor in effigy and put to death its Catholic king? Was it even possible for Pius VII to meet the bishops who had never formally abandoned the Civil Constitution denounced by Pius VI? Could he overlook not merely the Organic Articles by which Bonaparte had disfigured the Concordat, but the decrees by which Melzi, with Bonaparte's collusion, had extended to Lombardy the same secular control over the church?

Cardinal Consalvi, whom Pius in a moment of inspiration after his election at Venice had appointed Pro-Secretary of State—a man of tact and integrity, well suited to give form and strength to his more hesitating policy—agreed that the thing must be done, but believed that consent might be made conditional. The negotiations, conducted mainly by Consalvi and Fesch in Rome, and by Bernier and Caprara in Paris, turned partly on the conditions under which Pius might consent to come to Paris, and partly on the form of the coronation service. As to the first, he had to be content with Napoleon's promise—and he must have known by this time how little it meant—to do 'all he could compatible with his position, the interests of the state, and his duties,' to meet the Pope's wishes. As to the second, he received a definite undertaking from Fesch and Talleyrand (which, again, he must have known was of no value unless Napoleon confirmed it) that he should, as the *Pontificale* laid down, perform both the crowning and the anointing, that the Imperial oath should follow the same form, and that the religious rite should be entirely separate from any civil ceremony.

On September 29th Pius received a brusque letter from Napoleon, which read less like an invitation than a command to come to Paris: he was still hoping that the coronation might be held on November 9th, the anniversary of the 18th Brumaire. But this was now impracticable. It was all that Fesch could do to arrange for the Papal procession to start on November 2nd, and to make arangements for as speedy a journey as possible. The Pope, though the simplest and humblest of men, could not travel unattended: and his suite—6 cardinals, 10 bishops, 5 court officials, 5 abbés, a surgeon, 2 valets and others, 108 persons in all—occupied 3 convoys, comprising from 20 to 30 coaches and wagons drawn by some 130 horses. The passing of this procession out of the gates of Rome caused consternation amongst the people, who remembered the fate of Pius VI, and put the worst interpretation upon it. It caused no less sensation as it passed northwards and over the Alps.

They travelled by Florence, Pistoia, Modena and Parma to Turin; so rapidly that Napoleon's representatives were hardly in time to meet him there; then over the Mont Cenis, barely in time to escape the winter snows, which were late that year; but the oldest of the cardinals died at Lyon from the hardships of the journey. When at last the procession neared Fontainebleau, Napoleon made a point of meeting it casually as he was out hunting; but the Pope was honourably received, and three days later he was given apartments in the Pavillon de Flore, the southern wing of the Tuileries, recently vacated by Cambacérès, and redecorated on the model of those he was accustomed to in the Quirinal.[21]

10

When Ségur, the *grand maître des cérémonies*, had first consulted Napoleon about the coronation it had been assumed that the ceremony would
take place in the church of the Invalides. Napoleon then (July 25th) determined that, in view of the Pope's probable presence, and the crowds to
be expected, the only place suitable was Nôtre Dame; and elaborate
preparations were at once set on foot. First, extensive demolitions of
buildings round the cathedral; then the erection of a pseudo-Gothic annex to the west front—something like what was done at Westminster
Abbey for the last two coronations, and a covered way along the south
side of the nave to the Archbishop's Palace. Then, inside the building, the
choir screen was pulled down, with two altars, to make a big central
space; and arrangements were made for the designing and manufacture
of appropriate costumes for those taking part in the ceremony, and the
provision of altar plate, thrones, chairs and a hundred other properties
for what was becoming a theatrical production on an unprecedented
scale. One way and another Napoleon's coronation cost very much the
same as that of George IV, which was thought excessively extravagant—
about £250,000. But where an economy could be made, it was: for instance, the *dais* was to be that used a short time before at the funeral of
the Archbishop of Paris. As for the procession to the Cathedral, that
would involve thirty or forty new coaches (of which Napoleon's alone
cost £5700), and three teams of matched horses for the Emperor, the
Empress, and the Pope.

The most important items of all, perhaps, were the regalia—the crown,
sword, sceptre, globe and other emblems of Empire with which Napoleon
was to be invested. The genuine antiques, said to go back to the corna-
tion of Charlemagne, were kept at Nuremberg, and Francis was not likely
to lend them to his rival. A reputed sword of Charlemagne was brought
from Aix-la-Chapelle. Certain other relics—there are generally several
specimens of such things—had been removed from Saint-Denis during
the Revolution, and were found in museums or in private ownership. One
way or another the necessary articles—a 'job lot,' some old and some newly
made—were collected. By the time the Pope arrived in Paris, everything
was settled, except the essential points of the coronation rite itself. No
doubt Napoleon thought it would thus be easier for him to secure Pius's
consent to the alterations he was determined to make in the actual service.

The coronation had been fixed for Sunday, December 2nd. During the
intervening three days, whilst Napoleon was busy discussing with Isabey,
over plans and miniature figures, the final details of the ceremony, the
Pope had to make some hurried decisions.

First, Joséphine had lost no time in telling Caprara that her marriage with Bonaparte, eight years ago, had been only a civil ceremony. Napoleon was hoping to keep this dark; she calculated that if their union now secured the blessing of the church it would be more difficult in future for him to divorce her. Pius, horrified to learn that the Emperor to whom he was about to give the sacramental unction of coronation was, in the eyes of the church, living in sin with 'my dear daughter in Christ, Victoria Bonaparte,' insisted that he could take no part in the coronation unless a religious marriage first made them man and wife. Napoleon had to give way; and on the afternoon before the coronation Fesch performed the necessary rite.

Secondly, Pius had come to Paris with the intention of anointing and crowning Napoleon; and he had been assured by Fesch and Talleyrand that the two acts would be inseparable. But Napoleon strongly objected to receiving his crown at the hands of the church. It was therefore agreed on both sides, only a few hours before the ceremony, that the Pope should anoint the Emperor, but that Napoleon should place the crown on his own head.

Thirdly, Napoleon refused to take the second part of the coronation oath, which emphasized the dependence of the Emperor on the Pope; whilst the Pope refused to be present during the civil oath 'to maintain the laws of the Concordat and the liberty of worship (des cultes),' which recognized the Organic Articles and the state support of Protestantism.

Lastly, Napoleon would not carry his concessions to Catholicism so far as to communicate at the Mass which was the centre of the service. He did not want the Pope to 'make a good Catholic' of him. He shrank from making his confession; and he knew that to every peasant in France and to every man in the army the act of communion meant much more than any public ceremony of worship.

In the end, since neither the Roman *Pontificale* nor the French rite used for so many centuries at Rheims was acceptable to Napoleon, or indeed practicable in circumstances for which there was no real precedent, these and other amendments were embodied in a new Order of Coronation drawn up by Portalis and Cambacérès and accepted by the Pope.[22]

II

Jean-Louis David, portrait-painter and pageant-master of the Revolution, had been commissioned by Napoleon to produce a series of four paintings recording the events of the coronation. For that of the *Sacre* itself he was given a position in Nôtre Dame, as is shown by such of his preliminary sketches as remain, on the south side of the high altar, viewing the central figures of the ceremony in profile. The moment he intended to commemorate was that at which Napoleon placed the crown on his own head—following the ritual arranged beforehand, not snatching it, as is so often said, from the hands of the Pope. Pius was to be sitting a little behind the Emperor, supported by his legate, Caprara, by his relation Braschi, and by a 'Greek bishop,' whom one supposes David introduced for reasons of symbolism, as Holman Hunt inserted a Parsee sunworshipper into his picture of May morning on Magdalen tower. Further back was a group of ambassadors, and in front Lebrun, Cambacérès, Berthier and Talleyrand in cloaks and plumed hats, Eugène, Caulaincourt, Bernadotte and Fesch. On the left of the central figures came a group of generals and officials, then members of the Bonaparte family—Joseph and Louis (but not Lucien or Jèrôme, who were in disgrace) with their sisters and brothers-in-law, Hortense, and the young Prince Napoléon; and in the north gallery, looking down on the ceremony, Madame Mère (who was in Italy at the time), with her ladies-in-waiting; and behind her again, by further artistic licence, David himself, with his wife and daughters.

For many of the two hundred figures in his vast canvas David had to paint separate portraits, as he had done for his picture of the Tennis Court Oath in 1789; and in this he encountered, as might be expected, many difficulties and delays, although armed now with a decree naming him the Emperor's *premier peintre*. The Turkish ambassador refused to be painted. Louis Bonaparte objected that he was not given prominence enough, and ordered a replica of the picture showing himself in a different costume. Then a studio had to be found large enough for a canvas thirty feet by nineteen—nothing less would be worthy of such a scene—a disused church near the Sorbonne, where the artist and his assistants were at work for three years.

During this time David's friends would drop in to see how the picture was going; and one of them suggested an alteration which was adopted by the painter. He had represented Napoleon placing the crown on his head with his right hand, whilst his left grasped the hilt of his sword, and pressed it to his heart—a piece of theatrical symbolism he had already used for his picture of the Tennis Court Oath, in which Robespierre presses both hands to his heart, in token of total devotion to his country. It was his pupil Gerard who suggested that a far better effect could be got by painting Napoleon placing the second crown on the head of Joséphine, whilst she knelt before him. To this change Napoleon, to his credit, agreed; and everyone can see the admirable result. The figures are beautifully drawn, though Napoleon looks taller than his 5 feet 2 inches, and Joséphine more girlish than she was at forty-one.

But here is a real stroke of genius and irony in the picture. The face that catches the eye is not that of the Emperor, the centre of all its theatrical pomp, or of any of the self-conscious and overdressed ambassadors and generals, but that of the Pope, who sits behind, in his simple white vestment, and with downcast eyes. David took more trouble with Pius than with any other of his sitters, painting two likenesses of him, and a third with Caprara, which are amongst the masterpieces of portraiture. The Jacobin artist was deeply impressed by the modesty and simplicity of a man whose face seemed to belong to a quiet world lost sight of in the bustle and display of revolutionary France: consciously or not, he has put the contrast into his picture. But one more alteration had still to be made. When Napoleon saw the picture he said, 'The Pope didn't come all the way to Paris to do nothing,' and insisted that his right hand should not be drawn resting on his knee, but slightly raised, as though blessing Joséphine. So history is made to order.[23]

During the weeks that followed the coronation—for he did not leave Paris until the end of March—Pius had many strange experiences of the city he had dreaded to visit, and of the people he had supposed savagely hostile to the claims of Rome. What surprised and pleased him most was not the fulsome homage of the Senate, the Tribunate, or the *Corps législatif*, not the eloquent addresses he listened to from the Jacobin de Neufchâteau, the atheist Lalande, Fourcroy, Marat's successor in the Convention, and the author of the secular educational system, or Dr. Guillotin, the inventor of the machine which had put to death a Catholic king and queen, but the evident affection and reverence of the common people: the crowded churches, the throngs who came to mass, the wearing of rosaries and wedding rings that he had blessed. He discovered, as Napoleon never could, the soul of the French people. To one of the few who showed hostility to him, he is said to have remarked, 'Monsieur, you have nothing to fear: no one was ever the worse for an old man's blessing.' To Fouché, who asked him how he had found France, he replied, that he had passed everywhere through a people on its knees.

So, whilst Napoleon courted popularity by fêtes and fireworks (with a great set piece of the crossing of the St. Bernard); whilst he sent up a coronation balloon to be blown across the Alps to Rome (and by an Imperial miracle it came down there twenty-four hours afterwards), Pius was binding a more potent spell which, ten years later, brought the Emperor to his feet.

IX

ENGLAND

(1802-1810)

I

THE FOURTEEN MONTHS between March 25th, 1802, when the plenipotentiaries, Cornwallis and Joseph Bonaparte, put their signatures to the
Treaty of Amiens, and May 17th, 1803, when Whitworth and Andréossy,
the retiring ambassadors, met at Dover, determined the course of history
for the next twelve years, and the pattern of European politics for more
than half a century. The episode might be looked at in two ways: either
as an inevitable clash between two national traditions and temperaments,
or as an avoidable imbroglio of policies and personalities. It was in fact
both. George III's disposition to tolerate a revolutionary government in
France, so long as it did not upset the balance of power on the continent,
or interfere with Britannia's rule over the waves, was perhaps incompatible with Bonaparte's determination to make the French Republic powerful and respected on land and sea. Yet if the terms of the Treaty of
Amiens had been more wisely drawn, peace might have been preserved
between the two countries long enough to work out a *modus vivendi* in
a world still full of opportunities for expansion and civilization. It was not
in the breaking of the treaty that the tragedy of the affair lay so much as
in the making of it.

Britain was over-sensitive, in the early days of 1802, of her political
isolation, her economic difficulties, and her need of a breathing-space;
France was over-aware of her First Consul, her Concordat, her imposition
of new governments on Holland and Italy. It was likely enough that,
with only Addington behind him, the easy-going Cornwallis would be
outdone at the council-table by Bonaparte's brother, with Talleyrand and.
the First Consul himself at his elbow. Bonaparte was conscious of a
revolution behind him, a republic beside him, and an empire ahead of
him. He resented the patronizing air of an old aristocracy. He would not
be 'put on probation' for his good behaviour in Europe. He would
recognize no monopolies, whether of commerce or colonies or political

respectability. Having tied Britain down to the terms of a treaty unex-
pectedly favourable to himself, he would hold her to them at all costs,
reckoning that what stupidity had promised honesty would perform. He
failed to allow for the inherent realism which would enable a gentleman
to break his word rather than to persevere in a fatal mistake.

Would it be going beyond the evidence to suppose that, behind these
reasons for refusing accommodation with ,England, there lay a radical
dislike—all the more so for being unreasoned and unconscious—for the
British way of living and thinking? When, at the time of Brumaire, Mme
de Staël, who was almost an Englishwoman, said she believed in liberty,
Bonaparte asked peevishly 'What does she *want*?' 'It is not what I want,'
she replied, 'but what I *think*.' He never understood how anyone could
put ideas before needs. It was Mme de Staël again who wrote: 'The
English particularly irritate him, as they have found the means of being
honest as well as successful, a thing which Bonaparte would have us
regard as impossible.' He admired the English army and navy, and often
said so; but never the English way of life.

The fourteen months' period of the Amiens interlude falls into three
parts. The first runs from the signing of the Treaty on March 25th to the
arrival of Andréossy in London on November 3rd, 1802. During these
seven months British opinion steadily hardened against France, as in one
field after another Bonaparte seemed to be using the peace to gain advantages that he could not have won in war. Cornwallis's signature had
already been jeopardized by the proclamation of the new Republic of
Italy on January 23rd. During the summer and autumn this was followed
by a series of acts of political aggression: the proclamation of the Republic of Valais, and the guaranteeing of the construction of a military route
over the Simplon Pass (August 26th); the annexation of Elba (August)
and Piedmont (September 2nd); the failure to evacuate the French
troops from Holland, as required by the Treaty (September 23rd)—they
were kept there 'until ships could be provided' to transport them to
Louisiana; the proclamation of Bonaparte's intention to dictate a constitution to Switzerland (September 30th), followed by the French invasion
of that country (October 15th); the incorporation of Parma in the French
Republic (October). Whatever might be thought of these acts, none,
except the minor matter of the Dutch garrison, could be brought within
the terms of the Treaty. The British protest against the invasion of
Switzerland might be ignored or resented as a gratuitous interference in
matters which were no concern of a third party. When Andréossy arrived in London as ambassador at the beginning of November, he was
received with official favour (was he not an aristocrat of the old regime, a
general and an author?), but with less show of popular enthusiasm than
his predecessor, at the time of the Peace.

Andréossy's Instructions were (1) to prevent the British government from interfering in continental affairs, (2) to secure good terms for French commerce, (3) to press for the evacuation of Malta, and (4) to urge the expulsion from England of the Bourbon princes, and the suppression of press attacks upon Bonaparte.

Lord Whitworth, who arrived in Paris ten days later, was a less acceptable ambassador than Andréossy. He represented the reaction against the treaty and the conciliatory policy of Cornwallis; he was (unfortunately) married to that Lady Dorset who had been hostess at the embassy in the pre-revolutionary days of Louis XVI, and who did not conceal her distaste for the manners of the republican Tuileries; and one cannot read his dispatches without forming the impression that he took a narrow and prejudiced view of Bonaparte.

Whitworth's official Instructions were (as usual at that date) those of an accredited spy: but the covering letter from Lord Hawkesbury (November 14th) defines five duties: (1) he is to express King George's desire to keep the peace, (2) he is, however, to 'state most distinctly his Majesty's determination never to forego his right of interfering in the affairs of the Continent,' especially 'in any case which might lead to the extension of the power or influence of France,' (3) he is to bear in mind the principle of 'compensation' admitted by the French government [but not in the Treaty], by which any refusal of France to give up territory gained during the war justifies Britain in claiming an equivalent: this principle already applies to Holland and Switzerland under the treaties of Lunéville and the Hague [but again, these treaties had not been reaffirmed at Amiens], (4) if complaints are made about attacks on France in the unofficial English press, he is to point out that the attacks on England in the official *Moniteur* are worse, (5) if the question of Malta is raised, he is to 'avoid committing his Majesty as to what may be eventually his intentions with respect to that island.'

Evidently, then, by the end of 1802 the peace is wearing very thin. On the questions of continental interference, press attacks, and Malta the two governments are already at a deadlock. The difference in their attitudes is that, whilst Bonaparte is claiming his pound of flesh under the Treaty, George is appealing to an overruling principle of 'international law' under which he hopes to escape the penalty of his rash promises, and to earn the gratitude of Europe.[1]

2

This explosive situation was detonated by Bonaparte's publication of Sébastiani's report in the *Moniteur* of January 30th, 1803. Colonel Sébastiani was a fellow-countryman of Bonaparte, who had fought by his side in Corsica in 1793, at Arcola in 1796, and at Marengo in 1799. In September 1802 he had been dispatched to the Levant with instructions to visit Tripoli, Alexandria, Jaffa, Acre, Smyrna, Zante, Cephalonia and Corfu. Everywhere, especially in Egypt and Palestine, he was to inquire into the state of the country, the British garrisons and fortifications, and the grievances of the Christian population. Everywhere he was to plant, or prepare the way for, French *commissaires*; and he was to send home from Alexandria an *aviso* 'with all available news with regard to the position of the English, and anything which might interest us as to the state of Egypt.' Some concern was felt in England when Sébastiani started; but it was as nothing to the sensation caused by the publication of his report four months later. In it Sébastiani had revenged his cold reception in Egypt by insulting the commander there, General Stuart, by representing the Egyptian Pacha as powerless, and by saying that the few British troops still there, and the ruinous fortifications, could easily be overcome by 6000 Frenchmen.

This report was published within five days of Sébastiani's arrival in Paris. It had been hurriedly revised by Bonaparte himself, who toned down some passages, but left its main drift, and the reference to Stuart, untouched. A comparison of dates suggests that he did so in anger at recent attacks upon himself by Sheridan and Sir Robert Wilson, and the libels which led to the trial of Peltier three weeks later (February 21st). He may also have believed that such 'shock tactics' would alarm Addington and his friends, and speed up the Malta negotiations. It is hardly credible that he meant to provoke England into war. His view, expressed in an *Exposé de la situation de la République* to the Senate and *Corps législatif* on February 20th, was that there were in England two parties: one 'sworn to implacable hatred of France,' and one which 'had made the peace and intended to keep it.' Whilst this was so, France must remain armed; but 'the government can assert with just pride that England by herself cannot at present go to war with France.' What Bonaparte did not understand or take into account was the growing resentment of public opinion across the Channel (there was no such public opinion in France) against his aggressive policy, with the consequent drawing together of parties and stiffening of the government's attitude.[2]

Whitworth's first reaction to the Sébastiani report was not alarmist; especially as, at a dinner on February 2nd, its author 'recanted everything he had said disrespectful to General Stuart,' and Talleyrand assured him that Bonaparte was 'heartily tired of Egypt, and had no other views than those which were purely commercial.' But in London, in St. Petersburg, and at Constantinople (where Sébastiani had been treated as a friend) the Francophils were horrified, and the Francophobes rubbed their hands. The Foreign Office need no longer pretend that it was only waiting for the appointment of a Grand Master to surrender Malta to the Order. It could now instruct Whitworth to say (February 9th) that 'it will be impossible for His Majesty to enter into any further discussion relative to Malta unless he receives a satisfactory explanation on the subject' of the report. On the 18th Bonaparte talked loudly to Whitworth (as his habit was with ambassadors) for over two hours in the strain of his *Exposé* of the 20th: England, not France, was playing with fire: if Malta were not surrendered, war would follow; and France was readier for it than England.

On March 4th matters were brought to a head by the long expected appointment of a Grand Master of the Knights of Malta. England must now either withdraw from the island, or shoulder the guilt of breaking the Treaty. Her answer was given in George III's speech from the throne on March 8th. It did not mention Malta, but it informed the Commons that 'as very considerable military preparations are carrying on in the ports of France and Holland, he has judged it expedient to adopt additional measures of precaution for the security of his dominions.' Thus the third part of the fourteen months' period opened with the first overt move towards war. The seriousness of it was well understood on both sides of the Channel. 'I fear there is no compromise to be made with the pride and hatred of the First Consul,' wrote Whitworth to Hawkesbury on March 10th: 'I should mislead your Lordship were I to give any hope that we shall be able to retain Malta without fighting for it.'

Talleyrand's reply to the King's speech (March 12th) protested that the expedition preparing in the Channel ports was for America, that France was conscious of no offence that would justify a threat of war, and that 'it cannot really be imagined that England has any serious intention of avoiding its obligations under the Treaty of Amiens by resorting to arms. Europe knows well that attempts might be made to partition France, but never to intimidate her.' Bonaparte's less diplomatic remarks to Whitworth the next day at the Tuileries, 'loud enough to be overheard by two hundred people who were present,' had to be apologized for. Evidently he was disconcerted as well as surprised by what was in effect an ultimatum. He had not thought Britain was ready to risk war. He did not realize how far the Tsar of Russia, already jealous of the advance of French influence in the Netherlands and south Germany, had been alienated by Sébastiani's report, and was now prepared to back the British retention of Malta.

Having committed itself to breaking its promise under the Treaty, the British government now pressed its advantage. France, wrote Whitworth on March 21st, 'must be convinced that we are in earnest; that we have not adopted the present vigorous measures with a view solely to intimidate, but that our unshaken resolution is Malta or war.' No one can be so self-righteous as the man of principle who has found good reasons for doing wrong. No wonder Bonaparte was indignant. He was in no mood to pay attention to the warnings he received from Andréossy (April 2nd and 4th); nor does his failure to do so make him solely or even mainly responsible for the breach of the peace.

3

During the two months between March 12th and May 12th last-minute attempts were made to find a compromise which would prevent war; or what the British government called 'securities' to be offered by Bonaparte which would justify them in not wholly repudiating their treaty obligations. The story of these negotiations, as they appear in Whitworth's dispatches, is bewildering and sometimes fantastic. It can hardly be studied without the growing conviction that most of the demands were on the British side, and most of the concessions on the French; that England was trying to find reasons for war, and France conditions for peace.

On April 3rd Hawkesbury presents what Andréossy calls an ultimatum: England to keep Malta, France to evacuate Holland and Switzerland (there was no such undertaking in the Treaty), England to recognize the French settlement of Etruria, Elba, and the Italian republics, France to give satisfaction for the Sébastiani report (a new demand). On April 9th Bonaparte offers England Corfu or Crete in return for the evacuation of Malta; alternatively, he proposes the garrisoning of Malta by an international force, or its retention by Britain for a term of years.

On April 11th it 'occurs' to Whitworth (and Hawkesbury agrees) that the control of the island might safely be left to the Order, provided its fortifications were 'garrisoned for ever by troops of His Majesty'; or even that we might consent to hold Malta for not less than ten years, if we were enabled to acquire also the neighbouring island of Lampedusa. Whitworth, talking to Joseph (April 18th) took it on himself to stiffen this demand to twenty years. On the 23rd Hawkesbury made a final offer: Malta to be occupied for not less than ten years, and then to be given up, not to the Order, but to its inhabitants (a new point); Lampedusa to be ceded: Holland to be evacuated (but not Switzerland); and the Italian republics to be recognized only if compensation is provided for Sardinia and Switzerland (another new requirement). If these terms were not accepted within a week, Whitworth was to ask for his passports—in fact, it was another ultimatum.

Feeling that the French government was really anxious to prevent war, Whitworth stayed on in Paris, keeping in close touch with Joseph Bonaparte, Regnault, Malouet, Fouché and other members of the 'peace party.' On May 1st Talleyrand had received from Bonaparte a warning that he must stiffen his back (*Montrez-vous y froid, altier et même un peu fier*), and insist that France is not to be bullied by using the term ultimatum (*faites-lui sentir que cette manière de négocier est d'un supérieur à un inférieur . . . que jamais on n'obtiendra de nous ce que l'on a obtenu des dernières années des Bourbons*). Accordingly on May 4th he wrote that France had no power to cede Lampedusa, which did not belong to her; that the proposal about Malta was inconsistent with the terms of the Treaty, and must be submitted to the other signatories, Spain and Holland, as well as to Russia, Prussia and Austria, who guaranteed the stipulations as to Malta; and that to do this was the duty of the power proposing to vary the Treaty. He added that Holland would be evacuated as soon as the terms of the Treaty were carried out. In an additional note he suggested that, for greater security, Malta might be handed over to one of the three Powers, preferably Russia. Hawkesbury's only reply (May 7th) was that the limitation of our occupation of Malta to not less than ten years might be admitted in a secret article, and made dependent on the occupation of Lampedusa as a naval station: and this, once more, was an ultimatum: if it were not accepted Whitworth must leave Paris within thirty-six hours.

On May 9th Whitworth reported that Joseph believed his brother might agree to these terms, if the occupation were for not more than three or four years. Whitworth refused to consider less than five. A last proposal was that if Britain had Lampedusa France should have Otranto (May 12th). Again Whitworth refused, and at 8.30 the same evening left Paris, protesting that he had been 'delayed much longer than he wished by the infamous chicanery and difficulties which have occurred.' From Breteuil, thirty-six hours later, he sent on the Otranto proposal, as drafted by Joseph after a 'severe conflict' with the First Consul. When Hawkesbury read it he described it as 'wholly inadmissable.' On May 17th Dover Castle, which has seen so many famous comings and goings, looked down on the meeting of Whitworth and Andréossy—the representatives of Reason and of Right: it was a momentous turning-point in the history of their two countries, and in the destiny of Europe.[3]

4

Bonaparte was not caught unprepared by the breakdown of the negotiations. Two months before he had written to the Tsar and the King of Prussia about his intention to resist the English demands, and had told Frederick William that in the event of war he would attack Britain 'wherever her flag floated and wherever he could get at her.' This was a hint that he had not forgotten the three alternative fields of attack upon English power that he had discussed in his report of 1798—the Channel, Hanover, and Egypt. The Channel stood for the traditional scheme of direct invasion: it had only been postponed, and was now to be revived:

Egypt had been tried, and might (as Sébastiani's report suggested) be tried again: Hanover meant not so much a blow to British dynastic prestige as an attempt to blockade the mouths of the Elbe and Ems, and so to close the German North Sea ports to British shipping.

For Bonaparte well knew that a crossing of the Channel, or a fresh expedition to the Levant, could not permanently succeed until the British fleet was mastered; and that (he reckoned) would take him ten years. He knew that the British army—if there were such a thing—was unlikely to land on the continent in defence of Hanover. But the very strength of Britain, her command of the sea, was her weakness; for it had encouraged her to build her economy and her national prosperity upon overseas trade: and the closure of a foreign port against her shipping was like the destruction of one of her organs of sight, sound, or taste.

So he wrote to Decrès, his Minister of Marine, on March 13th, asking, 'What is the best way, in the event of war by sea, to do the greatest possible amount of damage to English commerce?' Not that he had much doubt about the answer. There were plenty of men amongst his advisers who knew the long history of economic warfare between the two countries—how, with the one exception of the Eden Treaty of 1786 (and that repudiated within seven years), both countries had combined the total exclusion of each other's goods with a prosperous pursuit of piracy (called privateering) and smuggling. Plenty of economic experts (as they would think themselves) were ready to discourse on the parlous state of a nation whose rich men lived on commerce, and whose banks had for the past six years refused payment in anything better than the paper *assignats* which had brought France to bankruptcy.

Bonaparte knew something of all this, for he knew something of everything. But whilst his advisers could tell him where to look for a weapon against England, only he could tell them how to use it. 'All you *idéologues* (he is reported as saying to Dalberg in 1806) act according to ready-made theories: I'm a practical man; I make the best of what opportunity offers.' That was his special gift. He would not, like Kersaint or Brissot in 1793, be content with threats. He would not reinforce the impracticable Navigation Act of that year, or the suicidal Law of Nivôse, five years later, which it had been one of his first acts in 1799 to repeal. He would proceed step by step, as opportunity offered, to close the outlets of British trade on the continent of Europe, and to drain England of her life-blood—the gold by which she bribed the Powers to coalesce against him.

To his acute but limited mind—the mind of a soldier, most accustomed to the conditions of war—it seemed certain that a policy of blockade, if it could be extended to a continental scale, closing all or most of the ports of Europe, would bring England to ruin in one of four ways, if not in all.

First, he argued, France is a self-sufficient country, living upon its own
produce, and that of its overseas possessions, as a cottager lives upon the
produce of his field and of his garden; it does not derive its wealth from
outside sources except in the form of forced contributions from countries
it has recently conquered. But Britain is a manufacturing and trading
country, producing a surplus of goods which it carries and sells overseas,
mainly on the continent of Europe; and, like other traders, it 'makes
money' in the form of cash paid for those goods, and for their carriage.
If it can be prevented from carrying on this trade, its supply of cash will
dry up; it will go bankrupt; and it will be unable to pay for the continuance of the war, either by itself or its allies.

Secondly, England must accumulate cash (in the form of gold) to pay
interest on the enormous national debt it is incurring, and to back the in-
flated paper currency with which it is financing its daily affairs. This debt
in fact amounted in 1802 to £507 millions, only £80 millions less than it
was on the outbreak of war in 1914, and the interest payable on it averaged £18 millions a year. The gold reserves at the Bank of England had
sunk almost as low as £1 million in 1797, and might be reduced to danger-
point again, if, instead of exporting goods for cash, England could be
prevented from exporting, or forced to pay out cash for goods imported.

Thirdly (Bonaparte argued), France, since the Revolution, had assimilated its social classes and unified its government upon the basis of
agriculture, citizenship, and a First Consul who knew what the country
wanted, and controlled all the means of achieving it. But in Britain political power was still disputed between the monarchy, the aristocracy,
and the farmers and shopkeepers; the country was torn by the rival interests of the landlords and the city of London, and still liable to commercial bankruptcy, labour troubles, and dangerous fluctuations of food
prices—all the symptoms which had preceded the revolution of 1789; and
these difficulties were supposed to be aggravated by the recent expansion
of cheap manufactures beyond the country's needs. In such a situation
the closing of foreign markets might well produce commercial bankruptcy,
unemployment, and political unrest enough to force the government to
sue for peace.

These were the ideas behind what is generally called the Continental
Blockade. 'Continental,' because only so could it be made effective, and
because Bonaparte's was the first French government in a position to
make it so. But why 'Blockade'? It was an old German word, but it bore
an English meaning. It signified the weary months spent by British naval
officers and men sailing to and fro off French ports to prevent the exit
of enemy ships of war, and to intercept and capture enemy merchantmen—a system whose boredom and hardships were inadequately repaid

by the prize-money earned by officers and crews. It meant too the 'paper' blockade of ports which it was impossible to police in this way, but whose ships, if they ventured to sea, were regarded as equally liable to capture.

But the intention of Bonaparte's 'blockade' (as he told his brother Louis in 1806) was to conquer the sea from the land (*par la puissance de la terre*), and was designed not to stop ships going out, but to prevent their coming in. It was an embargo, not a blockade; or, if you will, it was a self-blockade, an attempt to prevent trade with one's own country, in order, even at the cost of a lesser inconvenience, to cause a greater inconvenience to the enemy.

The paradoxes of the system did not end there. The blockade by itself could only effect the first of Bonaparte's aims—stop British exports. How was he to achieve the second—force England to export gold for goods? Only by admitting the very ships he was excluding, provided they took back goods for which they paid in cash. So the self-blockade must be self-broken: and if the Britisher will not pay for what he wants in gold, he may at least provide something that France requires—raw materials for its factories, or boots and overcoats for its armies—in exchange for French luxury goods. So Adam Smith's new doctrine of wealth-making exchange was superimposed willy-nilly upon Colbert's 'mercantile' basis of the blockade; and a plan for destroying one's enemy's industries became a plan for encouraging one's own.

Once more: if it was France's plan to exclude British goods from the continent, it must be Britain's plan to force their entry, and that by organized smuggling. And so it was; the more so as her new manufactures included many articles easy to smuggle, and she had a monopoly of colonial goods such as sugar and coffee, which remained, whatever Bonaparte might do, in urgent demand on the continent. Besides, it was impossible to enforce a strict watch on all the ports and coasts of Europe. So in the end Bonaparte found it worth while to connive at smuggling, so long as the sale of 'licences' was sufficiently profitable, and the smuggled goods paid a heavy enough tax.

Such an attempt to interfere with the accepted economy of Europe, even in its rudimentary state a century and a half ago, was certain to involve political consequences: not only those that Bonaparte himself hoped to bring about in Britain, but also many that he only half anticipated in other countries—in the continental states upon which he was already able to impose his system, or upon which he would impose it by diplomacy backed by war; upon the neutral countries of Europe and the Levant; and upon the colonies and the independent states of America beyond the western ocean.

For the blockade did not end at the coast-line of Europe. As its effects spread outward over the sea-roads of the Baltic, the Atlantic and the

Mediterranean, so they permeated inwards by every road and river route from the coastal ports to the business centres and the capitals of Europe. If Britain held a monopoly of the seas, France must hold a monopoly of the land. The passing and repassing of British fleets and convoys round the continental coast-line must be matched by the marching and counter-marching of Bonapart's armies behind the garrisons and customs officials that constituted his first line of defence. Holland, Prussia, Russia in one direction, Spain, Portugal, Italy, the Balkan peninsula in the other, must be forced to close their harbours and watch their coasts. Countries which had no coast-line must nevertheless be persuaded or forced to put up with the deprivation of British goods. Nor could neutral ships be allowed to lend themselves to the breaking of the blockade. America must not let its flag be used to cover cargoes of British origin, or carried from British ports. Or, since the British counter-blockade interfered even more than the French with the liberty of the sea and the rights of non-belligerents, Bonaparte must endeavour to profit by this circumstance, and incite the neutral powers to defy and declare war on their common enemy.

Thus with the closure of a few Channel ports began a struggle which spread to the whole Western world, and into which two great nations threw all the resources they possessed—of fleets and armies, of money and allies; and not till the end of eleven years was it clear that Bonaparte's grandiose scheme had failed.[4]

5

The main incidents of these years, as they could be read in the laws, decrees, and regulations issued by either side, as they were discussed in the council-chamber, or decided on the battlefield, had best be put in their chronological order.

1803	May	18	Declaration of war.
	May		Bonaparte occupies the chief ports of Italy.
	June	20	Bonaparte closes all French ports to British or British-borne colonial goods, and, if landed, orders their confiscation; he closes them also to neutral ships which do not either carry a certificate from the French representative at their port of origin, or undertake to carry back French goods of equal value.
	June	28	and July 26. England declares a blockade of the mouths of the Elbe and Ems.
1804	Aug.	9	England declares a blockade of all French ports in the English Channel and North Sea.
1805	Oct.	21	The battle of Trafalgar secures British monopoly of the high seas.

1805	Oct.	21	The publication of Stephens's *War in Disguise* leads to the re-enactment of the 'Rule of 1756' preventing the carriage of enemy cargoes under a neutral flag.
	Dec.	2	Battle of Austerlitz: Dec. 26. The Peace of Pressburg extends the blockade to the Adriatic.
1806	Jan.		British occupation of the Cape of Good Hope.
	May	16	England declares a blockade of the European coast from Brest to the Elbe.
	June	27	British capture of Buenos Ayres.
	Oct.	14	Battle of Jena. The collapse of Prussia enables Bonaparte to extend the blockade of the German coast.
	Nov.	21	The Berlin decree declares a blockade of the British Isles, imprisons all British subjects in French-occupied territory, with confiscation of their property, and closes every port on the continent to vessels coming from or calling at any port in England or its colonies.
1807	Jan.	7	The first British Order in Council prohibits any trade by sea between one French-occupied port and another.
	July	7	The Treaty of Tilsit brings Russia into the blockade.
	Sept.	2	The bombardment of Copenhagen alienates Denmark from England: the seizure of Heligoland provides a base for organized smuggling.
	Nov.	11	A British Order in Council declares all European ports from which British ships are excluded to be under blockade.
	Nov.	23	Bonaparte's first Milan decree and second Milan decree (Dec. 17) regulate and extend the working of the Berlin decree.
	Dec.	22	The American Embargo Act prohibits American ships from trading with European ports, and the Non-Importation Act prohibits foreign ships from landing goods in American ports.
1808	April	17	Bonaparte's Bayonne decree authorizes the seizure of any American ships entering French, Dutch or Italian ports.
	Aug.	1	The British landing at Lisbon prevents the extension of the blockade to the Spanish peninsula.

1809	Jan.		British annexation of French Guiana: in April, of Martinique.
	March	1	The American Non-Intercourse Act limits the Embargo Act of 1807 to Britain and France.
	July		British annexation of San Domingo and Senegal.
	July	5	Battle of Wagram.
	July	18	The Schoenbrunn decree closes the Franco-German frontier.
	Oct.	14	The Peace of Vienna brings Austria into the blockade.
1810	Jan.	6	Sweden joins the blockade.
	Jan.	12	Importation of forbidden goods into France is allowed on payment of a duty of 40 per cent when in captured ships.
	March	23	The Rambouillet decree authorizes the seizure and sale of American ships arriving in French ports.
	May	1	Abrogation of the American Non-Intercourse Act.
	Aug.	5	The Trianon Tariff regulates the decree of Jan. 12, imposing duties on various articles.
	Oct.	18	The Fontainebleau decree increases the penalties for smuggling, and orders the confiscation of colonial goods, and the destruction of prohibited goods.
	Dec.		British annexation of Guadeloupe, Mauritius, and Réunion.
1811	March		The first Luddite riots in England.
	March	2	An American Non-Importation Act partly restores the Non-Intercourse Act of 1809.
	Aug.		British occupation of Java.
1812	May		Napoleon invades Russia.
	June	19	The U.S.A. at war with England.
	Nov.	26	The Beresina: failure of the Russian expedition.
1813	June	21	Battle of Vittoria: the French driven out of Spain.
	Oct.	16	Battle of Leipzig: the French driven out of Germany.
1814	April	11	Napoleon's first abdication: end of the blockade.

6

Before considering the working and the results of Bonaparte's Continental Blockade, it will be as well to put side by side with it his scheme for an invasion of England; this was at first an independent plan, but it soon became an essential part of the main design. The idea of invading the British Isles was older than that of blockading them. To go no further back, four times within the last ten years French ships had crossed the Channel, to land troops on British soil—the Channel Islands in 1793, Bantry Bay in 1796, Fishguard in 1797 and Killala in 1798. True, all these attempts had miscarried; but that might well be because they had no Bonaparte to organize or to lead them. His report of February 1798, had only postponed, not negatived, the idea of crossing the Channel. The outbreak of war brought it at once into active operation.[5]

Bonaparte saw four advantages in invasion. First, considered in isolation, it was the quickest and most effective way to complete victory. A revolution in Ireland, backed by a French expeditionary force—still better, a revolution in England itself, caused by a surprise landing and a swift march on London, might end the war in a week. Secondly, if, for any reason, the invasion failed, the panic caused by the attempt might still force the British government to ask for terms. Thirdly, the continued menace of an invading force only twenty miles from Dover would perpetuate 'a war of nerves'; and this would double the effectiveness of the blockade. Fourthly, the threat of invasion would probably draw off the blockading squadrons in the Mediterranean and the Bay of Biscay. So the renewal of war in 1803 was marked by immense activity in the Channel ports and shipyards, which, whatever its subsidiary aims, was certainly meant to lead to an actual invasion.

At the end of 1802 the British Admiralty had 39 ships of the line, 13 smaller vessels, and 120 frigates in commission: France had only 13 ships of the line ready for sea, but could within a short time put another 50 or so in commission. Within six months, however, the tables were turned: Britain had 189 ships of the line, 37 smaller vessels, and 197 frigates, whereas Bonaparte, with all his efforts, could only add 14 ships of the line and 12 frigates, with the possibility of some help from the Dutch and Spanish navies. But he did not anticipate facing the whole British fleet. His plan was to divide or divert it for just long enough to throw an invading force across the Channel in an armada of small craft: and these he proceeded to build and equip, in vast numbers, and to a meticulous specification, at specially prepared bases all along the coast from the Texel to Brest, and from Brest to Bordeaux. Into all these preparations he plunged with his usual disregard for first principles and genius for detail, with demands upon his subordinates which drove them to despair, and with an optimism which took every design for a *fait accompli*.

'We must have a model of a flat-bottomed boat,' he writes to Decrés on May 29th, 'able to transport 100 men across the Channel. There would be a mortar (*obusier*) in the bows and stern. Such a boat should not cost

more than £200-£250.' Fifty *chaloupes canonnières*, 170 *péniches*, and 90
bateaux must be built within twelve months. Three months later he sends
Decrès another specification for *bateaux canonnières* carrying 80 men and
chaloupes carrying 56. In October he orders a company of *guides-inter-
prètes* to be formed (Irishmen eligible) to accompany the invading troops;
and draws up an elaborate hand-book of instructions for the crews of the
péniches, telling them how to use the oars which are to be provided for
a crossing in calm weather; what orders will be given (*embarquez* ...
préparez-vous à nager ... *babord descendez* ... *à droite marche*) and
how they should be obeyed. One day (November 17th) he stands on the
cliffs at Ambleteuse, and writes home to Cambacérès, 'I have seen the English coast as clearly as one can see the Calvary (at Fontainebleau) from the
Tuileries. One could pick out the houses, and see people moving about.
The Channel is a mere ditch, and will be crossed as soon as someone has
the courage to attempt it.' He did not perhaps reflect that his preparations might be seen from the other side. It was not many months later
that the Duke of York, inspecting the defence works at Dover, described
the view of the French camp on the opposite shore as 'a harmless pano-
rama.'

A few days later Bonaparte ordered Chaptal, Minister for Home Affairs, to 'get a song written, to go to the tune of the *Chant du départ*,
for the invasion of England. And while you are about it (he added) have
a number of songs written on the same subject, to go to different tunes.'
There was already a song popular among the troops, with the refrain
J'ai bien vu l'Angleterre, j'ai vu: Bonaparte had banned the revolutionary
Ça Ira and *Carmagnole*, but they were still sung *sotto voce*. The *Marseillaise*
had been written for an invasion of Germany; what was needed was
something similar for England.

Meanwhile Bonaparte did not drop the idea of an attack on Ireland. In
January 1804 he encouraged the Irish leaders, Thomas Emmet and
Thompson, to form a corps of United Irishmen to assist a French expeditionary force, promising that he would never make peace with England
unless the terms included the independence of Ireland. A rebellion in
Ireland would assist the invasion of England, as the invasion would assist
the blockade. In September, again, he writes to Decrès that 'the Irish
invasion has been decided upon'; that there are transports at Brest sufficient for 18,000 men, whom Augereau will land in Ireland; if the people rise, well and good; if not, he must wait till Marmont joins him with
reinforcements, 'and until the *grande armée* (that is, the force invading
England) has landed.' But as this dispatch seems to have fallen into British hands, along with another two days later announcing naval expeditions to Martinique, Surinam, and St. Helena, it is possible that these
schemes were designed to distract attention from the Channel crossing,

and to keep up during the winter the 'war of nerves' rather than as serious proposals. There is still talk of an invasion of Ireland in December 1804.[6]

In point of fact, Napoleon at this time had neither the ships nor the men for any invasion. In the summer of 1804 there were only 600-700 transports for 100,000 men, as against the 2000 he had estimated as necessary. Many of them were shut up in harbour by the British blockade of Brest, Rochefort, Bordeaux, Ferrol, and Toulon. All the winter of 1803-04 he had been devising plans to shake off this bull-dog grip, and to mobilize his capital ships within striking distance of the 'western approaches.' Towards the end of May 1804 he thinks Latouche-Tréville will be able to slip the blockade at Toulon, join another French squadron at Ferrol, and Truguet's ships at Brest, and enter the Channel. He now definitely planned the invasion for the late summer of 1804. He harried the camp commandants—Berthier at Bruges, Soult at Saint-Omer, Ney at Montreuil, Marmont at Utrecht—with instructions and demands. He wrote to Decrès every other day about the *flotilles*, the port defences, or the building of an arsenal at Antwerp. 'We must have a fleet,' he insisted, 'and we can't be considered as having one till we have 100 ships of the line.' 'In a country like France one ought to be able to get anything one wants done'—build thirty ships a year, if necessary.

In the middle of July he left Saint-Cloud, and made a royal progress (for he was Emperor now, and had signed himself *Napoleon* since May 18th), to Clermont, Amiens and Boulogne. All the rest of that month he was at Pont-de-Briques, visiting the flotilla bases. In his enthusiasm he would venture afloat, and was nearly captured by the enemy. He ordered a review in weather so bad that several ships were wrecked, and 200 men drowned. And it was now, apparently, that he ordered a medal to be struck with a figure of Hercules wrestling with a Triton, and the boastful inscription *Descente en Angleterre: Frappée à Londres en 1804.*

But on August 20th Latouche-Tréville died, and left no obvious successor; and Napoleon's relations with Russia and Austria were becoming unfriendly at a moment when he should have isolated England from her possible allies. The favourable moment had passed. A ceremonial distribution of crosses of the Legion of Honour (August 16th) compensated the army for deeds they could not now perform; and four days later the Emperor left Boulogne for a tour into Belgium and the cities of the lower Rhine. On October 12th he was back at Saint-Cloud, and a month later at Fontainebleau, to entertain the Pope, and to make preparations for his coronation.

His visit to Boulogne and his intention to invade England are still commemorated by the 'Column of the Grand Army' which rises 150 feet in the air by the road from Boulogne to Calais. Its foundation-stone was laid by Soult on the anniversary of Brumaire (November 6th, 1804), but only a third of it had been built ten years later, and in 1815 the statue of Napoleon which should have crowned it was broken up. Under Louis XVIII (1819) work was begun again to make it a 'Column of the Bourbons' (it was under scaffolding when Wordsworth visited it next year); but in 1841 Louis-Philippe commissioned a new statue of Napoleon, and this was finally erected in 1845.

During the winter of 1804 fresh plans were devised for an invasion in June or July 1805, supported by a Franco-Spanish fleet, which would try to draw off the British defence by a dash to the West Indies and back. There was a moment in December when Villeneuve, appointed to the Toulon command, with Lauriston at the head of the troops on board, seemed to have broken out into the Mediterranean; but he was soon back again. Meanwhile £3¼ millions were to be spent on improving the arterial roads to the frontiers, special priority being given to those from Paris to the Channel ports—Brest, Cherbourg, and Boulogne.[7]

7

Bonaparte's visit to Italy in 1805, his first journey outside French territory since Marengo, lasted three months (April 1st-July 11th). He was in close touch all the time with events in France, and never for a moment forgot the plans which he had set on foot for the invasion of England. Just as he was starting (March 30th), Villeneuve, now in command of the Toulon squadron, successfully evaded the blockade, and sailed into the Atlantic. On March 24th Ganteaume had sent a *dépêche télégraphique* from Brest saying that his squadron was ready to sail, but that there were fifteen British ships waiting outside the harbour: should he risk a fight ('success is certain')? Bonaparte had ruled against it: Ganteaume's role was to join Villeneuve intact; *Sortez sans combat*, was his reply. Villeneuve's eleven ships of the line, with Gravina's eight from Cadiz, Gourdon's four from Ferrol, and two more from Rochefort, together with Ganteaume's twenty-one, would make an armada of more than forty ships of the line (at one hopeful moment Bonaparte adds them up to over fifty).

Ganteaume's Instructions, drafted on March 2nd, were to evade the Brest blockade, join up with the squadron at Ferrol (destroying the seven or eight British ships off that port) and with the Spanish fleet at Cadiz, and then to sail for Martinique. There he would join Villeneuve from Toulon and Missiessy from Rochefort. The combined fleet would then sail for Europe, avoiding the ordinary route, and not touching land, till it arrived off the mouth of the Channel; there sweep aside any British opposition there might be, and head straight for Boulogne. It should arrive there between June 10th and July 10th, in time to convoy the invading forces across the Channel.

Whilst Villeneuve joined up with the Spaniards and the Rochefort

squadron at Cadiz, Nelson, supposing him to have sailed east from Toulon (as in 1798) was setting off from Sicily for Egypt. But on May 2nd
Nelson was reported to have turned back west for Gibraltar. The hunt
was up once more. Villeneuve had three weeks' start. What would
happen?

During the whole of April, May, and June Bonaparte bombards Decrès
with letters about the naval situation—twenty-seven in April, thirty-eight
in May, and another thirty in June; speculating as to what may be happening in the Mediterranean or the Atlantic, drafting new Instructions for
Villeneuve, when he arrives back, with four possible alternatives; making
out (probably from the *Naval Chronicle*) an *état exact* of the number of
British ships on home and foreign stations; asking for a fresh plan for an
Irish invasion—only a raid, but sufficient to draw off British ships from
the Channel; and so on. When Decrès, distracted by this constant interference, urges him to return to Paris, and look after things on the spot,
he replies, shrewdly enough, that nothing is so likely to mislead the English as to his real plans as his continued absence in Italy.

But on July 8th he leaves Turin, crosses the Mont Cenis, and hurries
back post-haste to Fontainebleau, travelling incognito, and taking four
days over a journey that, coming out, had occupied three months. He has
not forgotten that the invasion of England is timed for June 10th-July
10th, and he hopes to take the British Admiralty by surprise. But things
have gone wrong. He spends three weeks at Saint-Cloud, writing again
and again to Decrès, to Villeneuve, to Ganteaume, and to Allemand (now
in command of the Rochefort squadron), repeating his instructions for
the voyage up the Channel, or alternatively the circumnavigation of Scotland: give him only four days, three days, twenty-four hours, twelve
hours of protection from the British fleet, and the thing is done. 'Europe
is holding its breath whilst the great event is preparing.' 'With God's
help I will put an end to the future and very existence of England.'

On August 3rd he is at Boulogne; and there, for another month, he
waits from day to day for the favourable issue of his fantastic gamble—
fantastic, for he can no more control the movements of his admirals than
the winds and tides of the Channel. The tides exasperated him as much
as they exasperate those who try to swim across. There had been no tides
at Ajaccio, at Valetta, or at Alexandria. Why should they obstruct him
now? By this time, too, another plan is forming in his impatient mind.
'The information I receive from Italy,' he writes to Talleyrand on July
31st, 'all points towards war, and it is clear that we can do no more with
Austria': and on August 12th the minister is instructed to tell Cobenzl
that, failing a satisfactory reply to his demands for disarmament, he will
strike camp at Boulogne and march into Switzerland: unless the troops
in the Tyrol are withdrawn, *je commence la guerre*. Next day, the 13th,

he seems to be at the point of decision. He writes to Villeneuve, 'If you appear here for three days, or even for twenty-four hours, your job will be done'; and to Talleyrand, 'I have made up my mind (*mom parti est pris*): I am going to attack Austria, and shall be at Vienna before next November'—unless (there is still a loophole) Austria leaves him free to invade England undisturbed: for if Austria were to strike while his army is in England, he might be cut off again as he was in Egypt.

On August 22nd the news he has been so long waiting for comes at last. Villeneuve, returning from Martinique, and headed off from the Channel by Calder's blockading squadron off Brest, has arrived at Ferrol. There, Napoleon assumes, he will get his budget of instructions, and will carry out the plan for the meeting at Boulogne. But will he? Has he the necessary energy? If he joins Ganteaume off Brest, should not the latter take command? He consults Decrès again, and tells Ganteaume, 'If Villeneuve arrives, don't let him anchor off Brest, but sail at once for the rendezvous. There's not a moment to lose. I count on your character.' At the same time he writes a final appeal to Villeneuve, to be given him at Brest: 'Start, without losing a moment, and sail up the Channel with all the ships you have. England is ours. We are all ready: every man is on board. Appear for twenty-four hours, and the thing is done.'

Yet the very next day he writes again to Talleyrand in the strain of his letter of the 12th: save that the ten days' disappointment is turning an ultimatum into a declaration of hostilities: 'My fleet left Ferrol on August 14th (he did not know that it had turned back a few days later) with twenty-four sail. If it obeys orders, joins the Brest fleet, and sails up the Channel, there is still time; England is mine.' But if Villeneuve fails, the time is so short, and the threat from Austria so menacing, that he may at the last moment have to change his plans. He already sees himself (and perhaps with relief) embarking on a purely military campaign. 'I am off at full speed. I am striking camp . . . and there I am, on September 23rd, in the middle of Germany, with 200,000 men . . . I march on Vienna, and refuse to lay down arms till I have nothing more to fear from Austria . . . I don't return to Paris till I have reached my goal.'

And so it was. On September 3rd, tired of waiting for Villeneuve, he posted back from Boulogne to Malmaison. On the 24th he left Saint-Cloud for Nancy and Strasbourg. In the first week of October (only a week behind his time-table) he was in Germany. On October 19th he forced Mack to capitulate at Ulm. On December 2nd he defeated the Austrians and Russians at Austerlitz. On the 26th he dictated the Treaty of Pressburg.[8]

But two days after the surrender at Ulm, Nelson at Trafalgar had annihilated the combined navies of France and Spain. For ten years Bonaparte's invasion flotilas lay rotting in harbour, as those of Hitler did after 1941. Though as late as November 1811 he might be instructing Decrès to keep 500 of his *péniches* in good repair, since this 'will always be one of the most powerful means of influencing England,' yet in fact the scheme was dead.

The question whether an invasion might have succeeded need not concern us. That Napoleon believed it would can hardly be doubted. On his voyage to exile at Elba in 1814 he 'frequently spoke of the invasion of England,' and said that 'he never intended to attempt it without a superiority of fleet to protect the flotilla. This superiority would have been attained for a few days by leading our fleet out to the West Indies, and suddenly returning. If the French fleet arrived in the Channel three or four days before ours, it would be sufficient. The flotilla would immediately push out, accompanied by the fleet, and the landing might take place on any part of the coast, as he would march direct to London . . . He had 1,000,000 [this should read 100,000] men, and each of the flotillas had boats to land them: artillery and cavalry would soon have followed, and the whole could have reached London in three days.'

Asked what he would have done when he arrived in London, he admitted that this might not have ended the war; but he would certainly have separated Ireland from Great Britain, and the occupation of the capital would have been a death-blow to our funds, credit, and commerce. In one of his conversations at St. Helena, reported (perhaps with some improvements) by O'Meara, he added a few amendments to this design. He would have held command of the Channel with seventy ships of the line, besides frigates, for two months instead of three to four days; he would have landed 'as near Chatham as possible,' with twice as many men, and he would have reached London in four days. He supposed the result to have been more decisive. 'I should have proclaimed a republic, the abolition of the nobility and house of peers, the distribution of the property of such of the latter as opposed me amongst my partisans, liberty, equality and the sovereignty of the people. I should have allowed the House of Commons to remain; but should have introduced great reforms. I should have published a proclamation, declaring that we came as friends to the English, to free the nation from a corrupt and flagitious aristocracy, and to restore a popular form of government, a democracy . . . The hope of a change for the better, and a division of property, would have operated wonderfully amongst the rabble, especially that of London. The *canaille* of all rich nations are nearly alike. . .' When the British fleet came back 'they would have found their capital in the hands of an enemy, and their country overwhelmed by my armies.' [9]

8

There is no end to the complications of the Continental Blockade, and it would be impossible to deal with them adequately without going outside the scope of a biography and the scale of a portrait. The only point that concerns this chapter is the effect of Bonaparte's measures upon Great Britain. How much damage was actually done to her economy? How far was her fighting power reduced? How near did the commercial war come to forcing her to sue for peace? The answer to these questions is to be found, first, and most conclusively, in the statistics of British commerce from 1803 to 1814, and secondly in evidence which cannot be expressed in figures or graphs (but is no less real for not being mathematical) as to the movement of public opinion in England, and its effect upon the policy of the government.

Anyone who studies the statistical evidence will soon be struck by three points: the ineffectiveness of the blockade previous to the Milan Decrees of 1807; the crisis of 1809-11; and the part played by Napoleon's Spanish and Russian adventures in the breakdown of the system.

From 1803 to 1810 the embargo that Napoleon enforced in the French and Dutch ports, at the mouths of the Ems and Elbe, and, after 1806, in the German Baltic ports, did not seriously hamper British trade. The total exports of home-produced goods were valued at £41 millions in 1805, £44 millions in 1806, £40½ millions in 1807, £40¾ millions in 1808, £50¼ millions in 1809, and nearly £50 millions in 1810. The value of 'colonial' goods re-exported from England during the same years was, in 1805, £10 millions, in 1806 nearly £10 millions, in 1807 exactly £10 millions, in 1808 £9 millions, in 1809 £15¾ millions and in 1810 £12¾ millions. If, then, England lived on her export trade, Napoleon's attempt to destroy it was remarkably unsuccessful. It might be said that this was because, during the years in which the continental ports were increasingly shut against her ships, she was able to develop new markets overseas. To a great extent this was so; and it was a point which Bonaparte had overlooked in his calculations. Nevertheless the figures, when analysed, show that the proportion of our exports to Europe remained at a consistently high level. In 1805, 37.8 per cent of British-made goods went to Europe, in 1806, 30.9 per cent, in 1807, 25.5 per cent, in 1808, 25.7 per cent, in 1809, 35.4 per cent and in 1810, 42 per cent; whilst of foreign and colonial goods re-exported from England 78.7 per cent went to Europe in 1805, 72.9 per cent in 1806, 80 per cent in 1807, 71.1 per cent in 1808, 83.1 per cent in 1809 and 76.9 per cent in 1810. In its main endeavour, therefore, the Continental Blockade was, up to 1810, a complete failure.

But what of the other expected result of the embargo on British exports—the flooding of the home market with unwanted and unsaleable goods, to be followed by unemployment, political discontent, and so forth? Statistics again show what was happening. Between 1805 and 1810 the imports of coffee into Great Britain went up from 219,000 to 829,000 cwt., sugar from 3,186,000 to 4,809,000 cwt., raw cotton from 58,812,000 to 132,489,000 lb., wool from 6,021,000 to 10,936,000 lb., flax from 295,000 to 512,000 cwt., and raw silk from 804,000 to 1,341,000 lb. This glut of goods in 1810-11 coincided with a number of big bankruptcies amongst firms unable to recover payments for their exports, especially to South America, with the 'teething troubles,' social and financial, of the Industrial Revolution (the first Luddite Riots broke out in 1811), and with the serious falling-off of trade with North America.

The commercial depression of 1811 appears at once, if we pursue the statistics already given for 1805-10 a year further. The total value of exports of British-made goods from England in 1810 was nearly £50 millions: in 1811 it was just below £35 millions; and if this figure is analysed it is seen that the drop in the exports to northern Europe, including France, was no less than from £7,700,000 to £1,500,000, and in the United States from £10,920,000 to £1,840,000. In foreign and colonial goods re-exported the total drop was from £12,730,000 in 1810 to £9,020,000 in 1811, with similar heavy losses on northern European and U.S.A. trade, but with an even more remarkable drop in the trade with the rest of America from £2,040,000 to £900,000. The situation was critical enough; but it was saved by the rise in the value of exports to countries which the French blockade could not reach—Portugal, the Levant, Ireland, Guernsey, etc., and above all by the very step Napoleon took to complete the Continental System—the invasion of Russia in 1812.

The importance of the part played by America in the blockade is shown by the proportion of British exports that went to the New World—of British-made goods (during the years 1805-11) £60¼ millions value to the U.S.A., and £91¼ millions to the rest of America, altogether £151½ millions, or just a half the total of £301¾ millions. The sudden drop in these exports to the U.S.A. in 1808 from £11¾ to £5¼ millions was compensated for by a rise in the similar exports to the rest of America from £10½ to £16½ millions; and the same thing happened in 1810-11, when the exports to the U.S.A. fell from nearly £11 millions to a little over £1¾ millions (i.e. from 23.9 per cent of our total exports to 6.2 per cent), and those to the rest of America only dropped from £15¾ to £12 millions. Nevertheless 1811 was a black year, and the country came through the crisis only by its imperturbable temper, and through the adaptability of its commercial system—an adaptability derived from its varied and inventive industries, its command of the seas, and the individual enterprise of its people, which played as large a part in a half-world war then as government control did in a whole-world war a century later.[10]

9

But if the Continental Blockade failed in its direct effects, what of the indirect results upon which Napoleon counted? Three points call for special consideration: shipping losses; over-production leading to unemployment; and food shortages.

Although, partly from the outbreak of war, and wholly after Trafalgar, French merchantmen were excluded from the high seas, and only a precarious coastal trade (*cabotage*) survived, yet the naval squadrons and privateers which from time to time slipped through the blockade did more damage to British shipping than would be expected, and caused the ruin of many rich ship-owners. Between 1803 and 1814 the number of British ships captured by the enemy rose from a little over 200 to nearly 400 in 1804, 500 in 1805 and 1806, nearly 600 in 1807, 1808 and 1809 and reached the climax of 619 in 1810. In twelve years the total losses were no less than 5324, or at the rate of 444 a year. As against this, the British captures of French frigates and privateers (when there was little else to capture) averaged only 40 a year. But of course one fox killed was worth a good many chickens. Besides, the losses were abundantly made up for by the seizure of neutral vessels, which were added to the strength of the British mercantile marine. The number of these, during the same seven years, 1805-11, was 22,483, or an average of 3212 a year.

It would be possible to find statistics of other things that formed and moved British public opinion during the blockade—the ebbing tide of production, the rise in prices, the number of bankruptcies, the increased amounts spent on the relief of the poor, and so forth. But statistics are at their best a post-mortem on what was once alive, and at their worst an average which corresponds to no single experience, and points to no unexceptional law. What can safely be said is that the population of Great Britain went on growing during the war, and yet was able to get wages and food out of employers embarrassed by diminishing markets; that Napoleon had many admirers in London drawing-rooms, and the war many opponents in the House of Commons; but that neither party had much influence on the country's policy; that, though the workers smashed up the machinery they blamed for unemployment, they did not break the windows of the 'war-mongers'; that the manufacturers and merchants put more trust in new methods of production, and in smuggling and dumping, than they did in 'government interference' with commerce—for all parties believed in *laissez-faire*; and in short that, whilst Byron travelled round the Levant, and Jane Austen wrote *Sense and Sensibility*, and Leigh Hunt went to prison for insulting the Prince Regent, and Haydon studied the Elgin marbles, and John Keble became a Fellow of Oriel, the government took advantage of the complacent and confident mood of the 'ruling classes' to 'muddle through' to victory.

The most serious danger to British economy during this period was due, by another of the paradoxes of the blockade, not so much to an excess as to a deficiency of imports. This was felt to some extent in the diminishing supply of raw materials for industry—wool from Spain and Germany, silk from Italy, or timber for naval construction from Scandinavia. It was felt more seriously when, in years of bad harvest, the proportion of wheat that Britain normally imported from the Baltic ports—Königsberg, Elbing, and especially Danzig—was not available. This proportion apparently averaged during the years 1801-10 not more than 6½ per cent of our whole consumption, and its purchase cost us some £2 millions a year; to be totally deprived of it would not mean starvation. But when, in 1801, during the League of Armed Neutrality, the price of wheat rose from the normal 50s. or 60s. a quarter to 156s., or again in 1812, during the Moscow campaign, to 155s., and the cost of purchasing supplies from abroad rose from £2 millions to £20 millions a year, the results were felt by all classes, particularly by the poor, and the government was driven to remedies as unprecedented as they were unpopular: not bread rationing (though the French Revolution provided a precedent for it) but a Bill prohibiting the sale of new bread, a royal proclamation asking for economy in the use of bread, and the so-called Brown Bread Act of 1800, together with measures to suspend the corn duties, or to prevent the distillation of spirits and the manufacture of starch. Both in 1800 and in 1812 there were bread riots, but never of great political significance; nor was there ever any danger of the country being starved into surrender.

In view of what happened later in two world wars, the question has naturally been asked whether it ever occurred to Napoleon to reverse his policy, and to attempt to starve England instead of to glut her. It is an academic question: partly because the facts as to British production and consumption are too little known; and partly because, though he had played with the idea, Bonaparte was never in a position to deprive us of more than a small proportion of our overseas supplies: he could not, for instance, touch American wheat, which might have been diverted from Spain to England; and he would have found it difficult even in the Baltic to prevent exports for which we were ready to pay so high a price. In point of fact, he was so anxious to make money by exporting any surplus of grain there might be, after satisfying his own country, that he willingly sold to the highest bidder, whoever it might be.

There remains the more practical question, whether Napoleon's attempt to deprive us of the gold by which we subsidized the Coalition was at all successful. The answer seems to be that it did contribute to a serious drain on our gold reserves, which fell from £8 millions in 1808 to £2 millions in 1815, whilst imports of bullion fell from an average of £2 millions a year before 1800 to nil in 1811. Certainly this made it difficult to supply the £200,000 a month that Wellington needed in the Peninsula: but it was still possible to meet these and other commitments on the continent by exporting either such goods as were of direct use to the troops, or such as could be readily sold or exchanged by them in the country under occupation; or, as in the Peninsula, by taking advantage of business credits and bills of exchange in a foreign country. The amount of our cash subsidies to our allies during the six years 1807-12 was under £15 millions—a very small proportion of the total expenditure in goods and services overseas.

Nor was either the blockade or the payment of subsidies the main cause of the fall in our gold reserves, but rather the depreciation of our currency, which had been in the form of irredeemable paper since 1797, and which, after 1808, lost its value on the foreign market (at Paris, for instance, or at Hamburg) by amounts varying from 21 to 44 per cent. This process was not due to Napoleon's policy, and could have been arrested by the British government. The credit system on which we carried on the war—national debt, paper money, bills of exchange and so forth—was never seriously endangered. In fact, the experiences of 1803-15 provided a precedent and engendered a confidence which carried us through the much greater trials of 1914 and 1939.[11]

According to Gourgaud, the least untrustworthy of those who publicized the conversations at St. Helena, Napoleon maintained to the end the error which his experience of the blockade should have disproved: 'England,' he said, 'is insatiable, and goes on manufacturing goods till she has more than she needs: so her people get accustomed to luxury, and when their produce can find no more markets, they rebel.' But he also admitted, 'If we had only possessed half the national spirit of the English, they would never have been able to fight us.' 'Had I had an English army,' he once said, 'I should have conquered the universe.' He could appreciate the courage of a soldier: he could not understand the self-respect of a civilian. He shared the Frenchman's notion of patriotism as love of a social status and a political order rather than of a way of life: if those were not to one's liking, one would rebel, or go into exile. He did not understand the patriotism which clings to its country at all costs, and supports its government in an emergency, whether right or wrong. He was defeated by all the things he distrusted most: decentralization, aristocracy, landlordism, parliamentary government, a community of business men and shopkeepers. He was the victim of a fatal misjudgment.[12]

10

The history of Napoleon's relations with Spain and Portugal has commonly been treated by English writers as a narrative of the Peninsular War. These campaigns have, indeed, a special interest for military historians. Napoleon himself was only present in the Peninsula for two months out of the five years that his armies spent there. The generals whom he left in command were as much hindered as helped by the orders which he sent them from Paris or Vienna, from Prussia, Poland, or Russia, and which often arrived after the situation had so changed that they could not be carried out. The country, more resembling in its configuration and climate north-west Africa than any part of Europe known to Frenchmen, was mountainous, with few roads; its barren uplands topped by rocky *sierras* and cut by *wadis* either waterless or unnavigable; its scattered villages as primitive and impoverished as any in Ireland, its occasional cities walled like castles; only here and there an oasis-like valley or a coastal plain producing semi-tropical fruits and vegetation; its people proud, cruel, and accustomed to hardship, little capable (indeed) of political unity or military discipline, but easily incited by a fanatical hatred of foreigners and a superstitious dread of heretics (whom they recognized not in British Protestants but in French 'atheists') into every atrocious form of guerrilla warfare.

In such conditions the experience of the French armies in Italy, Germany, or even Egypt, was of little use to them. Scattered into the four corners of a country larger than France, far from their bases and without safe communications, they could not always deal with such forces as the Spanish *juntas* raised against them, and were quite unable to contain the successive raids and retreats of the small but highly disciplined British army, centrally situated on an almost inaccessible coastal plain, and supplied from the sea. Moreover, as Wellington said, 'there was never so perfect a system of espionage as the one he had in Spain; all the *curés* were in his interest, and the French never did or said a single thing that he did not know, and it never was suspected by the enemy.' For 'the power of the priest is immense in Spain; the priest is the resident gentleman of every parish; the bishops reside in towns, where their influence very much exceeds that of the *cabildo* or civil magistrates.'

Had Napoleon chosen to stay in Spain, he might have found an answer to these problems. He would at least have gained first-hand experience of Wellington's skilful and tenacious strategy, and of tactics which defeated his generals, and were to win the day at Waterloo. But the impulse which took his arms into the Peninsula petered out into the sands, like the streams of that desiccated land. The reasons which seemed to demand invasion became inoperative when the invasion began to fail. The pride which forbade an ordered retreat forbade risking the failure of a personal intervention. So the arming of Austria took Napoleon away from the pursuit of Moore in January 1809, as it had from the invasion of England in August 1805; and he never returned.

Yet it is not true that he had no later opportunities of resuming the command in Spain. He was in Paris from October 27th, 1809 to April 4th, 1810, from June 2nd, 1810 to May 16th, 1811, and again from June 5th to August 23rd the same year; he was there again from November 12th, 1811 to May 8th, 1812—nearly two years in all. No: he preferred to write off Spain as a partial loss, rather than to risk losing everything there. Some 600,000 men including 100,000 veterans served there during the five years of the occupation, and perhaps half of them never returned. But he could still win Essling and Wagram. He still had Frenchmen enough to form the spearhead of his cosmopolitan army of 1812. Baylen had been a serious setback for his reputation: what would be thought if it were followed by an evacuation of the country?

Bearing all this in mind, English historians would do well not to exaggerate the importance of the Peninsular War in the drama of the fall of Napoleon. To him it was a growing embarrassment, but not a cause of serious alarm—a running sore, but not a fatal wound. To us it was what in the First World War was called a 'side-show'—not a wasteful or futile one, like the Walcheren campaign of 1809, for it engaged a large force of the enemy, and by its growing successes enheartened our own people and our allies: but nevertheless not a field of ultimate decision.

The fact that Bonaparte exchanged some shots with the Spanish fleet at Toulon in 1793, and had some dealings with Spanish diplomats during his Italian campaign of 1796-97, gave him no special knowledge of Spain —the country, the people, or the government. He assumed, as most Frenchmen did, that there were three ways in which Spain could be useful to France, by supplying her with the three commodities of which she never had enough—ships, troops, and cash. As to how the Spanish government was to be induced to co-operate: that was a matter which only time and experience could show.

The Spanish government meant in effect one man—not the stupid and ignorant King Charles, nor the vulgar and sensual Queen Marie-Louise (though *Los Reyes* were unlucky in employing the ironic genius of Goya to hand down their likeness to posterity), but their Secretary of State, Manuel de Godoy, a gross, domineering and deceitful man, whose influence over the Queen kept him in power, like Talleyrand, long after his dismissal from office. The story of Franco-Spanish relations from 1799 to 1807 is in effect a series of attempts on the part of Napoleon to tie Godoy down to his engagements for the supply of ships, troops and cash, and of

Godoy's attempts to evade them, without exasperating his ally to the point of armed intervention, or involving Spain in the coalitions against her. Throughout these negotiations Napoleon made the mistake of treating Spain cavalierly, as though she were (as indeed she was, to his military mind) a state of second-rate importance, and of sending to represent France at Madrid persons for whom he had no further use in Paris—his brother Lucien, the inexperienced Vandeul, the stupid Beurnonville, or Joséphine's *émigré* brother-in-law, François Beauharnais.

Lucien, in point of fact, achieved three Conventions (1801) which, if they had been carried out, would have brought pressure to bear on Portugal, speeded up the Spanish naval programme, and regulated the tricky question (though of minor importance) of Parma. But he undid these services, in his brother's eyes, by allowing Portugal to buy off the Franco-Spanish offensive of 1801 (the *guerre des oranges*, they called it), and so to secure a breathing-space by the Treaty of Madrid (September 1801), almost coinciding with the Peace of Amiens a month later: in fact, Portugal remained immune from attack for another six years.

When war broke out again in 1803 Spain had to pay heavily for the 'protection' of her powerful ally. Napoleon bullied, and Beurnonville blundered. At last, on October 19th, Godoy promised to contribute 6 million *livres* a month (about £3½ millions a year) to the French treasury, so long as the war lasted; and this became Napoleon's principal source of revenue. But at the end of six months more than half the promised payment was still owing. When the collection of the debt was farmed out to the *Compagnie des négociants réunis* things went more smoothly for France, but more roughly for Spain: at best (e.g. in 1804) twice as much was owing as had been paid. Napoleon was not the first to be deceived by the promise of Spanish gold.

Spain also paid in men and ships: and disastrously. For in 1805 Napoleon induced Godoy to speed up his ship-building and refitting programme to such effect that the Spanish fleet became involved in the grandiose scheme for the invasion of England, and was almost wholly destroyed, with the loss of over 1000 men killed, in the defeat of Trafalgar. Not only so. Spanish troops were summoned to garrison Florence and the distant port of Hamburg, and to fight in the Polish campaign of 1807. They were even present, where some mutinied and more perished, on the Russian expedition of 1812.

There remained the question of Portugal. The position in which matters had been left by Lucien's treaty of 1801 could no longer be tolerated, now that Jena and Friedland had extended the anti-British blockade from the Bay of Biscay to the White Sea—the more so since, in the autumn of 1806, Godoy, believing that Napoleon contemplated the annexation of Spain north of the Ebro, had asked the allies to come to his assistance.

Spain must be punished by being forced to deny her harbours to British shipping, and to join in coercing Portugal to do the same. This was the object of the Treaty of Fontainebleau (October 29th, 1807). Portugal had already (July 19th) been required to close her ports, under threat of French military occupation, and had rejected the ultimatum. Already French troops were marching through the north-western parts of Spain, strung out (from lack of provisions) from Burgos to the Portuguese frontier, which they reached by November 11th. Early in 1808 there were 20,000 in Portugal, 40,000 in northern Spain, and 12,000 in Catalonia.

But now an unexpected occurrence upset Napoleon's plans. In October 1807 an intrigue was on foot in which the French ambassador Beauharnais was deeply involved, and to which Napoleon himself may have given his consent, to re-marry Ferdinand, the heir to the Spanish throne, whose first wife had died in 1806, to a French bride, Mlle de Pagerie. This plan was discovered by Godoy, and caused a constitutional crisis which did not end at the doors of the Escorial, but excited popular feeling against France, already disquieted by the passing of Junot's men in the north-west, and by the replacement of Spanish troops serving abroad by foreign garrisons.

Ferdinand's opposition to *Los Reyes* and their Secretary of State was so popular in the country that the King and Queen took alarm and talked of sailing to America, as their cousins of Portugal had done. But with a French squadron off Lisbon, and French troops under Murat marching on Madrid, Charles abdicated in favour of the Prince of the Asturias (March 19th, 1808). For a month the court was in chaos, one party regretting abdication, and the other unready for accession. At the end of April Napoleon had induced all the leading characters of the 'Escorial affair' to meet him at Bayonne. There, on May 5th, both kings signed away their claims to the throne, and were put under the super-vision of Talleyrand at Valençay, like Pius VII at Savona, whilst Godoy, like Pacca, went to prison. Joseph was summoned from Naples, and pro-claimed King of Spain.

The theatrical colours in which history has embellished the Escorial and Bayonne affairs need not be allowed to distort what to Napoleon might well seem the only solution of an impossible situation. Like most French-men of the time, he had no reverence for royalty, unless it was of his own making. Princes, he thought, should spend their time hunting—it was a piece of advice he followed, too, in his spare time: if they were clever, they became a public danger; if they were stupid, they were unem-ployable. Spain was an ally; and its duty to France in wartime was to provide men and money, particularly money, as required. If the govern-ment proved itself unfit to keep its engagements, and if it was found conniving with Napoleon's enemies, he would deal with it as he had dealt with the rulers of other less important states, by deposing its head, and substituting one of his own family, whom he could control. The thing was done by trickery; but trickery is not always treachery, nor a blunder always a crime. Napoleon honestly believed (if the common phrase be allowed) that Joseph's regime would not only benefit France, but also Spain: the country in all Europe most backward, most ill-governed, and most priest-ridden; an ideal field for the reforms that had renovated France, Italy and Egypt. His mistake was to forget that Spain was— Spain.[13]

II

Joseph Bonaparte, the nominal head of the family, was the only one of his brothers for whom Napoleon felt a steady affection, and in whom all through his life he kept the habit of confiding. Joseph, for his part, though a rich man, who liked nothing better than the life of culture and social enjoyments he led in Paris or at Mortefontaine, shared the family liking for public display, and was glad to get away sometimes from his plain virtuous wife and many daughters: nor was he unwilling to sacrifice his comfort to oblige his younger brother, though he never hesitated to criticize his policy or to quarrel with him over points of family honour. He was not the ablest of the brothers, but he was the most agreeable: the one who best knew how to make himself pleasant to an angry politician, a jealous general, or a pretty woman. He played the part of a devout Catholic with more conviction than his brother, and whilst Napoleon antagonized the church (December 4th, 1808) by abolishing the Inquisition and closing two convents out of every three in the country, Joseph made himself popular both with the superstitious mob of Naples and with the fanatical clergy of Seville.

It was the knowledge of Joseph's success as King of the Two Sicilies which induced Napoleon to transfer him to the throne of Spain. He imagined that the Spaniards were like the southern Italians, Madrid another Naples, and that its people would soon reconcile themselves to a kindly and conciliatory ruler, though a foreigner, and backed by a foreign army. He might have discovered, as George Borrow did thirty years later, that, 'notwithstanding the misrule of the brutal and sensual Austrian, the doting Bourbon, and above all the spiritual tyranny of the court of Rome, Spain can still maintain her own, fight her own combat, and Spaniards are not yet fanatic slaves and crouching beggars. Spain has undergone far more than Naples had ever to bear, and yet the fate of Naples has not been hers. There is still valour in Asturia, generosity in Aragon, probity in Old Castile.'

Joseph had hardly crossed the frontier when he was undeceived. 'No one has as yet told Your Majesty the real truth,' he wrote from Vittoria on July 12th: 'the fact is, not a single Spaniard is on my side, except the few who are travelling with me. The rest, who arrived here and at other places before me, went into hiding, for fear of the unanimous opinion of their compatriots': and from Burgos, a few days later, 'I haven't a single supporter here.' When he entered Madrid on July 20th the streets were empty, and the *largesse* he threw to the crowd lay untouched on the ground.

During these first months Joseph had to contend not only with the hostility of the people, but with the hatred caused by the misconduct of his troops, and with the patriotic enthusiasm roused by Dupont's surrender to the native troops at Baylen, only one day before his entry into Madrid, and by the news of the Convention of Cintra a month later. But when he returned to the capital at the end of the year, and set himself to win over public opinion by disciplining the army, improving the streets and buildings, attending bull-fights, and professing devotion to the church; still more when in 1809 he toured the southern provinces and was received with acclamation at Cordova and Seville, it looked as though, becoming sincerely attached to his new kingdom (like the Austrian Charles V two centuries ago), he would make a success of what might have been thought an impossible task.[14]

But all this time the northern and central provinces were really irreconcilable, in a state of unorganized revolution; and a Spanish revolution was something with which Frenchmen were quite unprepared to deal. It was as little like a French revolution as anything could well be. As in Belgium, the only country north of the Pyrenees with a Catholicism of almost southern intensity, it would be a reaction against new institutions and ideas, a movement for loyalty to the old order: to the hereditary crown of the Most Catholic kings, which Napoleon, an excommunicated enemy of the Pope, had put on the head of a Frenchmen; to the Catholic church, persecuted by republicans who had desecrated churches, murdered priests, and enforced a *loi des cultes*; and to local and provincial rights and privileges threatened by an efficiently centralized government. Almost from the first moment the Asturian parliament and the *junta* of Seville declared war on the French; and soon patriots in all parts of the country were spreading insurrection and mobilizing armies. These were in the long run easily routed by French troops better disciplined and led; but not before, at Baylen, on July 22nd, 1808, Dupont had allowed himself to be cut off, and surrendered with 18,000 men: a disgrace for which Napoleon, who was generally very easy with his generals, degraded him, and put him in prison. (Dupont had his revenge when in 1814, as Minister of War, he controlled the defences of Elba.)

That autumn Napoleon himself visited Spain for the first and last time. Now that Russia had been brought into the blockade by the Treaty of Tilsit, Portugal was the only front door onto the continent that had not been shut against English trade, and the only way to shut it was by conquering Spain. But Napoleon did not take the trouble to understand the country or the people of the Peninsula, and his intervention was marked by a series of mistakes.

His first mistake was to suppose that he could march a French army across Spain to attack Portugal without rousing Spanish resentment. His second mistake was to back the unpopular regime of Charles IV and Godoy, instead of the popular Ferdinand; an error which became irretrievable when he deported Ferdinand, put Joseph in his place, and then thought the position might be mended by restoring him with a French wife. His third mistake was to scatter his armies in attempts to capture and close Spanish-held ports, whilst the one essential port, that of Lisbon, was open, and in English hands. Junot's hold on the place was so feeble that Wellesley, on his first landing, beat him at Vimiera, and his 26,000 men were shipped back to France (August 30th, 1808).

Again, if the pursuit of Moore at the end of that year had been pressed, his force might have been annihilated, and we might have given up an expensive and unpopular campaign. Napoleon admitted at St. Helena that he ought to have stayed another month in Spain, and thrown Moore into the sea. If Soult had advanced straight on Lisbon from Oporto the following spring, the only other British force in the Peninsula might have been forced to re-embark. When at last, in the spring of 1810, Masséna, the ablest French general, was sent in sufficient strength to capture Lisbon, he moved so slowly that Wellington had time to construct the impregnable 'Maginot Line' of the Torres Vedras; and with that security behind him forced the French back into Spain.

In the spring of 1810, whilst Joseph was making his triumphant progress through Andalusia, Napoleon committed an even greater blunder. On February 8th, without consulting his brother, he set up independent military governments in the provinces of Catalonia, Aragon, Navarre and Biscay. He may have supposed Joseph's mild methods unsuited to these troublesome frontier provinces. He may have discounted the pacification of the south as contributing nothing to the policy of blockade. He may even have been jealous of Joseph's success, and have feared the erection of a semi-independent Spain, as he feared the possibility of a united Italy under another conciliatory relative, Eugène. Whatever his motive, his policy was fatal to that of his brother, and undid all the good he had accomplished. Joseph begged to be allowed to abdicate, but, after a short visit to Paris for the baptism of the King of Rome, returned to Madrid, with promises of redress and reinforcement which Napoleon never carried out.

At this point, in the spring of 1811, Napoleon made his final mistake.

Instead of evacuating a country he could not effectively hold, and abandoning a plan of blockade he could not enforce, he kept some 300,000 troops locked up in the country for another two years, only substituting raw recruits for the 60,000 veterans whom he needed for his Moscow campaign; and he left Joseph with no better military adviser than the elderly and incompetent Jourdan. The inevitable result soon followed. A year later, on August 12th, 1812, Wellington defeated Marmont at Salamanca, and entered Madrid. In June 1813, after reorganizing his troops in Portugal during the winter, he advanced again, won a decisive victory over Joseph at Vittoria and forced the French to retreat across the Pyrenees.

Meanwhile, what of the Peninsular blockade, for the sake of which the Peninsular War had been undertaken? The British exports to Portugal, of home products, increased from £430,000 in 1808 to £800,000 in 1809, £1¼ millions in 1810, and nearly £4¾ millions in 1811; and of colonial goods, from £170,000 to £320,000, £920,000 and £1½ millions in the same period; whilst Spanish imports of home products had similarly grown from £860,000 to £2½ millions, £1½ millions and £1¼ millions; and of colonial goods from £260,000 to £660,000, £340,000 and £270,000. These figures show both how ineffective the blockade was, and how little it was worth trying to enforce it; for, apart from military supplies, the Spanish market hardly repaid us the trouble of exploiting it. It would have been far easier for Napoleon if, instead of invading the Peninsula, he had closed the Pyrenees frontier—300 miles of almost impassable mountains as compared with 3000 miles of open coast-line—across which alone British goods could have been smuggled into Europe.

But this was not the whole extent of Napoleon's failure. The flight of the Portuguese royal family to Brazil in 1807, and the Anglo-Spanish alliance from 1808 onwards, opened to British commerce important new markets in Mexico, the West Indies, and the newly liberated states of South America. Figures again are eloquent. Whilst our exports to the U.S.A. declined between 1807 and 1809 from £11¾ millions (home products) to £7¼ millions, and from £250,000 to £200,000 (foreign and colonial goods), the corresponding exports to the West Indies and the rest of America rose from £10½ millions to £18 millions, and from £900,000 to over £1¾ millions.

The Peninsular War, then, stands as the greatest condemnation of the Continental Blockade, the final disproof of Napoleon's belief that he could defeat British sea-power from the land.

It was also taken at the time, and has been represented by historians (perhaps overestimating popular initiative and underestimating the influence of the clergy and of the crown) as a spontaneous national rising against the French invader. Napoleon's Spanish enterprise, Madame de

Staël wrote, 'was his first step towards ruin; for there he was faced with national resistance, the only kind that he could not deal with by diplomacy or bribes. He realized well enough the danger of village and mountain warfare, but he never understood that a war might be a crusade (*la puissance de l'âme*). He relied on cold steel—of which there was little in Spain before the arrival of the English armies. He never reckoned with the one power that no arms could overcome—the enthusiasm of a whole people.' This much is true: the fire that was kindled in Spain spread to the Tyrol, where it was with difficulty put out—only to blaze up again symbolically, three years later, in the burning of Moscow.[15]

12

Napoleon's great victories on land—Marengo, Austerlitz, Jena, Friedland, Wagram—carried with them political and territorial changes which seemed to alter the face of Europe; but the results did not last, and the work had to be done over again. Aboukir Bay and Trafalgar had no such obvious effects on policies or peoples; but they won for Britain the mastery of the Mediterranean and the Atlantic, and for France they were irremediable disasters. Yet it would be a mistake either to underrate Napoleon's naval designs and achievements during 1799-1805, or to ignore the naval operations of 1805-14.

It was by accident rather than intention that Bonaparte became a soldier. His power of organization, his generalship, and his personal magnetism would have made him as great a leader on sea as on land. His inventiveness and gift for extemporization were in fact applied even more to naval than to military affairs; partly, no doubt, because he had not the professional sailor's experience of what could not be done. It was fortunate for England that even he was unable to extemporize a navy efficient and experienced enough to win command of the sea.

Something has been said of Bonaparte's experience of 'amphibious operations' between Toulon and Corsica, when he learnt the weaknesses of a navy whose ships—relics, for the most part, of the Bourbon navy of the American War—put to sea undermanned by untrained and undisciplined crews, and with gunners who, when it came to close fighting, aimed too high. It has been seen how, in the Egyptian expedition, he assumed command of a fleet as large as Nelson's, with a huge convoy, outwitted our ablest admiral, and landed an army on the beach at Alexandria without a shot fired. True, his fleet was destroyed at Aboukir Bay; but he could not be blamed for more than a landsman's share in that disaster.

He took charge again of the voyage home to France, with the same confidence—a gambler's confidence—in his good luck; and again outwitted the navy that should have intercepted him. He may well have thought, when Brumaire put him at the head of the state, that the organization of a French navy capable of defeating that of Great Britain was within his capacity, and not beyond the resources of the country.

One of his first acts was to appoint a Minister of Marine—not a Board of Admiralty—to carry out his commands; then Prefects of Marine (*préfets maritimes*) in sole command of Havre, Lorient, Dunkirk, Rochefort, Toulon, Brest, Boulogne, Antwerp: some of them naval men, but others men of business, or with pre-revolutionary experience of naval arsenals, such as Malouet. For his admirals he chose the best men he could find, whether Jacobins or royalists. He made Sané, who had designed the fine French ships of the American war period, his inspector-general of naval construction; and was himself constantly suggesting new ideas in ship-building—special types of craft to break the Egyptian blockade, or to be employed in the invasion of England. Decrès was reproached, in May 1808, for not having more ships built: 'it seems that if I want a single schooner to put to sea I shall have to design it myself!' Indeed, he was prepared to do so; for again, two years later, he proposes the construction of 74-gun ships of specially light draught, suitable for the shallow channel of the Texel. Whilst in exile at Elba he is still regulating every detail of expenditure (the total of the naval budget is £30) on 'My cutters.'

Again, Napoleon is well aware that a fleet in harbour deteriorates no less surely than an army in barracks; and he is constantly thinking out fresh expeditions to the West Indies, Madagascar, the Canaries, San Domingo, Brazil, India, Surinam, Trinidad, Algiers, the Levant, Martinique, Guadaloupe, Santa Lucia, St. Helena and the West African coast. Even after Trafalgar, in January 1806, he will have Decrès dispatch twelve cruisers to scout the seas from the Baltic to the Newfoundland fisheries, south to Martinique, west to Brazil, east again to the Mediterranean: every available vessel is to be used against British commerce; and in fact a month later four frigates are sent to intercept English, Swedish and Russian ships off Denmark, and three more to cruise in Irish and Icelandic waters.

The most ambitious of these enterprises was the Australian expedition of 1800, which Bonaparte fitted out on the lines of his own invasion of Egypt. Two corvettes, named *Géographie* and *Naturaliste* to fit the idea that this was not a naval but a purely scientific adventure, with twenty-three scientists on board, under Commodore Baudin, sailed from Havre to the Ile de France and Van Diemen's Land, as Australia was then called. There, in what is still named Encounter Bay, they met an English explorer, Captain Flinders of the *Investigator*, on his way back to Europe. Further east they made inquiries of a non-scientific kind as to the British claims on the new continent, and fell under suspicion of intending to hoist the tricolor on King Island, which commanded a route followed by British shipping. The expedition finally returned to France, after the death of its Commodore and other casualties, leaving a few French names on the map of Australia, and with a respectable number of scientific observations, which were published in 1807.

Privateering, or commerce-raiding, as it would be called now, went on throughout the war. It falls into three periods: 1793-1802, 1802-05, and 1805-15. During the first period, though ineffective in Home Waters, owing to British naval superiority and the convoy system, it had considerable successes on the routes of our traffic with India and the East Indies, where Lemême, Malroux, Broussais, and especially Surcouf and Sercey captured a number of rich prizes.

During the peace of Amiens Napoleon showed an activity in naval and colonial designs which had no little to do with the refusal of Britain to surrender Malta, and so with the resumption of hostilities. The reestablishment of French authority in Guadaloupe (1801-02), the failure to recapture San Domingo (1801-03), the dispatch of a squadron to the Ile de France, and a scheme for the destruction of piracy in the Mediterranean by occupying Algiers and Tunis, all belong to these years.

From 1803 to 1805 the ruling idea in Napoleon's mind was the invasion of England. But commerce-raiding still went on in the Indian Ocean, where Bergeret fought a brave action against odds, and the *Sémillante*, under commandant Motard, fought Nelson's old frigate *Terpsichore* to a standstill. As late as 1807-08 Surcouf started a new career as privateer in the same seas, and was followed by Bouvet, Duperré, Hamelin and others; till the British reinforced their ships in those seas, and sent an expedition to occupy the French bases on the Ile Bourbon and the Ile de France (1810).

Napoleon's head was as full of naval projects after Trafalgar as before; but inevitably they came to nothing: projects (mainly designed to please the Tsar) for the conquest of India; expeditions to Ireland, North Africa, Egypt, Brazil; or attempts to relieve the French colonies in the West Indies. This last enterprise led only to the destruction of the Lorient squadron (February 1809), and the burning of that at Rochefort (April 11th) before it put to sea. A third squadron under Troude was attacked and dispersed by Cochrane at Les Saintes a few days later. One after another, the French colonies in the West Indies fell into British hands (1808-10). Napoleon might triumph at Essling and Wagram: but his Minister of Marine could see nothing but disaster. 'It's all very well for you,' Decrès is reported to have said to Marmont; 'you look at everything through rose-coloured spectacles. But let me tell you the truth, and the future as I see it. The Emperor is mad, completely mad: he will turn us all head over heels: the end of it all will be utter disaster.'

But still, in 1808, 1809, 1810, Napoleon was strengthening the Channel ports; in 1811 he was reassembling the invasion flotilla of 1805, and watched from the shore a British attack on Boulogne; he visited Cherbourg with his new Empress, and made a gesture of putting out to meet the British. He still dreamed of naval superiority. Speaking on March 24th, 1811, he said: 'Louis XIV had no port but Brest: I have the whole coast-line of Europe. In four years' time I shall have a fleet . . . I can build twenty-five ships a year. When my fleets have been three or four years at sea, we shall have the measure of the English. I know I may lose three or four fleets: but we are brave, we are always ready for action, before ten years are up we shall succeed. I shall conquer England.'

And in fact, within three years, the French fleet numbered some 60 ships of the line, 40 frigates and 800-900 smaller vessels: but they lay at anchor in various ports from Hamburg to Bayonne and Cette to Ragusa; and outside cruised British blockading forces strong enough to destroy anything that might venture out. So ended all Napoleon's dreams of naval supremacy: he could neither blockade the sea from the land nor the land from the sea.[16]

X

ROME

(1804-1814)

I

How was it that in 1810, when the Emperor of the French wanted to divorce one wife and marry another, he did not, as his Catholic predecessors would have done, appeal to the Pope? It was because during the six years that had passed since the coronation of 1804 the consequences of that pretentious ceremony had worked themselves out into disillusionment, hostility, and open violence, till at the moment when Pius VII might have been blessing the union of the only two Catholic dynasties north of the Alps, his capital was occupied by French troops, and he languished in exile in a remote seaport of north Italy, the prisoner of a sovereign whose disregard for the church's marriage law was not the least of his offences.

Three months after the coronation, Pius travelled back from Paris to Italy a few days behind Napoleon and Joséphine, greeted, even at such a commercial and worldly centre as Lyon, with an enthusiasm that may well have troubled the Emperor. They had a final interview at Turin on April 24th, 1805. The Pope knew that he had failed to get any concessions of importance to justify his condescension to the supplanter of the Bourbons. The Legations (Bologna, Ferrara, and Romagna) were still alienated from the Papal States; the Organic Articles still violated the spirit of the Concordat with France, and a like danger might be anticipated from the *Loi organique sur le clergé italien,* which had become an Italian Concordat over a year ago (September 16th, 1803). Since the publication of Melzi's decrees (January 24th, 1804) the Pope might refuse to ratify this settlement, and the Emperor might retaliate by depriving him of his Temporal Power—his title and rights as head of a sovereign state. Those who had formerly favoured the Pope's journey to Paris now deplored it, and fanatical Catholics—Joseph le Maistre, for instance—declared that the crimes of the Borgias were less heinous than the apostasy of their successor.

It was at least certain that Napoleon had taken the courtesy of Pius for weakness, and believed that he could now proceed with his Italian designs without considering the susceptibilities of a simple-minded old monk and his outmoded advisers. There followed, during the summer and autumn of 1805, a number of incidents which put this theory to the test.

At Milan, on May 26th, the immense white marble Duomo, with its towering pillars and fretted roof, was the scene of a coronation even more impressive than that in Nôtre Dame. In the presence of the people of Lombardy the new Charlemagne was invested by the obedient Caprara and sixteen bishops with the sceptre, the globe, the sword and other insignia of the old Emperors, and placed on his own head the iron crown of Monza, with the traditional challenge *Dieu me l'a donnée, gare à qui la touche!* The act was greeted as of old with the acclamation, *Viva il Imperatore e Re!* 'I hope (he wrote to Cambacérès) that it will be prophetic.' There followed, for the Milanese, fireworks and illuminations, and for the French army a distribution of 2000 crosses of the Legion of Honour. Orders were given for the completion of the western façade of the Duomo, and a figure of Napoleon appeared amongst the holy statues on the roof.

But the Pope of Rome was not at the coronation; neither was the Emperor of Austria, the legitimate head of the Holy Roman Empire, so recently dispossessed of his inheritance. To the one this ceremony represented the usurpation of a throne—empty, indeed, but not to be occupied by another without offence: to the other it was a threat to destroy the oldest sovereignty in Europe, that of the successor of St. Peter, and to reduce Rome, the capital of the civilized world, to the status of the *chef-lieu* of a French *département*.[1]

2

Within four days of his second coronation Napoleon ordered that the Italian Concordat should come into operation as from June 1st. This was soon followed (June 8th) by a *statut de clergé* on the lines of the Organic Articles, and by the decision to introduce the *Code Civil* as from January 1st, 1806. Whatever pains Napoleon might take to conciliate the bishops and clergy, these measures were a mortal affront to the authority of Rome, and to the Catholic law of marriage.

The second point may seem unimportant to those who are accustomed to regard the ordering of marriage as an affair for the state, and the church's scruples about divorce as based, at best, on a doubtful interpretation of words never meant to be embodied in a law. But in 1805 it was still a plain issue between revelation and reason, the Catholic church and the Revolutionary state; and the marriage clauses of the Civil Code seemed to attack the moral principles of the Papacy in their very stronghold. Moreover two instances of what was involved were fresh in the Pope's mind.

In December 1803 Napoleon's youngest brother Jérôme, whilst in America, had married a Baltimore girl, Elisabeth Patterson. When Napoleon first heard of this, it suggested nothing more than some disparaging remarks about his relations. But a year later, now himself an Emperor, and his family a royal dynasty, he took it very differently. 'M. Jérôme,' he wrote to Cambacérès on May 6th, 1805, 'has arrived at Lisbon with Mlle Patterson, his mistress. I have ordered him to come and see me, and his mistress to be shipped off again to America': and to Madame Mère (April 22nd), 'If he shows no inclination to wash away the dishonour with which he has stained my name, by forsaking his country's flag on land and sea for the sake of a wretched woman, I will cast him off for ever.' 'Married abroad, the marriage contract not entered in any register, under age, no publication of banns—why, it's no more a marriage than that of two lovers who get "married" in a garden, on "the altar of love," in the presence of the moon and stars. They may say they are married; but when they fall out of love they will soon discover they are not.' In fact (as he was forced to admit) they had been effectively married by a 'Spanish priest who so far forgot himself as to give them his blessing'; but the girl was a Protestant and a commoner. From Milan, accordingly, two days before the coronation, Napoleon had written to the Pope, saying that it was most undesirable, in the interests of the French church, that there should be 'a Protestant girl so near the throne,' and asking for a Bull to nullify Jérôme's marriage.

The request came at an unlucky moment, when everything that Napoleon did was suspect; nor could Pius fail to remember that he had been kept in the dark, till Joséphine told him, about the nature of the Emperor's first marriage; he might well suspect that this had been a calculated attempt to make the divorce of Joséphine at some future date less difficult. At any rate he was not going to provide a precedent for it. He therefore refused Napoleon's request. A year later (October 1806) Jérôme's marriage was dissolved, at least to Napoleon's satisfaction, by Fesch and the Archbishop of Paris: they probably foresaw the use that would be made of their decision four years later.[2]

The affair of Lucien Bonaparte was equally painful to the Pope. When in 1805 Napoleon was considering Lucien as a candidate for royalty, he insisted that he must divorce his second wife, Mme Jouberthon, the discarded wife of a business man, and the mother of his illegitimate son. Lucien—older than Jérôme, abler than Louis, and as antipathetic to Napoleon as Joseph was submissive—steadily refused, and was supported by his mother and other members of the family. In the end he retired with his wife to the shelter of the Papal States. But Napoleon would not leave

him alone: in 1807 he offered to make him King of Naples, and to provide for his children, if he would divorce Mme Jouberthon, though he
might still live with her (as he had done before marriage) as a mistress.
Lucien again refused. In 1808 he abused him for remaining in Rome
under the French occupation, and told Joseph to remove him, if necessary
by force, to Florence, Pisa, or better still to America. In 1810 his name
was to be struck off the list of Senators because he 'had given himself
over to a shameful passion for a woman whose manner of life had raised
an insurmountable barrier between himself and all decency, and We decided that he could not be included in Our hereditary line.' In order to
escape arrest Lucien was forced to escape by sea, hoping to reach America: but he was intercepted by a British ship, and taken to England,
where he settled down as a country gentleman, and became an example
of moral principle: 'a Frenchman refusing a crown and declining to
part with his wife (wrote Walter Scott) is indeed one of the most uncommon exhibitions in an age fertile in novelties.' [3]

To these instances of Napoleon's cavalier attitude towards the authority of the church and the indissolubility of marriage were added stronger
proofs of his intention to exploit the Concordat and the Coronation for
the political ends of his regime.

At some point in his restless inquisition into the subjects taught in
Catholic schools he came across the Catechism—perhaps he remembered
it from his childhood. There were at the end of the eighteenth century
as many catechisms in use in the French church as there was dioceses,
and more—most of them derived from Bossuet's catechism of 1686; and
since 1785 more than one attempt had been made to standardize them,
particularly in the new composite dioceses. To Napoleon this was a
heaven-sent opportunity to turn an ecclesiastical reform to political uses.
Recourse was had, as in other church matters requiring delicate handling,
to Bernier; and his additions to the questions and answers on the fourth
commandment, as emended by the Emperor, left no doubt in the minds
of his young subjects (if needed they could understand what they were
saying) as to what the founder of Christianity really meant when he
said, 'Render unto God the things which are God's, and unto Caesar the
things which are Caesar's.'

Q. What are the duties of Christians toward the princes who
govern them, and what, in particular, are our duties towards
Napoleon I, our Emperor?

A. Christians owe to the princes who govern them, and we, in
particular, owe to Napoleon I, our Emperor, love, respect, obedience, loyalty, military service and the taxes ordered for the

preservation and defence of the Empire and his throne: we also owe him fervent prayers for his safety and for the spiritual and temporal prosperity of the state.

Q. Why are we bound in all these duties towards our Emperor?

A. First, because God, who creates Empires and apportions them according to his will, has, by accumulating his gifts upon him, set him up as our sovereign, and made him the agent of his power, and his image on earth. So to honour and serve our Emperor is to honour and serve God himself. Secondly, because our Saviour Jesus Christ taught us both by example and precept what we owe to our sovereign: for he was born under obedience to Caesar Augustus, he paid the prescribed taxes, and in the same breath as he said 'Render to God what belongs to God,' he said, 'Render to Caesar what belongs to Caesar.'

Q. Are there special reasons why we should be more deeply devoted (*plus fortement nous attacher*) to Napoleon I, our Emperor?

A. Yes, there are: for it is he whom God raised up in difficult circumstances to re-establish the public worship of the holy religion of our ancestors, and to be its protector. It is he who restored and preserved public order by his profound and active wisdom; he defends the state by the strength of his arm; he has become the Lord's Anointed by the consecration he received from the Sovereign Pontiff, the head of the Universal Church.

Q. What ought one to think of those who are lacking in their duty towards our Emperor?

A. According to the Apostle Saint Paul they would be resisting the order established by God himself, and rendering themselves worthy of eternal damnation.

Q. Do our obligations towards our Emperor apply equally towards his legitimate successors in the order established by the Imperial constitutions?

A. Yes, undoubtedly; for we read in Holy Scripture that God, by a supreme disposition of His will, and by His Providence, bestowes his empires not only upon particular individuals, but also on families.

Rome would never sanction this caricature of Christianity. But the complaisant Caprara authorized its use, and the bishops obeyed (May 1806).

Another cause of offence was now remembered. Several years before, Bonaparte had rediscovered (though not in any orthodox martyrology) the saint after whom he had been named by his pious parents, and had ordered that St. Napoléon's Day should be celebrated throughout the Empire on August 16th. Parisians noticed with more amusement than indignation that in the *almanach national* from 1802 the name of St. Roch had been replaced on August 16th by that of St. Napoléon. It was explained that Napoleon's birthday (August 15th) could not decently supplant the popular feast of the Assumption on that date, and that St. Roch had been sacrificed to mark the First Consul's disapproval of the recent refusal of the *curé* of Saint-Roch to give Catholic burial to Mlle Chameroy, a dancer at the Opéra. Bernier, again appealed to, arranged suitable devotions; Caprara once more approved; the protest from Rome came too late.[4]

The Papacy has always been willing to allow a good deal of latitude to governments which undertake to enforce Catholic teaching in their schools. But it was shocked by Napoleon's additions to the Catechism and the Calendar; and it was not reassured by the turn which he gave to religious teaching in the militarized *prytanées* and *lycées*, and by the overruling authority of the *Université impériale* (1808). It was only too obvious that at every turn religion was being subordinated to political ends. The object was to produce loyal soldiers and civil servants, not good Catholics.

But much more than this—though perhaps nothing more important, *sub specie aeternitatis*, as a philosopher might say—was at stake in the ten years' struggle that began in 1804 between the Tuileries and the Vatican.

3

To a modern traveller Rome, with all its ecclesiastical glamour and all its memories of antiquity, is a national capital, the political centre of a people and a state that have been united and independent for nearly a hundred years. Within that capital, and by agreement with that government, there exists a tiny cell of Papal autocracy, as it once existed within French territory at Avignon—a state in material means more analogous to San Marino, Monaco, or Lichtenstein than to any of the European 'Powers,' yet with a spiritual citizenship that covers the whole world, and under a sovereign of whose words and acts every government must take account.

In 1804 things were very different. The Italians were a people, with a language and a way of life; but Italy was not a state. Rome was a capital, but not of a nation. Its sovereign, the Pope, was at once the heir of the Caesars and the successor of St. Peter: the representative of what remained of a Universal Empire, and the spiritual ruler of what remained of a Universal Church. Italy had never been to the Caesars what France or Spain were to their sovereigns at Paris or Madrid—a national and frontiered state, but merely the innermost of a series of zonal provinces; and Rome the centre of a spider's web of roads, knotted and crossing at fortified *castra* and *coloniae*, by which generals and administrators came and went on their imperial duties. When the flood of barbarism covered first the outlying parts of the Empire, and then Italy, these points and lines of the Roman pattern of civilization still emerged; Rome still at the centre, Rome still the source of law, still the seat of church government, 'the ghost of the deceased Roman Empire sitting crowned upon the grave thereof.' And so Italy had remained, down to the end of the eighteenth century, when, once again after 300 years, a French invader came across the Alps.

To Napoleon, who had Italy in his veins as well as in his mind, it was a matter both of personal ambition and of national policy to mould and remodel this land of grand memories and infinite possiblities into a modern state. Into what shape, was determined by the example of France, revolutionary and imperial: by what means, would depend, as the course of his military campaigns depended, upon the political lie of the land, and the counter-moves of his ecclesiastical enemies. He knew— had he not exploited it?—the old municipal spirit of the Italian city-states, which set one against another, and preferred a foreign alliance to a united front against invasion. He was aware, as intelligent travellers were half a century later, of the political, cultural, economic and religious differences between cities that looked so alike: Naples lazy, immoral and superstitious; Florence artistic and independent; Venice luxurious and materialistic; Milan republican and anticlerical. He knew (though he never visited it) Rome, with its three hundred churches, its crowd of ecclesiastics, its pilgrims and its beggars—Rome, which so many devout travellers greeted with delight and abandoned in despair.

But to his military and imperial mind each city had its special importance: Milan and Turin as gateways of the Alps, and warehouses of silk and wine and market produce; Genoa and Venice for their ships and sailors; Leghorn, Civita Vecchia and Naples as ports which must be closed against British or Russian ships; Tarento and Ancona as harbours that an enemy might use to support military operations in the peninsula; and Rome itself, which had always stood as a barrier between north and south, the final obstacle to Italian unity, yet with its agents of uniformity in every parish in the land, and its sovereign with a prestige above that of princes, as the very citadel of the enemy.[5]

As soon as the coronation festivities at Milan were over, Napoleon spent a month touring round the cities of north Italy, to inaugurate his new government; one night at Cremona, four at Brescia, with manœuvres on the battlefield of Castiglione, two at Verona, now the eastern frontier of his Italian kingdom, four at Mantua, with another review outside the gates of the town, three at Bologna, one at Modena, one at Parma, two at Piacenza (another review) and a week at Genoa.

Genoe, the port for Spain and the gateway of Lombardy and the western Alpine passes, had been of vital concern to Napoleon ever since the campaign of 1796. In April 1802 his old friend Saliceti had been sent there, with instructions to enforce the Constitution of October 1801. This had been done; but now it was not enough. On the day of the Milan coronation, in the absence of the Doge and many senators, Saliceti had put through a measure incorporating Liguria in the French Empire as the three *départements* of Genoa, Montenotte, and l'Appennin. On June 30th Napoleon made a state entry into his new possession, and slept at the Palazzio Doria in the historic bed of Charles V.

At Bologna, a few days earlier, he had settled the fate of another state, the little republic of Lucca, which had for centuries prided itself on the golden word *Libertas* inscribed above its gateway. In 1801, again through Saliceti's agency, it had been given a new constitution; now (June 23rd, 1805), it became the Principality of Felix Baciocchi and his wife, Elisa Bonaparte.[6]

It was not surprising, then, that by the summer of 1805 the Papacy watched with growing apprehension the rising tide of French occupation, with its destruction of ancient rights, its secularization of marriage, its subordination of church to state, its economic exactions, the irreverence and brutality of its manners. Where would it all end? The question might have had a different answer if Napoleon had been able to carry out his invasion of England in July 1805. The arming of Austria and the invasion of Germany made it certain that Italy would be drawn into central European hostilities, and that it would become almost impossible for the Papal States to remain neutral.

For three centuries north Italy had been the southern half of the battle-field between France and Austria. To Vienna it seemed the most impor-tant half: but now Napoleon had decided otherwise; and whilst the Archduke Charles fought an indecisive battle at Caldiero (October 30th) and hurriedly retreated to carry help to Vienna, the capitulation of Ulm and the overwhelming victory of Austerlitz brought disaster to anti-French interests in all Italy from Lombardy to Calabria. The whole coast-line was open to British or Russian war-ships. Every port was a possible landing-place. Woe to any state that now favoured or even tolerated the enemy!

The first place to feel Napoleon's anger was Naples. The 'Kingdom of the Two Sicilies' was under the rule of the Spaniard Ferdinand and the Austrian Marie-Caroline, of whom the least that can be said is that he caricatured the failings of Louis XVI without his good intentions, and she the faults of her sister Marie-Antoinette without her charm. The treacherous ways of the court and the degraded character of the people had been sufficiently notorious in the years preceding the Peace of Amiens; since then, under the influence of General Acton, a de-naturalized Englishman who retained only his hatred of the French, and who for a quarter of a century controlled its policy, Naples had been bitterly hostile to the French Republic. When war broke out in 1803, Napoleon took the opportunity given by his military re-occupation of Otranto, Tarento, and Brindisi to set a watch on Naples. Ferdinand retaliated by making a secret alliance with England. Alquier, the new French ambassador to the Vatican, succeeded in securing Acton's dismissal (May 1804); but this did not prevent the Neapolitan court from planning a Russo-English landing to coincide with the outbreak of the war with Austria, or from signing its adhesion to the Third Coalition (September 10th, 1805). Ferdinand, like Frederick-William of Prussia, could not have chosen a worse moment to declare himself against France: a month before Ulm, three months before Austerlitz.

Within ten days of that victory Fesch was told that an army was marching to 'protect' the Papal States and to drive the Russians and English out of Naples. 'Don't talk to me about Naples,' Napoleon writes to Talleyrand on December 23rd: 'every courrier brings news of fresh outrages by this wretched queen: she must be deposed: they must pay an indemnity of £2½ millions.' A proclamation to the army, penned four days later, reminded the troops that a few months ago they had been at the gates of Naples. Three times the Neapolitans had been forgiven for their treason, and for their false neutrality. 'Shall we forgive them a fourth time? Shall we once more trust a court without faith, honour, or reason? No! No! The reign of the dynasty of Naples is at an end: its existence is incompatible with the peace of Europe, and the honour of my crown.'

But the march on Naples was delayed, and it was not till February 18th, 1806, that Joseph, now at the gates of the city, was told to publish there the proclamation of December 27th. By this time no one was left to oppose him. The allied troops and ships had retired on the news of Austerlitz. Ferdinand had fled to Palermo in mid-January. Marie-Caroline, after a grovelling appeal to Napoleon, had followed him on February 11th. Three days later the French army entered Naples.

St. Januarius, who had shown such Francophil tendencies since 1798 that the Queen had appealed from him to St. Anne (but in vain), was now honoured with a Cardinal's mass, and King Joseph put a diamond necklace round his neck, amidst the cheers of the *lazzaroni*. Providence, it seemed, was once more on the side of the big battalions.[7]

4

It remained to deal with Rome and the Papacy. Though few doubted that the completeness of Napoleon's Italian policy involved the incorporation of the Papal States in the French Empire, Napoleon himself may well have shrunk from a step which he guessed would be regarded as a kind of sacrilege, and would weaken his repute as a Catholic sovereign all over Europe. He preferred to adopt a policy of pinpricks, which might drive Pius into putting himself in the wrong, and at the same time to elaborate a historical and theological counterblast to the claims of the Vatican. The second method pleased his inventive mind, flattered his dynastic pride, and exercised his taste for Italian rhetoric. But it was the first method upon which—always a realist—he mainly relied, and which in the end provided a tolerably good excuse for carrying out the plan he had in mind.

Hostilities had in effect been declared between Emperor and Pope in the autumn of 1805, when, in view of the danger of a British naval descent on the Adriatic port of Ancona—from which an enemy force might cut Italy in half—Gouvion St. Cyr's army, on its march north from Naples, occupied its fortifications (October 18th), and made it a base for military operations in the valley of the Po. After a short evacuation it was reoccupied early in November, with the inflictions of billeting and requisitioning which always accompanied a French army.

As soon as Pius heard of this, he took a course which Napoleon had often adopted towards himself, and which, by its very breach of Papal precedent, emphasized the seriousness of the occasion; he wrote a private letter to the Emperor (November 13th), which Fesch was to hand on, without knowing the contents. In it he protested against Napoleon's repeated attempts, during the past year, to compromise the neutrality of the Papal States, and demanded the evacuation of Ancona. If this were not done, he would break off all communications with the French representative at Rome. Napoleon received this ultimatum at Vienna, between Ulm and Austerlitz, and left it for the time unanswered. But on January 7th, 1806, he returned a letter which was as uncompromising as the Pope's. 'Your Holiness (he said) should not lend his ear to ill advice, and write me such a tactless letter (*une lettre si peu ménagée*) . . . The occupation of Ancona is an immediate and necessary consequence of the military incompetence of the Holy See. It was better for Your Holiness to see that fortress in my hands than in those of the Turks or the English . . . I have always considered myself the protector of the Holy See; and it was in this capacity that I occupied Ancona . . . I shall continue to protect it, whatever the mistakes, ingratitude, and ill-will of men whom these last three months have unmasked. They thought I was done

for; but, by the success with which He favoured my arms, God has signal-
ly demonstrated His protection of my cause. So long as Your Holiness
consults the friends of true religion, and his own heart, I shall be his
friend . . . God knows, I have done more for religion than any other
prince alive.'

Napoleon signed this missive, 'Your devoted son, Emperor of the
French and King of Italy.' His covering letter to Fesch was decidedly less
ménagée than the Pope's: 'The Pope has written me a quite ridiculous
and lunatic letter . . . Make it clearly understood that I won't stand any
more of this nonsense . . . As these imbeciles see no harm in a Protestant
occupying the French throne I shall send them a Protestant ambassador.
Tell Consalvi that . . . he must either do what I have required of him,
or resign his post.'

Then, after ridiculing the idea of Papal neutrality, Napoleon used for
the first time the historico-theological argument which recurs with variations throughout this extraordinary correspondence. 'For the Pope's purposes, I am Charlemagne. Like Charlemagne, I join the crown of France
with the crown of the Lombards. My Empire, like Charlemagne's,
marches with the East. I therefore expect the Pope to accommodate his
conduct to my requirements. If he behaves well, I shall make no outward
changes: if not, I shall reduce him to the status of bishop of Rome . . .
Really, there is nothing in the world so unreasonable as the court of
Rome.'

If Pius knew of this letter to Fesch, his reply (January 29th) ignored it,
and confined the controversy to Papal rights in Italy, including the old
question of the return of the Legations. This drew another angry letter
to Fesch (February 11th), instructing him to insist on the expulsion of all
English, Russians, Swedes, or Sardinians at the court of Rome. He was
also to take possession—by force, if necessary, and in the name of the
King of Italy—of the Roman palaces belonging to Venice, Naples, and the
Farnese family.

In May the 'war of nerves' is resumed with demands that the Pope
shall recognize Joseph as King of Naples: otherwise Napoleon will cease
to recognize the temporal power of the Papacy. Let Pius remember St.
Louis, who was at war with the Pope, and Charles V, who seized Rome.
Even Elisa Baciocchi is told to inform Pius, when he protests against her
introduction of the Concordat (April 12th), that she will obey him only
in spiritual matters, and Napoleon in matters temporal: if he persists in
encouraging sedition at Lucca, he will be guilty of conduct unbecoming a
follower of Christ. Next month Eugène is ordered to seize Ostia, and to
close the Tiber against English commerce.

By this time Napoleon's Charlemagne thesis was ready for embodiment
in ambassadorial instructions; and on June 19th Talleyrand instructed

Alquier, Fesch's successor at Rome, accordingly. This is what Napoleon had dictated. 'I have to consider the Pope both in his temporal and in his spiritual capacity. As a temporal prince, he belongs willy-nilly to my Confederation. If he falls in with my ideas (*fait des arrangements avec moi*), I shall leave him the sovereignty of his present states: if he does not, I shall seize his whole coastline. As for his spiritual capacity, it must always be clearly understood that if the difficulties occasioned by the Kingdom of Italy are not smoothed out, I shall enforce the French Concordat there. It must be understood too that, since our religion is really true (*étant toute vraie*), and not a matter of convention, everything which, saves souls in France saves them in Italy, and nothing which cannot save souls in one country can save them in another; so that, it being equally possible to be saved under the French as under the Italian Concordat, the Pope's opposition to the latter is a mass of wretched quibbles (*de mauvaises chicanes*). Anyhow I shall not go back on what I have done.'

The replacement of Fesch by Alquier, and of Consalvi by Di Pietro and other less cautious advisers, intensified the quarrel. The relationship of Pius and Napoleon (it seemed) was no longer that of Leo III and Charlemagne, but of Gregory VII and Henry IV. But for nearly a year hostilities were held up by the Prussian and Polish campaigns; and it was not until the Peace of Tilsit (July 7th, 1807) that Napoleon was free to force the final issue. Now he was in fact as well as in theory the master of western Europe, with the right to call himself 'King and Emperor of the Romans.' Now he must, if his enterprise against England is to succeed, close every port against British shipping, from the Baltic to the Adriatic. It is the same double policy as before, but with a new urgency. Since Austria has been compelled to close Trieste and Fiume, and France controls Genoa, Leghorn, Naples and the ports at the heel and toe of Italy, only Civita Vecchia on the west coast and Ancona on the east remain neutral; and both are in Papal territory. But Ancona had been in French hands now since November 1805, and Civita Vecchia since May 1806: was that not enough? No: for the blockade was never efficient where it ended at high water mark. It needed the support of friendly authorities, the rule of French law, the fear of French troops: the whole hinterland must be organized to enforce it.

Nor could the blockade be isolated from the other uses that Napoleon would make of his Italian possessions; notably the assignment of 'Duchies' to generals and statesmen whom he wished to reward for their services. This scheme was launched in a letter to Eugène on March 31st, 1806: there were to be estates of three values—£6000, £10,000 and £15,000; but of two taken out of Papal *enclaves* in Neapolitan territory one worth nearly £25,000 went to Bernadotte, and another (surely an intentional insult in a Catholic country?) to the apostate and excommunicated Talleyrand.

In July 1807 Pius so far yielded to Napoleon's threats as to nominate the French Cardinal de Bayane to discuss the points at issue; but when, early in November, Napoleon seized the whole Adriatic coastline of the Papal States included in the Duchy of Urbino, the March of Ancona, and the provinces of Fermo and Macerata, the Pope withdrew his powers. He would not be intimidated.

This was the beginning of the end. On January 10th, after his visit to Venice, Napoleon ordered his troops to march, and on February 2nd they entered Rome. General Miollis's instructions were to occupy the castle of St. Angelo, in order to arrest 'brigands' arriving from Naples, as well as Neapolitan and English nationals; but to show all deference to the Pope. But Napoleon's whole mind was revealed to Alquier twelve days later. 'The Emperor (his letter said) is not ambitious for any extension of the territory of his Italian states, and does not really want to take anything away from the Pope; but his intention is to include the Pope in his system, and to exercise in his states the same control as he does in Naples, Spain, Bavaria, and the states of the Confederation. If however the court of Rome . . . commits fresh imprudences, it will lose its temporal states once and for all.' And this is likely enough to happen; for, the first time the Pope publishes a Bull or any such declaration, Napoleon will at once issue 'a decree quashing the Donation of Charlemagne, and annexing the states of the Church to the Kingdom of Italy'—a step justified by 'the evil that the sovereignty of Rome has done to religion, and the contrast between Jesus Christ dying on a cross and his successor making himself a king.'

A pretext for annexation was found within two months. On March 20th, on the ground that 'the Pope shows no accommodation to Napoleon's wishes,' Miollis is ordered to seize the temporal government, march his troops through the Vatican, and mount guard over the entrances of the Papal palace. The 'wishes' the Pope ignored were of course le sine qua non of Napoleon's policy—that the Papal States should join in the Continental Blockade of English commerce. 'If the Holy Father agrees to this, there is nothing more between us. If he refuses, it is a declaration of war against the Emperor.' Napoleon ends with characteristic obtuseness by saying that if the Pope loses his states, 'nothing will be lost of his spiritual rights: he will still be the bishop of Rome as his predecessors of the first eight centuries were.'

Pius now retired to the Quirinal, where he barricaded himself in, under the mouths of French guns: and it was from this imprisonment that he issued on June 10th the bull Quam Memoranda, excommunicating (but not by name) the authors of attacks against the Holy See 'whatever their honours or dignities.'⁸

5

This second act of defiance by the Pope reached Napoleon, like the first, at an unlucky moment. Then it was between Ulm and Austerlitz; now it was between Essling and Wagram. This time he sent an instant reply: one so momentous in its consequences, yet so often ignored or misquoted that it must be given in full. It was addressed to Joachim Murat, and dated Schönbrunn, June 19th. 'I have informed you (he wrote) of my intention that matters at Rome should be conducted with a high hand (*vivement*), and that no kind of resistance can be tolerated . . . If, contrary to the spirit of his position and of the Gospel, the Pope preaches revolt, and uses the immunity of the Quirinal to print circulars, he must be arrested (*on doit l'arrêter*). There is no time for more scenes. Philippe le Bel arrested Boniface, and Charles V kept Clement VII a long time in prison; and they had done much less to deserve it. A priest who preaches discord and war against the temporal Power, when he should preach peace, is abusing his sacred character.'

Upon this General Radet, who was second in command of the troops, was ordered by his senior officer, General Miollis, to arrest the Pope, and remove him from Rome. At 2 a.m. on the night of July 5-6th detachments of troops with scaling ladders forced their way into the Quirinal, broke down door after door in the dark, echoing palace. The 90 *Suisses* with their antique uniforms and halberds offered no resistance. At last Radet and his men found the Pope sitting at a table with five Cardinals standing behind him, and a number of ecclesiastics and officials at the end of the room. 'Holy Father,' said the General, 'I am sent by His Majesty the Emperor Napoleon to ask whether your Holiness is disposed to agree to the treaty whose terms have been presented to Him.' 'Dear Son,' replied the Pope (they both spoke in Italian), 'I cannot, I must not, and I will not do so.' 'Then,' said the General, 'I must put you under arrest.' Within half an hour a carriage was ready. They drove off into the night.

When Napoleon's plans went right, he took the credit: when they went wrong, someone else must bear the blame—Brueys for Aboukir Bay, Villeneuve for the failure of the English invasion, Talleyrand for the murder of the Duc d'Enghien, Ney or Grouchy for Waterloo. So now. The kidnapping of the Pope by his 'devoted son,' the Catholic Emperor of the French, was a scandal that could not be hid. In a series of letters— to Fouché on July 18th, to Cambacérès on the 23rd, to Fouché again on August 6th, to Miollis on the 10th—Napoleon declared that he never intended it. 'They ought to have arrested Cardinal Pacca, and left the Pope in peace at Rome'; 'It was without my orders and against my will that the Pope was removed from Rome'; 'my orders were to arrest Pacca, and not the Pope.'

To all these protestations of innocence the letter of June 19th is a sufficient answer. The afterthought, in the first letter to Fouché, 'But after all there's no remedy; what's done has been done,' and the outbreak to Miollis, 'Never again shall the Pope return to Rome,' show where Napoleon's real mind lay.

On the other hand he was not to blame, except by the vagueness of his orders in a matter which he would ordinarily have regulated to the tiniest detail, for the Pope's sufferings during his journey. He could not have thought it good policy to treat a venerable ecclesiastic in his seventieth year as Pius was now treated. He was forced to start without any change of clothes, and with only twenty-two *sous* in his purse. He slept in wayside inns, and, owing to the heat and the poor food, suffered from dysentery: the carriage was driven at full speed over bad roads, and once overturned. Nor was Pius likely to forget that his predecessor, similarly carried over the Alps ten years ago, had died of his hardships (August 29th, 1799), or that one of his own companions had succumbed on the way to Paris in 1804. The journey was needlessly prolonged, first over the Alps to Grenoble, before orders came to travel by the Riviera; and then south again by Avignon—an omen of Papal captivity—to Savona. Here at last, by his captor's orders, Pius was decently lodged in the bishop's palace, with nothing of the air of a prison. But he refused any amenities; would not drive out, or receive gifts of money; sewed on his own buttons and washed his own clothes; and passed his days, like the monk he was, in reading and prayer.

As for the unhappy Pacca, he was imprisoned in the fortress of Fenestrelle, and not allowed to see anybody. 'I make a great difference,' wrote Napoleon, 'between him and the Pope, both on the ground of position and of moral virtue. The Pope is a good man, though ignorant and fanatical. Cardinal Pacca is an educated man but a rascal (*coquin*), and an enemy of France: he deserves no consideration.' But when his *Memoirs* were read in Paris, Pacca had his revenge: his account of the Pope's sufferings horrified Catholics and Protestants alike.[9]

6

Travellers who knew Venice in the days before the first world war will remember how proudly three great Italian flags flew on Sundays and holidays in the Piazza di San Marco, before the west front of the Duomo. Then the Risorgimento was almost recent history; the national state was barely half a century old; and the shame of a foreign occupation seemed to have been banished for ever. The flags (though as yet without the arms of Sardinia) had been first hoisted in place of those of Austria,

on January 19th, 1806. Soon afterwards Eugène Beauharnais, Napoleon's
Viceroy of Italy, with his young Bavarian bride, arrived to inaugurate a
new government. They found Venice bitterly cold, but the Venetians
warm-hearted and enthusiastic: for though their pride was hurt by incorporation, as seven Frenchified *départements*, in a new-fangled Kingdom of Italy, their rulers were chosen from the old aristocracy, and bore
good Venetian titles; and though Napoleon cut out of their territory
twelve estates to recompense his French generals, he reunited their ancient
possessions in the Adriatic, the lovely islands and coastline of Istria and
Dalmatia.

Elsewhere in Italy the same process of absorption in the French Empire
was going on, though less spectacularly, and at less speed. The Kingdom
of Etruria, created in 1801, came to an end with the death of its Spanish
sovereign two years later—its reputation as a home of Enlightened
Despotism tarnished, the trade of its chief port, Leghorn (Livorno), now
in French hands, sadly diminished, and its affairs controlled by clerics and
intriguers. For another four years Queen Marie-Louise was left undisturbed, the fate of her regency dependent upon Napoleon's complicated
dealings with the Spanish court: but in November 1807 she was informed
that Etruria would be exchanged for part of Portugal, and went out by
one gate of Florence, whilst the French troops entered by another. Six
months later Tuscany (resuming its ancient name) became four new
departments of the French Empire; and in March 1809 it was incorporated with the Principality of Lucca as a Grand Duchy, under the
realistic rule of Elisa Baciocchi, the most Napoleonic of the Bonaparte
sisters.

Further south, Naples had been in French hands since March 1806 and
Gaeta surrendered in July; but not before its resistance had encouraged
the country people of Calabria to rise in arms against the French invaders, so that General Reynier had to scatter his forces up and down
the country to deal with guerrilla tactics—a foretaste of what they would
soon experience in Spain.

The opportunity for intervention was seized by the British in Sicily,
and on July 1st Sir John Stuart landed with an expeditionary force of
5200 men, convoyed by Sir Sidney Smith, in the Gulf of Eufemia. Reynier
hastily mobilized a force of 6400 to oppose them. After an exhausting
march of nine miles along the shore, the British, courting disaster, proposed to attack the French camp, which lay on high ground on the far
bank of a small river. At that moment the French came charging down
in the column formation which had always broken through an Austrian
defence, reckoning to throw the British into the sea. But the French left
—1600 men in two columns, of whom only the first two ranks, 240 in all,

could use their muskets—found itself faced by 700 Britishers in two lines, every man of whom was a trained marksman, and who held their ground until they could make their fire effective. After three volleys the French columns broke and fled; and this first clash decided the day.

The battle of Maida had no immediate sequel. It was an opportunist victory, with no plan behind it. The arrival of French reinforcements made it necessary for the expedition to return to Sicily. But a pattern of fighting had been laid down which carried British arms to victory in the following years all the way from Bussaco to Waterloo. For Napoleon, who never himself met British forces in the field, failed to appreciate the importance of what had happened, and allowed his generals to carry on to the end with the old tactics; but Wellington, before he went to Spain, had learnt the lesson of Maida. 'If what I hear of their system of manœuvres is true (he said to Croker in June 1808), I think it is a false one as against steady troops. I suspect that all the continental armies were more than half beaten before the battle was begun. I at least will not be frightened beforehand.'

Another moral might have been drawn; but Napoleon disliked think-ing of it: he could no more cross the straits of Messina than the English Channel. Sicily in Bourbon and British hands remained a constant menace to his Kingdom of Italy: a second Malta, and only two miles away. He comforted himself with the fact that the whole peninsula, together with the east coast of the upper Adriatic, was now in French hands, and could at last be organized and exploited as a source of raw materials for his manufacturers, and a military outpost on the Mediterranean.[10]

It also was his own country: its rhetorical language on his tongue, its operatic extravagances in his veins: but behind the actor's pose and the make-up of a condottiere he had inherited something of the Roman bigness of mind that built aqueducts and empires. Here, more clearly than in Egypt or Spain or Germany, can be seen the pattern of Napo-leonic statesmanship.

Except that Piedmont was now cut off from the rest of the Po valley, and treated as part of the Alps, the new divisions of the country were geographical. The Apennine backbone of the peninsula separated the western coastal plain, now part of France as far south as Rome, from the northern and eastern plain, stretching from Milan to Ancona, called the Kingdom of Italy. Everything further south was the Kingdom of Naples. East of the Adriatic were the Illyrian provinces. Rome was no more than the *chef-lieu* of a *département*: it had ceased to be an obstacle to unity.

This unity was political, financial, administrative, military, economic, ecclesiastical—everything except national. Its sole ruler, under whatever name, was Napoleon; the sole motive of his rule, the predominance of France. The departments of the north-west were administered like those on the French side of the Alps, by prefects appointed and controlled from Paris, and they fell within Fouché's wide-flung police net. The Viceroy of the Kingdom of Italy was Napoleon's step-son, Eugène Beauharnais, only twenty-three at the time of his appointment, and allowed so little discretion that Napoleon pursued him with twenty-one letters of advice and instruction during his first week of office, and harassed him with constant interference afterwards. Neither Joseph nor his successor Murat at Naples (with Caroline Bonaparte as consort) dared diverge far from the policy laid down by the head of the family.

Napoleon believed that he understood better than anyone the Italian character, and (of course) the art of government. His first letter to Eugène, dated Milan, June 5th, 1805, two days before he was appointed Viceroy, illustrates both beliefs, and may stand as a frontispiece to the book of his Italian statesmanship.

'You are still at an age (he writes) when one does not realize the perversity of men's hearts: I cannot therefore too strongly recommend you to be prudent and circumspect. Our Italian subjects are more deceitful by nature than the citizens of France. The only way in which you can keep their respect and serve their happiness is by letting no one have your complete confidence, and by never telling anyone what you really think of the ministers and high officials of your court. Dissimulation, which comes naturally at a maturer age (*Napoleon was thirty-six to Eugène's twenty-three*), has to be emphasized and inculcated at yours. If you ever find yourself speaking unnecessarily, or *con animo*, say to yourself, "I have made a mistake," and don't do it again. Show respect for the nation you govern, and show it all the more as you discover less grounds for it. You will come to see in time that there is little difference between one nation and another . . . In any position but that of Viceroy of Italy you may boast of being a Frenchman: but here you must forget it, and count yourself a failure unless the Italians believe that you love them . . . The less you talk, the better: you aren't well enough educated, and you haven't enough knowledge, to take part in informal debates (*as Napoleon did*). Learn to listen, and remember that silence is often as effective as a display of knowledge . . . So long as a prince holds his tongue his power is incalculable: he should never talk (*especially at State Councils*) unless he knows he is the ablest man in the room. Don't trust spies: they are more trouble than they are worth. Your military police make sure of the army, and that is all that matters. The army is the one thing you can deal with personally, and from your own knowledge . . . You must take the greatest care not to expose yourself to any sort of affront. If anything of the kind occurs, don't stand it. Prince, ambassador, minister, general—whoever it may be, even if it is the Austrian or Russian ambassador, have him arrested on the spot . . . Don't show too much attention to foreigners: there is nothing to gain by it. An ambassador will never speak well of you, because it is his business to speak ill. Ministers of foreign countries are, in plain words, accredited spies. Give me a daily account of your doings: by degrees you will come to see how I look at things. Don't show my letters to a single soul, under any pretext whatsoever . . . One last word. Punish dishonesty ruthlessly. The exposure of a dishonest accountant is a victory for the government. And don't allow any smuggling in the French army.[11]

Why did Napoleon end on what might seem such a small point? Because the defeat of England, his first and last enemy, by systematic blockade, was still in Italy, as elsewhere, the be-all and end-all of his policy. Political centralization, to make his viceroys subservient to his will; financial exactions, to pay for his troops and his ships; military organization, to conscript and mobilize his armies; ecclesiastical discipline, to reinforce his secular policy with the sanctions of religion: all were devoted to the master-design of excluding England from a self-sufficient Tariff Union of all Europe.

Yet it might well be argued that Napoleon's Italian adventure brought him, in the long run, little more advantage than his adventure in Spain. The Kingdom of Naples, at least, and Illyria, were hardly worth the trouble that it cost to occupy them. It might have been better for France if a tariff wall had been erected along the line of the Pyrenees, and the near side of the Papal States; if the northern ports had been firmly held, and Lombardy exploited, but southern Italy left, as Spain in effect had to be left, as a British market: a poor one at best.

There was no more thought now of the republicanism of 1796, or of the constitutionalism of 1802. Each had served its turn, whilst it was necessary to conciliate north Italy or to disintegrate the centre and south; whilst an army fighting in Lombardy might be attacked from Naples, or its communications cut by British fleets based on Corsica or Leghorn. Now every port of the peninsula was in French hands; there was a French garrison in every city; the Viceroy of Italy, the King of Naples, and the Princess of Lucca and Piombino were all members of the Bonaparte family. The government was as centralized as that of France; with Civil Code and Concordat, conscription and censorship, prefects and police, and a show of popular representation to cover an arbitrary regime of *arrêtés*, *décrets* and *sénatus-consultes*; all reinforced by a spate of letters in which the proportion of *plaintes* and *reproches* increases as time goes on, and 'republican frankness' is freely mixed with the special rudeness that Napoleon reserved for members of his own family.

7

The Kingdom of Italy, the richest part of a poor country, well illustrates the character of Napoleon's regime in Italy. By taxation and conscription, tariff and blockade, its social and economic life was ruthlessly sacrificed to the interests of France. Its six million inhabitants paid from 1806 onwards an annual tribute of £1½ millions to the French treasury; from time to time other contributions were exacted—£120,000 in 1804 for shipbuilding; in 1805 the whole expenses of the army fighting in Lombardy; in 1806 the upkeep of the Franco-Italian forces in Dalmatia—to be paid in cash—£1 million in two years, till there was no more currency in the country. By 1810 the number of troops to be supported had risen to 100,000. When at the end of this year Eugène protested that the Kingdom was unable to find a penny more, Napoleon transferred to it the debt of the Papal States. It was not surprising that the budget, after producing a surplus of nearly £800,000 in 1804, showed a deficit of £400,000 on the next seven years' working. Where did the money go to? In 1811, out of a total revenue of £6½ millions, £1½ millions went in the annual tribute to France, and £2¼ millions to the army and navy; and this did not include another £1½ millions special contribution towards the expenses of the campaign in Russia: so that on the year's working there was a deficit of £250,000.

In the bad old days of Austrian control Lombardy had raised a volunteer militia for local service. Now the Kingdom of Italy was required to supply a conscript army rising from 30,000 to 55,000 men—an army, moreover, which sent 20,000 of its strength to fight in Germany, 10,000 to Spain, 3000 to Illyria, and in 1812 (when a special levy was made) nearly 60,000 to Russia. The result was both a direct drain on the labour market, and the indirect evils of desertion, brigandage, and emigration.

An internal tariff barrier cut off the Kingdom of Italy from the provinces to the west that were within the French economy. The grain and fruit-producing areas of Italy now became vast French allotments. The raw silk of Lombardy, which used to go in part to Germany and England, was pre-empted for the French market. It was made possible for the silk manufacturers of Lucca to compete with those of Lyon. Meanwhile the goods that Italy could no longer get from abroad owing to the blockade were supplied by France. Italy was in fact treated under the Napoleonic Empire much as the transatlantic colonies had been treated under the Bourbon monarchy.

When Eugène protested against this system, Napoleon replied with sophistication and threats. 'I cannot agree with your observations (he wrote on August 23rd, 1810). My principle is *France first*. If English commerce is supreme on the high seas, it is due to her sea power: it is therefore to be expected that, as France is the strongest land power, she should claim commercial supremacy on the continent: it is indeed our only hope . . . It would be short-sighted not to recognize that Italy owes her independence to France—that it was won by French blood and French victories, that it must not be misused, and that nothing could be more unreasonable than to start calculating what commercial advantages France gets out of it . . . I understand Italian affairs better than any-one else. It is no use for Italy to make plans that leave French prosperity out of account: she must face the fact that the interests of the two countries hang together. Above all, she must be careful not to give France any reason for annexing her: for if it paid France to do this, who could stop her? So make this your motto too—*France first.*'

8

In his after-thoughts at St. Helena, as edited and improved by Las Cases, Napoleon outlines a plan for Europe. 'One of my grandest ideas (he is represented as saying) was *l'agglomération*: the concentration of peoples geographically united, but separated by revolutions and political action. There are, scattered over Europe, 30 million Frenchmen, 15 million Span-iards, 15 million Italians, and 30 million Germans. My intention was to make each of these peoples into a separate national state (*corps de na-tion*) . . . As regards the 15 million Italians, *l'agglomération* had already gone far: it needed only time to mature: every day ripened that unity of principles and legislation, of thought and feeling, which is the sure and infallible cement of human societies. The annexation of Piedmont and Parma, Tuscany and Rome were only temporary expedients; the single aim was to guide, guarantee and hasten the national education of the Italian people.'

There is a passage in Montholon's *Memoirs* which gives the same idea in more detail. 'Napoleon (he writes) wanted to recreate Italy as a fatherland (*la patrie d'Italie*); to reunite the Venetians, the Milanese, the people of Piedmont, the Genoese, the Tuscans, the inhabitants of Parma and Modena, the Romans, Neopolitans, Sicilians and Sardinians into a single independent nation, frontiered by the Alps, the Adriatic, the Io-nian Sea and the Mediterranean . . . This great and powerful kingdom would have included, on land, the House of Austria; whilst at sea its fleets, in union with that of Toulon, would have dominated the Mediter-ranean, and protected the old commercial route to the Indies by Suez and the Red Sea. Rome, the Eternal City, would have been the capital of this state, protected by the triple barrier of the Alps, the Po and the Apennines. . . ."

Did his imagination stop here? When he named his son the King of Rome, when he decreed that Rome should be the second city of the Em-

pire, and the scene of yet another coronation, and when he commissioned
the building of an Imperial palace on the Capitol, was he not dreaming
(in a practical way as usual) of a Roman rather than a French Empire,
the Carolingian ideal at last realized, an Empire of the world once more
in being?

If Napoleon thought these things, he seriously misread history. Italy
had never been a *patrie*. Rome had never been its capital. He might
dream, as Mazzini did, of a united Italy designed by Providence with one
foot of its compasses in Rome and the other on the Alps; he might be
ambitious, as Mussolini was a century and a half later, of a Roman Empire in the Mediterranean, and an imperial capital on the Tiber. But such
an Italy must be created by its own efforts, and such an empire could
never again be the civilized world, fighting against barbarism; only one
national and political way of life trying to impose itself on others with an
equal right to existence. There is not a sign in Napoleon's actual policy
that he cared at all for Italian national unity or aspirations. The only
'unity of thought and feeling' he aimed at was unanimous submission to
French laws, French conscription and French taxes. He was as conscious
at Marengo as his nephew was at Solferino fifty years later of the danger
of creating an independent power in the Mediterranean. If a centralized
administration, a Concordat, Civil and Commercial Codes, an Italian
army and an Italian flag pointed the way to the Risorgimento, and laid
down the pattern of nineteenth-century Italy, then it was done without
intention or design; indeed, the patriotic movement which shaped Italy
into a national state was inspired by hatred of almost everything Napoleonic.[12]

9

Napoleon understood Italy; but he never understood Rome. He never
visited his new capital. He relied upon what Fesch told him, or Caprara,
or Alquier. One might as well hope to understand France without knowing Lyon, Marseille, or Bordeaux; or Spain, knowing only Madrid. Indeed the misjudgement was much worse: for Rome was the soul, not the
body, of Italy, and the Pope's dual character, as secular ruler of a tiny
state and ecclesiastical dictator of half the world, could not be dissolved
into its component parts by any facile distinction between the spiritual
and the temporal powers. Pius VII was the 147th Pope since the time of
Charlemagne, a thousand years ago. For a thousand years the Papacy had
claimed to rule Rome as the spiritual capital of the Holy Roman Empire.
Neither the constant feuds between Emperor and Pope, nor any schism
between Pope and Anti-Pope, nor the capture and sacking of Rome by
German or French armies, had weakened the conviction that the international authority of the Papacy involved its territorial independence of any

European state—its sovereign possession of however small an area of the world's surface. Napoleon, as great a realist as any Pope, might have agreed with this claim, if it had not interfered with his passionate aim to be *rex totius Italiae*. Perhaps he realized its truth in 1814, when he made it a condition of his abdication that he should retain the territorial sovereignty of the little island of Elba. Perhaps 'General Bonaparte' would have died content if he had been recognized as sovereign of St. Helena.

But at the moment (January 1810) Napoleon could see nothing except that the temporal power of the Papacy had been destroyed, and that Pius was a prisoner. He reckoned that it would not be difficult to coerce or persuade this weak old man, deprived of counsellors, of communications, and even of the ordinary comforts of society, to give up his useless antagonism.

As it was part of his purpose to make Paris the ecclesiastical as well as the political capital of his Empire, he first transported all the cardinals there, and the archives of the Quirinal. Then he set the comte Chabrol de Volvic, the prefect of the new department of Montenotte, to persuade Pius to a better state of mind; and, when that failed, and the Pope, though deprived of a secretary, still kept up 'a very mischievous correspondence,' he gave orders that no letters should be received or sent by the Papal household, and that Pius should have no intercourse with anyone except the prefect.

By the first week of January 1811 he was so incensed by the Pope's continued correspondence with the bishops, in spite of all precautions taken against it, that he wrote to Prince Borghese, Governor-General of the Trans-Alpine departments: 'As I desire to protect my subjects from the rage and fury of this ignorant and peevish old man, I hereby order you to notify him that he is forbidden to communicate with any church of mine, or any of my subjects . . . You will remove all suspicious persons from the Pope's household . . . You will not permit anyone of any kind to visit him . . . You will take care to have all the Pope's papers, books and documents taken from him . . . If the Pope should indulge in any extravagant behaviour, you will have him shut up in the citadel of Savona . . . As nothing will teach the Pope sense, he shall see that I am strong enough to do as my predecessors did before me, and to depose a Pope.'

These orders were carried out. Without chaplain, doctor, or valet, without pen, ink, or paper, Pius might at last seem reduced to impotence. But Napoleon had over-reached himself. A Pope who could not communicate with the outside world could no longer institute to their sees the bishops whom the Emperor required to fill vacancies in the episcopate. This was a more serious rebuff than the excommunication of 1809, and one that could not be concealed. Already in 1808 there were seventeen vacant sees, including that of Paris—for Archbishop Belloy had expired at this most inconvenient moment in his hundredth year.

If the Pope would not act, could the Emperor find another way out of the impasse? In 1809 he had summoned a *comité ecclésiastique*, consisting of two complaisant cardinals, Fesch and Maury, and seven other ecclesiastics and ecclesiastically minded laymen, to advise him about the Pope's bull of excommunication, and other matters. To his indignation their report, whilst declaring the excommunication invalid, added that no general questions of ecclesiastical government could be settled until the Pope was given complete liberty, and could preside over a General Council of the church. Meanwhile it might be possible for a National Council to regulate the Investiture of French bishops. Anything less would amount to repudiating the Concordat, and falling back into the schismatic regime of the Civil Constitution.

When the question of Napoleon's divorce and re-marriage came up and the *Officialité métropolitaine* annulled the religious marriage of Bonaparte and Joséphine, upon a declaration drawn up by Fesch and Maury that it had been solemnized without consent, and without witnesses, and that an appeal to the Pope was impracticable, the cardinals resident in Paris met to decide what they should do. Thirteen out of the twenty-seven (not counting Fesch, who was already committed, and Caprara, who was on his deathbed), refused to be present either at the civil or at the religious marriage ceremony. Napoleon was furious at what he took to be a plot against the imperial succession. He turned them out of the official reception at the Tuileries, publicly abused Consalvi and Opizzoni, whom he took for the ringleaders (even threatening to have Consalvi shot), forbade them to dress as cardinals (hence their nickname of 'Black Cardinals'), confiscated all their property, and exiled them, two by two, to provincial towns, with the offer of travelling money and an allowance of £2 10s. a month.

He then made a final attempt to break down Pius's resistance, sending first Lebzeltern, as from the Catholic Emperor of Austria, and then Spina and Caselli, two cardinals who had negotiated the Concordat. But Pius would make no concession, and when Maury was put in Belloy's place as archbishop of Paris, refused to recognize him. The *comitè ecclésiastique*, summoned again, again called for a National Council, rather as the Notables of 1788 had called for the States General: and to this Napoleon unwillingly agreed. But the only way the Council could suggest out of the Investiture problem was a modification of the Concordat, allowing an alternative method of Investiture if the Pope failed to act within a certain time: and this would need the consent of both signatories to the Concordat. Emery, the leading spirit in this decision, had the courage to argue the matter with the Emperor for two hours in the presence of the ministers, State Council, cardinals and bishops.

One more attempt was made at Savona, this time by three bishops, who were instructed to threaten Pius with the renunciation of the Concordat, and to bribe him with the offer of a return to Avignon, or even to Rome, if he would surrender his temporal claims. Pius indignantly refused to be tempted. But a week later (June 19th), under intolerable pressure, and the fear of throwing France once more into schism, he let it be assumed from his silence that he agreed to a new clause in the Concordat by which the power of investiture would pass, after six months' delay, to the archbishop of Paris.

Within twenty-four hours he recanted what he had never signed. His written retraction was concealed from the three bishops, who had set off post-haste for Paris. Napoleon had it, but suppressed it. The National Council met again, to endorse a decree embodying the Pope's concession. Led this time by Fesch, who had not forgotten the stand made by Emery, they defied Napoleon, taking one by one a solemn oath: 'I recognize the Holy Catholic, Apostolic, and Roman Church as the mother and mistress of all the churches. I promise and swear true obedience to the supreme Roman Pontiff, the successor of St. Peter, the prince of the Apostles, and the Vicar of Jesus Christ.' Napoleon dissolved the Council, but intimidated its members individually into giving their signatures to the decree. This 'unanimous decision' of the Council was at once reported to the Pope by a deputation of cardinals and bishops; and they asked for his signature. After three weeks Pius gave it, but with reservations that Napoleon would not allow.

10

The Emperor was now on the eve of his Russian campaign. He left Saint-Cloud on May 9th, 1812, expecting to be back in three months. He hoped that another victory would do what Marengo and Austerlitz had done. Meanwhile, he would have Pius moved from Savona to Fontainebleau, where he would be more accessible, and more amenable to personal pressure. So at midnight on June 9th, 1812, with every precaution of secrecy—in a carriage with darkened lights, muffled wheels, and the papal white mules blackened and unshod, the Pope was once more hurried across the Mont Cenis, where he became so ill that his doctor said he could not go on. But Napoleon's orders were inexorable: he was given the *viaticum*, and travelled on lying down. It was not till some weeks after his arrival at Fontainebleau (June 19th) that he had recovered from the journey.

Now he was back in the comfortable quarters prepared for him as an honoured guest in 1804; but he still behaved as though he were in prison, confining himself to reading and prayer. Day after day cardinals, bishops, and state officials repeated in his ears arguments he had grown tired of refuting. The conclusive proof of the Emperor's case never came. Four days after the Pope's arrival at Fontainebleau Napoleon crossed the Niemen. At the end of the three months he arrived in an abandoned Moscow. Three months later again he was back in the Tuileries, defeated and without an army.

He was still determined to have his way with the church. By the middle of January 1813, judging that the fortress of the Pope's constancy was so breached and weakened by three years' attacks that it was ready for the final assault, he determined to deliver this in person. His clerical Guard of bishops and cardinals, sent to prepare the way, had been beaten off, but with such cost to the garrison that Pius was almost too ill to argue any more. Now for six days he was subjected to everything that Napoleon could do, by charming or bullying, to bend him to his will. At last Pius, who had always liked his enemy, and was now sorry for him, consented to sign a document, which contained no more than the heads of a possible agreement, one of which was that after a delay of six months investiture might be performed by the Metropolitan archbishop of Paris.

But within twenty-four hours the Pope repented, as at Savona, of what he had done; and, as at Savona, Napoleon tricked him by ignoring his change of mind, by publishing the provisioned proposals as an agreed declaration, 'The Concordat of Fontainebleau,' and by ordering the singing of a *Te Deum* in honour of this happy reconciliation of church and state. The solemn retraction that Pius penned two months later was suppressed, and the Pope was once more subjected to almost solitary confinement, whilst Napoleon went off to seek in Germany the victory that had eluded him in Russia.

But Leipzig confirmed the verdict of Moscow. Napoleon was worsted in the very appeal to arms by which he had hoped finally to defeat the Pope. On January 21st, 1814, he gave orders that Pius should be taken back to Savona, and on March 10th that he should be restored to Rome.

Whilst Napoleon was travelling in custody across France, sometimes disguising himself, in fear of his life, from his angry subjects of Provence, to his exile in Elba, Pius was being fêted by enthusiastic crowds on his way from Fontainebleau to Turin, and from Turin to Rome; and ten days after the Emperor landed from a British ship at Porto Ferrajo, the Pope's carriage was drawn through the streets of his capital, greeted with enthusiastic cries of welcome, and accompanied by white-robed children carrying palm-branches, whilst all the bells of the city rang out, and the guns of St. Angelo fired their salute. After a visit to St. Peter's, Pius returned to the Quirinal, a sovereign once more. He found its walls redecorated for Napoleon (who had hoped to reside there in 1811) with a frieze

by Thorwaldsen and pagan goddesses in classical undress. 'We will give
them a little more to wear (he said) and make Madonnas of them.' [13]

An epilogue remained to be spoken. The Pope's message to the people
of Rome was, 'Let us forget the past.' There was much to forget, and
much to forgive—more than one might think forgivable. Three years
later, when Napoleon was languishing at St. Helena, Pius wrote to his
old friend and fellow-sufferer, Consalvi (October 6th, 1817): 'The Emperor Napoleon's family have informed us through Cardinal Fesch that
the rocky island of St. Helena is fatal to health (*this of course was untrue*) and that the poor exile is dying by inches (*se voit dépérir à chaque
minute*). We are deeply distressed to hear this, and you will certainly
share our grief; for we must both remember that to Napoleon more than
anyone, after God, is due the restoration of our Religion in the great
Kingdom of France. The pious and courageous initiative of 1801 has
long ago effaced the memory of later wrongs. Savona and Fontainebleau
were only mistakes due to temper, or the errors of an ambitious man: the
Concordat was the saving act of a Christian and a hero (*un acte chrétien-
nement et héroiquement sauveur*).' So he charged Consalvi to write to
the Prince Regent, and to ask him to lighten the unhappy lot of the exile.
'Nothing would give us deeper joy than to have done something to lessen
Napoleon's sufferings. He cannot now be a danger to anyone: we should
be sorry to think that he leaves behind him any feelings of remorse.'

Pius outlived Napoleon by two years. He, too, became a legendary figure. One reads without surprise of the effect he produced upon a young
English Catholic presented to him in 1818. Nicholas Wiseman was only
sixteen at the time; but he remembered and recorded forty years later
that 'whatever we had read of the gentleness, condescension and sweetness of his speech, his manners, and his expression, was fully justified,
realized and made personal'; for 'there was the halo of the Confessor
round the tiara of Pius, that eclipsed all gold and jewels.' [14]

XI

GERMANY

(1802-1810)

I

POLITICAL SCIENCE, basing itself upon the comparative study of institutions, would design a government for the ideal state. The Art of Politics, building on the science, must invent and develop institutions fitted for a particular people. Both science and art call for experience and experiment. The first demands a knowledge of history, the second a knowledge of human nature.

The difference—and it was immense—between Sieyès and Bonaparte in 1799 was that Sieyès had devised a constitution which satisfied all the requirements of an ideal state, whereas Bonaparte knew that in postrevolutionary France it would not work. The constitution which he substituted for it at Brumaire had two essential virtues: it suited him, and it suited the country. The later changes which he made in it, or carried through contrary to it, passed with little protest, not so much because his police system crushed opposition as because he trained public opinion to accept them, playing upon the strength as well as the weakness of the French character, until the nation came to identify itself with him—its glory with his ambition, its revolution with his reaction, the liberty and equality of 1789 with the Dictatorship of 1804-14.

Bonaparte understood France. It was, in the last resort, because he did not understand England that his Continental Blockade was a failure. It was because he did not understand Spain that his Spanish adventure ended in disaster. In Italy he understood the people, but not the Pope; and most of what he gained at Milan and Naples he lost at Rome. But Germany he believed, like most Frenchmen, that he did understand. For between France and Germany there stood no Alps or Pyrenees, no seapower or Papacy. The Rhine, for a thousand years, had been an open frontier. Always German affairs had been the pivot of French foreign policy. A good Jacobin, Napoleon knew that since Valmy the initiative

300

had passed again from the heirs of Frederick the Great into the hands of the French Republic.

2

How did it come about that in August 1805 Napoleon's plan for an invasion of England was suddenly changed into a plan for the invasion of Germany? What was the provocation; what the danger?

On July 5th, 1800, three weeks after the battle of Marengo, Francis II had written to the victor a letter which stated, once for all, with unusual frankness, and without the fulsome politeness customary in the Imperial correspondence, the Austrian point of view. 'I have never fought (he said) against any particular form of French government. I have been forced to take arms for the defence of my states, when twice attacked without provocation on my part. I fight as head of the German confederation (*corps germanique*) for the safeguarding of the Empire. But—I appeal to your loyalty—is it the same with the French nation as regards the necessity of war? Neither its territory nor its government is at stake. It is fighting far from its homes in order to retain its conquests, and to continue or to renew governments established by force against the will of their peoples; in other words, after condemning the ambitions of the Directory, France seems to have no other aim in continuing the war save to profit by the success of these very ambitions. So soon as a number of states combine to resist one, there is an end to the balance of power (*l'équilibre*) in Europe. What is to happen if this one power adds further to its previous preponderance, and by conquests of an extent hitherto unheard of claims a decisive influence over most of the other states of Europe? To propose peace on such conditions is not only useless for humanity: it proves that peace is not even intended.'

Since this letter, events had done nothing to diminish the fears of French aggression. For three years, Austria had suffered under the humiliating terms of the treaty of Lunéville. By a series of territorial changes which recalled nothing so much as the Peace of Westphalia a century and a half ago, she lost what little control she had then retained over the states of western Germany, and saw her clients enriched into rivals, and encouraged to become her enemies. Prussia had gained half a dozen ecclesiastical states with a population of 400,000, Bavaria another half-dozen with 300,000 inhabitants; Baden and Würtemberg had extended their frontiers—all at the expense of the Empire, all by the action of France.

As though this were not enough, the kidnapping of a Bourbon prince on German soil, and his execution as a warning to the old monarchies, had been followed by the proclamation of an Empire of the French in the person of the victor of Marengo—a challenge not to the King of Hungary and Bohemia, whom Napoleon was ironically pleased to see transformed into a junior Emperor (for he insisted on his own preceddence, and suggested that the King of Prussia might make a third), but to the Holy Roman Empire itself, that empty magnificence which for nearly four hundred years had been the proudest possession of the Habsburg rulers of Austria. Whilst Russia and Sweden had refused to recognize Napoleon's new title (indeed, the King of Sweden still referred to him as *Monsieur Napoléon Bonaparte*), Francis haggled for three months before submitting to the insult; and then gave way only because he could not fight without Russian troops and English gold.

If matters had gone no further, war, which was always in the air after the breakdown of the Peace of Amiens, might have been avoided. Napoleon, for his part, though deeply suspicious of the proceedings of Russia and her possible allies, was obsessed with his plan for invading England, and realized that it could not be safely carried out unless he was secure from an attack from the east. Yet he proceeded in his provocative policy. At Aix-la-Chapelle, in September 1804, he had a *Te Deum* sung in the presence of the relics of Charlemagne, the founder of the Holy Roman Empire; and at Milan, on May 26th, 1805, he placed upon his head the iron crown of Lombardy, the symbol of Habsburg supremacy in Italy.

Nor were these vain gestures. Napoleon made no secret of his intention to use Italy as the base for new adventures in the Levant—the reconquest of Egypt, and the partition of Turkey in Europe—a region in which Austria had regarded herself, ever since the seventeenth century, as having an exclusive right to quarrel with Russia. Nearer home, Francis was alarmed at the rumours which came from Maintz in September 1804, that Napoleon was thinking of setting up a Confederation of those Rhenish states which were already looking to France for help against the Empire. The result of all these moves or rumours of moves was what had been expected ever since the breakdown of the Peace of Amiens—the formation of a Third Coalition.[1]

The first step came from Russia, and was due to her apprehension of Napoleon's designs in the Near East—that dream which had haunted him ever since he stood on the Piazza at Venice, and which was one of the causes of his ultimate downfall. Whilst Tsar Paul was alive Bonaparte tried to play on his Mediterranean ambitions by suggesting a partnership in the reconquest of Egypt and the opening of a Suez canal (February 1801). But after the accession of Alexander a month later no such co-operation was possible. Alarmed hardly less than Francis had been by the First Consul's failure to respect the neutrality of Naples (under the secret treaty of October 1801) and by rumours of his intention to land troops in Albania and southern Greece, Alexander and his Francophobe Foreign Minister Czartoryski were encouraged by Pitt's return to power (May 1804) to open negotiations with England and Austria. The latter was indeed quite unready for war; yet, in November 1804, she signed a preliminary agreement with Russia to join in resisting Napoleon if he attacked Turkey, or was guilty of any further aggression in Naples or north Germany: Austria to supply twice as many men as her ally, provided they were paid for by England.

This dangerous commitment was followed by the setting up of a military *cordon sanitaire* along the southern frontiers of Austria, which looked more like a precaution against French military agression than against any plague in the Adriatic. Francis neglected the warning that this action evoked, and drifted into the Third Coalition, which came into existence with the Anglo-Russian alliance of April 11th, 1805; by this England undertook to pay £1¼ millions for every 100,000 men put into the field by her allies; it was completed by the definite adhesion of Austria on August 9th and of Prussia on November 3rd, 1805.

Napoleon, whose budget estimate for the year included £17¼ millions for war purposes (nearly two-thirds of the whole), had postponed his choice between an English and German war almost beyond the safety-point. Though assured by his ambassador at Vienna that Francis would not fight, he put more trust in his spies, and in such signs of aggression as the *cordon sanitaire*, the annexation of territory on the Suabian frontier, and the strengthening of garrisons in the Tyrol. He did not know for certain of the existence of the Third Coalition, which had been formed in the greatest secrecy, but he suspected it. In the third week of July he had asked the Emperor for a plain statement of his intentions. He believed himself, he said, to be at peace with Austria: but if troops continue to be mobilized and stores to be accumulated, he must assume that Francis means war, and would be compelled to march against her. This was followed (August 12th) by an ultimatum demanding the withdrawal of troops from the Tyrol, the reduction of garrisons in the Adriatic provinces, and a declaration to England of Austrian neutrality. He knew by this time that Austria could not comply; he wrote to Talleyrand that his mind was made up. Within a fortnight the Grand Army was on the march for the Rhine.

Now was seen the result of detaching the western states from the Empire, and strengthening them at the expense of their weaker neighbours. Bavaria, that old outpost of France in the Danube valley, and guardian of the gate of Austria, Baden, Würtemberg, and Hesse-Darmstadt, all were ready to join in the attack on their nominal overlord, and to give the war the false appearance of a movement for national independence. 'My heart bleeds,' Napoleon wrote to the Elector of Bavaria (August 25th) 'at the thought of the evils that must follow. God knows I am not to blame. But Austria is asking for war; and she will get it sooner than she bargains for.'[2]

3

During the month between August 23rd, when he finally made up his
mind to divert his army from England to Germany, and September 24th,
when he left Paris for the front, Napoleon was intensely occupied with
every detail of his new expedition, and wrote five letters a day to Berthier,
to Decrés, to Talleyrand, and to his generals, closing down the Boulogne
affair, trying to detach Prussia from Russia and Austria, sending out his
spies, and directing the march of his seven columns towards the Rhine.

The English invasion was to be postponed (no more) until he had
dealt with the Austrians. A force of 60,000-80,000 men and 500 barges
was to be maintained in the Channel ports, to conceal the departure of
the Grand Army, and keep the British apprehensive by occasional demonstrations.

Talleyrand was to make Austria understand that her threat of war could
only encourage England, and postpone the day of European peace. 'If the
Emperor commands his army in person, we shall probably have the
honour of meeting' (they did, but not till after Austerlitz). He was to put
articles in the *Moniteur* speaking of an Austrian invasion of Bavaria, and
exaggerating the mobilization in the Tyrol. Meanwhile Duroc was to
visit Berlin, and make sure of Prussian support; but he found the Austrian envoy there, too, and could not secure more than a temporary and
untrustworthy Prussian neutrality.

Next, the ground had to be surveyed, and the enemy's positions discovered. With his usual foresight and thoroughness, Napoleon had not
left this till the last minute. Not only was the French ambassador at
Dresden handing on information about the Austrian and Russian armies
supplied by observers at Prague, Cracow, and Lemberg; but in the previous autumn, anticipating an Austrian campaign, Napoleon had collected stores at Maintz, and instructed Berthier to prepare a map of
Suabia and the Black Forest, showing the state of the roads in the probable field of hostilities. As long ago as July 1804, Sébastiani, that accomplished spy, had been sent to travel round Bavaria as a tourist, and to
report 'anything interesting from a political or military point of view.'
Now Murat, disguised as 'Colonel Beaumont,' was sent to Mayence,
Frankfort, Würzburg and Bamberg to spy out the Bohemian frontier,
then south by Nuremberg, Ratisbon and Passau to Munich, Ulm and the
Black Forest, taking with him an account of Belle-Isle's retreat from
Prague (1742), and a friend who could talk German. Bertrand, too, was
instructed the same day (August 25th) to go to Munich, explore the
valleys of the Inn and Lech and return by Ulm; he was to pay special
attention to the Ulm-Rastadt and Ulm-Donauwörth roads, and to make a
reconnaissance très détaillée of Ulm. Both spies were given a fortnight in

which to finish their work; it was not till Napoleon received their reports on September 13th and 15th that he knew where the Austrian armies were, and could make his final plans.[8]

It was the situation of May 1796 over again. The Danube was the Po, but in reverse, with the Iller, Lech, Isar and Inn flowing north from the Alps instead of south, like the Ticino, Adda, Oglio and Adige. Ulm was Milan, Donauwörth was Piacenza, Vienna was Mantua. By striking for the north bank of the Danube at Donauwörth he could avoid the Black Forest and the river obstacles on the south bank, and either force Mack to retreat along that bank towards Vienna, or, if he delayed his retreat, cut him off.

To reach this position, Napoleon's seven columns—172,000 men in all— were to advance from the Rhine on roughly parallel routes, so as to keep in touch with one another, and draw on different zones of country (particularly in friendly Baden) for their supplies; for it was never supposed that they could live on the meagre rations prepared in such a hurry at Strasbourg and Mayence: Bernadotte and Marmont on the left, then Davout, Soult, Ney, Lannes, and Murat. The seven columns marched the four hundred miles from Boulogne to Ulm at the rate of nearly fifteen miles a day, keeping in touch with one another every night, and reporting their positions to Napoleon every twenty-four hours.

On September 24th Napoleon left Paris, and spent four days at Strasbourg and three at Ludwigsburg, receiving promises of support from the rulers of Baden and Würtemberg. From Strasbourg he wrote to Bernadotte, 'I am ready for all emergencies . . . If I have the happiness to find the Austrian army still asleep on the Iller and in the Black Forest for another three or four days, I shall have outflanked it, and I hope only the remnants of it will escape.' And to Masséna two days later, 'If I can rid myself quickly of this army on the Iller, which with God's help I hope to do, I shall fall on the Russians.'

Napoleon had no need to invoke the Deity. The Austrians themselves were arranging for his victory. A French officer who had served during the revolutionary wars with almost every army in Europe concluded that, with all its capacity for quick recovery, the Austrian army had inveterate vices which would always bring defeat at the hands of a resolute and energetic foe. Its officers served for duty and honour, its men to earn a living. Both were interested only in their own regiment, and did not care, so long as they stood firm, what might be happening on the rest of the battlefield. 'Old-fashioned, theoretical, brave, slow, and obstinately attached to its own methods, the Austrian army will fight our nephews as it fought our forefathers, and will consequently be beaten by the former as it was by the latter.' This army was now in a transition stage of unpreparedness—half reformed by its only capable leader, the Archduke

Charles, and its main strength lying south of the Alps. Its commander in the Danube valley was the rash and incapable Mack, who underestimated Napoleon's numbers, and proposed to meet him where he was not, in western Bavaria. The Russians were below strength, and not yet in the field, being in part behind the Inn, and in part still in Moravia. If Napoleon struck quickly, nothing could stop his advance to Vienna.

And so it happened. On October 7th, whilst Mack was preparing to stand at Ulm against a Franco-Bavarian advance from the west, Napoleon was at Donauwörth, nearly fifty miles lower down the Danube, and his circling armies had cut the Austrians off from their base. Plunging south on the 8th, Mack found Frenchmen at Wertigen: plunging north on the 9th, he found Frenchmen at Nordingen, and only a small part of his forces broke through. 'The Austrian army is almost completely cut off,' said the Bulletin of October 12th: 'it is in practically the same position as the army of Mélas was at Marengo.' 'Tomorrow,' Napoleon proclaimed on the 13th, 'will be a day a hundred times more famous than that of Marengo.' On the 14th, after an assault on the town, Mack surrendered with 27,000 men. The Austrian army had disappeared (Napoleon told Cambacérès) as though by the stroke of a magician's wand.[4]

As soon as the capitulation was completed, Mack was sent to the Emperor Francis—an ominous envoy—with a note urging him to surrender, and to be quick about it. The reply was a cringing note to *Monsieur mon Frère*, assuming that they both desired peace, but saying that he must first consult his ally the Tsar. Napoleon in return tried to separate the allies by insisting that his only real enemy was England, and that Francis need not consider Alexander's feelings. 'For Russia this is merely a *guerre de fantaisie*; but for you and me it is one which absorbs all our means, all our feelings, all our faculties.' But when it became obvious that Francis was only playing for time, Napoleon advanced from Vienna, which he had entered on November 14th, to Brünn (November 20th), threatening to chase the Russians off German soil, hoping that he might bluff them into a decisive battle, and save himself from an inglorious retreat.

The arrival of Alexander at Olmütz (November 25th), with the news that Prussia had at last been coerced into joining the Third Coalition (Treaty of Potsdam, November 3rd), determined the allies to stand and fight. Should 86,000 Russians and Austrians refuse battle to 70,000 Frenchmen? Accordingly they advanced to Austerlitz, half way on the road to Brünn, and ranged their forces opposite the French position, on ground that Napoleon had already surveyed. Their intention was to outflank his right and cut him off from Vienna. But Napoleon had anticipated this move. 'Whilst they march towards my right,' he said in an Order dated *Au bivouac*, the day before the battle, 'they will expose their flank.' If all goes well, he will direct the army from behind; but 'if victory is for a moment uncertain, you will see your Emperor risking his life in the fore-front of the battle; for there must be no faltering in our victory.' And so things turned out. The allied centre, weakened by the move to the right, was broken in half, and the whole army routed. It was an overwhelming victory: 18,600 Russian bodies were counted on the field, and only 900 French.

In a letter to his brother Joseph describing the battle, and in the thir-tieth Bulletin, Napoleon alleged that 'a whole column of the enemy threw itself into a lake, and most of them were drowned: the cries of the wretched men whom it was impossible to save still ring in our ears.' The story was repeated in a dozen or more French memoirs: but local evi-dence to the contrary was confirmed when the lake was drained, soon after the battle, and nothing found but twenty-eight or thirty cannon, 150 dead horses and two or three human bodies.

The only general killed on the French side, Valhubert, had his leg carried off by a cannon-ball: it was reported that he refused to be moved: 'Remember your orders,' he shouted in a voice of thunder; 'close your ranks. If you win, they will pick me up after the battle: if you lose, I shall not care to live': his dying words were singularly like those of Desaix on the field of Marengo.[5]

The battle of Austerlitz, fought and won on December 2nd, the anni-versary of Napoleon's coronation, had no need of legend to add to its completeness. Its effects were felt all over Europe. Whilst Francis begged for an interview with his conqueror, and Alexander was found in tears, retreating with the remnant of his army, Frederick-William of Prussia hastened to desert his new allies. The Third Coalition was at an end. Pitt might well say, 'Roll up the map of Europe: it will not be wanted these ten years.'

4

The *grande armée* of Ulm and Austerlitz was very different from the forces with which Bonaparte had beaten the Austrians in Italy ten years before. That was a volunteer, this a conscript army. That was ill-balanced, undisciplined, this organized and trained for a particular campaign—though not the one on which it was used. That was an army of libera-tors, owing allegiance to a republic, this one of conquerors bound in per-sonal loyalty to an Emperor. But the new army had grown out of the old, and shared its essential character. Its comradeship and its discipline were still those of the volunteers of 1792: it won its victories by the speed of its movements and the impetus of its attack—the virtues of irregulars: it was still, though professionalized, an improvised army.

The armies of the Empire were organized, like those of the Republic, on the principle of the *amalgame*, that is, a judicious mixture of veterans and recruits. Every other man in the army of 1805 had fought at Marengo:

one in four had served during the wars of the Revolution. Nearly all the officers and non-commissioned officers had seen active service: most of the former were still young, some of the latter were men of fifty or sixty.

The bulk of the rank and file was composed of recruits enlisted under the *loi Jourdan* of 1798. This was at once less oppressive and more unfair than any modern system of conscription. It might have been modelled on the pre-revolutionary method of taxation. Conscripts were designated in age-classes, from twenty to twenty-five; but by no means all were called up. A quota was fixed for each Department and selected by lot. Many exemptions were made by rule; heads of families, married men, and seminarists; and many more were allowed by *remplacement*—i.e. those who could afford to do so paid to be passed over. The result was that, of the 200,000 called up in September 1799, just over half reached the front, and that, in the seven years 1799-1805, out of over 2 million men classed for conscription (*portés sur les tableaux*) no more than 1¼ million were called up (*appelés*). Even of these another large proportion was exempted as unfit to serve by committees with medical assessors who were subject to all kinds of local pressure. On the average, one man in every four was rejected (*réformé*) as being under five feet—at that time the average height of Frenchmen (later the required height was gradually reduced to 4 feet 9 inches)—this at a time when the standard height in the British army was 5 feet 5 inches, and a fair proportion of the men topped 5 feet 9 inches; and one man in sixteen was rejected as physically unfit. That is not the whole story. Of the remainder finally passed for service, 250,000 defaulted before mobilization, or deserted afterwards. The result of all these losses was that out of the 2 millions classed during the seven years under review only 700,000 actually served in the army.

Bonaparte was well aware of these leakages, but would not at first risk making an unpopular system more oppressive than it need be. Soon, however, with the break-down of the Peace of Amiens, and the scheme for the invasion of England, it became necessary to regularize and centralize conscription. The recruiting authority was now to be the prefect, in whose hands the conditions of exemption and *remplacement* were stiffened up; the annual quotas were increased; severe steps were taken against defaulters and deserters; and levies were in future voted by the submissive senate. By these means the proportion of recruits reaching the army soon (1807) became nearly 100 per cent, and it was comparatively easy for the Emperor to raise fresh armies at will, as he did in 1813 and 1814.

Napoleon was not one of those who must always have the newest inventions. He never revived the *compagnies d'aérostiers* whose war balloons had accompanied Jourdan's and Moreau's armies in 1796-97. He was at his best when furbishing up old weapons. He would challenge Goliath with the arms he was accustomed to. His conscripts came straight from the village street and the town square. They learnt their drill during a week in barracks, or on their way to the front. When they reached the fighting line they were mixed with older men—*et voilà*! Their officers had risen from the ranks, and they might become officers in their turn. They said what they thought, did what they liked, fought for glory and loot, and won victories through the assurance that under Napoleon's leadership they could not be defeated. It was the great merit of the conscription system that it brought together men from all classes of society—a nation in arms. Military service was the only profession open to all, it was the surest way to win Napoleon's favour, it stood for comradeship, travel, adventure and perhaps wealth. And, being what they were, the republican armies had discovered means of enforcing discipline without the cruel punishments of the knout or cat-o'-nine-tails which degraded the Russian and British soldiery. But it is something of a shock to find Napoleon suggesting that the return of the Grand Army to Paris in February 1807 should be celebrated with 'Spanish bullfights or combats of wild animals,' on the ground that 'everything must be done to excite enthusiasm and to give militarism fresh prestige.'

Since all important orders came from Napoleon himself, and every movement was reported to him by roving members of his staff, the generals need not concern themselves too much with strategy, or the battalion commanders with tactics. They might be blind leaders of the blind; but their Emperor saw that they did not fall into a ditch. Their muskets were of a pattern thirty years old, which fired only four rounds in three minutes, and were effective up to 300 yards. Their guns belonged to Gribeauval's day, with cannon-balls of 4, 8, or 12 lb., that did good execution up to 600 yards; but in 1805 there were not more than twelve to a division.

Antoine Goerin, a soldier in the Grand Army, who enlisted in 3 Mess. An. XI (1803), carried a small book in a thick grey paper cover about seven inches square in which were recorded his name and description, an *extrait des lois militaires* (viz. the punishments to which he was liable), an account of all payments made to him, an inventory of his *effets de linge et chaussure* (1 *sac de peau*, 3 *chemises*, 3 *paires de guêtres*, 4 *paires de bas*, 2 *paires de souliers*, 2 *cols*, 2 *mouchoirs*, 1 *brosse*, 1 *peigne*, etc.), and a list of all uniforms and equipment issued to him, with the date of issue: thus '*Habit*, May 1812; *Veste*, ditto; *Bonnet*, May 1811; *Capot*, March 1812; *Pantalon*, ditto; *Schakot*, March 1811; *Pompon*, ditto; *Grande culotte*, ditto.' No detail was too small for the Emperor's attention. As for Antoine Goerin, his little grey book was as good as a passport to glory.

5

It has been said that three things are needed to found a militant church; and it may be that they are equally necessary to constitute a victorious army: an inspiring idea, an ancient liturgy, and an element of miracle or legend. The ancient liturgy of the *grande armée* was the tradition and weapons of the Bourbon army and of the revolutionary volunteers. Its inspiring idea was the *liberté, égalité, fraternité* of 1789. Its legend was that of its leader.

Napoleon's presence in the field, Wellington used to say in his precise way, was worth a force of 40,000 men. Thirty years after Austerlitz, and with all his own experiences in mind, he put on paper his reasons for this opinion; and the passage may stand as a verdict from which there is no appeal.

1. Napoleon was a grand *homme de guerre,* possibly the greatest that ever appeared at the head of a French army.

2. He was the Sovereign of the country as well as the Military Chief of the army. That country was constituted upon a military basis. All its institutions were framed for the purpose of forming and maintaining its armies with a view to conquest. All the offices and rewards of the State were reserved in the first instance exclusively for the army. An officer, even a private soldier, of the army might look to the sovereignty of a kingdom as the reward of his services. It is obvious that the presence of the Sovereign with an army so constituted must greatly excite their exertions.

3. It was quite certain that all the resources of the French State, civil, political, financial, as well as military, were turned towards the seat of the operations which Napoleon himself should direct.

4. Every Sovereign in command of an army enjoys advantages against him who exercises only a delegated power, and who acts under orders and responsibilities. But Napoleon enjoyed more advantages of this description than any other Sovereign that ever appeared. His presence, as stated by me more than once, was likely not only to give to the French army all the advantages above detailed, but to put an end to all the jealousies of the French Marshals and their counter-action of each other, whether founded upon bad principles and passions, or their fair differences of opinion. The French army thus had unity of action.

This omnipresent omnicompetent leader was already becoming legend-dary: he knew it and encouraged it. The legend of Lodi, the legend of the Pyramids, the legend of the St. Bernard, the legend of Marengo—they were medals on the breast of the victor of Ulm and Austerlitz. No one knew better how to make himself popular with his troops, and no one knew better how to advertise his popularity. 'It is raining heavily,' he wrote in the First Bulletin of the Grand Army, from Nordlingen, Oc-tober 7th, 1805, 'but that does not delay the forced marching of the Grand Army. The Emperor sets the example: he is on horseback day and night;

he is amongst his troops, and wherever his presence is necessary. Yesterday he covered forty leagues on horseback: he spent the night in a tiny village, without a servant or a scrap of baggage'—though he might have slept in a bishop's palace. 'Soldiers,' he told them on September 30th, 'your Emperor is in your midst: you are but the advance guard of the great people . . . We shall have forced marches to make, fatigue and privation of every kind to endure. But whatever obstacles we meet, we shall overcome them, and we shall not rest until we have planted our banners on the territory of our enemies.'

Battles have been won without such appeals, and by generals who had nothing magical or legendary about them. Napoleon's way was, however, the only way for the leader of a French revolutionary army, in an age of romantic illusions, when war had become a national adventure. His campaigns have been made a text-book of military science: his strategy will perhaps always be magisterial. But the essence of his victories was something in himself, something that only one other great captain of his age possessed—and he was a sailor.[6]

6

On the same day (December 23rd) as Talleyrand arrived at Pressburg to negotiate (or rather to dictate) terms of peace, Francis sent the Archduke Charles to Napoleon, to make a last appeal for clemency: perhaps, he thought, they will reverence my brother. Charles was, indeed, a fine soldier, and a man whom Napoleon might respect; they met on the 27th, and talked long of military matters: two years later, after Wagram, Charles wrote that he had been proud to meet the greatest captain of the age in the field, and that he was ambitious to meet him again 'either with a sword or an olive-branch in his hand.' It was a tragedy for Austria that the wrong brother sat on the throne. But nothing could now change Napoleon's intentions towards a paste-board Emperor who had consistently promised peace and plotted war. The terms of Pressburg, signed at 5 a.m. on the 27th, were meant to make another Austrian revival impossible. Austria was to lose the Tyrol, Vorarlberg, Breisgau, Ortenau, Constance (gaining only Salzburg) in Germany, and in Italy Venetia, Istria and Dalmatia; and to pay an indemnity of £2 millions.

Talleyrand, who signed these terms for Napoleon, had for two months past been warning him against the policy they represented. He had never believed in the possibility of a French domination of Germany. On October 17th, watching from Strasbourg the victorious advance of the French army, he had sent Napoleon a memorandum urging a conciliatory treatment of Austria. He would isolate, not antagonize, her; cut her off from Lombardy by depriving her of Venice, and from the upper Rhineland by detaching Suabia and the Tyrol; but turn her away from German interests by giving her, in compensation, Wallachia, Moldavia and Bessarabia; and by the same means embroil her with Russia, and Russia with England, in the Near East. France would then be free to fight out her duel with England undisturbed.

Again, three days after Austerlitz, Talleyrand protested: 'Your Majesty can now either break the Austrian monarchy, or restore it. Once broken, it will be beyond even the power of Your Majesty to reassemble the scattered fragments, and put them together again into a single whole. The existence of this whole is necessary: it is indispensable to the future safety of the civilized world.'[7]

This was no new idea. It was as old as the Peace of Westphalia (1648). Talleyrand had already outlined it to the Prussian ambassador, Lucchesini, and to his colleague d'Hauterive. Napoleon was quite ready to discuss the suggestion, as he did at Munich on October 27th: but it was only the second string to his bow. He wanted no partner in his adventure in the Near East: certainly not Austria—at best an unwilling ally —standing immediately in his way. He believed that he could dominate a federated Germany which was weak enough not to interfere with his invasion of England, and strong enough to keep Russia out of the West. He was already thinking, not nationally, but imperially. He was destroying the Empire of the Habsburgs, and creating an Empire of the Bonapartes. But would France be any more able than Austria to hold together the centrifugal states of Germany? Would the Empire be any more Holy or any more Roman in the hands of a Bonaparte than a Habsburg? Would it not be even more unsubstantial than its ghost enthroned in the Vatican? Was he not involving France in a *guerre de fantaisie* in which she was likely to be worsted by the one power in Europe which was too vast and too evasive to be overcome?

Austria might have forgiven Austerlitz: she would never forgive Pressburg. Napoleon, confident that she was powerless, and thinking it absurd to suppose that Prussia would venture on war alone, looked forward to a period of peace in which he could organize western Germany, consolidate his gains in Italy, and march his armies back to Boulogne. The states on the right bank of the Rhine, headed by the new Kingdoms of Bavaria and Würtemburg and the new Grand Duchy of Baden, were to be grouped into a Confederation of the Rhine (Hamburg, Bremen and Lübeck might be included) to form, under French protection, a barrier between France and the Netherlands on the west, and Prussia and Russia to the east. On July 12th, 1806, sixteen states came into this arrangement, stretching from the Elbe to the Alps. Thus was created a third German state, a rival to Austria and Prussia, which could be used against them both.

This, like the re-orientation of Austria, was no new idea, but part of the old Bourbon policy, taken up again during the revolutionary wars, revived by Talleyrand in 1799, by Bonaparte in 1802, and by Bignon, the French envoy at Cassel, in 1804: it may have been discussed between Napoleon and the German princes at Maintz that autumn. Talleyrand favoured an opportunity to make a fortune out of the bribes he received from the princes. Napoleon made sure that there was included in the measure a promise that the Confederation would contribute 150,000 troops in the event of any war in which he was engaged on the continent. Within a month of the forming of the Confederation, Francis, feeling that his last authority over the states of Germany had slipped from him, formally renounced his 'Imperial dignity as supreme head of the German Empire,' and remained 'Emperor of Austria'—the title he had assumed on September 10th, 1804.

Nor did the humiliation of Austria end in Germany. The loss of her Adriatic possessions meant the sacrifice of her ambitions in the Near East. Napoleon now held what he had always coveted—a sea and land base for an attack on the Turkish Empire. Yet it was for him a double error; for it made him at once the supplanter of Austria and the rival of Russia.

Again, Pressburg set him free to become, in Italy, the heir of the Habsburgs—and more. The Bulletin which announced the signing of peace with Austria also announced a French invasion of Naples. On January 13th the Bourbon sovereign of the Two Sicilies fled to Palermo. Two months later Napoleon's troops held the whole of the south. On April 6th his brother Joseph became King of Naples. What did it all mean? A fresh attempt to close the Mediterranean ports to British trade? A renewed attack on Egypt and Turkey, and an attempt to encircle Russia from the south? The dream of a federation of western Europe under Bonaparte kings and German princes deriving their powers from a hereditary Emperor of the French? 'My intention,' he told Joseph on January 27th, 'is to make the kingdom of Naples hereditary in my family: thus Naples, Italy, Switzerland, Holland, and the three German kingdoms will constitute my federated states, in fact the French Empire.' Perhaps Napoleon himself did not know which of these plans had the priority. But George III, Pius VII, and Alexander each felt himself singled out for attack; and not least the Emperor of Austria, whose defeat had become the source of all these threats and anxieties.[8]

7

Since the middle of the eighteenth century, when modern history really began, Prussia had been as much the traditional friend of France as Austria had been the traditional enemy. Frederick the Great's *volte-face* in 1756 and the French defeat at Rossbach in 1757 belonged to the old regime; the invasion of France in 1792 was due more to Marie-Antoinette than to the King of Prussia. Frederick-William III, who came to the throne (November 1797) in the first year of a new French alliance, was very conscious both of his inheritance of Frederick's organization and Frederick's army, and of the dangerous position in which his country stood, a scattered and frontierless state, between France, Austria and Russia. He was twenty-seven at the time of his accession (Queen Louise, whose beauty and early death made her an almost legendary figure of Prussian patriotism, was only twenty-one): a timid peace-loving man, born for neutrality, who showed, even in his congratulations to Bonaparte in 1799, his apprehension as to the First Consul's real intentions.

These for the next three years seemed so favourable (by the treaty of September 1802, Prussia gained a population of 400,000) that Frederick-William had every reason to congratulate his *Grand et cher Ami* on the Life Consulship—'the final homage paid by the French nation to the character and genius of its saviour.' Prussian opinion was generally pro-French, and favoured a Bonapartist degree of revolution; though it was noticed that this feeling was stronger in the more intelligent provinces west of the Elbe than in those east of it, where there was more friendliness to Russia.

The first blow to Frederick-William's uneasy optimism came with the break-down of the Peace of Amiens, and Bonaparte's occupation of Hanover and the ports of Cuxhaven and Ritzebüttel (Hanoverian and Hamburg territory) at the mouth of the Elbe (June 3rd, 1803). Bonaparte refused to withdraw, and all Frederick-William could do was to exchange with the Tsar Alexander resolutions to oppose any further French aggression in northern Europe. He refused Napoleon's suggestion—a compliment which carried a sneer—that he should call himself Emperor of Prussia, now that Francis was only Emperor of Austria, and advertise a third new-fangled title in the Gotha Almanac.

It was not long before he had fresh cause for suspicion that Napoleon was treating Prussia as though it were a state of second-rate importance. On the night of October 25th, 1804, a detachment of French troops kidnapped Sir George Rumbold, British envoy at Hamburg, on territory within the Prussian-directed Circle of Lower Saxony. This violation of neutral rights, following so closely the pattern of the d'Enghien affair six months before—Rumbold himself hourly expected the same fate—drew a long and, for him, violent protest from Frederick-William. Napoleon, having got what he wanted, packed Rumbold off to England, and sent the King a mild reply. But there was no relaxation of the blockade, which was already causing much discontent in Prussia. The incident was closed (March 1805) by an exchange of Orders between the two sovereigns: the Black Eagle of Prussia for the Grand Eagle of the Legion of Honour.

Eighteen months later the two countries were at war, and in one day's fighting Prussia was reduced to the position that Napoleon had always assigned her—that of a second-class power, useful to France as Bavaria was useful, but unfit even for the degree of independence granted to Austria. How did this come about?

The orders for the mobilization of the Prussian army were first issued on August 9th, 1806. By an unlucky coincidence a dispatch from Lucchesini, the Prussian ambassador at Paris, dated August 6th, was opened in the *cabinet noir*, and found to contain proof of Frederick-William's adhesion to the Third Coalition. Lucchesini was at once recalled; but Napoleon's shadowy belief in Prussian honesty was destroyed.

Even now he did his best to avoid war, as is shown by a 'Note on the present situation' which he addressed to Talleyrand on September 12th. 'It is not in my interest,' he wrote, 'to trouble the peace of the continent. Austria is not in a position to attempt anything. Russia and Prussia are kept apart by every kind of rivalry and dislike . . . It may be assumed that no considerable force of Russians can appear in Europe just yet. They might go to some lengths to attack the Porte: they might keep reserves in Poland: but I don't think they will again run the risk of sending 100,000 men into Germany. The idea that Prussia could take me on single-handed is too absurd to merit discussion. It is impossible for me to have a genuine alliance with any of the great European powers. Prussia is only my ally through fear. Her cabinet is so contemptible, her king so weak, and her court so dominated by young officers in search of adventure, that no one can depend on her. She will go on acting as she has acted—arming today, disarming tomorrow; standing by, sword in hand, while the battle is fought, and then making terms with the victor.'

The policy resulting from this shrewd and frank estimate of the situation was, first, that Prussia must be reassured, and given an opportunity to disarm—for obviously Napoleon does not want another continental campaign to interfere with his English invasion; secondly, Prussia will only disarm in 'a mood of reassurance touched with fear—that is the language she understands, that is the only form of appeal that really moves her.' Lucchesini's return to Berlin can be used to advertise the idea that the French army is on the alert. 'Instead of saying, "Disarm or fight," I shall say, "Disarm if you don't want me to reinforce." '

Napoleon had not misjudged the weakness and inconsequence of Frederick-William's policy; but he had underestimated his pride. The reply to Lucchesini's message took the form of a private letter to Napoleon, dated Naumberg, September 25th, just three weeks before the battle of Jena. Its 3000 provocative words—*cette espèce de pamphlet,* Napoleon called it—were due to Frederick-William's minister, Lombard; but they

did no more than express the accumulated grievances of three years which
had been rankling in the King's mind, and which he had hitherto lacked
the courage to put on paper.

Three times in three years (he protested) he had been on the point of
making a firm alliance with Napoleon, and every time he had been faced
with fresh demands. Napoleon had invaded Hanoverian territory, and
sacrificed Prussian interests to his martime war with England. He had
kidnapped a British minister on Prussian soil. He had taken no account
of Frederick-William's services with respect to Russia, or Sweden, or
'Louis XVIII.' The King had hoped that the partition of the 'intermediate
states' of Germany between 'our two empires' would have been followed
by peace on the continent, and that 'for the good of France the hero
would have been satisfied with more peaceful pursuits.' 'I do not speak
(he said: but he did) of the evergrowing advances of French power,
before which the most distant states tremble; nor of Switzerland, Holland, Genoa, and even Portugal purchasing an anxious neutrality by
weight of gold.'

The letter went on to remind Napoleon of Prussia's neutrality in 1805,
and her willingness to mediate, on the principle 'that I have heard you
proclaim time after time: *les traités, tous les traités, rien que les traités.*'
But when the war opened, Bavarian troops under Napoleon's orders
violated the Prussian territory of Ansbach; and when Austria was defeated the only treaty Prussia got was more loss than gain. Finally, 'at
the moment when I believe all your troops to be on their way home, and
Germany could have blessed me as her liberator, you (without consulting
me) turned the constitution of the Empire upside down.'

'Such, *Monsieur mon Frère,*' the letter ended, 'is the true picture of your
conduct towards me. I see in it no signs of the friendliness which I was
so anxious to have from you, and which, at great sacrifice to myself, I had
done so much to deserve. It is not resentment which dictates these words.
I shall always be ready to do justice to your great qualities, and, whatever
our future relations, you will always find me fair and modest . . . Please
God we shall come to an understanding on principles which, without
diminishing your prestige, leave other peoples their self-respect, and free
all Europe from the present plague of fear and anxiety, in which none of
us can reckon on the future, or know where his duty lies.'

Fine words! But what Frederick-William forgot to say was that ever
since June 1803 he had been intriguing with Russia against France, that
during the summer of 1805 he was involved in the negotiations that led to
the formation of the Third Coalition, and that on November 3rd, a fortnight after the capitulation of Ulm (which should have warned him) he
joined Russia and England in the alliance which was crushed at Austerlitz. Still less did the writer mention that in July 1806, he had signed a

secret pact with the Tsar, and that whilst signing himself *le bon frère, ami et allié* of Napoleon, he was in reality mobilizing his armies, and preparing to prove that the Prussia of Frederick-William III was still the Prussia of Frederick the Great.

Frederick-William might have called himself 'Emperor.' Prussia might have been the head of a confederation of north German states. She might have been a bulwark against Russia, as Bavaria was against Austria, and the mainstay of the continental system against England. In the summer of 1806, with Austerlitz behind him, and the Confederation of the Rhine in being, Napoleon really counted on an interval of continental peace—peace during which he might resume his struggle with England. Prussia made the double mistake of not joining him in 1805, and of turning against him in 1806—and that at the worst possible moment, whilst she was without allies, not fully mobilized, and before the Grand Army was even out of Germany.[9]

8

The pattern of the campaign of 1806 was that of the campaign of 1805, but foreshortened. As then Napoleon had marched for the 'liberation' of Bavaria, so now he marched for the 'liberation' of Saxony—Saxony which, he told the army in his proclamation of October 6th, was being attacked by the same war party which had incited the invasion of France in 1792. It pleased him to make fun of the Queen of Prussia, whom he knew to have played the part of Marie-Antoinette to Frederick-William's Louis XVI. 'She is at the front,' he said, 'dressed like an Amazon, wearing the uniform of her regiment of dragoons, and writing twenty letters a day to fan the flames of war.' The King of Prussia was advised, as Francis had been advised, to give up the struggle: he was only courting defeat.

This was the plain truth, though no Prussian would admit it. The army of Frederick the Great, fourteen years after its inglorious retreat from Valmy, was half composed of foreigners paid to fight, and half of peasants forced to do so. It had lost the habit of war, and its military ideas, like many of its officers, were septuagenarian. Above all, it lacked a leader; Frederick-William was a mere wraith of the man who had made it and led it to victory in two great wars, and who would have scorned the idea of a Queen riding at his side.

Instead of waiting for their Russian allies, the Prussians advanced to the attack, and enabled Napoleon to destroy them in detail. The two armies blundered into each other in the hill country of Thuringia. On October 14th Davout at Auerstadt won a battle against odds, helped by the death of the opposing general; and at Jena, the same day, Napoleon was able to outnumber and defeat a second army. The Prussians lost in all 27,000 killed and wounded. The rest were rounded up bit by bit over the northern plains. The fortresses surrendered. The civil authorities, bereft of military backing, collapsed. The people, without initiative, accepted a new regime, as they were to do at every turn of the coming century, at first with a puzzled stare and perhaps a stamping of the ground: then turned tail, and let themselves be driven in whatever direction the new sheep-dog determined. The Prussia of Frederick the Great had ceased to exist.[10]

9

Six weeks after the battle of Jena (November 25th) Napoleon marched east again from Berlin for the Polish campaign against Russia; he was at Warsaw on December 19th, fought the battles of Eylau (January 8th, 1807) and Friedland (June 14th), and met the Tsar on the Niemen (June 25th). After the signature of the Treaty of Tilsit he started home on July 9th, and was back at Saint-Cloud on the 27th.

During ten months of absence from France and campaigning in the north of Europe he was never quite free from the fear that Austria, who, in spite of her pacific professions, was still under arms, might attack his right flank. In September 1806 Francis had refused an invitation to enter into an alliance with France, thinking it enough to protest his neutrality. Napoleon doubted his sincerity, and asked that the Austrian army should be put on a peace footing. Vincent was dispatched to Warsaw with a letter from Francis explaining that his mobilization was merely protective (December 21st); Ferdinand of Würtemberg followed with another in the same sense (January 25th).

But Napoleon did not trust these empty assurances; and in the enforced pause after the battle of Eylau he tried to detach Prussia from her Russian ally, and (once again) to attach Austria to his own fortunes by a treaty of alliance that would safeguard his forthcoming attack on Russia, and set him free for the Spanish campaign that he was already planning for the summer. Francis replied to his letter of May 27th with his usual empty professions of peace and friendship (June 13th). But the news of Friedland and Tilsit changed his attitude, and on October 10th he accepted a postscript to the Treaty of Pressburg confirming and extending that agreement.

But Austria was still arming. What was more important, she had at last found a statesman who could turn the occasional provocations of Thugut, Cobenzl, and Stadion into a cautious but consistent collaboration with France's enemies for the overthrow of Napoleon. By birth and looks, character and experience, Clemens Wenzel Lothar, Prince Metternich, was the perfect diplomat of an age that was on the turn from dynasticism to democracy. Born in diplomacy, brought up in the little courts of old Germany, watching the French Revolution from Brussels and Maintz, and the Directory from London, married to a grand-daughter of the old anti-Jacobin statesman Kaunitz, he shared with Talleyrand and Castlereagh a European outlook based on a policy of national self-preservation.

At Dresden (1801-03), Berlin (1803-06), and Paris (1806-09) he studied at increasingly close quarters Bonaparte and the Napoleonic system. Equally adept at arranging a function or flirting with an ambassadress, as ready to share a safe secret as to conceal a dangerous one, using the naive vanity that shines through his Memoirs and portraits to cover a shrewd and calculating mind, he made himself for nearly half a century the most formidable enemy of the militant French Revolution. Watching Napoleon, he noticed that his victories, whether at home or in the field, were never final. He was a cardplayer who overcalled his hand; a gambler who staked all his winnings on another throw of the dice. One day his luck must turn, and everything he had gained be lost in a single stroke of fate. All that Austria need do was to wait and prepare for that opportunity of revenge.

At Dresden, the northern counterpart of Turin—the capital of a frontier state that could only exist by playing off its powerful neighbours against each other—Metternich realized that the last ten years had brought about a greater change in the traditional alliances of Europe than all the wars of the preceding century; and that Austria in particular would need a new and realistic foreign policy. At Berlin he read (as Mirabeau had twenty years before) the signs of Prussia's decadence: territorial gains which dissipated her strength as much as Austria's losses concentrated her own: a militarized state living on its reputation, unready and unfit for war: a weak, well-meaning king ill-advised by statesmen who covered their rival fears of France and Russia by empty professions of championing the peace of Europe.

Gradually there formed in his mind a policy for his country—for he was at heart a simple patriot, a devout believer in the destinies of Austria, and in the divine right of the house of Habsburg. 'Those who discerned in the conduct of the First Consul the coming Sovereignty of France (he wrote from Berlin in January 1805) are as well justified in foretelling where the progressive designs of the restorer of the Empire of Charlemagne will lead him; from summoning the Sovereign Pontiff, the legislators of the Italian republics, and as many of the German princes as are disposed to attend him, as a gesture of vassalage, at his Coronation, he will proceed to demand still stronger guarantees of supremacy by setting up the very military government and political principles which carried the Roman Empire to the monarchy of the world.'

During the campaign of 1805, Metternich did everything he could to induce Frederick-William—terrified of Napoleon, but outraged by the casual way in which he marched Bernadotte's troops through Prussian Ansbach—to sign the Treaty of Potsdam, and to take military action, even after the fall of Vienna and the disaster of Austerlitz, against the exposed French left. Whether or not the terms of this treaty were given away, as Metternich believed, by Haugwitz, Napoleon's mind as well as his army moved too fast and too straight for the Prussian and Austrian diplomatists; and he extricated himself by Austerlitz and Pressburg from what might have been a situation as dangerous for him as the weeks before Leoben.

Metternich had still something to learn. His scheme for an Allied Journal, as a counterblast to Napoleon's *Bulletins de la Grande Armée*, seemed to forget that almost daily propaganda distributed by a victorious army will always outsell an occasional magazine published by a refugee government. His outline of a *Plan politique* for the allies in January 1806 which envisaged a fortified line across Europe from the mouth of the Weser to the head of the Adriatic, with notice-boards (as it were) warning Napoleon to keep to the west, was hopelessly unrealistic. It included the suggestion that Austria should offer to give up her title to the Holy Roman Empire in return for the retention of Dalmatia. Six months later Francis renounced the Empire without compensation. It had no longer any market value.[11]

10

The years 1806-09, whether viewed from Paris or Vienna, contain the reasons for the Franco-Austrian war of 1809. At Vienna, the Emperor Francis, as feebly authoritarian as ever, was encouraged by his new Chancellor, Stadion, and his brother the Archduke Charles, now in full command of a reformed army, to hope for revenge. But abroad the nullity of Prussia since Jena, and the estrangement of Russia since Tilsit, and at home the lack of resources, made delay inevitable. From Paris Metternich's dispatches discussed each move in the Napoleonic policy, and promised to give the word when at last it might be safe for Austria to come into the open, and to declare hostilities against the oppressor of Europe.

It cannot be doubted that for Napoleon himself these years were a time of increasing difficulty. He was like a conjurer who has added another and again another ball to those already in the air, and is beginning to fear that he may have to drop one. Prussia, whom he never really took seriously—that was Frederick-William's deepest shame—he had bought off in December 1805, and February 1806, only to find her challenging him eight months later; so that he had the trouble of reducing her to a second-class power—disregarded, in spite of the appeals of her queen, in the arrangements at Tilsit. But even Prussia was to rise again.

Alexander, defeated at Friedland, and cajoled at Tilsit, had for the present renounced European ambitions, but could not look on indifferently whilst Napoleon resumed his Near and perhaps Far Eastern designs.

Austria and Russia would come together again to resist a French partition of Turkey. Francis was mollified a little by the Treaty of Fontainebleau (October 1807), but never stopped thinking of the next war.

And now there was a fresh ball in the air—Portugal, without whose harbours the blockade could never be complete; and, to reach Portugal, Spain, which must be added to the growing calendar of Bonapartist kingdoms, and for whose conquest and garrisoning part at least of the Grand Army must march across the Pyrenees.

Bonapartist, not French: for, as Metternich observed, the Parisians were by this time so accustomed to see old thrones crumbling and new states rising from their debris that the politicians of the cafés and drawing-rooms hardly noticed the fall of Prussia or of Spain. But it was different in the courts and chancelleries. Napoleon well knew—Talleyrand was slyly pleased to remind him—what Vienna or Petersburg was saying about Madrid. 'The catastrophe in which the throne of Spain is crumbling,' wrote Metternich to Stadion on April 27th, 1808) 'merely fills up the measure of Napoleon's cunning, destructive, and criminal policy—a policy which he has never ceased to follow since he came into power . . . The noise made by the fall of a throne is formidable and echoes round the world; though in principle it is no worse than the passage of a detachment to carry off a wretched Bourbon from sanctuary, and have him shot at Vincennes.'

On January 1st, 1809, Napoleon was pursuing Sir John Moore towards Corunna when he received a batch of letters from Paris. After reading them he went on slowly to Astorga, remained there two days; returned to Valladolid; waited there another ten days for a deputation from Madrid asking for the return of King Joseph to his capital; and on the 17th, posted at full speed to Paris, arriving there on the 23rd. Why did he leave it to others to carry on the pursuit, so that much of Moore's army escaped, and the English were encouraged to land again in the Peninsula? Two reasons have been given, and it matters little which had the priority: a plot against him in Paris, and a growing threat of war from Austria. The surprising thing is that he should have felt these reasons to be urgent enough to break off the Spanish campaign, for they were both affairs of long standing, and must have been discounted when he made up his mind, only two months before, to take command of his armies south of the Pyrenees. 'Was he disinclined *de se frotter* against Moore (it is Wellington who tries to explain the enigma)? Did he wish that Soult should try what stuff our people were made of before he risked his own great reputation against us? or did he despair of driving us out of Corunna? . . . My own notion is that he was not sure of the victory.'

There was at any rate nothing new in the situation in Paris. Austria had been re-arming ever since Austerlitz; during the summer of 1808 there had been persistent rumours, which Napoleon had done nothing to discourage, of preventive action by the French armies in Prussia; his generals were always itching for new campaigns and fresh titles and rewards; and in July he had travelled all the way from Bayonne to Paris for the sole object, apparently, of convening the ambassadors, haranguing Metternich, in their presence, on the Austrian re-armament (August 15th), and complaining of the personal unfriendliness of Francis, contrasted with the friendliness of Alexander.

Nor was there anything new in the opposition to Napoleon's designs amongst his own ministers. There were in 1808, says Metternich, two parties in France: on the one side Napoleon, with his determination to extend his power in Europe by force, both for his own ambition and for that of his family (nepotism in him came next to egotism), and backed by the military clique: on the other side 'the mass of the nation, inactive and unimpressed, like the lava-field of an extinct volcano,' but at their head Talleyrand, Fouché, and all those who feared the loss of their fortunes with the next turn of the wheel—and they thought they saw it beginning at Baylen and Cintra.

But Napoleon would not move unless he were sure of Russian support, or at least neutrality. He had therefore invited his dear friend the Tsar, and commanded his clients the princes of Germany, to meet him at Erfurt at the end of September 1808. Outwardly this was to be an *Exposition Universelle* of the Napoleonic Empire, such as to impress Europe and silence opposition: inwardly it was to produce diplomatic arrangements which would assure him a free hand for next year's campaign in Spain. But in everything except its receptions and its parades, its balls and its banquets, Erfurt was a disappointment. Alexander refused to do more than 'use his good offices,' as the phrase goes, to restrain Austria during Napoleon's absence in Spain; and Talleyrand took the opportunity to offer his services to Russia and Austria in any steps they might take to counter the further designs of the Emperor.

Napoleon, then, had returned to Spain like a man looking back over his shoulder; and when the operations against Moore did not seem likely to bring him any decisive victory (indeed they were reckoned a reverse in Paris), it needed only the disquietening news of January 1st, 1809, to hurry him back to France. The Opposition at home would be easily dealt with. He thought he had the measure of Talleyrand—a man as servile as he was treacherous, who would never sell himself except to the winning side. But the Austrian affair was more serious. Not that, as things were, Francis would declare war on France—the armed Confederation of the Rhine stood in his way. But the wastage and dispersal of the French armies contrasted unpleasantly with the growth and concentration of those of Austria; and he must either abandon the Spanish adventure, or wage a preventive campaign against Francis before the balance of power tipped dangerously against him.

During the ten days he spent at Valladolid before leaving for Paris he dictated letters furiously: in particular two intended to intimidate the Emperor of Austria. He had, he told Champagny and Caulaincourt, 400,000 men ready to march on Vienna, 150,000 in Italy, a like number on the Rhine, and 100,000 consisting of troops of the Confederation. He was raising another 80,000 conscripts. The guard was to march for Bayonne within a week. He could afford to leave 200,000 men in Spain, and yet have more than enough to deal with Austria.[12]

II

Five days after his return to Paris Napoleon attacked Talleyrand and Fouché, whom he accused of being at the head of a party of opposition to his government and to his dynasty. The next day, at a diplomatic reception, Metternich, who expected another lecture like that of August 15th, was passed by in silence, which he took to be an even worse omen; and Romanzov, the Russian ambassador, warned him in so many words that war had been determined.

Yet for nearly three months nothing appeared to happen, and Metternich's dispatches could only speculate on the reasons for delay, and the prospects of the coming campaign. Russia alone could prevent it; and Russia would not. The partnership of Tilsit still held, though Erfurt had not strengthened it. Alexander would not risk another Austerlitz. The more embarrassed Napoleon became by Austrian hostility, the easier it would be to deal with him. There was talk of a *garantie*, under which, assured by France and Russia that neither would attack her, Austria was to reduce her armaments. Francis, with Charles and Stadion behind him, would not dream of such a humiliation. Austria stood on her right to defend herself, and was confident that the verdict of 1805 could be reversed.

'Napoleon,' wrote Metternich from Paris, 'has provoked the present situation by his hot-headedness and excessive ambition. He thinks he has a good chance of winning; yet he has no illusions as to the nature of the struggle, or as to our considerable means of resistance. He bases his hopes of success on his military genius, and the spirit that animates his generals and soldiers. He is engaging for the first time in a huge struggle with inferior resources: he hopes to double them by superior mobility. He bases his hopes on the slowness of our movements, on our need to recuperate after an early success, or alternatively on our growing discouraged and losing our morale.' The war of 1805 had been unpopular enough in France: another in 1809 would be far more so. Then the Treasury was full: now it was half empty. Then the army was one of veterans and trained men:

now it was composed largely of raw conscripts and foreigners. If he meant to fight, Napoleon should have done so last year, or the year before.

It might seem that Austria had equally missed the opportunity of Napoleon's embarrassments in Poland in 1807 or in Spain in 1808. But it had needed Tilsit and Erfurt to enable Francis to represent his crusade against Napoleon as European, not merely Austrian, as a war of liberation, not of revenge: and it had needed Baylen, Cintra and Corunna to enlist hope under his banners. Even in the wars of the previous century it had been noticed that there was more national feeling in the Austrian than in the Prussian armies. This was now at its height, and the army, if not as ready as Charles could have wished, was yet larger and better trained than it had ever been before. Besides, the military talents of the Archduke had been wasted in the war of 1805. Now he was in supreme command of an army of his own making—the only man who counted in the country (*c'est le seul homme là*, said Napoleon); whilst Wellington regarded him as the best general of the age ('Why, he knows more about it than all of us put together').[18]

During the forty-five days preceding the opening of the campaign of 1809, Napoleon dictated no more letters than during the eighteen days preceding the campaign of 1805. Days spent in hunting, evenings at the opera, inspections of girls' schools—people began to wonder whether he shrank from the coming struggle, whether, even, he might have lost his taste for war. But there were good reasons for delay, and even for an appearance of unpreparedness. He knew every inch of the ground on which the campaign had to be fought. He remembered every incident of 1805. It was not yet the season for forced marches or quick manœuvres. His army had to be mobilized from north, south, and west: yet its march could not be co-ordinated to converge on an unsuspecting enemy. Meanwhile it would be all to the good if the Archduke Charles were tempted, as Mack had been in 1805, to advance from the narrow valley of the middle Danube into the open plain of the upper Danube, where there was room to out-manœuvre him. Asked for his plan of campaign—'*Mon plan de campagne?* (Napoleon replied) *Je n'en ai pas. Je n'en ai jamais eu.*' It must depend on the movements of the enemy.

At last, at 7 p.m. on April 12th, he heard that the Austrians had crossed the Inn: '*C'est la guerre,*' he exclaimed, and was off at once. He had dinner at nine, slept for two hours, and started for Strasbourg at 4 o'clock the next morning. Joséphine had only just time to pack up and go with him.

He had put off his arrival at the front dangerously late. Berthier, who was unrivalled in placing the pieces on the board, had no idea how to move them. The triangular battle-field, with its eastern apex at Linz, and its western base on the Lech, divided into three sectors by the Isar and the Inn, offered plenty of opportunities for cornering and destroying isolated forces. Davout with 60,000 of Napoleon's best troops was isolated on the north bank of the Danube at Regensberg (Ratisbon), Oudinot with a mixed German-Bavarian force stood on the Lech: the other French armies were not yet in the field. The Archduke Charles had avoided the chief mistake of 1805: the bulk of his army, 200,000 strong, was concentrated in the Danube valley: if only he had moved straight on Regensberg, he might have crushed Davout before help arrived.

With Napoleon's arrival at Donauwörth on April 17th the campaign began to take shape. It had three stages. In the first week the Archduke's army was rounded up in the battle of Eckmühl, and driven northwards across the Danube, with the loss of nearly half its effectives. In the second month Napoleon advanced straight on Vienna (May 12th), bridged the Danube below the city, attacked the Austrians on the north bank, was defeated at Aspern (or Essling) (May 22nd-25th), and had to retire with severe losses to the midstream island of Lobau. Six weeks later (July 4th) the third phase began with a surprise crossing on to the north bank, and the stubborn pitched battle of Wagram, and ended in an Austrian retreat and armistice (July 12th).

The campaign had lasted a month longer than that of 1805. Except at Eckmühl Napoleon had displayed more energy than genius. The losses on both sides had been exceptionally severe, and almost equal. The Austrian surrender, which was due as much to divided counsels as to military exhaustion, saved Napoleon from the most dangerous situation he had ever been in. The British had landed in Portugal, and in the Netherlands. The Tyrol was in revolt. The Russians had a large army in Galicia, and Alexander's attitude was increasingly unfriendly. Fouché was exploiting his temporary position as Minister of the Interior to set all Paris by the ears; and Napoleon, though he might profess to despise it, was always nervous about public opinion. When the Austrian negotiators, headed by Metternich, tried to drag out the peace talks, in order to give time for military recovery and Russian intervention, Napoleon grew impatient, and forced the signature of the Treaty of Schönbrunn (October 14th).

12

Austria expected worse terms in 1809 than in 1805, for then Prussia was in arms, and Russia was her ally; but she was appalled by the loss of 3½ million souls, and all of her Adriatic coast, with an indemnity of £3¾ millions. Less serious, but hardly less galling, was the recognition, which Francis had hitherto refused, of the Bonapartist crowns of Italy and Spain, the surrender of nearly 1000 books and manuscripts from the Imperial library, and the reduction of the Austrian army to 150,000 men.

Francis, with more spirit than usual, protested (September 20th) that these terms were 'fatal to the existence of Austria and the welfare of his people ... A peace upon such terms (he said) would leave my monarchy with no frontiers, my states with no outlets: it would deprive my provinces of their essential communications, and so destroy the foundations of the national industry and individual happiness of my people.' Napoleon's only reply was to point out that if Francis had accepted with good grace the settlement of Lunéville both countries might have been spared many sufferings.

His sympathy for the people of Vienna, so eloquently expressed in the *Proclamation à l'armée* of May 13th, did not outlive his need of their houses and their food for the troops that occupied the capital. He might set a guard of honour outside the house in which old Haydn lay dying —remembering, no doubt, the performance of *The Creation* at the Théâtre des Arts in Paris nine years before, when an attempt had been made on his life, and knowing that the Viennese nearly worshipped the author of their national anthem: yet it was only the gesture of a moment. He had always blundered in his dealings with a national, a European, almost a spiritual state. He had treated the Habsburg Empire as though it were of no more account than the upstart monarchy of Prussia, and civilized Catholic Vienna as though it were a mere centre of government like St. Petersburg or Madrid. He was already making the same mistake in Italy, where his treatment of the Pope was to rouse against him, alongside the nationalism of Spain and the Tyrol and the dynastic pride of Austria, the spiritual integrity of the Catholic church. Such things were not dreamed of in his philosophy.

That was what Talleyrand meant when he said to Alexander at Erfurt: 'The French are civilized, their sovereign is not. The sovereign of Russia is civilized, her people are not. Therefore the sovereign of Russia must be the ally of the French people.' For Talleyrand, though he was treacherous, venal and immoral, remained an aristocrat of the eighteenth century, regretted a *douceur de vivre* destroyed by the Revolution, and disliked the tawdriness of Napoleon's court, the vulgarity of his manners, and the violence that he employed in his foreign policy. He had felt much the same about Mirabeau, another man of constructive and comprehensive genius. But Mirabeau had weaknesses that made him vulnerable and unstable: Napoleon seemed always to be certain of himself, always efficient, always successful. You could not but admire him and follow him: but you were not fond of him; and you felt that his view of life was fundamentally false.

This insensitiveness, this devaluation of values, had been growing on him rapidly since his assumption of Empire. There had been a time, not much more than ten years ago, when his passion for Joséphine, with all its sensuality, gave him some insight into the meaning of existence; when he could curse the ambition and love of glory that separated him from 'the soul of his life'; when he could ask, 'What is the future? What is the past? What are we? What magic liquid is it that shuts us in, and hides from us the things that we ought most to know? We move and live and die in the midst of miracles.' But when disillusionment came, he had been quick to console himself for Joséphine's supposed unfaithfulness; and since the reconciliation at Brumaire, and the transformation of a one-sided love match into a partnership of habit and affection, he had drifted into the hard unimaginative middle age of business and organization, of functions and interviews, of flattery and insincerity, of the calculation of material loss and gain, of having always to be in the right, and to put everyone else in the wrong, which is the curse of dictators: he had become more brutal, more overbearing, more coarse in his judgments of men, women and affairs.

It can hardly be supposed, then, that any but worldly (that is, dynastic) motives were behind his determination to round off the Austrian episode, as he might now hope to call it, by divorcing Joséphine and marrying a princess of the house of Habsburg. The campaigns of 1805 and 1809 had taught him that though he might defeat Austria he could not hope to subdue her. He still refused Talleyrand's advice to encourage her Balkan ambitions: but he might take another step towards conciliating the Emperor of which both Talleyrand and Metternich approved, and which was so consonant with the Habsburg maxim: *Tu, felix Austria, nube.*

There were of course such minor matters to consider as the means of divorce, the form of re-marriage, and the religion of the bride. But Napoleon had by now come to make light of such obstacles. If reasons of state made an heir essential, and if this heir must be born and brought up in the purple, nothing less than the best would suffice. A way could always be found to get what he wanted. But here a horrid fear intervened. Was Napoleon's childlessness, after eight years of marriage and a series of mistresses, perhaps his own fault? In Bertrand's *Journal* at St. Helena there is a remarkably frank conversation *sur le divorce et le mariage de l'Empereur* in which his alleged impotence (upon evidence attributed to Joséphine) is given as the reason why the Tsar refused to let him marry his sister. Napoleon seems to have remained uneasy on this subject until the birth of an illegitimate son, afterwards called the Comte de Léon, in December 1807. (His son by Mme Walewska was not born till May 4th, 1810—too late to determine his mind.) It was almost certain now that Joséphine, who was forty-six, would not have another child. Hortense's eldest son, whom he had talked of adopting, had died in May. An Emperor who must have an heir could hardly be blamed for making fresh arrangements for the future of his dynasty. It was at this time that a list was drawn up, apparently by Fouché, of eighteen eligible princesses, Catholic and non-Catholic, aged from thirteen upwards, from which he might make his choice. But he had put the matter off for another two years, partly because his policy wavered between a Russian and an Austrian marriage, and partly, perhaps, through his affection for Joséphine.

She was the only woman for whom he had really cared. Mme Fourès, the succession of *actrices* and *lectrices*, la Grassini, Eléonore Denuelle (whom he would not see the year after she bore him a son), even Mme Walewska, and the mysterious Mme XXX, never took her place. Only Joséphine could amuse him by her indignation, and move him by her tears: she was his only refuge from his own family, the one person in the world to whom he could say what was really in his mind; with whom, in a world of make-belief, he could be his natural self. When he divorced Joséphine he cut his life in half, and threw away the better part of it.[14]

13

The first suggestion of divorce may have come in 1801 (as asserted in his *Memoirs*) from his brother Lucien: all the Bonapartes were against Joséphine. Talleyrand spoke of it again, suggesting a Baden princess as bride, in 1804; and it was her knowledge of this which prompted Joséphine to the admission which necessitated the Catholic marriage on the eve of the Coronation. Tilsit (where the two Emperors may well have discussed their matrimonial troubles) brought the idea from the back to the front of Napoleon's mind. On his return from Warsaw and Mme Walewska in 1807 (so Metternich told Stadion) he treated Joséphine coldly, and slept in a room apart. But he would not allow any public discussion of the matter, and was indignant with Fouché for mentioning it in such a way as to cause pain to the Empress. If Lucien were to divorce Mme de Jouberthon, it would make the business easier: Lucien's refusal (in Italy, at the end of 1807) made his course more difficult. He mentioned the subject again, it would seem, to the archiepiscopal Chapter of Bordeaux in 1808, and was put out by their refusal to agree with his ideas.

After his return from the Austrian campaign of 1809, with his mind full of Staps's attempt upon his life (not Francis's life, the man admitted, because he had heirs), his purpose became fixed. On November 30th, at the end of an interview with Napoleon and Eugène (whom he unfeelingly used to bring pressure to bear on his mother), Joséphine was told that she must consent to divorce; and on December 15th, at the Tuileries, in the presence of Mme Mère and all the available Bonapartes, Napoleon and Joséphine gave their formal consent to a document which was signed and witnessed by all present. Joséphine was in tears: Napoleon found the scene 'extremely interesting.'

This document was passed on to a meeting of the Senate next day, at which Eugène, again, was forced to make a speech expressing the consent of the family. The Senators, with their usual subservience, raised no objection, although the agreement transgressed two articles of the Imperial Statute—one forbidding divorce to members of the Emperor's household, and the other prohibiting divorce by consent when the wife was over forty-five: Joséphine was now forty-six. The same day she left the Tuileries, and went to live alone at Malmaison, Napoleon visited her there a few days later, and exhorted her to take it cheerfully. '*Je désire te savoir gaie*,' he wrote afterwards.

Already the new Empress had been chosen. The first proposal, made at Erfurt, to marry the Tsar's young sister Anne was opposed by her mother, the widow of Tsar Paul, a German by birth, a Francophobe by conviction and the girl's legal guardian. On December 4th Schwartzenberg wrote to Metternich saying that the choice lay between a Russian, a Saxon and an Austrian princess. Metternich saw at once a heaven-sent opportunity to secure a French alliance, and to safeguard Austria from a possible Franco-Russian attack, or a not impossible partition of the Habsburg dominions. When he heard of the divorce proceedings of December 15-16th he wrote at once to Schwartzenberg (December 25th): 'His Majesty (Francis) will shrink from nothing that may contribute to the welfare and peace of the state: he therefore authorizes you to follow up (the idea of an Austrian marriage), and not to reject any overtures that may be made to you on that subject.'

But Francis was a good Catholic, and insisted that Joséphine's divorce should cover the religious marriage of 1804 as well as the civil marriage of 1796. This was awkward. The only French precedents for the annulment of such a marriage (Louis XII and Henri IV) required an appeal to the Pope: but though Pius VII was at Savona (not so far away, it was pointed out, as Rome), he might as well have been at the Antipodes: he had refused to annul Jérôme's marriage: he had insisted on Napoleon's remarriage in 1804: it was useless to ask him to dissolve it. What was to be done? There still existed under the *régime concordataire* an *Officialité Métropolitaine*—the relic of an Ecclesiastical Court—attached to the see of Paris, with jurisdiction in questions about Catholic marriages. This body had pronounced Jérôme's marriage null and void, on the ground that it had not been correctly performed. Could it not do the same for Napoleon? On December 22nd (i.e. before Metternich's letter from Vienna) this body was approached by Cambacérès with the statement that the Emperor meant to marry a Catholic, and that he wished them to nullify his marriage to Joséphine. The *Officialité* were willing to do what they would do for any other French citizen, but doubted whether their jurisdiction covered the case of the Emperor. In any event, they asked, what grounds were alleged for annulment?

In his first application Cambacérès claimed that the marriage of 1804 had been performed without the presence of witnesses or of the parish *curé*, and that Napoleon had been 'forced' by Joséphine into a ceremony to which he attached no importance: it was therefore invalid. At his second application he alleged 'absence of mutual consent.' As it was evident that the *Officialité* thought poorly of these reasons, and stronger measures were needed, he added the opinion of a *commission ecclésiastique*, composed of two cardinals and five bishops whom Napoleon could trust, that the marriage was certainly invalid, and that it was within the competence of the *Officialité* to annul it.

The *Officialité* still insisted on hearing witnesses. Fesch, in a written statement (January 6th) said that he had performed the marriage without witnesses, because Napoleon insisted on it; but admitted that he had first obtained a dispensation (*toutes les dispenses*) from the Pope; and that (to Napoleon's great displeasure) he had given Joséphine a certificate of marriage. Of the other witnesses, Talleyrand urged the canonical irregularities, whilst the two laymen, Berthier and Duroc, said in effect that the marriage was invalid because Napoleon had intended it to be so. There was, in fact, little else they could say.

In view of this evidence the *Officialité* gave way and pronounced the marriage invalid. The *Moniteur* of January 14th, announcing this decision, thought it worth while to reassure its Catholic readers by adding a note to the effect that the action of the *Officialité* had the approval of the *comité ecclésiastique*, and was in accordance with 'the customs of the Gallican church and the decrees and canons of the Councils.'

All this may seem a very small matter compared to battles and blockades and the rise and fall of thrones. But a miniature is often a better likeness than a state portrait; and perhaps nothing shows better the deterioration of Napoleon's character under the stress of power and self-will than the way in which he carried through his divorce.[15]

14

After Metternich's letter of December 25th, 1809, Napoleon knew that he had only to ask Francis for his daughter's hand. But it was not till a dispatch from Caulaincourt on February 6th convinced him that it was no use to wait any longer for the Russian princess that he finally made up his mind. Then he acted with his usual impetuosity. The marriage contract with Marie-Louise was drawn up by the Austrian ambassador the same night, and sent off the next day: it returned with Francis's ratification on the 23rd. Lauriston was sent off the same day with a love letter to Marie-Louise and another in as friendly terms as Napoleon could think of to the Empress, whom he knew to be his enemy. Berthier, the indispensable chief of staff, followed next day to arrange a wedding by proxy, and to ask the Archduke Charles, Napoleon's recent antagonist, to act as bridegroom at the ceremony.

The marriage by proxy took place in Vienna on March 11th; two days later the bride was hurried off in her coach for Paris. On the 27th the impatient bridegroom met her at Courcelles, some miles short of the official meeting-place, and jumped into her carriage. At Compiègne, where they arrived at 9.30 that evening, he lost no time in consummating a marriage by proxy, which he was assured gave him all the rights of a husband. There followed a civil marriage at Saint-Cloud on April 1st; and the next day Fesch, who had tricked Joséphine into a form of marriage which his own evidence annulled, found no difficulty in bestowing the blessing of the church upon the Imperial bigamist.

As for Marie-Louise, she was a commonplace, insensitive, sensual girl, accustomed to obey her father; and she had led a sufficiently dull and economical life at Schönbrunn to look forward to the excitements of Paris and the stir of life at the Tuileries. The fate of her great-aunt, Marie-Antoinette, somewhat alarmed her, and she was never at ease in French society; but Napoleon, everyone said, had put an end to the Revolution, and she took philosophically enough her sudden betrothal to her country's arch enemy, if it could save her father's throne, and to the reviler of the Papacy, so long as he undertook—for she was a pious girl—not to interfere with her devotions. 'I am sorry,' she had said, 'for the poor princess he chooses to marry'; but when she was chosen she made up her mind to find satisfaction in obeying the will of Providence, and doing her duty as a wife as well as a daughter. The Vienna papers reported with impartial truth her happiness at the idea of her marriage, and a remarkable rise in the public funds. Otto told Champagny that she was looking forward to a chance of cultivating in Paris her taste for painting and music. Laborde sent home an enthusiastic account of her charms, and added: 'I am sure her children will be as strong and fresh as herself.'

Napoleon was delighted with his new toy, and for a fortnight left his letters unanswered and his secretaries idle whilst he amused himself with a simple-minded German girl more than twenty years younger than himself. It is only necessary to read her diaries, or his letters, to realize that, under her *naiveté* and school-girlish enthusiasms lay a commonplace character and an empty mind. As an Empress Marie-Louise could never match the poise or win the popularity of Joséphine: but she did the one thing demanded of her. The birth, within a year, of the King of Rome, as the Emperor proudly called his heir, seemed to justify the repudiation of a wife who was only a commoner, and of the republican way of life. The

Napoleonic star was still in the ascendant. Providence was still on the side of Imperialism.

With his usual insensibility Napoleon kept his discarded wife informed of her rival's pregnancy (*L'impératrice est effectivement grosse de quatre mois; elle se porte bien, et m'est fort attachée*), and boasted of the birth of a son with the family features: *Mon fils* (he wrote on March 22nd, 1811) *est gros et très bien portant . . . Il a ma poitrine, ma bouche, et mes yeux. J'espère qu'il remplira sa destinée.*

Three months after the wedding, whilst Napoleon and Marie-Louise were attending a ball at the Austrian Ambassador's house, an alarming and fatal fire broke out, and only his coolness saved her life. Superstitious Parisians, remembering the disaster that had marked Louis XVI's marriage festivities, shook their heads. They may have recalled this omen four years later, when Marie-Louise deserted the fallen Emperor and, whilst he was dying at St. Helena, bore three children to the Comte de Neipperg, whom Metternich had provided as her escort in exile. She was a worthless creature, after all.[16]

The Imperial wedding was unique: but it did not stand alone. The marriage of Louis to Hortense, of Jérôme to Catherine of Würtemberg, and of Eugène to Augusta of Bavaria were royal, if not imperial—extra-illustrations of the album of Bonapartist dynasticism. It was *à propos* of the last—the happiest of these political marriages (as that of Louis and Hortense was the unhappiest)—that Murat is said to have told Napoleon what was in the mind of good republicans: 'When France raised you to the throne, it believed it had found in you a popular chief, with a title that put you above all the sovereigns of Europe . . . But today you are doing homage to claims of sovereignty (*titres de pouvoir*) which are not yours, and which are opposed to our own: you are advertising to Europe your preference for something that none of us possess—distinction due to birth (*l'illustration de la naissance*).' 'M. le Prince Murat (Napoleon replied), I am always content when I see you at the head of my cavalry: but this is not a military operation: it is a political action, and one to which I have given much thought. You don't like this marriage? I do. I regard it as a great success—a success on a level with the victory of Austerlitz.[17]

15

What mark was left upon Germany by the Napoleonic invasions of 1805-1809? The question is perhaps too often asked with an eye to the territorial changes of the country, or the development of its ideas—matters which concerned chiefly the rulers or the thinkers; too seldom with respect to the ordinary citizen, whether townsman or countryman.

Territorially Germany had for so long been in a state of flux—states enlarging or contracting their frontiers by purchase or marriage, princes

with hyphenated or conglomerate titles, loyalties and even religions changing overnight—that citizenship in the smaller states was of parish, town-
ship, or county size, and even the bigger titles of Bavarian, Badener, and
Würtemberger marked differences more like those between the men of
Kent, Norfolk, and Yorkshire, than anything racial or national. At the
same time there was no such country as Germany—no inclusive state, no
over-riding patriotism. There were only certain units larger than others,
with older dynasties or better organized governments; congeries of estates
held together by custom, convenience, or fear; with a wisp of imperial
pedigree, perhaps, or an itch to over-run its neighbours. The predominance
of Protestantism in the north and Catholicism in the south favoured the
rivalry of two main powers, Prussia and Austria: the overlapping of
political loyalties and economic interests in the west enabled French influence to exploit the jealousies of a multitude of small rulers, and to build
up in the Rhineland what might in favourable circumstances become a
third power in Germany, and challenge the claims of Hohenzollern and
Habsburg.

To foster such a power had been the traditional policy of French rulers
from Henri IV to the Committee of Public Safety. Napoleon saw himself
as the successor of Richelieu and Mazarin, the executor of the Jacobin
heritage of a Ligue du Rhin. It was possible too—and this had obvious
advantages—to represent such a Third Power as the only purely German one on the continent (were not Austria and Prussia contaminated
with alien subjects, and Hanover an appanage of the British crown?),
and to raise the attractive and not yet dangerous cry of 'nationalism.' The
new Kings of Bavaria and Würtemberg, the Duke of Baden, Arch-Chan-
cellor Dalberg and the rest might each think himself the saviour of German independence, under the protection (no more) of the French armies:
not for them to realize that they were being incorporated with France and
Italy in an Empire of the West, all subservient to a new Charlemagne.

Territorially, then, the formation of the Confederation of the Rhine and
the Kingdom of Westphalia, following the readjustments of Rastadt, did
little more than put on the map the underlying tripartism which had been
the real political character of Germany since 1648: forming a transition
from the medieval kaleidoscopic pattern of small states to the three-
power rivalry of the nineteenth century. But though Napoleon may sometimes have played with the idea of reconstructing central Europe on these
lines, his immediate motive was the purely realistic desire to make the
western states of Germany as useful to France as possible: contributing
themselves, in return for 'protection,' the troops that protected them, and
the money by which they were paid: forming a military base for an attack
on Vienna or Berlin, and a first line of defence if Austria or Prussia were
to retaliate.

Bavaria, predestined by its geographical position to be the battle-field between France and Austria (as Belgium between France and Prussia), had long been accustomed to a weather-cock neutrality, inspired by fear or by greed. In 1805 its amiable, fussy, and ineffective ruler, Max Joseph, was only saved at the last moment from Austrian 'liberation' by the arrival of Napoleon's army of 'liberators,' and again from Prussian resentment at the violation of Ansbach by the victory of Austerlitz. Bavaria's reward (January 1806) was the proclamation of its Duke as King Maximilian I, and the marriage of his daughter Augusta to the Emperor's step-son, Eugène Beauharnais. Thereafter Max Joseph might make gestures of independence—he found reasons for not attending the coronation in Nôtre Dame; but in effect Bavaria was as indissolubly attached to the political and economic fortunes of France as were the Kingdoms of Holland or of Italy. The indignity of his position irked only Maximilian: the subservience of his foreign policy concerned his ministers and officials. But in three ways all his subjects felt the change—in the poorness and expensiveness of living under the continental blockade; in the burden of taxes, billeting and requisitioning laid upon them by the presence of French soldiery; and in the military service to which they were liable in time of war.

Time did nothing to lighten these burdens. Almost ruined by the war and invasion of 1805, Bavaria joined unwillingly in the campaign of 1806, professing pride that its 30,000 men were under the inefficient command of Jérôme Bonaparte. The victory of Jena was celebrated at Munich; but the troops, now under their own Prince Louis, marched on into Poland, and did not return until the end of 1807: 260 had been killed, nearly 1000 wounded, over 400 were missing or prisoners. It was expected that these services would be rewarded by the cession of Bayreuth to Bavaria; but nothing came of it, and feeling against France was only kept within bounds by suspicion of the designs of Austria, especially in the Tyrol. Thus, when Napoleon again invaded Austria in 1809, it was again to 'liberate' Bavaria, and that country was once more the victim of its own victory—devastated, impoverished and depopulated: the Tyrol in revolt, Regensberg burnt to the ground, and 10,000-11,000 military casualties. Such were the rewards of a French alliance.

The political fragmentation of western Germany which made it such an easy prey to French ambitions had other and more important results for the civilization of Europe. Like the city-states of Greece or Lombardy, many of the university towns and ducal capitals fostered an intellectualism which was little the worse for being parochial and self-satisfied. Foreign travellers, who in the middle of the eighteenth century had attended the parade ground at Potsdam, dined at Dresden, and danced at Tsarkoye-

Selo, now sought out Schiller and Schelling, visited the venerable Wieland, and listened at Weimar to Goethe's endless allocutions. Crabb Robinson from 1800 to 1805, and Benjamin Constant in 1804, directed their travels from study to study, and recorded the sayings of the wise men of Germany—men who were wise because they had for the most part no political preoccupations to direct their talents or to disturb their meditations. Kant, who died with the old Germany (February, 1804), had dreamed in the year before Bonaparte invaded Italy of a plan for lasting peace; Schlegel wanted to found a new religion; Fichte had propounded a scheme by which each country should secure its economic independence by introducing a coinage of no value elsewhere, and too heavy to be carried across the frontier. Their visitors mocked, but admired.

Meanwhile Mme de Staël hurried ahead of the invading armies (she was at Vienna in 1809 and at Moscow in 1812), collecting material for her *De l'Allemagne*, or trying to find a publisher, and talking—how these Frenchwomen talked!—against the tyrannical regime of Napoleon.

These cells of enlightenment actively at work in the placid bloodstream of German society were politically powerless, but they were the secret of its intellectual influence. Goethe himself, the most eminent and representative seer of them all, never believed in the political unity of Germany, which he thought could only come about at the expense of German culture, diffused over the land from its twenty universities, its hundred libraries, its seventy theatres, and its handful of philosophers and poets. As late as 1830 he was saying: 'We have no city, nay we have no country of which we could decidedly say—Here is Germany! If we inquire in Vienna, the answer is—This is Austria! and if in Berlin—This is Prussia! Only when we tried to get rid of the French (he admitted) sixteen years ago, was Germany everywhere.' That Germany, the Germany of 1814, was to become the Germany of the nineteenth century—Prussianized, militarized, nationalized: meanwhile the old Weimar system was to pass on its thought and art, from its great men (who left few heirs) to the non-German nations of Europe.[18]

To the mass of the German people neither the new frontiers nor the decay of enlightenment had much meaning. To them the all-important change brought by the Napoleonic regime was the blockade. During its early years, whilst no more than a coastal embargo on British imports, it did not seriously affect the economic life of the Rhineland. Consumers, no doubt, had to pay more for British and colonial goods that slipped through the meshes of the *douane*, and had to put up with beet-sugar, *ersatz* coffee, and home-grown tobacco: but producers of textiles or glass benefited by the absence of British competition.

When, however, the blockade extended, in 1806-07, along the whole northern coast-line, and in 1808-10 to the Spanish peninsula and the Adriatic, the states of the Confederation of the Rhine became the nucleus of a 'continental system,' in which the hinterland of central Europe had as important a part to play as the coast-line itself in the cold war against British commerce. When the Munichers saw English goods that they coveted thrown on bonfires by French officials, or when they were required to close the remote Zillerthal against goods smuggled from the Mediterranean, they realized how their economy was being sacrificed to the interests, not of Europe, but of France.

These effects were felt even more keenly in the Grand Duchy of Berg, the economic core of the Kingdom of Westphalia, which lay at the intersection of the lower Rhineland trade-routes from south to north and east to west, and coincided with the industrial area later known as the Ruhr. For Berg was not only hit like Bavaria by the coastal blockade, but it was also handicapped by the tariff barrier set up in 1806 between the right and left banks of the Rhine. Not only did its manufacturers suffer, with those of the Confederation, from the closure of the ports, and the impossibility of procuring raw silk or cotton for their factories, except in small quantities smuggled through at enhanced prices: their manufactured goods, too, were unsaleable in France owing to the protective tariff in favour of the silk-merchants of Lyon or the cloth-makers of Amiens. Their country was as firmly excluded as Italy or Russia from the economic benefits which were supposed to flow from the French alliance. They were to learn, as Eugène had learnt, that the motto of the Napoleonic empire was everywhere 'France first.' [19]

XII

RUSSIA

(1802-1812)

I

BEHIND AUSTRIA in 1805, behind Prussia in 1806, lay the enigmatic and half oriental power of Russia. What did Russia mean to Napoleon? Frenchmen of the eighteenth century were not particularly conscious of its area or population: it could not put more troops into the field than Austria, or even Prussia. There was no Russian music or literature to admire. But there was no 'iron curtain.' Central and eastern Europe merged almost unconsciously along that wavering line from the Baltic to the Aegean where once the eastern Empire of Rome had been divided from the west, and the Teutons had halted the Slavs, and the missionaries of Rome had competed for converts with the missionaries of Byzantium. Russia in the eighteenth century was embarrassingly anxious to become European. The visits of Peter the Great to London and Paris, like that of some African or Afghan chieftain in later times, informed the Western world that Russia had an army, a navy, and a government. Since the middle of the century Russian troops had appeared on European battle-fields, Russian diplomatists helped to partition Poland, and a Russian Empress, preaching the crusade of the cross against the crescent, claimed a right of way from the Black Sea to the Mediterranean.

An intelligent Frenchman who had served in the Russian army put on paper, just at this time, his impressions of the country and its people. 'It is impossible to judge (writes Comte Roger de Damas), how many reigns must pass before the different institutions in Russia assume the aspect of age common to the rest of Europe; everything in the place looks new. The effects of Peter I's haste to make himself a European have not yet disappeared: everything resembles a powerful sketch rather than a finished picture. The industries are all young; the houses are all frontage; the officials have had insufficient experience and have not learned their business. The costumes, which are Asiatic for the people and French in society,

337

look as if they had never been quite finished; ignorance still exists even among the upper classes; the national character is only muzzled, not tamed; the national genius is imitative to perfection, but not at all inventive. One meets a great many intelligent people, but very few agreeable ones. In short, the past seems to be in the act of retiring in favour of the present, and in consequence nothing is settled.'

To the First Consul in 1799 Russia was different from Poland or Turkey (important differences for him) chiefly in having an army that one must reckon with and a government that one could respect. He knew how much Frederick the Great had suffered from the one, and how anxious he had been not to antagonize the other. He remembered that Suvorov in Italy in 1798 had undone his work of 1796-97, and that the Turks he defeated at Aboukir had landed from Russian ships.

His hopes of Russian co-operation against England during 1800 which he called an alliance of 'the two most powerful nations in the world' (December 21st) had been brought to an end by the murder of Tsar Paul and the accession of Alexander in March 1801. Twelve days after he heard of this event (April 25th), Bonaparte dispatched Duroc on a mission to Berlin and St. Petersburg. At both capitals he was instructed to speak of Egypt as still strongly held by France, and of the British expedition there as a failure (though only a few months later the French army was forced to evacuate the country); any other issue would be a misfortune for all Europe. In a personal letter to Alexander he offered to sign a treaty of peace between France and Russia. When nothing came of this, he professed to be unmoved by Alexander's change of front, and was soon (October 10th) trying to win him over by the offer of the protectorate of Malta, and of the return of 7000 Russian prisoners of war by sea with flags and arms and new uniforms, to save them the march overland. Next year (February 16th, 1802), announcing the early conclusion of the Peace of Amiens, he suggested that France as well as Russia would favour the opening of the Dardanelles.

Since Alexander remained unmoved by these temptations, Bonaparte seems to have thought it worth while to try another approach more likely to appeal to the liberal-minded young Tsar. When the Peace of Amiens was in danger of breaking down (March 10th, 1803), and it became more important than ever to divide Russia and England, he sent Colbert to St. Petersburg. 'In your conversations with the Emperor (his instructions ran) you must discourse principally on liberal and philosophical subjects. You must represent the First Consul as hard at work designing canals, establishing manufactures, and dealing with matters of public education.' Colbert was also the bearer of a private letter in which Bonaparte explained the state of his negotiations with the British government. 'England (he said) has dropped the mask, and declared her intention of keeping Malta for seven years.' Such a breach of good faith must be without precedent in history. Bonaparte will never put up with it, and will do all he can to prevent it. Alexander, he is sure, will be interested to hear of this. During the last days of the negotiations (August 23rd), Russia was indeed drawn in as a possible intermediary, but Bonaparte insisted that he would allow no deviation from the terms of Amiens, and nothing came of it.

So matters remained for two years—the years of the Coronation, and of the attempted invasion of England. When, in August 1805, Napoleon embarked on his campaign against Austria, he sent Duroc once more to Berlin to prevent Russia forcing Prussia into the Third Coalition. The attempt failed; but Austerlitz did Duroc's work for him. Frederick-William, though allied to Russia and England, accepted a French treaty which embroiled him with England and outraged his self-respect. In 1806 he rushed into war without waiting for Russian help, and was defeated.[1]

2

Twice, then, in two years Russia had incited the continent to war against Napoleon: twice it had thwarted his invasion of England. Alexander had refused every invitation to desert his English ally. There might never be a better opportunity—with both Austria and Prussia under foot—to press home an attack on his last enemy on the continent, and to force Alexander not merely to break with Britain, but to join in the continental blockade against her which the occupation of the Prussian coast at last made feasible.

Napoleon's mind was at once made up. The day before his truimphal entry into Berlin (October 27th, 1806), he published a proclamation to the army, which, after describing the defeat of the Prussians, went on: 'The Russians boast that they are advancing against us. We will march to meet them and save them half their journey. They will find another Austerlitz on Russian soil.' He at once set about inciting and arming the Poles, not merely against the retreating Prussians, but also against the advancing Russians. Fouché was to send Kosciusko to the front from Paris: but he refused to 'liberate' his country for the French. Cambacérès was to compose a *manuscrit trouvé dans le cabinet du roi de Prusse* describing the shameful Partition of Poland. Davout was to tell the Poles that, once they were armed and organized, Napoleon would declare himself in support of their national independence.

Turkey, too, now comes into the picture as a possible source of embarrassment to Russia. From Berlin, as early as November 9th, Cambacérès is instructed to urge the Turkish ambassador to make military demonstrations on the Dniester front. From Posen (December 1st) Sébastiani, now French ambassador at Constantinople, is authorized to sign a secret treaty with the Porte, guaranteeing the integrity of Moldavia, Wallachia and Serbia in return for a Turkish advance on Choczim; and long before this threat can become effective Cambacérès is to announce it to the Turkish ambassador as an accomplished fact. The bulletins of the Grand Army are to be translated into Turkish and Arabic, for distribution throughout the ports of the Levant, together with an anti-Russian pamphlet entitled *Un vieil Ottoman à ses frères*. Indeed, Napoleon looks even further afield. The Shah of Persia is urged to seize Georgia, and to make a diversion on the Caucasus front.

But the Polish campaign of 1806-07 did not follow the pattern of Ulm and Austerlitz. Frederick-William, at first adopting the style of one soldier to another (*avec cette franchise qui doit caractériser tout militaire*), was soon reduced to fulsome flattery (October 15th, 1806); but he was so *péniblement affecté* by Napoleon's terms for an armistice—the surrender of all his lands between the Rhine and the Elbe, an indemnity of £5 millions, and help against England—that he refused to accept them, and fled to the Russian headquarters.

Napoleon was disappointed, too, in his hopes of the Polish patriots. 'They ask for too many guarantees before committing themselves. They are egoists, without a spark of patriotism. But I have grown old in the knowledge of human nature (he writes). My greatness does not depend on the support of a few million Poles.' They must make the first move. He is indeed short of troops, and sends for 14,000 Spaniards to garrison Hamburg. In any case, operations are held up by the weather, which, up to the end of December, is wet and warm beyond precedent, rendering the few roads of the country impassable.

At last an advance was possible, and at Eylau on February 7th-8th was fought a battle *fort sanglante, fort chaude*, in which French troops for the first time ran away, and in which victory could only be claimed because Napoleon remained in possession of the field. Even he admitted the loss of 1500 killed and 5000 wounded, and was painfully affected by his customary tour of the battle-field. 'A father who has lost his children (he wrote in a postcript to the 58th Bulletin) takes no pleasure in his victory. When the heart speaks, glory loses all its attractions.' Indeed, his correspondence for more than two months after Eylau shows him still harping on the battle; denying Russian accounts of it; dictating, as 'an eye-witness account, translated from the German,' the version he wished to go down to history; sending home specially prepared pictures of the engagement; exploiting the pessimism of a captured Russian general; and publishing, as the last words of a French captain, sentiments curiously reminiscent of those at Marengo and Austerlitz: 'I die content, since victory is ours, and I expire on the bed of honour, surrounded by guns captured from the enemy and by the debris of their defeat. Tell the Emperor that I have only one regret—that in a few moments I shall be beyond doing any more in his service and for the glory of *la belle France. À elle mon dernier soupir!*' So the legend grew of another Napoleonic victory.

As for the French losses, which (he complained to Fouché on April 13th), were still being exaggerated in the Paris press: 'What are 2000 men killed in a big battle? Not one of the battles of Louis XIV or XV but was much more costly.' He would have felt the need for excusing his set-back all the more if he had been aware that in Dumouriez's *Jugement sur Bonaparte*, written in England at this moment, Eylau was taken as evidence that Bonaparte's 'lucky and criminal career' was at an end. But the bitter jealousy of the older and unsuccessful military careerist, and his anger at Bonaparte's refusal to employ him seven years before, distorted his judgment: in the light of Friedland the book had to be rewritten, and was not published—and that anonymously—till 1809.

Victory or defeat, the campaign was not over; and for four months Napoleon remained in winter quarters at Osterode (February 21st-March 31st) and Finkenstein (April 1st-June 6th), drowning his disappointment in ceaseless activity. It is a little surprising that he did not return to Paris, which he had never left for so long before, and where he knew that the industrial effects of the blockade were causing considerable criticism and discontent. But he trusted Cambacérès and Talleyrand to carry out his orders on home or foreign policy; and prided himself on being able to deal, by a constant stream of letters, with any matter that might arise.

His official correspondence, and that far from complete, contains 159 letters during February (six a day), 340 during March (eleven a day), and 148 during April (five a day). It includes not only decisions on routine affairs, but also a decree constituting a *conseil de guerre* for the defence of the Empire while he is away from Paris; a long letter to his brother Louis, King of Holland, about his matrimonial troubles ('Your quarrels with the queen are becoming public property . . . You drill your young wife like a regiment of soldiers . . . Let her dance as much as she likes: she is just the age for it. I have a wife in the forties, and I write to her from the battle-field, telling her to go to balls. Do you expect a wife of twenty to live in a nunnery or in a nursery, with nothing to do but bathe her baby?'); a treatise on higher education, headed 'Remarks on a scheme for establishing a Faculty of Literature and History at the *Collège de France*'; another dated the same day on History and Criticism, in the form of 'Remarks on the Home Secretary's reports about the encouragement of literature'; and an elaborate scheme for the management and curriculum of the girls' school at Écouen. Never was Napoleon's inventive mind more alert.

Another reason for not returning to Paris was that he had determined to fight this campaign to a finish, as soon as the state of the ground allowed; and the necessary preparations could best be made on the spot. It was never more true than in 1807 that Napoleon's victories were won before his army came on the field. He did not trouble overmuch (though more than the Russians) about commissariat. But, in order to concentrate all the French troops under his immediate command, he summoned more Spaniards to garrison Antwerp, drafted *marins de la Garde* for special duty at Danzig, took in hand the training of recruits, and told Fouché that the minimum height of 4 feet 10 inches required for conscripts (of the 1808 class, called up before its time) might be further reduced if necessary. By these means he was able to increase his fighting strength between Eylau and Friedland from under 100,000 to over 200,000, and the total of all his forces in Germany, including Dutch, Polish and German contingents, to twice as many. Bennigsen, if not out-generalled, was at least to be outnumbered.[2]

There was a third consideration which kept Napoleon away from Paris, and reconciled him to a winter in Poland. Joséphine had gone to the front with him in 1805, and again in 1806. While she was at Strasbourg he had written to her on the average every four days, and had invited her to Munich for the wedding of Eugène and Augusta. Between October 5th, 1806, and January 25th, 1807, when at last she returned from Mainz to Paris, he wrote to her thirty-five times, or almost every three days; and between that date and his return to Paris (July 18th) fifty-one times.

But here is the difference. Up to January 3rd, 1807, Napoleon speaks as though Joséphine might join him: 'I only lack the pleasure of your company, but I hope that it will not be for long (November 2nd) . . . If the journey were not so long, you could come as far as this (Berlin, November 16th) . . . I will decide in a day or two either to invite you here or to send you to Paris (November 22nd) . . . You can prepare to start (November 26th) . . . I shall be at Posen tonight; then I will invite you to Berlin, so that we can both arrive there the same day (November 27th) . . . When our winter quarters are settled (in Poland) you could come; but you must wait a few days (December 3rd) . . . You must wait a few more days (December 9th)—I am off for Warsaw: I shall be back in a fortnight: then I hope I shall be able to send for you (December 15th).'

But on December 31st, at Poltusk, the last stage of his journey to Warsaw, he heard of the birth of a son to his mistress Eléonore Denuelle—a son who was undoubtedly his own: and next day, at a relay post on the Warsaw road, he saw Mme Walewska, the eighteen-year-old wife of a Polish Count of seventy, and was captivated by her youthful charms. He had been laughing at Joséphine's jealousy: 'One thinks little of beauties in these Polish deserts (December 3rd) . . . The beauties of Poland are not at all what you suppose (December 31st): he had professed *Je t'aime et*

*te désire . . . Il n'y a qu' une femme pour moi . . . Ces nuits-ci sont lon-
gues, tout seul* (December 2nd).' Now suddenly he knows what he wants.
He meets Mme Walewska again at a Warsaw ball. 'I saw no one but you,
I admired no one but you, I want no one but you. Answer me at once
(he writes), and assuage the impatient passion of N.' . . . Again: 'Grant a
few moments' pleasure and happiness to a poor heart that is only waiting
to adore you' . . . Very soon she became his mistress.

Now there was additional cause for telling Joséphine that the Polish
roads were impassable, and for urging her to return to Paris (January 3rd,
7th, 18th, 23rd, 25th, 26th); additional reason, too, for exchanging the discomforts of the *mauvais village* of Osterode for the *très beau château* of
Finkenstein, with its open fireplaces (Napoleon loved a wood fire), where
he could entertain his new mistress. Joséphine of course heard what was
happening, and did not conceal her jealousy; and he was in such a good
temper that he tried to joke her out of it: 'My little Joséphine is the only
woman I love: she's as kind as she is sulky and capricious, and her quarrels are as graceful as all she does; she is always adorable—save only when
she's jealous: then she's a regular little devil.' Marie Walewska was only
a diversion; but she meant more to him than his Egyptian camp wife,
Mme Fourès. She was with him at Paris in 1808, at Vienna in 1809, and
at Paris again in 1810; and she visited him at Elba in 1814. Their son,
Alexandre Walewski, born on May 11th, 1810, made history under Napoleon III.

So the winter months passed, and the alternation of frost and thaw at
last gave way to weather fit for campaigning. The outlying fortresses had
fallen one by one into French hands: Danzig, the Mantua of Poland, on
May 24th. It was to save the old East Prussian capital of Königsberg, the
base of his supplies, that Bennigsen in the early days of June advanced to
the attack. At Heilsberg, on the 10th, he was victorious, but retreated: at
Friedland, on the 14th, he was caught on the wrong bank of the Alle, and
totally defeated—not so much by the skill of Napoleon's dispositions as by
his remembering to fight on the anniversary of Marengo. It was in this
same country of forests and marshlands that Russian troops suffered an
even more disastrous defeat, a century later, at the battle of Tannenberg.[3]

3

Historians on the look-out for picturesque scenes have everything provided for them in the meeting of Napoleon and Alexander at Tilsit on
June 25th, 1807. Nothing could be more symbolical, nothing more theatrical, than the tented raft that French engineers moored midstream in
the Niemen, with its flags and mirrors, its table and twin arm-chairs, to
which the sovereigns of East and West were rowed out simultaneously,
whilst to imaginative onlookers the river seemed to stay its current, and

the very air to hold its breath. They met, and embraced, then disappeared from view for half an hour's secret talk; embraced again, parted, and rowed back to their opposite banks, whilst guns fired, and trumpets blew, and drums rolled, in honour of their reconciliation and the peace of Europe.

This ritual was repeated next day; but in the evening Alexander returned to the west bank, dined with Napoleon, and took up his quarters in the town, in the same street as his host. Tilsit had a few good houses, and wide streets; but even Frenchmen accustomed to the *pavé* and *égouts* of Old Paris found its mud and stepping-stones (such as might still be found in Siberian towns a century later), intolerable, and the three weeks that they had to spend in the place infinitely boring. Berthier was reduced to reading *Corinne*.

The town was divided up into a French, a Prussian, and a Russian quarter, each with its own garrison and sentries. The two Emperors met every day, talked, and studied the map of Europe. From the first they had taken to each other: for they had much in common. Both belonged to a transitional generation, half sceptical and rationalistic, half mystical and romantic. Both were seductive double-dealers. 'I have just been seeing the Emperor Alexander,' Napoleon wrote to Joséphine on the day of their first meeting: 'I like him very much: he is young, friendly, and very good-looking; and he has more intelligence than is commonly supposed.' The good impression did not fade: at Erfurt, two years later, Napoleon wrote again: 'I like Alexander, and he ought to like me: if he were a woman, I should fall in love with him.' There was in fact something feminine in a youth who had been brought up under the rival affections of his father and his grandmother: a feminine intuition, a feminine guile. He would seem to give his confidence easily; but even those who knew him best were puzzled as to his real mind. As for Napoleon, no one could be more charming when he chose: 'There was something in his voice and face and manner (says Caulaincourt) as seductive and persuasive as his mind was fine and flexible.' But if Alexander, too, was attracted by Napoleon, he would not easily be taken in by him.

Frederick-William was quite outside these imperial confidences: he could tell a plain diplomatic lie, but anything subtle was beyond his intelligence: he was neither a romantic nor a rationalist; the plain Calvinism of his Hohenzollern ancestors was good enough for him. If the Emperors went riding, or held a review, the King of Prussia might be seen on horseback with them, but generally following behind. He was never invited to the conferences with which they ended the day. But when his queen came to Tilsit on July 6th, Napoleon, who knew she was his real enemy, and liked talking to a pretty woman, paid her a two-hour call, and invited her to dine with the sovereigns. She did her best to charm him, and to get better terms for her country. 'She was a woman of wit and intelligence,' he told Gourgaud at St. Helena, 'and of courage, too, for she was always interrupting me.' She thought, perhaps, that she had succeeded: but next day Napoleon was inexorable, and referred her to Talleyrand for the pitiless terms which Frederick-William was forced to accept.

The Treaty of Tilsit, about which so many theories have been propounded, is best understood if considered from the point of view of the Continental System, as the utmost that Napoleon could do at the moment to drill European commerce into an army of attack on England. Russia was the only power he feared: in order to use its influence (as an ally, though a disillusioned one) on the English government, and to secure the closure of its ports against English trade, Alexander must be flattered and tempted. Prussia was the power Napoleon most despised; he thought of it as a bigger Bavaria, and believed he could make better use of it as a barrier against England, and as a buffer between western Germany and Russia, if he occupied it as an allied state than if he ruled it as a province of France. Poland too was to be a buffer along with Turkey south of the Danube; but he had no desire to see the Russians on the Vistula; so Warsaw should be neither his nor Alexander's. Moldavia and Wallachia would compensate Russia for this loss; but the Danube was to be as firm a limit as the Niemen, and Constantinople as sacrosanct as Danzig.

Frederick-William, then, lost his Polish provinces in the east, and his German provinces west and north of the lower Elbe. Berlin was now in a far corner of Prussia, and within sixty-five miles of its frontier on every side, except up the Oder Valley into Silesia, or along the coastal corridor to Königsberg. Eastwards, Warsaw was the capital of a Frenchified Duchy under Napoleon's client, the King of Saxony; and the only outlet of its trade, the port of Danzig, nominally a free city under Prussian and Saxon protection, was held by a French garrison. Westwards, the old Confederation of the Rhine and the new Kingdom of Westphalia constituted, as Napoleon had long intended, a third power in Germany, threatening both Austria and Prussia.

As for Russia, she was encouraged to look towards Finland and the Black Sea instead of towards Poland and the Adriatic. At the same time Alexander was to use the threat of a blockade of the Baltic ports to induce England to make peace: more than that; if England did not accept his mediation, or did not within five months restore her conquests, and recognize the 'freedom of the seas,' he would declare war on her; it being understood that in any hostilities engaged by either party to the treaty (e.g. against Turkey, as against England) France and Russia would stand together. The secret clauses contained another provision that had momentous consequences. If England refused to come to terms, then Denmark, Sweden and Portugal were to be forced to join in the war and the blockade against her. Nothing could show more clearly the real aim of the whole settlement, and its place in the pattern of Napoleonic states-manship.

It must at once occur to the historian—why did Alexander assent to terms so apparently one-sided? Was it the defeat of his army, and his dread of invasion? Was it his grudge against England for failure to help him during the campaign, either with subsidies or arms (there had been talk of a landing in the Baltic, but no more)? Was it relief that Napoleon had forgone his design to restore the independence of Poland? Was it greed for Finland or Turkey? Or was it perhaps a longer calculation of the opportunity that might come in a few years to fight again?

These and other suggestions have been debated by successive historians, from Thiers to Tarlé, and various solutions propounded. They do not necessarily exclude one another. It is known that many suggestions were made, memoirs drawn up, and pleas presented: it is not known what the two negotiators said about them as they leant together over the map of Europe. The only minute of their discussions is the wording of the treaty. By that their intentions must be judged. Though each accused the other afterwards of double dealing, it would not be good history to regard the whole affair as a clash of personalities, and no more. Both were respon-sible rulers, bargaining for the best terms they could get for their coun-tries. Both had much to gain by a few years of peace; both more to lose by continuation of the campaign. To both, though not to the same degree, British sea-power and commercial monopoly were a burden hard to be borne. It really seemed probable that such an alliance as theirs, a co-opera-tion of East and West, might at last conquer the sea from the land, and restore the peace and liberties of Europe. [4]

4

It took Napoleon and Alexander five years, not to discover (for they had suspected it from the first), but to admit that they could not permanently collaborate on the basis of Tilsit. During the last two years of the five their wish to remain allies turned into a conviction that they must be-come enemies. It was only one step, though a long one, from the treaty of 1807 to the war of 1812.

At first circumstances seemed to be favouring the new alliance. True, England did not seem to appreciate the opportunity given her for repent-ance, and rudely anticipated the time-limit by three months when, after an investment of the city, the British fleet bombarded Copenhagen, and compelled the surrender of the Danish navy. Napoleon was all the more indignant at this action because he had intended, if necessary, to do the same thing in another way. 'I am deeply incensed at this horrible crime,' he wrote to Alexander, and he suggested that the courts of Europe should break off relations with 'a people that tramples the most sacred rights of humanity under foot.'

Whilst any direct attack upon England must be postponed until the Spanish question is settled, Russian ambitions in the East need not be delayed. In a letter of February 2nd, 1808, Napoleon propounded a fantastically ambitious scheme for a joint expedition into Mesopotamia, which by threatening India 'would put England into a panic, and make her beg for mercy.' Both Emperors would no doubt prefer 'the pleasures of peace, and a life spent in the midst of their vast empires, regenerating them and making them happy by the arts and blessings of good government'; but this 'the enemies of the world will not allow.'

Alexander was not taken in by such an obvious attempt to distract him from his Balkan ambitions; and the imperial relations became strained. The Tsar could, however, be congratulated on his success against Sweden, and informed of Napoleon's policy in Spain; and it was gratifying to hear in return (July 20th) that, in the event of war with Austria, Napoleon could count on Russian support. This was no more than had been agreed upon at Tilsit, but its reaffirmation was evidence that Alexander still professed to value their alliance.

It was in order to re-examine and if possible strengthen this understanding that the two Emperors met at Erfurt on September 27th, just fourteen months after their return from Tilsit: it was perhaps designed to be the first of a series of meetings. Three weeks were spent in dinners and dances ('Alexander dances, but I don't,' Napoleon told Joséphine; 'forty is forty'). The Comédie française, summoned from Paris, performed a series of plays chosen by the Emperor to impress an audience of princes: Mithridate, Iphigénie, Phèdre, Mahomet, Rhadamiste, even (a little risky —it was banned in Paris) La mort de César. There could have been no greater contrast to the barbarous conditions of life at Tilsit, or to the company, which now, to impress the Tsar, included almost all the royalties, real or hypothetical, in Europe. Goethe was there, too, and entertained Napoleon at Weimar. Another day there was a trip with the Imperial guests—characteristic of Napoleon's insensibility—to the battle-field of Jena. The arrival of Vincent, the envoy of Francis, on September 28th, was made the occasion of a state picture of all the distinguished visitors standing round a table, at which Napoleon, with his left hand thrust into his white gilet, and his cameo-like Roman profile turned to the artist, receives from the obsequious ambassador the letter of a junior Emperor.

Napoleon and Alexander met and talked affectionately enough. But their minds were full of suspicion and doubt. Prussia had evaded the payment of her indemnities, and was still occupied by French troops. Austria was once more defiantly arming. England had not sued for peace. Napoleon's promise to help Russia in Scandinavia had come to nothing, and his offer to partition Turkey denied Alexander what he chiefly valued—an outlet to the Mediterranean. With the proposal to renew this uneasy partnership came the suggestion that Napoleon might look to the Tsar's family for an Empress to replace Joséphine. Talleyrand, with his Austrian sympathies, whilst officially forwarding both projects, was secretly working against them. He admitted to Wellington in later years—and the Tsar himself confirmed it—that 'he used to visit Alexander secretly at night, and furnish him with every argument, reason, or pretence which he could invent or discover against Buonaparte's plan.'

In these circumstances the formidable *Convention d'Alliance* dictated by Napoleon before the Conference began, and signed by Champagny and Romanzov at the end of it (October 12th), did little more than re-assert the undertakings of Tilsit. The preamble expressed the wish to 'make the alliance (between the two Emperors) more and more definite and durable,' and to lay down the principles (a good word, Napoleon thought) that would guide them in all future steps against 'their common enemy and the enemy of the whole continent, England.' They accordingly promised not to make a separate peace with Britain (Art. 1 and 7), but to negotiate together for terms on the *uti possidetis* basis (Art. 2-4); to demand English recognition of Russian gains in Finland and Turkey, and of the French occupation of Spain (Art. 5-6); and if nothing came of these negotiations the Emperors would meet again within a year and plan new steps against Britain (Art. 12). The other articles concerned the partition of Turkey (Art. 1-18), and the compensation of Denmark for its sacrifices in the common cause (Art. 13).

On the same day as these articles were signed a letter was dispatched to George III signed by the two Emperors (with a covering letter from Romanzov to Canning), pleading with him to 'listen to the voice of humanity, silence that of passion, and seek to reconcile all interests, and so assure the happiness of this generation at whose head we have been placed by Providence.' So the decencies of diplomacy were observed.

During the ten days Napoleon spent at Paris on his way back from Germany to Spain he told the *Corps législatif* (October 25th) that the meeting at Erfurt had confirmed the unanimity of Alexander and himself, either for peace or war, and their determination to restore 'the benefits of maritime commerce to the hundred millions of men we represent.' He lost no opportunity during the winter to emphasize the alliance, and next spring (February 14th) reminded the Tsar personally of his promise to co-operate against both England and Austria. For by now his suspicions of the last few months had hardened into the certainty that he would have to fight another Austrian campaign. Again, on March 21st, Caulaincourt was instructed to ask that, on the first warlike move of Austria, the Russian ambassador should be withdrawn from Vienna, and to hint that a Russian military threat to Galicia would effectively prevent war.

But in fact the campaign of 1809 showed how little Napoleon had come to expect from Tilsit and Erfurt. As late as June 27th, only a week before Wagram, he 'supposed' the Russians to be at Cracow, and 'hoped' they would advance on Olmütz. But the little that happened on this front had no effect on the main course of the campaign. If Napoleon was angry at the Tsar's failure to support him, he concealed it beneath a remark to Champagny that 'it is never clear what the Russian government wants,' and by a series of polite letters to Alexander telling him of Wagram and the armistice, and hinting that if hostilities are resumed he counts on immediate and active help. Finally, when it is all over (October 10th), he hopes that the Tsar will be pleased with the moderate terms of the treaty with Austria, cries down English military action in Spain, and ends with the phrase *nôtre système*, as a reminder to Alexander of the designs of two years ago. Even with Austria off the field, he cannot afford to offend Russia: he trusts her ruler less than ever. 'I no longer know what you want,' he writes to Alexander on December 31st. 'I cannot slay chimaeras and fight phantoms. I leave Your Majesty to judge which of us still uses the language of alliance and friendship. The moment we begin to distrust one another, we might as well forget Erfurt and Tilsit.'[5]

5

Napoleon's failure at Erfurt either to charm or to intimidate Alexander was well understood in the chancelleries of Europe. Already, in 1810, both sides were preparing for the war of 1812.

On December 15th, 1809, Joséphine had publicly consented to her divorce. On the 25th, as soon as he heard of it, Metternich had offered the hand of Marie-Louise: but Napoleon was still playing with the idea of marriage with Alexander's sister when, on February 6th, 1810, a dispatch from Caulaincourt convinced him that the Russian court would never give its consent. The abrupt way in which he broke off the negotiations, and the jubilant speed with which his Austrian marriage was celebrated, only two months later, could not but be offensive to the Tsar, who saw in it, rightly enough, a political *volte-face*, and the first step towards an attack on his country.

Other signs of war soon followed. In August the movement of French troops from southern Germany to the Baltic coast was a reminder that Napoleon had not evacuated Prussia, and did not intend to do so: its occupation was still to be a military threat against Russia. In December he annexed, along with other territories between Holland and Hamburg, the Grand Duchy of Oldenburg, in spite of Alexander's protests on behalf of his sister Catherine, the wife of the heir apparent. Catherine remained the most stubborn enemy of France at the Russian court. It was not an accident that Alexander chose this moment (December 31st, 1810) to publish an *ukase* putting up his tariff against imported French wines and luxury goods. That this was a deliberate challenge is clear from the Tsar's letter to his sister (December 26th), saying 'It is only too probable that we shall have to face fresh bloodshed': again, six months later: 'How can one expect Napoleon to be reasonable? It is not in him to forego conquest unless by constraint of arms.' Alexander falls back on the belief that 'things cannot possibly go on as they are: all classes in Germany, and even in France, are suffering so much that their patience must soon be exhausted.'

However this might be, the Tsar well knew that the patience of his own people was fast running out. The liberal reforms that he had played with during the first five years of his reign might have been forgiven him as a return to the policy of his grandmother, Catherine the Great: they had come to grief on the same obstacle as hers, the eternal problem of serfdom. But in the second period of his rule the double military disaster of Austerlitz and Friedland had brought the indignities of the French alliance, the hardships of the continental blockade, and Speranski's programme of Napoleonic reforms and finance, which offended the aristocracy without giving any real relief to the people. The only two classes in Russia with any political influence were the landlords and the merchants. The landlords had forced Alexander to make terms at Tilsit, because they feared that a French invasion would mean the liberation of their serfs, and the loss of their estates. The merchants deplored the terms of Tilsit, which forced them to refuse British imports, and to accept French goods without profit.

Remembering (nor was he allowed to forget it) his personal responsibility for the defeat of Austerlitz, and knowing that his generals despised him as a soldier, the Tsar dreaded another war. But his character became stabilized under misfortune; and 1810 was his climacteric year. Though disposed to admire Napoleon, as his grandfather had admired Frederick the Great, he could never forgive him the accusation of parricide, the defeat at Austerlitz, the humbling of Prussia, or the invasion of Poland. He remembered the theatrical oath he had taken with Frederick-William by the tomb of the great Frederick, in the presence of the patriot Queen of Prussia; he had not forgotten their visit to St. Petersburg in January 1809. Though he had done little for the Prussian crown at Tilsit, he regarded himself still as the heir of the Prussian cause, the champion of the liberties of Europe.

If 1810 was a year of decision, 1811 was a year of preparation, on both sides, for a war that had now become inevitable. Up to the autumn of 1810 Napoleon continued to pretend that Alexander was co-operating in the blockade, and in the attempt to compel England to sue for peace. The most significant of a series of letters is that of October 23rd, 1810, in which he describes the industrial and financial crisis in England: 'daily bankruptcies are throwing the City into confusion: the manufacturers cannot provide employment: the warehouses are crammed with unwanted goods.' He declares that 600 so-called British ships in the Baltic are making for Russian ports. If Alexander were to seize them and impound their cargoes, 'it would be a terrible blow to England.' Again on December 2nd, 'England is showing signs of distress: there are more bankruptcies than ever: the exchange has fallen 25 per cent: it is no longer possible to doubt that her manufacturers and bankers are alarmed.'

What Napoleon did not tell Alexander was that France, too, was passing through a serious economic crisis during the years 1810-11; for the very success of the blockade measures against England meant new hardships for the French people, and new grievances for their allies; and these were insufficiently offset by the preferences granted to the middle-class manufacturers and traders, whose influence finally pulled the Emperor from his throne. Napoleon's correspondence at this time contains many schemes for providing work for the Paris unemployed; and the Minister of Police is accused of being afraid—of what, unless of that which the Emperor himself feared: popular insurrection? [6]

Against this background comes the Oldenburg affair, and the *ukase* against French trade. Napoleon recalls his ambassador Caulaincourt, whom he regards as pro-Russian, and sends Lauriston in his place. The whole tone of the correspondence changes. Napoleon's sentiments towards Alexander (he assures him on February 28th, 1811) have not altered; but 'I can't pretend that Your Majesty any longer feels friendly towards me (*n'a plus d'amitié pour moi*)'; and 'in the opinion of England and Europe our alliance has ceased to exist.' Lauriston's Instructions are very significant (April 5th, 1811). He is to talk of peace, but to think of war. He is to bear in mind what is described as Napoleon's 'ultimatum.' He will not make war for Poland, so long as the Tsar does not touch the Grand Duchy; nor for the blockade, although the new *ukase* is contrary to the engagements of Tilsit; nor for Turkey, so long as Alexander is content with the left bank of the Danube. But if Russia goes beyond the Danube, or intervenes in Serbia, or if she 'tears up the Treaty of Tilsit, and makes peace with England,' then it is war. Nor is Lauriston to make any secret of Napoleon's military preparedness, or reserves of wealth, but rather to stress them: but of course they are purely defensive, and due to the Tsar's 'secret' war preparations.

Reading the letter of February 28th and the Instructions of April 5th side by side, it is evident that real *casus belli* in 1812 was the suspicion that Alexander was deserting the French for a British alliance, and the knowledge that he was challenging Napoleon's claim (as at Tilsit) to dictate limits to Russian power in the Baltic, in Poland and in the Balkans. 'As for myself (Napoleon protests) my feelings are what they were; but I am struck by the evidence of Your Majesty's acts, and by the thought that Your Majesty is fully determined, as soon as circumstances permit, to come to terms with England; and that is equivalent to kindling war between our two empires. Once Your Majesty abandons the alliance and burns the conventions of Tilsit, it is obvious that war follows.'

But the *casus belli* is not always the real cause of a war. *A propos* of Balachov's mission with a letter from the Tsar (Vilna, June 30th), asking the reasons of Napoleon's invasion; Caulaincourt reports the Emperor as saying openly: 'Alexander is making fun of me (*se moque de moi*). Does he suppose I have come all the way to Vilna to negotiate commercial treaties? I have come to make an end once and for all to the Colossus of the barbarian north (*le colosse des barbares du nord*). My sword is drawn. These barbarians must be driven back into their Arctic ice-fields (*leurs glaces*) so that for the next twenty-five years they shan't come and interfere in the affairs of civilized Europe.' They should never have been allowed to partition Poland: it must be made a barrier against them. The war must go on till peace is signed at Moscow. 'Ever since Erfurt Alexander has been above himself (*a trop fait le fier*). The acquisition of Finland had turned his head. If he wants victories, let him fight the Persians, and not interfere in Europe. Civilization rejects these northerners. Europe can manage its affairs without them.'

Once again the Emperor explained his policy, namely the necessity of crushing England in the person of the only strong power remaining on the continent which might cause him anxiety by joining her. He spoke of the utility of banishing Russia from European affairs and establishing in the centre (of the continent) a state to act as a barrier against invasions from the north; adding that the moment was opportune, and that later on there would not be time, and that he must strike this last stroke in order to secure general peace, and 'years of repose and prosperity for us and our children.'

There can be little doubt—there are other passages to prove it—that, as in Spain, in Italy, in Austria, in Prussia and in the East, so in Russia, too, the particular reasons in Napoleon's mind for a military enterprise gave way, in the excitement of the event, and as the hope of victory opened out new vistas of adventure and power, to sheer acquisitiveness and the greed to dominate and direct the world: a world in which it became increasingly certain that the Napoleonic Empire could tolerate no rivals.

As for the assertion that Napoleon's military moves in Prussia, and particularly his garrisoning of Danzig, were purely defensive (as reasserted by Champagny to Kourakin on March 29th), it is only necessary to read his letter to Davout of March 24th, in which he says that he is afraid, when Russia is free from the Turkish war, she will turn towards Warsaw; he is therefore strengthening his forces in Prussia beforehand, so as not to be taken unawares. 'Thus I shall be ready to take the offensive, with Danzig well provisioned, well armed, and strongly enough garrisoned, and yourself with nearly two divisions at Stettin; so that if the Russians make the slightest move I shall be at the Vistula as soon as they are.'

To Napoleon then, as to Alexander, 1810 was a year of decision. It has been called by historians the climax of his power; but it seemed to contemporary observers full of omens of disaster; and the very persistence with which he pursued his fading star into the east showed to what a degree he had become the slave of a theory, the victim of a blind belief in his destiny.

The invasion of Russia was to be a final answer to pertinacious critics of the invasion of Spain. There would be no underestimate of the enemy, or of the difficulties of the campaign: no Convention of Cintra, no Baylen, no Saragossa. The invading army would be of such a size—that alone is enough to show the deterioration of a military genius—as to preclude failure. Its French nucleus was to be swollen to half a million men by contingents from dependants and allies—citizens of the Rhenish Confederation, Poles, Lithuanians, Austrians, Hungarians, Dutchmen, Prussians, Italians, Croats, Illyrians, Swiss, even Spaniards and Portuguese. Yet these were not merely to impress the world; they were to be hostages for the good behaviour of their discontented peoples, whom they left disarmed behind them.

Far-sighted persons were by no means sure of a French victory: not Talleyrand, who for three years at least had been reinsuring against his master's defeat: not Caulaincourt, who constantly warned him against the Russian adventure: least of all Vorontzov, the Russian ambassador in London, whose Cassandra prophecy may still be read, in a letter of June 5th, 1812: 'Even if, at first, military operations go against us, we can win, by persistent defence and retreat. If the enemy begins to pursue us, it is all up with him: for, the further he advances from his bases of supply and munitions into a trackless and foodless country, starved and encircled by an army of Cossacks, his position will become more and more dangerous; and he will end by being decimated by the winter, which has always been our most faithful ally.'

Can it be supposed that Napoleon did not reckon with these difficulties? Was he so confident of an early victory that he was content with the massing of supplies on the Niemen front, and had made no provision for the march of 550 miles from Kovno to Moscow? No: for his librarian Barbier had been instructed (December 19th, 1811) to send him 'some good books with the best information about Russian and especially Lithuanian topography, dealing with marshes, rivers, woods, roads, etc.' He had specially asked for 'the most detailed French account of the campaign of Charles XII in Poland and Russia.' (. . . *Depuis Grodno*—Voltaire had written—*jusqu'au Borysthène, en tirant vers l'orient, ce sont des marais, des déserts, des forêts immenses; dans les endroits qui sont cultivés on ne trouve point de vivres; les paysans enfouissent dans la terre tous leurs grains, et tout ce qui peut s'y conserver: il faut sonder la terre avec de grandes perches ferrées pour découvrir ces magasins souterrains. Les Moscovites et les Suédois se servirent tour à tour de ces provisions; mais on n'en trouvait pas toujours, et elles n'étaient pas suffisantes . . .*) Later (May 7th, 1812) he had asked for 'a work by the English Colonel Wilson on the Russian army,' of which he had apparently seen a French translation in MS. in Mounier's office; and he thinks there may be other such MSS. there, including one by M. de Plotho on the organization of the Russian army.

No again: for he had with him in Russia—it was stolen from his carriage at Vilna during the retreat—a 500-page *aide-mémoire* on the resources of Russia which warned him against the badness of the roads and other difficulties, and said that his invasion was no more likely to succeed than the old inroads of the Scythians and Parthians.

He did not disregard these warnings. His food supply and transport arrangements were on a scale unprecedented in his previous campaigns. Huge purchases were made of wine and spirits from Italy. Immense stores of grain were accumulated at Danzig, Thorn, Elbing, and fifty other places. Water transport was organized up the Niemen to Kovno, and thence by the Vilia to Vilna. Napoleon's every other letter during the advance into Russia deals with questions of commissariat. It was in the end neither the cold, nor the Cossacks, but the food shortage—sheer starvation of men and horses—which destroyed his army. He had not calculated on the Russians in their retreat drawing him so deep into the country, and eating or burning up their crops and provisions. He had not realized that in such a land and climate his transport would be unable to keep up with the troops. He had not calculated on the loss of horses which disorganized the supplies, nor on the amount of sickness amongst his men, nor on the indiscipline, especially of his foreign troops, whose deserters and stragglers, even before the entry on Russian territory, disordered his communications, and consumed his stores.

But if Napoleon was unprepared for many of the difficulties of the campaign, he was at any rate in sole command, and could co-ordinate the movements of an army at least twice as strong as any that the Russians could put in the field. Against him was an Emperor who knew nothing of war, and had followed the advice of one Phull—a German military theorist, a strategical Sièyes—in pinning his faith to a fortified camp at Drissa, a Russian Torres Vedras, which (it was supposed) would block the French advance both towards Moscow and St. Petersburg. When the Tsar was persuaded to dismiss Phull, and to betake himself to St. Petersburg (where he spent the rest of the campaign) he left Barclay de Tolly in command of the largest and central army, Bagration of a smaller southern army, whilst Tormassov and Wittgenstein with still smaller forces blocked the Austrian front and the road to St. Petersburg.

Barclay was a man of method, but the Scotch caution in his blood made him disliked by Bagration, a Georgian by birth, with dark features and dangerous eyes, who had learnt soldiering under the eccentric genius Suvorov, and was happiest in desperate adventures. To make matters worse, Barclay's chief of staff, Ermolov, encouraged Bagration's refusal to obey orders, and the personal feud between the generals became an issue between two parties in camp and court. The quarrel was only settled, after the armies united at Smolensk, by the appointment of an even more distinguished and popular pupil of Suvorov, General Kutusov; a man of 74, 'a *bon vivant*, polished, courteous'—so Wilson describes him—'shrewd as a Greek, intelligent as an Asiatic, well instructed as a European,' and so fat that he had to be driven about the field.

Russian officers had a reputation for incompetence, corruption, and cruelty to their men; but these vices were more obvious on the parade ground than in the field; and there were occasions, as at Vitebsk and Smolensk, on which they led desperate ventures with skill and courage. The rank and file—serfs lent by their landlord owners for twenty-five years to the government, paid a shilling a month, and allowed to cut off the beards which were the sign of serfdom—were without initiative, but more inured to cold and starvation than Frenchmen, and would sooner die than be dislodged from a position they had once taken up. They were supported by an artillery superior to that of Napoleon, and by great numbers of extremely mobile but ill-armed Cossack horsemen: Mme de Staël, on her way from Kiev to Moscow, saw them going to the front 'without order or uniform, with a long lance in their hand, and a kind of grey dress, whose ample hood they put over their head.' [7]

6

'War is the last word in diplomacy.' Clausewitz, the great military theorist, learnt this maxim from Napoleon, as he learnt many rules of war in the Moscow campaign, in which he took part on the Russian side. When Napoleon had received sufficient information about Alexander's preparations from his agents at Danzig, Warsaw, and Vilna; when Tchernychev of the Russian embassy at Paris had fled, fearing the discovery of his knowledge of the French army returns, whilst his accomplice Michel, of the French General Staff, was apprehended and guillotined (May 2nd, 1812); when the veteran Kurakin (April 27th) had made the Tsar's last offer to Napoleon, demanding only the withdrawal of French troops from Prussia; when Napoleon had advertised his strength and self-confidence to the world by his fortnight's court at Dresden (May 16th-29th); and when Narbonne, who remembered being Louis XVI's War Minister, had been politely received and dismissed by Alexander at Vilna (May 19th)—then nothing remained (for there was no formal declaration of war on either side) but for the French army to cross the Niemen, Napoleon's Rubicon.

The central reach of the Niemen, running for a hundred miles from Grodno in the south to Kovno in the north, was the most easterly section of the frontier between Prussian and Russian Poland, and the centre from which roads diverged in three directions: north-east (400 miles) to St. Petersburg, the 'head' of Russia, south-east (300 miles) to its 'foot,' Kiev, and east (500 miles) to its 'heart,' Moscow. From the Niemen to Moscow was about as far as from Brighton to Edinburgh, via London (Vilna), York (Vitebsk) and Darlington (Smolensk): the battle of Borodino was fought as far away as Berwick. The country was a vast gently undulating plain, its dry dusty soil alternating with marshlands, and diversified by pine, birch, or beech woods. The roads were cart-tracks, the rivers as often as not unbridged, the towns scattered at intervals of fifty or more miles apart, the villages mere groups of wooden huts, with no more cultivated ground than would feed their few inhabitants, a barn or two, a threshing-floor, and a church, whose gilded cupola rode like a buoy upon the endless ocean of green and grey.

Here, on the Niemen, in the centre of the invading force, were three corps of French troops, 145,000 in all, the pick of the army and the head of its attack. Further north were 30,000 men, mostly Prussians, who remained on the left wing, and took no part in the main advance. Southwards came first two more corps, one of 45,000 Italians and the other of 25,000 Germans, who were grouped with the centre; and three more, 70,000 strong, forming the right wing. In addition there was a cavalry reserve nominally 40,000 strong, 30,000 Austrians far away to the south, and the picked men, infantry and cavalry, of the Old and Young Guard, numbering some 45,000. This gives a probable total of 430,000, of which something like 250,000 may be taken as an effective attacking force.

The Russian army opposing the invasion—not counting for the moment the detached forces of Wittgenstein and Tormassov—consisted of some 120,000 men under Barclay covering the 100-mile front from Grodno to Kovno, and barring the roads to Moscow and St. Petersburg, and perhaps 40,000 men under Bagration, guarding the gap between

Grodno and the Pripet marshes, which effectively limited the field of battle southwards.

It was at Grodno (Napoleon no doubt remembered) that Charles XII and his 43,000 Swedes had crossed the Niemen on their ill-starred adventure in September 1708. During his reconnaissance of the river on June 23rd, Napoleon was thrown from his horse. The ill omen was not forgotten; for the campaign which opened that night was nothing but a long series of miscalculations and mistakes.

Napoleon's evident intention was to bring both Russian armies to battle as soon as possible, and destroy them in detail. Whether or not, as one amateur strategist asserts, the three army corps on the French right were not to attack Bagration direct, but to drive him northwards towards the central army, at any rate both attacks failed to hold or to divert the Russian retreat. Jérôme, who was in command of the right wing, and refused to take orders from his old enemy Davout on his left, was bitterly reproached by his brother for the slowness of his advance: but Napoleon himself equally failed to prevent Barclay from retreating along the Vilna-Smolensk road. This was a first, and, as it proved, a fatal mistake.

A week after crossing the Niemen the French entered Vilna unopposed. They remained there from July 1st to 17th. This halt was a second major mistake, for it enabled the two Russian armies to make good their retreat, and to converge on Smolensk, 250 miles further east. What was the reason of this delay? Was Napoleon waiting, as he asserted, for news of Jérôme's progress? Did the army need rest, after a week's forced marching in heat and dust such as old soldiers had not experienced since the Syrian campaign? Did the sudden change from drought to torrential rain, which occurred at this moment, so disorganize transport that it was impossible to proceed? This last certainly; and it made matters worse that the failure of supplies led to straggling, looting and other offences which so alienated the country people that the French were dreaded as brigands rather than welcomed as liberators.

Vilna, the seat of a University, and the last outpost of European culture and education against Russian barbarism, was to be the advanced base of the expedition, the chief link between the Emperor and his capital. Maret, his Foreign Minister, and Bignon, his *commissaire impérial*, were there, with the diplomatic representatives of Prussia, Saxony, Denmark, Baden, Austria, and even the United States. Couriers came and went every day between Paris (in ten days) and Moscow (six). Many of the inhabitants had fled, but the foreign residents organized theatrical shows, dinners and dances, and duly celebrated the festivals of the Imperial calendar. Some of the diplomats—the only war correspondents of the time—may have spread gloomy forebodings; but it was not till mid-October, when Napoleon left Moscow, that Vilna began to reflect not victory but defeat.

There was another reason for the delay at Vilna. It was the capital of Lithuania—that is, of the Lithuanian provinces of Poland which had been annexed by Russia in 1794, and which had supplied two generals and many volunteers to the Polish legions serving with the French armies in Italy in 1797, and again in Prussia in 1806-07, always hoping to be rewarded with the liberation of their country, and always—at Lunéville, at Pressburg and at Tilsit—disappointed and disillusioned. During the last two years the eastern Poles had been courted by both sides; and it was not till the crossing of the Niemen—a compelling argument—that they decided to throw in their lot once more with France. But they welcomed Napoleon with less enthusiasm than Alexander, who had left the town three days before. They distrusted him, and he them. They could not forget Tilsit, which they called the Fourth Partition of Poland. They knew in their hearts that he did not care a fig for their independence. He was already disappointed with the response of the western Poles to his demand for troops—the Duchy of Warsaw, with a population of 4 millions ought, he held, to produce 70,000 men, not a mere 30,000; and he was irritated afresh by the conditions the Lithuanians tried to attach to miliary assistance.

Much time too was taken up, not only with the defences of the town and the accumulation of stores for the army, but with the organization of a provisional government for Lithuania—a government which, for all its employment of national leaders and institutions, pleased neither the 'French' nor the 'Russian' party; neither the adherents of the absentee and unpopular King of Saxony, the nominal head of the Duchy of Warsaw, nor his rivals amongst the great nobility; with a constitution and a code too liberal for the landlords and clergy, and meaningless to the common people, whose ideas of emancipation could not rise above serfdom or military service. Yet Russian Poland was designed to be the base from which Napoleon's army would set out, and to which it would return; and his failure to understand or conciliate the country was one of the main causes of his disaster.[8]

At last, at midnight on July 23rd, after scraping together ten days' rations for the Guard, Napoleon was off again, riding by day and driving by night; for there were few hours of darkness in these high latitudes. On the 24th he crossed the Dvina, and on the 28th entered Vitebsk. Here, again, he was disappointed to find the town undefended; but it was now only a week's march to Smolensk, where he was confident that the combined Russian armies must make a stand. Yet here again, for more than a fortnight, he held up the pursuit. Again, why? There had been a serious clash with Barclay's rear-guard at Ostrovno, outside

Vitebsk. The enemy were not far ahead on the road to Smolensk. The French troops were tired, but in good heart. Was it not imperative to press on, and give Barclay no time to halt? The indecision of Vilna seems to have seized Napoleon again, and more fatally. He called a council of generals, and put the case to them. Almost all were against proceeding; and Daru (who knew best about this) urged the impossibility of keeping the army supplied in a country already devastated by the retreating Russians. Napoleon was shaken, and declared that he would set up a government of eastern Russia at Vitebsk, and wait for Alexander to sue for terms. But, with the soldier's desire for a decisive battle, and the gambler's trust in luck, he soon changed his mind; and on August 13th the pursuit was resumed.

On August 16th Napoleon stood within sight of Smolensk: a Spanish-looking town (Wilson thought) with an eighteen-foot brick wall and thirty towers, rising on the far bank of the Dnieper: a famous, almost a sacred city, a second Moscow; and the meeting-point of the enemy's two lines of retreat—a position which the Russian generals would almost certainly make the scene of their last stand. The place seemed to be full of troops; its camp-fires shone at night as the gilded cupolas of its churches shone by day. Napoleon sent Junot round to cut the Moscow road, and ordered a bombardment of the city, to be followed by a frontal assault. For two days the ancient walls crumbled under cannon-fire, but as slowly as those of Acre; and for two days every assault was beaten off by the defence. On the night of the 17th, with much of the city already in flames, Barclay ordered retreat, taking with him the sacred *ikon* of the Virgin, which had inspired the defence: next morning his troops could be seen retiring along the Moscow road. Here Junot should have blocked the way: but he moved slowly, and arrived too late—another disastrous mistake.

Even to the most hardened soldier the experiences of Smolensk were terrible, and the exhausted troops made little attempt to pursue the Russians beyond Valutino, on the road to Viasma and Moscow. Napoleon, once more out of touch with the elusive Barclay, did not know that his retreat was dictated by necessity, and began to think that it was a deep-laid plan; particularly when reports came in that every village found on the line of march had been plundered and burnt. Still less did he know that Bagration's constant intrigues were at this moment resulting in the dismissal of Barclay, and the appointment (August 17th) of the veteran Kutusov as generalissimo, with the understanding that he would bring Napoleon to battle for the defence of Moscow.

At Smolensk Napoleon had even better reasons for calling a halt to the campaign than at Vitebsk. This was where Charles XII had turned south in 1708, to seek food and an ally in the Ukraine. (. . . *Le Vain-*

queur—he read again—*était toujours dans le grand chemin de la capitale de la Moscovie. Il y a de Smolensk, auprès duquel se donna ce combat, jusqu'à Moscou, environ cent de nos lieues françaises: l'armée n'avait presque plus de vivres . . . Au grande étonnement de toute l'armée, le roi quitta le chemin de Moscou et fit marcher au midi . . .*) But Napoleon could not imitate Charles. If he pressed on towards Moscow he must remember that he would be leaving the relatively friendly territory of what had once been Poland, where he could represent himself to the doubtful peasantry as a liberator, and entering on native Russian soil, where every man's hand would be against him, where the village *papas* were already denouncing him as a heretic and excommunicate, and where (as he soon found) the burning of villages and supplies was no longer an occasional expedient but a matter of strategy. He found that even Murat was against going further, and is said to have announced, 'The first Russian campaign is over.'

But how could this burnt-out shell of a city, empty of food and piled with dead bodies, become the winter quarters of the Grand Army? Nor was there any Mazeppa offering food and allies, if he turned south towards the Ukraine. He was much more than half way to Moscow, where he could winter in comfort, and dictate an honourable peace. This time he only hesitated a week. On August 25th the march was resumed: 200 miles still to go.

7

On the 30th the French reached Viasma, treading close on the heels of the Russian read-guard. Pressing on by the Moscow road, which here ran about fifty feet above the left bank of the little Kalotza, a tributary of the Moskva, they soon came in sight of the position which Kutusov, with the advice of Bennigsen, was hurriedly fortifying for his last stand. On the right, across the Kalotza, the village of Shevardino stood on a shoulder 150 feet high (a mountain in this flat land) which had originally formed the left end of the Russian position, but had been abandoned for a fresh line further back, and left as an outpost to delay the French advance. Napoleon at once (September 5th) attacked this position, and the Russians lost some thousands of men in its defence; but they gained a day's respite for the main body, which was now digging itself in on a line running along a ridge two miles south from the village of Borodino on the Kalotza to some woodlands on higher ground east of Shevardino. Kutusov, remembering Austerlitz, had fortified his centre with a turf redoubt bristling with guns, and there were lighter works of the same kind at either end.

This re-aligned Russian position was a formidable one, and Napoleon thought he had not enough men to outflank it. He was committed to a frontal attack on a fortified camp, which gave the enemy, with his stronger artillery and stubborn defence, every advantage. He knew it would be a costly affair, and was in a state of depression aggravated by an unaccustomed chill. September 6th was spent in preparations, and in hoping that the Russians would not again retire.

At half past five on the morning of the 7th Napoleon took up his position on the captured point of Shevardino. As the sun rose he said, 'See, it is the sun of Austerlitz!' But though the battle-fields were not alike, nor the proportion of forces (for each side had some 120,000 in the fight), and though he was faced by Kutusov and Bagration, whom he had defeated at Austerlitz, and Bennigsen, whom he had defeated at Friedland, yet the battle that followed showed little skill or initiative on his part, and could only be claimed as a victory because the French were left in possession of a field on which one in every four of their army lay dead or wounded.

If it was a mistake to attack such a position, what else could he do, short of retreating? If it was a mistake to make a frontal assault, would it have been possible, as Davout suggested, to concentrate his best troops on the right, occupy the higher ground there, and roll up the Russian position from its left? If it was a mistake not to throw his Guard into the action, as his best generals demanded, he had to consider that its intervention might not be decisive, and that if it suffered heavily there would be less possibility of pursuit in the event of victory, or (in case of retreat) the less protection for himself, the brain and will of the whole army.

For twelve hours, under the incessant clamour of 1200 guns, two half starving armies fought hand to hand, by incessant charge and counter-charge; first round the redoubt on the Russian right, which only yielded, with the fatal wounding of Bagration, at midday; and then round the central redoubt, which was not captured till the sun of Austerlitz was setting. All day long Napoleon walked to and fro in front of his Guard, almost apathetically, well out of range, watching the battle through his glasses, receiving and sending off messages, whilst the Guard's band played *Allons, enfants de la Patrie!* and other Republican march music. When the din of firing at last died down, and such wounded men as could walk straggled back to their camp-fires, the whole Russian position was found covered with dead and dying men. It was neither a French victory nor a Russian defeat, but another Eylau—a massacre, in which both armies lost the power to strike again. 'The enemy's losses,' said Napoleon's letter to Marie-Louise the next day, 'can be estimated at 30,000: I had a number of men killed and wounded.' In fact the Russian casualties were nearer 58,000—half their army, including forty-three generals; the French casualties nearly 30,000—a quarter of their army—and fifty generals. The ambulance arrangements on both sides were utterly inadequate, and wounded men were left to die among the dead.

What follows would be hard to believe, were it not in the letter of a French Colonel written on the spot. 'When it was all over (*après l'affaire*) I saw Napoleon riding over the battle-field; I followed him everywhere: he was beaming (*rayonnant*) and rubbing his hands: "There are five dead Russians—he said it repeatedly with satisfaction—to every Frenchman." I suppose he took Germans for Russians.' Such was Borodino, the most horrible battle of the Napoleonic wars.[9]

8

A week later (September 14th) Napoleon looked down from the last wave-top of the Russian plain upon the walls of Moscow, and the golden cupolas of the Kremlin. Kutusov had given orders that the city should not be defended. His troops marched through the streets and away to the south: the civil population poured out of the gates to take refuge in the country round. They went unmolested. In the evening the French army moved into an empty and silent city. Next day Napoleon rode into the Kremlin, the heart of Old Russia, with its ancient walls, its gates and towers, and the lovely churches where Tsars had been crowned and buried, the tall bell-tower of Ivan, and the mosaic palace of Peter the Great. He had reached the city of his dreams.

That night he was awakened by the cry of 'Fire!' From the first hour of entry the careless bivouacking and plundering of his own soldiers had set light to a half-wooden town. Now whole streets were ablaze. Were the few remaining inhabitants deliberately burning down the sacred city rather than let it be desecrated by his presence? Had Rostoptchin, the boastful and eccentric Governor of Moscow, left incendiaries behind, and taken the fire-engines away? Whatever the cause, the city was on fire in every quarter, and sparks, driven by a high wind, were beginning to fall on the Kremlin. Napoleon was at last persuaded to escape, and to take refuge outside the city. For five days the fire raged, whilst the soldiery pillaged the burning palaces and churches of valuables of every description. 'I had no idea,' Napoleon wrote to Marie-Louise on the 18th, 'of the wonders of this town. It had five hundred mansions as fine as the Elysée, with French furniture and incredible luxury, a number of imperial palaces, barracks, and magnificent hospitals. The whole place has disappeared. For four days the fire has been consuming it. All the small middle-class houses are of wood, and catch fire like matches. It was the Governor and the Russians who set this beautiful city on fire: the respectable inhabitants, 200,000 of them (*an obvious exaggeration*) are in despair, and are reduced to wandering wretchedly in the streets. However there is enough left for the army, which has found all kinds of valuables; in the present confusion everything is for loot.' 'The soldiers have found abundance of provisions and commodities (he adds later); food, and quantities of French brandy.'

But in effect Moscow remained hardly more fit for winter quarters than Smolensk. The Kremlin was saved by its circuit of walls. Outside, only 5000 houses were still standing out of some 25,000. There was plenty of strong drink in the cellars, but little to eat. Foraging parties found that the peasantry would not sell supplies which they could ill spare for false *rouble* notes brought from Paris. Stragglers outside the city—and inside, too—were found murdered. It was imperative that Napoleon should induce Alexander to make peace before winter prevented the possibility of retreat. Moscow had lost its military value; but it was still, he believed, a political asset to bargain with. It took him five weeks to realize what he might have learnt in five minutes' conversation with any Russian patriot: that his occupation of Moscow was the unforgivable sin, and that no armistice would be granted to invaders whom the peasantry (as Kutusov told Lauriston) regarded as 'no better than a marauding force of Tartars under Gengis Khan.'

Napoleon made three attempts to approach the Tsar: by entrusting letters to Toutolmin, the director of the Moscow Foundling Hospital, and to a rich Muskovite, Iakovlev, and by sending Lauriston to Kutusov for a pass to St. Petersburg. To the letters there was no answer: Lauriston's request was refused. A message from Kutusov to Berthier (October 20th) made it clear that the only thing about which the Tsar and his generals were agreed was that there should be no parleying with the enemy. Alexander had 'declared upon his honour (reports Wilson) that he would not enter into or permit any negotiation with Napoleon as long as an armed Frenchman remained in the territories of Russia. His Imperial Majesty said he would sooner let his beard grow to his waist, and eat potatoes in Siberia.' Sometimes Napoleon talked of marching on St. Petersburg—a threat which Alexander at least took seriously: but he knew in his heart that it was impossible, with a disorganized and half-starved army, and winter rapidly coming on.

A little snow fell in Moscow on October 13th. The next day Napoleon issued preliminary orders for retreat: the wounded to be evacuated, reinforcements to be halted; whilst, for a bluff, his allies were to publish exaggerated accounts of the strength of their forces. He would establish winter quarters he said, in Poland. He even suggested to Marie-Louise that she might visit him there. But he must have known the perilous state of his 500-mile communications, and the unlikelihood that at Smolensk, or any other town in Poland, he would find food and accommodation for 100,000 men. He was in a desperate position, winter or no winter, and he knew it. In his anger, he left Mortier behind for four days to mine and blow up the Kremlin. Fortunately the work was badly done, and the main buildings remained standing. But it increased the hatred of the Russian people; and his retreat was harried at every turn not merely by Cossack cavalry, but also by organized bands of *franc-tireurs*, and by indignant peasantry, who waylaid and murdered any Frenchman who fell out of the line. Tolstoy's *Dolokhov* was drawn from life.

In some undated *Notes* included in the official Correspondence there is evidence that Napoleon considered a plan by which his retreat from Moscow might be given the appearance of a fresh offensive. A force of reserves from Smolensk would advance towards Polozk and Vitebsk, at the same time as Napoleon led the main army from Moscow along a more northerly route than that of the invasion to Velikije Luki, 100 miles north of Vitebsk, where he could be supplied from Polozk and Vitebsk. Meanwhile the remainder of the army could return by the old route; and all would foregather in the Vitebsk-Polozk-Velikije Luki triangle: the most suitable district for winter quarters, and (Napoleon even tried to persuade himself) constituting such a threat to St. Petersburg as might force the enemy to sue for peace.

But in fact the only practicable plan, and he knew it, was to escape by the shortest possible route to Smolensk and Vilna. Yet the first part of the journey, at least, might be varied with advantage, if he started by the road which led south-westwards towards Kaluga; because Kutusov was there, with a growing army that it would not be safe to ignore, and because, if he could force back this army beyond Malo-Jaroslavetz, sixty miles away on the Kaluga road, he would be able to reach Viasma on the old road by a route not devastated during the invasion, and to avoid the battlefield of Borodino; if the enemy were to retreat south of Kaluga, he might even have the use of an alternative road all the way to Smolensk.

So on the night of October 19th the army set off in that direction—some 100,000 of them, encumbered with a huge train of carts and carriages, in which small supplies of provisions were hidden under heavy loads of loot, the plunder of Moscow's burnt-out palaces and churches. With the army went a crowd of French residents from Moscow, with their families, and Russian prisoners, most of whom were destined to perish miserably on the road.

Sergeant Bourgogne tells us what was in his knapsack when he set out on his 500-miles march: several pounds of sugar, some rice, some biscuit, half a bottle of liqueur, a woman's Chinese silk dress, several gold and silver ornaments, amongst them a part of the silver gilt casing of the great cross of Ivan the Great (in its centre a solid gold cross about a foot long), a woman's riding cloak lined with green velvet, two silver pictures in relief, one of the Judgement of Paris, the other of Neptune in a chariot drawn by sea-horses, several lockets, and a Russian prince's spittoon set with brilliants: in a large pouch hung at his side by a silver cord was a crucifix in silver and gold, and a Chinese porcelain vase. He adds, almost as an afterthought, his powder-flask, fire-arms and sixteen cartridges.

9

Kutusov was determined, whatever the Tsar and his generals might say, to avoid another Borodino. He was not even anxious to capture Napoleon, or to defeat his army: he was interested only in the fate of Russia, not of Europe. He allowed Bennigsen to attack Murat at Tarutino on October 18th, and Dokhtourov to defend Malo-Jaroslavetz on the 23rd; but when Napoleon accepted this check, and rather than face the whole Russian army, turned north again on to the old Viasma-Smolensk road, he contented himself with marching parallel to the line of retreat, further south, several miles in the rear; he would leave the destruction of the French army to starvation and guerrilla warfare.

Napoleon's turn northward at this moment—the real beginning of his retreat—was a mistake due to necessity. If he had been able to push Kutusov a few miles further south, he would have had the choice of two alternative routes, both of which would have taken him through country hitherto unplundered by either army. But he had lost some 10,000 men at Malo-Jaroslavetz, and was alarmed by the strength of Kutusov's army. But nothing could have been worse for the spirit of his troops than to begin their march over the field of Borodino, still covered with the dead bodies of their fallen comrades.

The fine weather held for the 280 miles' march to Smolensk: there was no frost, and no snow fell, until a few days before reaching it. Yet already the retreat was a disaster. Every mile men fell out from exhaustion or starvation, to be murdered by the peasantry or captured by Cossack horsemen. In their hunger they would eat dying horses, or even human flesh. There was, too, a serious rear-guard action at Viasma on November 3rd, in which the French suffered 6000 casualties, and lost 2000 prisoners.

Smolensk, reached on November 8th, was not better than Moscow: it was much worse. Most of its supplies had been eaten up by reinforcements going east, or by wounded men and deserters going west. What was left was looted in a few days by Napoleon's starving and undisciplined troops. On the 17th the retreat was resumed. At the crossing of the Dnieper a heroic action by Ney's rear-guard, to which Napoleon gave no support, enabled the Emperor and the Guard to hurry on. It was imperative to reach the Beresina before the Russians could bar his passage. Alexander's military advisers at St. Petersburg, incited by Kutusov's critics in the field, had drawn up a plan for trapping him there, between his pursuers and the forces under Tchitchagov and Wittgenstein, which were on the far bank. According to all the rules of war it should have been an easy operation: military historians have never quite agreed why it failed. Was it because Napoleon remembered Charles XII's crossing there in 1707, and used the same strategem to mislead Tchitchagov as to the place of crossing? (... *Charles posta quelques régiments sur le bord de la Bere-zine, à l'opposite de Borislou, comme s'il avait voulu tenter le passage à vue de l'ennemi. Dans le même temps il remonte avec son armée trois lieues au delà vers la source de la rivière; il y fait jeter un pont, passe sur le ventre à un corps de trois mille hommes qui défendait ce poste, et marche à l'armée ennemie sans s'arrêter* ...) Was it because Wittgenstein came up too late? Was it because Kutusov still believed himself too weak (he had no more than 27,000 effectives) to risk a major engagement, and held to his policy of letting the French escape?

At any rate Napoleon succeeded in throwing two bridges across the river (that it was not hard frozen showed how mild the winter had been), and in getting about 60,000 of the army across, including the Guard, which still kept its ranks, and marched stolidly along, defying attack, amid a crowd of disarmed soldiers, wounded men and stragglers. When the Russians caught up with his rear-guard, he ruthlessly ordered the bridges to be burnt down, and left behind some thousands of unarmed or wounded men, with many women and children who had followed the army from Moscow, to perish on the bridges or the breaking ice, to be killed by Russian gun-fire, or to remain behind at the mercy of the pursuing Cossacks. Perhaps 10,000 never came back alive. But again the Emperor and the Guard were saved.

Yet now, as though outraged Nature had only reserved her fire, the weather suddenly worsened, and the last fortnight's frost carried off a higher proportion of victims than the preceding six weeks of starvation.

(*Dans cette extrémité*—Napoleon might read again—*le mémorable hiver de 1709, plus terrible encore sur les frontières de l'Europe que nous l'avons senti en France, détruisit une partie de son armée. Charles voulait braver les saisons comme il faisait de ses ennemis; il osait faire des longues marches de troupes pendant ce froid mortel: ce fut dans une de ces marches que deux mille hommes tombèrent morts de froid sous ses yeux. Les cavaliers n'avaient plus de bottes, les fantassins étaient sans souliers et presque sans habits: ils étaient réduits à se faire des chaussures de peaux de bêtes, comme ils pouvaient; souvent ils manquaient de pain ... Cette armée, auparavant si florissante, était réduite à vingt-quatre mille hommes près à mourir de faim. ...*)

The sufferings of the retreat were now as horrible as anything imagined in Dante's Circle of Ice. With the temperature 30 degrees below zero, and 'a subtle, keen, razor-cutting, creeping wind that penetrated skin, muscle, and bone to the very marrow,' men dropped and froze by the roadside, or lay down and froze round the camp-fires at night. Yet still the Guard marched on through snow and ice, unperturbed by the attempts of the guerrillas to break its ranks, 'like a hundred-gun warship (a Russian witness wrote) amidst a fleet of fishing-boats.'

Vilna was now the one hope. Vilna, where there might still be food, and shelter, and a defence against the constant attacks of the pursuers. But when the remnant arrived there, on December 8th, they were no more an army, but a horde of desperate savages, who beat their way into the town, plundered the terrified inhabitants, looted the stores, and by their indiscipline made any attempt to defend the place impossible. Two days later Murat (now in command) ordered evacuation, and marched on to Kovno. By a final blow of fate, all the remaining guns and baggage had to be abandoned on an icy hill outside Vilna, which the unroughed horses could not surmount. At Kovno the confusion was even worse than at Vilna, and nothing remained but to cross the Niemen, which was now so frozen as to be useless for defence, and to seek escape northwards towards Gumbinnen and Königsberg. It was thus that, on the evening of December 14th, Ney, who had fought a series of stubborn rear-guard actions since Krasnoi on November 7th, was the last Frenchman to leave Russian soil. The 350 tattered and exhausted men who returned with him over the ice were all the effectives left of the 250,000 who had led the invasion across the river six months before.

10

'All is lost, save honour.' But whose honour? Napoleon was not there. After his escape at the Beresina he feared for his life and for his throne. On October 21st a Polish force had been defeated at Slonim, and communications with Paris were cut for the first time. A month later the Russians took Minsk, and closed in on Vilna, which was now in danger of isolation. It was rumoured in England that our enemy would not come back alive; and an Oxford Common Room betting book contains the entry: 'Mr. Senior bets Mr. Jenkins four Bottles to one that Bonaparte is not dead this day Dec. 1st 1812.' Mr. Senior won his bet. For on November 29th Napoleon ordered Maret to evacuate the diplomatic corps, and told him of his intention to return to France: for he had heard of Malet's attempt to seize the government of Paris, and believed his immediate presence necessary there to save the state. He could not save the army: there was no army to save.

On December 4th he sent for Hogendorp, the governor of Lithuania, and ordered relays of horses for the journey. On the night of the 5th, at Smorgoni, forty miles short of Vilna, he dictated the 29th Bulletin announcing the defeat and dissolution of the Grand Army; he then took leave of his officers and set off: a sleigh for his Polish interpreter, Wonsowicz, a carriage for himself and Caulaincourt, and two more for Duroc,

Mouton, Lefebvre-Desnottes and three valets. There was a cavalry escort of Frenchmen, Poles, and Neapolitans; the bodies of some of the last, in smart new uniforms, were found frozen outside the gates of Vilna. Even Napoleon shivered under the fur coat and hood and boots that Caulaincourt had provided for him. After crossing the Niemen the carriage could go no further; but a comfortable *berline* on runners was found, and in this he travelled on by Warsaw to Dresden; and thence, in a carriage lent by the King of Saxony, to Erfurt and Mainz, and reached Paris on December 18th.

During most of the journey Napoleon talked and talked—*il témoignait avant tout le besoin d'épanchement*, says Caulaincourt—about his Polish policy, about England, about the government of France, about his mistresses, about anything that came into his head. But one thing emerges from his companion's hour-by-hour report of their fortnight's *tête-à-tête* which is more significant than any record of policy and opinions; and that is, Napoleon's seeming insensibility to the disaster from which he has just escaped, and to the fate of the army that he has left behind; the lack of any sense of responsibility, let alone remorse, for the sufferings and death of a quarter of a million men. (... *Cependant cette armée suédoise, sortie de la Saxe si triomphante, n'était plus; la moitié avait péri de misère, l'autre moitié était esclave ou massacrée. Charles XII avait perdu en un jour le fruit de neuf ans de travaux, et de près de cent combats: il fuyait dans une méchante calèche, ayant à son côté le major-general Hord, blessé dangereusement; le reste de sa troupe suivait, les uns à pied, les autres à cheval, quelques-uns dans des charrettes, à travers un désert où ils ne voyaient ni huttes, ni tentes, ni hommes, ni animaux, ni chemins ...*) Caulaincourt, indeed, thought this indifference a mark of Napoleon's greatness. 'Anyone else (he writes) would have been cast down (*accablé*). The Emperor showed himself superior to his misfortunes. His adversities, instead of depressing him, brought out all the more the energy of his great character ... He rose superior to every event, and proved his fitness to dominate everyone—if only he had not been so misused by fortune, men, and glory. The hope, nay the mere chance of success inspired him (*l'enivrait*) more than the worst reverse put him down.'

But it is Caulaincourt again who provides an unflattering pendant to this picture of a hero, and disproves yet another legend—that of Napoleon trudging along in the snow, sharing the sufferings and privations of his men, and surviving the horrors of the march by his physical and moral superiority. For he tells us how throughout the campaign the Guard had the best of everything; how, just before Borodino, where the rest of the army went into battle half starved, a convoy arrived from Paris with special food for Napoleon, and 'abundance reigned at Headquarters, where Clos-Vougeot and Chambertin were drunk at table'; how, whilst guns and wagons had to be left behind because the baggage animals were not roughed or could not be fed, Napoleon's transport had been carefully seen to, and of the thirty-two saddle-horses taken for his private use twenty-two came back alive; how, when the road was 'covered with the bodies of wounded men who had died of hunger, cold and misery,' Napoleon would leave his carriage and walk for a while two or three times a day, leaning on the arm of one of his suite; or how 'the Emperor alone had always been given proper meals (*bien servi*) during the retreat: every day he had clean table linen, white bread, Chambertin, good oil, beef or mutton, rice and beans or lentils—his favourite-vegetables.' Whatever pains Napoleon might take in his daily letters to the Empress to conceal the true facts about the campaign, there was one thing that he could always say with perfect candour: 'My health is excellent.'

There are writers who assert that the Moscow expedition shows a falling off in Napoleon's powers, and that this was due to indisposition, mental exhaustion, or the beginnings of the disease from which he died nine years later. There is really no evidence for this, and nothing in the events of 1812 which cannot be better accounted for by other causes. The inordinate size of Napoleon's army, the inclusion in it of so many disaffected and undisciplined foreigners, the miscalculation of means to ends in the commissariat, the delay which enabled the enemy to avoid battle, the failure to provide against a winter campaign, or to organize winter quarters at Vilna or Smolensk, the false belief that the Tsar would come to terms—all of these were errors due not to any unusual deficiency in Napoleon's powers, but to over-confidence, belief in his good luck, refusal to take advice, and misjudgment as to the probable scope and conditions of the whole operation. For all this he, in the last resort, and no one and nothing else was to blame. He came to admit at last, at St. Helena, that this was so. *J'étais le maître, et c'est à moi qu'incombe toute la faute.*

The year 1812 was a crisis in Napoleon's life: but the change came after Moscow, not before. Chaptal, who knew him as well as anyone, says that 'after his return from Moscow those who saw most of him noticed a great change in his physical and moral constitution . . . I confess that after this unhappy period I did not find the same consistency in his ideas or the same strength in his character; one noticed only inconsequent leaps of imagination. There was not the old taste and faculty for hard work. As I had often said, out of the hundred nerve-centres (*fibres*) that composed his brain, more than half were no longer sound.' Riding tired him: he needed more sleep: he began to like good food. He was the only person not to realize the change in himself; and if things went wrong he was more than ever disposed to blame others for it.

Yet his belief in his 'star' was still, Caulaincourt would have us believe, unshaken. Ever since his easy capture of Malta in 1798 he had felt, like

Samuel Butler's hero, that 'as luck would have it, Providence was on his side.' Aboukir Bay seemed to confirm this faith, because it led to his return to France, and made possible Brumaire. Might not even Moscow offer additional proof of it—another army abandoned, another providential return to Paris? 'This idea never left his mind (says Caulaincourt), and gave him not merely a confidence, but a kind of superstition; a belief that he could not define; for without being an atheist, he was not a religious man.' Colossal egoism! [10]

XIII

THE RHINE

(1813-1814)

I

THE HOSTILITIES of 1813 and 1814 are commonly described as a campaign for the reconquest of Germany and a campaign for the defence of Paris. But the real issue of both, in the minds of most Frenchmen, and by the grudging admission of their Emperor himself, was the Rhine frontier of France. In 1813 they fought to secure it, in 1814 to defend it. No Frenchman now wanted to march eastwards again. Few Frenchmen ever wanted to defend Paris, which the provinces viewed with envy and dislike. But the Rhine was the traditional frontier of the fatherland; two hundred yards of grey water as important to Frenchmen as twenty miles of blue water are to Englishmen. For eighteen centuries and a half it had defended a Roman civilization from the relative barbarism of central Europe, its nearer bank fortified by cities which still remembered their Latin names—Augusta Rauricorum, Argentoratum, Moguntiacum, Colonia Agrippina; only its upper reaches, which turned too near to the heart of France, defended on the east bank by a precarious *limes* (afterwards a barrier of satellite states) drawn to the upper Danube. No attempt to bring the west and east together into a Rhenish state had succeeded for long, or would ever succeed. No one living east of the Rhine could really be a Frenchman: no one living on the other side of it could really be anything else.

Napoleon was not a Frenchman; but he knew his history, and he had a good eye for a map. When he dined in 1797 at the Three Kings, whose balconies overhung the Rhine; when he crossed the bridge beyond Strasbourg, or slept at Mayence, or reviewed the garrison at Cologne in 1804 (spied at a distance by Henry Brougham from a Rhine passenger boat), he must have felt as Frenchmen did about the most important frontier in western Europe.

He would fight for this on the far bank, with his back to it, as long as

371

he could; for he always preferred an attacking campaign, and one not fought on French soil: but if that failed he would fight behind it—not along its whole impossible length, but in the district where the routes from the Rhine crossings converged on the capital. He would fight, and he would negotiate with one end in view—the retention of the whole natural, original, and revolutionary frontier, from Basle to Cologne, and from Cologne at least to Antwerp. As a last resort he would defend Paris: but Paris for the sake of the Rhine.

2

'All they that take the sword shall perish with the sword.' The ruler of a state may, if reason fails to gain his end, appeal to force; but if force fails, he cannot again appeal to reason. Such was the predicament in which Napoleon found himself in December 1812. Nor was that all. The invasion of Russia was not an isolated act, but the culmination of a line of policy which he had pursued for ten years. He had come to rely on victory in the field to clinch his diplomatic arguments and to enforce his political demands. Marengo, Austerlitz, Jena, Friedland, Wagram had convinced him that his plans could not fail. Moscow was a shock to this personal faith; as though the imperial Providence on whom he had counted to oversee and applaud his exploits had suddenly frowned, and, in the sight of all Europe, turned down his thumb. For the moment he could not believe that it was really so. His present mood of elation ('I never remember seeing him so gay,' writes Caulaincourt) was a defiance of fate. He would create another army: he would fight again: he would win a great victory: he would force Providence to revise a mistaken verdict. Everything would go on as before. But in his heart he no longer felt sure of success. The shadow of Moscow lengthened ahead of him. He found himself using the word *if*. 'I shall win victories and get peace this year,' he wrote on February 14th: 'but what if my plans go wrong and I suffer defeat? . . . But that is still a long way off.'

To Europe as a whole—to Napoleon's unloving allies and unforgiving enemies, to the statesmen who calculated on his fall and the generals who needed peace to enjoy their gains, to the Jacobins who longed for liberty and the royalists who said masses for a restoration, to the manufacturers whom he had regimented and the merchants whom he had ruined—the news from Moscow was 'as the lightning cometh out of the east and shineth even unto the west'; and the eagles would soon be gathered round the carcass of the French Empire.

Napoleon spent four months at home between his return from Russia and his fresh start for Germany (December 19th-April 15th). Every day he was busy with his ministers, or at meetings of committees and councils: he received ambassadors, he held reviews, he visited the theatre, he went hunting. But it is not difficult to read between the lines of the old routine the new preoccupations which filled his mind. Another army had to be raised. Another war had to be paid for. Allies had to be reassured, enemies intimidated. In every country of the continent the spirit of 1789, which twelve years of government and conquest had sown and rolled in, was now rising from the ground. The cry was now for liberation, not from the Old Regime but from the New—from the regime of militarism, of regimentation, of state control. How would Napoleon deal with it? He only knew and understood one way—the soldier's way, by war.

A new army? Napoleon began by dreaming that the remnants of the old army would be able to reform behind the Niemen. Did he forget that the river was frozen, and afforded no defence? Did he suppose that Alexander would be content with Kutusov's policy, and halt the pursuit at the frontier? Optimistically he estimated this remnant at 150,000. A new class of recruits, those for 1813, were already under training: 140,000 more. The National Guard, reconstituted against considerable opposition, and only for home service, could by a stroke of the pen be sent abroad: 100,000 strong. Total, nearly 400,000. There were still the armies in Spain (but on the run before Wellington), certain contingents of allies too timid to break away, and detached garrisons in Prussia and elsewhere.

But on December 30th Yorck's Prussian corps on the lower Niemen signed the capitulation of Tauroggen, and was allowed by the Russians to return home. The remnants of the French centre were too few and demoralized to make a stand. The Niemen line had ceased to exist. Then let it be the next river. 'The Grand Army has taken up its winter quarters on the Vistula,' Napoleon told Jérôme on December 23rd. But soon Frederick-William made it known to the Tsar that if the Russians appeared on the Oder he would join in the attack on France. At Vienna Metternich talked of peace and prepared war; the more securely, as Napoleon still believed that his new father-in-law would not turn against him, and calculated (not altogether wrongly) that he was more afraid of Russia than of France. Then, by the Convention of Zeycz, the Austrian army followed Yorck's example, and retired from the war—thus uncovering the line of the Vistula, and enabling the Russians to seize Warsaw.

As the prospect worsened Napoleon invented new ways of raising troops. He would call up those belonging to the classes of the last four years who had been lucky enough to escape enlistment. This would give him 100,000 more. And as soon as the youths of the 1813 class had finished their training he would call up the boys of 1814: another 150,000. Both steps were bitterly resented. There was no open resistance: but it was noticed that the number of young men who secured exemption from service on the ground that they had been recently married nearly doubled between

1812 and 1813; whilst the price paid for a substitute (*remplacement* was still allowed) reached in 1812 the unheard of figure of £750. If the worst came to the worst, there were still 8000 men in the French navy who could be drafted into the army to save the state.

Napoleon could only think of one more way of raising fresh troops. It appeared from the various negotiations that had gone on between England and France for the exchange of prisoners taken during the last ten years that there were, in 1810, some 41,000 French prisoners in England and 11,000 English prisoners in France. The Morlaix negotiations of that year had broken down through Napoleon's unaccountable refusal of a favourable offer by Britain. At that time we had been more anxious to recover our 11,000 men than to refuse him his 41,000. Now, in 1813, the positions were reversed, and he suddenly reopened the question, endeavouring to throw into the scales 17,000 Hanoverians, who were not really in his hands; only to find that we had no intention of presenting him with a possible reinforcement of 28,000 men.

Supposing that, by hook or crook, he could raise a new army of half a million men, how was it to be paid for? The balance-sheet of the Russian campaign showed an expenditure of £2¼ millions, and a credit in hand of £675. Nothing more could be extracted from direct taxation (now efficiently collected); nor from the unpopular indirect taxes which, abolished under the Revolution, had been gradually restored under the Empire; nor from the local *octrois* and *centimes* (which we should call rates) to which a large share of public expenditure had been transferred; nor from the forced contributions of Italy, Holland, and the confederated states of Germany, already fully pledged for the expenses of their governments and the upkeep of troops, both French and their own; nor from the *trésor de l'armée*, formed of the war contributions of conquered countries, of which all but £100,000 in gold had been abandoned on the icy road outside Vilna; nor even from the *domaine extraordinaire*, the revenues of estates seized in Italy and elsewhere. But war had paid; and war could be made to pay again.

Meanwhile, Napoleon exploited to the full the revenue drawn from the Continental Blockade in the form of tariffs, licences, and fines for smuggling; and he finally hit upon the expedient of seizing the funds of the municipalities (*biens des communes*), compensating them with government stock (*rentes d'état*): this gave him £18 millions for his immediate needs. Characteristically, as he had refused to sacrifice his Guard at Borodino, so his personal wealth—the *trésor des Tuileries*, as it was called (£16 millions) and the *trésor personnel* (£6 millions, most of which lay in the form of cash in the cellars of the Tuileries)—was left untouched.

3

What had Napoleon to hope or fear from his former enemies and allies?
By the time that he was ready to join his new armies in the field (he left
Paris on April 15th, and was at Erfurt on the 25th) the position was becoming clear and ominous. With the Russians, Alexander's determination
to pursue his advantage, and to drive Napoleon back across the Rhine,
had prevailed over Kutusov's view that his punishment might be left to
Providence. Russian troops had invested Thorn and Danzig, and pushed
on across the Vistula and Oder as far west as Hamburg, whilst Eugène,
with forces quite inadequate to hold so forward a front, fell back behind
the line of the Elbe. Prussia was balanced between the wish of her generals for revenge, and the caution of her statesmen, who would not declare
against Napoleon so long as Berlin was in French hands, and the attitude
of Austria was undeclared. It was not till March 17th, after significantly
moving his court to Breslau, that Frederick-William signed an alliance
with Russia. Then the passion for liberation which had begun in the
Universities spread like a forest fire through all the country east of the
Elbe: and it was not an impotent or misdirected movement, but one
inspired by the reforms of Stein and embodied in the military organization of Scharnhorst and Gneisenau, in which old traditions inherited
from Frederick the Great blended with new ideas borrowed from the
French Republic and Empire.

The King of Saxony, whose territories astride the middle Elbe were
open to attack from both east and west, hesitated which side to join till
the news of Lutzen brought him back post-haste from Prague to Dresden,
and forced him into unwilling subservience to Napoleon. Jérôme, now
King of Westphalia, was expected to defend the lower Elbe. Mecklenburg,
on the north-east bank, joined the Allies. Further north again, Sweden,
under the jealous and ambitious Bernadotte, made a Russian alliance in
April. On May 29th Denmark declared for France, and Danish troops
helped Napoleon to regain possession of Hamburg (June 1st), where
Davout was soon shooting and fining the citizens for their temporary
surrender to the enemy. All the confederated states of West Germany
sent contingents to Napoleon's new army; but unwillingly, and with the
intention of deserting his cause on the first sign of defeat. If they did not
share the Prussian passion for revenge, they were equally determined to
free themselves from the burden of French occupation, French military
demands, and the Continental System.

And Austria? There was Napoleon's greatest danger, Europe's greatest
hope. There was the hook baited with a family alliance, and the memory
of two disastrous defeats, carefully disguised by those affectionate letters
from his father-in-law that Napoleon was getting to know so well (how

he must have longed to tell Francis what he really thought of him!), and the line held in the cunning hand of his most formidable enemy, Metternich. One of these letters, dated December 20th, was brought to him by Bubna a few days after his return to Paris. In it Francis expressed his sympathy over the Russian affair, all the more so as his own 'brave army' was involved in the disaster, and his own 'provinces were exposed' by the retreat. But his real object was to sound Napoleon as to the conditions on which he would consider making peace. Napoleon's reply (January 7th: it is omitted from the official Correspondence) pointed out how strong the French army still was, or would be, but said that Napoleon had no objection to any steps Francis might take towards 'a peace that could be honourably accepted by all the belligerents.'

Francis's later letters during the summer of 1813 are variations on this theme. 'Twenty years of a reign troubled by disasters unexampled for centuries' have taught him that his people above all desire peace. He wishes to mediate, but with an army at his back—an army whose commander (though he forgets to mention it) has followed the Prussian Yorck's example in arranging an armistice with the Allies and dropping out of the war. He is already bitten by Metternich's anti-Jacobinism, and opines that 'any prolongation of the war, or any temporary settlement, which did not enable the sovereign to devote serious and sustained efforts to the extirpation of the Jacobin menace would soon threaten the very existence of their thrones.' Right up to the end of August the two Emperors solemnly exchange notes on their good health (Emperors, it seems, do not ask, 'How are you?' but say how well they are), and profess to be working side by side for a peace which is the supreme desire of both their peoples. The bait is still on the hook; the line is still in Metternich's watchful hand; he will know better than anyone whether the movement of the float means a nibble or a bite; he will be ready for exactly the right moment to haul in the catch.

Everything would in fact turn, as Napoleon clearly saw, on the issue of the coming campaign. Victorious, he might reimpose his rule at least as far east as the Oder: defeated, he would have to give up everything beyond the Rhine. And would it end there? Since 1793, Frenchmen had learnt to assume that the Rhine throughout its length from Basle to Belgium was the 'natural' frontier between France and central Europe, and had added Ostend and Antwerp to the line of Channel ports under their control. But would England, who had allowed this claim at Amiens, put up with it now? To accept the frontier of 1792 was to affirm the *ancien régime*, and to deny the Revolution. Could an Empire founded on Valmy and Jemmappes survive such a humiliation? This uncomfortable doubt was in Napoleon's mind all through the fighting of 1813—and, for that matter, of 1814 too.[1]

4

The course of the fighting in 1813—a summer campaign of a month from May 1st to 30th, and a two months' autumn campaign from August 16th to October 19th—was determined by the configuration of the battle-field. It was a parallelogram about 200 miles from east to west and 100 miles from north to south, limited on the north by the Prussian frontier and on the south by the mountain circuit of Bohemia: a country of wood and pasture, traversed by numerous rivers flowing from south-east to north-west, tributaries of the Oder, which formed its eastern boundary, or of the Elbe, which cut through the middle of it from the Bohemian frontier to Dresden and Magdeburg. Between these two places, thirty miles west from the Elbe, lay Leipzig.

Three Allied armies were advancing from the north, east and south sides of this parallelogram—Bernadotte from the north, Wittgenstein from the east, Schwartzenberg from the south. It was Napoleon's intention, advancing from the west, to divide these armies, and deal with them separately. But he had not been able to choose his ground, or to send out his spies; and his army was deficient in cavalry. He was like Nelson in the Mediterranean in 1798: a fleet without frigates. The Allies were little better off; and at first it was a game of Blind Man's Buff; Napoleon at Leipzig, with his eyes bandaged, waiting for one of his enemies to make an incautious move. Nor was such an opportunity unlikely, when dealing with a polygot enemy under a divided command.

'I long to hear the first cannon shot,' wrote the Duke of Cumberland to the Prince Regent from Strelitz, where he was serving with the Prussians, 'and everyone in this part of Germany burns with the same desire; I expect everything from the spirit of enthusiasm which pervades this part of the Empire.' But he goes on to deplore the quarrels between the Allies: 'I pity Schwartzenberg from the bottom of my soul.'

At Lutzen (or Grossgorschen) ten miles south-west of Leipzig on May 1st Ney encountered Wittgenstein, and a battle was fought which resulted in heavy losses on both sides. In Paris the *Te Deum* was sung for a great victory: and the Bulletin of May 2nd said that during the twenty years that he had commanded French troops the Emperor had never seen such bravery or devotion as that of his young recruits. But the Allies retired unmolested to Dresden. Napoleon attacked them again at Bautzen (or Wurschen), thirty miles east of Dresden, on May 20th: another costly and indecisive victory.

Ten days later, unable to press his advantage, and believing that time was on his side, he accepted an offer of the Austrians to mediate for a Franco-Russian armistice; and this was concluded at Plasnitz on June 4th. It was originally meant to last till August 1st, but was later extended to August 10th. 'This armistice (he explained) halts the tide of my victories: but I have decided in favour of it for two reasons—my lack of cavalry, which prevents my striking decisive blows, and the hostile attitude of Austria.' He hoped during the armistice to reinforce his cavalry, and to place armies in positions (both in Italy and Germany) from which they could prevent an Austrian declaration of war.

During the armistice Napoleon increased his forces to some 400,000 men, including 12,000 of the Old Guard from Spain; but the bulk of his reinforcements were untrained conscripts called up before their time. True, not much training was needed to hold a musket by the right end and to discharge it at an enemy 150 yards away; but these young troops had not the physique or the experience to march and fight like veterans. And meanwhile his enemies were reinforcing and regrouping for the next campaign, and could put, perhaps, half a million men in the field. Above all, the diplomatists were at work, and two new decisive forces—Austria and England—entered the field against him. Hitherto he had counted on the friendly neutrality of Francis, and on George III's not interfering in the diplomatic exchanges of the continent. But now Metternich and Castlereagh, more formidable enemies than Blücher or Bernadotte, were to direct the blows and dictate the terms of the Fourth Coalition.

Neither of them was pledged to Napoleon's deposition: Metternich, with his eye on Poland, Saxony, and the Balkans, was more afraid of Russian and Prussian aggrandizement than of a French *revanche*. Castlereagh was prepared for almost any settlement which would enable Great Britain to contract out of continental affairs. They both aimed at a balance of power, a European settlement which would leave no clear predominance, create no new demands, offer no temptations to another world-conquest. Their influence—Austria's army, England's gold—would be thrown into the balance not only against a French revival, but also against the natural but selfish desires of Russia and Prussia for compensation and revenge.

Up to the end of May Napoleon seems to have believed that Austria would not intervene. But at Reichenbach on June 24th Metternich, following up approaches he had already made to Russia and Prussia, persuaded Alexander and Frederick-William to sign a treaty by which the three allies were to present an ultimatum to Napoleon: if he did not accept it, Austria would declare war. The four conditions were that he should surrender the Duchy of Warsaw (to Russia), consent to the restoration of Prussia, cede Illyria to Austria, and restore the independence of the Hanseatic towns and parts of north Germany. Seeing the actual condition of affairs, one might think these terms generous and tempting. But Metternich knew Napoleon too well to suppose that he would readily surrender an inch of territory, least of all to a threat from a professing ally whom he had constantly defeated in the field. So when he accepted an invitation to Dresden it was less in the hope that the terms of Reichenbach might be accepted than in the confidence that they would be rejected, and that their rejection would show the world that the Allies were forced to go on fighting, not France, but Napoleon.

The famous interview in the Marcolini palace at Dresden on June 26th has come down to history in two accounts. Because that recorded in Metternich's *Memoirs* is more circumstantial and dramatic, it does not follow that it is truer than the 'official' version given in Fain's *Manuscrit de 1813*; fortunately both agree on the essential point that Napoleon refused to make any concessions except perhaps in Illyria, but that he consented to the calling of a conference at Prague. The conference sat from July 12th to August 12th; but nothing was done. Napoleon would make no concessions, preferring as ever, the appeal to arms: England had signed a subsidy agreement with Russia and Prussia (June 14th), and promised similar help to Austria if she declared war: the news of Vittoria (June 21st) stiffened the backs of the allied generals. On August 12th Metternich decided that Austria's 'zero hour' had come, and Francis for the third time in eight years threw his armies against Napoleon.

At Trachenberg on July 12th a meeting of allied leaders had already settled a plan of campaign. There were to be three armies of mixed nationality: in Prussia under Bernadotte 125,000 men, in Silesia under Blücher 104,000 men, and in Bohemia under Schwartzenberg, accompanied by the three allied sovereigns, the main army of 244,000 men. It was determined not to risk a general engagement with Napoleon in person, but to turn his strategy against himself by defeating his forces in detail.

During the first fortnight of the autumn campaign, between August 23rd and September 6th, Napoleon established himself successfully at Dresden, but suffered a series of defeats on the edge of his now semicircular front: at Grossbeeren and Hagelberg in the north, at Katzbach in the east, and at Kulm in the south. His forces were terribly reduced, too, by sickness: already on July 3rd he was ordering accommodations at various centres for 24,000 sick men and 11,000 convalescents: 30,000 more were to be lost by a typhus epidemic during the retreat.

The Allies now closed in on him, aiming to outflank Dresden on the north (Blücher) and south (Schwartzenberg); and this manœuvre was so successful that the French had to retreat on Leipzig, which had only been prepared for local defence against Cossack raids, and where they were almost surrounded. The second and decisive struggle began with Napoleon's resolve to make his final stand here (October 14th). On October 16th the 'Battle of the Nations' opened, and fighting went on for three days. On the 18th the Saxons went over to the allies, Bernadotte's army came into action, and the rout began. On the 19th the French streamed westwards through the town, only to find the gates hopelessly congested, and the Lindeman bridge blown up too soon. The Pleisse was a second Beresina. As before, Napoleon and the Old Guard crossed safely, and led the retreat. But a fifth part of the army (chiefly foreign troops), with thirty generals and most of the guns and transport, remained behind. The Poles were forced to surrender. The Italians and Germans deserted to the Allies.

At Hanau on October 30th a retreating action against the Bavarians, who had joined the enemy by the treaty of Ried three weeks before, made it possible for what was left of the French army—some 40,000 men—to cross the Rhine. On November 9th Napoleon re-entered the palace of Saint-Cloud. For the second time within twelve months he had abandoned an area twice the size of France and lost an army of close on half a million men.

This time he could not blame the country, or the climate, or the misconduct of his foreign troops. He had been outnumbered: but he had also been outmarched and outmanœuvred. He had relied on the patriotic and personal loyalty of French fighting for the glory of their Empire. It had been matched and worsted by the patriotism of Germans, Russians, and Swedes fighting a *Befreiungskrieg*—a war for the liberation of Europe.[2]

5

The Empire was now breaking up, under outward pressure and inward discontent, into a hundred fragments. The Grand Duchy of Warsaw was in Russian hands, and must pay court to an eastern instead of a western liberator. Saxony once more fell to Prussia, which would not let it go. One after another, dynastic scruples fighting in vain against public demands, the states of the Confederation came over to the allied cause: Bavaria, Würtemberg, Baden, Hesse, Frankfort. Further north, Westphalia and Berg, which had felt the full impact of Imperial exploitation, put to flight their French rulers, and turned their forces towards the Rhine.

The cautious Dutchmen waited for their country to be invaded by Bülow with part of Bernadotte's army; and it was not till a week after his return to Paris that Napoleon heard of the revolt of Amsterdam, the flight of Lebrun, and the loss of the country which was the key of the Continental system. Belgium, intensely Catholic and half French, still offered a barrier and a battle-field. Switzerland valued her dependence on Napoleon so long as it spelt neutrality. Fouché had abandoned Illyria, and taken refuge at Venice. Since Vittoria (June 21st) the French armies in Spain had been streaming back across the Pyrenees: the whole peninsula was lost irretrievably. Only in Italy was Eugène able to stand with a considerable army on the line of the Adige. But Murat was already scheming to exploit the French defeat by conquering all Italy from Naples to the Po, if not to the Alps, and saving, out of the wreck of the Napoleonic empire—was it for France, or for himself?—that United Italy which Napoleon had dreaded, though it was the consequence of his designs.

The flood of French occupation had thus flowed back from the continent, all the way from Königsberg and Cadiz, and from the Moskva to the Rhine: but a number of stranded garrisons (over 200,000 men in all) still held out: Dresden till November 11th, Torgau till December 26th, Stettin till November 30th, Danzig till December 2nd, Zamosk till November 22nd, Modlin till December 1st, and Magdeburg till May 6th, 1814. Hamburg (where Davout had 100,000 men) gave itself up undefeated to Louis XVIII after the Restoration.

6

Napoleon spent eleven weeks at Saint-Cloud and the Tuileries between the end of the retreat from Germany and the opening of the campaign for the defence of the Rhine (January 25th). It was a bitterly cold winter. The Thames was frozen thick at London Bridge, and as Castlereagh drove from the Hague to Frankfort his carriage windows were 'covered with frost which no sun could dissolve.' But the frost which bound the Seine and covered the windows of the Tuileries was of a different and deeper kind. It came from a winter of discontent, almost of despair.

How desperate the financial situation had become can be judged from a letter from Napoleon to Mollien on November 3rd, in which he proposes means for raising, by increased taxation, direct and indirect, and by confiscating all the *octrois* in the country, an additional £25 millions. He still spoke of victory as certain. Yet, whatever way he looked at it, the position was far worse than it had been a year ago. The army that he had lost in the field at Lutzen, Bautzen and Leipzig, the army that had wasted away by disease in Saxon hospitals and on the banks of the Rhine, was a French army, drawn with difficulty from a country which after twenty years of war was just beginning to feel the full weight of conscription. Napoleon had already, in August, raised 30,000 men from those hitherto exempted in the call-up of classes from 1808 to 1814 to replace his veterans in Spain; and in October another 120,000 from the same source. He would now call up, by anticipation, the class of 1815 (the usual quota should yield 160,000 boys), as well as 150,000 spread over classes as far back as 1803, and another 40,000 squeezed from the 1808-14 contingents. There might be other expedients, such as the *Guides d'Honneur* that were raised by the prefects for ceremonial occasions in provincial towns. But there was too little time to carry out all these plans; none of them yielded as many men as was expected—they never did. Last year many of the recruits had gone to the front untrained and ill-equipped; and many were killed in battle still wearing civilian dress. It was even more difficult now to find uniforms and arms. The officers, especially of the higher command, were sick of war, and uncertain of victory. Yet in the rank and file of the army disloyalty was countered by the thought that France was being invaded, and that, for the first time since 1792, French soldiers were fighting against the 'Kings' of old Europe in defence of the 'cottages' of the new Republic.

But what support had the army amongst the people? A study of the reports and correspondence of the commissioners whom Napoleon sent round the country at this time (they were distinguished men, whose evidence cannot be gainsaid, such as Roederer, Ganteaume, Caffarelli, Monge, Chaptal) shows that public spirit in France had slipped back, during the last few years, into the insecurity and disillusionment of the Directory. Only in the frontier provinces, as might have been foreseen from the experiences of the Revolution, was there still a warlike temper. Elsewhere people asked only for peace.

Yet it was a moment at which, if he had not been inhibited by ten years of camp life and court etiquette, Napoleon might have made himself the First Citizen of a French Republic, and have led such a popular rising as would have made it impossible for any invader to subdue or hold down the country. But he could not do it. The *levée en masse* which he tried to initiate in the eastern departments in the early months of 1814, to supply *corps francs* and to carry on guerrilla warfare on the flanks and rear of the invaders, was made unpopular by its connection with professional soldiers and imperial *commissaires*; in some districts it was sabotaged by the nonjuror or royalist clergy; it remained unspontaneous, ineffective.

Thus it was that, a professional soldier to the end, Napoleon led a military forlorn hope against immense odds, and prolonged a useless struggle beyond expectation, whilst French citizens, who might have been defending the country-side, as the Spaniards had done, or the Tyrolese, hid themselves from the recruiting sergeant, refused to pay taxes, and looked on sullenly at foreign troops marching through their streets and occupying their *hôtels-de-ville*. Only where atrocities had been committed by the invaders the country people might waylay a few Cossack stragglers, cut their throats and thrust their bodies down the village well.

One more attempt at accommodation was made, and failed. Just when Napoleon returned to Paris, the French Minister at Weimar, Saint-Aignan, arrived at Frankfort. Metternich, playing out of the same hand as at Prague, persuaded Nesselrode and Aberdeen, the Russian and British representatives (November 9th), to agree to his being sent to Caulaincourt with proposals to treat on the basis of what came to be called the Declaration of Frankfort. The essential paragraph of this document (December 1st) was: 'The Allied Powers are not making war on France, but against that much advertised predominance (*prépondérance hautement annoncée*) which, unhappily for Europe and France, the Emperor Napoleon has for a long time exercised beyond the frontiers of his Empire . . . The Powers are still willing to recognize an extension of French territory which the country never knew under its kings (*Les puissances confirment à l'empire français une étendue de territoire que n'a jamais connue la France sous ses rois*).' But they will not lay down their arms until they have secured a 'fair balance of powers (*juste équilibre*) in Europe.'

If words meant what they should mean, this was an offer to make peace on the basis of the 'natural frontiers' of France, i.e. to recognize the conquest of Belgium by the revolutionary armies of 1793, and to include this country within the frontier of the Rhine. But if so, why not say so, unless (as Napoleon might well suspect) the object was to start negotiations on an ambiguous formula, a formula which might enable Metternich either to save Napoleon or to destroy him? For if Napoleon accepted this offer outright, Austria would be spared another campaign, and Russia deprived of another triumph; whereas, if he refused it, he could be accused before all Europe of prolonging an unnecessary war. Metternich himself half hoped that Napoleon would accept; but he was more than half certain that he would refuse.

Since the breakdown of the Prague conference Napoleon had suspected any offer from Austria. He wanted, he declared on August 17th, 'a congress of all the powers, great and small, to discuss everything'; and he did not mind how long this might take. The fighting need not stop, any more than it did during the peace conferences of the mid-eighteenth century. But if it were still possible to treat on a firm offer of the 'natural' rather than the 'ancient' frontiers, and thus to retain Belgium and Antwerp (not to mention Savoy and Nice), it would be madness to refuse outright. Unfortunately, as at Prague, he delayed his answer and missed his opportunity. The letter 'dictated by His Majesty to be written by Caulaincourt to Metternich,' and accompanied by a private note from Besnardière saying, 'The point His Majesty has most insisted upon, *and has most often repeated*, is the necessity of France keeping her natural frontiers. That, he tells me, is a condition *sine qua non*'—this letter was not written till January 16th, a month too late.

By the time Napoleon's answer arrived, both Britain and Russia had disowned Metternich's terms: Britain because Holland was now liberated, and she could not allow French control of the Belgian ports; and Russia because the Tsar was determined to dictate terms of peace from Paris. Castlereagh, as soon as he heard of Metternich's proposals, had written to Aberdeen, saying, 'This nation is likely to view with disfavour any peace which does not confine France within her ancient limits . . . I must particularly entreat you to keep your attention upon Antwerp. The destruction of that arsenal is essential to our safety. To leave it in the hands of France is little short of imposing upon Great Britain the charge of a perpetual war establishment.' The Cabinet gave approval to this view by sending Castlereagh himself to replace Aberdeen. His arrival at Châtillon in the third week of January stiffened, with the inherent stiffness of an unright character and a forthright policy, the Allied attitude against Napoleon.

But the Emperor still had hopes of using Metternich's fear of Russia to secure better terms. In a flattering letter on January 16th he proposed an armistice—and without attaching any conditions to it; but when the armistice was accepted (January 19th), he added that it could lead to peace only on the 'natural frontiers' basis. This again came too late. Castlereagh was already on his way to Basle with the declaration of the British cabinet, and with a free hand to secure its acceptance by what means he could. This policy was embodied in the so-called 'Langres protocol' of January 29th, and formed the basis of six weeks' futile discussions at the Châtillon conference (February 1st-March 12th): futile, because they were conducted to the sound of gunfire, and every throw of the military dice meant a change of position on the diplomatic board; futile, because the Allied leaders were not really agreed on their terms either for the surrender of France or for the settlement of Europe; futile also because Caulaincourt, whose embarrassments at Châtillon cannot but be pitied, could never induce Napoleon to consider any peace proposals promptly or seriously so long as there remained a chance of dividing and defeating his enemies in the field.

At a moment of Allied success on February 5th, Caulaincourt had been given *carte blanche* to do his best to save Paris, and to prevent a battle. He had offered the 'ancient frontiers,' and the Allies might have accepted them. But the French victories at Montmirail and Montmoreau a few days later caused such confusion in the Allied counsels at Troyes that Napoleon was encouraged to disown Caulaincourt's *démarche* (February 17th), and to forbid him to sign anything in future without authorization. 'I would rather lose Paris,' he wrote, 'I would rather see the Bourbons in France on reasonable terms, than accept the infamous proposals you send me.' To his brother Joseph he expressed himself even more frankly: 'If I had signed peace on the ancient frontiers basis (he said) I should have declared war again two years later, and should have told the nation that it was not a peace I had signed, but a capitulation.'

By March 1st the Allies were ready to advance again, strengthened by Castlereagh's Treaty of Chaumont, which defined their territorial claims, bound them in a twenty years' Grand Alliance, and guaranteed British subsidies. A week later (March 8th) Metternich offered Napoleon a last opportunity to avoid a *guerre à extinction*. In reply (March 17th)—he had just heard of Wellington's capture of Bordeaux—the Emperor authorized Caulaincourt to make any concessions that would keep the negotiations open, and to find out what was really the Allies' ultimatum; but all that he offered was to consider the independence of Belgium under a French prince, and some addition to the territories of Holland—still without any mention of Antwerp.

If this were Napoleon's ultimatum, Metternich answered, peace was impossible; and on March 19th the Conference of Châtillon closed its last session with a statement that Napoleon's failure to reply by March 10th to the Allies' proposals of February 17th must be taken as a refusal to treat on that basis; that Caulaincourt's counter-proposals came too late; that Britain's willingness to return the French colonies justified her refusal to let France retain Antwerp (the name was not mentioned); and that the blame for the failure of the Conference rested on Napoleon.

If any verdict is to be passed on the relative responsibility for the breakdown of these negotiations, perhaps Caulaincourt's is the fairest. 'I was given a little more freedom (he means during the last stages of the Congress), but not enough to make peace, even supposing (which was very doubtful) that the plenipotentiaries themselves still wanted it. The Emperor did not see, or rather would not see, his true position. He deceived himself on every head—about the Congress, and about his own strength. He could not forget that he had once dictated to Europe, or reconcile himself to the idea of being dictated to in his turn: he could not bear having an inexorable *sine qua non* written at the foot of every article of a treaty which he had to sign at such a time on such a day.'[3]

7

On the day the Congress closed (March 19th) Napoleon began a movement intended to cut the Allies' communications north of the Marne. A letter telling the Empress of this plan fell into their hands. Alexander seized the opportunity to urge an immediate march on Paris. On the 25th Marmont and Mortier at Fère-Champenoise tried in vain to stop the advance. On the 28th Paris suddenly realized the danger. Whilst Joseph tried to improvise a defence, the Council of Regency met to decide whether the Empress should or should not leave the capital—i.e. in effect, whether the Government should be dissolved. The matter was decided by a letter from the Emperor refusing to leave his wife and son at the mercy of the enemy. Next morning, the 29th, Marie-Louise set out for Rambouillet. Talleyrand spoke against this step, calculating (he said afterwards) that the Empress would act against his advice. Fouché, who arrived too late to do anything, claimed that he would have saved the Council, and set up a National Regency for the defence of Paris. But it was not to be. On March

30th there was fighting in the suburbs. At 2 a.m. on the 31st Marmont, as commander of the defence, signed the capitulation of Paris—a city that had never learnt how to defend itself.

That it had taken the Allies so long to reach Paris was due to the skill with which Napoleon had made use of his central position east of the city, in country which he knew well, where there were plenty of roads and bridges, and in which his troops could always find food, shelter and information. From this point of vantage he had struck out at the enemy columns converging from Belgium, Lorraine, and the Langres plateau, one by one. But no amount of skill could do more than postpone defeat. Instead of the admiration with which they have described Napoleon's military movements during the 'defence of Paris,' historians might better have called attention to the obstinacy which, by refusing to treat, had made such a course necessary, and imposed useless sufferings on a misguided people.

Napoleon was hurrying towards Paris when, at 6 a.m. on the 31st, he heard of its fall. He returned to Fontainebleau, still talking of peace and thinking of war. Caulaincourt was to negotiate for peace: Berthier was to mobilize such troops as could still be counted upon to fight again. But his fate was already being determined: Providence had deserted him for the Allies.

When Marie-Louise abandoned Paris on March 29th, or again when Marmont capitulated on the 31st, Talleyrand might have been expected to leave the capital. But he stayed behind. Now at last his opportunity had come to free France from the tyranny of Napoleon. His reputation for bribery and intrigue was already, and has since remained, so bad that he has received little credit for a policy which, whatever its motives, was true to the best interests of his country. On the morning of the 31st, together with Nesselrode and Dalberg, representing the Allies, and his secretary de Laborie, he drafted a Declaration, which was approved by Alexander and published the same night. This announced that the Allies had occupied Paris, and that they would refuse to treat with Napoleon or any of his family, but that they would recognize the integrity of pre-revolutionary France: 'they may even go further (added the Tsar), for it will always be their principle, for the happiness of Europe, to keep France great and strong': so the terms of the Declaration of Frankfurt might still be attainable.

At midday the Allied troops, led by Alexander, Frederick-William, and Schwartzenberg, made their formal entry into Paris. The Tsar, upon a rumour that the Elysée was mined, took up his residence in Talleyrand's house; and there a Council authorized the Declaration, and discussed the next step. Here Talleyrand's advice was conclusive. France, he insisted, would never tolerate another Bonapartist regime, nor a sovereign im-

posed by a foreign power: there was nothing for it but to recall the
Bourbons, the only legitimate dynasty, in the person of Louis XVIII.
When at last a hearing was given to Caulaincourt, who had posted from
Fontainebleau, it was to turn down decisively Napoleon's proposal to
abdicate in favour of his son, the King of Rome, especially as news had
just come that Marmont's troops had declared for the Allies. But it was
agreed that he might be allowed to retire to the sovereignty of the Island
of Elba. The business of the day thus disposed of, the two sovereigns
dined together, and went to the Opera, where they were received with
acclamation, and listened to a song written in honour of their conquest
of Paris: *Vive Alexandre, Vive ce roi des rois! Vive Guillaume, et ses
guerriers vaillants!*

The Senators, summoned to meet next afternoon at the Luxembourg,
appointed a Provisional Government consisting of Talleyrand, Beurnonville, Jaucourt, Dalberg, and Montesquiou: the wits said that four of the
five were Talleyrand's habitual whist party: his secretary de Laborie completed the circle. This Provisional Government issued next day (April 1st)
an Address to the army absolving it from allegiance to Napoleon (*Vous
n'êtes plus les soldats de Napoléon: le Sénat et la France entière vous
dégagent de vos serments*).

On the 3rd a Provisional Ministry was set up, and Lebrun was commissioned to draft a Constitution: that of 1791, perhaps, with the addition
of a Senate? On the 6th his document was ready: the only clause that
interested the public was that which said: 'The French people freely
summons to the throne Louis-Stanislav-Xavier de France, brother of the
last King, and, after him, the other members of the house of Bourbon in
the old order.'

On the same day Napoleon at Fontainebleau, finding that none of his
marshals would take part in any further resistance, signed an uncondi-
tional abdication. On Easter Sunday, the 10th, in the Place de la Concorde,
on the site of the guillotine at which Louis XVI and Marie-Antoinette
had perished, an altar was set up, a *Te Deum* sung in the presence of the
two kings, and the Catholic crowd blessed by priests of the Orthodox
church. On the 11th the Treaty of Fontainebleau settled the future of the
Bonaparte family. The same day the Comte d'Artois, as *lieutenant-général
du royaume*, in the absence of his brother Louis XVIII, made a ceremonial entry into Paris.

8

Within a short time Paris was flooded with inquisitive Englishmen in
numbers such as had not been seen since 1802. Whilst a good proportion
of those who had been interned at Verdun and elsewhere hurried home,
some five hundred new visitors crossed the Channel. 'It might be said,'

wrote the enthusiastic and observant Haydon, 'that when we arrived at Paris the ashes of Napoleon's last fire were hardly cool: the last candle by which he had read hardly extinguished; the very book he had last read was to be seen turned down where he left it . . . We could be admitted to his palaces, to his bedroom; we could see the table he had leaned upon and inked, the chairs which he had sat upon and cut, the bell-ropes he had pulled, the servants who had served him.

'In the middle of the day the Rue St. Honoré was the most wonderful sight. Don Cossack chiefs loosely clothed and moving as their horses moved with all the bendings of their bodies visible at every motion—the half-clothed savage Cossack horseman, his belt stuck full of pistols and watches and hatchets, crouched upon a little ragged-maned, dirty-looking, ill-bred, half-white, shaggy pony—the Russian Imperial guardsman, pinched in at the waist like a wasp, striding along like a giant, with an air of victory that made every Frenchman curse within his teeth as he passed him—the English officer, with his boyish face and broad shoulders —the heavy Austrian—the natty Prussian—and now and then a Bashkir Tartar, in the ancient Phrygian cap, with bow and arrows and chain armour, gazing about from his horse in the midst of black-eyed *grisettes*, Jews, Turks and Christians from all countries in Europe and Asia. It was a pageant that kept one staring, musing and bewildered from morning to night.'

Haydon noticed, alongside a 'popular hatred and dread of England,' the 'extraordinary ignorance of the French people as to their own political position and that of other nations'—Napoleon's censorship had kept them 'so brutishly vacant.' Yet 'the French had a more martial air than the English'— 'there was scarcely a driver of a *fiacre*, a waiter at a *café*, or a man in middle life, who had not been in a battle, served in a campaign, or been wounded by a shot.' Such was the result of twelve years' military dictatorship.

And what of that eastern city, a blackened ruin, whose destruction had destroyed its conqueror? When Alexander revisited Moscow in 1816 a beginning had been made in the reconstruction of its 6000 burnt-out buildings. In later years visitors could count in front of the Arsenal 875 guns captured in the campaign of 1812, half of them French, and most with the Imperial 'N' on the breach; outside the Borovitski gate, by which Napoleon entered and left the Kremlin, rose the magnificent new cathedral of Our Saviour, built to commemorate the deliverance of Russia from the invader.[4]

XIV

ELBA AND WATERLOO

(1814-1815)

I

'HALLELUJAH!' wrote the Duke of Cumberland to the Prince Regent (rather incoherently) when he heard of Napoleon's abdication: 'thank God you have succeeded now in all your endeavours, and you in England have gained the day, for she alone never did recognize that wretch, and I think the baseness he has shown at the end proves him to be baser than any man that ever has existed. France must feel itself humbled at having submitted so long to the despotism of such a man; had he fallen gloriously in battle, had he rushed when he saw he could do nothing to the cannon's mouth, one might have said he was great in his end, but to submit tamely and ask for his treasure proves a soul as mean in his misfortune at it was cruel in prosperity.'

The abdication of April 6th, 1814, was the real end of Napoleon's career. For ten months he was to be sovereign of Elba; for four months Emperor of the French again, but at home an embarrassment, and abroad an outlaw. For a second time he suffered the humiliation of defeat and deposition. He survived for nearly six years more, and died a prisoner and an exile. But this was no longer the same man. In Elba the pigmy ruler of a miniature state; in France playing a part which he had not rehearsed, and in which he could never succeed; at St. Helena transforming history into legend—the real Napoleon had died in 1814; it was his shadow which returned to Paris in 1815; his ghost in 1840.

The Treaty of Fontainebleau, signed on April 12th by the representatives of Russia, Austria, Prussia, and France (but not England), provided for the future of the deposed Bonapartes. Napoleon and Marie-Louise might still call themselves Emperor and Empress; his mother, his brothers and sisters, and their children remained Princes and Princesses. For Napoleon the island of Elba was to 'form during his lifetime a separate principality which he shall possess in full sovereignty and property.' He was to receive from the French Government a pension of two million francs

(£100,000) a year. He was given a detachment of the Guard to escort him to Saint-Tropez, and a corvette to carry him to Elba: and this vessel was to remain in his possession. He could take with him, as bodyguard, 400 officers and men. The Powers even undertook that the Elban flag (which had still to be designed) should be respected by the Barbary pirates. Marie-Louise was given the Duchy of Parma-Guastalla, with reversion to the 'King of Rome': Joséphine, Eugène and other members of the Beauharnais family were provided for.

To a generation which remembers 1918 and 1945 such treatment of a dictator whose armies had overrun Europe for ten years may seem fantastically generous. It needs historical imagination to put oneself in the position of sovereigns and statesmen to whom the acquisition of one another's territories, without leave asked of their inhabitants, needed no apology; to whom war was still, in spite of modified conscription, a professional affair, with more than a dash of romance in it; and in which the sufferings of the civilian population were local and incidental. There was little that Napoleon had done which would not have been thought excusable if he had been a Bourbon or a Habsburg. His armies had committed no atrocities which had not been equalled by Russian guerrillas, or even, under occasional provocation, by British soldiers in Spain. There were no recognized or enforceable rules for the treatment of wounded men or prisoners. If the shooting of civilians, the burning of villages, and the taking of hostages were deplored as evidence of a more ruthless method of war introduced since the French Revolution, there was no international tribunal at whose feet the Allies could throw down their clothes before stoning the offender.

Yet it was of immense significance for the future that a Quadruple Alliance of states had undertaken to deal with the Napoleonic menace, and that a dynasty had been deposed, however considerately, whose continuance in power threatened the peace of Europe. Napoleon's policy in Spain and Germany had cheapened the divine right of kingship. Now his own punishment, which that policy had brought upon him, became a warning to all heads of states, divine or democratic. An idea that 1814 laid down, and 1815 confirmed, gradually became a conviction of civilized society: its results were seen in 1870, in 1918, in 1945: and it will not easily be given up.

Napoleon was shrewd enough to take advantage of the Allies' generosity—though he did not trust the French Government to carry out their part of the bargain: but he was deeply humiliated and distressed. Humiliated, not by his military failure, for he never had been (he was convinced) and never could be defeated by his own fault in the field—always someone or something else was to blame: but by the suggestions the Allies made for his 'imprisonment.' True, Alexander, who admired whilst he hated, had offered him an asylum in Russia, and Castlereagh had talked of Fort St. George in the Highlands. Corsica had been spoken of, and Corfu. It was to the Tsar that he owed Elba—Elba which less charitable judges thought too near to France, and to Italy, where Eugène still had an army and Marie-Louise a Duchy. *The Times* had said that 'such a wretch' as Napoleon 'would be a disgrace to Botany Bay'; Talleyrand would have sent him to the Azores; and Metternich would have liked to see him as far away as that remote Atlantic island, St. Helena.

Yes; there were possibilities at Elba which Napoleon had in mind when he stipulated in his peace proposals of March 15th to surrender all sovereignty beyond the Alps, *l'île d'Elbe exceptée*. It was an island, like Corsica; its inhabitants could be organized, ruled, and made to pay taxes; it was within a few hours' sail of the Italian coast and a few days' of the French. Napoleon would soon be making Porto Ferrajo an island Paris, and the Casa dei Mulini a miniature Tuileries.

What distressed him during the fortnight he spent at Fontainebleau was his betrayal (as he regarded it) by those whom he had calculated to hold to his cause by interest, if not by affection. Not Talleyrand, whom he had long known to be working against him; not Murat, nor Bernadotte, whose ambitions he had reckoned with: but Marmont, who had prevented his last blow for Paris, Joseph, who had surrendered the city, and his marshals, Ney and Augereau, who had transferred their allegiance to the new government. Even his valet and his Mameluke had deserted him. Above all, Marie-Louise had been persuaded by her family to put herself and her son into Austrian hands. 'He referred to the separation from his wife and child,' says Campbell, 'and the tears actually ran down his cheeks. He continued to talk in this wild and excited style, being at times greatly affected.' Another witness who observed him at mass in the palace chapel says that he appeared 'in the most perturbed and distressed state of mind—sometimes rubbing his forehead with his hands, then stuffing part of his fingers into his mouth, and gnawing the ends of them in a most agitated and excited manner.'

More than this. Since the publication of the detailed account of the incident in Caulaincourt's *Memoirs*, it is scarcely possible to doubt that on the night of April 12th Napoleon tried to commit suicide by taking a dose of poison which he had carried with him ever since he nearly fell into Cossack hands at Malo-Jaroslavetz: it was of the same kind as that which Condorcet had taken in prison in 1794. His strong stomach rejected the dose. It is strange, as Caulaincourt himself thought, that he did not disdain such an escape from a humiliating position, for he more than once condemned suicide. As he remarked three weeks later, in a more sensible state of mind, his well-wishers would have gained nothing by his death, and his evil-wishers would have been only too pleased.[1]

2

In general (it has been remarked), Napoleon was never more at his ease than when travelling. Of the journey to Elba in 1814—a week by land (April 20th-27th) and a week by sea (April 28th-May 4th)—only the second part confirms this thesis. He set out in comfort, in a sleeping-carriage (*dormeuse de voyage*) with Bertrand, the most faithful of his followers, and a procession of fourteen vehicles, escorted by detachments of the mounted Guard: a baggage train of a hundred wagons went ahead. They reckoned to cover about fifty miles a day, and to sleep at local inns: thus the night of the 20th was spent at Briare, the 21st at Nevers, the 22nd at Roanne; when he stopped, Napoleon would send for the local authorities, and inquire about the state of public opinion in the district.

As far as Nevers he was received with loyal demonstrations; but at Moulins, in the next department, white cockades were being worn, and there were cries of *Vive le roi Louis XVIII!* After that experience he slept in his carriage, passing through Lyon and Vienne by night. But worse was to follow. When he crossed the border into Provence, Napoleon entered a district which had suffered from the depredations of the *armée du Midi*, and whose people were celebrating the restoration of the Bourbons. At Donzière (April 24th) there were cries of *À bas le tyran! A bas le boucher de nos enfans!* At Avignon (writes Campbell), 'the carriages which preceded us by one day were stopped, and the eagles defaced: if Napoleon had been there, he would have been destroyed.' At Orgon he was forced to see himself hanged and shot in effigy, with more cries of *Vive le roi!* and *Mort au tyran!* Aix on the 26th was passed by night. At St. Maximin and Brignoles the travellers were protected by the local authorities. It was not till they reached Le Luc that evening that all danger of assault and perhaps assassination was over.

It is not necessary to believe that a plot to waylay and kill Napoleon had been hatched by royalists in Paris; the evidence rather suggests spontaneous local demonstrations, never amounting to attempted murder. But this was enough to rouse Napoleon's natural fear of mob violence—a fear just as real as his soldier's courage in the field—and this fear took surprising forms. After the experience at Orgon he disguised himself as an Austrian officer, and rode ahead, galloping through two villages where trouble might be expected. At the inn at La Calade 'he trembled at the least sound, and changed colour,' and when he left, disguised himself again in clothes borrowed from the Russian and German Commissioners, who travelled with him, and who were surprised by his lack of courage and self-control.

Near Valence on April 24th Napoleon had an embarrassed meeting with Marshal Augereau, in command of the *armée du Midi*—Augereau who had issued a proclamation to his troops, welcoming the end of the 'tyrannical yoke' of Napoleon, and releasing them from allegiance to 'a man who, after immolating millions to his cruel ambition, did not know how to die as a soldier.' 'Let us hoist the genuinely French flag,' he had exhorted them, 'and banish every symbol of a revolution which has now been abolished.' Napoleon could not abide a traitor; but he spoke politely, almost humbly, to a soldier whose services at Castiglione eighteen years ago he never forgot.

On the night of April 21st A.-C. Thibaudeau, the prefect of Bouches-du-Rhône, had been driven from Marseille by an outbreak due to the economic depression of the blockade, the burden of conscription, and the news of the fall of Paris. Whilst still within sight of the port he had seen its citizens (as he thought) already exchanging friendly signals with English cruisers in the bay: it was the story of Toulon over again. At Nîmes, too, he found all the people in the streets, sporting white cockades, and carrying white banners: a royalist reaction was in full swing. As his journey progressed, he was obliged to wear now the royalist and now the republican colours according to whether foreign or French troops were in control.

Finding himself at Nevers on the same night as the ex-Emperor—'both of us fallen, but his a worse fall than mine: he an Emperor, but proscribed, and a prisoner: I an unhappy and obscure traveller, but a free man'—Thibaudeau did not call on Napoleon, who was no great friend of his, but watched him pass the inn when his carriage set out next day: 'The people shouted *Vive l'Empereur!* He looked serious, indeed severe, and seemed to see nobody.'

At Le Luc, on the afternoon of April 26th, Napoleon found his favourite sister Pauline: she had his good looks and his charm, and would throw herself into *l'amour* with the same wantonness that her brother threw himself into *la guerre*. She was on her way to a watering-place, but declared that she would share his exile at Elba. When he left next day he wrote a message to a M. Aune, apparently the steward in charge of the Château de Luc, thanking him for his consideration to his sister and to himself—'one who tried to make France the first country in the world, but has failed.'[2]

3

From the first days of his journey Napoleon had varied the plan prescribed by the Treaty and entrusted to the Allied Commissioners: Baron von Köller for Austria, Count Truchsess von Waldburg for Prussia, Count Shuvalov for Russia and Colonel Sir Neil Campbell for England. He would not go by the 'high road' originally selected via Auxerre and Grenoble, but insisted on the 'low road' via Roanne and Avignon: hence the dangers into which he ran. (He avoided this mistake on his return in

1815.) He would not embark at St. Tropez, but at Fréjus, partly because it was more accessible, partly because he had landed there on his providential return from Egypt in 1799. Finally, he would not sail on the ship the French government had contracted to provide for him, because he thought himself safe from insult, let alone assassination, in British hands. Campbell, therefore, went ahead from Roanne to Marseille, with a verbal message from Napoleon and a written authorization from Castlereagh 'to call upon any of His Majesty's cruisers . . . to see him safe to the island of Elba.' He arrived there at the very time when Captain Ussher of the *Undaunted*, who was cruising off shore, had seen the place illuminated on the arrival of the news from Paris (this was what Thibaudeau took for 'signals'), had sailed into the bay, and was being enthusiastically welcomed by the royalist Municipality.

Ussher, who had been hoping for just such an opportunity as Campbell now offered him, at once set sail for St. Tropez, where (it was still supposed) Napoleon would embark. Arriving off that port at 8 o'clock next morning, he found the French frigate *Dryade* and the brig *Inconstant* already there, under the Comte de Montcabrié, with orders to carry Napoleon to Elba: but almost at the same moment a messenger from Campbell came aboard to tell him that the rendezvous had been changed to Fréjus. He sailed at once, and anchored off St. Raphael, the roadstead of Fréjus, at 3:30; when the Frenchman arrived at 7 he found Napoleon's baggage already going on board the British ship.

Napoleon himself was staying at the local inn, the *Chapeau Rouge*; there, 'dressed in the regimentals of the Old Guard, and wearing the star of the Legion of Honour,' he received Ussher 'with great condescension and politeness,' and questioned him (as his way was) about his ship and the passage to Elba. In the evening they dined together, with the Commissioners; and 'he talked to us with unusual frankness about the plans for French aggrandizement which he still had in mind . . . If he had attacked England (he said) as determinedly as he had attacked the Continent he would have conquered her in two years.' He was already his old self again and Bertrand was instructed to write home for more books and for a fresh supply of presentation snuff-boxes.

The same evening Napoleon had a brusque interview with Montcabrié, whose 'rotten old brig' (*un vieux brick pourri*), he said, was a poor return to one who had given France a navy, and he would refuse to sail under the white flag of the Bourbons, 'even if they flew the tricolor in their hearts.' In the end Montcabrié sailed back to Marseille, and posted to Paris, where he was easily excused for not carrying out his orders. But the *vieux brick pourri* remained to serve as the flagship of the Elban navy, and brought Napoleon back to France ten months later.

Next evening, after a day's delay due to the Emperor's indisposition (he had eaten too much lobster at dinner), and to his hope that something might yet turn up to save him, he drove to the beach at St. Raphael, rowed out to the *Undaunted*, where he was received with a royal salute, and was accommodated in the captain's cabin. Next morning (April 29th) they were at sea, and the French coast was fading from sight.

Only two of the four commissioners accompanied Napoleon beyond Fréjus; and of those, Köller left Elba again soon after landing. Campbell had instructions from Castlereagh to convey him to the island: whether his mission ended there (he writes) was to 'depend on Bonaparte's wishes and my own management.' It was fortunate, both for Napoleon and for his biographers, that he remained. Neil (more properly Niall) Campbell, a member of a famous Scottish family, had fought in Spain under Wellington, had seen Napoleon through his telescope on the field of Bautzen, and had been wounded almost to death at La Fère-Champenoise. He was a man of experience and integrity. He accepted the task put upon him, when it was refused by Lord Burghersh, at a few days' notice, though scarcely fit to travel, from a sense of duty and lively interest. He made himself very useful to Napoleon; and left behind an intelligent and sober account of his mission. His position was difficult, for he had responsibilities without powers. He was thought to be the police-man of the Allies; but he was at Elba on sufferance, and could only see its sovereign when invited to do so. It is quite untrue to say that he 'carried out with smiling hypocrisy the part of a gaoler and a spy.' Both parties employed spies; and at most he was out-manœuvred by a more experienced hypocrite.

'The (late) Emperor of the French,' as the muster of the *Undaunted* describes him, thoroughly enjoyed his voyage to Elba. He was a good sailor. He knew more than most landsmen about ships and the way of life at sea. He was amongst personal friends (Bertrand, Drouot) whom he could trust, and professional enemies (Campbell, Ussher) who respected him. He had shaken off the depression of Fontainebleau and the fears of Provence. Throughout the voyage he 'conducted himself (says Campbell) with the greatest condescension and cordiality towards us all. He re-marked himself that he had never felt in better health, and officers of his suite observed that they had never seen him appear more at his ease.' When, on May 2nd, a contrary wind drove the *Undaunted* for shelter under the Corsican shore, 'Napoleon took great delight in examining it with his glass, and told us many anecdotes of his younger days.' When, next day, they shaped course for Elba, he was eager for a sight of it, and urged Ussher to set every stitch of canvas. 'When the man stationed at the masthead hailed the deck that Elba was right ahead, he became exceedingly impatient, went forward to the forecastle, and as soon as the land could be seen from the deck was very particular in inquiring what colours were flying on the batteries.'

This was an all-important point. There was no certainty that Napoleon's new kingdom would be available for his possession. The French officer in charge of the island, General Dalesme, had been without news of the outside world for some weeks, until, on April 27th, two British ships appeared off Porto-Ferrajo, informed him of the abdication of Napoleon, and summoned him to surrender the island, not to Louis XVIII, but to George III. If he had done so—and his Italian garrison was in a state of mutiny—Napoleon might have been exiled elsewhere. But he refused; the British ships sailed away; and he hoisted the Bourbon flag only forty-eight hours before the arrival of the *Undaunted*.[3]

4

The first act of the new sovereign of Elba was to send General Drouot ashore with a letter to General Dalesme, saying that 'circumstances had led him to renounce the throne of France,' but that he had 'kept for himself the sovereignty of the island of Elba . . . with the consent of the Powers.' Dalesme must, therefore, hand over to Drouot 'the said island, with its stores of munitions and food, and such properties as belong to My imperial domain,' and 'make known to the inhabitants this new state of affairs, and the choice I have made of their island for My residence, on the ground of the mildness of their manners and the clemency of their climate. They will be (he ended) the constant object of My liveliest interest.'

These sentiments were repeated at greater length to a deputation of the inhabitants who boarded the *Undaunted* a little later. 'He gave a short narrative of the misfortunes of France . . . When he spoke of the circumstances which had robbed him of victory his speech became really animated. His sentiments burned with patriotism. He declared his intention of devoting himself henceforth to the happiness of the people of Elba.' His landing next day coincided with Louis XVIII's official entry into Paris.

In Lieutenant Smith's picture of the landing the Elban flag is shown flying for the first time from the forts of Porto-Ferrajo and from the stern of Napoleon's barge. When he left Fréjus no one knew what it might be. He invented it on the voyage, choosing, from a book of Tuscan flags, one that he fancied with a red band on a white ground, and adding to it (with the help of the ship's tailor) three bees, an emblem that he had chosen for his new kingdom because it was associated with the pre-Bourbon dynasty of Childeric the father of Clovis.

Porto-Ferrajo means 'Iron-port'; and, long before he came in sight of the capital of the island, Napoleon's eye must have been struck by the green and tawny colouring of its encircling hills, which had been valued since Roman times for their iron ore. The island was about the same size as Malta, eighteen miles from east to west, and of almost identical area, but rising steeply to a rocky ridge four times as high (Monte Capanne, almost equals Snowdon), indented with landlocked bays, and providing, especially on the south-east coast, natural sun-traps where almost anything —grapes, olives, oranges, pomegranates—could be cultivated.

A few weeks after landing (June 24th) Napoleon drew up a *Budget des domaines* in which he put down the profits of the mines as £18,000 a year, saltpans, £1000, and tunny-fisheries, £1400; the toal revenue of his new kingdom would be £20,400; its outgoings he put at £5500. But this was optimistic. His estimate of revenue for 1815, after adding £4350 for taxes and £500 for sundries, still amounted to only £22,350; and the paltry sum for taxes must be extracted from poor and unwilling peasants at the cost of rioting (at Capoliveri, November 16th) which had to be put down by the military, but without the shooting and burning of other days.

The iron-mines had since 1809 been under the management of Pons de l'Hérault, a Jacobin of the Left (had he not changed his Christian names to 'Marat Lepelletier'?) and the most important civilian on the island. The profits of their working had hitherto gone to the funds of Napoleon's Legion of Honour: but he had lost interest in that now, and claimed them as part of his Elban revenue. Pons, who had no liking for dictators, refused to give them up; until he arranged with the French government to have a corresponding sum deducted from the annuity which it had promised to pay to Napoleon but which he never received. Thereafter they lived on the friendly terms which are reflected in Pons's *Souvenirs*.

5

The day-by-day diary of Napoleon's nine months' regime at Elba can best be read in the 114 letters and documents printed in the official correspondence, and the 182 added in Pélissier's *Registre*. They show the same Imperial pattern as the huge canvas of 1810, but in miniature; as though the business of Buckingham Palace, the Houses of Parliament, and White-hall were suddenly to shrink to the local affairs of the Isle of Wight. There is the same multiplication of departments and offices: a *directeur des domaines*, an *ingénieur des ponts et chaussées*, a *grand maréchal du palais*, a *commandant des écuries et des canots*, a *commandant de la maison*, a *garde des citernes de Porto-Ferrajo*, and so on. There is the same preoccupation with military matters: barracks and latrines for 600 men of the Guard, the garrisoning and fortifying of the little island of Pianosa ('Flatholm' in the Bristol Channel), the strengthening of the forts (but they had no guns or gunners) defending Porto-Ferrajo and Porto-Longone, accommodation for officers, and, if necessary, the shooting of deserters: whilst he doubles the size of his army by adding a Corsican battalion, and, later, a new Polish detachment formed of men from Eugène's disbanded army of Italy.

The Elban navy, proudly flying the Elban flag, consists of the ('rotten old') brig the *Inconstant*, the *Caroline*, a fast Maltese boat used for postal service with the mainland, two *feluccas*, *l'Abeille* and *la Mouche* ('Bee' and 'Fly') from the mines, three *canots*, a third *felucca* used to chase smugglers, and *l'Etoile*, a *chebek* used to transport grain: the whole personnel, including a crew of sixty for the brig, was 129 men. But if Decrès had been on Elba he would have been kept busy all day with orders for the repairing, arming, and equipping of these vessels: 'The provisional grant under this head will be £30, assigned as follows: For a copper compass for My cutter, £2 10s.; for cushions, tapestry, curtains, etc., £22 10s.; for greasing the *Caroline*, painting the cutters, and other necessary expenses, £5.'

Napoleon had lost nothing of his passion for palaces. The Mulini palace at Porto-Ferrajo, filled with furniture commandeered from his sister Elisa's house at Piombini, and with plate and books from Fontainebleau, was walled off from publicity landwards, and had on the seaward side a garden terrace from which Napoleon could turn his telescope on any vessel entering the bay. But soon he must add a country estate and house at San Martino, two miles out of the town, with a new road to it, a bedroom painted to look like a tent, a *salon* with a picture of two doves symbolizing his affection for the absent Empress, and an Egyptian room decorated with palms, camels and minarets, with the hopeful motto *Ubicunque felix Napoleo*; and everywhere the open fireplaces that reminded him of the winter he had spent with Marie Walewska in Poland. Nor was that all: for at Marciana, 2500 feet up on the cool northern slope of Monte Capanne, he took possession of a small hermitage, La Madonna del Monte, for a summer residence. Though more than 50 per cent of his annual expenditure still went to his army and navy, Napoleon, scrutinizing every detail, lavished large sums on these imperial residences. They fed his hunger for constant activity and his thirst for public display. And if other sovereigns went hunting, then so must he; and by walling off the Capo di Stella, a mile-long promontory on the south coast of the island, he constructed a sporting estate, a Bourbon *capitainerie*.

But it was dull, after all, being alone, in a throng of obsequious servants, and surrounded by uniformed officials who dared not sit down in his presence. He needed the easiness of family life; he missed the admiring attentions of pretty women. His sister Pauline came, as she had promised, on May 31st, but, with the capriciousness of a *malade imaginaire*, only stayed two days. It was for her return that he bought and decorated San Martino. When she came back on October 30th, it was to a round of balls, dinners and theatrical performances: the month's carnival in January-February 1815 surprised and shocked Elban society. So, in a different way, did Napoleon's attendance at an entertainment in honour of George III's birthday given on board the *Undaunted* on June 4th.

'Madame Mère,' after a short visit at the end of May, came back to stay early in August, lodging in Porto-Ferrajo, befriending Corsicans, and helping Napoleon to pay for extravagances he could not afford. But the visit that excited him most, and caused most speculation, was that of Madame Walewska and her (and his) child, a boy of four, on September 1st. She came by night, stayed only a few days at the remote La Madonna, and went away again as secretly as she had arrived. Napoleon had never advertised his amours. He did not discourage the rumour that his visitors were really the Empress Marie-Louise and the King of Rome, whom he had hoped in vain to welcome to his new kingdom. He had in fact written to her on August 9th and had tried to give it out in Paris that her arrival was expected.

There were other visitors, 'mysterious adventurers and disaffected characters from France and Italy' (says Campbell), and inquisitive Englishmen who came on the chance of seeing, and if possible interviewing, the exiled Emperor: Lord Ebrington, Major Vivian and Mr. Wildman, Lord John Russell, Captain Smith, with four friends, Mr. Vernon and Mr. Fazakerley, Mr. Darling and Mr. Murray: and several of these wrote accounts of their experiences. Napoleon was much more easy-going now than he became at St. Helena, and talked freely to his visitors, asking them the inevitable string of questions, describing his career, defending his policy, excusing his treatment of British nationals, maintaining that his invasion of England would have succeeded, professing that he had always been ready to make peace, but not upon terms humiliating to France, and seldom failing to express admiration for the British people. For, failing the conquest of England, Napoleon sometimes envisaged, in almost Churchillian terms, a *mariage politique* based on the co-operation of the French army and the British navy, and a *unité de législation politique des deux nations*.

Most of his interlocutors were surprised to find him a fat little man with a chubby face, very chatty and amiable: but Captain Smith soon noticed that 'his eye is remarkably expressive and quick; his eye and voice inspire respect, and his manner indicated great talent . . . My companions were unanimous (he ends) in the opinion that he has more the appearance of a clever, crafty priest than of a hero.' (So, at St. Helena, the officers of the 66th Regiment, who interviewed Napoleon in September 1817, thought that 'his general look was more that of an obese Spanish or Portuguese friar than the hero of modern times.')

It would be a mistake to dismiss Captain Smith's impression as the delusion of a benighted Protestant. It is borne out by many portraits of the later Napoleon. Twenty years of fighting, organizing, persuading, bullying and pretending had altered his whole aspect. Long hours of office-work, even when on campaign, and of good living, even when his tastes were still simple and his meals hurried, had made him stout and sleek. Clever he had always been; crafty he had become: how else could he have survived the intrigues of the Directory, the flatteries and jealousies of the Consulate, the diplomatic entanglements of the Empire? A priest? He would have repudiated the idea: but was there not a likeness of character as well as a partnership in power between the Empire and the Church? Was not Napoleon's conviction that soldiers were superior to civilians, that it was for the government to order the life and thought of the people, and that the heart of heresy was opposition to Authority, essentially Catholic? Did he not feel, throughout his contest with the Papacy—concealing it even from himself in a cloud of words—that Pius was the only man in Europe who might defeat him with his own weapons, with a counter-claim to world-conquest backed by an international army? [4]

6

But here and now, in February 1815, his craftiness had a more immediate aim. It was in his mind to return to France, and to make one more bid for Empire. He is said to have promised, when leaving Fontainebleau, to return next spring; and the violet, the spring flower, was adopted by his adherents as an emblem of this hope. Meanwhile he must pretend to be dead to any European ambition—*Je suis homme mort*, he was fond of telling Campbell—and to be planning nothing more than the government and defence of a couple of small islands in the Mediterranean. This was all that was seen by casual visitors to Elba, all that could be inferred from the stream of Orders issued to Drouot and Bertrand, and from the elaborate budgets drawn up with Peyrusse. Still, in the middle of February 1815, he was discussing roadbuilding, hospital arrangements, and the local *biscotterie* (bakery): on the very day that he ordered repairs to the ship that was to take him to France he prescribed to Peyrusse a new form for the Elban Budget for 1815.

But people who knew him well, such as Talleyrand, Fouché and Metternich, or good observers like Campbell, were not deceived. Mariotti, the French consul at Leghorn—a Corsican whom a star of the Legion of Honour had not kept faithful to Napoleon—was only one of a series of spies in the Italian ports, who did their best to stop all communications between Elba and the continent, and to report what went on at Porto-Ferrajo. Napoleon, too, had his counter-espionage service, organized by Fesch at Rome, Bartolucci at Leghorn, and elsewhere. It proved impossible to prevent communications crossing a channel only half the width of the straits of Dover. Leghorn soon became what Lisbon was during the second world war—a centre of international spying and intrigue. Nevertheless little beyond rumours ever reached the ears of the Allies at Vienna, or of the commanders of the British and French ships that constantly patrolled Elban waters; and even Campbell, who believed Napoleon was planning escape, thought he would try to join Murat at Naples.

When and why did Napoleon form the idea of returning to France? 'When?' is not easily answered. Probably from the moment of leaving Fréjus, if not Fontainebleau. Certainly soon after his establishment at Elba. He had given no parole. He was not a prisoner, but a sovereign. His 'army' could occupy Pianosa and Palmejola without a shot fired by the *Partridge* or the *Fleur-de-lys*. His 'navy' could enter Italian harbours with as much right as those of George III or Louis XVIII. He had only to wait for a good opportunity, and to slip through the blockade, as he had done fifteen years ago, to some port of Provence.

As for 'Why?': he had his grievances: the failure of the French government to keep its promises (personally affirmed by Louis) under the Treaty of Fontainebleau—they had not only refused to pay a penny of his pension, but they even proposed (December 18th) to confiscate the whole of his family property. He had his fears, too: of assassination, perhaps; of deportation certainly—for it was discussed at Vienna—maybe to the Azores, or even to St. Helena. He may well have read such dangers between the lines of Fouché's strange letter advising him to escape to America. He had his invitations, both from Italy (not Naples, but Milan, where they still remembered his promise of a united Italy), and from France, where almost every act of the restored Bourbons alienated the army and revived the national republicanism of 1789 and 1792. But above all he had the feeling of boredom and frustration inevitable in any man suddenly deprived of publicity and power—a feeling doubly strong in a self-made Emperor at the height of his talents, with unrivalled experience of affairs, and still, at forty-six, as ambitious as any starving lieutenant of twenty-five.

7

Quite suddenly, in the middle of February 1815, every circumstance conspired in favour of Napoleon's designs. On the 11th he heard from Murat—though the news was premature—that the Congress of Vienna was breaking up. On the 15th Campbell noted in his *Journal* the arrival, 'under the guise of a sailor from the Bay of Spezzia,' of an individual calling himself by the odd name of Pietro St. Ernest: this was in fact a Frenchman, Fleury de Chaboulon, with a message from Maret, who could not be suspected of rash intrigue, saying that public opinion was calling for Napoleon's return to France, and—what was more imperative

—that Fouché was plotting to substitute an Orleans sovereign, the liberal Louis-Philippe, for the reactionary Louis XVIII. This last piece of news was decisive.

The very next day had, as it chanced, been chosen by Campbell for one of his periodic visits to the mainland—for his health, he said, and to consult a doctor at Florence about his eyesight. He was to be away ten days, and Captain Adye of the *Partridge* must take him to Leghorn and fetch him back. During his absence Adye had orders to sail off Elba, and to visit Palmajola, 'a small rock' a mile off Elba with 'a surface of not many square yards, on its summit' which Napoleon had recently garrisoned. Adye, as he reported later, after leaving Campbell at Leghorn, cruised off Elba, and anchored in the harbour at Porto-Ferrajo on the night of the 23rd; went ashore on the 24th, called on the Bertrands, heard that Napoleon was there, and was planning a summer holiday at Marciana, walked about the town, and saw 'the soldiers of the Imperial Guard all busy in carrying earth and planting trees in front of their barracks.' The *Inconstant* was not in harbour. Next day, sailing to Palmajola, he was a little surprised when he sighted her manœuvring shyly in the offing: but when he passed the port at sunset he could see her topmasts: she was back at anchor again.

Evidently a trustful soul, Adye repeated these facts to Campbell, when they met at Leghorn on the 26th, as proof that Napoleon was still at Elba. Campbell had, however, just received a budget of spies' reports from Ricci and Mariotti which convinced him that 'Napoleon was on the point of embarking a military force with stores and provisions,' probably for Gaeta or Civita Vecchia: he was in a fever to return, and know the truth. When at last, delayed by light winds, he landed at Porto-Ferrajo on the 28th, he was met by 'Mr. Grattan, an Englishman,' who described how he had seen Napoleon board the *Inconstant* and put to sea, with a flotilla of small craft, on the evening of the 26th.

For Napoleon's star was again in the ascendant: Providence was once more on his side. On January 12th the *Inconstant*, the one ship on which his fortunes depended, had been driven ashore off Porto-Ferrajo in a gale, and had since lain in harbour, partly repaired, but not yet fit to go to sea again. On February 17th, as soon as Campbell was out of sight, Napoleon wrote to Drouot: 'Give orders for the brig to be put into wet dock (*la darse*) and heaved down (*viré sur quille*), to have her copper bottom inspected, her leaks stopped, her hull careened, and everything done to make her seaworthy. Have her painted (i.e. with black port-lids) like an English brig. You must have plans for all this ready for me by tomorrow. The brig must be re-armed, and stored with biscuit, rice, vegetables, cheese, drink—rations, half of brandy and half of wine, and three months' water supply for 120 men. There must be a fortnight's supply of salt meat. You must see to it that there is timber on board, and in short nothing whatever lacking. My wish is that she may be in the roads by the night of the 24th-25th of this month with everything ready as above. For economy's sake the wine can come from my cellar: the rice, biscuit and oil will be provided from store. Tell me how many boats she can carry: I want to have as many as possible.' At the same time two *feluccas* from the Rio iron-works, the biggest available, were to bring cargoes to Porto-Ferrajo, one of timber needed for repairs, or for stopping leaks: they too would take part in the projected expedition.

Then followed one of those episodes in which the stars in their courses seem to be fighting on behalf of an incredible adventure, but one which is easily understandable in the conditions of sea warfare a hundred and fifty years ago. On the night of the 26th, with a bright moon and a gentle breeze from the south, Napoleon's flotilla set sail—*Inconstant, Saint-Esprit* (a recently purchased merchantman), *l'Etoile, Saint-Joseph, Caroline* and the Rio *feluccas*, with a complement of 1050 soldiers and *gendarmes* and 100 civilians.

Their chances of slipping through might seem to be small. The *Partridge*, it so happened, was becalmed at Leghorn, fifty miles to the north, till 4 a.m. next day; but less than thirty miles to the north-west, off the island of Capraia, in the direct course for France, three French ships were cruising on the look-out: the *Zéphyr* to the west, the *Fleur-de-Lys* to the north-west, and the *Melpomène* to the south-west. The *Fleur-de-Lys* and the *Partridge* were both sighted, but neither recognized the *Inconstant*: she was intercepted and hailed by the *Zéphyr*, whose captain, having no definite orders, accepted his friend Captain Taillade's assurance that the *Inconstant* was on a routine trip to Genoa, and had left Napoleon safe at Elba. (He wrote afterwards to the Emperor to say that he well knew what he was doing.) So he got through. It was the third time that he had narrowly escaped capture in these waters.

Campbell was convinced by what he heard at Porto-Ferrajo that Napoleon had gone north, not south. But he pursued him in vain. On March 2nd he was becalmed: on the 3rd he spoke to the *Antelope*, a French schooner, and on the 4th H.M.S. *Wizard*, and learnt nothing. On the 5th a Sicilian ship from Genoa said it was reported there that Napoleon had landed near Antibes; and this was confirmed by H.M.S. *Aboukir* on the 7th. At Antibes on the 8th he was a week behind the fugitives, and could only wait for the expected news of their capture by royalist troops. On the 13th he heard to his dismay that Napoleon had arrived in triumph at Grenoble, and hurried back to report to his government. Everywhere he found it believed that he had connived at the Emperor's escape.

Napoleon's flotilla anchored in Juan Bay, between Fréjus and Antibes, and he and his company came ashore at 3 in the afternoon of March 1st.

They stayed there unmolested till sunrise next day. Corsin, the Governor of Antibes, was picnicking with friends on the neighbouring island of St. Marguerite, and noticed their proceedings with some surprise: the band played *Où est-ce qu'on peut être mieux que dans le sein de sa famille?*— the French equivalent to *Home Sweet Home*—whilst Napoleon sat or walked in his grey coat under the trees: his officers approached him hat in hand: at night he slept on a mattress on the ground. Patrols were thrown out; but no violence was offered or suffered, save the capture of a handful of men sent against Antibes. At Cannes a butcher got out his musket with the determination of going to Juan Bay and killing Napoleon; but the inhabitants surrounded him and begged him to desist, or their houses would be burnt down, and they would all be sacrificed. At daybreak on March 2nd the invaders started off for Grasse and Grenoble.[5]

8

The mountain road followed by Napoleon and his 'handful of heroes' from Cannes to Grenoble, imperfectly marked on maps of the period, is now a coach-route frequented by tourists, and, to faithful Bonapartists, almost a *Via Sacra*—the course of the eagle, which (as the Emperor put it) 'would fly with the national flag from steeple to steeple till it perched on the towers of Nôtre Dame.' The official *Relation de la marche de Napoléon de l'Ile d'Elbe à Paris* misses no touch of romance, though it is reticent about the famous gesture at Laffrey, where Napoleon is said to have thrown open his great-coat ('bared his breast') to the hostile garrison from Grenoble, with the words: 'Soldiers, if there is one among you who wishes to kill his Emperor, he can do so: here I am!'

The historical interest of the eighteen days' march—an episode which Napoleon was never tired of recounting—lies in the methods by which he appealed to the army, to the French people, and to Europe—in that order of importance. To the army he said, upon landing on French soil: 'Soldiers, we have not been beaten, but betrayed . . . Shoulder once more the standards that you carried at Ulm, at Austerlitz . . . at Montmirail'; and in old age (he promised them) they would be 'proud to say, 'I too belonged to the Grand Army . . . which conquered Vienna, Rome, Berlin, Madrid and Moscow, and liberated Paris.' To the people of the departments that welcomed him (he was careful to avoid those which had abused him during his flight ten months before): 'You are right (he said) to call me your Father.' In the decree issued from Lyon dismissing Louis XVIII's parliament, and convoking an *Assemblée extraordinaire du Champ de Mai*, he proposed (with an eye on the Liberals and anti-Bourbons) to 'improve and change our constitutions according to the interests and will of the nation: and at the same time (for there must be no mistaking the dynastic character of the new regime) to take part in the coronation of the Empress, Our dear and well-beloved spouse, and that of Our well-beloved son.'

For the benefit of the European Powers he assumed in his first manifesto (*Au peuple Français*, March 1st) the title *Napoléon par la grâce de Dieu et les constitutions de l'état, Empereur des Français*, explaining that his abdication had been a voluntary retirement, and that he returned by invitation to a national sovereignty designated by twenty-five years of revolution, and demanded by the French people. Since he is raised to the throne by their choice, everything done without their sanction is illegitimate. 'For the last twenty-five years France has had new interests, new institutions, a new fame: these cannot be guaranteed by any but a national government and a dynasty born under the new conditions.' This idea of a national and revolutionary monarchy he expounded in greater detail in his answers to addresses from the *conseil d'état* and the *Cour de Cassation* (March 26th). No monarchy is legitimate, he told them, or has any right to be hereditary, 'unless the interests of the country make it so (*l'intérêt des peuples l'exige*). Only a dynasty created in the conditions which have created so many new interests, and whose concern it is to maintain all the new rights and properties, can be called natural and legitimate.'

There was hardly a class in the country, as Napoleon well knew, which was not anxious to be rid of the Bourbons; and it was a question about which the Allies themselves were divided. What everyone wanted to know was the nature of the Napoleonic regime which would take their place. Would it be a restoration of the Empire of 1810, but limited to the frontiers of 1814; and could it be the same, if so limited? Would it accept the essential changes of 1814, and be a constitutional Monarchy like that of 1791? Or would it be (as, for instance, Thibaudeau desired) a revolutionary and military dictatorship, to resolve itself, as soon as the country was liberated from the enemy, into something like the Consular Republic of 1799?

There was a curious sentence in Napoleon's *Réponse* to the *conseil d'état* which might seem to give the answer: 'I have renounced the ideas of the Grand Empire, whose foundations—no more—I had been laying for fifteen years. In future the aim of all my thoughts will be the happiness and the consolidation of the French Empire.' What was to be the difference, then? The old Empire, but 'French' instead of 'European'? Just acceptance of the 'natural frontiers'? Or did the word 'happiness' (*bonheur*) mean that the French people would be given more control over their own affairs, through liberal institutions? And did 'consolidation' (the same word in French) mean that the Empire would in future concentrate on a peaceful collaboration with the other nations of Europe, and mind its own affairs? The Allied Sovereigns, at least, who had struck commemorative medals in 1814 with the motto *Gallia reddita Europae* ('France restored to Europe') might read it so. But were not Napoleon's real intentions better expressed (or, as Talleyrand would have said, concealed) by his words to the Ministers: *Tout à la nation et tout pour la France. Voilà ma devise*: which might be translated, 'I live wholly for the nation and act solely for France.' Such a motto might bear a dozen interpretations, each according to the need or the desire of the moment; Napoleon himself being its only interpreter.

The news of Napoleon's landing had reached Paris on March 5th. Louis XVIII was not alarmed. He believed that his troops at Lyon and in the Midi, under the nominal command of the Comte d'Artois and the Duc de Berry, would easily intercept him, and that officials and civilians alike would answer his appeal against an adventurer and a rebel (March 6th). But the events at Grenoble altered everything. Macdonald and Gouvion Saint-Cyr arrived at Lyon too late to prevent the defection of the royal army. Ney, who might be supposed immune against a cause he had deserted the year before, was won over by a simple appeal from Napoleon —'Come and join me at Châlons. I shall receive you as I did on the morning after la Moskowa'—and by a repugnance against raising the standard of civil war. At every stage of the march the defence collapsed—Villefranche, Macon, Tournus, Châlons, Autun, Auxerre. When Napoleon arrived at Fontainebleau on the 20th, it was to hear that Louis had already left Paris.

The news of the journey from Elba reached Metternich at Vienna on March 7th, at a moment when the Congress was in danger of breaking up over disputes about the settlement of Germany. War was decided upon in 'less than an hour.' Within a week (March 13th) the Allies unanimously declared that Napoleon had broken the treaty of Fontainebleau (they ignored the fact that France had broken it, too), had placed himself 'outside the pale of civil and social relations,' and was an enemy and disturber of world peace (*il s'est livré à la vindicte publique*—of which the nearest modern equivalent would be, 'He has made himself Public Enemy No. 1'). His claim (*lettre circulaire aux souverains*, April 4th) that he had been restored to the throne by the 'irresistible power, the unanimous wish of a great nation,' meant nothing to them. A week later they reconstituted their Grand Alliance, and took steps to do the work of 1814 over again.[6]

9

It only needed the declaration of outlawry—and it is the crux of the case against him that he cannot really have expected anything else—to confirm Napoleon's appeal to the French nation. His protestations of peaceful intention repeated within a fortnight of Waterloo (April 4th) went unheeded. War, as he must have known from the moment he left Elba, was inevitable: and it would be a war in which the scales were tipped so heavily against him that, whatever temporary successes he might win, the last result was almost certain to be defeat. He had in two years lost two great armies. The Allies had been victorious in two campaigns. No less than 148 French generals had fallen since 1805: half of those who survived were no longer loyal to their old leader. Great parts of the country were disaffected. Even the official correspondence reveals that there was a state of civil war in the Vendée, and that it had become necessary to set up special committees and courts to arrest and try disloyal mayors, sub-prefects and other officials. Punitive measures had to be ordered against Marseille. Letters not included in the official publication provide evidence of widespread opposition in the Civil Service, the clergy, and the authorities of the Midi: royalist and *émigré* agitators, prefects who do not back up the appeal for recruits, and so forth.

Above all, there was defection and what would nowadays be called defeatism amongst those whom Napoleon himself had made the 'governing classes.' Not much store could be set by the 'loyal addresses' sent up by ministers, peers, representatives, judges and electoral colleges: they served only as pegs on which to hang declarations on Napoleon's part of his devotion to the country, his hope of victory and his desire to rule constitutionally. The plain fact was that both he and they were changed from what they had been a year ago. 'Whatever the personal prestige of the Emperor,' writes that staunch Jacobin and Bonapartist, Thibaudeau, 'when defeated and dethroned, he was not the same man when he returned to power. He had been struck by lightning, and carried the scar. France, too, was changed. In its transitory course the royal restoration had awakened in some the love of liberty, and rewarded others for their treachery. What hold could the Empire retain on marshals, generals, ministers, senators and notables of all kinds who, whether by calculation or chance, were stained, in a single year, with a double defection? Even sincere Bonapartists were divided. Some acclaimed the Emperor, raising him on their shields: "We are your men (they cried), but on conditions: there must be no more despotism, but liberty, a constitution, guarantees!" The Emperor too posed as a Liberal, compulsorily, against his will; like a man self-mutilated (*il se mutilait*). Caught between two fires—that of his own nature and habits and that of the necessities of the situation— virtue had gone out of him (*il était affaibli*). He was no longer himself.' If only he could have made a clean cut with the past! But he could not.

With the old Empire came back 'the old company of dignitaries, ministers, state councillors, marshals, grooms, and chamberlains most of whom were more than dubious friends, discredited by public opinion, and little disposed to sacrifice themselves for him or for the country.' The best and most loyal of them all was Carnot; and he—the professional soldier, the organizer of victory—was sacrificed to the policy of the moment, and be-came Comte Carnot, Minister of the Interior, his duty to organize the National Guard, to look after roads and buildings, agriculture and the Post Office, industry, commerce and education.

If only Napoleon could have appealed over the heads of the official class to the people—to a nation which (he told the Electors) 'had never shown more energy or unanimity.' But again he could not. True, when the faubourgs of St. Antoine and St. Marceau—those hot-beds of revolu-tionary violence—sent their *fédérés* to the Tuileries to tell him that they preferred him to the Bourbons 'because you are the man of the nation, the defender of the fatherland, and we count on you for a glorious inde-pendence and a wise liberty,' Napoleon replied: 'It is men born in the upper classes of society who have dishonoured the name of France: patriotism and regard for national honour survive unimpaired in the towns-people, the men of the countryside, and the ranks of the army.'

But he still felt the same inhibition, that of a professional soldier, against amateurs under arms. *Corps francs* might be organized, and be allotted guns, to harass the rear of the invader. The National Guards might defend the capital, or even the frontiers. The *fédérés*, formed into twenty-four battalions of sharp-shooters (*tirailleurs*), might help them to man the defences of Paris. Prefects might organize *Compagnies de ré-serve*, as in 1814. But school-boys of eighteen from the *lycées* (he thought) were more to be trusted to serve the guns than either *fédérés* or National Guardsmen. Only in the event of defeat in the field, only as a last resort (he tells the Chamber), will he appeal for a truly national effort (*c'est alors surtout que j'aimerais à voir déployer toute l'énergie de ce grand peuple*). It was the crowning irony of Empire that in the moment of need Napoleon should distrust the revolutionary enthusiasm which had won Bonaparte his victories in Italy twenty years before.

It is significant that four out of five of Napoleon's letters during the Hundred Days are addressed to the Minister of War. But three important acts show that he was alive to the need of backing his appeal to arms by implementing his profession of constitutional government: the *Acte Ad-ditionnel* of April 22nd, the *Champ de Mai* of June 1st, and the Opening of Parliament on June 7th. It was the opinion of those best able to judge that all three rang false, and failed to rouse national enthusiasm.

The 'Appendix to the Constitutions of the Empire' was an attempt to graft the *Chartre* of Louis XVIII onto the stem of the Napoleonic dic-tatorship, as that had been grafted onto the trunk of the revolutionary Republic. The operation was carried out by Mme de Staël's clever but inconsequent friend Benjamin Constant, who had just penned a bitter attack upon Napoleon, but was persuaded by Fouché (the association shows to what straits the Emperor was reduced) to join the *conseil d'état*, and to become the Sieyès of the new regime. But the *Benjamine* (as the Additional Act was nicknamed) pleased nobody. Jacobins resented its reaffirmation of 'the constitutions of the Empire,' i.e. the modifications of the settlement of Brumaire introduced by subsequent acts of the Senate; the House of Peers they considered was not merely anti-republican but English. The royalists objected to the articles enabling Napoleon to confiscate the property of his political enemies, and prohibiting any return of the Bourbons. Napoleon himself disliked the whole document, and regarded it merely as a concession to popular opinion. 'The constitution,' he assured the Representatives on June 11th, 'is our rallying-point; it must be our pole-star in hours of tempest.' But the 'liberty' he wanted France to enjoy must be limited through fear of anarchy, and 'freedom of the press' involved, as things were, 'repressive legislation.' There can be little doubt that, as he told Gourgaud at St. Helena, he would have taken the opportunity of his first victory in the field to denounce the Additional Act, and to dismiss the Chambers.

The *Champ de Mai* was intended to be a solemnization of the national monarchy, a fête like that of Federation in 1790, at which both the Emperor and the people, represented by the electors, would take an oath of loyalty to the new constitution. As a show it was magnificent: coaches, uniforms, liveries, satins and embroidery, jewels and gold, Mass and *Te Deum*—nothing had been seen like it since the Coronation of 1804. But the troops were puzzled, and the electors were not impressed. Thibaudeau was there, and describes 'the well-known figure of Napoleon, usually so handsome, noble, calm and composed in his simple undress, now anxious and shrunken (*contractée*), with the severity of Nero, in his imperial finery.' The painful impression remained with him all his life.

When the Chambers met (June 11th), elected or nominated under the rules of 1802, to work a constitution ratified by no more than a third part of the electorate, it was to manifest their hostility to the Emperor, and to be told to mind their own business—the implementation of the Additional Act—whilst the army took the field. It was the old familiar pattern of 1800, of 1805, 1806, 1809, 1812: politics and diplomacy waiting on the result of war.

Meanwhile at St. James' they had read unmoved Napoleon's conciliatory decree of March 29th abolishing the Slave Trade; at Vienna Talleyrand had passed on to the Emperor Francis a letter in which Napoleon tried to tempt him back into his service—could anything have shown his fortune at a lower ebb?—and at St. Petersburg the Tsar, though indignant to hear of the secret treaty by which Britain and Austria had bound themselves to resist his designs on Poland, nevertheless did not

weaken in his determination to be done with his rival. On April 4th
Wellington took command at Brussels of the army which was to save
Europe.[7]

10

From the moment of Napoleon's outlawry by the Congress of Vienna
war was inevitable. But where, between what forces, and with what
prospects of a final decision?

The position of the Allied armies was determined by their lines of
retreat after the occupation of Paris in 1814. Those of Russia and Austria
were too far away to intervene effectively before the third week in June.
But Blücher's Prussians, 120,000 strong, stood along the banks of the
Sambre and Meuse from Charleroi to Liège; and on their right this line
was sketchily continued by Wellington's mixed force of British, German
and Dutch-Belgian troops, numbering 94,000 in all, strung out between
Brussels and Mons. Behind the Sambre a road from Namur ran westwards to Nivelles and Braine-le-Comte on the high road from Paris to
Brussels; and this road intercepted at three points Napoleon's possible
lines of advance from the south: Nivelles, Quatre-Bras, and Ligny. If
Blücher and Wellington had been thinking in terms of defence, this
road would have linked up their lines. But they were not: they wanted
to attack Napoleon before he was ready. They were more concerned with
parallel advance than with latitudinal support. When the fight came at
Ligny on June 16th, a quarter of Blücher's army was out of reach on the
left at Liège, and at Waterloo on the 18th a fifth part of Wellington's
was out of reach on the right, watching the Tournai-Brussels road, to
prevent a *coup-de-main* against Ghent.

Unfortunately for the Allies (though they might have remembered it)
Napoleon never waited to be attacked. His whole strategy was based on
a sudden and overwhelming offensive: and he was always lured by a
capital. Brussels was within 180 miles of Paris. It was still marked French
on the maps. Both Blücher's and Wellington's troops were, to patriotic
Frenchmen, invading their fatherland. The capital of Belgium was to be
his objective. He would mass his 125,000 men on the Charleroi road, pretend (such a report reached Wellington) to be on the defensive, then
suddenly hurry to the front, and attack the Allied line at its weakest
point, where the Prussians and British did not quite meet; separate them,
and annihilate them in detail. It was his favourite move. It had rarely
failed. It very nearly succeeded again.

On June 12th Napoleon left Paris. On the 13th, at Avesnes, he issued an
Ordre du jour, fixing the positions of his troops for the next day. On the
14th he published a *Proclamation à l'armée*, reminding his men that it
was (as he had no doubt designed) the anniversary of Marengo and
Friedland, victories 'which had twice decided the destinies of Europe.' On

the 15th the Allies, taken by surprise, hurriedly concentrated for defence, knowing now that an attack was coming, but uncertain on which of the three crossroads the blow would fall. Wellington was so out of touch with reality that he ordered his troops to concentrate on a curved front from Brussels to Nivelles, and lingered till 3 a.m. on the 16th at the Duchess of Richmond's ball. Of the Prussians, Ziethen's 32,000 had pushed forward to the Sambre at Charleroi; during the 15th they were driven back in a north-easterly direction towards Ligny, where they were able to join their comrades, hastily brought up from Namur, and prepared to make a stand there next day. Meanwhile the French left had swung round almost as far north as Quatre-Bras, where they were checked by Dutch-Belgian troops under the Prince of Orange, nominally second in command to Wellington. Thus the stage was set for two fights on the 16th—at Ligny on the east and at Quatre-Bras on the west; and Napoleon might confidently count on driving back both Wellington and Blücher along divergent roads towards Brussels and Liège, and then slipping in between. Why did this not happen?

At 11 o'clock on the morning of June 16th Napoleon, who had failed to make his usual early reconnaissance, surveyed from a windmill at Fleurus the Prussian position at Ligny, decided (wrongly) that he only had Blücher's one corps to deal with, and was in no hurry to attack. Meanwhile, at another windmill at Bry behind Ligny Wellington, who had ridden over early from Quatre-Bras, was conferring with Gneisenau, the Prussian Chief of Staff (Blücher himself could not speak French or English), and when pressed to send help, said that he would if he were not too heavily attacked himself.

It was fortunate for the Allies that, owing to Napoleon's misunderstanding of the position, the attack both at Ligny and Quatre-Bras did not open till 2 or 3 p.m. For at both points they were so roughly handled that they had to retreat, and, given more time, might have been routed. At Ligny Napoleon found himself up against three corps instead of one, and the fighting, in which he lost nearly as many men as his opponents, went on till sunset. At Quatre-Bras Wellington had time to bring up reinforcements enough to save the situation: but he too lost nearly 5000 men out of the 21,000 engaged. Fortunately the pursuit was not pressed, and the two allied armies did not retire in divergent directions, as Napoleon had assumed they would; for whilst Wellington fell back towards Brussels (where the guns of Quatre-Bras were clearly heard during the evening of the 16th), Gneisenau, in order to concentrate all his forces for the defence of the capital, ordered the Prussians to retreat on Wavre, fifteen miles north, on a course roughly parallel to that of the British.

When, eight years later, Wellington read in Las Cases's *Mémorial* the 6000-word *Relation de la campaigne de Waterloo, dictée par Napoleon,* in which he was convicted of having been surprised by the French advance, and of having 'violated all the rules of war' in fighting at Waterloo, 'D—n them,' he said with great animation, 'I beat them, and, if I was surprised, if I did place myself in so foolish a position, they were the greater fools for not knowing how to take advantage of my faults.'

Wellington, though he might appear casual, was completely confident. 'He had not for an instant (he said) felt more dread of Bonaparte than of any other general'; though he admitted 'he never had taken such pains in occupying a position,' and that 'he had placed every regiment himself,' yet, having done that, 'he was quite tranquil as to the issue.'

June 17th therefore found Wellington's forces, though tired and reduced in strength, taking up a new line at Mont St. Jean, on the main road fifteen miles south of Brussels, and Blücher, now strengthened by Bülow's corps of 32,000 men, which had not been engaged on Ligny, moving up towards them from the south-east; whilst Napoleon, thinking he had dealt with the Prussians (they were reported to be retreating on Namur), thought he had plenty of time and strength to annihilate the British. Accordingly Grouchy was sent off with 27,000 infantry and 6000 cavalry, and spent the day pursuing north-eastward toward Gembloux and Liège a Prussian force which was in reality marching to the northwest.

The tables were now turned. Napoleon's favourite manœuvre was being used against himself. At Waterloo the French army was divided, and that of the Allies united. For, at a conference on the night of the 17th, Blücher, barely recovered from 'being twice rode over by the cavalry,' and still 'smelling most strongly of the gin and rhubarb' he had taken for a remedy, had improved upon Gneisenau's strategy by insisting that the only hope for the Prussians was not merely to remain in touch with the British, but to come actively to their help next day by marching against the right flank of the French. Early on the 17th Wellington had sent word that he would stand where he was if he were sure of the help of a Prussian corps. At 3 a.m. on the 18th the reply came that at dawn not one but two corps would move from Wavre by St. Lambert against Napoleon's right wing.

II

This, then, was the position on the morning of June 18th. Wellington's polyglot army of 67,000 Dutch-Belgians, Nassauers, Hanoverians, Brunswickers, and British (including the German Legion) was in a moderately strong position astride the Brussels road—a slight hill, with a sunken road behind it (such as he favoured for concealing his troops from enemy observation and gunfire), and protected on each wing by a strong group of farm buildings, Hougoumont on the right and La Haye Sainte on the left. On the opposite hillside lay Napoleon's 74,000 Frenchmen. And whereas these were all of one language and military training, mostly veterans of many battlefields, the others included some who had no heart in the affair, and many raw recruits—'the worst equipped army (its common-sense commander himself described it) with the worst staff, ever brought together.' Napoleon, too, was greatly superior in the number, if not the quality, of his cavalry and artillery. The unknown but crucial factor was the position of the Prussians. Wellington had calculated on their covering the ten miles to the battlefield, however bad the roads might be after 'the most terrible storm of rain' that he had ever seen, by midday. Napoleon did not even hear of their approach till 2 in the afternoon. Their first effective attack on the French right came at half past four, after fighting had been in progress for five hours.

To visit the battlefield of Waterloo is to be reminded how little the practice of war had altered between the seventeenth and the nineteenth centuries. It is not much larger than those few acres of fields and hedgerows which contained the battles of our Civil War. The cannon had a longer range, the muskets were more efficient: but infantry fought face to face with swords and bayonets: cavalry rode at one another and struck with lances and swords: the biggest battle was (as Napoleon said) an *escarmouche* (a scrimmage). Banners waved, trumpets blew, and rival generals, spying each other through glasses a few hundred yards apart, led their men to the attack with gestures and shouts. It was a hand-to-hand *mêlée* in which physical fitness and courage won the day. 'Never did I see such a pounding match,' was Wellington's own description of Waterloo.

What were the decisive moments of that day-long struggle? The defence of Hougoumont or of La Haye Sainte? The flight of the Dutch-Belgian troops? The charge of the Inniskillings, or of the Scots Greys? Ney's cavalry attacks on the British squares? The Prussian advance on the flank, which during the last two hours of the battle reduced the force attacking Wellington by 14,000 men? The final charge and rout of the Old Guard? The general advance of the British line? Every incident of the battle has been debated to and fro in so many Memoirs and histories that hardly any detail is indisputable, and hardly any theory can be ruled out of court.

To a biographer of Napoleon it is less necessary to establish exactly what happened than to inquire what he thought about it. As to this there can be no doubt: he had never been so confident of victory, and was hard put to it to account for defeat. He always spoke of the battle with an air of bewilderment. He could never imagine what went wrong. Grouchy was to blame, or Ney, or D'Erlon. If only Mortier had been there, or Lannes, or Bessières! If, above all, he could have had the trusty Berthier to issue his orders, instead of that idiot Soult, who sent one messenger when he would have sent six! Certainly the English fought well: they were so well-disciplined that 'they could advance thirty paces, halt, fire, retreat, fire and advance thirty paces again, without losing their ranks.' Perhaps he should have concentrated on their right instead of their left? But no: it remained to the end of his life an inexplicable affair, *journée incompréhensible!*

Wellington's view was that Napoleon 'was certainly wrong in attacking at all. There were four armies going to enter France, before the harvest, and in a country much exhausted by the last campaign. We should have been reduced to many straits for subsistence . . . Napoleon might have stationed himself somewhere on the Meuse with nearly 300,000 men. He might have played again the same game which he had played so admirably the year before—that campaign of 1814 I consider the very finest he ever made . . . Instead of this, by Waterloo he put an end to the war at once. But the fact is, he never in his life had patience for a defensive war.' Nevertheless, as Wellington admitted to Creevey next day, it was 'a damned nice thing—the neatest run thing you ever saw in your life.'

What, if it had gone the other way? It can hardly be supposed that, with a ring of armies closing in on the country, and its will to fight weakened by his abdication, Napoleon would have survived another summer's campaign. Waterloo is rightly regarded as one of the decisive battles of the world; but if it had not been, another 'battle of the nations' would have done its work.[8]

12

Wellington never said, 'Up, Guards, and at 'em!' Cambronne never cried, *La Garde meurt et ne se rend pas.* History must remain satisfied with a homelier and more symbolical moment. 'Blücher and I (Wellington used to say) met near La Belle Alliance; we were both on horseback; but he embraced and kissed me, exclaiming, *Mein lieber Kamerad*, and then *Quelle affaire!* which was pretty much all he knew of French.'

Both French and British were exhausted: Wellington left the pursuit to Blücher and his Prussians. Napoleon, barely escaping capture, drove off through the night, and reached Paris in the early morning of June 21st. He published an official account of what had happened in the *Moniteur* the same day: as after the Beresina, he hoped to forestall rumour, and to prepare the minds of the Parisians for fresh sacrifices. With a characteristic rebound from despair to optimism he had written to Joseph from Philippeville on the very morning after the disaster, 'All is not lost. I suppose that, when I reassemble my forces, I shall have 150,000 men. The *fédérés* and National Guards will provide 100,000 men, and the regimental depots another 50,000. I shall thus have 300,000 soldiers ready at once to bring against the enemy. I will use carriage-horses to drag the guns, raise 100,000 men by conscription, arm them with muskets taken from royalists and from National Guards unfit for service, organize a mass levy in the Dauphiné, in the Lyon district, Burgundy, Lorraine, Champagne, and overwhelm the foe.'

But 1815 was not 1812. Though the news of Waterloo had only reached Paris on the night of the 19th, public opinion was in such a state of alarm that thirty-six hours were enough for a clever man with a clear policy to carry through the final destruction of the Empire. A year ago Napoleon's fate had depended on Talleyrand. Now it depended on Talleyrand's rival, the Emperor's once accredited minister and now acknowledged enemy, Fouché. In 1814 Fouché had favoured a military dictatorship to prevent a Bourbon restoration: in 1815, when Napoleon proposed a military dictatorship, he worked for a Bourbon restoration, but in such fashion as to make it more acceptable to the country than it had been a year ago. Louis XVIII must not be reimposed by the Allies, but by the representatives of the French nation. The agents of the new regime must not be royalists or reactionaries, but the revolutionaries of 1789, the constitutionalists of 1791, the regicides of 1793.

To work this transformation Fouché had recourse to a technique which he had already employed (was he conscious of it?) in 1794. Then, in order to bring about the fall of Robespierre, he had worked upon the moderate members of the Convention, representing Maximilien as a dictator who threatened their liberties, and had found enough supporters amongst the deputies to secure his outlawry. Now he must persuade the Chamber that Napoleon intends to dismiss them, and to set up a military dictatorship, whilst making the Emperor think that the representatives are plotting his deposition. Agents for this double plot were ready to hand: at the Elysée Carnot and Davout, Regnaud and Caulaincourt—men loyal to Napoleon, but who saw no other remedy; at the Palais Bourbon a group of old constitutionalist and republican deputies elected under a constitution which neither he nor they believed in, representatives of a nation which was sick of a war that no longer brought victory, and which passionately desired peace, if it could be had without dishonour.

These men found a leader in one who still imagined himself to be standing in the National Assembly of 1789—'a sufficiently stout figure, dressed like a well-to-do farmer, with nothing that recalled the slim and elegant Marquis who once commanded the National Guard': Lafayette. So, whilst the Elysée talked, the Palais Bourbon acted. It was Lafayette who, warned by Fouché that Napoleon might dissolve the Chambers, carried the resolution 'that a State of Emergency exists (*qu'on déclarât la patrie en danger*), that both Houses declare themselves to be in permanent session, and that anyone who attempts to dissolve or prorogue them is guilty of High Treason.' It was almost the Tennis Court oath that some of them remembered swearing under Bailly's uplifted hand just twenty-six years ago. It was followed by a demand for Napoleon's abdication.

Thibaudeau and two others went to the Elysée to tell him so. Napoleon insisted, as in 1814, that he could only abdicate in favour of his son: and published a 'Declaration to the French People,' saying: 'My political life is over, and I proclaim my son Napoleon II, Emperor of the French.' Thibaudeau's companions were in tears. 'For myself (he wrote afterwards) no tears, or sighs, or words could express what I felt. Bonaparte had exhibited a glorious career, and won immortality. But we—France—the Revolution—how had we profited? What was to become of us?'

This was for long uncertain. A half-hearted attempt to proclaim the King of Rome as 'Napoleon II' was brushed aside. A Provisional Government, set up on June 22nd, with Fouché at its head, sent a message to Blücher, who was advancing at full speed on Paris, telling him of the abdication, and asking for an armistice. This he refused, unless Napoleon surrendered in person. On the 25th Fouché asked Napoleon to leave Paris, and he obeyed, going for the last time to Malmaison and the sad ghost of Joséphine. On the 29th Blücher was near enough to make an attempt to kidnap his enemy—he was in a mood to have him shot: but Fouché again baulked him, by ordering Napoleon away to Rochefort. On the day he arrived there (July 3rd) Blücher granted an armistice, on condition that Paris was not defended. The city surrendered on July 4th. On the 8th Louis XVIII made his second entry into his capital.[9]

XV

ST. HELENA

(1815-1821)

I

On June 21st, 1815, Napoleon had returned to Paris from Waterloo, defeated and without an army, but still calling himself Emperor of the French, and with every intention of carrying on the national resistance. A month later he was on board a British ship in Torbay. Four months later he landed at St. Helena, 'General Bonaparte' once more, but with no career to make, no world to conquer, only a past to reconsider and a renown to reconstruct. Another man might have been able to live quietly, and to forget. But to Napoleon thinking, talking, and ordering had become a habit that he could not forego. The more his body was forced into inactivity, the more restless grew his mind. Of his garrulity—that prominent upper lip the sign of it—wherever he was, whatever he might be doing, there seemed to be no end. If there were no longer even an Elban army or navy to organize, yet the etiquette of the Tuileries must be kept up in the inn parlour at Rochefort, and the wooden *Salon* of Longwood: the pretensions of Empire must be preserved amidst the *ennui* of exile.

The first three weeks were spent in pitiful indecision. He stayed on three days at the Elysée, after signing his abdication, in the hope that perhaps, after all, he would be asked to lead the cheering crowds outside against the advancing Prussians, yet more and more convinced that he had no future in France, and must start a new life elsewhere. But where? A year ago he might have found a home in Russia, or in Scotland. But would the Allied Sovereigns trust him now, after the escape from Elba? England, perhaps; for his most inveterate was his most generous foe; and England meant ships, naval officers, an old aristocracy, a peaceful country life: just such a society and surroundings as (he liked to fancy) would suit his tastes in retirement. Lucien had been well received in England: why should not Napoleon reside, as 'Colonel Muiron' or 'Duroc,' at some old place not too far from London? Marie-Louise would be content in the country. The boy might go to Eton? . . .

Or, if not England, then America. It would be a new world to explore —west instead of east. He had been reading Humbolt's *Voyages aux contrées équinoxiales du Nouveau Continent*; and he wrote off from Malmaison to his librarian Barbier, telling him to bring tomorrow 'some works on America,' to make up an up-to-date 'travelling library' (like those he had taken to Egypt and to Spain), and to consign it 'to some American house, which will forward it via Havre to America.'

Fouché played up to this idea, telling Napoleon to go to Rochefort, where two fast frigates waited for him, and promising to ask for a British safe-conduct to America. On the 29th, a last offer to fight rejected by the government, and only a few hours ahead of Blücher's cavalry, he left Malmaison with Fouché's friend General Becker (whose name he took as an incognito), Savary, and Bertrand, and drove off by Rambouillet, Chartres, Tours, Poitiers and Niort to Rochefort, where he arrived early on July 3rd. Gourgaud followed in a carriage full of money, books, and arms. There were no such hostile demonstrations as on the journey to Fréjus the year before: at Tours he is said to have passed unrecognized except by an English traveller, W. S. Landor; and in the coastal districts, at Niort and Rochefort, he was cheered by crowds who still thought of him as a liberator from the Bourbons.

Four days were spent at Rochefort, waiting in vain for the safe-conduct to America, and for a respite from the westerly wind, which might make it possible for a corvette from Royan, a few miles south, at the mouth of the Gironde, to carry the refugees through the British blockade. On the evening of July 7th Becker received orders from Paris to save Napoleon (it might be from the Prussians, it might be from the Bourbons) by putting him on board one of Fouché's frigates. So next day he moved to the Île d'Aix, and went on board the *Saale*. There he found himself barred from the mainland, but free to communicate with Captain Maitland of the *Bellerophon*, which lay between him and the open sea. On the 10th he sent Savary and Las Cases (who could speak English, but pretended not to) on board the British ship with a letter from Bertrand, to sound Maitland as to the intentions of the British government.

2

It is important to fix the course of these negotiations, for upon them was based a main structure of charges against our treatment of the fallen Emperor.

Maitland was in a difficult position. He had left Plymouth Sound on May 24th with routine blockade orders 'to send back into port all armed vessels belonging to the Government of France.' On the 30th he had been told to proceed to Rochefort to see what ships might be there, and to 'prevent a corvette from putting to sea' which was thought to be carrying proposals from Bonaparte to the West Indies. The Basque roads west of Rochefort cover an area of some 160 square miles, and are divided by the big islands of Ré and Oléron into three passages, by any of which a fast frigate might hope to slip past the slow-moving *Bellerophon*: meanwhile it could lie under cover of the little Île d'Aix only three miles off shore. By the time of Napoleon's *démarche* of July 10th the *Bellerophon* had been brought into a position three miles north-west of the Île d'Aix, where she could watch the frigate, whilst *Cyrus* and *Daphne* barred the northern and southern exits from the bay. But Maitland still did not feel certain that he could intercept both frigates, if they made a dash for it.

Three days before (July 7th) he had heard from his commanding admiral, Sir Henry Hotham, stationed at Quiberon, that Napoleon had left Paris for Rochefort, to embark there for America. 'I have to direct (the order went on) you will use your best endeavours to prevent him from making his escape in either of the frigates at the Île d'Aix.' Next day he heard that the application for a safe-conduct to the United States had been refused; Napoleon would probably make no move till he heard of this, but if and when he did, 'the orders from the Admiralty are that the ships which are looking out for him should remain in that service *till further orders, or till they know him to be taken.*' 'I depend on your using the best means that can be adopted (Hotham concluded) to intercept the fugitive, on whose captivity the repose of Europe appears to depend.' At the very time that Napoleon's two ambassadors, Savary and Las Cases, were on board the *Bellerophon* (July 10th) Maitland received yet another dispatch from Hotham repeating these orders, and adding that if he were 'so fortunate as to intercept him,' he was to keep Napoleon in careful custody, and return with all speed and secrecy to the nearest British port.

Bertrand's letter, handed to Maitland by Savary and Las Cases, asked three questions: (1) whether the safe-conduct had arrived, (2) whether the British government intended to put any obstacle in the way of Napoleon's voyage to the United States, and (3) whether Maitland would allow him to sail in a neutral vessel. Maitland's answer was, 'I cannot say what the intentions of my government may be (*Hotham's 'captivity' was a vague word*); but, the two countries being at present in a state of war, it is impossible for me to permit any ship of war to put to sea from the port of Rochefort (*he is quoting his orders of May 24th*).' As for the last question, he must refer it to his commanding admiral (*and the delay, he reckoned, might give time for reinforcements to come up*). Then he made a suggestion: 'Why not ask for an asylum in England?' Various objections were raised at the moment: but Napoleon's emissaries returned to think it over.

Four days later Las Cases came aboard again, this time with General Lallemand, whom Maitland had known in Egypt, and repeated the question about a neutral ship for America. Maitland said he had received no reply yet from Hotham; but (he went on) 'I think I may venture to receive him (Napoleon) into this ship, and convey him to England. If however he adopts that plan, I cannot enter into any promise as to the reception he may meet with, and I shall be acting on my own responsibility, and cannot be sure it will meet with the approbation of the British Government.' 'He was lying,' says the French historian Aubry, and he enticed Napoleon on board with a sham promise that he would not be treated as a prisoner. No. Maitland had clear orders to use 'the best means that can be adopted' to 'take' Napoleon. If he represented these orders as a private offer on his own responsibility, that was in fact less than the truth, but it implied no promise, as he more than once pointed out in the presence of witnesses (and got Las Cases's own assent to it) that Napoleon would be treated as anything but a prisoner of war; if he voluntarily surrendered, his life would be spared, but all else must rest with the British government; and they had not declared their intentions.

On this Las Cases retired; but he was back by 7 o'clock the same evening, to say that Napoleon would come on board the next day. 'If the admiral sends you the safe-conduct for the United States, His Majesty will go there with pleasure: if it is not available, he will go to England voluntarily as an ordinary individual (*volontiers, comme simple particulier*), there to enjoy the protection of the laws of your country.' He asked that Gourgaud should be sent on with a letter from Napoleon to the Prince Regent: a letter that must be quoted, because its date (July 13th) and wording show that the writer was relying, not on any undertaking by Maitland, but on a generosity which he hoped to find in the British government and people.

'Your Royal Highness (he wrote): Victimized by the factions which divide my country, and by the hostility of the great European powers, I have ended my political career; and I come, as Themistocles did, to claim a seat by the hearth of the British people. I put myself under the protection of British law—a protection which I claim from Your Royal Highness as the strongest, the stubbornest, and the most generous of my foes.'

Next morning, after an anxious night spent in arranging accommodation on the *Bellerophon* for the thirty-three members of Napoleon's company, and wondering whether they might not after all slip away in the dark, Maitland was relieved to see the brig *Épervier*, with a flag of truce flying, coming slowly out from the Île d'Aix. At the same time the *Superb*, Admiral Hotham's flagship, was sighted sailing up the bay. Being anxious, as any junior officer might be, to finish the affair for himself, Maitland sent off the captain's barge and brought Napoleon on board.

'When he came on the quarter deck, he pulled off his hat, and addressing me in a firm tone of voice said: I am come to throw myself on the protection of your Prince and laws. I shall probably (he added) spend the remainder of my life in England.'

A fortnight later (July 31st) the British government decided that 'General Bonaparte' should be deported to St. Helena. Within a few hours Sir Samuel Romilly received a letter from Savary, who knew him to be a skilled lawyer and liberal reformer, protesting against the proposal—as he took it to be—to hand over himself and Lallemand to the vengeance of Louis XVIII. He enclosed a copy of a letter from Maitland to Lord Melville agreeing that Savary and Lallemand 'threw themselves under the protection of the British flag,' and that he had 'acted in the full confidence that their lives would be held sacred.' This appeal Romilly passed on to the Lord Chancellor, and it was effective. The 'protection' guaranteed to Savary and Lallemand would apply also to Napoleon—no less, and no more. The document which Savary forwarded at the same time, entitled *Considérations sur Napoléon Bonaparte et sa situation civile et politique en abordant en Angleterre*, could add nothing more to the point. Even if Maitland had exceeded his instructions, and promised more than he had any right to do, the government were not bound by his *ipse dixit*. But he had not.

Savary's arguments were beside the point. Napoleon had no more right than any other foreigner to claim the liberties of a British citizen. His life was secure under the British flag: where the remainder of it might be spent was entirely at the discretion of the British government. This was in effect the answer that Romilly himself gave to a subsequent letter from Savary, raising the same point, a year later.

The British government did not stand alone in this attitude. They were acting for the Allies. It was the Russian cabinet (and the Tsar was the Allied Sovereign who most wished to treat his fallen enemy with respect) which drew up the memorandum annexed to the protocol at Aix-la-Chapelle (November 13th, 1818) which insisted that by his return from Elba Napoleon had lost all right to be considered the Emperor of the French; that he could only be regarded as 'a disturber of public peace, a rebel, a vagabond and a refugee'; and that though on board the *Bellerophon* he might be under the British flag, he was also under the jurisdiction of the international court of Europe (*il dépendait de la justice de l'Europe*).

Nor must it be forgotten,—it was familiar enough to every member of the British government—that public opinion, as expressed in the columns of *The Times*, was at this moment denouncing Bonaparte as a poisoner, an assassin and an incendiary, and was demanding that he should either be delivered up 'to the justice of an injured sovereign, and of a country which he has involved in every species of ruin,' or be placed on trial for 'the murder of Captain Wright' who, imprisoned as an accomplice of Cadoudal, had been 'found dead' in his cell at the Temple ten years before (October 25th, 1805): such might be the unreckoned result of appealing to 'the protection of British law.'

There was, then, no perfidy, and no unfairness, on the part of the British government: only some lack of consideration in the way in which they carried out the Allies' resolve. On the part of Napoleon there was a complete failure or refusal to face realities: a blindness, which by now had become inveterate, to the idea that the Emperor of the French was subject to the normal rules of right and wrong, or that the reprobation of Europe might justly be visited upon one who had for so many years been a disturber of international peace.[1]

During the two days that .the *Bellerophon* was anchored in Torbay (July 24th-26th) Napoleon was a public spectacle to anyone who could hire a boat to row round the ship, and was fortunate enough to get a sight of him; and it may be that, confusing publicity with popularity, he took these demonstrations as evidence that he could appeal from the British government to the British people: a delusion that remained in his mind throughout his exile at St. Helena. When at last orders came from the Admiralty that he should be transferred to the *Northumberland* for the voyage to St. Helena, it had to be decided who should accompany him. After much agitation and heart-burning he was permitted a suite of twenty-six persons: Bertrand with his wife, three children, and two servants, one with a child of her own: Montholon with his wife, one child, and a servant; Las Cases and his son; Gourgaud; Marchand and two other *valets de chambre*; two *valets à pied*; a *chef d'office, cuisinière, maître d'hôtel, huissier* and *lampiste*. A Pole, Piontkowski, who had been with Napoleon at Elba, was allowed to follow him two months later.

The voyage from Torbay to St. Helena occupied an uneventful nine weeks. Napoleon soon became, as usual at sea, companionable and knowledgeable. True, he would not take wine with the officers after dinner, preferring to read in his cabin—one of his books was a life of Nelson; but he would walk the deck with the admiral, play chess with one of the officers, or talk about himself. On his birthday they all drank his health, and let him win eighty *napoléons* at *vingt-et-un*. Later he gave up this game for *wisth et piquet*. It was noticed that he habitually kept his hands in his pockets, unless it was to take snuff, and that he never offered his box to anyone he might be talking with. At dinner he preferred meat and coffee, and would eat a mutton cutlet with his fingers. The officers were struck with his uncommonly 'large, full, and pale' face, and his way of talking without any movement of the skin or muscles, so unlike the general way of Frenchmen. He sometimes smiled, but was seldom seen to laugh. One day Gourgaud measured his height in his cabin, and made it 5 feet 2½ inches.[2]

3

When the *Northumberland* entered James Bay, Las Cases wrote in his diary that as the anchor touched ground it 'formed the first link in the chain that bound the modern Prometheus to his rock.' The legend of St. Helena had begun.

The island is much the same size and shape as Jersey, but far more mountainous, for its central spine rises to three peaks of about 2500 feet, and on most sides it thrusts great cliffs into the sea. 'It rises abruptly,' wrote Charles Darwin, 'like a huge black castle from the ocean.' But the grim rockiness of its first appearance somewhat belies its real character.

'This is a very queer place, I assure you,' wrote Major Gorrequer to his friend Lieut.-Col. Fergusson; 'it is the *vice-versa* of all others. All the verdure and cultivated parts are at the summit of immense mountains— the lower regions resembling cast iron more than anything else; it blows continually in the same direction, and is always raining; the shores of the island are frightful precipices without any beach. Bonaparte calls it the Island of Desolation, and says (with truth) that it is the driest and at the same time the wettest country in the universe. . . .'

The *Esquisse de la Flore de Sainte-Hélène* with which Antommarchi filled the last 200 pages of his *Mémoires* includes, besides a great variety of flowers, nutmegs, dates, pears, coconuts and other plants good for food; on the upper slopes there were still traces of the semi-tropical forest which once covered the whole island. To Darwin the vegetation seemed surprisingly British, and the 'English, or rather Welsh character of the scenery' was 'kept up by the numerous cottages, and small white houses, some buried at the bottom of the deepest valleys, and others mounted on the crests of the lofty hills.'

The fauna of the island was specially rich in birds and fish. When Gourgaud followed *la chasse*, he bagged plenty of pheasants, pigeons and partridges; mountain goats and wild peacocks gave good sport, and there was sea-fishing off the rocks—all the more so because, as a measure of precaution against escape, all fishing-boats had been forbidden to put to sea.

The only port, Jamestown, was at the mouth of a narrow valley at the north-west corner of the island. From this point a winding road climbed inland for three miles to Hut's Gate, then turned left north-eastwards for another mile and more to Deadwood, the only large piece of level ground on the island, and to the house called Longwood. If one turned to the right at Hut's Gate a tortuous road led in two miles to Plantation House, the Governor's residence, and thence downhill in another three miles back to Jamestown. This part of the island, with the coast east of Longwood, was all that was familiar to Napoleon and his company, and all that is seen by most modern travellers, who are content to visit the places where Napoleon lived and was buried. Sandy Bay on the south coast, 'a place of indescribable beauty,' the forest-clad mountain ridges, the 'green valleys down which burble little streams,' or the riot of budleia, hibiscus and honeysuckle growing amidst bananas, tree-ferns and olives—little of this would be inferred from the despondent pages of Gourgaud, O'Meara, or Las Cases.

As for the weather, Napoleon was fond of pointing out to Antommarchi how many wet days there were, and how few fine, proving his point from meterological observations made at Longwood in the early months of 1816 and 1817. Certainly there were extremes of wind, sudden changes of temperature and mists such as that which had obscured Halley's sight of the transit of Venus in 1676; yet not more than might be expected in any small mountainous island so near the tropics.

But was all this, at its worst, injurious to health? It was part of the Longwood case against the British government that the climate caused Napoleon's death, or at least hastened it. According to a contemporary resident 'the climate of St. Helena is unquestionably one of the most temperate and salubrious in the universe.' The island was commonly used as a hospital and convalescent home for troops going to and from India; and sick men landed there soon benefited from its good air, fresh water and wholesome food. A recent investigator has also made out that, of eleven persons resident at Longwood with Napoleon, seven exceeded the expectation of life at that time by a total of fifty-seven years, and four fell short of it by thirty-six years; whilst, of thirteen residents at Jamestown, ten exceeded the expectation of life by a total of 126 years, and only three fell short of it by twelve years. These figures should not be taken to mean that Jamestown was more healthy than Longwood—admittedly it was less so—but that the Jamestown people were residents of long standing in the tropics, whereas those at Longwood had newly arrived from Europe.

This is the explanation, too, of the figures given by two doctors, Henry and Baxter, as to the health of the regiments quartered at Longwood. Henry, thinking of the 1st battalion of the 66th, which was already seasoned by service in India, speaks of St. Helena as 'for a tropical climate certainly a healthy island, if not the most healthy of this description in the world'; whereas Baxter says of the 2nd battalion of the same regiment, which came straight from England, that in nine months over 900 men had been in hospital, and twenty died, 'dysentery and liver inflammation being most fatal.' Compare this last remark with the mistaken diagnosis of Napoleon's disease by O'Meara and Antommarchi: it was the local medical theory.

But if St. Helena had been Paradise itself, Napoleon would have found his third island ugly and unhealthy. In Corsica he was a native, and a noble. At Elba he had been a sovereign ruler. Here, whatever he might pretend, he was a prisoner. Every other grievance—and it was not difficult to find grievances—began and ended there. He had persuaded himself that he had voluntarily surrendered to the British government, when he might have gone free to America, trusting British generosity and hospitality; and that his trust had been misplaced, his confidence abused. St. Helena was a garrisoned fort, Longwood a prison, the Governor no better than a warder. Every official notice that spoke of his 'detention,' every rule made for his 'safety,' every limitation put on his movements or his correspondence, even the refusal (a useless and therefore gratuitous offence) to call him 'Emperor,' was construed as an insult, and answered with hard words, and obstructive actions.[3]

4

But this was not so at first; for after one night on shore at Mr. Porteous's house in Jamestown, Napoleon was content, during the next two months, to live by himself in a pavilion in the garden of 'The Briars,' a small house with 'a compact pleasant estate' three miles out of the town, and occupied by Mr. W. Balcombe, a business man, with an invalid wife and three children. This pavilion was a single large room, used for parties, or for passing guests. Wellington had slept there in 1805 on his way back from India, and wrote to Admiral Malcolm from Paris on April 3rd, 1816, 'You must tell "Bony" that I find his apartments at the Elysée Bourbon very convenient, and I hope he likes mine at Mr. Balcom's.' 'The Briars' was free of the noise and publicity of Jamestown; and Napoleon—to the scandal of Las Cases—seemed positively to encourage the friendly impudence of the Balcombe children, especially Betsy, a precocious and lively girl of fourteen. He was happier in this interlude of Empire and the enforced discomforts of a picnic, with bad cooking, undrinkable coffee, and no table linen, than his companions at Jamestown, who were for ever complaining of their uncomfortable town lodgings, and inciting him to compose letters of protest against the *horreur et misère* of their exile. He had got out of uniform, and begun to dictate his memoirs, and might even have settled down to an incognito retirement, and to the kind of country life he had so often said that he desired.

But there were times when he dreamed and talked of a possible return to France, where he fancied he might soon be wanted to keep the Jacobins and *idéologues* in order. And always there rankled in his mind the role of prisoner, and the title of 'General Bonaparte,' upon which the British government, which had never recognized him as Emperor, insisted. If 'Bonaparte' (he argued), then 'Napoleon': if 'General,' then 'Emperor.'

His career, like the Revolution that it consummated, was a *bloc*: it must stand or fall as a whole. To insist on being called Emperor, and to keep up the externals of a court, was not a personal fad, but a political manifesto, a vindication of historical fact. He owed it to France and to Europe. A private grievance is never so dangerous as when it can be identified with a matter of principle.

So the move to Longwood on December 10th was no gain in real happiness. True, he was now able to have the services of his own *chef*, and to enjoy his first hot bath since leaving Malmaison. But once more, as on the day he landed at Jamestown, he appeared in full uniform, with medals and stars, and became an Emperor again. His companions found themselves subject to all the etiquette of the Tuileries: they must stand in his presence, or, when allowed to be seated, remember not to get up if Mme Montholon came into the room. A routine which had been tolerable enough in a spacious life of constant activity and changing interests became unbearable when contracted into a few rooms where there was nothing whatever to do. They could not be called a happy family party (admits Las Cases): 'we still quarrelled over the few remains of our life of luxury, and the relics of our ambitions': more than once Napoleon had to exhort them to cheerfulness and unity. The most characteristic entry in all Gourgaud's *Journal* is, '*Juin 25-30. Mardi 25, Ennui, Ennui. Mercredi 26, Idem. Jeudi 27, Idem. Vendredi 28, Idem. Dimanche 30, Grand ennui.*'

Longwood, the country seat of the Lieutenant Governor, stood 1700 feet above the sea in 'the most eligible situation on the island,' surrounded by a walled and planted estate. 'Viewed from a short distance (wrote Darwin) it appears like a respectable gentleman's country seat. In front there are a few cultivated fields, and beyond them the smooth hill of coloured rock called the Flagstaff, and the rugged square black mass of the Barn.' The house itself, described by a contemporary as an 'insufficient dwelling, a set of rooms thrown together at different times without attention to order or convenience,' was in fact a four-roomed bungalow, enlarged for Napoleon's use by the addition of two sizable wooden apartments at right angles to the original building.

One entered this extension from the north by a small veranda, and passed through the *parloir*, a long room with six windows, and the *salon*, a little smaller, into the four original rooms, which were now, from left to right, the library, the dining-room, the Emperor's study, and his bedroom; all were small, and the dining-room dark. Behind came a courtyard surrounded by outbuildings: on the left a pantry (*argenterie*), on the right a kitchen and linen-room, at the back a *pharmacie*, and two rooms for Las Cases and his son; finally, in an extension running southwards, rooms for the British *officier de surveillance*, for Gourgaud and O'Meara, and two large apartments for the Montholon family. Only Bertrand, of the inner circle, remained outside, and lived in a cottage at Hut's Gate till a house could be built for him close by. The new part of Longwood was cheerful enough, with its veranda and big windows, a garden on either side, and a fifty-foot walk (*tonnelle*) beneath an elaboarte pergola. The rest had the elegant stuffiness of any eighteenth-century country lodge; but there were the open fireplaces which Napoleon always liked, and the study had a door with steps down into the garden.[4]

5

'But what shall we do *dans ce lieu perdu?* (asked the Emperor)—Sire; replied Las Cases, we will live on the past; read about Caesar and Alexander, or better (he added) we will re-read *your* life, Sire!—Of course! (was the reply) We will write Our own Memoirs!' But Las Cases and his companions were not content to transcribe from Napoleon's dictation: they kept private diaries, in which they recorded, day by day, the small events of their exile, and Napoleon's studied and unstudied conversation.

The canon, as it may not unfairly be called, of the St. Helena scriptures has never yet been investigated with the full care of literary criticism— indeed this cannot be done until the whole of Bertrand's *Journal* is available. Of this the most careless reader is soon aware; for many topics recur in various forms: and they need to be collated and compared, before one can be at all sure what Napoleon really said, and how far the variations are due to careless reporting, copying, or deliberate editing.

The chronological sequence of the St. Helena canon may be set out thus. For the voyage to St. Helena and the first months of residence there, we have Gourgaud's *Journal*, O'Meara's *Voice from St. Helena*, and the *Mémorial* of Las Cases. From the time of the arrival of Lowe in April 1816 to the departure of Gourgaud in February 1818, there is also Bertrand's *Journal*. After O'Meara and Las Cases go in July and November 1818, this is still the main authority (but only part of the work is at present available); for Montholon's *Memoirs* were not published till 1847, and Antommarchi's *Derniers Moments* borrowed much from O'Meara's and Las Cases books, which preceded it: both these sources have some value as narratives of events, but little as records of Napoleon's conversation.

Las Cases has been called the Boswell of St. Helena. It is true that the *Mémorial* contains much the same number of words—about half a million —as the *Life of Johnson*, that it throws into literary form the daily life and conversation of a great talker, and that it is based on notes made at the time. But there the likeness ends: for Las Cases's editorial habits destroy one's trust in his truthfulness. He groups together the events of several days at a time; he gives summaries covering several months; he inserts long excursuses which owe less to Napoleon's words than to his own researches; but above all he makes the Emperor talk—and talk at immense length—in a style which is not that of the dictated *Correspondance*, but Las Cases's own: literary, not conversational, rounded and balanced, not rhetorical. This is not like Boswell's occasional 'improvement' of some Johnsonian turn of words, but a constant translation into another kind of language, the expression of a different type of mind: as though Wellington's table-talk had been paraphrased by Coleridge.

Seeing himself as a literary man, Las Cases was also ready to devote his talents to publicizing the attitude which his hero adopted towards his present captivity and his past career. It may be doubted how far this attitude was the natural reaction of a great man in retirement planning an Apologia—literature is rich in such works—or how far it was a deliberate attempt to create for the benefit of Napoleon's possible successors the legend (which a series of historical accidents ultimately made effective) of an Empire founded on the principles of Liberalism, Pacificism, Nationalism, and Religious Toleration. Some readers may be content with the verdict of one of Creevey's correspondents on Las Cases's book: 'the most delicious effusion of sentimental old French twaddle that ever was read'; others may feel that through all its extravagances they get something of Napoleon's real mind.

Gourgaud was a soldier, not a literary man: he had neither the intelligence to invent a 'legend' nor the skill to express it. Like Las Cases, he diligently wrote up his diary day by day, but kept the events and conversations of each day distinct, and eschewed summaries and compilations. Having no style of his own, he did his best to record Napoleon's own words; and time after time the reader recognizes (as he seldom does in Las Cases's version) the authentic tone of the official *Correspondance*. The *Journal* is half as long as the *Mémorial*; but it has twice as much of the real Napoleon in it.[5]

6

The historian who wishes to get at the truth about Napoleon's thoughts and feelings during the five and a half years of his exile on St. Helena will not pay undue attention to his resentment against the precautions taken to prevent his escape. It may be said, St. Helena was the safest prison in the world, and that he might have been allowed perfect liberty within it. It is 1200 miles distant from Africa and 1800 from South America: the nearest island is Ascension, and that 600 miles away. Though it was on the main route of traffic to and from India and the Cape, and 150 ships called there during 1816-21, vessels could not easily approach it, owing to the prevalent winds, except from the south-east, and could be sighted from the hills long before they were liable to interception by the frigates that constantly circled the island. In any case there were few possible landing-places, and those as hard of access from the land as from the sea. Nevertheless the Governor could not ignore the possibility of an attempt at rescue (Montchenu's papers alone contain sufficient evidence that such a plot was on foot in South America); he was amply justified in limiting Napoleon's movements, and requiring daily evidence (by signal from the barracks at Longwood to Plantation House) of his presence on the island. When Wellington was asked, in the autumn of 1818, *à propos* of O'Meara's *Voice from St. Helena*, whether it was necessary to limit Napoleon's movements on the island, 'By God!' he replied in his usual manner, 'I don't know. Bonaparte is so damned intractable a fellow, there is no knowing how to deal with him.' But it was a pity that the government of the island was taken out of the hands of Colonel Wilks, the representative of the East India Company, a rich, well educated and hospitable man, and put into those of Sir Hudson Lowe, an Irishman 'wanting in education and judgment (said Wellington), a stupid man, suspicious and jealous.' With Wilks, as with Cockburn of the *Northumberland* and Malcolm, the Admiral of the station, Napoleon had got on well enough: with Lowe he was at loggerheads from the first. He objected to the rigidity with which the new Governor interpreted his orders and carried out his rules. He resented what seemed an unnecessary emphasis on his status as a prisoner. But, though he entered with some zest into the popular game of Lowe-baiting, and was even prepared to sacrifice his health and comfort rather than comply with the Governor's demands—this applies particularly to the later period, after Las Cases was sent home for trying to smuggle a letter out of the island (November 1818)—yet this whole question, which French writers discuss with such passion, was of little importance to Napoleon except as anti-British propaganda: he knew well enough that a prisoner must be imprisoned. The pity of it was that one who knew only how to command should be the prisoner of one who knew only how to obey.

If he gradually gave up the walks and rides, the jaunts into the country, the interviews and the dinner-parties of the earlier days at Longwood; if he would not attend the amateur theatricals at Jamestown, the races at Deadwood (which he watched through his telescope), or the ball given by *La Kricket-Society*; if he soon got tired of shooting with Gourgaud because he 'expected the birds to wait for him'; if he became more and more a recluse, spending long hours in bed, or in his bath, reading, dictating, and talking; it was mainly because he was growing bored, and tired, and ill. He had given up any idea of escape, or of a recall to Europe. Five months of Bourbon misrule had been enough to guarantee his return from Elba. It would need more like ten years now; and by then he would be too old. There was nothing to look forward to; and what had he ever done but look forward? He could now only look back. He would write his memoirs. He would explain to the world what he had done, and what he had meant to do. There was nothing else to keep him alive.

But he was not an old man, even as the expectation of life went a century and a half ago. He had never 'retired.' He could not dissociate the man he was from the man he had been. His memoirs, like the lamentable writings of the proscribed Girondins in 1793, or of the 'collaborators' of 1940, dealt with matters still *sub judice*, and were speeches for the defence. That is why historians show little interest in the eight volumes of *Mémoires pour servir à l'histoire de France sous Napoléon*, the two volumes of *Campagnes d'Egypte et de Syrie*, and the six volumes of *Commentaires* published between 1830 and 1867, and are cautious in their use of the conversations recorded by Las Cases.

There were certain topics to which Napoleon returned again and again: his Corsican childhood, the Egyptian expedition, the return to France in 1799, Marengo, Austerlitz, 1812, the return from Elba, 1815. He was fond of talking about his Austrian marriage, of comparing Marie-Louise with Joséphine, of recounting his amours, often with a freedom offensive to polite taste: and he could not describe too often the circumstances of the birth of the King of Rome. When the events of his own life failed he would talk about books, which he devoured with a speed and a gusto like Dr. Johnson's—72 volumes of Memoirs in one year; and his criticisms were often shrewd, though unimaginative.

Often too (it seems) he would discourse about science and religion, the meaning of life, and the nature of reality. These topics did not interest Las Cases: they hardly fitted into the 'legend.' But if instinct and experience are right in expecting something more from a man than mere efficiency in the business of life, if greatness is to be reckoned in terms of mental integrity and moral principle, then it is to these conversations that we shall look for evidence of Napoleon's real mind.[6]

7

Consider a series of speculations recorded by the diligent Gourgaud as to the origin and nature of human existence.

'1817. January 6th. What are electricity, galvanism, magnetism? There lies the great secret of nature. Galvanism works silently. I believe myself that man is the product of these fluids and of the atmosphere, that the brain circulates these fluids and so gives life, that these fluids compose the soul, and that after death they return into the ether, whence they are circulated by other brains.

'1817. January 28th. I believe that man issued from the slime (*a été produit par le limon de la terre*) when heated by the sun and combined with electric fluids. What are the animals—an ox for example—but or-

ganized matter? Very well! When you see that we are constituted in
almost the same way, is there not good ground for believing that man is
only matter better organized, his condition almost that of material perfection? Perhaps at some future time there will appear beings of even
greater material perfection. Where is the soul of an infant? or of a mad-
man? It is an accompaniment of physical growth in youth. Does it decay
with age? If it is immortal, it must have existed before us: then why
does it remember nothing? . . . Look at it another way. How is one
to explain thought? Why, at this moment, whilst I am talking to you,
I am back in France; I can see the Tuileries, I can see Paris. All the same,
nothing is simpler than the idea of a God. Who made everything? There
is a veil we cannot lift; something beyond the utmost reach of our soul
and understanding; a higher order of being. The simplest idea is to
worship the sun, the universal fertilizer (*qui féconde tout*) . . . I have
often discussed these things with the Bishop of Nantes. Where do animals
go after death? He told me they have a special kind of soul, and go to a
limbo of their own.

'December 17th. When I see a pig or a dog with an appetite and digestion, I say to myself: if I have a soul, so have they. Show a savage a watch,
and he will think it has a soul. If man is a thinking being, it is because his
nature is more perfect than that of a fish. When my digestion is out of
order I don't think so well as when it is working properly. Everything
is material.'

It would be possible to sweep all this aside as a second-hand version of
ideas derived from d'Holbach and Diderot; and if we knew more about
Napoleon's reading we might be able to point to chapter and verse of its
origin. But that would not account for the element of personal experience
in it, nor for the prominence given to these conversations by Gourgaud,
the most faithful witness, and the one who, as a simple Catholic, must
most have disliked them; still less, for the way in which Las Cases, in his
anxiety to show that Napoleon really believed in the religion he professed, and the altars he re-established, tries to explain away this
unfortunate manifesto of infidelity. The only part of the conversations reported by Gourgaud which reappears in the *Mémorial*—the question put
to the bishop of Nantes about the souls of animals—is attributed to a
casual questioner (*lui disait-on*). Instead of the arguments for materialism,
Napoleon puts forward those for religious belief: 'A man launched into
life asks himself—where do I come from? Who am I? Where am I
going? There are so many questions of this kind that force us towards
religion. We hurry to meet it—that is our natural tendency. But then
comes education, and history: they are the great enemies of the true
faith, distorted as it is by human imperfection . . . Such, exactly, has
been my spiritual development. I needed faith, and I found it: but it was

shaken and unsettled as soon as I began to learn and reason, and that happened early enough, when I was thirteen. Perhaps, God willing, I shall become a simple believer again. Certainly I am not fighting against faith: there is nothing I should like better; I regard it as a true and great happiness. One thing I can affirm—that in times of storm, and of casual temptations to immorality, I have never been influenced at all by lack of religious faith, and have never doubted the existence of God. If my reason could not comprehend Him, I was none the less deeply conscious of Him. My feelings were in sympathy with the faith.'

Is this kind of talk compatible with the sceptical conversations recorded by Gourgaud? If it had been authentic, would he not have reproduced it? If it is Las Cases's interpretation of Gourgaud's account, is it a fair one? Does it sound like Napoleon? Was this the spirit in which the Concordat was negotiated, or the Coronation carried through, or the Pope deported to Savona and Fontainebleau, or the religious affairs of the Empire administered? The most that can safely be supposed is that it represents the nostalgic mood in which Napoleon sometimes remembered the faith of his childhood—the mood which induced him to accept the ministrations of a Corsican priest on his death-bed, and to die, like Voltaire, in the 'arms of the Church.'

No. Napoleon's attachment to religion might have been better defended as Dr. Johnson defended that of his friend John Campbell: 'I am afraid he has not been in the inside of a church for many years; but he never passes a church without pulling off his hat. This shows that he has good principles.' Napoleon was as irreligious as any man could well be; but no one was more forward to recognize the established church in any country he wished to control—Mohammedanism in Egypt, Catholicism in Italy or Spain, no doubt Orthodoxy if he had established himself in Moscow and Anglicanism if he had succeeded in crossing the English Channel. His religion was a matter of policy, not conviction.

It is not irrelevant to bear in mind that a similar tendency is apparent all through the *Mémorial* to interpret Napoleon's career according to a formula of which there is little or no trace in Gourgaud's *Journal*: a formula which recurs in so many of the St. Helena writings that one must suppose that it originated in Napoleon himself, and that Gourgaud alone was either too stupid or too sincere to be taken in by it. Napoleon the champion of the principles of 1789; Napoleon the defender of national rights, in Italy, Germany, Switzerland, Poland; Napoleon the friend of peace, forced into war at every turn by the animosity of England; Napoleon the family man, the founder of a new dynasty; Napoleon the French patriot, the lover of Paris: such are the main headings of a legend invented at Longwood, elaborated in the Château de Ham, and immortalized under the dome of the Invalides.[7]

8

Some men are born to become legendary: others have legends thrust upon them. Napoleon was of such stature that he could not have been hid. Physically indefatigable; mentally capable of wide grasp and intense concentration; with a memory mathematical in its mastery of detail; and with the power to charm and persuade others whilst remaining insensible to any feelings or interests but his own—Napoleon had every gift required to found a real renown and to create an imaginary one.

'He talked of anatomy,' says Gourgaud one day, 'and assured us that no one had ever been able to hear his heart beating; he might as well not have had one at all.' Gourgaud's unusually courtly reply was that His Majesty carried his heart in his head. It was true. He was prodigal of his senses towards Joséphine, but thrifty of his heart: he had both well under control in his other amours, and in his second marriage. When Gourgaud had taken offence at some slight rebuff (as he was too fond of doing) and excused it by his affection for Napoleon, the reply was, 'Sensibility? Bah! what silliness! You must be a man. You don't know the way of the world. You should scoff at everything: you mustn't take things so seriously.' Again: 'You must take things as you find them (*paraître complaisant*); promise as much as you like, but never keep your promises. That's the way of the world. You take everything too seriously. You're just a big baby!' 'After all (he sums up his own character) I only care for people who are useful to me, and as long as they are useful. What does it matter how they think about me—or what they say?' *N'est-il pas vrai, Gourgaud* (he said one day) *qu'on est heureux d'être égoiste, insensible?*

Such insensibility and hardness of heart would be no bar to the admiration and loyalty that Napoleon won, not merely from the common people, and the ranks of the army, but from his almost equals—men of capacity and ideas. Such men admired his great qualities, followed his inspiring leadership, but did not, for all that, entirely like him or trust him. Amongst his family, his ministers, his generals, he found in the end more enemies than friends. One cannot imagine his commanding the personal reverence that made Jane Carlyle go up behind Wellington in a crowded room, when she thought herself unobserved, and kiss his shoulder. One woman, Joséphine, and perhaps two men, Bertrand and Caulaincourt, never wavered in their attachment to him. But rulers need clever servants even more than close friends; and Napoleon was eminently skilful in choosing and keeping able men for his service—the Fouchés and the Talleyrands—dominating them by his knowledge and energy, allowing them liberty without trust, and forgiving more often than punishing their mistakes. He might have adopted the title of the strongest of Bourbon kings—*Bien Servi*: he would have valued it more than that of the most popular of them—*Bien Aimé*. 'When a king is said to be a good fellow (he told his brother Louis) his reign is a failure.' He had the dictatorial mind and morals to perfection. *Il voit les choses tellement en masse et de si haut* (wrote Las Cases) *que les hommes lui échappent. Personne ne peut prendre d'empire sur moi* (Gourgaud reports him as saying); *vous voudriez être le centre de tout ici, comme le soleil au milieu des planêtes. C'est moi qui doit être le centre.*

Yet this hardness, this ruthlessness, this egoism—not so much that of a cruel man as of one who will let no consideration interfere with his life-work—to what cause was it devoted? To the consummation of the revolution of 1789? To the military and naval defeat of Great Britain? To setting up a French Empire in the Mediterranean and Near East? To the establishment of enlightened government and economic self-sufficiency in Europe? Each of these, perhaps, at one time or another, was more prominent in his mind than the rest. None contained the single unselfish motive that might have given high purpose and consistent greatness to his career.

9

For a hundred years the nature of Napoleon's disease and the cause of his death were in dispute between writers more anxious to attack or defend the British government than to study the medical evidence. When that is done, there need be little doubt about the true answer to both questions.

The doctors who attended Napoleon at St. Helena were (1) from October 1815 to July 1818, O'Meara, (2) from September 1819 to May 1821, Antommarchi: but (3) during the interregnum between O'Meara and Antommarchi, Stokoe, the surgeon of the *Conqueror*, paid five visits, and (4) from April 21st, 1821, till Napoleon's death Arnott, the senior army surgeon on the island, was called in to consult with Antommarchi. (5) Daily reports on Napoleon's condition, based on what was said by the doctors, were made to the Governor by Dr. Baxter; these reports provide the best evidence by which to check the published accounts of O'Meara and Antommarchi, and to arrive at the facts. (6) At the post mortem, besides Arnott and Antommarchi, five English doctors were present: Shortt, Burton, Mitchell, Livingstone, and Henry.

There were two rival theories as to Napoleon's illness: that of the 'French' party, that it was due to a disease of the liver, brought on by the climate of St. Helena; and that of the 'British' party, either that the symptoms were hypochondriacal, or that, if Napoleon was really ill, it was due to a cancer of long standing. None of the medical men diagnosed the gastric ulcer which had long existed, and which, by neglect and improper treatment (such as merciless doses of rhubarb and calomel), became malignant. 'The cancer which killed Napoleon (such is the recent conclusion of a doctor who carefully and impartially studied all the available evidence) was secondary to a chronic ulcer, from which he must have suffered for a considerable time, and in the edges of which it originated.'

This was the disease from which Napoleon believed his father and sister to have suffered, and of which he expected to die. Its beginnings would not compromise a steel constitution, unaffected by the heat of Syria or the Russian cold: it might account for the occasional attacks of vomiting, followed by lethargy, which some writers have turned into evidence of epilepsy. His condition was no doubt worsened by the boredom and depression of life at Longwood, together with his refusal for a great part of the time to go out, or to take exercise. But it was not directly due to the climate of St. Helena, or to his treatment by the British government.

So now he was dying: slowly, inevitably: nor had he any wish to go on living. 'If I ended my career at this moment,' he told Bertrand on March 28th, five weeks before the end, 'it would be a happiness. There are moments when I wish I were dead. It would be a happiness for me to die within a fortnight. What have I to hope for?' Then, a little later: 'On the whole I don't wish to die, I don't want to; but, as things are, life has little value for me. I blame myself for some mistakes, but for no crimes. It would surely be better to die than to go on vegetating here as I have done for the last six years.'

His mind was active and inquisitive almost to the end. Bertrand's notes of his conversations during the last weeks contain constant references to topics already recorded by Gourgaud and Las Cases: he carries on a long medical discussion with the doctors on the anatomy and physiology of his disease; and, when his memory is at last failing (April 28th-29th) there recur two of those long *questionnaires* to which he subjected his interlocutors, but now endlessly repetitive. One of the iron camp-beds upon which he had slept during so many campaigns was brought into the *salon*, where Bertrand, or Montholon, or the valet, Marchand, could be at hand by day and night. 'Tears came into my eyes (it is Bertrand who says it) when I saw this formidable man, proudly accustomed to absolute obedience, begging for a spoonful of coffee, asking leave to drink, obeying like a child, begging again and again, and taking refusal without resentment . . . There lay Napoleon the Great, humble and pitiful.'

At times he would feel a little better. 'For the last three days' (it is April 18th), 'he always has his windows opened; and commonly, when he sits in his chair, he says "Good morning, sun! Good morning, sun, my friend!" or nods it a greeting.'

During the last of these intervals, less than a month before his death, he dictated his will to Montholon, and added from time to time fresh codicils: he seemed to forget no one, to provide for everything. Certainly he did not forget or forgive his enemies. 'I recommend my son (he wrote) never to forget that he is a French prince by birth, and never to let himself become an instrument in the hands of the Triumvirate which oppresses the peoples of Europe.' Again: 'I die prematurely, assassinated by the English oligarchy and their murderer' (*sicaire*—he means Lowe). Even less pardonable, perhaps, is the codicil which leaves £500 to a certain Cantillon who had been acquitted on a charge of attempting to assassinate the Duke of Wellington: 'He had as much right to assassinate that oligarch as he had to send me to perish here on the rock of St. Helena.'

For the last few days Bertrand's journal is little but a painful record of *lavements, crachements, vomissements, évanouissements*. On May 1st the abbé Vignali, under conditons of some secrecy, administers Extreme Unction. On the night of the 2nd the Emperor tries to get up, and then falls back on his bed muttering *Mon Dieu, Mon Dieu, Mon Dieu!* On the 3rd he drinks a little wine, and says 'Good, bon, very well.' He is very weak, with death in his eyes: he looks at Marchand with a pitiful expression, as though to say, Why do you torment me so?

On May 4th he lay with his hands crossed on his breast, his eyes half closed, his pulse weakening. On May 5th he was like a corpse, *très calme, immoblie*; only from time to time a tear fell on his cheek. During the night he had pronounced his son's name, *Napóléon*, and the words, *A la tête d'armée*. In the evening, as the sun was setting, he sighed four times, and died.[8]

10

During the last hours the curtains had been drawn back, the windows opened; sixteen members of the household stood in silent groups (imperial etiquette still forbade any other attitude) watching the Emperor die, whilst in the next room Vignali could be heard at prayer. At the moment of his last breath, someone stopped the clock on the mantelpiece. It was 5.51. Within a few minutes Lowe (who had spent the day at New Longwood, close by) received the news, and had the death attested by the English doctors, Shortt and Mitchell: Arnott stayed in the room all night, and the abbé remained at prayer. At seven o'clock next day the Governor returned, with a dozen companions, and confronted the Frenchmen across the body of the prisoner who had at last escaped him. 'Do you recognize him?' he asked Montchenu, the only remaining representative of the Powers, who had been commissioned to guarantee his presence on the island, and who now saw him for the first time in five years . . . 'Yes (he said), I do.'

In a letter to Lowe two years afterwards, Dr. Henry wrote: 'The face presented a remarkably placid expression, indicative of mildness and even sweetness of disposition, which afforded a most striking contrast with the active life and moral character of the deceased. The features were regular, and even might be considered beautiful. The head . . . was of large size . . . The forehead was very broad and full; the organs of combativeness, philo-progenitiveness, and causativeness were strongly developed . . . The skin . . . was very white and delicate, as were the hands and arms. Indeed the whole body was slender and effeminate. There was scarcely any hair on the body, and that of the head was thin, fine and silky.'

But now the doctors, each anxious to prove his theory of the cause of death, were gathered round Antommarchi, as he dissected the Emperor's body: that at least he could do efficiently. The report of the post mortem exists in several forms: the original draft by Shortt, as the principal medical officer on the island, including a sentence to the effect (this was his particular theory) that the liver was larger than natural, afterwards crossed out and altered in the margin; this amended report, signed by Shortt, Burton, Mitchell and Arnott, with a note saying the omission was made by order of the Governor; and several copies of this document, with the addition of Livingstone's signature. Antommarchi refused to sign any of the reports, because he had never diagnosed the ulcerated stomach which was now shown to be the site of the disease, and would not admit his mistake.

Several drawings were made of the dead Emperor lying on his narrow bed; the best of them by Captain Marryat, who happened to be at Jamestown at the time. There were several attempts too to make a cast of the face: the only successful one was Dr. Burton's; it disappeared soon afterwards, removed, as was supposed, by Antommarchi, and was used by him to produce the 'death-masks' that he put on the market seven years later.

For two days the body lay in state, and hundreds of those on the island came to see dead one whom they had never seen alive. On May 9th it was carried on the shoulders of British grenadiers, beneath flags bearing in gold letters the names of Minden, Talavera, Albuera, Pyrenees, Orthez, and was buried under a group of weeping willows in the Valley of the Geranium. But it was buried anonymously: for Hudson Lowe, meticulous to the last letter, would not allow the name *Napoleon* to be put on the coffin, and Montholon would have no other.

Meticulous, but not ungenerous. 'Well, gentlemen,' he said afterwards, 'he was England's greatest enemy, and mine too: but I forgive him everything. On the death of a great man like him we should only feel deep concern and regret.' But in London the news of his death 'made much less sensation than the death of Lady Worcester: nobody talks of it, and the only feeling is pleasure that we are saved the expense of keeping him.'

Twenty years later Louis-Philippe, the last king of France, thought to win popularity and outbid the Bonapartists by restoring Napoleon to the city where he would be: for during his last illness he had quoted the lines of Voltaire:

Mais à revoir Paris, je ne dois plus prétendre,
Vous voyez qu'au tombeau je suis prêt à descendre;

and in his will he had written: 'I wish my remains to rest on the banks of the Seine, amidst the French people that I loved so well.'

The King of Rome was dead. The Bonaparte brothers, scattered over two continents, looked askance at the only member of their family who claimed the imperial succession. But others were still loyal. Antommarchi, O'Meara, and Vignali were dead. Las Cases was too ill to go, but sent his son. Bertrand, at sixty-seven, would not be refused, nor Gourgaud. With them went Marchand, and five of the old domestics. The leader of the expedition was Louis-Philippe's third son, the Prince de Joinville. Their ship was the frigate *Belle-Poule*.

They landed at Jamestown on October 9th, 1840, almost the anniversary of Napoleon's arrival there twenty-five years before. On the 14th at midnight work was begun at the tomb; early next day the innermost of the four coffins was opened, and the body found almost untouched by time—that of a young man, it seemed, with unwrinkled face, beside his now aged companions, Bertrand, Marchand, Gourgaud. The coffin was closed again, placed in a new outer case brought from France, and covered with a pall bearing the initial 'N' and a crown. Three days later the *Belle-Poule* set sail, carrying the Emperor's body in a mortuary chapel constructed below deck.

At Cherbourg, on November 29th, the coffin was transferred to a river boat, taken to Havre and up the Seine. At Rouen, as it passed under the bridge, the people threw laurels on the deck, and the archbishop pronounced a blessing. At Paris, on December 14th, the body was received by old Soult, as President of the Council. Next day it was drawn on a magnificent hearse by six horses under the Arc de Triomphe, along the Champs-Elysées, and across the Seine, amidst the firing of cannon and ringing of bells, to the Invalides. There the Prince de Joinville handed over his trust to the King, and Gourgaud placed on the bier the sword that Napoleon had worn at Austerlitz. And there in the Invalides, in St. Jérôme's chapel, the body lay, till, twenty years later, it was placed by Napoleon III where it now lies, beneath the lovely dome of Louis XIV; its first *gardien* Santini, who had followed the Emperor ever since he enlisted as a drummer-boy in the Grand Army of 1805. A heavy sarcophagus of Finnish granite, given by a successor of Alexander I, is surrounded by twelve colossal figures of Napoleon's victories, fifty-four flags taken at Austerlitz, and ten bas-reliefs representing the legend of 'Napoléon le Grand,' as interpreted by 'Napoléon le Petit.' In a reliquary rest his hat, his sword, and his grand chain of the Legion of Honour. In the surrounding chapels are monuments of Joseph and Jérôme, of the King of Rome, of Vauban and Turenne, of Bertrand and Marshal Foch.

Here, one evening in 1855, Queen Victoria and the Emperor Napoleon III stood side by side; and the Queen, putting her hand on the shoulder of the small boy who was to be Edward VII, said, 'kneel down before the tomb of the great Napoleon.'

It was Foch who, a hundred years after Napoleon's death, wrote his truest epitaph, and best summed up the causes of his rise and of his fall: 'He forgot that a man cannot be God; that above the individual is the nation, and above mankind the moral law: he forgot that war is not the highest aim, for peace is above war.'[9]

APPENDIX

Napoleon's Correspondence

THE *Correspondance de Napoléon* published by order of Napoleon III between 1858 and 1870 falls into two series covering the dates 1793-1808 and 1808-1815. The contents of each volume are:

Vol. 1   1-1018 (Oct. 25/93–Sept. 21/96)
   2   1019-1746 (Sept. 22/96–Apr. 19/97)
   3   1747-2425 (Apr. 20/97–March 4/98)
   4   2426-3364 (March 5/98–Sept. 21/98)
   5   3365-4383 (Sept. 22/98–Oct. 15/99)
   6   4384-5332 (Oct. 15/99–Jan. 29/01)
   7   5333-6258 (Feb. 2/01–Aug. 18/02)
   8   6259-7129 (Aug. 19/02–Sept. 23/03)
   9   7130-8065 (Sept. 24/03–Sept. 29/04)
  10   8066-8960 (Oct. 1/04–June 28/05)
  11   8961-9740 (July 1/05–Feb. 3/06)
  12   9741-10546 (Feb. 4/06–July 24/06)
  13   10547-11331 (July 25/06–Nov. 30/06)
  14   11332-12248 (Dec. 1/06–March 31/07)
  15   12249-13094 (Apr. 1/07–Aug. 31/07)
  16   13095-13744 (Sept. 1/07–Apr. 13/08)
  17   13745-14382 (Apr. 15/08–Oct. 14/08)
  18   14383-15203 (Oct. 19/08–May 13/09)
  19   15204-15955 (May 19/09–Oct. 15/09)
  20   15956-16742 (Oct. 16/09–July 3/10)
  21   16743-17534 (Aug. 2/10–March 31/11)
  22   17535-18244 (Apr. 1/11–Nov. 6/11)
  23   18245-18877 (Nov. 7/11–June 30/12)
  24   18878-19626 (July 1/12–Feb. 27/13)
  25   19627-20323 (March 1/13–July 31/13)
  26   20324-21054 (Aug. 1/13–Dec. 30/13)
  27   21055-21680 (Jan. 1/14–Feb. 26/15)
  28   21681-22067 (March 1/15–Aug. 3/15)

29 ⎫
30 ⎬ Napoleon's dictated works at St. Helena.
31 ⎭

32 Notes on St. Helena, and Napoleon's *Testament.*

In the first series (vols. 1-15) the Index is in the form of a *Table des pièces*, summarizing the contents of each letter: in the second series (vols. 16-28) it is a *Table analytique*, listing the letters under countries and topics.

NOTES

CHAPTER I

1. Boswell, *Account of Corsica* (1768); cp. *Letters of James Boswell to the Rev. W. J. Temple* (1908), pp. 51, 109.

2. Villat, *Le Corse de 1786 à 1789* (1925); Dumouriez, *Mémoires* (ed. Barrière, 1886).

3. Larrey, *Madame Mère* (1892); Masson and Biagi, *Napoléon inconnu* (1895); Chuquet, *La Jeunesse de Napoléon* (1897-99); bibliography in Villat, *La Révolution et l'Empire*, II (1936); cp. Decaux, *Létizia, mère de l'Empereur* (1950); for the Greek ancestry, *Notes and Queries*, III, xi, 307 f.; for the speech of 1938, *Révolution Française*, 1939, 5.

4. Pichard, *Napoléon à Auxonne* (1847); *Some account of the early years of Buonaparte at the military school of Brienne, by Mr. C. H., one of his school-fellows* (1797); Thomazi, *Napoléon et ses marins* (1950), p. 2; Decaux; Las Cases, *Mémorial de Sainte-Hélène*, August 27th-31st, 1815.

5. Lenôtre, *Vieilles maisons, vieux papiers*, I, 175; Chuquet.

6. Bonaparte had evidently been reading Roustand's *Offrande aux autels* (1764). To this period may belong the four love-letters to 'Emma' described in *N. and Q.*, XIII, v, 20.

7. To this period may belong the sketch of an imaginary correspondence between Theodore, the ex-King of Corsica, and 'Milord Walpole'; also the plan of a romantic novel in which an Englishman landing on an island off Corsica, finds there a Corsican Prospero and Miranda, refugees from the hands of French oppressors.

8. For Strasbourg cp. the Memoirs of L. Grucker, a German student there, who says 'Zu H. Prof. Lorentz kam auch mit mir Buonaparte Napoleon als Student.' The story in the Memoirs of the Duchesse d'Abrantès of Bonaparte's passion for the actress Saint-Huberti, who was playing there at that time, is less trustworthy.

9. Whilst at Auxonne Bonaparte probably wrote a love story, *Ellison et Eugénie*, in the Rousseauist manner. v. Garros, *Itinéraire de Napoléon Bonaparte* (1947), p. 76.

10. The letters quoted are in Masson and Biagi, I, 79, 121; II, 69, 127, 203, 208, 387, 392, 396. English versions in Thompson, *Letters of Napoléon* (1934).

CHAPTER II

1. Pietri, *Lucien Bonaparte* (1929); Nabonne, *Joseph Bonaparte* (1949); Godechot, *Les commissaires aux armées sous le Directoire* (1937).

2. Designed for propaganda, the *Souper de Beaucaire* was printed the same year by Tournal of Avignon and Aurel of Valence.

3. Pons de l'Hérault, *Mémoire pour servir à l'histoire de Toulon en 1793* (1825); *London Gazette*, esp. September 13th, 1793; *Gentleman's Magazine*; *Life and Letters of Sir Gilbert Elliot*, II (1874); *Nelson's Despatches* (ed. Nicolas), I; *commissaires'* reports in Aulard, *Recueil des actes du comité de salut public* (1889-1911); *le Moniteur* (réimpression, 1863-70).

4. Other (less trustworthy) accounts of Bonaparte's appointment are in his Memoirs, and elsewhere.

5. Sir Sidney Smith's *Life and Correspondence* (1848) gives a highly coloured account of the burning of ships and stores.

6. Michon, *Correspondence de Maximilien et Augustin Robespierre* (1926), p. 229.

7. *Correspondence de Napoléon* (referred to as *Corresp.*)—from this point onwards the essential source. See Appendix for account of it and guide to its use. Joseph Conrad's *The Rover* has a good account of the Hyères country.

8. *Corresp.*, under dates given in text; Debidour, *Recueil des actes du directoire exécutif* (1910-17, ends in February 1797); Colin, *L'éducation militaire de Napoléon* (1900); Krebs and Moris, *Campagnes dans les Alpes* (1891-95); Godechot.

9. Michon; Reinhard, *Le grand Carnot* (1950).

10. *Revue de études napoléoniennes*, September 1930; Garros, pp. 72-4; Godechot, I, 240; Pietri, pp. 54-6.

11. Thomazi, *Napoléon et ses marins* (1950).

12. Thibaudeau, *Mémoires sur le Convention* (1821), chap. xvi.

13. *Mémoires de la reine Hortense*, 11; *Mémoires de la duchesse d'Abrantès*; Lenôtre, 1er serié; Garros, p. 87; *Napoleon's letters to Joséphine*, ed. Cerf (1928), or Bourgeat (1941); *N. and Q.*, I, vi, 265, 177, 380; *The Creevey Papers*.

CHAPTER III

1. *Corresp.*, as before under dates in text.

2. Saliceti has been appreciated by Godechot, *Les Commissaires*, I, 237 f; Chaptal, *Mes souvenirs* (1893), 204.

3. Kircheisen, *Napoleon* (E. T.), p. 79.

4. The Italian campaigns are best followed in *Corresp.* (under dates in text), and *Moniteur*. Bibliography in Villat, *La Révolution et l'Empire* (1936), I, 389.

5. Ferrero, *l'Aventure* (1936), with controversy in *Rév. Fran.*, 1937, 221; 1938, 1, and Garros, p. 50; for diplomatic background, Guyot, *Le Directoire et la paix de l'Europe* (1911).

6. These 'defeatist' ideas were represented in Paris by Buonarroti, and lost official support when he was implicated in the Babeuf plot.

7. Walter, *Le Comte de Provence* (1950); for Fructidor, Mathiez in *Annales Historiques*, November-December 1929.

CHAPTER IV

1. *Corresp.* under dates in text; Lacour-Gayet, *Talleyrand* (1928); Desbrière, *Projets et tentatives de débarquement* (1900); Correspondence of W. A. Miles, II, 332.

2. De la Jonquière, *L'Expédition d'Égypte;* Rose, *Napoleonic Studies* (1904) App. 1; *Nelson's Dispatches* (ed. Nicolas, 1844); Lacroix, *Bonaparte en Égypte* (1899).

3. *Corresp.* 2618-2697.

CHAPTER V

1. Leibniz, *Projet d'expédition d'Égypte* (1672) in *Œvres*, v (1864); Savary, *Letters on Egypt* (E.T. 1786); Volney, *Travels through Syria and Egypt in the years 1783, 1784 and 1785* (E.T. 1788); other reports in de la Jonquière; Lacroix, *Bonaparte en Égypte* (1899).

2. Lacour-Gayet, *Talleyrand* (1928); *Ann. Hist.*, March-April 1933; Villat, I, 396-7.

3. *Corresp.* 2778, 2765; *Copies of original letters from the army of General Bonaparte intercepted by the fleet under the command of Admiral Lord Nelson* (London, 1798); Berthier, *Relation* (An. VIII).

4. *Orig. Let.*, II, 110, with facsimile.

5. *Corresp.* 2850, 2907, 3238, 3423; Charles-Roux, *Bonaparte gouverneur d'Égypte* (1936).

6. *Corresp.* 2853, 2937, 3399, 3589, 3542, 3268, 3320-3, 3416, 3456-7, 2736, 2559-60, 2947, 3509, 3654, 3756, 3857, 3904-5; *Annuaire de la République Française calculé pour le méridien du Kaire, l'an IX de l'ère Française* (Imprimerie nationale, Cairo).

7. *Corresp.* 3117; Charles-Roux.

8. *Corresp.* 3091.

9. De la Jonquière, II, 83; *Corresp.* of July 3rd, 27th, 30th, August 19th; *Naval Chronicle*, I, 521; *Logs of the great seafights*, II, (1900) p. 1; Rose, *Napoleon and seapower* in *The Indecision of modern war* (1927); Douin, *La flotte de Bonaparte sur les côtes d'Egypte* (1922).

10. *Corresp.* 3280, 3439, 3528, 3595, 3633, 3677, 3729, 3744, 3775-6, 3936, 3259, 3767, 3938, 3955.

11. *Corresp.* 3076-7, 3282, 4001, 4022, 4025, 4063, 4026, 3605; Smith's dispatches in *Naval Chronicle*, II, 620; Rose, *Napoleonic Studies*, App. II. For the Jaffa incident, Kircheisen, *Napoleon*, 184.

12. Haydon, *Autobiography* (World's Classics).

CHAPTER VI

1. Desaix, who followed from Egypt six months later, was taken by a British frigate off Hyères. Ganteaume commemorated the fortunate outcome of the voyage by having his notepaper engraved with two frigates sailing towards a star in whose centre was the letter 'B,' with the motto, *Nous gouvernions sur son étoile.* In 1807 Napoleon ordered the *Muiron* to be specially preserved in the arsenal at Toulon, with an inscription saying *Elle ramena en 1799 le sauveur de France*; and there was a model of her in his bedroom at Malmaison. v. Thomazi, *Napoléon et ses marins* (1950).

2. Benjamin Constant, *Mémoires.*

3. Aulard, *Paris pendant la réaction thermidorienne et sous le Directoire* (1898-1902).

4. Madelin, *Fouché* (1923), and his *Mémoires*, ed. Madelin (1945).

5. Lacour-Gayet; Bonaparte's first letter to him is in Kerry, *The First Napoleon*, p. 286 (with facsimile).

6. Neton, *Sieyès* (1900).

7. Bourdon, *La Constitution de l'an VIII* (1942).

8. Miot de Melito, *Mémoires*, I, 242.

9. *Corresp.* 4403, 4404, 4439, 4442, 4393, 4414, 4438, 4396, 4398, 4447.

10. Aulard, *Histoire politique de la révolution française*, p. 707.

11. Thiry, *Le Sénat de Napoléon* (1949); Gourgaud, *S. Hélène*, I, 325; Durand, *Études sur le Conseil d'état de Napoléon* (1949); Thibaudeau, *Mémoires*; Chaptal, *Souvenirs*, 55.

12. *Corresp.* 4474.

13. For the prefects, Aulard, *Études et leçons*, 2ième série, 186.

14. Mollien, *Mémoires*; Gaudin, *Mémoires.*

15. Garros, *Itinéraire*, 165; *Corresp.* 4533-4.

16. *Relations secrètes des agents de Louis XVIII*, p. 410.

CHAPTER VII

1. *Corresp.* 4473, 4506, 4744, 4657, 4720.
2. *Corresp.* 4445-6, 4449, 4538, 4614, 4670, 4726, 4599, 4634, 4649.
3. *Corresp.* 4623, 4708, 4722, 4710-1, 4729, 4738, 4731-2.
4. Garros; *Corresp.* 4911, 4952, 4846.
5. *Corresp.* 4729, 4784, 4761, 4786, 4792, 4825, 4904, 4883, 4894, 4807, 4814, 4833, 4838, 4845, 4849, 4881, 4892-4, 4908, 4897; Thiry, *Marengo* (1949). For another legend of Marengo v. Byron's *Letters* (Everyman ed.), p. 137. Bonaparte was not at Maggiore at this time.
6. *Corresp.* 4938, 4940, 4955.
7. *Corresp.* 5417, 4949, 4958, 4964-5, 5047, 5034, 5099, 5103.
8. *Corresp.* 4927; Pitt's speeches in *Orations on the French War* (Everyman's Lib.); *Henry Crabb Robinson in Germany*, ed. Morley, pp. 53, 89.
9. Gazier, *Études sur l'histoire religieuse de la révolution française* (1887).
10. Aulard, *Études et leçons*: 2ième série, p. 186. For the pre-Concordat church, Latreille, *L'Église catholique et la révolution française*, 1 (1946); for the *Eglise concordataire*, 11 (1950); Leflon, *La crise révolutionnaire* (*Histoire de l'église*, Tom. 11) (1949): this covers the Concordat too.
11. Latreille, *Napoléon et le Saint-Siège* (1934); Boulay de la Meurthe, *Documents sur la négociation du Concordat* (1891-97 and 1905); *Mémoires du Cardinal Consalvi* (1864); *Corresp.* 6032, 6042. For the Tuileries chapel, 6045, 6075. For Strasbourg, Reuss, *Histoire de Strasbourg* (1922), 375 f.
12. *Corresp.* 6121, 6103, 6311, 6345, 6531, 6534; *Annales Historiques,* 1926, March-April.
13. *Corresp.* 6408. For Fesch, cp. Latreille, *Napoléon et le Saint-Siège*; for de Cicé, Lévy-Schneider, *L'application du Concordat par un prélat d'ancien régime, Mgr. Champion de Cicé* (1921).
14. *Corresp.* 5059, 5131, 13896, 13939; Text from *nouvelle édition* of 1810. cp. Villeneuve de Janti, *Bonaparte et le Code Civil* (1934); Sagnac, *La législation civile de la révolution française* (1898); De Montmorency in *Napoleon Supplement* to *The Times* (May 5th, 1921).
15. This letter was reproduced in *The Times* of November 11th, 1921.

CHAPTER VIII

1. The biographer of Napoleon is in the unique position of being able to say where he was and what he was doing on almost every day of his life. Schuerman's *Itinéraire général de Napoléon I* (2nd ed. 1911) can now be supplemented and corrected from Garros's *Itinéraire* (1947).
2. For convenience of reference to the Correspondence, the reader will find in Appendix A a synopsis of the volumes, showing what documents are to be found in each. English translations of 292 select letters will be found in Thompson, *Letters of Napoleon* (1934). Lecestre's additional collection was translated by Lady Mary Loyd as *New Letters of Napoleon I* (1903).
3. Garros.
4. Lefebvre, *Napoléon* (1935); Pariset, *Le Consulat et l'Empire* (1921).
5. *Corresp.* 6230; Necker, *Dernières vues de politique et des finances* (1802). For Jeremy Bentham v. Alger, *Napoleon's British Visitors*, p. 85. For the d'Enghien affair, *Corresp.* 7636, 7639; Villat, 11, p. 68.

6. De Staël, *Considérations sur la révolution française* (ed. 1820), 4ième partie.
7. De Staël, 3ième partie.
8. cp. Pariset, *Le Consulat et l'Empire*.
9. *Corresp.* 5257, 5259, 5719, 7090, 6519, 5679, 5437, 5904, 4993, 5058, 5094, 5946, 5980, 6132, 6454, 6573, 6834, 5978, 6291, For the *Nautilus*, 5477; Thomazi, *Napoléon et ses marins* (1950), p. 91; Alger, *Napoleon's British Visitors*, p. 128.
10. *Corresp.* 6490, 5083, 5117, 6010, 6141, 7130.
11. *Corresp.* 5086, 5004, 5359, 4980, 4940, 5835, 6156, 6633, 5095, 5745, 7080, 5350, 6619. For the courts and executions in 1802 v. *The Life of Sir Samuel Romilly* (1842), I, 410; Lefebvre; Pariset; for the committee of the Senate, Aulard, *Études et leçons*, 3ième série; Las Cases, *Mémorial*, p. 47.
12. cp. Sorel, *Essais d'histoire et de critique* (*La censure et les censeurs sous le premier Empire*); *Corresp.* 5645, 5681, 6780-1, 9769, 12285; cp. Gallois, *Histoire des journaux et des journalistes pendant la révolution française* (1845).
13. For the Baron de Pommereul, v. Lenôtre, *En suivant l'Empereur* (*Censure*). For art, Benoit, *L'Art français* (1897), pp. 157 f.; *Corresp.* 6576, 6855, 5972, 8821, 4706, 5586, 9905, 9915. cp. Vauthier in *Revue des études napoléoniennes* (1919), p. 108; Lecestre, p. 40. For the Argus, v. Alger, *Napoleon's British Visitors*, pp. 105, 206; *Correspondence of George IV*, I, 147. *Corresp.* 5535, 8790, 11287.
14. *Corresp.* 8505, 5602, 8328; cp. Brunot, *Histoire de la langue française* (1931), Tom. IX; references in Villat, II.
15. *Corresp.* 8328, 12415-6.
16. *Corresp.* 12585. Napoleon's original idea (1805) was to found schools for the education of daughters of members of the Legion of Honour. The castle of Ecouen was taken over for this purpose in 1806, and Madame Campan was appointed *directrice* in 1807. The same year Hortense became *Protectrice de l'Institut des maisons impériales Napoléon*; and by 1810 there were six *maisons impériales d'orphelines* under her patronage; v. her *Mémoires*, II, 121.
17. *Corresp.* 10291, 10538, 11320; cp. Anchel, *Napoléon et les Juifs* (1928).
18. cp. Maxwell, *The English traveller in France*, 1698-1815 (1932); Alger.
19. The later history of the Vendôme column is instructive. In 1814 the statue of Napoleon was replaced by a gigantic *fleur-de-lys*; in 1853 by a new statue of the Emperor, but in civilian dress; in 1863 by a copy of the original statue. This was pulled down during the Commune of 1871 and again replaced in 1874.
20. cp. Bertier de Sauvigny, *Le comte Ferdinand de Bertier* (1948).
21. Walter, *Le Comte de Provence* (1950), pp. 336, 362. v. Latreille, *Napoléon et le Saint-Siège*; cp. Leflon, *La crise révolutionnaire*; *Mémoires du Cardinal Consalvi*.
22. v. Masson, *Le sacre et couronnement de Napoléon* [E.T., *Napoleon and his coronation* (1911).] The expenses came to about £250,000.
23. v. J-L-J. David, *Le peintre Louis David* (1880); cp. *Revue des études napoléoniennes*, January-February 1919, p. 26.

CHAPTER IX

1. Deutsch, *The Genesis of Napoleonic Imperialism* (1938); Browning, *England and Napoleon in 1803* (1887); Coquelle, *Napoleon and England, 1803-1813* (E.T. 1904); Dechamps, *Les Îles Britanniques et la révolution française* (1949); de Staël, *Années d'Exil* (E.T. *Ten Years' Exile*, 1821).
2. *Corresp.* 6276, 6308, 6951; *The Trial of John Peltier, Esq., for libel against Napoleon Bonaparte* (London, 1803).
3. Browning; Coquelle; de Mesmay, *Horace Sébastiani* (1948).

4. *Corresp.* 6629, 6632; Heckscher, *The Continental System* (E.T., 1922), Dunan, *Napoléon et l'Allemagne* (1948).

5. Desbrière, *Projets et tentatives de débarquement aux Îles Britanniques* (1902); for the Bantry Bay and Fishguard affairs, v. Stuart-Jones, *An Invasion that failed*, and *The Last Invasion of Britain* (both 1950).

6. *Corresp.* 6774-5, 7026, 7165, 7187, 7279, 7333, 7475, 8048, 8060, 8213; Rose, *Pitt and Napoleon* (1912).

7. *Corresp.* 7030, 7832, 7723, 7704, 7731, 7861, 8206, 8209, 8309, 8430. For the medal, *N. and Q.*, IX, VI, II. For the Boulogne Column and marching songs, v. Nicolay, *Napoleon and the Boulogne Camp* (E.T. 1907).

8. *Corresp.* 8480, 8379, 8542, 8570, 8568, 8583, 8700, 8794, 8809, 8813, 8985-9027, 9107-17. It has been argued (e.g. by Desbrière) from the number of these orders and counter-orders, that Napoleon was merely hoping to mystify the British Government, and never seriously intended an invasion; they are rather evidence of his anxiety to try all possible ways of carrying it out.

9. Ussher's *Narrative* in *Napoleon's last Voyages* (ed. Rose, 1895); O'Meara, *Napoleon in Exile* (1822), I, 349.

10. Heckscher, pp. 242, 245, 324-5.

11. Cunningham, *British Credit in the last Napoleonic War* (1910).

12. Gourgaud, *Sainte-Hélène* (3rd ed.), II, 447; I, 435; Rosebery, *Napoleon, the Last Phase* (1900), p. 176.

13. Cp. a conversation with Flahaut in Kerry, *The First Napoleon* (1925), p. 6.

14. *Corresp.* 14527-8. v. Fugier, *Napoléon et l'Espagne* (1930), esp. correspondence printed in II, 459. For Borrow v. the preface to *The Bible in Spain*; Villat, p. 166.

15. de Staël, *Considérations sur la révolution française*, 2ième partie, p. 364; Heckscher; Fugier.

16. *Corresp.* 5276, 6774, 13960, 17034, 5097, 5284-5, 5292, 5327, 5859 f., 6188, 6379, 8060 f., 9725, 9853-4; Pélissier, p. 354; *Voyages de découverte aux terres australes sur les corvettes le Géographie et le Naturaliste* (ed. Péron, 1807-15), cp. Thomazi, *Napoléon et ses marins*; Rose, *Life of Napoleon I*.

CHAPTER X

1. *Corresp.* 8796, 8803; cp. Latreille, *Napoléon et le Saint-Siège*.

2. *Corresp.* 7699, 8690, 8720, 8781; Lecestre, *New Letters*, p. 23. For Miss Patterson, cp. *N. and Q.*, 169, 51f.

3. Lecestre, *New Letters*, pp. 81, 96, 275, 290, 331; Pietri, *Lucien Bonaparte*, and *N. and Q.*, XII, V, 30. cp. *The Croker Papers*, I, 33.

4. v. Latreille, *Le catéchisme impérial de 1806* (1935). For St. Napoléon, *Relations secrètes des agents de Louis XVIII*, p. 199; cp. *N. and Q.*, III, 1, 13 f.

5. cp. Renan, *Correspondance avec M. Berthelet* (1849).

6. *Corresp.* 8873; cp. Fugier, *Napoléon et l'Italie* (1947).

7. *Corresp.* 9016, 9041, 9176, 9566, 9625, 9848.

8. *Corresp.* 9655-6, 9806, 9717, 9720, 9784, 10237, 10266, 10392, 10399, 10377, 10038, 13441, 13477, 13666; cp. *Mémoires du Cardinal Consalvi* (1864), II, 420.

9. *Corresp.* 15384, 15555, 15578, 15615, 15634, 15815; cp. *Memoirs of Cardinal Pacca* (E.T. 1828); Narrative of Rossignoly in *Révolution Française*, July-September 1925.

10. v. Oman, *Studies in the Napoleonic Wars* (1929); Croker, p. 13.

11. *Corresp.* 8852.

12. *Corresp.* 16824; Las Cases, *Mémorial de Saint-Hélène* (ed. 1842), p. 247; Montholon, *Memoirs*, p. 247n, cp. Tarlé, *Le Blocus continental et le royaume d'Italie*

(1928); Bourgin et Godechot, *L'Italie et Napoléon* (Cahiers de la révolution française, IV).

13. Lecestre, *New Letters*, pp. 216, 218, 223; *Corresp.* 17656; cp. Consalvi's and Pacca's *Memoirs*.

14. Wiseman, *Recollections of the last four Popes* (1858).

CHAPTER XI

1. *Lettres personelles des souverains à l'empereur Napoléon Ier (I)* (ed. le Prince Napoléon, 1939).

2. *Corresp.* 5417, 8350, 9038, 8286, 9134; cp. Deutsch, *The Genesis of Napoleonic Imperialism*.

3. *Corresp.* 9207, 9125-6, 8075, 8277, 7859, 9133-4, 9205, 9219, 9380-1, 9122, 9274, 9286, 9380-1.

4. *Corresp.* 9254, 9233, 9348; *Memoirs of Count Roger de Damas* (E.T. 1913), p. 214.

5. *Corresp.* 9013, 9550, 9410, 9452, 9464, 9503, 9533, 9550, 9538. For the Austerlitz legend, Rose, *Napoleonic Studies* (ed. 1906), Appendix VII.

6. v. Hargenvilliers, *Compte général de la Conscription* (ed. Vallée, 1937); cp. *Annales Historiques*. Nov.-Dec. 1937 (563); *Edinburgh Review*, XIII, 427; *Corresp.* 7344, 9348, 9293; Lefebvre, *Napoléon*, p. 191 f.; Stanhope, *Notes of Conversations with the Duke of Wellington* (ed. 1888); Gronow, *Reminiscences* (1892), I, II, II, 186; Goerin's *Livret* is in the Curzon collection in the Bodleian. For the *aérostiers* v. *Annales Historiques*, May-June 1931. For the bull-fights, *Corresp.* 9832.

7. *Lettres personelles*; *Lettres inédites de Talleyrand à Napoléon*, 1800-09 (ed. Bertrand, 1889).

8. *Lettres personelles*; *Corresp.* 9713; Deutsch.

9. *Lettres personelles*; Metternich, *Memoirs*, II; Lecestre, p. 31.

10. *Corresp.* 10948, 10967, 10990.

11. *Corresp.* 12661; Kerry, *The First Napoleon*, 7.

12. Lecestre, 389-90. The *Croker Papers*, I, 354.

13. Metternich, *Memoirs*, II; Stanhope, *Notes of Conversations*.

14. Geiringer, *Haydn* (1946); Metternich, *Memoirs*, II; *Lettres personelles*; Caulaincourt, *Mémoires*, II, 383; Kerry, *The First Napoleon*, p. 208; Masson, *Napoléon et les femmes* (ed. 1894); Bertrand, *Cahiers de Saint-Hélène*, p. 46.

15. *Corresp.* 13329, 13373, 13379; Welschinger, *Le divorce de Napoleon* (1889). For a modern parallel, the divorce between King Peter and Queen Milan of Serbia, 1888. For Staps, *Corresp.* 15935, and *Revue des études napoléoniennes*, March-June 1922.

16. *Diaries* of Marie-Louise; *Letters* of Marie-Louise to Napoleon (E.T. 1935); *Lettres de Napoléon à Joséphine*.

17. Dunan, *Napoléon et l'Allemagne* (1942).

18. *Henry Crabb Robinson in Germany*, 1800-05 (ed. Morley, 1929); Benjamin Constant, *Journal Intime* (ed. Mistler, 1945); Eckerman, *Conversations with Goethe* (ed. Everyman's Lib.).

19. Schmidt, *Le Grand-Duché de Berg* (1905); Fisher, *Napoleonic Statesmanship*.

CHAPTER XII

1. *Corresp.* 5232, 5545, 5550, 5589, 5791, 5830, 5957, 6624-5, 7032, 7034; *Memoirs of Comte Roger de Damas* (E.T. 1913), p. 90.

2. Corresp. 11093, 11153, 11328, 11247, 11251, 11216, 11337, 11434, 11651, 11476,

11502, 11518, 11951, 11791, 11800, 11815, 11897, 11913, 12160, 11907, 12361; *Lettres personelles*, p. 326 f.

3. *Lettres de Napoléon à Joséphine*; Garros; Masson, *Napoléon et les femmes*.

4. Villat, II, 122 f.

5. *Corresp.* 13086, 13744, 13778, 14069, 14170, 14248, 14372-3, 14413, 14778, 14933, 15508, 15557, 15592, 15676, 15926, 16099. For Erfurt, Lacour-Gayet, *Talleyrand*; Garros; Croker, p. 335.

6. *Corresp.* 17699, 17700, 18236; Viennet, *Napoléon et l'industrie française* (1947); Caulaincourt, *Mémoires*, I, 302.

7. *Brief Remarks on the Character and Composition of the Russian Army, and a Sketch of the Campaign in Poland in 1806 and 1807*, by Sir Robert Wilson (1811), who was with the Russian army at Eylau and Friedland; de Staël, *Dix Années*; Voltaire, *Histoire de Charles XII* (ed. Garnier).

8. Tarlé, *La campagne de Russie, 1812* (French trans., 1950); Dundulis, *Napoleon et la Lithuanie en 1812* (1940). Mansuy, *Jérôme Napoleon et la Pologne en 1812* (1931) ch. v; *Corresp.* 18289. Zoltowski, *Border of Europe* (1950).

9. *Corresp.* 18892 f. (but many documents are missing); Tarlé, *La campagne de Russie*; *Revue des études napoléoniennes* (May-June, 1914), p. 420; Wilson, *Narrative of events during the Invasion of Russia by Napoleon Bonaparte* (1860). For Borodino, Tolstoy, *War and Peace* (E.T. World's Classics) II, 242 (with plan of Russian position); Kinkiel in *Revue des études nap.*, Jan. 1929, p. 10 (agreeing with Tolstoy).

10. Caulaincourt, II: for the theory of Napoleon's failing powers, Wolseley, *The Decline and Fall of Napoleon* (2nd ed. 1895); *Memoirs of Sergeant Bourgogne* (E.T. 1926).

CHAPTER XIII

1. *Corresp.* 19583, 19621, 19396; Lecestre, p. 265; Caulaincourt, *Mémoires*, II; Chaptal, *Mes souvenirs sur Napoléon* (1893), p. 331.

2. *Corresp.* 19951, 20072, 20084, 20175, 20219; Lecestre, pp. 284, 299.

3. *Corresp.* 20853, 21601, 20395, 21101, 21179, 21325, 21407, 21505, 21293; Rose, *Napoleon*, II, 372; Fain, *Manuscrit de 1814*; Lacour-Gayet, *Talleyrand*, II; Caulaincourt, III, 36; Benaerts, *Les commissaires extraordinaires de Napoléon Ier en 1814* (1915); Borrey, *L'esprit public chez les prêtres francs-contois pendant la crise de 1813 à 1815* (1912). For Metternich in 1813, Sorel, *Essais d'histoire et de critique* (1883) p. 139.

4. *Autobiography of Benjamin Robert Haydon* (ed. World's Classics), chapter XII; Gerrare, *Moscow* (1900).

CHAPTER XIV

1. Fain, *Manuscrit de 1814* (1823); *Correspondence of George IV* (1938), I, 429; Caulaincourt, *Mémoires*, III; Campbell, *Napoleon et Fontainebleau and Elba* (1869).

2. Thompson, 'Napoleon's journey to Elba' (*Amer. Hist. Rev.*, October 1949; January 1950, with authorities); Campbell; Thibaudeau, *Mémoires, 1799-1815* (1913), chap. XXIII; Bertrand's letter in Caulaincourt, *Mémoires*, III, 410. For Augereau, *Corresp.* 21343.

3. Ussher, Napoleon's deportation to Elba, in *Napoleon's Last Voyages* (ed. Rose, 1906); Campbell; Thompson.

4. Pons de l'Hérault, *Mémoire aux puissances alliés* (1899), *Souvenirs et anecdotes sur l'Ile d'Elbe* (1897); for the Elban flag, Thompson; cp. *N. and Q.* I, VII, 535 f. *The early correspondence of Lord John Russell*, I, 181.

5. *Corresp.* 21566, 21574, 21581, 21599, 21604, 21611, 21640, 21649, 21651, 21663, 21674-5, 21677; Pélissier, *Le registre de l'île l'Elbe* (1897); Pons de l'Hérault; Campbell; Norwood Young, *Napoleon in exile at Elba* (1914); Las Cases, *Mémorial, November 6th,* 1815; Fouché, *Mémoires* (ed. Madelin, 1945). For the violet, *N. and Q.,* IV, XI, 134; for the *Zéphyr,* Gourgaud, *Journal,* February 21st, 1817.

6. *Corresp.* 21681-2, 21715-7, 21689, 21769.

7. *Corresp.* 21945, 21921, 21709, 21728, 21905-6, 21831, 21814, 21943, 22010, 22023, 22039, 21743. For generals killed, Charavay, *Les généraux morts pour la patrie* (1893).

8. Couderc de Saint-Clamant, *Napoléon et ses dernières armées;* Stanhope, *Notes of conversations with the Duke of Wellington* (2nd ed. 1888); Gourgaud, I, 347, 502; II, 84; Rose, 'The Prussians at Waterloo,' in *Napoleonic Studies* (1906); Creevey; Croker, p. 72.

9. Lecestre; II, 1225; Thibaudeau; Fouché.

CHAPTER XV

1. *Corresp.* 22064, 22066; Aubry, *Sainte-Hélène* (1938); Maitland, *Narrative of the Surrender of Buonaparte and of his Residence on board H.M.S. Bellerophon* (ed. 1826); cp. Correspondence (unpublished) of Maitland and Lord Keith; *Life of Sir Samuel Romilly* (ed. 1842); *History through The Times* (1937). For Landor, Horne, *A new Spirit of the Age* (World's Classics), p. 113. For Capt. Wright, Alger, *Napoleon's French Visitors,* p. 73. cp. Becker's *narrative in* Croker, pp. 68, 328.

2. Warden, *Letters written on board H.M.S. Northumberland* (ed. 1816); Glover, *Taking Napoleon to St. Helena,* in *Napoleon's last voyages* (ed. Rose, 1895).

3. Darwin, *The Voyage of the Beagle* (ed. 1845); Capt. John Barnes, *A Tour through the island of St. Helena* (1817).

4. Aubry; Darwin; *Illustrated London News,* May 7th, 1921.

5. Rosebery, *Napoleon, the last phase* (1900); Gonnard, *Les Origines de la légende napoléonienne* (1906); Chaplin, *A St. Helena's Who's Who* (1914); Henry, *Events of a military life* (1843).

6. Forsyth, *History of the Captivity of Napoleon at St. Helena* (1853); *The Creevey Papers,* p. 288; Watson, *A Polish exile with Napoleon* (1912); Brice, *Les Espoirs de Napoléon à Sainte-Hélène* (1938).

7. Gourgaud, under dates in text; Villat, II, p. 282.

8. Chaplin, *The illness and death of Napoleon Bonaparte* (1913). Bertrand, *Cahiers de Sainte-Hélène* (ed. Fleuriot de Langle, 1949). For the 'French' view *v. Revue des ét. Nap.,* May-June, 1933.

9. Rohan-Charlot's reports in Firmin-Didot, *La Captivité de Sainte-Hélène* (1894) *Napoleon Supplement* to *The Times:* May 5th, 1921.

INDEX